SCMAD Exam Guide

Exam CX-310-110

Sun Certified Mobile Application Developer

SCMAD
Exam Guide
Exam CX-310-110

Sun Certified Mobile Application Developer

Ko Ko Naing
Development Manager
Itorama Consulting, Thailand

Sathya Srinivasan
Technical Architect
BearingPoint, Inc., USA

Chad Davis
CEO
Blackdog Software, Inc., USA

Sivasundaram Umapathy
Technical Architect
Sella Synergy India Ltd, India

Tata McGraw-Hill Publishing Company Limited

NEW DELHI

McGraw-Hill Offices

New Delhi New York St Louis San Francisco Auckland Bogotá Caracas
Kuala Lumpur Lisbon London Madrid Mexico City Milan Montreal
San Juan Santiago Singapore Sydney Tokyo Toronto

Tata McGraw-Hill

Published by Tata McGraw-Hill Publishing Company Limited,
7 West Patel Nagar, New Delhi 110 008.

ISBN (13): 978-0-07-070453-4
ISBN (10): 0-07-070453-8

Managing Director: *Ajay Shukla*
Head—Professional and Healthcare: *Roystan La'Porte*
Publishing Manager—Professional: *R Chandra Sekhar*
Junior Sponsoring Editor—Computing: *Ritesh Ranjan*
Asst. Manager—Production: *Sohan Gaur*
Manager—Sales & Marketing: *S Girish*
Product Manager—Science, Technology & Computing: *Rekha Dhyani*
Controller—Production: *Rajender P Ghansela*
Asst. General Manager—Production: *B L Dogra*

Typeset at Text-o-Graphics, B1/56 Arawali Apartment, Sector 34, Noida 201 301 and printed at
Adarsh Printers, C-50-51, Mohan Park, Naveen Shahdara, Delhi-110 032

Cover Printer: SDR Printers

Cover Design: Kapil Gupta, New Delhi

RZALCDLFDXDYX

The McGraw-Hill Companies

Preface

The complicated nature of Java ME, with its specification intensive architecture and nebulous base of target devices, inspired us to write a Sun Certified Mobile Application Developer (SCMAD) exam guide. The Java ME presents an open-ended, conceptual architecture that provides a flexible set of specifications that can be combined to make an ad hoc version of the Java platform to meet the needs of a specific set of devices.

The SCMAD exam covers the Java Technology for the Wireless Industry (JTWI). More specifically, it covers a version of the Java platform built to serve mobile phones. At first this may sound simple enough, but it is actually an umbrella specification containing many component specifications, such as Connected Limited Device Configuration (CLDC), Mobile Information Device Profile (MIDP), Wireless Messaging API (WMA), and Mobile Media API (MMAPI). To locate all of the information covered by the exam, you need to read all five component specifications, as well as the modifications made to each of them by JTWI itself.

Just collecting all of the documents demands a substantial amount of effort—locating each specification one by one in Java Community Process (http://www.jcp.org), downloading them all, and printing them out. The worst is that Mobile Media API specification is not available in PDF format from the JCP website; it's only in HTML format. And, to add a touch of intrigue, some specifications simply can't be located—perhaps they are top secret. So we finally decided to write this book to overcome the difficulties mentioned earlier.

Our goal is to provide a single book that covers all the necessary information to help aspirants prepare for the SCMAD exam. You can be confident that you won't miss any part of the exam objectives by reading this book. But keep in mind that *practice makes one perfect.* So make sure you practice writing a lot of Java ME code while reading the book.

ABOUT THE BOOK

The topics included in the book are based on the SCMAD exam objectives provided by Sun Microsystems Inc. The exam objectives are important as the questions in the SCMAD cover only the topics that are reflected by the exam objectives. While you need not study beyond the scope of the exam objectives provided by Sun, it is strongly recommended that you learn all the topics within the scope of the exam objectives.

Background

Before reading the main details about the book, let's take a look at background information related to the topics that the book is based on.

Portability and Network Centricity

The Java platform was born and matured in the age of Internet. Naturally, the conceivers of the platform sought to integrate portability and network centricity into the core of their new technology. Over the years, the platform has remained true to these core principles. During these years, Internet and other networking technologies have enlarged the standard application deployment target from individual laptops and desktop computers to a vast distributed realm of well-connected, heterogeneous machines all sharing in the creation and consumption of data and functionality. Increasingly, the new target for deployment is no less than the world itself. In this setting, successful applications must be portable, and they must be seamlessly integrated into the networked environment. On-demand, network available, portable computing has become de rigueur.

Although no one could have predicted exactly how things would have developed, the Java folks were certainly right about portability and network-centric technology. As we have said, the Java platform is built on these principles. The Java platform consists of a set of components that provide a complete run-time environment for Java applications. These components include key items such as the Java Virtual Machine, the Java language, and a vast array of APIs that provide a staggering amount of built-in functionality.

The reference implementation (RI) is the development kit that you can download from Sun if you want to develop for the platform. It typically includes an implementation of the JVM, a compiler built to the language specification, and the APIs. While these actual implementations are more concrete and useful, in a practical sense, the document based specifications provide the mechanism to create magic. Sun's core mode is based on producing specifications that detail precise characteristics, requirements, and parameters of a compliant implementation.

While it may seem intuitive that the JVM would be the product of a specification process, the APIs are also specification driven. Not only are the behaviors of the APIs specified but the selection of APIs to be included in the platform is itself a key function of the specification process. The built-in APIs include all the functionalities that one might reasonably think of as fundamental to modern applications. Certainly, applications need to be network capable, and one can certainly expect to find plenty of network-related packages in the platform. But the dividing line between core and optional functionality changes continuously. By following a rigorous specification process, that produces new versions every few years, the APIs can respond to new demands of what the industry considers core functionality. For example, in recent years, the XML functionality of the platform has grown tremendously as various XML technologies and techniques have become core software elements.

Three Editions of Java

In response to the overwhelming range of computing environments and intents, in 1999, Sun restructured the Java technology into three editions to target specific markets:

- Java Platform, Standard Edition (Java SE), having core API and API for creating desktop applications (via Swing and AWT packages)
- Java Platform, Enterprise Edition (Java EE), providing robust data processing, concurrency, interoperability and other functionality demanded by the enterprise environment
- Java Platform, Micro Edition (Java ME), providing support for devices having tight resource constraints

These editions are shown in Fig. P.1.

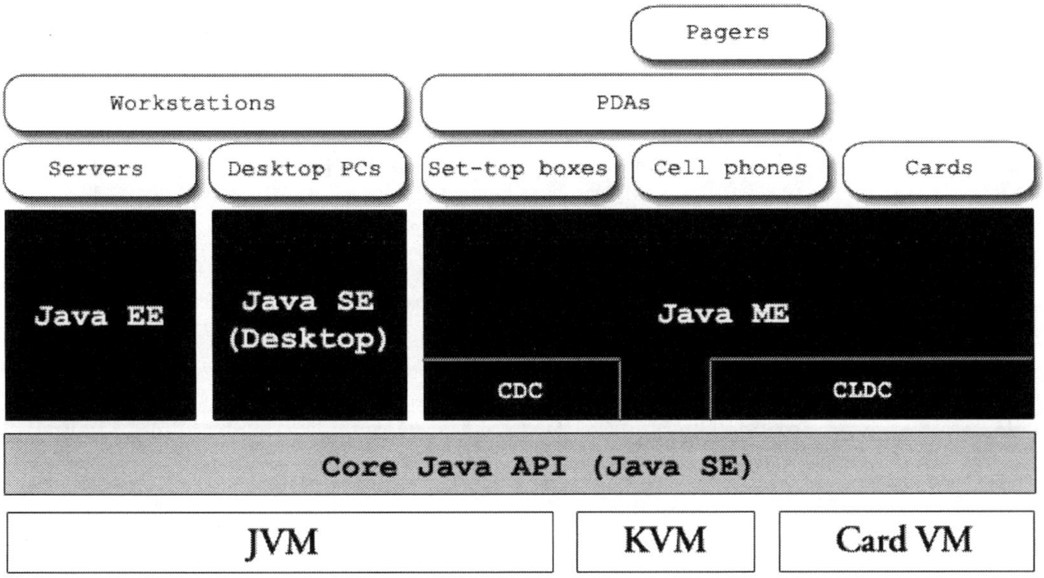

Fig. P.1 Java flavors and corresponding devices

As you can see from Fig. P.1, a combination of these three APIs covers a wide variety of applications and hardware applied in various domains. If we examine the layered diagram, we can see how the Java platform supports various devices by components that reside in the three layers of platform. For instance, we can see that Java SE and EE sit on top of the core APIs and the standard JVM and support various PCs. Similarly, Java ME combines a modified virtual machine with the core APIs and some other elements.

Who Should Read this Book?

This book is for SCMAD exam aspirants, who want to prepare for SCMAD certification exam. Java programmers who want to learn how to develop mobile applications in Java ME platform should read this book to build a strong Java ME knowledge. While expert Java ME application developers will find this book essential for the exam preparation, beginners can expect step-by-step explanations of each topic with of code examples. This book is also written in a way that it can be useful even after passing the exam and/or as a reference to mobile application development in Java ME platform.

How is this Book Organized?

This book has four parts:

Part	Title	Topic	Chapters
1.	Getting Started	Basics of Java ME and concepts of JTWI	Intro through 2
2.	Mobile Application Essentials	Essentials of mobile application development—CLDC and MIDP	3 through 4
3.	Creating Mobile Applications	Core MIDP APIs: MIDP UI, Networking, MIDP Game, RMS and Security	5 through 9
4.	Working with Optional Features	Optional Java ME packages: MMAPI and WMA	10 through 11

The first part of the book, *Getting Started*, covers Java ME basics and explains the purpose and scope of JTWI subset of Java ME. The second part, *Mobile Application Essentials*, covers low-level platform details, including virtual machine and core APIs. Then *Creating Mobile Applications* delves into the actual environment and APIs that support application development. Finally, *Working with Optional Features* covers some additional APIs that, while officially known as optional in the scope of the Java ME as a whole, are absolutely required for the SCMAD.

How is each Chapter Organized?

Starting from Chapter 2, each chapter starts with an “Exam Objectives” section, where the exam objectives that correspond to the topics that we are going to learn in the chapter, and the corresponding section numbers at the end of each exam objective have been provided. In some chapters, the order of the section number may not exactly follow the order of the exam objectives. This is to organize the topics in a logical way, in order to help the readers follow a learning path set by the related topics of the chapter.

The next section is the "Introduction" to the chapter, in which you will be provided with preliminary concepts and basic ideas before you get down to the main concepts and advanced topics of the chapter. While you are going through the main sections of a chapter, you will encounter several "Exam Tips" and some "Notes". Both of these are very important from the exam viewpoint. While an "Exam Tip" reminds you of what to remember from the previously learned topics, a "Note" emphasizes important concepts and/or points out the pitfalls.

While the purpose of the "Summary" section is to help you recall the topics that you have learned from the chapter, and to give you a quick review on the important concepts of the chapter, those of the "Review Questions" and "Review Answers" sections is to let you test your knowledge on the chapter and to measure up your readiness on the topics of the chapter. In some chapters, there is a section called "Exercises" to help you practice implementing the concepts that you learned from the chapter.

At the end of each chapter, you will see "Exam Notes" section that can be used as a quick recap of all the exam objectives that correspond to the topics of the chapter. The notes are primarily from the famous SCMAD exam notes prepared by Sathya Srinivasan, and known among the SCMAD exam aspirants as "*Sathya's Notes*".

Conventions Used in this Book

Some of the conventions used in this book are as follows:

Italic typeface is used to introduce new terms.

`Courier` typeface is used to represent programming code, including attributes, method names, classes, interfaces, and other identifiers.

`Bold courier` is used to represent important parts of the code listings.

Line continuations are indented.

ABOUT THE EXAM

The saying "Small is good" is true. While big things like Java EE and Java SE rocks, we shouldn't ignore the best things that a small thing like Java ME can provide us. Therefore, Sun created Sun Certified Mobile Application Developer (SCMAD) certification exam for the Java ME platform, and made Sun Certified Java Programmer (SCJP) certification as a prerequisite for SCMAD exam.

SCMAD covers only a narrow range of the Java platform. Since SCMAD is specific to the Java ME it eliminates two-thirds of the Java world. The Java ME provides Java platforms for a range of consumers and embedded devices that include PDAs, cell phones, set-top boxes, and their kind. Although we must understand Java ME in order to be good developers under the scope of the SCMAD, we do not need to master the entire micro-universe. In fact, we are concerned with only a very specific subset known as Java Technology for the Wireless Industry (JTWI). Let's take a quick overview of the Java certification exams provided by Sun.

Sun Java Certification Exams

Sun created Java platform in three different editions—Java Platform, Standard Edition (Java SE), Java Platform, Enterprise Edition (Java EE), and Java Platform, Micro Edition (Java ME). So far, Sun has developed various certifications for all three editions—Sun Certified Java Programmer (SCJP) for Java SE, Sun Certified Web Component Developer (SCWCD), Sun Certified Business Component Developer (SCBCD), Sun Certified Developer for Java Web Services (SCDJWS) and Sun Certified Enterprise Architect (SCEA) for Java EE, and Sun Certified Mobile Application Developer (SCMAD) for Java ME. Figure P.2 illustrates the categories of Sun Java certification exams based on the editions of the Java platform.

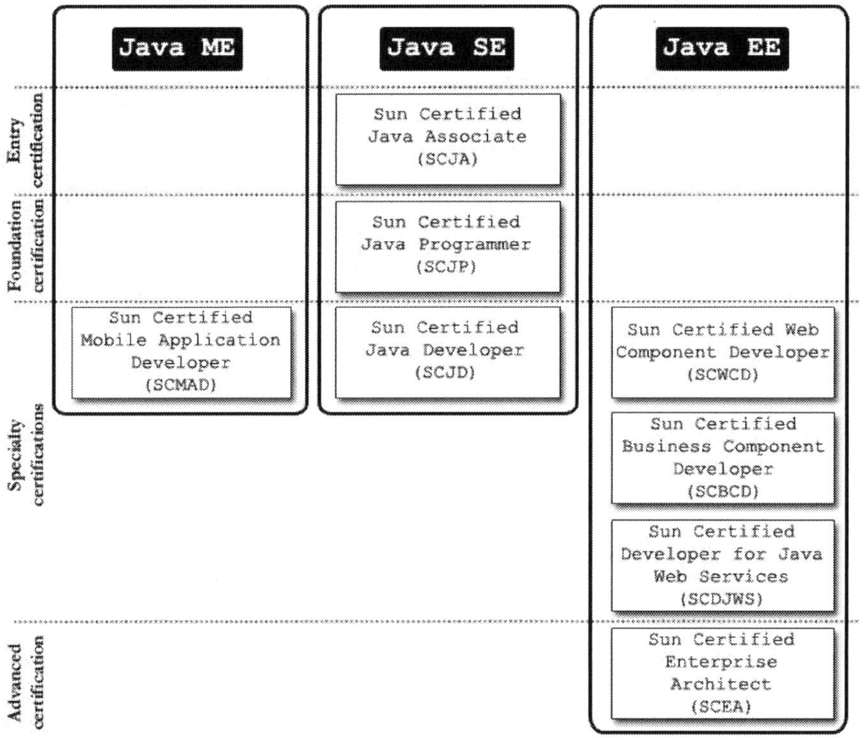

Fig. P.2 Certification map that illustrates the categories of Java certifications provided by Sun Microsystems, Inc.

While SCEA and SCJA do not have anything as a prerequisite, all the specialty certifications (SCMAD, SCJD, SCWCD, SCBCD and SCDJWS) require SCJP as a prerequisite. We believe that you already have SCJP by now and are planning to take the SCMAD exam to get certified in Java ME application development field. Let us take a quick look at the checklist that we need while preparing for the exam.

Preparing for the Exam

As an SCMAD exam aspirant, you need the following items to prepare for the exam:

- A copy of SCMAD exam objectives—Since the exam requires you to know only the items listed in the exam objectives, it is very important to stick with the exam objectives provided by Sun and make sure you don't miss any of them while preparing for the exam. We have also provided related exam objectives at the beginning of each chapter to inform you of the topics that you are going to learn in the chapter, and at the end of each chapter along with the exam notes. You can also take a look at all the exam objectives in one place at the SCMAD certification homepage (http://www.sun.com/training/catalog/courses/CX-310-110.xml).
- A copy of related specifications needed for the exam—The SCMAD exam is based on the following specifications: Java Technology for the Wireless Industry (JTWI) 1.0, Connected Limited Device Configuration (CLDC) 1.1, Mobile Information Device Profile (MIDP) 2.0, Wireless Messaging API (WMA) 1.1, and Mobile Media API (MMAPI) 1.1. This book can be used to prepare for the exam, instead of reading all the topics included in all those specifications. However, those specifications can be learned as references in case you want to learn something beyond the exam objectives and/or find out more about the related technologies. You can download all the specifications from Java Community Process website (http://www.jcp.org).
- Sun Java Wireless Toolkit—You will need this software to practice coding. Since the exam never asks questions related to device-specific topics, the toolkit is logically the best software for you to get hands-on experience. One of the most important things to remember while preparing for the exam is 'never stop coding'. Try to play around with the code examples provided in the book and try something beyond the code examples. Appendix A contains all the information you need to know where to get the toolkit from, how to install it, and how to run code examples from the book.
- Exam simulator—An exam simulator is needed to test your readiness before taking the exam. Though it is not a must, you should measure up your knowledge that you've learned so far using an exam simulator. An exam simulator can provide you a very similar exam environment that you will see in the exam room. It contains various question types—the single-choice questions, multiple choice questions, and drag and drop questions.

Taking the Exam

You will need to take only one exam for the SCMAD certification, while certifications such as SCJD and SCEA require more than one exam to pass in order to get certified. Some important facts about the exam are provided as follows:

Place: Authorized Worldwide Prometric Testing Centers

Prerequisites: Sun Certified Programmer for the Java 2 Platform (any edition)

Exam type: Single choice, multiple choice, drag and drop

Number of questions: 68

Passing score: 55% (38 correct items of 68)

Duration: 150 minutes

Exam cost: $300 (The cost may vary upon the location of the testing centers worldwide)

Languages available: English, Simplified Chinese, Japanese

You will need to take a survey at the beginning of the exam session. The survey contains the questions related to your expertise level and working experience on the different technologies covered by the SCMAD exam. The time spent on the survey is not a part of the actual exam.

After taking the survey, you are ready to go with the actual exam. The exam includes single-choice questions, multiple-choice questions, and drag-and-drop questions. For choice-based questions, the exact number of options to be selected is given in the question statement. For drag-and-drop questions, it is very important to note down your drag-and-drop answers. Because whenever you review the questions of drag-and-drop type, the previously-entered answers will get erased. Some questions have the Exhibit button that you can click to see the code fragments. The code fragments usually provide more information that you need to know to be able to answer a question. During the exam you can revise your answers whenever you want using the navigation buttons provided in the application interface.

As per the instructions by Sun, the duration allowed for the exam is 150 minutes. Since Sun sometimes changes the time limit, make sure to verify it before taking the exam at the SCMAD certification homepage (http://www.sun.com/training/catalog/courses/CX-310-110.xml), and double-check the time displayed on the screen at the beginning of the exam.

The following is the typical process to take the exam:

First of all, you need to buy an exam voucher from a local Sun Education Services in the country you are going to take the exam. Since the exam voucher is tied to country, you must take the exam in the country, in which you buy the exam voucher. You may also buy an exam voucher online at http://www.sun.com/training/certification/register/index.html.

After getting the exam voucher, you can schedule the exam. Before scheduling the exam, you need to know the exam center and exam time that you prefer. You can check the exam centers and available exam time at a center by visiting http://securereg3.prometric.com/. Once you are ready to register for the exam, you can go ahead and contact a local Prometric center near you or visit the same site mentioned earlier (http://securereg3.prometric.com/).

On the exam date, you should arrive at the exam center at least 15 minutes before the test, and must identify yourself with two forms of identification. One of them must have your photo on it.

After completing the test, you will be able to see the exam result on the computer screen, and the exam center will also give you a printed document with detailed percentage that you received in each section of the exam objectives.

Within a month or two, you will receive the SCMAD certificate from Sun through mail if you pass the exam.

All the best for the exam!

KO KO NAING
SATHYA SRINIVASAN
CHAD DAVIS
SIVASUNDARAM UMAPATHY

Acknowledgements

This book could not have been completed if we hadn't received help from certain people. We are very thankful to them and appreciate their help.

Note from Ko Ko Naing

First of all, I would like to thank God for giving me such a great opportunity to co-author the book and guiding me to success.

And my special thanks go to Sathya for introducing me to this project, and providing me his greatest support towards the completion of the project. I have always been impressed with his contribution to the field of SCMAD exam.

I thank Hanumant Deshmukh for giving me an opportunity to work on Enthuware's SCMAD exam simulator, JMADPlus, and for providing me guidance.

I am really grateful to my lovely and supportive wife, Saengwan Mankhongwaja, for her constructive criticisms, creative ideas, and for all of her greatest support.

Many thanks go to my parents for providing me ethical guidance and moral support in my life. I could never have reached at this level without their support throughout my life.

Note from Sathya Srinivasan

First, I would like to thank the editorial and production teams at McGraw-Hill Education for their support and perseverance in getting this book published.

Next, I would like to thank my co-authors, Ko Ko, Siva, and Chad Davis, for taking the reins when I was swamped with official work during the last stages of the book. Their timely help ensured the successful publication of the book.

I would also like to thank my wife Srividya for her encouragement throughout the book-writing process and my brother, cousins, and friends for their constant support and enthusiasm. Most importantly, I would like to thank my parents, Srinivasan and Brinda for imbibing in me the habit of reading books right from childhood, thus creating a strong base for authoring a technical book.

Finally, thanks to my BearingPoint colleagues, Ravi and Sachi who had supported me during times of hectic activity in professional as well as personal front when I was writing this book.

Note from Chad Davis

It has been a pleasure to work with everyone involved, from the co-authors to the editors at McGraw-Hill Education. I would like to thank my wife Mary for making all the money while I put time into such a fiscally unwise venture as book writing. And I would like to thank my mother and father for their love and support.

Note from Sivasundaram Umapathy

I thank our publisher for trusting us with this project. Without their belief, support and patience, the project wouldn't have taken its current form. A special mention goes to Ritesh Ranjan of McGraw-Hill Education for being with us.

I thank my co-author Sathya Srinivasan, who was always influential in the SCMAD arena, right from the beta days. He was instrumental in kick-starting this project and supported me whenever I required help. I would also like to thank Ko Ko and Chad Davis, who helped us in meeting the goals.

I would like to thank my parents, Umapathy and Vijayalakshmi, for their love and virtuous upbringing. I specially thank my wife Preethi for her love, encouragement and patience. Last but not least, my friends Raji, Vinu, Krishna, Vinay and other colleagues at SSIL deserve a big thanks for their support and incessant motivation.

Contents

Preface *v*
Acknowledgements *xv*

Part-1 Getting Started 1

Chapter 1 Understanding Java ME 3

Introduction *3*
1.1 Specifying Portability: The Java Nirvana *4*
1.2 The Underlying Technology *5*
1.3 Understanding Java ME Architecture *6*

Chapter 2 Java Technology for the Wireless Industry (JTWI) 13

Introduction *13*
2.1 Methodology of JTWI *16*
2.2 Requirements of JTWI *20*
2.3 Requirements and Clarifications on Component Specifications *24*
2.4 Trusting Applications *32*

Part-2 Mobile Application Essentials 41

Chapter 3 Connected Limited Device Configuration (CLDC) 43

Introduction *43*
3.1 Understanding the Goals, Requirements and Scope *45*
3.2 Knowing CLDC Application Contract *49*
3.3 Differences between CLDC 1.0 and CLDC 1.1 *50*
3.4 Kilobyte Virtual Machine *52*
3.5 CLDC Library *55*
3.6 Handling Exceptions and Errors *60*
3.7 Managing Memory and Garbage Collection *65*

Chapter 4 The MIDlet: A Different Kind of Application 77

Introduction *78*
4.1 Building MIDlet *79*
4.2 Packaging Applications *83*
4.3 Describing MIDlet Suite *84*
4.4 Journeys of MIDlet Suite *90*
4.5 Platform Request API *93*
4.6 Playing around with Events and Notifications *94*

Part-3 Creating Mobile Applications 125

Chapter 5 A Face to Remember–The MIDP User Interface API 127

Introduction *128*
5.1 MIDP User Interface Model *128*
5.2 Creating High-level User Interfaces *132*
5.3 Issuing Commands *133*
5.4 Creating User Input Forms *137*
5.5 Other High-level UI Components *152*
5.6 Creating Low-level User Interfaces *157*

Chapter 6 Playing Games Using the MIDP Game API 182

Introduction *182*
6.1 GameCanvas: Setting Stage for the Game *183*
6.2 Layer and LayerManager: The Game's Backdrop *192*
6.3 Sprites: The Game's Actors *195*
6.4 TiledLayer: A Scene for Our Play *208*
6.5 Optimizing Game Size and Performance *210*

Chapter 7 Connecting to the Outside World 222

Introduction *222*
7.1 GCF at a Glance *223*
7.2 MIDP 2.0 Protocol Implementations *236*
7.3 Working with Connection *241*
7.4 Network Troubleshooting *270*

Chapter 8 Persisting Data Using the Record Management System (RMS) 282

Introduction *282*
8.1 Record Stores *283*

8.2 C.R.U.D! *291*
8.3 Advanced Features *296*
8.4 Putting It All Together *301*

Chapter 9 Securing Wireless Applications **331**

Introduction *331*
9.1 CLDC Security Provisions *332*
9.2 Untrusted and Trusted MIDlet Suites *335*
9.3 Signing and Authenticating MIDlet Suites Based on X.509 PKI *345*

Part-4 Working with Optional Features **359**

Chapter 10 Working with Multimedia: MIDP 2.0 Media API and Mobile Media API (MMAPI) **361**

Introduction *362*
10.1 Understanding MMAPI *362*
10.2 Generating Simple Tones *364*
10.3 Defining Source of Media *365*
10.4 Getting Media Player *371*
10.5 Playing Media *373*
10.6 Controlling Player *383*
10.7 Differences between MMAPI and MIDP Media API *401*

Chapter 11 Sending Messages Using the Wireless Messaging API **415**

Introduction *415*
11.1 WMA Package Overview *416*
11.2 Understanding SMS Adapter Support *431*
11.3 Understanding CBS Adapter Support *437*
11.4 Back to WMA in General *439*

Appendix A Developing Mobile Applications Using Sun Java Wireless Tool Kit **456**
Appendix B A Sample Java Application Descriptor (JAD) File **462**
Appendix C Over-the-Air (OTA) Provisioning **464**
Index **477**

Part-1

Getting Started

As the name implies, this part of the book leads you along the path you should take before diving into the pool of Java ME-related technologies and specifications. The topics in this part include the birth and architecture of Java ME; and the goals, characteristics and requirements of JTWI specifications.

Let's take a look at how Java ME was born and how it is architected with various technologies and specifications. Then we'll go further with an umbrella-like specification, JTWI, which mandates various technologies of Java ME in order to create a more stable platform for portable application deployment on mobile phones. If you are already familiar with the basics of Java ME, you can go ahead with the JTWI part.

1

Chapter

Understanding Java ME

INTRODUCTION

This book starts with a short chapter that introduces Java ME, the complicated world on which the SCMAD test is based. Many Java developers won't be aware of the difference between Java ME and the subject matter of SCMAD. A lot of confusion can be cleared by discussing all these in this chapter. If you already have understanding about the platform Java ME and SCMAD, you can skip it. This chapter lays the groundwork for easy comprehension of the whole book.

Java ME represents an attempt to provide a stable and fully portable platform for small electronic/computing devices. Defining this set of devices for Java ME platform puts us continually at a loss, meaning that we can't literally limit the range of devices that Java ME will cover. These devices include cell phones like BlackBerries and PDAs. Sun Microsystems includes both cell phones and printers in this inclusive grouping and suggests that this is only the tip of the iceberg. I have even heard rumors that the unofficial list of devices includes personal broiling devices, otherwise known as toasters. The range is so elusive that we might be better off defining the set by what it is not. We might not be wrong to suggest that Java ME seeks, ultimately, to cover the entire range of computing devices that exists outside of the relatively rigid and stable confines of those familiar devices we refer to as personal computers.

Personal computers, as used here, include any of those desktop, laptop, or workstation machines that have become an integral part of our existence. While it once seemed that the differences between Apple and Intel architecture, or between a Unix and Windows environment, were real boundaries, the overabundance of consumer and embedded devices that exist on the frontiers of computing technology put old versions of hardware incompatibility to shame. When the target hardware runs from cell phones to, nearly, toasters, we can easily see the challenges facing developers of truly portable Java ME applications.

Lucky for us, SCMAD does not take up all the challenges of Java ME. In fact, the subset of Java ME covered by SCMAD seems downright easy after all that scary talk of printers and toasters. The SCMAD focuses, basically, on cell phones. And while cell phones can also cover a pretty broad range of devices, browning slices of bread will probably not be found as one of the marketplace's proprietary whistles and bells. If, by chance, there is an optional API for controlling a broiling device, rest assured that it is not covered by the exam. However, we do need to familiarize ourselves with the conceptual architecture of Java ME so that we can understand the dynamics in play within SCMAD specifications.

1.1 SPECIFYING PORTABILITY: THE JAVA NIRVANA

As discussed in the introduction, the Java platform depends heavily on specifications. It is through these specifications that a portable and stable target environment can be created. Sun seems to be a company that respects solid engineering principles. For computing, standardization may be the most important engineering principle. Standardization defines specific and exact requirements for various technical and non-technical components of the domain from Internet protocols to hardware-level form factors. The standards are published and, if everyone conforms to the specifications, we can be confident that the various implementations of various components will work together.

Without standards, we would not be able to write protocol stacks to enable our computers to communicate over networks. And we would not be able to run down to the mall and buy a new power supply that is guaranteed to fit our box. If there were two or three proprietary Internets from which to choose, what good is a fragmented Internet? Recognizing the importance of standardization, Sun has adopted a policy of standardization through specification. Java has always been specification-based, and over the course of the past few years, Sun has developed a highly formalized process for the creation of specifications.

The Java specifications are the products of the JCP. This process aggregates the knowledge, energy and market intentions of various representatives of the industry to help guide the development of the Java platform. When a new technology seems imminent, someone usually submits a Java Specification Request (JSR). Then a group of experts and stakeholders is assembled to develop the actual specification. Ultimately, the group creates the final specification along with a Reference Implementation (RI) and a Technology Compatibility Kit (TCK). At this point, the mechanisms are in place for interoperable computing. Device manufacturers can build compliant devices. Software engineers can develop compliant software, and everything should work just fine. It's almost magic. If you're excited by all these, you're an engineer. If you're a little bored, you're a developer. Try to hang in there.

For Java SE and Java EE, the specifications define a JVM and a set of APIs geared toward the application domain. The SE provides desktop application APIs and the EE provides such things as servlets to support enterprise-level applications. This seems almost straightforward. In some sense, each of these editions can be thought of as a specific environment you can set up on your computer. The SE provides a specific environment for developing desktop applications, and the EE provides a richer environment that adds many tools specific to the enterprise application domain such as JSPs and Web services.

Unfortunately, Java ME complicates things a bit. Instead of defining a single target environment, it defines a number of technologies and specifications from which it may be possible to build a variety of target environments. This almost sounds like a break down in the engineering practices. But it's not. Perhaps, the concept of an edition is a bit taxed by Java ME and it actually contains several editions of the Java platform, while Java SE and EE truly represent single editions. At any rate, just keep this in mind as you encounter any lack of clarity. Ultimately, due to the underlying instability of the range of devices covered by Java ME, we should not be surprised that its architecture must be a bit more flexible than those of the other editions.

1.2 THE UNDERLYING TECHNOLOGY

Why do we need a separate edition when there is already a well-defined and proven Java SE? The target devices of Java ME are completely different in terms of their capabilities and requirements. For example, the memory in these devices is measured in terms of kilobytes, and running a full-fledged Java SE that requires megabytes of volatile and non-volatile memory is impossible given these constraints. Another example would be the limited screen capabilities of a device. A Java SE user interface API like the Abstract Window Toolkit (AWT) would overpower the tiny screens of these devices. And the typical pointing mechanisms used in a desktop world just don't make sense in this micro domain. Also, the mode of deployment varies widely. Java ME applications can be downloaded and installed easily by the customer.

Thus, Java ME originated as a separate edition with its own virtual machine and libraries. Theoretically, you can call Java ME a subset of Java SE, since the byte code of a Java ME application is also a valid Java byte code. However, you cannot expect a Java ME class to run as it is in a Java SE virtual machine. Some of the required Java ME libraries may not even be present in Java SE.

As the platform is targeted for heavily resource-constrained devices, the designers of Java ME had to rethink the way Java applications are run and installed. As a result, applications running on resource-constrained devices, such as a mobile phone, use a different virtual machine called the Kilo Virtual Machine (KVM). The KVM is a subset of a JVM and derives its name from its more diminutive allocation of memory. Also, the supported set of libraries will be limited. In a way, this provides the developers of the Java ME application a sense of satisfaction and thrill, since the demands of such a restricted environment insist that applications be designed with careful use of resources in mind—a skill not always found in other realms of Java development. In short, the limited and varying nature of the target devices demands a more robust platform. Next, we'll take a look at the architecture that strives to satisfy these demands.

1.3 UNDERSTANDING JAVA ME ARCHITECTURE

The specifiers of Java ME have a tough engineering task. They must make the platform work for low-end devices with limited memory, low-resolution display and unreliable network connections as well as high-end devices with more memory, color display and permanent connections. A low-end device doesn't need support for an expensive graphics routine but a high-end device loses a sizeable chunk of its value without that support. Instead of adopting any one-size-fits-all or least-common-denominator solutions, Java ME is designed to be modular and flexible, allowing you to mix and match the components depending on the potentials of a particular device. We will see later in this section how this flexibility has often caused confusion and how the Java Community Process has responded to it.

For now, let's look at the details of Java ME. According to Sun, Java ME is

> a collection of technologies and specifications that implementers and developers can choose from and combine to construct a complete Java runtime environment that closely fits the requirements of a particular range of devices and target markets.

As with all good technical writing, the amount of information to be taken from this single sentence resists the efforts of the casual glance. It's the kind of sentence that at first appears to say nothing, but upon deeper reflection contains the secrets to the kingdom. Almost it reminds a legalese—clearly written by an engineer.

In particular, we need to pay attention to the following notions packed in this quote.

- The Java ME is a collection of technologies and specifications.
- They can be chosen from and combined to construct a stable platform.
- All these must be done with a mind toward a particular range of devices and target markets.

In other words, we are forewarned that this is a shifty ground—quicksand perhaps. And only through careful consideration, we can expect to have any success in developing portable applications for even a specific set of devices. With Java SE or Java EE, we just look it up in the API and write the code. That is not the same here. This is a specification in action. Now we're being asked to carefully pick, choose and assemble our own Java platform. I'm pretty sure, that is not in my job description.

Thankfully, somebody else has done this for us. Actually, the process of assembling a version of the Java platform for mobile devices built on the architecture of Java ME has been ongoing for several years. Intermediate stages of the platform have been implemented and applications have been deployed. During these intermediate stages, various problems have been identified. The primary difficulty has been found in achieving adequate stability in these platforms. As the platforms have not been tight enough in their scope and requirements, the platforms have suffered from a high degree of what is politely termed API fragmentation. Basically, this means that the platforms have not proven stable enough for the development of truly portable applications; the development target has been a moving target. In response to this, the engineers created another specification through the JCP that addresses the looseness and pins down a nice stable development target. Don't think that this implies that the Java ME architecture did not accomplish its goals. On the contrary, the flexibility of the architecture was intended as a mechanism for just such a process. This new specification is the JTWI, the subject of the next chapter as well as the main subject of the SCMAD. With this new specification, we finally have a stable platform for developing and delivering portable, powerful Java applications to a broad base of mobile phones.

But before we go on, we need to pause for a moment on Java ME itself. For this exam, we ultimately don't have to concern ourselves with Java ME, but, rather, a specified subset of it. But while we don't have to understand the entirety of Java ME for the task at hand, we clearly need to get a feel for how it works. We need to understand the conceptual vocabulary of the specifications and technologies from which the platform that is the subject of this book, and exam, has been constructed.

1.3.1 Conceptual Elements of Java ME

The term *conceptual architecture* may send the developers running for a fresh cup of coffee, but I promise that this abstract term will prove to be clear, concrete and highly useful in understanding the material of this book. Just hear me out. The engineers are, of course, riveted. The flexibility of the Java ME stems from the careful design of its conceptual architecture. In order to provide a more modular architecture, the specification defines three conceptual elements—*configurations*, *profiles*, and *optional packages*. Each of these will be covered in detail as we proceed, but a quick glance at Fig. 1.1 shows how these elements are combined to create a target environment for an application. Don't spend too much time trying to take this diagram in just yet. We will refer back to it in the upcoming paragraphs, and it will soon be all clear.

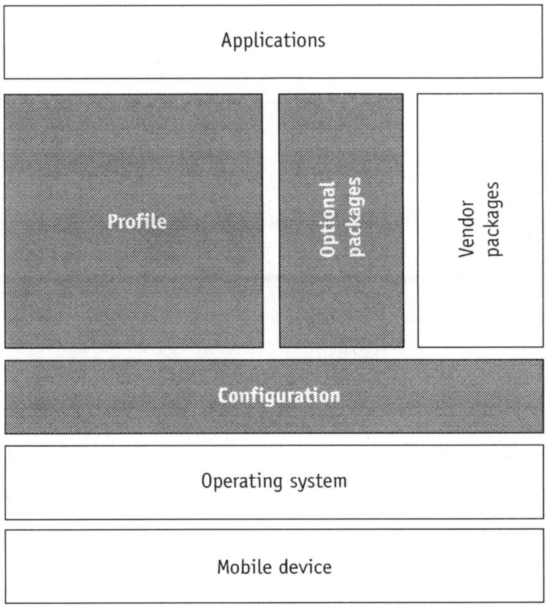

Figure 1.1 Java ME architecture

The terms—configurations, profiles, and optional packages—were invented by the JCP folks who wrote the specifications. If we think of a data bus, we instantly picture the wires on our motherboard that carry the electrical currents from component to component, thus allowing our computer to work. But even a bus was once just an abstract concept invented and matched to a somewhat arbitrary bit of vocabulary by a long forgotten engineer. The particular names used in Java ME attempt to solidify some rather new architectural concepts. While it might take a bit of effort to become comfortably familiar with these new concepts, eventually we will be able to make these elusive concepts become a rock hard, stable platform. Take a quick look back at the definition of the Java ME we went through. We need to recognize that these configurations, profiles and optional packages are precisely the technologies and specifications referred to in that quote. And from these, we will choose a set of components to construct a complete Java platform.

So, the configurations, profiles and optional packages are the lego blocks of Java ME. Next we need to understand the special purposes of each type of building block. We need to start trying to understand why the specifiers drew the boundaries where they did when sectioning off the things that make up each of these conceptual building blocks. We'll start with the lowest-level building block—configurations.

1.3.2 Configurations

A configuration is a specification that defines a JVM and a set of core-level APIs for a given set of similar devices. In other words, there is more than one configuration in Java ME. Each configuration targets a subset of devices from the universe of devices covered by the entire Java ME. This subset of devices is presumed to be a group of devices with a fairly similar set of resources, such as memory and Internet connectivity. As you can see in figure 1.1, the configuration is positioned above the operating system and below the profile and optional packages. We can think of it as a low-level, or core, layer of the Java platform. Naturally then, the configuration specifies a JVM and core set of APIs that must be implemented. The JVM and the APIs are typically subsets of the full JVM and APIs found in Java SE, although this is not a requirement for a configuration.

It turns out that there are only two configurations actually defined, although there could be many more in the future. Java ME defines the concept of a configuration and then leaves the door open for an open-ended number of configurations to be specified, as necessary, to meet the needs of emerging categories of devices. For now, we have the Connected Device Configuration (CDC) and the Connected Limited Device Configuration (CLDC). CDC aims at the devices such as set-top boxes, home appliances, and high-end PDAs, while CLDC is primarily designed for the devices such as mobile phones, pagers, and low-end personal organizers. Figure 1.2 illustrates the relationship between CDC and CLDC as well as that between the configurations and Java SE. As it turns out, we only need to be concerned with CLDC. So, for our purposes, once we understand the role of a configuration within the conceptual architecture of Java ME, we can then narrow our scope to the details of just CLDC. The Java ME is already getting simpler. Try not to lose that feeling.

Incidentally, we only focus on the CLDC because it is the configuration component chosen, in the context of SCMAD, to be the configuration layer. As per the language of our oft-cited Java ME definition, you are witnessing the construction of a Java platform.

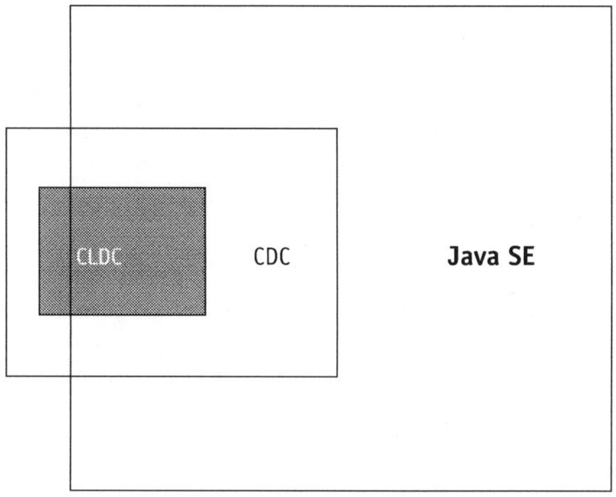

Figure 1.2 The relationship between the configurations and Java SE

1.3.3 Profiles

The next building blocks we need to understand are profiles. In Fig. 1.1, we see that they are on top of the configuration and make up part of the layer upon which the applications directly sit. Again, there can be many different profiles in Java ME, but only one is used at a time. Perhaps the best way to think of it is that they are higher-level APIs added to the configuration to provide all of the good stuff for writing applications. In fact, Sun refers to the combination of a profile and a configuration as the creation of an *application environment.* The functionality provided by a profile includes application lifecycle, data persistence, and user interface support. Although the APIs of a profile are not considered as core as the APIs of a configuration, they provide the necessary foundation of functionality required by applications. For the developer, profiles are fundamental; you rarely would find yourself writing applications for a configuration without the benefit of the additional APIs of a profile.

Like configurations, only a few profiles have actually been defined. More importantly, we will be concerned only with Mobile Information Device Profile (MIDP). Again, Java ME becomes simpler—at least for us. While we do not need to learn the details of the other profiles, we must understand the concept and position of profiles and know that they can be theoretically many, but our profile is the MIDP.

If you are wondering why we separate the functionality of the Java platform into two pieces, a configuration and a profile, then you are certainly thinking like an engineer now. It's certainly a good question. The specifics of the precise location of the line drawn in the APIs is probably best answered by the JCP people who created the idea of configurations and profiles, but it seems a safe bet that they had a good reason for creating a logical layer between a certain set of APIs and a more fuller set of APIs. We do know from the specifications that define the conceptual architecture itself that the configurations are meant to provide base-level functionality, and profiles are meant to provide support for applications. Perhaps it's a bit like the division between services incorporated into an operating system kernel and those left on the outside in user space. Some of the stuff in user space, although not included in the sacred space of the kernel, definitely remains indispensable to applications. Indeed, if we consider a Unix-based OS, we have the example of the windowing system. This system is used by every application but remains at a higher level than the kernel services that support such things as network connections. Indeed, Java ME similarly puts the user interface packages in the profile layer rather than in the configuration, and it puts the network connectivity in the configuration. Here, as anywhere in computer science, layering provides flexibility and helps manage complexity. These issues of layer creation are probably deeper questions than we need to concern ourselves with, but knowing what the big questions always help clarify even the least profound minutia.

1.3.4 Optional Packages

The last conceptual piece of Java ME is the optional packages. They provide more APIs addressing specialized functionality that we don't expect every device to implement in a profile. In short, they are optional. Optional packages of Java ME include support for such things as graphics, multi-media, Web services and wireless messaging. Over the years, there have been optional packages to Java SE as well. It's perhaps not always clear what makes a package optional or part of the main platform. However, in the case of Java ME, it's perhaps a bit clearer. Due to the inherent resource constraints of the base technologies, there is clear motivation to limit the APIs required for conformity with a given profile. Again, this makes sense. For now, the notion of optional packages seems rather straightforward.

There are many optional packages defined in Java ME. Some of the more common optional packages include support for such things as Wireless Messaging, Mobile Media, Bluetooth, and Location API. As with profiles and configurations, we are not required to concern ourselves with the full range of optional packages available. We are required only to know the Wireless Messaging API (WMA) and the Mobile Media API (MMAPI).

☞ **Note:** WMA and MMAPI packages are only optional in the scope of the Java ME conceptual architecture. They are optional because they are not deemed essential enough to be included in a configuration or profile-level component. However, if they are selected in the process of constructing a complete Java platform, they may become required components for the purposes of that newly constructed platform. Keep this in mind as we move forward.

1.3.5 Putting It All Together

Now we know what we will need to learn in the context of the SCMAD exam, let's put everything together to form the Java ME architecture in the context of the SCMAD exam as in Fig. 1.3. In fact, the figure is just a more specific version of Fig. 1.1.

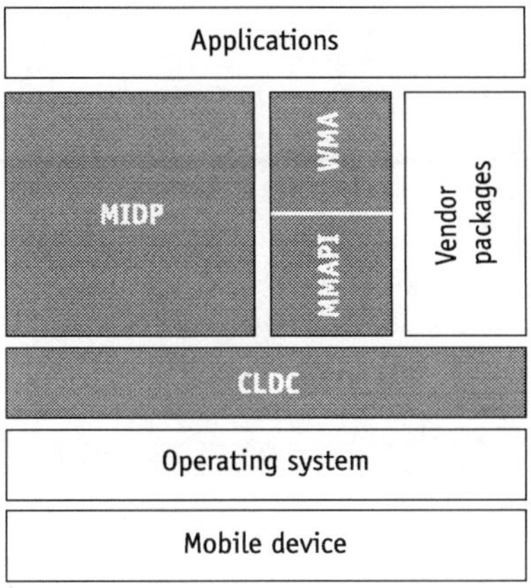

Figure 1.3 Java ME architecture in the context of the SCMAD exam

As we have discussed above, we are going to learn CLDC for the *configuration* level, MIDP for the *profile* level, and WMA and MMAPI for the *optional packages* level. While the *applications* level will contain all the mobile applications that we develop, the *operating system*, the *mobile device*, and the *vendor packages* levels are beyond the scope of this book as well as the exam.

Summary

Now, you have had your quick course on Java ME. So, are you an engineer or are you a developer? I think I'm kind of a hybrid myself. If the quick course has done its work, you should now understand the way Java builds cross-platform portability through the use of specifications. Although it seems a bit abstract at times, the principles of standardization and specification, while important throughout Java and computing in general, seem to be of an even more critical nature in the technological space addressed by Java ME. This is an exciting field. These are the early days of micro computing. One day everyone will take it for granted that you can write software for a toaster, but for now it's bleeding edge.

We've seen that Java ME is a bit different from the other editions of Java in terms of the flexibility and adaptability of its architecture. You should understand that this fluidity is a reflection of the high rate of change in the technologies that constitute target devices of Java ME. Hopefully, you understand how the conceptual elements of Java ME—*configurations*, *profiles* and *optional packages*—can be used as building blocks to construct stable target deployment environments. But you won't have to do that, thank goodness.

Several times we mentioned that Java ME covers a lot more material than what you learn for the SCMAD exam. We also mentioned that the looseness of the early attempts to assemble Java platforms for mobile phones, using the architecture of Java ME, had led to some problems such as

API fragmentation. Basically, it was determined that the flexible architecture was working well, but the early platforms left too much unspecified and that further clarifications needed to be made in order to guarantee a stable deployment environment. Again, this process of platform building, if you recall once again our beloved definition of Java ME, was pretty much the intention of Java ME creators. There's no need to slander the engineers. This leads us to our next chapter, which introduces JTWI. Building upon the work of the earlier attempts at building a Java ME-based platform for mobile phones, JTWI narrows the scope and tightens the requirements of these earlier platforms. JTWI and the platform it constructs is the subject of SCMAD.

References

1. Official Java ME website
   http://java.sun.com/javame/
2. A survey of Java ME today
   http://developers.sun.com/techtopics/mobility/getstart/articles/survey/

2

Chapter

Java Technology for the Wireless Industry (JTWI)

Exam Objectives

1.1 Identify the goals and characteristics of the JTWI specification (JSR 185), including:
- ❖ The mandatory specifications
- ❖ Conditionally required specifications
- ❖ The minimum configuration

Compare the relationship and differences between JTWI and other wireless Java technologies. (Section 2.1)

1.2 Develop portable applications that are compatible with the requirements and restrictions an application programmer must adhere to, in order to ensure compatibility with a JTWI-compliant device, including:
- ❖ Resource minimums (e.g., standard-size application)
- ❖ Clock resolution
- ❖ The use of preferred MIME names as applicable to CLDC 1.0/1.1, MIDP 2.0, WMA 1.1, and MMAPI 1.1)

(Sections 2.2, 2.3 and 2.4)

INTRODUCTION

In Chapter 1, we discussed about Java ME. In particular, we learned that Java ME represents an attempt to construct a version of the Java platform for the broad range of computing devices that fall outside, or perhaps beneath, the bounds of the standard laptop and desktop computers. In general, the Java platform represents an attempt to construct a stable runtime environment to allow for the development of fully portable applications. Java ME brings the same goals of interoperability to the realm of resource-constrained micro devices.

We also learned that Java ME, in an attempt to deal with the overwhelming variety of micro devices, introduces a uniquely flexible approach to the Java platform. Instead of defining a specific target environment for applications, Java ME specifies a flexible architecture of *configurations*, *profiles* and *optional packages* from which various elements can be selected to suit one's needs. This allows a variety of platforms to be constructed—all of which can meet the variety of target devices in this consumer-oriented sector of the technology market.

The advantage of the flexibility lies in the architecture's ability to anticipate and adapt to the rapid change, while providing a Java platform for now. The disadvantage of flexibility lies in the challenge it presents to full interoperability. Its patchwork architecture, combined with the multitude of optional functionalities, often results in applications that are developed to a too rigid platform. For instance, to develop a cell phone application that could send Short Message Service (SMS) messages, we would have to construct a platform using MIDP, the profile appropriate for cell phones, and WMA, an optional package of Java ME. As a testament to the adaptability of the architecture, this is easily done. The only drawback appears when one tries to download this application to a cell phone that doesn't implement the optional WMA. This is a minor case of API fragmentation. Things get much worse when more features are added to an application.

Is this a fault of Java ME design? No, this isn't. Before we jump to the conclusion that the optional package is at fault, we need to recall that Java ME covers a wide range of devices. Due to the wide range of devices supported, tight requirements would only exclude devices. As we noted in the introduction, it may be best to think of Java ME as containing an unknown number of editions of the Java platform unlike the tightly focused Java SE and EE. The problem remains, though. Flexibility and optional packages seem to be at odds with the concept of truly interoperable applications.

But it only seems this way. If we recall again that the architecture of Java ME intends for us to create platforms that are assemblages of its flexible components, we realize that the flexibility is the very thing that allows us to build stable platforms upon which interoperable applications can then be built. Building new platforms generally takes the form of new specifications. In our case, the Java platform for mobile phone is defined in JTWI.

At this point, all the engineers cheer, and all the developers groan. JTWI attempts to fix a stable development target within the moving space of Java ME. JTWI does a very simple thing. It reduces the range of devices that will be covered to the very specific set of devices known as mobile phones. Although the title is vague, it refers to the wireless industry. The language of the specification itself makes it very clear that it targets mobile phones. The stated goal of JTWI is to provide "a set of services to develop highly portable, interoperable mobile phone applications".

Perhaps, if you're an engineer, you will be able to identify the critical mechanism in specifications. It's quite simple really. If you want to tighten the specification, and thus stabilize a platform, you merely tighten the range of devices covered. In this case, JTWI reduces the range of devices to mobile phones. Suddenly, the motivation for a hyper-flexible architecture has been eliminated. If you are wondering how they made the decision to focus on mobile phones, rather than some other specific devices, you are not business-oriented. That particular choice was made by money. Recall that the expert groups that craft the specifications include key players from the wireless industry, and cell phone is one of the hottest consumer items in the history of the planet.

With the identification of a single target device, we can start nailing down precise definitions for all elements of the platform without the cost of excluding large portions of our target device base. We no longer have to be concerned with widespread coverage. Instead of offering a choice of profiles and configurations, we specify a single configuration and a single profile. Furthermore, we start eliminating the optional elements. As we mentioned earlier, the main goal of JTWI is to create a stable platform for mobile phones. Keeping this in mind, the JTWI specification has the following to say regarding optional elements:

> From the perspective of developers, system integrators, manufacturers and operators, each option increases the difficulty of understanding what is available on a particular device. Generally, JTWI seeks to reduce the number of options.

This makes the strategy of JTWI quite clear; all specifications should make themselves so clear. In order to make it possible for developers to start making highly portable, and thus marketable, applications, we need to focus on a single device, the mobile phone. Once we have a single device in mind, we start tightening the specifications by eliminating choices and options.

We need to be clear about one thing though. There's nothing wrong with Java ME. In fact, we can see JTWI as a demonstration of the strength and appropriateness of the flexible architecture. The flexible architecture lays the framework for the construction of more specific and more stable platforms as the need arises. Since the micro device market will probably remain richly innovative for some time to come, we can be thankful that there's a flexible edition of the Java platform ready to anticipate and quickly adapt to whatever demands those new devices might present. In the coming years, we can certainly expect to see other high-level specifications, similar to JTWI, that come along and attempt to create a stable platform for another more specific sector of devices.

Now we are ready to move on to discuss about the details of JTWI. Before that, we should point out that JTWI serves as an umbrella over a range of materials which will be covered in more detail through the book. Due to this, you should probably read this chapter now and then read it again after you go through the book. Although it makes sense to you now, it will be even more informative after you complete the book and have more knowledge about the specific technologies that fall within the scope of JTWI. All the pieces should fall into place. Also, you can refer to this chapter whenever you come across the relevant sections in the following chapters. We cover JTWI first because it is the organizational structure of all the rest of the material. Also, it is the subject of SCMAD exam. On the exam, you must be able to understand the other materials in the context of JTWI.

2.1 METHODOLOGY OF JTWI

In this section, we will examine more closely the strategies that JTWI employs. As we said before, the JTWI's main goal is to create a more stable platform for portable application deployment on mobile phones. So how exactly does JTWI achieve this? Mostly it identifies existing specifications from within the space of Java ME and then it attempts to tighten those specifications. JTWI does three things:

1. It identifies component specifications.
2. It upgrades certain optional elements of those component specifications to mandatory.
3. It clarifies areas that, under the component specifications alone, lack the specificity necessary for full portability.

In the next three sections, we will examine each of these three methods of platform building.

2.1.1 Component Specifications

The first thing that JTWI does is identify component specifications. JTWI can be thought of as an umbrella specification. By this, we mean that it doesn't in itself create any new features or technologies *per se*. Rather it defines a specific assemblage of existing specifications. Recall Sun's own language regarding the intent of the Java ME's flexible architecture:

> a collection of technologies and specifications that implementers and developers can choose from and combine to construct a complete Java runtime environment that closely fits the requirements of a particular range of devices and target markets.

JTWI embodies this concept. It combines a set of technologies and specifications from Java ME to construct a stable platform for mobile phones. JTWI refers to the elements that it aggregates as *component specifications*. Figure 2.1 illustrates how JTWI chooses a set of component specifications from within the space of Java ME.

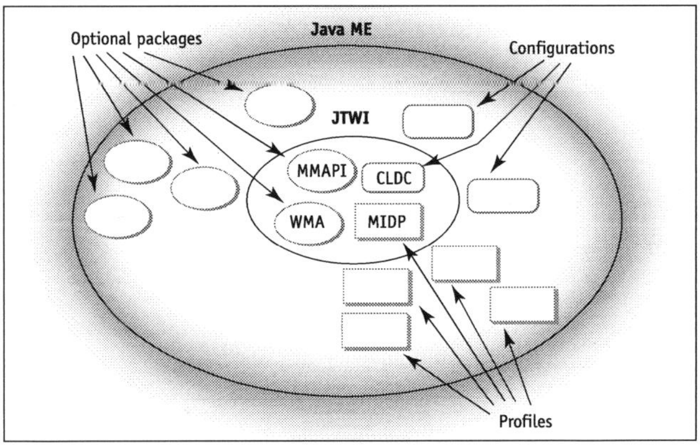

Figure 2.1 The JTWI's choice of component specifications client

JTWI distinguishes between three classes of component specifications: *mandatory*, *conditionally required* and *minimum configuration.* Mandatory specifications are those that must be implemented if the device is to be compliant. Conditionally required specifications are those that must be implemented on compliant devices when a certain condition holds true. Such a condition might include the presence of certain media functionality of the device. The third type of component specification is the minimum configuration specification. This type of specification identifies a minimum requirement that must be met. Table 2.1 lists the component specifications of JTWI, identifies its type and summarizes the role that it plays in the construction of a complete Java platform for mobile phones.

Table 2.1 JTWI component specifications and their purposes

Specification	*JSR*	*Category*	*Purpose*
CLDC 1.0	30	This specification is the *Minimum Configuration* for a mobile device. The device should be built upon this configuration.	Provides a common platform for basic functions like networking, utilities, etc. CLDC 1.1 is also acceptable.
MIDP 2.0	118	This specification is *Mandatory*. All JTWI-compliant devices must use this profile.	Provides API for user interface, security, persistence, gaming, simple audio support, and application lifecycle management API.
WMA 1.1	120	This specification is *Mandatory*. All JTWI-compliant devices must implement this API.	Provides support for CBS and SMS messages.
MMAPI 1.1	135	This specification is *Conditionally Required*. If a device supports rich multimedia capabilities (like polyphonic tones, MP3 playback, video capture, etc.), then it should support this API. If the device does not have such capabilities, it need not implement this API in order to be JTWI compliant.	Provides support for rich audio and video recording and playback. (Conditionally required).

For the configuration component, JTWI identifies the CLDC 1.0 as the minimum configuration. In Java ME, you could choose your own configuration depending on the needs of your target device. Now that the target device is no longer a big question mark, JTWI can focus on a specific configuration. Since we are working only with mobile phones, we can safely name CLDC as the configuration. Since this component specification is a minimal specification, we can use other configurations that satisfy all of the CLDC 1.0 requirements. For instance, we can use the CLDC 1.1 since it is superset of the CLDC 1.0.

For the profile component, JTWI mandates that the MIDP 2.0 be used. This is a non-negotiable mandatory component specification. However, with the focus on mobile phones, it is also the obvious choice for a profile. It is the MIDP after all. The other mandatory component specification of JTWI is WMA. Since wireless text messaging has become very popular (particularly in Asia and Europe), JTWI mandates the inclusion of WMA which defines API for messaging services such as SMS.

JTWI names one component specification as a conditionally required component specification. MMAPI specifies an API for exposing the underlying media capabilities of the device. Although some mobile phones might not have, or might not expose, existing media, the mobile phones that do choose to expose such media must do so by implementing MMAPI.

Exam Tip

Remember which specifications are mandatory and which are optional. It is also important to remember the version of each specification. Especially, remember that the minimum requirement for JTWI 1.0 is CLDC 1.0.

2.1.2 Promoting Optional to Mandatory

After identifying the component specifications, JTWI goes on to impose further tightening on each component specification. We noted earlier in this chapter that when specifications include optional requirements, this creates a barrier to the concept of portable applications. As we said before, JTWI strives to eliminate as much optionality as possible. We should note that we are now talking about a level of optionality that resides within the component specification themselves. Do not confuse this with the higher level optional packages of the Java ME architecture itself. This higher level optionality is eliminated when the platform builders choose their component specifications. You might have noted that a couple of these optional packages, WMA and MMAPI, are identified as component specifications by JTWI. Once chosen, they are no longer optional within the scope of JTWI.

But JTWI goes even further. In its effort to remove as much optionality as possible, it examines the internal details of each component specification in an effort to find optional requirements within the component specification itself. If possible, it removes this lower level optionality by making the requirements of the component specification stricter than they would be if the component specification stood by itself. A specific instance of this can be seen in the case of MIDP 2.0. JTWI identifies this profile as a component specification. As we can see in Fig. 2.2, the MIDP 2.0, standing on its own, specifies exactly that a compliant device must implement format support for PNG (Portable Network Graphics) image. Support for other image formats such as JPEG is optional.

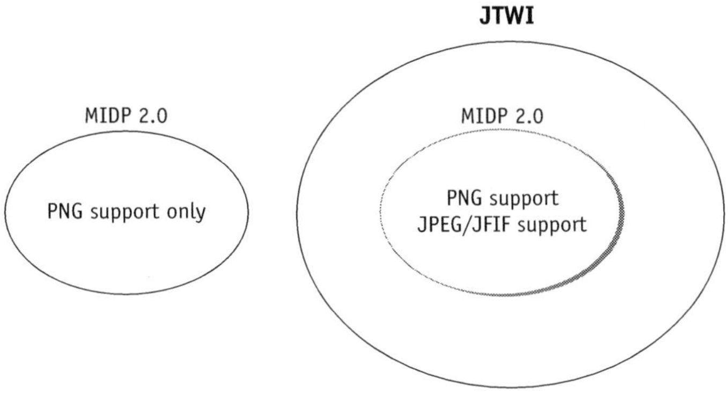

Figure 2.2 Reducing optionality in JTWI

JTWI eliminates this laxity by stating that compliant devices must implement support for both PNG and JPEG (Joint Photographers' Expert Group) /JFIF. We can see in Fig. 2.2 that when the MIDP 2.0 enters the space of JTWI, it must adhere to certain stipulations made by its host. This process of imposing tighter requirements within the space of the component specifications is the second method JTWI employs to tighten the specifications and create a stable platform. When we discuss each component specification in detail later in the chapter, we will know exactly where JTWI makes further impositions upon some of its constituency.

2.1.3 Clarifications

Lastly, JTWI sometimes clarifies certain concepts or requirements. Perhaps the component specifications left something a bit open-ended, or simply didn't address the subject. Much of JTWI focuses on eliminating areas of fuzziness by clarifying all requirements that might interfere with the creation of a stable platform for portable applications. JTWI, seeking to be transparent in its mechanisms, explains that "an overriding consideration for the inclusion of any single requirement was its impact on compatibility and interoperability."

Many of the clarifications pertain directly to some elements of one of the component specifications. These clarifications will be presented with the per component specification discussion that comes later in this chapter. Others clarify things that, though they might be loosely connected to a component specification, for one reason or another are best treated on their own. These items include such things as recommended system resources, application sizes and persistent storage details. The JTWI requirements for these will be treated in detail in the upcoming sections of this chapter.

Exam Tip

JTWI does not define any new features by itself. It only mandates or clarifies features already found in other specifications.

2.1.4 Technology Compatibility Kits

As with all Java specifications, a JTWI-compliant device is responsible for implementing all the requirements. For JTWI, this means that the compliant device must meet the requirements of each of the component specifications. In the world of Java specifications, a TCK provides the test suite for verifying compliance with a given standard. For JTWI, a compliant device must pass the tests of the TCKs for each of the component specifications.

2.2 REQUIREMENTS OF JTWI

The later chapters in this book discuss the requirements of the component specifications. Each of these component specifications is a mature specification of Java ME that has been implemented in devices long before the arrival of JTWI. Keeping that in mind, the later chapters will be dedicated to the specifics of each of these specifications and the ways in which they work together to provide a complete Java runtime environment. However, we said that JTWI makes some clarifications and further requirements in the space of these component specifications. The remainder of this chapter outlines the details of these additional requirements that JTWI introduces. You could think of the material covered by the rest of this chapter as the cement that JTWI uses to bind its component specifications together.

Earlier, we said that some of the requirements of JTWI extend beyond the scope of the component specifications. These requirements clarify things that might fall between the cracks if we limit ourselves strictly to the reach of the component specifications. So before we discuss the additional requirements imposed on the component specifications themselves, let's start with some requirements that don't exactly pertain to a certain component specification. Let's start with the device requirements.

2.2.1 Physical Device Requirements

One of the problems encountered in Java ME, which was not that apparent in desktop machines, is the varied form factor of the devices. Since mobile devices are consumer-oriented rather than business-oriented, the device manufacturers try to come up with creative ways to sell the devices. As a result, there are a number of models that vary significantly in their screen size and keyboard layout. While this is great for consumers, it's a nightmare for an application developer because he would have a hard time to ensure that his application is displayed properly across these screens and takes input in a user-friendly manner.

While MIDP covers these issues to certain degree, JTWI, which focuses on mobile phones, tries to clarify and tighten the requirements in this area. JTWI specifies strict requirements on some of the basic capabilities on a device. These requirements, as shown in Table 2.2, ensure that the applications written for a compliant device would behave similarly as on devices by various manufacturers.

Table 2.2 Device requirements

Feature	*Requirement*	*How to verify?*
Screen size at full screen mode	125 x 125 pixels	`Canvas.getHeight ( ) > = 125` `Canvas.getWidth ( ) > = 125`
Color depth	4096 colors (12 bits)	`Display.numColors ( ) > = 4096`
Pixel aspect ratio	1:1	
Volatile memory for Java runtime	256 KB	

If compliant devices meet these minimal requirements, developers can be more certain of the behavior of their applications. Devices can certainly exceed these requirements, but these are the minimum.

2.2.2 Standard-size Applications

JTWI also tries to clarify some requirements related to the deployment of the applications. Unlike a standard Java application, which is deployed as a JAR file, a Java ME application package is made of two files. One is the standard JAR file, which is a compressed version of all the class files that make up the application, and the other is a meta-information file called Java Application Descriptor (JAD) file that provides information about the installable. The JAD file is optional, but it is recommended that it be provided. The rationale behind a JAD file is quite simple.

Wireless data transfer is quite expensive (at least for now). Hence, it would be beneficial for a consumer to first check the size and details of an application that he wants to install in his device before downloading the whole thing. The JAD file is exactly that. It is a very small file (typically a few kilobytes) that tells the device installer about the size of the accompanying JAR file, general details about the vendor, and any specific features that the device must support for the application to work properly. The user can view this information and decide whether the JAR file is worth downloading.

In order to achieve smooth deployment and execution, JTWI makes some requirements on the size of the application JAR, accompanying JAD, and Record Management System (RMS). The requirements for applications that run on the devices, as shown in Table 2.3, focus on the maximum size that the device will support without complaining. While most devices support applications that are larger than the minimum sizes listed, the programmer must try to stay within limits to ensure maximum compatibility.

Table 2.3 Application requirements

Feature	*Limit*	*Description*
Java Application Archive (JAR) file size	64 KB	The size of an application JAR file up to which the device guarantees to support (sizes beyond this value may be supported by some devices, but not required to do so).
Java Application Descriptor (JAD) file size	5 KB	The size of a JAD file up to which the device guarantees to support (sizes beyond this value may be supported by some devices, but not required to do so).
Record Management System (RMS) data size	30 KB	The maximum size of data that each application can store in its RMS area without having issues (sizes beyond this value may be supported by some devices, but not required to do so). This works in conjunction with another attribute called `MIDlet-Data-Size`, which we will see in the next section.

When installing an application on the device, the device will check if the sizes of various artifacts in the application meet the minimum requirements as shown above. If not, then the application will not even be installed in the device.

☞ **Note:** These are the minimum requirements for the maximum sizes of different artifacts. This means that while a JTWI-compliant device may accept an application size that exceeds these minimums, you shouldn't develop to larger sizes if you want to guarantee portability, which is the whole point after all.

Exam Tip

JTWI specifies only the minimum requirements for various aspects of a device and the application that is installed on the device. This means that the compliant device must at least support these requirements and may optionally provide more than what is needed.

Some exam questions might test your knowledge in this area. Also, remember that there is a difference between the MIDP minimums and the JTWI minimums. In fact, you could just forget the MIDP minimums as far as SCMAD is concerned. The exam focuses only on JTWI with regard to minimum requirements.

2.2.3 Storing and Retrieving Data

Part of the size requirements pertain to the data storage available to the application. Java ME devices that use the MIDP profile use RMS to store application-specific data. Compared to a traditional database, RMS is a relatively simple mechanism to store and retrieve data. This is mainly due to the limited resources available in the underlying device.

Each application that is installed on a device can specify the minimum amount of memory required for its data store by using the `MIDlet-Data-Size` attribute in the JAD file. JTWI mandates that the value specified should not be greater than 30 KB. This amount, and no more, is guaranteed by the platform. The device will then check whether that space is available in the system. If it cannot satisfy this requirement set forth by the application, the device will not install the application. If the device has the space, it will reserve that space for the application after installing it. Even if the application does not use all of it, the space requested will still be reserved and will not be given out to other applications.

Hence, care must be taken to specify this value. If you specify a value too high, newer applications might be rejected during installation due to lack of space. On the other hand, an application can store more than what it requested after installation. The device will allow the application to do so as long as it has space to spare. However, if there is no space, then it is the application's responsibility to handle the error. Figure 2.3 illustrates the tradeoff of setting the `MIDlet-Data-Size` value high and low.

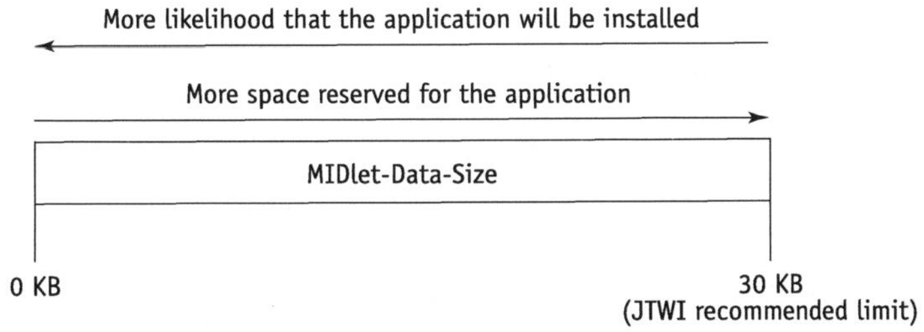

Figure 2.3 The tradeoff of setting the `MIDlet-Data-Size` value high and low

The application can use the `RecordStore.getSizeAvailable()` method to retrieve the size (in bytes) allocated by the device for the application's record store to check whether enough space is available to store more records during runtime. This must be greater than or equal to the application's `MIDlet-Data-Size` value.

An application must also be able to create at least five record stores, provided there is enough space. That is, a system should not limit the application to create less than five record stores if it has enough space to accommodate them. Of course, it can always allow more than five record stores to be created. We will discuss this in detail in Chapter 8.

☞ **Note:** JTWI-compliant device must support a minimum of five record stores.

2.3 REQUIREMENTS AND CLARIFICATIONS ON COMPONENT SPECIFICATIONS

The last few sections discussed the bonding that JTWI uses to hold its component specifications together. These are the requirements that JTWI defines outside the scope of its component specifications. In all, JTWI doesn't make many requirements of this nature. Now we will look at the clarifications and additional requirements that JTWI imposes on the component specifications.

2.3.1 Requirements on Minimum Configuration: CLDC

A configuration provides fundamental language support to a Java ME application along with some basic functionalities like network support. As JTWI 1.0 is targeted for wireless devices that may have very little memory or processing power, it defines CLDC specification, which has been specially defined for devices with such constraints, as its minimum configuration. Since this is a minimum specification, a compliant device could implement any superset of the CLDC 1.0, such as the CLDC 1.1 or any other configuration that meets the superset requirement.

Now, let's look at how JTWI imposes some further stipulations on its component configuration. First of all, JTWI identifies a condition under which the minimum configuration changes from the CLDC 1.0 to the CLDC 1.1. If a device supports floating point operations and exposes that functionality through Java APIs, the device must implement CLDC 1.1, which includes floating point support.

Exam Tip

A JTWI device must support CLDC as its configuration. At least version 1.0 must be supported. Any higher versions may also be optionally supported.

The following sections cover a few more requirements made upon CLDC. These mostly fall under the category of clarifications of things not specifically pinned down by CLDC.

System Requirements

CLDC, as a configuration, is concerned mainly with system-level operations. The requirements mandated at this level by JTWI are given below.

For Multi-threaded Applications Any elaborate application with a complex UI scheme would almost always require multiple threads in order to provide a smooth interface to the user. Since the ability of the Virtual Machine installed on a device varies with the device's capacity to provide this, JTWI enforces certain minimums so that the applications can at least rely on a reasonable set of threads that would be available across all compliant devices.

Applies to

`java.lang.Thread` instances

Requirement

At least 10 threads should be able to run simultaneously.

Rationale

The application should be able to run at least 10 threads simultaneously. This is independent of the requirements on `Timers` that will be explained in "Working with `Timers`" section.

For Clocks Keeping time is not only harder for humans but is harder for computers also. Depending on the quality of the timing system installed inside a device, the accuracy of internal clock might vary. Hence, JTWI provides a requirement based on probability rather than a requirement based on an absolute value for clock resolution.

Applies to

`System.currentTimeMillis()`

Requirement

Maximum allowed difference between two successive `System.currentTimeMillis()` calls must be not more than 40 ms for at least 80 percent of the time.

Rationale

8 out of 10 times, the difference in time noted between two successive time calls should not be greater than 40 ms.

> **Exam Tip**
>
> The requirements mentioned previously are the most commonly used and hence would be tested more in the exam. There are other less common features in CLDC that have been clarified by JTWI.

Using TimeZones

`TimeZone` is a class provided in the CLDC API that can be used to represent various time zones. Since mobile devices can be truly international and an application can often be operated in different time zones, having such a class can be quite useful. We shall discuss more about this class in the CLDC chapter. For now, do remember that CLDC 1.0 and 1.1 mandate only GMT (00:00) for the `Time Zone` class. JTWI expands it further and provides specification for providing custom time zones. If the time zone is not specified, or the string does not match the syntax shown below, GMT is assumed.

A `TimeZone` instance can be created as follows.

```
TimeZone zone = TimeZone.getTimeZone(timeZoneString);
```

where `timeZoneString` is of the format `GMT{+|-}nn<:>nn` and `n` is a number from 0 to 9 and the colon between < and > is optional.

For example,

```
GMT+0000
GMT0010
GMT+05:30
+8
```

You can always get this `String` back from a `TimeZone` object using the `zone.getID()` method. The returned value will have a colon (:) between the hours and minutes. If the sign is not given or if the `String` does not begin with 'GMT', then the value defaults to 'GMT'.

Encoding Strings

Encoding generally defines the character set that is used by a `String` object. This mechanism is used by Java to support strings based on different character sets. This is normally specified in a `String` or in a data stream in order to decipher the characters properly. Some common encodings are UTF-16 and US-ASCII.

There are several encoding schemes defined by the Internet Assigned Numbers Authority (IANA). Most encodings have a preferred MIME name. JTWI requires that a device must always understand the preferred MIME name when available for the character encodings supported by the device.

The standard Java API supports the full Unicode 3.0 (and now Unicode 4.0 since Java SE 5) to support internationalization. Since the wireless device memory is quite small, the CLDC API had to cut corners to keep its footprint small. As a result, the CLDC API supports only a subset of the Unicode character set as a minimum. Among the characters specified in Unicode, JTWI mandates that a device must at least support "Basic-Latin" and "Latin-1 Supplement" blocks, which are located in ISO Latin-1 range. As always, a JTWI-compliant device may choose to support more character sets.

2.3.2 Requirements on Profile: MIDP

As JTWI caters to mobile phones, MIDP is the mandated profile. This profile is designed for mobile devices such as cell phones and other wireless devices that have a small screen and small memory size. JTWI requires that a compliant device should support at least version 2.0 of the MIDP specification.

Additionally, JTWI makes some extra requirements in the space of MIDP. These additional requirements primarily pertain to optional features of MIDP. JTWI tries to eliminate as many optional elements as it can by upgrading them to required, thus stabilizing the platform and increasing portability. Let's have a look at the requirements imposed by JTWI on MIDP.

Exam Tip

At least MIDP version 2.0 must be supported by a device to be JTWI-compliant.

General Requirements

These requirements define some constraints or mandates on existing features. The constraints are mainly imposed to ensure that an application can find out if the device complies with JTWI specifications, some basic requirements on storage and network connectivity, and support for event-based handlers.

The `System.getProperty(String)` method in the standard edition of Java, which is useful to get various pieces of information pertaining to JVM, CLDC also comes with a `System` class that contains a `getProperty(String)` method that, not surprisingly, can be used for the same reason. JTWI specifies that at least one property should be present—the one that identifies its version.

Applies to

`System.getProperty(String key):String`

Requirement

The value returned by the key "`microedition.jtwi.version`" must be "`1.0`".

Rationale

This is similar to Java version number in Java SE applications. This is pretty useful in finding if the device is JTWI-compliant or not dynamically. This method will be discussed more in the CLDC chapter.

Networking Requirements

Wireless devices that support Java ME, at the least, require an Internet connection. Not only is a connection useful for supporting applications that have richer features than simple standalone applications (maybe except gaming), they are also used for transferring applications from a server to the device. JTWI requires that for various download features, including application download and other media download as might be required by applications, a compliant device must support the standard HTTP protocol.

Applies to

The classes in the `javax.microedition.io` package

Requirement

Minimum HTTP version support for media content download must be 1.1.

Rationale

Device must at least support HTTP 1.1 according to the MIDP 2.0 specification. This will be explained further in the Networking chapter.

Push Registry Alarms

Push Registry is a very interesting feature that has been added in the second version of MIDP. In short, it allows an application to perform some event-based operations (far beyond a simple `Timer` class) over a network connection. For example, you can start an application if some data comes to a particular port in your device. We will elaborate on this feature further in the MIDlet chapter.

Applies to

`javax.microedition.io.PushRegistry` class

Requirement

Alarm-based push registry events must be implemented with MIDP 2.0 security mechanism or explicit user permission.

Rationale

MIDP 2.0 introduces a cool feature called Push Registry that allows an application to be 'waken up' based on some events. JTWI requires that this feature must be supported by compliant devices.

Since the automatic 'waking up' can be used inappropriately, JTWI also mandates that such events must be declared using the MIDP 2.0 security mechanism or if such a mechanism is not available, explicit permission from user is required before getting activated.

Imaging Requirements

It is possible to represent images in a MIDP application using the `javax.microedition.lcdui.Image` class.

MIDP 1.0 supported only PNG, a lossless format. Lossless formats represent pixels in an image as they are, and consume more memory. On the other hand, lossy formats normally use some algorithm to compress the pixels in order to make the image size smaller. As mobile devices are already memory-constrained, this is definitely preferable.

Hence, JTWI included a requirement to support JPEG/JFIF—a lossy format—for MIDP 2.0. Among the many variations and algorithms that come under the JPEG umbrella, only baseline, non-differential, Huffman coding is required to be supported by the device. The device is also expected to support a color depth of up to 32 bits (in increments of powers of 2), with a support for up to 32,768 pixels for each color depth.

As some of the encodings might have some licensing requirements, JTWI also provides an escape clause. It says that if the format, at any point, becomes licensed, then the device does not need to support that format from then on.

Also, an important point to note is that even if the phone does not have a color display, it must still be able to process color images. While this might look a bit awkward at first, this would not be a problem because currently, almost all the JTWI-compliant phones are color phones anyway.

Working with Timers

The `Timer` class provided in the `java.util` package in the MIDP API provides features that would allow an application to perform event-based actions, such as alarm, stop clock and so forth. Since the time-keeping mechanism and the accuracy may vary from device to device, it would be hard to specify an absolute requirement. Hence, the JTWI proposes a requirement based on probability as shown in Table 2.4. Since a `Timer` also works using a `Thread` as it has to run in the background, the JTWI provides restrictions on the minimum number of threads that must be available exclusively for the `Timer` feature.

Table 2.4 Timer class requirements

Feature	*Requirement*	*Description*
Timer resolution (applies to the `firstTime, delay,` and `period` parameters of `java.util.Timer.schedule` method)	not more than 40 ms	The requirement for resolution is similar to the system time resolution in CLDC. That is, the resolution should be honored at least 80% of time, because in some cases, garbage collection might mess up the resolution times.
Minimum `Timers` (applies to `java.util.Timer` class)	5 instances	The device should allow an application to create at least five `Timer` instances. Since each `Timer` is normally run on a separate thread, this requirement is independent of the minimum requirements for a `Thread`.

User Interface Requirements

Probably the most obvious and eye-catching feature of an application would be its user interface. If a user interface is not friendly or simple, a user may simply be put off from using the application. One other typical function that a user interface performs aside from being pretty is to validate the user input so that he does not send junks to the application, causing it to crash.

Since mobile devices are even more sensitive to user interfaces compared to standard desktop systems because of their limited size and since the types of data that the user can enter typically fall within a pre-defined set of fields (Phone number, Email, etc.), JTWI stipulates tight requirements on these features. These specific requirements are summarized in Table 2.5.

Applies to

`javax.microedition.lcdui.TextBox` and
`javax.microedition.lcdui.TextField` classes

Requirements

Table 2.5 MIDP user interface requirements

Constraint	*Requirement*
`TextField.PHONENUMBER`	A compliant device must implement a mechanism for picking a number from the device's phone book, if it is available and accessible. (But the phone book itself should not be accessible to the application, only the numbers, and that too for lookup only.)
`TextField.ANY`	A compliant device must support the following Unicode characters (but no need to memorize for the exam): U000A (line feed) U0020–U007E (standard keyboard characters) U00A1, U00BF (inverted characters) U00A7 (section mark) U00A3–U00A5, U20AC (currency signs) Additional characters may also be supported, but this is the minimum requirement.
`TextField.EMAILADDR` `TextField.URL`	A compliant device must allow the same characters as those of `TextField.ANY`.

Rationale

These extra specifications are provided to ensure that the user input mechanisms are consistent across different implementations. These will be explained further in the MIDP UI chapter.

2.3.3 Requirements on Messaging Support: WMA

One of the most common and popular uses of mobile phones has been messaging. Although it has not caught the fancy that much in the United States yet, sending text messages is hugely popular in Asian and European countries. Keeping this in mind, JTWI mandates WMA as a required component specification. Additionally, JTWI makes some further requirements in the space of WMA, such as promoting some optional elements to mandatory status.

JTWI 1.0 specification emphasizes that a JTWI-compliant device must support the WMA 1.1 specification and that:

> If the phone is based on GSM/WCDMA technology, it must support SMS protocol as specified in the WMA 1.1 specification

and

> If the phone supports Cell Broadcast Service (CBS), it must follow the specification as in WMA 1.1.

A combination of text messaging support with the Push Registry mechanism (as discussed earlier) can be very powerful. For example, an application provided by a vendor installed on the mobile device can be started by sending a message to that device. This feature can be very helpful for providing updates, notifications, and even product advertisements.

JTWI specification also emphasizes that GSM-based devices must support Push handling for the SMS protocol. However, one must also be aware that most service providers charge a fee for SMS support, either as a subscription or as a per-message fee. Hence, spamming might prove to be very expensive. As a result, JTWI specifies that if a proper security mechanism is not provided by the device, the Push Registry support for SMS must not be allowed without explicit user permission.

2.3.4 Requirements on Multimedia Support: MMAPI

MMAPI is a package that provides support for rich multimedia functions like MIDI playback support and video capture. While the MIDP 2.0 provides some basic multimedia functions like support for monotones, MMAPI is much more flexible and has much more features. Since one cannot expect all mobile devices to have video support, this API is conditionally required component specification of JTWI. That is, if the device has features specified in the MMAPI (like video), and the device wants to expose these features to the Java platform, this exposure must be through the MMAPI. Additionally, if the MMAPI is implemented, certain further requirements are imposed within the space of that API.

Getting Data to Device

As mentioned earlier, the device must at least support media content download via HTTP 1.1 protocol. MMAPI does not define any protocol. This has been tightened in JTWI.

Hearing Sounds

Since the MIDI format provides reasonable support for sophisticated audio with a very small memory requirement, JTWI mandates that MIDI file handling and playback must be supported. This would be very useful for gamers and ring tone developers.

Apart from MIDI format, JTWI also mandates support for the Tone Sequence file format, a much simple format that can be used to generate monotones.

MMAPI provides an ability to control the audio and video streams using an interface called `Control`. Among the several possible controls, JTWI mandates that a device must at least support the `VolumeControl`, for obvious reasons.

Exam Tip

While JTWI requires support for MIDI playback, it does not require the device to support the `MIDIControl` interface.

Seeing Things

MMAPI supports video capturing and viewing. These features have been designed for devices that have in-built cameras capable of capturing images or short videos.

JTWI requires that the JPEG format must be supported for video capturing.

2.4 TRUSTING APPLICATIONS

We have covered the requirements that JTWI makes on its component specifications. But we have one last topic to cover. It is so important that it must have its own section. Since the beginning, Java has been known for its tightly-integrated support for security. This becomes all the more important in mobile devices as some features in a device may incur a huge cost to the user if not properly authenticated. With this in mind, the MIDP specification includes classes that can be used to provide security to the application in terms of installation, access and functionality.

Again, JTWI seeks to tighten the platform by imposing some further requirements on the existing specifications. In this case, security is already defined in the MIDP 2.0's own *Recommended Security Policy for BSM/UMTS Compliant Devices.* For the more specific needs of JTWI, this policy is not clear enough on several issues. In particular, the realm of untrusted applications needs much clarification.

2.4.1 Trusted and Untrusted Applications

It is possible that an application that is being installed on a device may or may not provide its security constraints. An application that is signed using the security mechanism in the form of encrypted certificates specified in MIDP 2.0 is said to be trusted. Such an application normally specifies what it would do with regard to security-sensitive features such as network access using specific parameters (`MIDlet-Permissions` and `MIDlet-Permissions-Opt`) in the descriptor file.

An application that is not signed is said to be untrusted. When such an application tries to access network resources, it should get permission from the user explicitly. JTWI 1.0 expands this particular section of the MIDP 2.0 security mechanism and provides strict guidelines for the behavior of an untrusted application. Also, it must be noted that JTWI 1.0 only provides specification for GSM/UTMS based devices and only recommends the same (but not mandates) for devices using other technologies.

JTWI 1.0 requires that the application must let the user know if the application is trusted or untrusted. If it is not trusted, it must notify the user explicitly and provide enough information to the user about the source of the application so that the user can decide whether or not to install the application or to allow the application to do some security-sensitive action, like connecting to the Internet.

Exam Tip

JTWI clarifies the security requirements only for untrusted applications because the requirements for trusted applications are clearly defined in MIDP 2.0 specification.

2.4.2 Security Permissions

Security requirements for an application can be provided by the user in the descriptor files (JAD and manifest) that accompany an application. In general, the constraints are broadly divided into three groups, as described in Table 2.6. JTWI 1.0 classifies various security-sensitive features in the following categories:

Table 2.6 Security requirements

Group	*Features*	*Description*
Network	Net access	Features that need a network connection
	Messaging	Features that send and/or receive SMS, MMS, or other equivalent messages
	Auto invocation	Features that allow an application to be started automatically based on some event (like push, timer, etc.)
	Local connectivity	Features that connect to a local port like IrDA, Bluetooth, etc.
User privacy	Media recording	Features that record audio, video, or capture images
Other		Anything that is not covered in the above two categories

The idea of having groups is that in devices that have a small display, it might not be user-friendly to show all features under a specific group to the user and ask if it's OK for the application to carry on. Instead, the user can just view the groups and their summary and decide whether what the application is trying to do is acceptable to him or not.

Also, if the user wants to create new security groups, care must be taken to ensure that it is not redundant with other groups, as it might end up cluttering the user interface that displays the groups.

Individual security permissions are covered thoroughly in the chapter on MIDP 2.0 security.

Summary

Now you should be able to understand the beauty of Java ME and the engineering cleverness it manifests. Java ME attempts to provide a flexible architecture that contains a set of building blocks from which a Java platform may be constructed on an overwhelming range of resource-constrained devices. JTWI takes up the challenge and constructs a platform from these building blocks tailored specifically for mobile phones. It doesn't define any new technologies; it merely assembles a platform from the flexible elements of Java ME.

Since JTWI narrows the scope of supported devices to mobile phones, it takes advantage of this to eliminate much of the looseness that is inherent in the broader scope of its component specifications. JTWI clarifies and tightens requirements both within the space of these component specifications and in some of the gaps that they don't cover. But, as we have seen, these gaps are not actually that large.

For the exam, you certainly need to know the component specifications of JTWI. You should be able to differentiate between the various types of component specifications, such as those that are mandated and those that are conditionally required. You will also need to know the additional requirements and clarifications that JTWI imposes on the component specifications. And, of course, you'll have to know the details of each of these component specifications themselves. The rest of the book gets down to business and covers the nuts and bolts of how the component specifications are used to build portable applications. Enough with the engineer geek stuff, let's get on to the developer geek stuff.

References

1. Java Technology for the Wireless Industry (JSR-185)
   http://www.jcp.org/aboutJava/communityprocess/final/jsr185/
2. Understanding JSR 185 by Jonathan Knudsen
   http://developers.sun.com/techtopics/mobility/midp/articles/jtwi/

Exercises

1. Write a small program that will print out the following details in the default output console. Use an emulator to run the program. You can take a small peek at Chapter 5 (MIDP UI) to get started, or you can come back and complete this exercise after finishing the MIDP UI chapter.
   a. The value of the property "`microedition.jtwi.version`"
   b. Width of the screen at full screen mode
   c. Height of the screen at full screen mode
   d. Number of colors supported by the device
   e. Size available for a record store

   After looking at the output, do you think your device emulator satisfies the JTWI requirements for the tested properties?

Review Questions

1. Which Java ME configuration is the minimum requirement for JTWI 1.0 compliance?
   a. CLDC 1.0 b. CLDC 1.1
   c. CDC 1.0 d. CDC 1.1
2. JTWI 1.0 specification mandates that a device must support at least 5 simultaneous threads, including those used for `Timers`.
   a. True b. False
3. Which protocol must be supported by a JTWI 1.0-compliant device to download media content?
   a. HTTP 1.0 b. FTP
   c. HTTP 1.1 d. Bluetooth/OBEX
4. Which of the following statements are true regarding JTWI 1.0's clarifications on the MIDP 2.0 security model?
   a. JTWI 1.0 clarifies statements in MIDP 2.0 for applications that are trusted and untrusted.
   b. JTWI 1.0 is concerned only with GSM/UTMS based phones and does not mandate anything for phones based on other technologies.
   c. If a user tries to access a feature that is sensitive or might incur a cost to the user, then the device that is JTWI 1.0 compliant must explicitly ask the user for permission.
   d. A device implementing JTWI 1.0 need not have any security constraints.
5. What would be the maximum file size that a JAD file can have in order to be safely supported by a JTWI 1.0-compliant mobile device?
   a. 2 KB b. 5 KB
   c. 30 KB d. 64 KB
6. Which of the following image file formats must be supported by a JTWI 1.0 compliant device?
   a. PNG b. TIFF
   c. JPEG d. BMP
7. Which control interface must be supported by a JTWI 1.0-compliant device that supports MMAPI 1.1 specification?
   a. `MIDIControl` b. `RecordControl`
   c. `VideoControl` d. `VolumeControl`
8. The supported character set for a `TextField` object having the constraint `TextField.EMAILADDR` is all alphanumeric characters along with the special characters @, _, and . (period).
   a. True b. False

9. What is the minimum number of colors that should be supported by a device that conforms to the JTWI 1.0 specification?
   a. 256
   b. 4096
   c. 32768
   d. 65536
10. Which of the following statements would characterize a JTWI 1.0-compliant device?
    a. The device implements MIDP 2.0 specification.
    b. The device is not Internet ready.
    c. The device can play MIDI files.
    d. All applications installed in the device will be trusted applications.

Review Answers

1. a. CLDC 1.0 is the minimum configuration that must be supported by a device that is JTWI 1.0 compliant. While JTWI 1.0 suggests that CLDC 1.1 can also be supported by compliant devices, it is not mandatory.

   JTWI 1.0 is intended mainly for wireless devices such as mobile phones. CDC targets more powerful devices such as PDAs and TV set-top boxes and hence, is not covered under JTWI 1.0 specification.
2. b. JTWI 1.0 mandates that a compliant device must support at least 10 simultaneous threads regardless of the number of `Timer` threads (which must be at least 5).
3. c. While MMAPI 1.1 does not specify a particular protocol that must be implemented by a device to support media download, JTWI 1.0 mandates that the device must at least support HTTP 1.1 protocol for media content download.
4. b and c. JTWI 1.0 clarifies the security requirements only for the untrusted applications. Trusted applications must follow the guidelines specified in the MIDP 2.0 specification. JTWI 1.0 also focuses only on GSM/UTMS devices. Devices based on other technologies are out of the scope of the specification, but are recommended to follow a similar security model.
5. b. JTWI 1.0 requires that a compliant device must support JAD files at least up to 5 KB. Files greater than this size may be supported by the device, but is not required to do so.
6. a and c. MIDP 1.0 requires that implementing devices must support PNG format for images. This is a lossless format. That is, data is stored without any compression. As most of the devices are resource-constrained, JTWI 1.0 added the JPEG/JFIF file format, a lossy format as a part of the image support requirement.
7. d. JTWI 1.0 requires that if a device supports the MMAPI 1.1 specification, then it must at least implement the `VolumeControl` interface.
8. b. If a `TextField` has the constraint `TextField.EMAILADDR` or `TextField.URL`, that instance must support all characters supported by the constraint `TextField.ANY`, which is more than the three special characters mentioned in the question.

9. b. A device that complies with the JTWI 1.0 specification must support at least 4096 colors.
10. a and c. Since JTWI 1.0 requires that a device must implement WMA 1.1, which requires an Internet connection, the device must be Internet ready. Applications installed in a JTWI 1.0-compliant device may be untrusted, as long as the device explicitly asks for user permission when the application tries to access sensitive information or connect to the Internet.

Exam Notes

☞ Identify the goals and characteristics of the JTWI specification (JSR 185), including the mandatory specifications, conditionally required specifications and the minimum configuration. Compare the relationship and differences between JTWI and other wireless Java technologies.

Goals and Characteristics of JTWI

The goal of the JTWI specification is to improve the compatibility, interoperability and completeness of Java ME technology implementations in mobile phones.

- The specification specifies a set of component specifications that must or should be implemented by compliant devices.
- The specification mandates some of the optional sections of the component specifications to improve compatibility.
- The specification clarifies some portions of the component specifications.

Mandatory Specifications

- These specifications must be implemented for a device to be JTWI-compliant.
- MIDP 2.0 (JSR-118) and WMA 1.1 (JSR-120) fall under this category.

Conditionally Required Specifications

- As the name implies, these specifications are required based on certain conditions. For example, if a specific feature is going to be provided by the device, the related specification must be implemented fully by the device. If the feature is not going to be provided, the device does not need to implement the specification.
- MMAPI (JSR-135) falls under this category.

Minimum Configuration Specifications

- This specification is the minimal specification needed for a JTWI-compliant device to run.
- CLDC 1.0 (JSR-30) falls under this category.

Relationship between JTWI and Other Specifications

- The JTWI specification is a specification on top of specifications. It is used to clarify other specifications and to mandate some of the optional elements in those specifications.
- Future versions of the given set of specifications are also acceptable for JTWI compliance. For example, a device may implement CLDC 1.1 and still be JTWI 1.0 compliant.
- JTWI version obtained using the key "`microedition.jtwi.version`" must be 1.0.

Specification	*Required?*	*Details*
MIDP 2.0	Yes	Some requirements are clarified. Some optional elements are made mandatory.
WMA 1.1	Yes	JTWI does NOT mandate specific underlying technology to implement (GSM/CDMA). GSM/CDMA (UMTS) phones *must* support the GMS SMS service and *must* also support Push Registry mechanism. If a security mechanism is not present, the SMS push function *must not* be allowed without explicit user permission.
MMAPI 1.1	No	JTWI mandates certain media types to be supported. Separate requirements have been specified for audio-only devices and audio-video devices. If implemented, MMAPI 1.1 *must* be the minimum version. MIDI file playback and tone sequence format *must* be supported. `VolumeControl` must be implemented. If video image capturing is supported, JPEG encoding in video snapshots *must* be supported.
CLDC 1.0	Yes	JTWI uses CLDC 1.0 as the minimum configuration. CLDC 1.1 is also usable.

☞ Develop portable applications that are compatible with the requirements and restrictions an application programmer must adhere to, in order to ensure compatibility with a JTWI-compliant device, including resource minimums (standard-size application), clock resolution, and the use of preferred MIME names as applicable to CLDC 1.0/1.1, MIDP 2.0, WMA 1.1 and MMAPI 1.1.

Resource Minimums

Resource	*Method to use*	*Minimum requirements*
Screen width	`Canvas.getWidth()`	125 pixels
Screen height	`Canvas.getHeight()`	125 pixels
Color depth	`Display.numColors()`	4096 colors (12 bits)
Pixel aspect ratio		1:1

Volatile memory for runtime		256 KB
JAR size		64 KB (at least up to this size)
JAD size		5 KB (at least up to this size)
RMS data size	`MIDlet-Data-Size` property can be used for specifying a minimum reservation.	30 KB (at least up to this size)
Minimum thread count		10 threads
Minimum clock resolution	`System.currentTimeMillis()`	40 ms (the least difference between two calls 80% of the time)
Record stores		5 record stores (at least)
Media content protocol		HTTP 1.1
Image formats		ISO/IEC JPEG or JFIF must be supported to be JTWI-compliant. PNG must be supported to be MIDP 2.0-compliant.
User interface		Selection of phone numbers from a phone book for the `TextField.PHONENUMBER`
`Timers`		5 `Timer` instances (at least)

Preferred MIME Names

- Implementations must support at least the preferred MIME names as defined by IANA for the supported character encodings. Some examples are
  - US-ASCII
  - UTF-16
- Compliant implementations must provide support at least "Basic Latin" and "Latin-1 Supplement" encoding. Other encodings may be supported optionally.

Content type	*MIME name*
JAR file	application/java-archive
JAD file	text/vnd.sun.j2me.app-descriptor
WML	text/vnd.wap.wml
MIDI file	audio/midi
Tone sequence	audio/x-tone-seq
MP3	audio/x-mpeg
AU	audio/basic
PNG	image/png
JPEG	image/jpeg

Part-2

Mobile Application Essentials

CLDC and MIDlets play very important roles in developing applications in Java ME platform. In this part of the book, you'll learn the goals, requirements, scope and characteristics of CLDC (a configuration on which mobile applications are built) and the lifecycle of a MIDlet and the MIDP application model, as specified by the SCMAD exam objectives.

Let's go ahead and begin to explore these fundamentals.

3

Chapter

Connected Limited Device Configuration (CLDC)

Exam Objectives

2.1 Identify correct and incorrect statements or examples about the requirements and scope of the CLDC specification, including the differences between 1.0 and 1.1. (Sections 3.1 through 3.3)

2.2 Describe the ways in which a CLDC virtual machine does and does not adhere to the Java Language Specification (JLS) and the Java Virtual Machine specification. (Section 3.4)

2.3 Identify correct and incorrect statements or examples about CLDC classes including those derived from Java SE, and the CLDC-specific classes, including identifying which core Java SE classes are NOT included in CLDC, or have different behaviors (for example, java.lang.String and io classes). (Section 3.5)

2.4 Given the differences and limitations of exception/error handling with CLDC devices, handle exceptions correctly. (Section 3.6)

2.5 Write code that effectively manages memory and garbage collection. (Section 3.7)

INTRODUCTION

In the conceptual architecture of Java ME, a complete Java platform is built from the choice of a configuration, a profile and a set of optional packages. Each of these elements plays an important and specialized role in the creation of a complete Java runtime environment. The role of the configuration is to provide low-level core functionality. The role of the profile is to remain on top of the configuration and provide higher level functionality through higher level libraries. The role of optional packages, perhaps obviously, is to provide functionality that isn't common enough to be considered as a fundamental ingredient of the platform. In Fig. 3.1, we can see the layering of these elements. In this chapter, we look at the details of the configuration element chosen by JTWI.

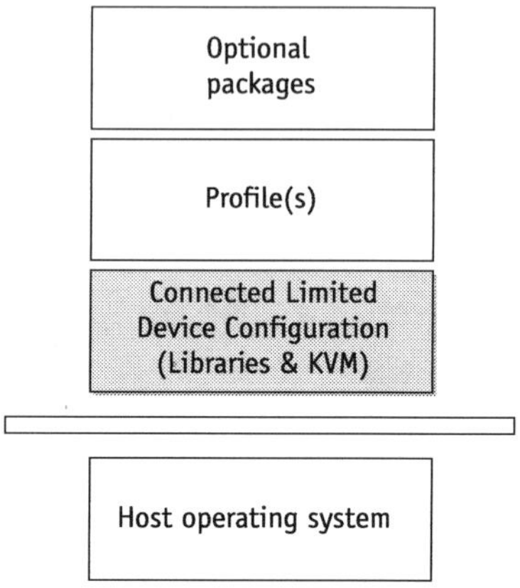

Figure 3.1 High-level architecture of Java ME using a CLDC configuration

The main components of a configuration are its implementation of a JVM (commonly referred to as KVM), typically a subset of the full JVM of Java SE, and a set of libraries that provide core functionality, typically a subset of the core libraries of Java SE. The core functionality provided by the configuration includes such critical elements as networking, installation and low-level management of applications, and security. JTWI, in building a Java platform specifically for mobile phones, identifies CLDC as its configuration.

The main goal of CLDC is to provide a configuration for a class of devices characterized by restricted memory, restricted processing power, restricted power supplies and restricted network connectivity. From this we can see the derivation of the configuration's name. The device is limited in resources and connected to the Internet. One should note that CLDC covers a much broader range of devices than JTWI which covers only mobile phones. CLDC covers, in addition to mobile phones, devices ranging from PDAs to home appliances. Indeed, the role of a configuration within the conceptual architecture of Java ME is to provide the core of the Java platform for a very broad range of devices. By definition, core functionality should be consistent across a wide range of cases, thus we should expect that a single configuration element meets the needs of a variety of devices. As in most layered architectures, specialized functionality is implemented in higher layers. The scope of the functionality provided by a configuration aims to be as inclusive as possible. Keeping this in mind will help you understand the logic that places some libraries in the profile rather than in the configuration. It will also help you understand the logic that JTWI employs when articulating its clarifications and further requirements upon the component specifications.

Exam Tip

Connected Limited Device Configuration (CLDC) = Core Libraries + Kilobyte Virtual Machine (KVM)

As mentioned before, JTWI defines the CLDC 1.0 as the *minimum configuration.* Any configuration providing at least the functionality of the CLDC 1.0 would be compliant. Specifically, the CLDC 1.1 can be used, and must be used, if the implementation desires to provide floating point support. For the exam, it is important to understand the requirements and the scope of the specification along with the difference between the 1.0 and 1.1 versions. The floating point support is the biggest addition, and 1.1 remains fully backward compatible with 1.0.

☞ **Note:** Since 1.1 is a minor revision of 1.0 (i.e. there aren't many differences), and the exam objectives include knowing the differences between 1.1 and 1.0, we will focus on 1.1 in this chapter. Our reasoning is that if you know 1.1 and its differences with 1.0, you know 1.0 by default.

We will cover a lot of terrain in this chapter, so let's start with a road map. First, we will look at the ways in which CLDC fulfills its role as a configuration as defined by the conceptual architecture of Java ME. We will see how CLDC makes certain concessions to the limitations of the target devices while still trying to provide them with a powerful Java core. Finally, since the configuration layer is the home of garbage collection, we will even take a look at some memory management techniques that will help you write efficient code. In other words, we will start with some abstract engineering lingo and end with some practical tips for writing fast, real world code. Enjoy the ride!

3.1 UNDERSTANDING THE GOALS, REQUIREMENTS AND SCOPE

As a configuration, CLDC aims to define the minimal set of features that provide a complete Java platform. The broad range of micro devices that are the targets of CLDC shares a common set of constraints and needs. These common characteristics drive the goals, requirements, and scope of CLDC.

3.1.1 High-level Goals

As we have already seen, the main goal of CLDC specification is to standardize a highly portable, minimum footprint Java application development platform for resource-constrained, connected devices. The primary goals of CLDC specification are:

- **Smaller footprint**

  The target audiences for CLDC devices are price-conscious customers who will shy away from the devices if it turns out to be too expensive. So, one of the primary goals of CLDC is to make sure that CLDC could run on devices without the need for any expensive hardware and software, thereby keeping the increase in per-unit price of the device to a minimal level. Thus, the memory requirements of the CLDC-compliant devices are set as low as possible.

- **Application programming platform**

  For the devices covered by CLDC, the Java platform provides the means to deploy user-oriented applications and not system-level applications. This allows CLDC to target its included libraries towards a higher level development interface. Such APIs might expose the transfer of data on the Internet at the file level rather than at the protocol level.

- **Dynamic delivery of content and third-party applications**

  Most devices covered by CLDC are not extensible beyond the default factory implementation. However, the consumers expect dynamic behavior and applications in the devices. The dynamic addition of user applications to the device provides much of the incentive for devices to be compliant with Java specifications. With this in mind, one of the main goals of CLDC is to support the dynamic installation of Java applications.

3.1.2 Requirements

As CLDC applies for a wide range of devices with varying capabilities, it is not possible to define a strict common hardware and software requirements. For example, a mobile phone may offer only a limited display, non-multitasking kernel with no persistent storage where as a PDA could have a better display, multitasking OS with a proprietary file system. Since CLDC has to run on both these extreme conditions, CLDC does not lay down any fixed rules.

Exam Tip

CLDC specification defines only minimum limits.

Hardware Requirements

In an effort to be as inclusive as possible, CLDC remains agnostic towards the underlying hardware and specifies only requirements for the amount of memory ultimately available to the Java platform:

- At least 160 kilobytes of non-volatile memory is available for the virtual machine and CLDC libraries.
- At least 32 kilobytes of volatile memory is available for the virtual machine runtime.

Non-volatile memory does not go away when the device is powered down. This chunk of the memory must be permanent to store the JVM and libraries. The volatile memory can be used for runtime needs. It is not that device implementation must follow the exact ratio (160:32) that CLDC 1.1 specification assumes. Depending on the target device and the role of the Java platform in the device, the ratio may vary. It is just the recommendation of the CLDC 1.1 that, of 192 kilobytes minimum memory budget, 160 kilobytes should be available for non-volatile memory usage, and 32 kilobytes for volatile memory usage. Figure 3.2 illustrates this.

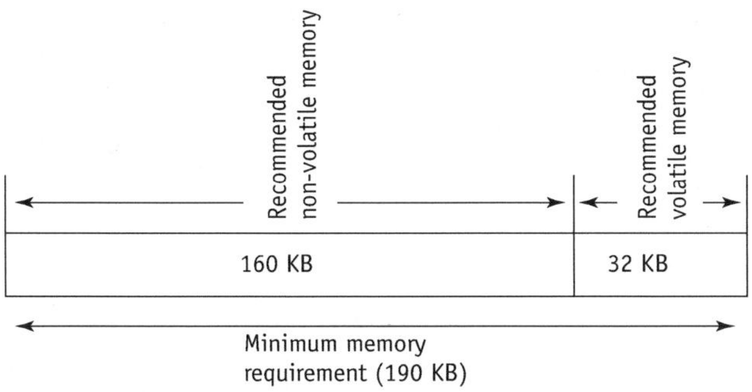

Figure 3.2 Recommended memory allocation in CLDC 1.1

Exam Tip

Remember these numbers inside out.

Software Requirements

CLDC places similarly low requirements on the underlying operating system of the devices. Indeed, almost nothing is required except that the JVM be run. In particular, CLDC assumes only:

- The presence of a minimal host operating system or kernel to control the device resources
- A schedulable entity (A task or a thread) to run JVM

  And, notably, the following common features of more robust operating systems are not required:
- Support for separate address spaces or processes
- Real-time scheduling or latency behavior guarantee

Java ME Requirements

Some other guiding principles in the design of CLDC are motivated by the conceptual architecture of Java ME itself. As a Java ME configuration, CLDC must service the intent of a configuration as defined by the Java ME architecture. With this in view, CLDC complies with the following three architectural constraints.

- As per the definition of the configuration, CLDC is allowed to define only the "common minimal" or "lowest common denominator" features to support the wide range of devices. This implies CLDC as such cannot leverage the complete potential of the target devices and it requires the specific profiles to unleash the complete feature set of the device. A device-specific profile built over a generic configuration is the ideal combination for Java ME devices.

- CLDC should not define any optional features as it compromises the promise of portability and interoperability. As one expects, the optional features are specified by the profiles.
- As a configuration is a subset of Java SE, CLDC should be compatible with Java Language Specification (JLS) and Java Virtual Machine Specification (JVMS), and any deviation or difference from this behavior should be properly specified by the CLDC specification.

3.1.3 Scope

As we have discussed at length, the functionality of a full Java ME runtime environment is divided between a configuration and a profile. This division between the two stems from the architectural goals of Java ME. We will now discuss the scope of CLDC as it applies to this division of functionality. As CLDC is the first layer above the host operating system, it defines the following basic functionalities needed by higher layer APIs:

- Java language and virtual machine features
- Core Java libraries (`java.lang.*, java.util.*`)
- Input/Output (`java.io.*`)
- Security
- Networking (`javax.microedition.io.*`)
- Internationalization

Apart from the features listed previously, other remaining areas are covered by either the profiles or the optional packages. Some common examples of such features are shown in Table 3.1.

Table 3.1 Examples of features not defined by CLDC but implemented by other mechanisms

Feature	*Typical implementation by*
High-level application (i.e. MIDlets) installation and lifecycle management	Profiles
User interface functionality	Profiles
Event handling	Profiles
High-level application model (the interaction between the user and the application)	Profiles
Multimedia support	Optional package
Wireless connectivity	Optional package
Access to Bluetooth network	Optional package

Exam Tip

CLDC defines only bare minimal features. Anything that looks lavish on the features probably isn't defined by CLDC.

As you can see in Table 3.1, the configuration leaves non-core functionality to the other elements of the Java ME architecture. These non-core things include support for higher level application models, which provide more convenient abstractions that allow software developers to create richer applications in shorter periods of time. They also include obviously non-core functionalities such as support for device-specific multimedia bells and whistles. Core can be a relative notion, but by now you should be getting a sense of what ground is covered by the configuration and what types of things are left to the profiles and optional packages.

3.2 KNOWING CLDC APPLICATION CONTRACT

The CLDC defines the concept of an application. When the CLDC talks about the concept of an application, it is talking about a low-level version of an application. This means it defines an application at the level of the basic units of Java execution. What does the JVM recognize as a executable unit of Java code. This key concept is the start of everything, especially security. Luckily, a CLDC application's contract is very simple. Like in Java SE, any CLDC class with a method named `main` which is *public, static* and *void* defines the entry point of a CLDC application.

Before we go any further, we should address a potential point of confusion regarding the concept of an application. (I apologize as we're certainly entering engineer territory again, but, alas, what else can we do?) In the scope of JTWI, there are actually two concepts of a Java application: a high-level one and a low-level one. At the configuration layer, we definitely are referring to the lowest level idea of an application, as defined in the previous paragraph. However, when we get to the profile level, we will meet with a higher level abstraction of the concept of an application. These higher level applications are similar to applets or servlets. They do not have a `main` method entry point. They execute on a higher level of abstraction defined by a set of managed lifecycle methods. In the sense of the low-level application defined in the previous paragraph, they are not true Java applications. The true low-level applications, in these cases, are the server that starts the servlet and the Java Runtime Environment (JRE) plug-in that starts the applet. The higher level application used in JTWI, the MIDlet, will be discussed at length in Chapter 4.

Exam Tip

An executable CLDC class must have a `public static void main(String[] args)` method.

3.3 DIFFERENCES BETWEEN CLDC 1.0 AND CLDC 1.1

As we said before, the CLDC 1.0 is the minimum configuration for JTWI but you can focus on the CLDC 1.1 as long as you know the differences between the two. The CLDC 1.0 specification was well-accepted by the market except for a few shortcomings such as the lack of floating point support and weak references. The CLDC 1.1 specification adds the crucial features and does not differ much from CLDC 1.0 specification in terms of the core architecture and feature set. It is fully backward compatible. The exam does not require the knowledge of CLDC 1.0 specification but requires you to understand the incremental features that were added in CLDC 1.1 specification. The new features can be categorized as:

- **Floating point support**

  Floating point math was not present in CLDC 1.0 since it was a processor intensive operation. Starting from CLDC 1.1, floating point operations are supported with the addition of `Float` and `Double` classes and the addition of various methods in the other library classes to handle floating point operations. The CLDC VM now supports the complete set of floating point byte codes.

- **Minimum memory requirement**

  Because of the addition of floating point support, the minimum total memory (i.e. Volatile + Non-volatile) got increased from 160 Kilobytes to 192 Kilobytes.

- **Addition of weak reference support**

  A weak reference aids in a better garbage collection by maintaining references to elements in a table of canonical objects. If memory becomes low, any of the weakly reachable objects (that are referred to by the table and not referred to anywhere else in the application) are garbage-collected.

- **Error handling**

  The `NoClassDefFoundError` present from JDK 1.0 is now added to signal the condition when the JVM tries to load the class definition and it could not be found. In addition, the error handling requirements have been clarified to remove the ambiguity present in the previous version.

- **Thread handling**

  CLDC threads can now have a name like their Java SE counterparts. This results in addition of couple of constructors and a method to return the name. Table 3.2 shows the new constructors and methods.

Table 3.2 New additions in `java.lang.Thread` class of CLDC 1.1

Constructor/Method	*Description*
`Thread(Runnable target, String name)`	Allocates a new `Thread` object with the given target and name.
`Thread(String name)`	Allocates a new `Thread` object with the given name.
`public String getName()`	Returns the thread's name.
`public void interrupt()`	Interrupts the thread.

- **Better alignment with Java SE**

  The utility classes `Calendar`, `Date` and `TimeZone` have been redesigned to be more Java SE-compliant.

- **Miscellaneous changes**

  The specification text is less ambiguous than before and obsolete sections have been removed to precisely convey the meaning. In addition, the class verification is explained in detail and minor changes like addition of new methods in the `String` class are in place. Table 3.3 lists the methods and fields that have been newly added to the CLDC 1.1.

Table 3.3 New methods and fields added to the CLDC 1.1

Constructor/Method	*Description*
`String.intern()`	Returns a canonical representation for the `String` object.
`String.equalsIgnoreCase()`	Compares the `String` to another `String`, ignoring case considerations.
`Random.nextInt(int n)`	Returns a pseudorandom, uniformly distributed int value between 0 (inclusive) and the specified value (exclusive), drawn from the random number generator's sequence.
`Date.toString()`	Converts the `Date` object to a `String`.
`Thread.interrupt()`	Interrupts the thread.
`Boolean.TRUE`	The `Boolean` object corresponding to the primitive value `true`
`Boolean.FALSE`	The `Boolean` object corresponding to the primitive value `false`

Apart from the methods listed in the previous table, CLDC 1.1 also includes various methods to handle floating point operations in various classes as mentioned before.

Exam Tip

It is very important to be able to identify which methods are available only in CLDC 1.1. The exam usually contains questions that ask the examinees to identify the methods/classes/fields in a way or another.

3.4 KILOBYTE VIRTUAL MACHINE

Since the configuration layer provides core functionality, we should be surprised to find a virtual machine at the heart of every configuration. KVM is the virtual machine used by CLDC and is a derivative of the standard JVM written with an aim to provide modular, extensible and a fast implementation with a smaller footprint. JRE for a Java SE distribution had grown into enormous proportions over the years, and Java SE versions definitely cannot be used in resource-constrained devices. Thus, the Java SE virtual machine was rewritten as KVM for the mobile environment where kilobytes are still the yardsticks for storage capacity. It was written from the scratch using the C language.

Supporting the entire feature set defined by JLS and JVMS requires more resources than available to the devices supported by CLDC. Hence, the KVM (also known as CLDC VM) designers consciously decided to avoid certain troublesome or unnecessary features to keep up with their aim of smaller footprint VM. The exclusion of certain features was guided by the high-level goals of CLDC as discussed earlier in this chapter. Although the exam does not require you to understand the specifics and internals of KVM, you still need to know how the KVM differs from JLS and JVMS.

3.4.1 Non-adherence to JLS

The CLDC environment tries to be as compliant as possible with JLS. Nonetheless, some concessions have been made due to the resource constraints of the target devices. The points of deviation from the specification are as follows.

Object Finalization

Finalization helps in cleaning up resources before getting garbage-collected. But is it an unreliable mechanism since the order in which finalizers are run and whether they would run depends on the underlying JVM implementation? Hence, they are not advised as a routine cleanup mechanism and should be used only in rare cases like cleaning up memory allotted in native methods or as a fallback cleanup mechanism for releasing resources.

The finalization mechanism defined by JLS requires some complex processing to be done by JVM during the garbage collection of the instances. Since it is rarely useful even in the context of Java SE and the cost of implementation is heavy, CLDC avoids this feature altogether and therefore you will neither find `finalize` method in `java.lang.Object` nor `runFinalization` in `java.lang.System` and `java.lang.Runtime` classes in CLDC.

Exception and Error Handling

The `Exception` class hierarchy in Java SE is huge and many of them may not be applicable to the resource-constrained Java ME environment. So, only a limited number of `Exception` classes are supported by CLDC. The exception handling mechanism remains the same with the exception (no pun intended) of *asynchronous exceptions* such as `InternalError`. Since they are expensive to implement, CLDC avoids them. On a similar line, support for error handling is very much limited due to the resources required to implement a 100 percent JLS-compliant error recovery mechanism.

We will discuss more about the exact exceptions and errors supported by CLDC later in this chapter. Till then, remember that the exception and error handling is limited in CLDC.

☞ **Note:** Most of the exceptions are synchronous in nature, as they are triggered by the actions of the thread in which they occur and at a specific point where there is a possibility for the exception to be thrown. On the other hand, asynchronous exceptions (like `java.lang.InternalError`) can occur at any point of time during the execution of an application. Asynchronous exception handling mechanism is complex to design and luckily, KVM avoids it.

3.4.2 Non-adherence to JVMS

JVM is an abstract computing machine and JVMS defines the instruction set, file formats and verification mechanisms supported by it. Due to the lack of a full-fledged security model in CLDC, many features have been eliminated from the CLDC virtual machine. These include features like user-defined class loaders, thread groups and daemon threads, finalization of class instances and support for asynchronous exceptions. Two-phase class file verification has been added in JVM to efficiently perform class file verification.

User-defined Class Loaders

CLDC does not support user-defined class loaders. Any class required by the application shall only be loaded by the built-in bootstrap loader which cannot be modified, configured or replaced by the application.

In addition, the class lookup order cannot be modified. In Java SE, you can typically alter the class lookup order using the `classpath` environment variable or similar mechanism. This is not possible with CLDC. You will understand these features better when the CLDC security is discussed later in the Security chapter.

Exam Tip

Class lookup order cannot be modified. It just means that there is no `classpath` variable, which you can use to alter the loading order of your classes.

Thread Groups and Daemon Threads

CLDC provides support for threading, but does not allow the creation of thread groups or daemon threads. So you will not find any methods like `setDaemon(boolean daemon)` or

ThreadGroup ridden constructors in the Thread class of CLDC like its Java SE counterpart. The absence of ThreadGroup is really not a limitation as you can mimic the behavior by manually creating a collection object to hold your group of threads.

Class File Verification

The Java SE VM verifies that the classes loaded are satisfying the constraints of the language to prevent any possible problems. Similarly, the CLDC VM also verifies the class files so that invalid class files are rejected. The standard Java SE class file verification's memory requirements are expensive and the load on the processor for the complex iterative dataflow algorithm is enormous for resource-constrained devices. So an efficient two-phase verification process is implemented for CLDC VM. This uses lesser memory and a linear algorithm that is less demanding on the processor. The verification happens as shown in Fig. 3.3.

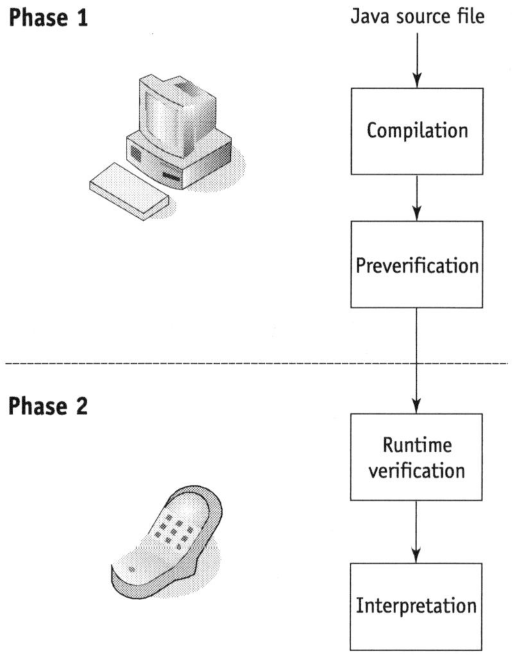

Figure 3.3 CLDC class file verification

Phase 1: Preverification (Off-device)

The class files are run through a preverifier, which inlines all subroutines, removes certain byte codes and add special StackMap attributes to facilitate runtime verification. The developer generally performs this preverification phase with a tool on his workstation.

Phase 2: In-device verification

The runtime verifier uses the augmented `StackMap` attributes to perform a linear scan on the byte code and completes the verification. This process happens in the device when it tries to load a class.

Exam Tip

The exam does not require the detailed knowledge of the CLDC class file verification. Just remember that it is different from the standard behavior and happens in two phases.

3.5 CLDC LIBRARY

Now that we have covered the JVM implementation of CLDC, we need to look at the core set of libraries that it defines. These libraries provide the low-level functionality of the Java platform. In addition to providing core programming support, the creators of CLDC identify connectivity as a high-priority goal of the core libraries of CLDC. Every Java programmer is familiar with the core packages of Java SE such as `java.lang` and `java.util`. Many of these packages are included in CLDC as well. However, stripping down to a minimal subset, in an effort to meet device resource requirements, is not as easy as just choosing a desirable subset of functionality. Extricating the subset of the highly interdependent full set of packages can be difficult. Due to this, some of the basic classes have been rewritten to work within the new limited environment. Hence, the libraries of CLDC can bc divided into two groups. First, there are the libraries that are directly inherited from Java SE. Second, there are the libraries that are specific to CLDC.

Table 3.4 Summary of CLDC libraries

Origin	*Package(s)*

Derived from Java SE	`java.io`
	`java.lang`
	`java.lang.ref`
	`java.util`

CLDC-specific classes	`javax.microedition.io`

The exam requires a thorough knowledge of classes that belong to CLDC and those which are derived from Java SE and the way they differ from the Java SE counterpart. We will see them one by one, grouped according to their functionality, in the following sections. As you can see in Table 3.4, CLDC defines its own dedicated I/O package. The `javax.microedition.io` package will be dealt in detail when we discuss about CLDC networking in a later chapter. For the moment, remember that any class you see from the package`javax.microedition.io` exclusively belongs to CLDC.

3.5.1 System Classes

Table 3.5 lists some of the fundamental classes of CLDC. As there is no support for finalization, the `java.lang.Object` lacks the `finalize` method. Also since cloning is not allowed, there isn't any clone method in the `Object` class. Reflection is not supported and hence a number of methods that support reflection have been omitted in the `java.lang.Class`. Accessing of native code libraries, running native programs, accessing and modifying of security manager are all prohibited by the VM and hence you will not find the corresponding methods in classes like `java.lang.Runtime` and `java.lang.System`. But both these classes support the famous `gc()` method for signaling the garbage collector to reclaim unused objects. Methods for setting the daemon flag and constructors with thread group names cannot be seen in `java.lang.Thread` class. Starting from CLDC 1.1, the `java.lang.String` and `java.lang.StringBuffer` classes contain methods that support float and double data types.

Table 3.5 System classes and interfaces

Class/Interface in CLDC	*Limitations/ Differences w.r.to corresponding Java SE class*
`java.lang.Object`	No `finalize` method No `clone` method
`java.lang.Class`	No support for reflection API
`java.lang.Runtime`	No support for executing commands using `exec()` No support for shutdown hooks No support for running finalizers
`java.lang.System`	No support for native library invocations No support for accessing/mutating security manager No support for running finalizers
`java.lang.Thread`	No support for daemon threads No constructors with `ThreadGroup` functionality
`java.lang.Runnable`	Same as in Java SE
`java.lang.String`	Minimal support for internationalization CLDC 1.1 defines support for `float` and `double` data type conversions CLDC 1.1 defines `equalsIgnoreCase()` method CLDC 1.1 defines `intern()` method
`java.lang.StringBuffer`	CLDC 1.1 defines support for `float` and `double` data type conversions No support for `substring()` or `replace()` operations
`java.lang.Throwable`	No support for dynamic stack traces No support for exception chaining

3.5.2 Data Type Classes

Table 3.6 lists the data type classes available in CLDC. Each of the listed classes is a subset of the corresponding Java SE class. Since floating point operations are supported from CLDC

1.1, two new data type classes, `java.lang.Float` and `java.lang.Double`, have been added.

Table 3.6 Data type classes

Class in CLDC	*Limitations/ Differences w.r.to corresponding Java SE class*
`java.lang.Boolean`	CLDC 1.1 defines `Boolean.TRUE` and `Boolean.FALSE` constants
`java.lang.Byte`	
`java.lang.Short`	
`java.lang.Integer`	
`java.lang.Long`	
`java.lang.Float`	Since CLDC 1.1
`java.lang.Double`	Since CLDC 1.1
`java.lang.Character`	Conversion operations and properties are valid only for ISO-Latin 1 character set

3.5.3 Collection Classes

The support for collection classes in CLDC reminds the collection classes supported in Java Development Kit (JDK) 1.1. The Java SE collection framework is completely avoided due to resource constraints and hence the collection classes do not inherit from a common interface like in Java SE. Table 3.7 shows the collection classes that are available in CLDC.

Table 3.7 Collection classes and interfaces

Class/Interface in CLDC	*Limitations/ Differences w.r.to corresponding Java SE class*
`java.util.Vector`	Few missing methods like `add`, `clear` and `toArray`
`java.util.Stack`	Same as in Java SE
`java.util.Hashtable`	The load factor is always 0.75 (75%) and cannot be modified
`java.util.Enumeration`	Same as in Java SE

3.5.4 Input/Output Classes

CLDC supports reading and writing of byte streams as well as character streams. `java.io.ByteArrayInputStream` and `java.io.ByteArrayOutputStream` can be used to read and write byte arrays from the stream using an internal buffer. The `java.io.DataInputStream` and `java.io.DataOutputStream` can be used to read and write primitive Java data types in a portable way. The `java.io.InputStreamReader` and `java.io.OutputStreamWriter` are used for reading and writing characters from a byte stream. The supported character encodings varies with the implementation. Table 3.8 summarizes the list of input/output classes and interfaces of CLDC.

Table 3.8 Input/Output classes and interfaces

Class/Interface in CLDC	*Limitations/ Differences w.r.to corresponding Java SE class*
`java.io.InputStream`	Subset of Java SE
`java.io.OutputStream`	Subset of Java SE
`java.io.ByteArrayInputStream`	Subset of Java SE
`java.io.ByteArrayOutputStream`	Subset of Java SE
`java.io.DataInput`	Same as Java SE
`java.io.DataOutput`	Same as Java SE
`java.io.DataInputStream`	Subset of Java SE
`java.io.DataOutputStream`	Subset of Java SE
`java.io.Reader`	Subset of Java SE
`java.io.Writer`	Subset of Java SE
`java.io.InputStreamReader`	If encoding is not specified, value defined in the `microedition.encoding` system property is used. If encoding is not available, `UnsupportedEncoding Exception` is thrown.
`java.io.OutputStreamWriter`	Subset of Java SE
`java.io.PrintStream`	Subset of Java SE

Figure 3.4 illustrates the hierarchy tree that contains all the I/O classes that are located in the `java.io` package of CLDC 1.1.

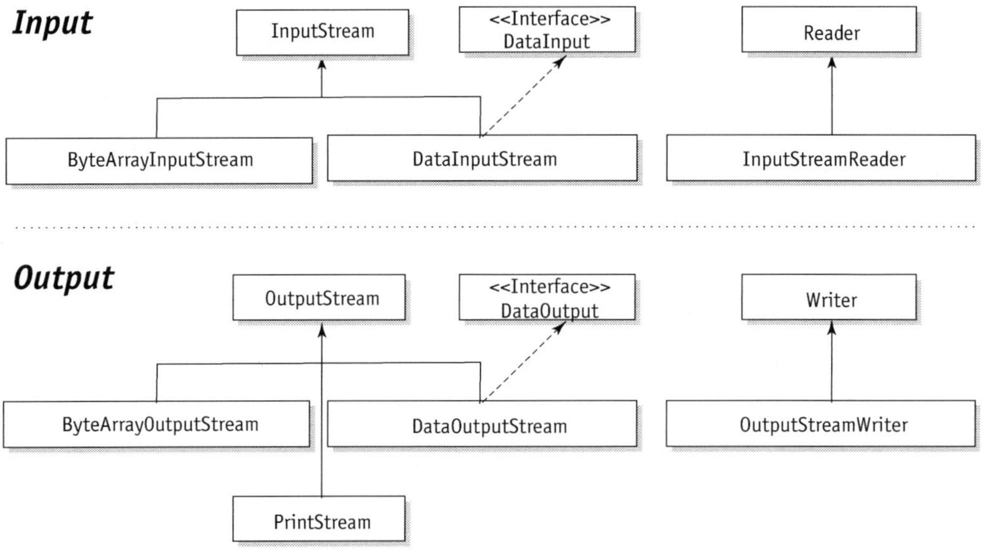

Figure 3.4 I/O hierarchy of `java.io` package in CLDC 1.1

3.5.5 Calendar and Time Classes

There is limited support for calendar and time, with the three classes that are listed in Table 3.9. CLDC supports only one time zone and by default, it is set to the Greenwich Meridian Time (GMT). The CLDC implementations may provide additional time zones but they must be compatible with the time zones supported by Java SE.

Table 3.9 Calendar and Time classes

Class/Interface in CLDC	*Limitations/ Differences w.r.to corresponding Java SE class*
`java.util.Calendar`	A subset of the JDK 1.3 counterpart
`java.util.Date`	A subset of the JDK 1.3 counterpart
`java.util.TimeZone`	Only GMT is required to be supported. The rest are optional.

3.5.6 Additional Utility Classes

Table 3.10 lists the `java.util.Random` class, which is a pseudo-random number generator, and the `java.util.Math` class that offers standard mathematical functions such as minimum, maximum and absolute. The `java.util.Math` class supports the trigonometric functions, square root calculation, floor and ceil operations starting from CLDC 1.1. Also, new overloaded versions of the existing functions to support `float` and `double` data types have been introduced in CLDC 1.1.

Table 3.10 Additional utility classes

Class/Interface in CLDC	*Limitations/ Differences w.r.to corresponding Java SE class*
`java.util.Random`	Subset of Java SE
`java.lang.Math`	Only basic math operations are defined.
	In CLDC 1.1, basic trigonometric methods (`sin`, `cos`, `tan`) have been added.
	In CLDC 1.1, constants have been added for PI and E.

There is no `random` method in any of the utility classes.

3.5.7 Weak Reference

As we have already seen in Section 3.3, the following two classes that are listed in Table 3.11 have been added in CLDC 1.1 to provide weak reference support in the CLDC VM.

Table 3.11 Weak reference classes

Class/Interface in CLDC	*Limitations/ Differences w.r.to corresponding Java SE class*
`java.lang.ref.Reference`	Since CLDC 1.1
`java.lang.ref.WeakReference`	Since CLDC 1.1

3.5.8 Property Support

In CLDC, there is no `java.util.Properties` class as in Java SE to deal with system-related properties such as the version of the operating system, the version of the virtual machine and so forth. Due to the limited capability of the CLDC devices, a limited set of properties is available to the application to retrieve. Table 3.12 lists the available system properties in CLDC that the application can retrieve using the method `System.getProperty(String key)`.

Table 3.12 System properties available in CLDC

Key	*Description*
`microedition.configuration`	Name and version of the current configuration
`microedition.encoding`	Default character encoding of the system
`microedition.platform`	Name of the host platform
`microedition.profiles`	List of profiles separated by blanks

The properties listed in Table 3.12 are just the ones that are defined in CLDC. More properties might be available at the profile level. In addition, vendors may store their own vendor-specific properties in the system and make them available through the application. But vendor-specific keys should be prefixed with the same package name that the vendor-specific classes use, for example, "`com.scmadkit.propertyname`", because the words "`microedition`", "`java`" and "`javax`" are reserved for the official Java ME configurations and profiles.

Now we have learned all the classes of CLDC that are derived from Java SE, but the exception- and error-related classes. We are going to learn the mechanism that CLDC applies to handle exceptions and errors in the next section.

3.6 HANDLING EXCEPTIONS AND ERRORS

An exception is an event that disrupts the normal flow of instructions during the execution of an application. It can occur due to any reasons ranging from logical bugs in the application (such as violating business rules) to serious hardware errors (such as running short of resources). In Java, an exception is represented by an instance of the `Throwable` class or one of its subclasses. This exception object can then be treated by an exception/error handler constructed using a `try-catch-finally` mechanism.

The `RuntimeException` class and its subclasses, and the `Error` class and its subclasses are called unchecked exceptions. All the other exception classes are checked exception classes and need to be declared as a part of the method contract using the `throws` clause of the method. With this introduction, let us see the CLDC's support for exception and error handling.

3.6.1 Exception Handling

The CLDC exception handling is very similar to the behavior defined by JLS except the lack of support for asynchronous exceptions. Table 3.13 summarizes the CLDC supported exception classes classified into different categories along with brief descriptions.

Table 3.13 CLDC exception classes

Application management	
Exception class	*Description*
`java.lang.RuntimeException`	Superclass of the exceptions that can be thrown during the normal operation of JVM
`java.lang.SecurityException`	Thrown to indicate a security violation
`java.lang.ClassNotFoundException`	Thrown when the definition for the specified class is not found while loading a class
`java.lang.InstantiationException`	Thrown when an application is unable to instantiate an object because the specified class is an abstract class or an interface
`java.lang.IllegalMonitorStateException`	Thrown to indicate that a thread has attempted to wait on an object's monitor or to notify other threads waiting on an object's monitor without owning the specified monitor
`java.lang.IllegalThreadStateException`	Thrown to indicate that a thread is not in an appropriate state for the requested operation
`java.lang.InterruptedException`	Thrown when a waiting, sleeping or paused thread is interrupted by another thread
Language	
Exception class	*Description*
`java.lang.IllegalAccessException`	Thrown when there is an attempt to access a class that is not public and in another package
`java.lang.ClassCastException`	Thrown when there is an attempt to cast an object to a subclass of which it is not an instance
`java.lang.NullPointerException`	Thrown when there is an attempt to use `null` in a case where an object is required
`java.lang.IllegalArgumentException`	Thrown when an argument passed to the method is illegal or inappropriate
`java.lang.NumberFormatException`	Thrown when there is an attempt to convert a string that does not have the appropriate format to one of the numeric types

Collection and utility

Exception class	*Description*
`java.lang.ArithmeticException`	Thrown when there is an exceptional arithmetic calculation like "divide by zero"
`java.lang.IndexOutOfBoundsException`	Thrown to indicate that an index to an array, a string or a collection class is out of range
`java.lang.ArrayIndexOutOfBoundsException`	Thrown to indicate that an index to an array is out of range
`java.lang.StringIndexOutOfBoundsException`	Thrown to indicate that an index to a string is either negative or greater than or equal to the size of the string
`java.lang.ArrayStoreException`	Thrown to indicate that there is an attempt to store the wrong type of object into an array of objects
`java.lang.NegativeArraySizeException`	Thrown when there is an attempt to create an array with negative size
`java.util.EmptyStackException`	Thrown to indicate that the stack is empty
`java.util.NoSuchElementException`	Thrown by the `nextElement` method of an `Enumeration` to indicate that there are no more elements in the enumeration

Input/Output

Exception class	*Description*
`java.io.IOException`	Thrown when there is a general I/O failure
`java.io.EOFException`	Thrown to indicate that an end of file or end of stream has been reached while reading the input
`java.io.InterruptedIOException`	Thrown to indicate that an I/O operation has been interrupted
`java.io.UnsupportedEncodingException`	Thrown to indicate that the given character encoding is not supported
`java.io.UTFDataFormatException`	Thrown to indicate that a malformed UTF-8 string has been encountered while reading the input
`javax.microedition.io.ConnectionNotFoundException`	Thrown to indicate that a connection target cannot be found or the specified protocol is not supported

Figure 3.5 illustrates the exception hierarchy tree that contains all the exception classes that are located in various packages of CLDC 1.1. And the root of the hierarchy is the `java.lang.Exception` class.

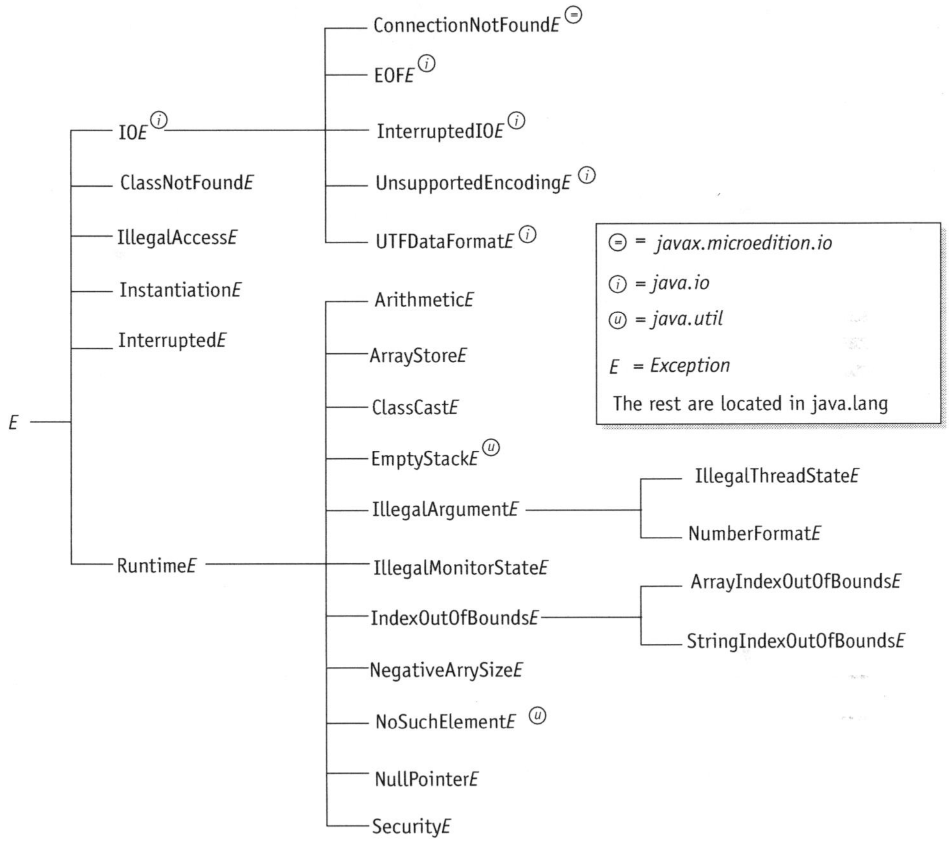

Figure 3.5 Hierarchy tree of the CLDC exception classes

Exam Tip

The exam requires a thorough knowledge of which exception classes are supported in CLDC. Understanding the context in which an exception would arise helps in remembering the exception hierarchy.

3.6.2 Error Handling

As discussed earlier, the support for error handling is somewhat crippled with limited number of error classes. The reason for this is two-fold:

- In embedded systems, error recovery mechanism is highly device-specific. Incorporating these into the standard libraries will be against the purported generic nature of CLDC. In addition, this would make the application programmers worry about the system programming issues.
- Implementing the complete error handling mechanism as defined by JLS would be expensive and unnecessarily complicate the virtual machine design.

So you cannot find the myriad of error classes in CLDC. A blessing in disguise, since you have only lesser number of `Error` classes to remember for the exam. Table 3.14 discusses the four error classes defined by the CLDC library.

Table 3.14 CLDC error classes

Error class	*Description*
`java.lang.Error`	The root class of the error hierarchy and the subclass of the `Throwable` class
`java.lang.NoClassDefFoundError`	Thrown to indicate that JVM is unable to load the definition of a class and no definition of the class could be found. This error class is newly added in CLDC 1.1
`java.lang.OutOfMemoryError`	Thrown to indicate that JVM is out of memory
`java.lang.VirtualMemoryError`	Thrown to indicate that JVM is broken or enough resources aren't available

Figure 3.6 illustrates the error hierarchy tree that contains all the error classes that are located in CLDC 1.1. The root of the hierarchy is the `java.lang.Error` class and all the other error classes are also located in the `java.lang` package.

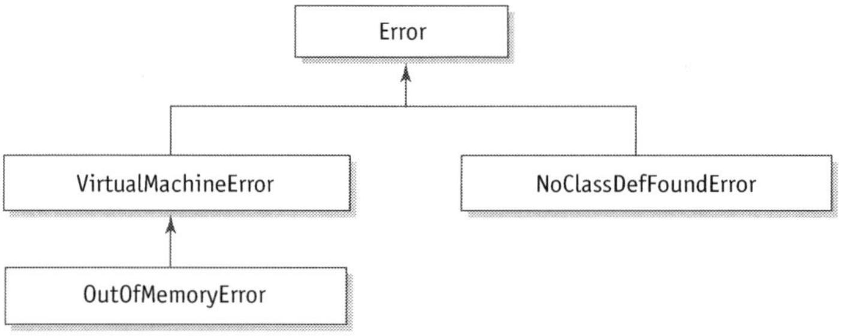

Figure 3.6 Hierarchy tree of the CLDC error classes

So, the next obvious question would be, "What does the KVM do when an error occurs that is not supported by the CLDC library?" In this case,

- Either, the VM will halt in an implementation-specific way such as showing user-friendly messages, logging and forgetting the error, rebooting the system and so on.
- Or the VM throws an `Error` that is the nearest CLDC supported superclass of the `Error` that must be thrown as per the JLS, meaning that any of the four error classes listed in Table 3.14 is thrown for all kinds of possible errors.

3.7 MANAGING MEMORY AND GARBAGE COLLECTION

Garbage Collection (GC) is always boasted as one of the prime features of Java language. In languages like C where there are no automatic memory management, you would create an object by manually allocating the memory and need to release the memory once you create the object. If you don't do the second part properly, you would end up in loosing the memory, which leads to memory leakage. With Java, there is automatic memory management, so you can create new objects and set them to `null` once you finish. When the runtime memory runs low, the GC kicks in and reclaims the memory occupied by objects, which are not referenced or referenced only in a cyclic way by other unused objects.

Things would have been simple, if they are so easy. Although GC ensures a healthy system, it is not a silver bullet for all kinds of situations. GC could potentially slow down an application's responsiveness, as the algorithms employed by GC are computationally expensive and could steal precious processor cycles. Coupled with a resource-constrained KVM, the problem with GC is simply magnified. Similarly, as you have seen, the CLDC runtime memory budget is limited. Therefore, care should be taken to keep the storage and runtime memory requirements to a minimal level. Let us see various techniques to write effective code in terms of runtime memory usage and efficient GC.

Minimize Object Creation

A proper object-oriented design favors creating multiple objects with well-defined responsibility for a better clarity. However, frequent object creation is not so performance-friendly due to two factors. First, if an object is complex and has a heavy initialization, it increases the time taken to create new objects and thus slowing down the overall performance. Second, you loose some memory. So care should be taken to minimize the object creation whenever possible. Developers should read this correctly. We advise developers to write code that places performance ahead of principles of object-orientation.

Use Primitive Data Types Whenever Possible

Try to avoid creating wrapper objects such as `Long, Integer` when the problem can be handled by the corresponding simple primitive data types.

Reduce and Reuse

If an object can be reused without affecting your application's logic, you should probably reuse it. A classic scenario for object reuse is a user-interface object such as a cancel button, which is often repeated in each screen of the application. Another most often usage is the reuse of MIDP `GameCanvas` object since it is a heavy object with a buffer area created in memory for each object.

Depending on the application's complexity, you could also go for an object pool to get and return the objects. This would reduce the load on GC and time taken for the application to create a new object. However, beware that the object pools can sometimes underperform for your requirement. So take all this advice with a pinch of salt and a good profiler should help you out in picking up the right strategy. For the exam, just remember to avoid larger number of short-lived objects and reuse objects as often as possible.

Favor StringBuffer for String Concatenation

This is often a repeated tip for improving performance during string concatenation even in a lavish Java SE environment. `String` is an immutable object and thereby string concatenation will result in new object. If this is done frequently, you can be rest assured that you will deplete the memory heap sooner than you would expect. Therefore, any string concatenation should use the mutable `StringBuffer` thereby avoiding the creation of numerous intermediate objects.

Lazy Instantiation

Create the objects only when you require them. A complex object that has been created during application initialization but used later can increase the responsiveness of the application at the cost of occupying the memory for a longer time.

Free Unused Objects

If there is no scope for reusing the object, you should set the object reference to `null` as soon as possible so that the GC can reclaim in its next cycle.

Verifying Free and Total Memory

The `Runtime` class offers two methods which can be used to verify whether your application's memory requirements can be met. They are `freeMemory()` which returns the amount of free memory available to the system and `totalMemory()` which returns the total amount of memory in the virtual machine. You could gracefully shutdown the application if free memory is below a threshold limit or request the GC to run by calling up `Runtime.gc()` or `System.gc()`.

Avoid GC Hang-ups

GC runs in a low-priority thread but when it starts recollecting memory, it's placed in the driver's seat and slows down your application's threads substantially. Probably you could have witnessed this behavior in Java SE/EE environment where your application becomes unresponsive for few moments during load. This could be avoided by using the above-discussed memory handling practices so that GC is not invoked very often or by voluntarily invoking GC during safe periods, when we know for sure that the application isn't busy doing any heavy task.

Optimize Storage Size

When packaging the final deployable JAR file, include only the files that are required for running the application. Often, when using a third-party library, we may use only a subset of functionality and hence not all the classes of the library need to be packaged. Techniques such as code obfuscation can also reduce the size of the classes by eliminating unnecessary data and by translating long identifiers into shorter ones.

Exam Tip

Minimize the object creation, avoid memory leaks by nullifying unused objects and reduce the load on GC so that it doesn't run for a longer time.

Summary

Now, you should be pretty comfortable with the concept of a configuration, the role it plays in the conceptual architecture of Java ME, and in particular, you should understand the specifics of CLDC. JTWI specifies a minimum configuration of CLDC 1.0. As a minimum requirement, any superset will satisfy the requirements of JTWI. In particular, the CLDC 1.1 adds floating point support, as well as some other minor revisions. The exam requires you to understand CLDC and its role as the configuration for JTWI.

CLDC was chosen for JTWI because it defines a small footprint VM along with libraries that are suitable for the resource-constrained devices such as the target mobile phones of JTWI. You should now understand the nature of CLDC and its subset implementations of the Java platform's standard JVM and core libraries. For example, we saw that the CLDC's JVM does not support finalization, user-defined class loaders, thread groups, daemon threads and asynchronous exceptions. You should also understand the minimum requirements that CLDC places on the underlying device, such as memory minimums. We also toured the core libraries offered by CLDC. You should understand the two types of libraries defined in the CLDC: those inherited from Java SE and those that are specific to CLDC. We covered most of these but left the CLDC-specific, network-related libraries for a later dedicated chapter.

We have now embarked upon the detail-oriented section of this book. This chapter and the following ones will make you commit many details to memory. What is the minimum requirement for Java dedicated memory on a CLDC 1.1 device? Sometimes details can be difficult to manage. It's much easier if you can understand the design logic and architectural motivations behind the details. As you read through the exercises and review questions, try to not only answer the questions but see whether you can determine the architectural goals and motivations that drove the requirements in question. Early in this chapter, we discussed the motivations for the structure of CLDC. Some of these motivations stem from the market goals of the target devices, some come from the resource limits, and some come from Java ME architectural imperatives. Understanding these goals and how they manifest will make the details much easier to remember.

References

1. Connected Limited Device Configuration versions
   http://java.sun.com/products/cldc/
2. White Paper - The K Virtual Machine (KVM)
   http://java.sun.com/products/cldc/wp/index.html
3. CLDC and KVM FAQ
   http://java.sun.com/products/cldc/faqs.html

Exercises

1. Write the classic "Hello World" application using CLDC classes.
2. Use a CLDC-specific class in your application and see how the compiler responds. Repeat the same by using some of the unsupported features such as finalization, custom class loaders and so on.
3. Modify the same application to include the new features in CLDC 1.1. Run the same code using a CLDC 1.0 VM.
4. Use the `System.freeMemory()` and `System.totalMemory()` to measure how much memory is used for creating a `Vector` of 100 `Long` objects in your CLDC application. Modify the code to use an array of `long` data type and verify the results once again. Do you see a reduced memory usage?

Review Questions

1. What is the minimum memory budget for non-volatile memory for a CLDC 1.1 implementation?
   a. 192 Kilobytes
   b. 160 Kilobytes
   c. 32 Kilobytes
   d. 128 Kilobytes
2. CLDC 1.1 does not support `ThreadGroup` where as CLDC 1.0 did.
   a. True
   b. False
3. Which of the following is supported by CLDC VM?
   a. User-defined class loaders
   b. Daemon threads
   c. Multithreading
   d. Loading of native libraries
4. In a CLDC VM, which of the following environment variable is used to alter the class loading behavior?
   a. `classpath`
   b. `microedition.classpath`
   c. `cldc.classpath`
   d. The class loading behavior cannot be modified
5. Identify the method(s) that are not present in `java.lang.Object` of CLDC?
   a. `clone()`
   b. `finalize()`
   c. `notifyAll()`
   d. `toString()`
6. Identify the package that is newly added from CLDC 1.1.
   a. `java.beans`
   b. `java.lang.ref`
   c. `java.math`
   d. `java.util.jar`
7. What are the software requirements for the CLDC VM?
   a. Presence of an operating system or a kernel
   b. Multiprocessing capability
   c. Real-time scheduling behavior
   d. At least one schedulable entity to run the VM
8. Identify the true statements about CLDC class file verification.
   a. It's the same as Java SE class file verification
   b. It happens in two phases
   c. The class file verification can be switched off for a better performance
   d. It uses a special attribute named `StackMap` to speed up the process

9. Which of the following classes are not present in the `java.util` package of CLDC?
   a. `ArrayList`
   b. `Vector`
   c. `TreeMap`
   d. `Stack`
10. In CLDC, event handling is defined by the classes present in
    a. `java.io`
    b. `java.lang`
    c. `java.event`
    d. None of the above

Review Answers

1. b. The minimum memory budget is 160 kilobytes for non-volatile memory and 32 kilobytes for volatile memory. This is only the minimum recommendation and hence a device's actual memory can be more than this.
2. b. CLDC never supported the `ThreadGroup` concept although this can be mimicked by the application programmer using collections.
3. c. All the others are not supported by the CLDC VM.
4. d. Class lookup order cannot be modified in CLDC. Hence, there is no concept of `classpath` environment variable as you would find in Java SE.
5. a and b. Both the `clone()` and `finalize()` are not present in the `Object` class and hence not available to any class in CLDC.
6. b. Support for weak reference has been added from CLDC 1.1. Hence, `java.lang.ref` has been introduced from CLDC 1.1
7. a and d. The only requirements are the presence of an operating system or a kernel and a schedulable entity to run the virtual machine.
8. b and d. CLDC class file verification is different from Java SE's verification. It is done in two phases, which includes an off-device preverification process that inlines all subroutines, removes certain byte codes and adds special `StackMap` attribute to speed up the in-device verification.
9. a and c. In CLDC, `java.util` package supports only `Hashtable, Vector, Stack` classes and `Enumeration` interface.
10. d. Event handling, UI handling, application lifecycle management are typically defined and implemented by profiles.

Exam Notes

☞ Identify correct and incorrect statements or examples about the requirements and scope of the CLDC specification, including the differences between 1.0 and 1.1.

Requirements of CLDC Specification

- Hardware requirements
  - At least 160KB of non-volatile memory is available for the VM and CLDC libraries
  - At least 32KB of volatile memory is available for the VM runtime
- Software requirements
  - A host OS and one schedulable entity to run the virtual machine

Scope of CLDC Specification

- What are in scope?
  - Java language and VM features
  - Core Java libraries (`java.lang.*` and `java.util.*`)
  - Input/Output libraries (`java.io.*`)
  - Security
  - Networking (`javax.microedition.io.*`)
  - Internationalization
- What are not in scope?
  - High-level application installation and lifecycle management
  - User interface functionality
  - Event handling
  - High-level application model (human-device interaction)
- The items that are not in scope are typically addressed in the profiles

Differences between CLDC 1.0 and CLDC 1.1

- Floating point support
  - Classes `Float` and `Double` have been added
  - Various methods have been added to other classes to handle floating point values
- Weak reference support
- Redesigned `Calendar`, `Date` and `TimeZone` classes
- Clarified error handling requirements, and one new error class (`NoClassDefFoundError`)
- Thread naming support
- The new fields and methods as follows:
  - `Boolean.TRUE` and `Boolean.FALSE`
  - `Date.toString()`
  - `Random.nextInt(int n)`
  - `String.intern()`
  - `String.equalsIgnoreCase()`
  - `Thread.interrupt()`

- Minimum memory budget raised from 160 to 192 kilobytes, mainly because of the added floating point functionality

☞ Describe the ways in which a CLDC virtual machine does and does not adhere to JLS and JVMS.

Differences between CLDC VM and JLS

- Class instances cannot be finalized, meaning that there is no `Object.finalize()` method
- Limited error and exception handling facilities
  - In short, the error and exception classes are limited in CLDC and if an implementing VM performs more checks than those mentioned in CLDC, it is expected to throw the nearest appropriate `Error` to the application
  - Asynchronous exceptions are not available such as `InternalError` in JLS

Differences between CLDC VM and JVMS

- No user-defined class loaders
- No thread groups
- No daemon threads
- Two steps class file verification (a preverifier which is run on the development system, like your PC and a runtime verifier which is run on the device during the installation of the application)
  - The verification is a linear pass on the code and does not have complex algorithms like in JVM
  - An application cannot be installed on a device without running it through the preverifier
- No modification on class file lookup order
  - Application programmer cannot modify CLDC, MIDP, or vendor-specific packages

☞ Identify correct and incorrect statements or examples about CLDC classes including those derived from J2SE, and the CLDC-specific classes, including identifying which core J2SE classes are not included in CLDC, or have different behaviors (for example java.lang.String, io classes, etc.)

Comparison between CLDC and Java SE Classes

All or most of the classes defined in CLDC that have a counterpart in Java SE have a subset of functionalities.

- Localization not supported
- Only *Basic-Latin* and *Latin-1-Supplement* character sets required

System Classes

- `java.lang.Object`
- `java.lang.Class`

- `java.lang.Runtime`
- `java.lang.System`
- `java.lang.Thread`
- *`java.lang.Runnable`* (interface)
- `java.lang.String`
- `java.lang.StringBuffer`
- `java.lang.Throwable`

Datatype Classes

- `java.lang.Boolean`
- `java.lang.Byte`
- `java.lang.Short`
- `java.lang.Integer`
- `java.lang.Long`
- `java.lang.Float`
- `java.lang.Double`
- `java.lang.Character`

Collection Classes

- `java.util.Vector`
- `java.util.Hashtable`
- `java.util.Stack`
- *`java.util.Enumeration`* (interface)

Calendar and Time Classes

- `java.util.Calendar`
- `java.util.Date`
- `java.util.TimeZone`

Additional Utility Classes

- `java.lang.Math`
- `java.util.Random`

Input/Output Classes

- `java.io.InputStream`
- `java.io.OutputStream`
- `java.io.ByteArrayInputStream`
- `java.io.ByteArrayOutputStream`

- *java.io.DataInput*(Interface)
- *java.io.DataOutput*(Interface)
- java.io.DataInputStream
- java.io.DataOutputStream
- java.io.Reader
- java.io.Writer
- java.io.InputStreamReader
- java.io.OutputStreamWriter
- java.io.PrintStream

Weak References

- java.lang.ref.Reference
- java.lang.ref.WeakReference

Property Support

- Retrieving system properties using System.getProperty(String key)
- microedition.configuration to retrieve the current configuration information
- microedition.encoding to retrieve the default character encoding information
- microedition.platform to retrieve the host platform information
- microedition.profiles to retrieve the supported profiles information
- The "microedition", "java", "javax" prefixes are reserved for the Java ME configurations and profiles

☞ Given the differences and limitations of exception/error handling with CLDC devices, handle exceptions correctly.

Exception/Error Handling in CLDC

- A new Error called NoClassDefFoundError added in CLDC 1.1
- When an error other than those defined in CLDC occurs
  - ♦ The VM may halt in an implementation-specific manner, or
  - ♦ The nearest CLDC-supported Error is thrown
- No asynchronous errors and exceptions support
- SecurityException can be thrown for any operation that needs permission (like opening a network connection)
- InterruptedIOException can be thrown by any data transfer operation, if the connection is lost during data transfer. This exception may also be thrown if the application had requested to be notified of connection timeouts, although this is not guaranteed.

Errors

- `java.lang.Error`
- `java.lang.NoClassDefFoundError`
- `java.lang.OutOfMemoryError`
- `java.lang.VirtualMemoryError`

Application Management Exceptions

- `java.lang.RuntimeException`
- `java.lang.SecurityException`
- `java.lang.ClassNotFoundException`
- `java.lang.InstantiationException`
- `java.lang.IllegalMonitorStateException`
- `java.lang.IllegalThreadStateException`
- `java.lang.InterruptedException`

Language Exceptions

- `java.lang.IllegalAccessException`
- `java.lang.ClassCastException`
- `java.lang.NullPointerException`
- `java.lang.IllegalArgumentException`
- `java.lang.NumberFormatException`

Collection/Utility Exceptions

- `java.lang.ArithmeticException`
- `java.lang.IndexOutOfBoundsException`
- `java.lang.ArrayIndexOutOfBoundsException`
- `java.lang.StringIndexOutOfBoundsException`
- `java.lang.ArrayStoreException`
- `java.lang.NegativeArraySizeException`
- `java.util.EmptyStackException`
- `java.util.NoSuchElementException`

Input/Output Exceptions

- `java.io.IOException`
- `java.io.EOFException`
- `java.io.InterruptedIOException`
- `java.io.UnsupportedEncodingException`

- `java.io.UTFDataFormatException`
- `javax.microedition.io.ConnectionNotFoundException`

☞ Write code that effectively manages memory and garbage collection.

Garbage Collection in CLDC

- Minimize object creation
- Use primitive data types whenever possible
- Reduce and reuse
- Favor `StringBuffer` for string concatenation
- Lazy instantiation
- Free unused objects
- Verifying free and total memory
- Avoid GC hang-ups
- Optimize storage size

4

Chapter

The MIDlet: A Different Kind of Application

Exam Objectives

5.1. Explain the specification guarantees for:
- ❖ Browsing for MIDlet suites
- ❖ Transferring MIDlet suites using HTTP
- ❖ Push registries
- ❖ Basic authentication
- ❖ Installing and updating MIDlet suites
- ❖ Invoking MIDlet suites
- ❖ Deleting MIDlet suites

(Section 4.4)

5.2. Identify correct and incorrect statements or examples about the MIDP application model, including:
- ❖ The MIDP execution environment
- ❖ MIDlet suites
- ❖ MIDlet suite packaging (including the manifest and the application descriptor)
- ❖ Discovering available services on the device
- ❖ Discovering which version of MIDP/CLDC is on the device

(Sections 4.1 and 4.2)

5.3. Develop applications that correctly reflect a MIDlet's application lifecycle, including:
- ❖ The purpose of the MIDlet class
- ❖ Communication with the application management software
- ❖ Platform request API
- ❖ Valid MIDlet states and transitions
- ❖ The behavior that should and should not be implemented within different lifecycle methods (including the constructor)

(Sections 4.1.1 and 4.5)

5.4. Deploy a MIDP 2.0 application with the correct use of JAD files and manifests. (Section 4.3)

5.5. Given an installation failure, analyze the problem and develop possible resolutions. (Section 4.4.3)

5.6. Given a set of requirements, develop applications that correctly implement MIDP 2.0 support for delayed or scheduled activities using timers and background threads. (Section 4.6.1)

7.1. Explain MIDP 2.0 Push Registry benefits and limitations, and describe its use in applications. (Section 4.6.2)

7.2. Develop applications that correctly use MIDP 2.0 Push Registry including:
- Discovery
- Dynamic vs. static
- Recognizing the types of connections that can and cannot be accepted

(Section 4.6.2)

INTRODUCTION

Engineers, now you fasten your seat belts and put your trays in an upright position, we are coming back down to earth. This is where the true developer stuff starts. This chapter will start showing how to actually write applications for mobile phones. If a configuration is like the skeleton of the human body, the profile forms the rest of the body—the skin, muscles and so on. Following this analogy, sunglasses, tattoos and jewelry would translate to bluetooth support, video capture and other technological bling—the optional packages. This chapter focuses on the profile.

JTWI names the MIDP 2.0 as the mandatory profile.

☞ **Note:** There is a version 1.0 of MIDP, but JTWI mandates the use of 2.0; don't get confused with the CLDC requirement. The requirement of using version 2.0 of MIDP is not optional; 1.0 doesn't work.

MIDP forms the flesh of most of the stuff you will need to develop full-featured applications for mobile phones. Like all profiles, MIDP aims at providing a complete application development platform by specifying a set of APIs that makes possible the efficient development of secure and portable applications. It defines APIs for user interface, gaming interface, security, storage and even some basic multimedia functionality.

As developers in the realm of JTWI, most of your time will be spent coding to the specifications of MIDP. In fact, the bulk of the remaining chapters of this book cover the features of MIDP in detail, with many code examples. This chapter introduces the application architecture of MIDP. As we discussed earlier, CLDC defines, at the configuration layer, the concept of an application. At the configuration layer, an application is a set of classes with a single entry point defined by a `main` method. That application is the low-level idea of an application, the one that actually executes on the virtual machine. The application that developers, and MIDP itself, are most concerned with is a higher level entity. We discussed the differences in these two concepts of an application when we covered CLDC. This is an important matter.

The higher level application defined by MIDP is MIDlet. If you are a seasoned Java guru, you probably already understand the concept by noting the resonance of the nomenclature. We will go through it just to be clear though. A MIDlet is a high-level conceptual application that is much parallel to Java servlets and applets. These applications do not contain main method entry points like the lower level applications. These higher level applications are executed by being deployed in some other lower level application, such as a servlet container or a JRE plug-in.

The execution of MIDlets, servlets and applets occur according to the strict guidelines of a lifecycle definition. Each application type defines a set of lifecycle methods, usually something like `init()`, `start()`, `stop()` and `destroy()`. The low-level application within which the application is deployed is responsible for managing the lifecycle of the high-level application. As can be seen in Fig. 4.1, the lifecycle methods of the high-level applications are invoked by the containing application. In this case, we can see a servlet container invoking a servlet's `service()`, and the Application Management Software (AMS) invoking a MIDlet's `startApp()`. We can say that the containing applications manage the lifecycle of the high-level applications they contain.

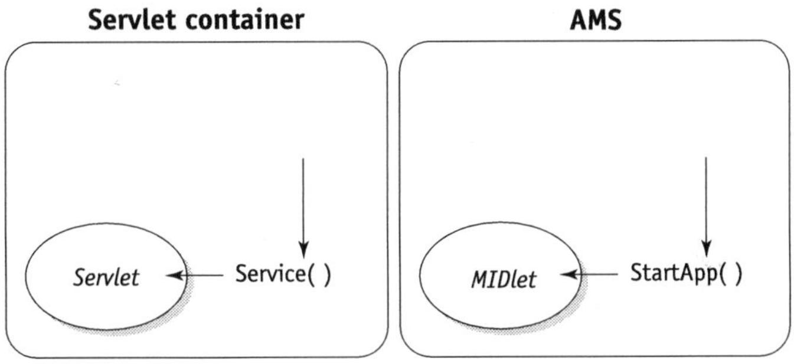

Figure 4.1 Lifecycle management

Managing a lifecycle amounts to invoking the lifecycle methods at the appropriate time to cause execution. Take the servlet lifecycle as an example. The servlet container will invoke its appropriate lifecycle method, `service()`, when an HTTP request arrives with a URL that maps to the servlet. Similarly, an applet has its appropriate lifecycle method, `start()`, invoked by the JRE plug-in when the browser displays the page that contains the applet. In this chapter, we will become very familiar with the lifecycle of the MIDlet.

4.1 BUILDING MIDLET

Typically, the process of building a Java application starts with a `main` method as an entry point to the application. The process of building a MIDlet is different from the typical one. It does not start with a `main` method. As we have said, a MIDlet is more similar to an applet than an application. Much as an applet relies on the browser plug-in to start it, and a servlet has the servlet container to start it, a MIDlet has AMS. AMS is responsible for managing the applications installed in a device. It provides facilities for the user to install, look up, select, start and even uninstall the application.

That is said, now let's get our hands dirty. We're about to make up for all the engineering talk by leaping head first into some real code. The first thing to do to create an application is to create a class that will override the `javax.microedition.midlet.MIDlet` class. To illustrate this, let us take the traditional "Hello World" application in Listing 4.1.

Listing 4.1: A "Hello World" MIDlet

```
package com.scmadkit.ch04;
import javax.microedition.midlet.MIDlet;
public class HelloWorldMIDlet extends MIDlet {
  protected void startApp()
    throws MIDletStateChangeException {
      System.out.println("Hello world!");
  }                                                        (1)
  protected void pauseApp() {
  System.out.println("Hold on for a second, world!");     (2)
  }
  protected void destroyApp(boolean unconditional)
  throws MIDletStateChangeException {
                                                           (3)
      System.out.println("Good Bye world!");
  }
}
```

(1) **Starts the MIDlet**

(2) **Pauses the MIDlet**

(3) **Destroys the MIDlet**

We will discuss the details of this code in the upcoming sections. But, for now can you glean anything for yourself? For instance, from our discussion of high-level applications, can you infer anything about this class? Lifecycle-based applications don't have a `main` method. What are the important methods of a MIDlet?

4.1.1 MIDlet Lifecycle

Let's try to analyze this tiny program. In particular, we will use this basic program as a demonstration of the lifecycle methods defined by MIDlets.

The line `public class HelloWorldMIDlet extends MIDlet {` implies that this program is a Java ME program based on the MIDP profile because it extends the `MIDlet` class. This is similar to an applet extending the `Applet` or `JApplet` class. This class controls the lifecycle of the application.

```
public void startApp()
  throws MIDletStateChangeException {
    System.out.println("Hello World!");
}
```

When the user selects the application in the device and starts it, AMS will look for the associated class that extends `MIDlet` class. Once it finds that, it will invoke the `startApp()` method of the class to start the application. The application also gets a chance to let AMS know if it is ready to be started or not (say, it could not get a network connection that it needs) by having the option to throw back a `MIDletStateChangeException` if needed.

```
public void pauseApp() {
  System.out.println("Hold on for a second, world!");
}
```

In mobile devices, there might normally be some events that would warrant the user's immediate attention even if s/he is in the middle of playing an interesting game of Solitaire. For example, the user might get a call (after all, that's why cell phones are there in the first place). In such cases, AMS would have to switch to the native phone application and resume the game once the call is complete. That's when it calls the `pauseApp()` method—to pause the application and resume it later. A developer can use this method to store the state of the application before it is paused. This would also be a good time to release all the resources that the MIDlet holds, like closing a network connection.

```
public void destroyApp(boolean unconditional)
  throws MIDletStateChangeException {
    System.out.println("Good Bye World!");
}
```

Finally, when it is time for the application to be destroyed, AMS calls the `destroyApp (boolean)` method. Notice that this takes a flag as a parameter. This flag is used by AMS to indicate if it wants to terminate the MIDlet immediately or not. If the flag passed is set to `true`, then AMS will terminate MIDlet regardless of any protest from the application. If it is set to `false`, the MIDlet can make a plea to live by throwing a `MIDletStateChange Exception`. In such cases, AMS will let the application live for some more time and call the method later. Figure 4.2 shows the lifecycle of a MIDlet application.

You might notice one thing in the diagram that was not mentioned earlier—the use of the `new` call. Who calls it? Well, AMS calls the constructor to create an instance of MIDlet. As you might have guessed by now, AMS should have access to the no-argument constructor. Since the application is never going to call the constructor of `MIDlet`, the developer does not have any reason to write his own constructor for a `MIDlet`.

Now, a related question, what happens if we have a standard `public static void main(String[] args)` method in the program? It will be ignored. Along the same note,

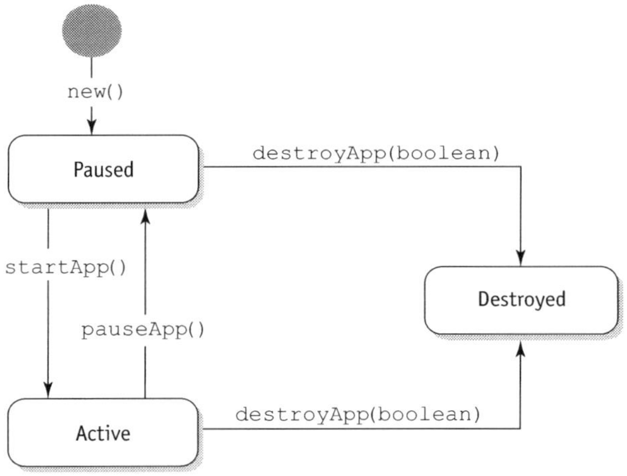

Figure 4.2 MIDlet lifecycle and signals from AMS

the application also must not call the `System.exit()` method. If it dares to do that, a `SecurityException` will be thrown by AMS in return. Remember, this is a higher level application. All of its execution should be controlled via the lifecycle methods and their invocation by AMS.

☞ **Note:** As indicated by the state chart diagram, each method call in the `MIDlet` class changes the state of the application. As a result, you should ensure that the method calls return quickly and hence, should not have any complex, time-consuming logic to improve user-friendliness.

4.1.2 AMS Notifications

The lifecycle methods we have just discussed are the methods that AMS uses to manage the MIDlet's lifecycle. These are not usually invoked by the application programmer. However, if the developer wants to affect its lifecycle transitions, there is a way. The `MIDlet` class provides a mechanism for the application itself to request certain lifecycle state changes. These are the notification methods. Three notification methods can be used by the application to make requests to AMS for a lifecycle state change. Figure 4.3 is a modified version of Fig. 4.2 along with the signals sent by MIDlet to AMS to change its lifecycle state.

`public final void notifyDestroyed()`

This can be used by the application to let AMS know that the application wants to be destroyed. On receipt of this notification, AMS will not call the `destroyApp()` method of the application but will simply kill it, assuming that the application has done all the cleanup work that it would have performed had it destroyed MIDlet normally.

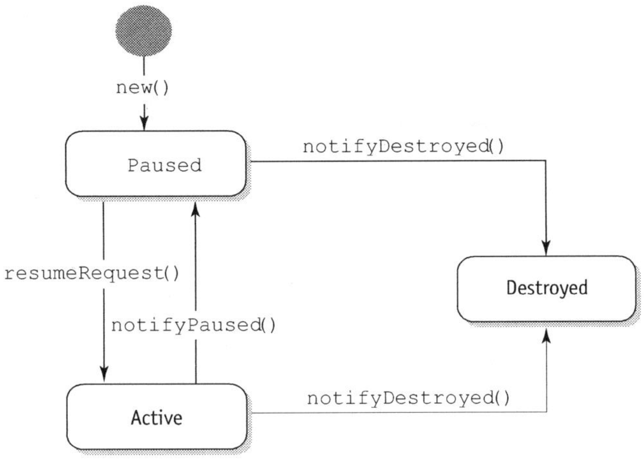

Figure 4.3 MIDlet lifecycle and signals to the AMS

`public final void notifyPaused()`

This is similar to the previous one, except that MIDlet notifies AMS that this time it is going into the paused state.

`public final void resumeRequest()`

This method is complementary to the `notifyPaused()` method. By invoking this event, the application indicates AMS that it is raring to go once again. When AMS thinks it is ready to let the application loose, it will call the application's `startApp()` method.

4.2 PACKAGING APPLICATIONS

Now that we have covered the basics of MIDlet lifecycle management, we need to consider the packaging of our MIDlets for deployment. Again, as with servlets and applets, a standard packaging structure, defined by the MIDP specification, is utilized for deployment of MIDlets. Servlets are deployed in Web Application Archive (WAR) files, a special kind of Java Application Archive (JAR) file with a specified internal directory structure that identifies specific locations for specific components of a servlet-based application. MIDlets are also packaged in a JAR file with a specified structure and an accompanying descriptor file.

So, we have written our application, it is now time to package it and deploy it in a mobile device. If you do not have a JTWI-compliant mobile device, you can do the next best thing—test it in an emulator. You can either use an emulator that is available from a device manufacturer or Sun Java Wireless Toolkit. You can download the wireless toolkit from Sun's Java site. We shall be using the wireless toolkit to prepare for the exam. (Appendix A covers everything you need to know about Sun Java Wireless Toolkit to be able to test the code examples.)

MIDlet applications are normally packaged as MIDlet suites. A MIDlet suite may contain one or more applications, which essentially means that the suite can have one or more classes that extend the `javax.microedition.midlet.MIDlet` class. Each MIDlet suite contains the following:

- A JAR file (which contains the class files and a manifest file) and
- A JAD file

Figure 4.4 illustrates the anatomy of a MIDlet suite as discussed above.

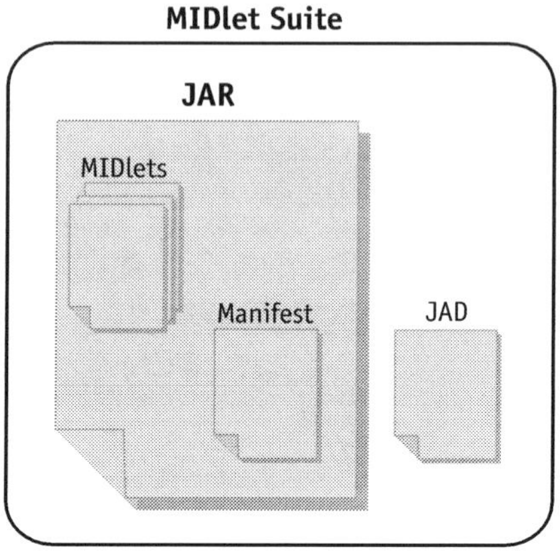

Figure 4.4 Inside a MIDlet suite

In order to package and deploy a MIDlet application, the following steps need to be taken:

1. Compile the class files
2. Create a JAR file with a valid manifest file
3. Create a JAD file
4. Deploy the application to the device (using WAP, Bluetooth or any other connections)

4.3 DESCRIBING MIDLET SUITE

As with other high-level applications, such as servlets, MIDlets must contain self-descriptive documents to help AMS understand the contents of the application. For instance, the servlet *deployment descriptor* is the `web.xml` file bundled into the WAR file. The information about a MIDlet can be provided in two places—in the manifest file of the JAR (which is always present in the location `/META-INF/manifest.mf` in the JAR file) or in the associated JAD file.

MIDlet suites are usually downloaded over-the-air (OTA) using the device's in-built WAP (Wireless Access Protocol – similar to HTTP) browser, or using other data transfer technologies like IrDA (infrared) or Bluetooth.

Exam Tip

A device must at least provide support for HTTP 1.1 for transferring the MIDlet suite and the Java Application Descriptor (JAD) file OTA for installation.

In case of OTA, transfer of data usually comes at a price, in the form of data transfer charges set by the service provider. By the way, we are talking about dollars here, not performance costs. It will be a shame to download an application and then find out that it does not work with the device or it is not the one the user is looking for. This is similar to someone downloading a huge application using a dial-up modem and then finding out that it is not compatible with his machine or that it is not the one he is looking for.

In order to avoid this scenario, the MIDlet suite normally comes with a descriptor file known as the JAD file. This file provides some general details about the application, like who created it, what type of network access is required by the system, how large the associated suite is, etc. The user can first download this information (which is normally much smaller than the application itself) and then decide whether he wants to download the associated application or not.

The JAD file is a simple text file containing attribute name-value entries of the form "`name:value`". Let us now take a look at the most commonly used attributes. The values in the JAD and the manifest files can be read dynamically by the application in the suite by using the `public String getAppProperty(String key)` method of the `MIDlet` class.

Exam Tip

The MIME type of a JAD file is "`text/vnd.sun.j2me.app-descriptor`". The extension for a JAD file must be, not surprisingly, "`jad`".

Here's the JAD file for the "Hello, World!" example that we wrote earlier.

```
MIDlet-1: HelloWorldMIDlet, ,com.scmadkit.ch04.HelloWorldMIDlet
MIDlet-Jar-Size: 100
MIDlet-Jar-URL: SCMADKit.jar
MIDlet-Name: SCMAD Exam Guide
MIDlet-Vendor: McGraw-Hill
MIDlet-Version: 1.0
MicroEdition-Configuration: CLDC-1.0
MicroEdition-Profile: MIDP-2.0
```

Exam Tip

A MIDlet JAR file must not contain packages defined in MIDP or CLDC. It must also not contain any classes that can invoke native libraries.

☞ **Note:** There can be two descriptor documents for a MIDlet that both contain the same information: the JAD file and the manifest file.

The natural question is, why the duplication? The first reason is that in some cases, it might not be possible to have a separate JAD file. In such cases, AMS will look for the manifest file to get some information about the suite. The more critical motivation lies in the costs, performance-wise and cents-wise, of downloading large amounts of data on a limited device.

If the application doesn't have a JAD file, it can still be downloaded and installed. There are consequences however. MIDlet suites that do not have a JAD file are implicitly assumed to be untrusted by AMS. Trusted and untrusted applications will be handled more elaborately in the Security chapter.

4.3.1 Mandatory Attributes

Now we will examine some of the details of the application descriptors. These details pretty much hold true whether the attribute is contained in the manifest or in a JAD. There are a couple of differences dependent upon the use of a JAD or manifest, but these will be covered at the end of this section.

MIDlet Suite Attributes

The following attributes describe the MIDlet suite and the applications inside the suite. The first three are mandatory both in the JAD file and in the manifest file.

`MIDlet-Name`

This attribute can be used to provide a readable name for the suite. This will normally be presented to the user when he is browsing for applications in the device.

> **Exam Tip**
>
> The exam usually asks whether the `MIDlet-Name` attribute refers to the name of a MIDlet or that of a MIDlet suite. Do remember that it is of a MIDlet suite.

`MIDlet-Version`

This attribute specifies the version of the suite, if the suite happens to have different versions. It is mandatory even if you think that a certain application will have only one version. In general, it is always a good practice to version your applications. You never know when you will extend it.

Apart from being a good practice, AMS also uses this number to determine if a MIDlet suite having the same name as another MIDlet suite that is already installed is newer or older. The version numbers must be of the format `x.y[.z]`, where x represents the major version, y represents the minor version and z represents patch number. The patch number is optional. If no value is given for this attribute, the default will be "`0.0.0`".

`MIDlet-Vendor`

This attribute specifies the person or company that created the application. The consumer would typically use this information to determine the source of the application (not too safe, but there is the security model to take care of that problem!).

`MIDlet-Jar-URL`

This attribute specifies the URL from where the JAR file corresponding to the JAD file can be downloaded. As you can guess, this attribute is mandatory for a JAD file, but is optional for a manifest file.

`MIDlet-Jar-Size`

This attribute specifies the size of the JAR file. Once again, this is mandatory for a JAD file, but optional for a manifest file. AMS would typically use this information to provide a feedback mechanism to the user while it is downloading the application.

MIDlet Attributes

The following attributes are used to describe the applications present inside the MIDlet suite and the requirements for those MIDlets to run successfully. The JAD or the manifest file must contain them.

`MIDlet-<n>`

This is the most important attribute. This attribute is used to specify classes in the suite that extend the `MIDlet` class. If there is more than one class that extends the `MIDlet` class in the suite, multiple entries must be specified, each describing one class.

The value of this attribute must be in the following format:

```
MIDletName, MIDletIcon, MIDletClass
```

Among these, the `MIDletIcon` is optional, but the commas on either side must still be present. If not, the AMS will mistakenly read the class as the icon, resulting in a possible error. It would be similar if you ignore the class name. However, if you don't specify the name, the application will not even show up on the list of applications available in the suite.

There are some important restrictions to observe regarding this attribute:

- The number <n> specified must be sequential, beginning with 1.
- If there is a break in the sequence, any entry after that number will be ignored. For example, if the descriptor looks like this,

```
MIDlet-1: App1,,com.scmadkit.ch04.App1
MIDlet-2: App2,,com.scmadkit.ch04.App2
MIDlet-4: App4,,com.scmadkit.ch04.App4
```

only applications App1 and App2 will be considered by the AMS. Even if App4 is perfectly valid, it will be ignored, which essentially means that it won't be displayed on the screen as an option and hence, the user will not be able to run it.

`MicroEdition-Profile`

This attribute can be used to specify the MIDP versions required to be implemented by the device in order to successfully run the application. Multiple profiles or profile versions may be specified with a space as the separator. If the device does not have all the specified profiles installed in it, the application will not be installed.

The value specified in this attribute must have the same format as that of the value of the system property "`microedition.profiles`". For example, MIDP 2.0 will have the value "`MIDP-2.0`".

`MicroEdition-Configuration`

This is similar to the previous attribute, except that this specifies the configuration to be implemented by the device for this application to run successfully.

The value specified in this attribute must have the same format as that of the value of the system property "`microedition.configuration`". For example, CLDC 1.0 will have the value "`CLDC-1.0`". As a device can have only one configuration, this attribute will have only one value (anything beyond a space will be ignored).

4.3.2 Optional Attributes

The following attributes are optional in both the JAD file and the manifest file.

Additional MIDlet Suite Attributes

The following attributes are normally used to provide additional information about the suite or its provider.

`MIDlet-Icon`

This attribute can be used to point to a small icon that can be used in conjunction with the application. This is normally displayed by the AMS along with the name of the application while the user is viewing a list of installed applications. The image format must be PNG.

`MIDlet-Data-Size`

This attribute is used to specify the minimum memory space in byte required by the MIDlet suite to install successfully. The default value for this attribute is zero.

`MIDlet-Description`

This attribute is used to provide a more elaborate description about the capabilities of the suite.

`MIDlet-Info-URL`

This attribute can be used by the provider to specify the URL that gives further description about the MIDlet suite (say, support website).

Security Attributes

The following attributes can be used by the application developer to let the device know about the security requirements for the application. If the requirements provided cannot be satisfied by the device, the suite will not be installed. More information about these attributes will be provided in the Security chapter.

`MIDlet-Permissions`

Requirements specified in this attribute are "must-have" for the suite. If they cannot be met, the suite must not be installed.

`MIDlet-Permissions-Opt`

Requirements specified in this attribute are "good-to-have" for the suite. The applications in the suite will run even if some or all of these requirements cannot be met (potentially in a reduced-functionality mode), but it will be great if the device fulfills it. For example, if the suite mentioned a network requirement in this attribute but the device does not have any network access, then the applications in the suite may run in a stand-alone mode.

Notification Attributes

These are some attributes that an application provider can use to get notifications about the installation of the application on the device.

`MIDlet-Install-Notify`

While selling an application over the Internet, an application provider might be interested in knowing if someone has installed the application. This attribute is provided for that purpose. The application provider can specify a destination URL using the HTTP protocol that can accept POST requests. Once a suite is installed, the device will attempt to send a notification message to this URL.

The important point to note is that even if the device is not able to communicate to this URL, the suite must be installed, as long as there is nothing else wrong with it.

`MIDlet-Delete-Notify`

This is the same as the previous attribute, except that this is used during the uninstallation process.

`MIDlet-Delete-Confirm`

This attribute can be used by the application provider to customize the delete confirmation message for the suite. When the user attempts to uninstall the suite from the device, this message will be prompted to the user for confirmation.

Therefore, the application provider can say something like, "If you uninstall this application, you will get seven years of bad luck. Do you still want to continue?"

Push Registry Attributes

The `MIDlet-Push-<n>` attribute can be used to register a MIDlet to handle inbound connections. The `<n>` portion works the same way as in the `MIDlet-<n>` attribute. Registering the MIDlet using these attributes is called static push declaration mechanism and will be covered in detail in Section 4.6.2 (Push Registry).

Table 4.1 summarizes the various configuration attributes that can be put in the manifest or JAD file. The table indicates, for each type of configuration file, whether the given attribute is mandatory or optional.

Table 4.1 MIDlet descriptor attributes present in JAD and/or manifest files

<table>
<tr><th>Attribute name</th><th>JAD</th><th>Manifest</th></tr>
<tr><td>MIDlet-Name</td><td colspan="2" rowspan="3">Mandatory in both files</td></tr>
<tr><td>MIDlet-Version</td></tr>
<tr><td>MIDlet-Vendor</td></tr>
<tr><td>MIDlet-<n></td><td colspan="2" rowspan="3">Mandatory in one of the two files, preferably the manifest</td></tr>
<tr><td>MicroEdition-Profile</td></tr>
<tr><td>MicroEdition-Configuration</td></tr>
<tr><td>MIDlet-Jar-URL</td><td rowspan="2">Mandatory</td><td rowspan="2">Not applicable</td></tr>
<tr><td>MIDlet-Jar-Size</td></tr>
<tr><td>MIDlet-Icon</td><td>Optional</td><td>Optional</td></tr>
<tr><td>MIDlet-Data-Size</td><td>Optional</td><td>Optional</td></tr>
<tr><td>MIDlet-Description</td><td>Optional</td><td>Optional</td></tr>
<tr><td>MIDlet-Info-URL</td><td>Optional</td><td>Optional</td></tr>
<tr><td>MIDlet-Permissions</td><td>Optional</td><td>Optional</td></tr>
<tr><td>MIDlet-Permissions-Opt</td><td>Optional</td><td>Optional</td></tr>
<tr><td>MIDlet-Install-Notify</td><td>Optional</td><td>Optional</td></tr>
<tr><td>MIDlet-Delete-Notify</td><td>Optional</td><td>Optional</td></tr>
<tr><td>MIDlet-Delete-Confirm</td><td>Optional</td><td>Optional</td></tr>
<tr><td>MIDlet-Push-<n></td><td>Optional</td><td>Optional</td></tr>
</table>

4.4 JOURNEYS OF MIDLET SUITE

The MIDlet suite that we created in the last section goes through several distinct phases during its lifetime. We already saw one of them—creation. Once the suite has been created, it needs to be deployed to some customer-accessible locations, such as a website. Once the application has been deployed to a website, it just remains there and waits for a customer.

The excitement comes when a customer comes browsing for applications. The customer might have seen an advertisement and decided to purchase the application. After he has discovered the application in this manner, he would then proceed to the website, download the application and finally install it on his device and run it. At a later stage, he might also want to download updates to the application. Finally, when he is tired of the application or has found something better, he might remove the application altogether from his device. Figure 4.5 illustrates the journeys of a MIDlet suite.

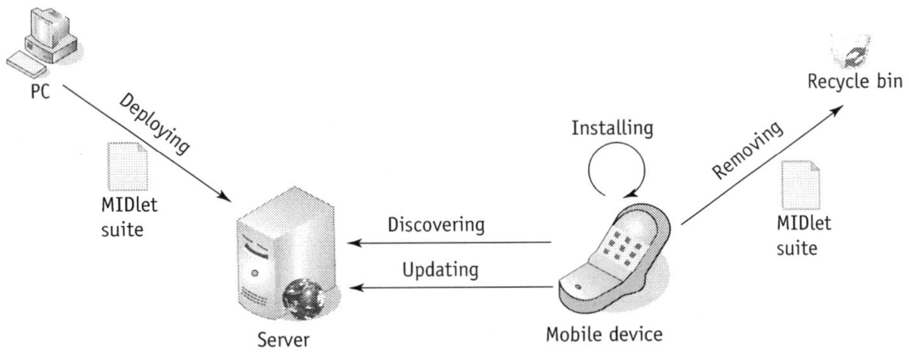

Figure 4.5 Journeys in the life of a MIDlet suite

We will discuss each stage of this process in detail in the following section.

4.4.1 Deploying Applications

Once the JAR file and the JAD file are created for the MIDlet suite, the next step would typically be to make it available for public consumption. The most common way to do this is to make the JAD file available on the Internet. As mentioned earlier, the JAD file must have the Multipurpose Internet Mail Extensions (MIME) type "`text/vnd.sun.j2me.app-descriptor`" and must have the extension "jad".

4.4.2 Discovering Applications

Now that the suite has been made public, a device can simply go to the Internet site using a native browser. The user can download the application to his device. When the link is selected, the JAD file is downloaded to the device. This allows the device to learn about the application before downloading the whole thing. AMS checks if the conditions set forth in the JAD file for successful installation of the MIDlet suite (like network requirement, data size, etc.) can be met. In case the conditions cannot be met, the AMS would display an appropriate message giving reasons as to why the application cannot be installed on the device.

If all conditions can be met by AMS, it proceeds to download the JAR file using the link provided in the JAD file (`MIDlet-Jar-URL`). Before downloading, the AMS also checks with the user if it's OK to download so many bytes (`MIDlet-Jar-Size`). Once the user accepts, AMS proceeds to download the application and install it on the device.

AMS must support at least HTTP 1.1 protocol for downloading data from the Internet. In case of secure web pages, the server may return a 401 (unauthorized) or 407 (proxy authentication required) error code. If that happens, AMS will prompt the user for a username and password to send to the server for authentication. At least Basic Authentication (RFC-2617) will be supported by AMS to achieve this.

4.4.3 Installing Applications

During the installation, the user will always have an option to cancel the application download/installation.

If the installation fails for any reason, AMS will supply a status code indicating the reason for the failure. Table 4.2 shows some of the possible status codes that can be returned by AMS and the reasons behind them.

Table 4.2 MIDlet installation status codes

Status code	*Reason*
900	Suite installed successfully
901	Insufficient memory
902	User cancelled the installation
903	Loss of service (Signal became weak, etc.)
904	JAR size mismatch (The size specified in the JAD file did not match the size of the downloaded file.)
905	Attribute mismatch (The attributes "`MIDlet-Name`", "`MIDlet-Vendor`" and/or "`MIDlet-Version`" specified in the JAD file and the manifest file did not match.)
906	Invalid descriptor (The JAD file is not well-formed or could not be parsed properly or contains invalid values for some important attributes.)

Exam Tip

You don't need to memorize the status codes listed in Table 4.2. The table is just to demonstrate the usage of status codes and their descriptions as an example.

A MIDlet suite author or the website administrator may want to be notified if someone downloads and installs it on their device. For example, this might be a part of the registration process. As mentioned earlier, this is possible by providing a URL in the "`MIDlet-Install-Notify`" attribute of the JAD file. If provided, AMS would then send a notification with the status code and the status message using HTTP POST method. If the URL specified uses a protocol other than HTTP, it may be ignored by AMS. In return, the website can respond with a "`200 OK`" message. The response must not contain anything else. If it does, it will be ignored to save network bandwidth.

After installation, AMS will provide a screen to the user where he can select the newly installed suite from a list of suites installed in the device.

4.4.4 Updating Applications

If a version of a MIDlet suite being installed already exists in the device, the installation is considered by AMS as an update to the existing version. Regardless of whether the version downloaded is older, newer, or the same as the existing application, AMS will prompt the user for confirmation before installing the application. AMS uses the "`MIDlet-Version`" attribute to determine if the application is older, newer, or the same as the existing one.

As a part of the installation, AMS will try its best to preserve the associated data (persistent stores). But there is no explicit guarantee that it will be preserved.

4.4.5 Removing Applications

Finally, the user may remove a suite already installed in a device. AMS will confirm the action before proceeding with the removal process. As mentioned earlier, the suite author may provide a customized message to be displayed when a MIDlet suite is being removed using the "`MIDlet-Delete-Confirm`" attribute in the descriptor. If present, this message will be displayed to the user as a part of the confirmation. When a suite is being removed, all the applications in the suite as well as the associated record stores will be removed.

4.5 PLATFORM REQUEST API

Now we begin to examine some of the APIs that provide essential functionality to a MIDlet. One of the most interesting features in the `MIDlet` class is the platform request API. Since MIDlets cannot access the device-specific functionality, such as dialing phone numbers, a special method has been provided in the `MIDlet` class to perform some basic functions. While this method has been written in a generic form so that any functionality could theoretically be invoked, only a few functions are defined by MIDP. The method for invoking such functionality takes a very generic form:

```
public final boolean platformRequest(String url)
  throws ConnectionNotFoundException
```

The default implementation supports three functions via this method.

1. The ability to install another MIDP application
2. The ability to update the application that is invoking the method
3. The ability to initiate a voice call

Manufacturers may provide additional features, which are not supported by the specification. If the program passes an URL that cannot be interpreted by the implementation, it will throw a `ConnectionNotFoundException` back to the application. The return value indicates if the application should be stopped before the appropriate action can be made (say, a phone call).

4.5.1 Installing MIDlet

If the `url` parameter points to a JAD or JAR file, the method call is interpreted to be an installation request. The application will hand over the information to AMS and will go to the background. AMS will then use the standard procedure (as explained in previous sections) to install the application and once done, it will resume the paused application (the one that initiated the call).

4.5.2 Updating MIDlet

If the `url` parameter refers to a JAD or JAR file that represents the application invoking the method, the method invocation is interpreted to be an update request to the current application. In that scenario, AMS will stop the currently running application and then go ahead with the update using the standard procedure. AMS will not automatically restart the application. It has to be done manually.

4.5.3 Making Phone Call

If the `url` passed is in the format

```
tel:<RFC2806-number>
```

the method invocation is treated as a request to start a voice call to the provided number. AMS uses the device's native application to initiate the phone call. The number supports both domestic and international calling facilities. The number URL must be in the format specified by the IETF's RFC 2806.

4.5.4 Restrictions

As the execution of this `platformRequest(String)` method call may incur a cost to the user (data transfer or voice call), the user will be explicitly prompted for confirmation before the appropriate action is taken. The user can either accept or reject the request.

The method is non-blocking. That is, the implementation happens on a separate thread and the method itself returns immediately. The implementation is not expected to queue multiple requests. If multiple requests are made, it will honor only the last request.

If the resources required to execute the method are not available immediately, AMS may wait until the application exits before taking the appropriate action (say, making a phone call). In such cases, after the application exits, the appropriate application will be shown to the user right away.

4.6 PLAYING AROUND WITH EVENTS AND NOTIFICATIONS

Another important feature available to the MIDlet programmer is the APIs that support a couple modes of event notification. Most applications will need to handle events that occur outside the logic of the main thread of execution. These events might be externally triggered or they might be scheduled, by the application itself, to occur at a given time in the future. These events are called notifications to signify the mechanisms by which the application will be notified of their occurrence. MIDlets have two such mechanisms at their disposal. If the MIDlet wants to schedule an event for the future, the APIs provide a Timer mechanism. The mechanism for being notified of externally triggered events is the Push Registry.

4.6.1 Timers and Background Threads

`Timers` can be used to run some tasks of an application at a scheduled time. Most Java developers would have used this `Timer` before as it is the same one as found in the Java SE. A `Timer` uses threads in the background and ensures that its operation does not affect the rest of the application. The `Timer` itself is thread-safe. Therefore, multiple threads can access a `Timer` object without having to do any synchronization.

Scheduling a Task

There are four possible ways to use a `Timer`:

- ❑ Start a task at a specified time
- ❑ Start a task after some delay relative to the time when the task was created
- ❑ Start a task at a specified time and keep repeating it at constant intervals
- ❑ Start a task after some delay relative to the time when the task was created, and keep repeating it at constant intervals

Figure 4.6 illustrates the above four possible ways to create and execute a task.

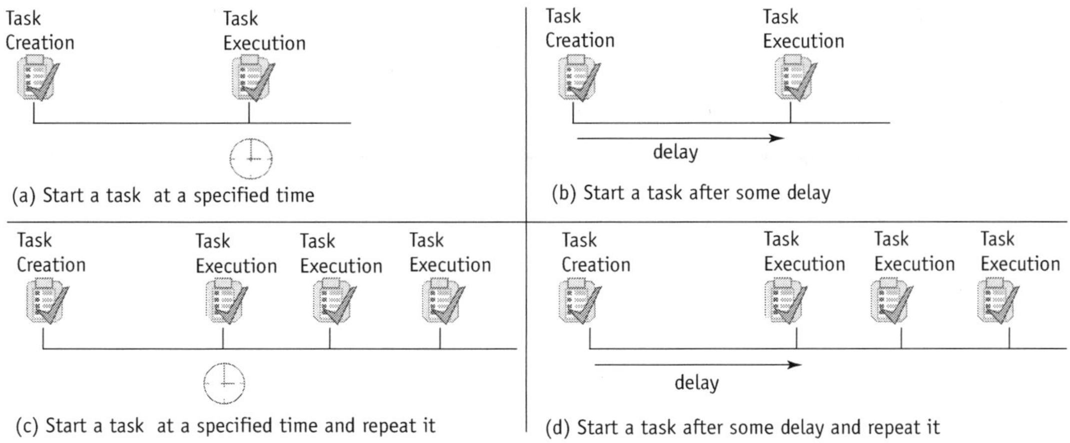

Figure 4.6 Four possible ways to create and execute a task

The application must use a `TimerTask` object to represent the task that needs to be executed by the `Timer`. A `TimerTask` is a simple, abstract object that can be put in a `Thread` (it implements the `Runnable` interface). To give the `TimerTask` the code that it should execute when it is invoked, you override its `run()`.

Canceling a Task

If it is a one-time task and has already been executed, the associated `TimerTask` object will be cancelled automatically to ensure that it does not run again (well, it cannot be because a task can either be scheduled using a fixed date or using a relative time, and both cannot happen more than once).

In case the application wants to cancel a task before its scheduled execution or cancel a recurring task, it just has to invoke the `cancel()` method of the `TimerTask` object. This method returns `true` if the invocation affects any future tasks. If the task is already completed, or has not yet been scheduled, or is already cancelled, this method will return `false`. If a task is running while the method is called, the task will run till it ends. But it will not run again (even if it is scheduled as a repeated task).

Canceling a Timer

The `Timer` object also has a `cancel()` method that does not return anything. As with a `TimerTask`, if a task associated with this `Timer` is already running while this method is called, that task will execute completely. After that, no more tasks associated with this `Timer` will be run.

It is possible to invoke both the `cancel()` methods within the `run()` method of the `TimerTask` object. If so, then this will absolutely guarantee the task (in case of a `TimerTask.cancel()`) or any other task (in case of a `Timer.cancel()`) will never run.

Exam Tip

Be wary of tricky questions that might confuse you with the `cancel()` methods in the `Timer` and `TimerTask` classes. As always, read the question very carefully—more so in this case.

Alarm Clock Application

Let us see the practical use of a `Timer` by creating a simple alarm clock application. The application should be capable of storing a time entered by the user and then displaying a "*BEEP* *BEEP* *BEEP*" message when the time requested reaches.

In order to write this application, we need three screens—one to show normal activity when there is no alarm, one to get the alarm time from the user, and one to display the message upon alarm event. To spice things up a bit, we also want to show a constantly ticking clock on the screen where the alarm time is being set. Figure 4.7 shows how the program would look when installed in a mobile device.

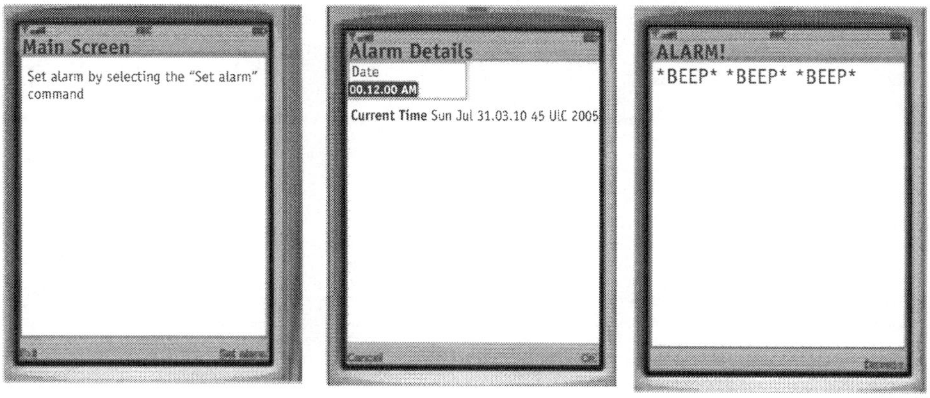

Figure 4.7 Screens for the alarm clock application

Let's get our hands dirty with the code for the alarm clock application displayed above.

☞ **Note:** Don't worry when you see a bunch of User Interface (UI) classes in upcoming listings. They will be covered in detail in Chapter 5 (A face to remember—the MIDP User Interface API). For now, let's focus on the alarm-related code.

Listing 4.2 represents the main screen for the application. This screen simply provides some information about the current status of the application.

Listing 4.2: The main screen

```
package com.scmadkit.ch04;
import javax.microedition.lcdui.*;
/**
 * This is the main screen for the application. This screen simply
 * provides some information about the current status of the
 * application.
 *
 * @author Sathya.Srinivasan
 */
public class MainScreen extends TextBox {
 /** Command to set the alarm */
 public static final Command SET_ALARM_COMMAND
             = new Command("Set alarm", Command.SCREEN, 1);      ❶
 /** Command to stop the application */
 public static final Command EXIT_COMMAND
                  = new Command("Exit", Command.EXIT, 2);
 private static final String MESSAGE
             = "Set alarm by selecting the \"Set Alarm\" command.";
 /**
 * Creates a new instance of MainScreen.
```

```
    */
    public MainScreen() {
      super("Main Screen", MESSAGE, 100, TextField.ANY);
      this.initialize();
    }
    /**
    * Initializes this screen with necessary UI objects.
    */
    private void initialize() {
      this.addCommand(SET_ALARM_COMMAND);
      this.addCommand(EXIT_COMMAND);
    }
}
```

(1) The command to set the alarm

Upon clicking on the command provided in Listing 4.2 to set the alarm, we'll be forwarded to the screen where we can set the alarm time. Listing 4.3 represents the screen that is used to take user input regarding the time when the alarm should be set.

Listing 4.3: The screen for setting the alarm time

```
package com.scmadkit.ch04;
import java.util.Calendar;
import java.util.Date;
import javax.microedition.lcdui.*;
/**
 * This screen is used to take user input regarding the time when the
 * alarm should be set.
 *
 * @author Sathya.Srinivasan
 */
public class AlarmSetForm extends Form implements TimeDisplay {
    /** Command to set the time */
    public static final Command OK_COMMAND
                                   = new Command("OK", Command.OK, 1);
    /** Command to go back to the main screen */
    public static final Command CANCEL_COMMAND
                              = new Command("Cancel", Command.CANCEL, 2);
    private DateField dateField
                         = new DateField("Date", DateField.TIME);          (1)
    private StringItem stringItem
                  = new StringItem("Current Time", new Date().toString());
    /**
    * Creates a new instance of AlarmSetForm.
    */
   public AlarmSetForm() {
      super("Alarm Details");
      this.initialize();
```

```
  }
  /**
   * Initializes this screen with necessary UI objects.
   */
  private void initialize() {
   // Adds UI Objects.
   this.append(dateField);
   this.append(stringItem);
   // Adds Commands to this screen.
   this.addCommand(OK_COMMAND);
   this.addCommand(CANCEL_COMMAND);
  }
  /**
   * Gets the time that was set by the user.
   */
  public Date getAlarmTime() {
   // Gets the time set by the user.
   Date dateValue = dateField.getDate();
   // If no time has been set by user, return null.
   if(dateValue == null) {
     return null;
   }
   Calendar cal = Calendar.getInstance();
   Calendar ref = Calendar.getInstance();
   cal.setTime(dateValue);
   cal.set(Calendar.MONTH, ref.get(Calendar.MONTH));
   cal.set(Calendar.YEAR, ref.get(Calendar.YEAR));
   cal.set(Calendar.DAY_OF_MONTH,
            ref.get(Calendar.DAY_OF_MONTH));
   return cal.getTime();
  }
  /**
   * Sets the current time.
   *
   * @param time The current time.
   */
  public void setTime(Date time) {
   stringItem.setText(time.toString());
  }
}
```

❶ The field where the user can input the alarm time

❷ Since the user sets only time, we need to get the month, day, and year when the alarm was set also. We don't want to get this from the user as it would be an inconvenience. Get it from the Calendar instead.

Listing 4.3 makes use of the `Calendar` class to set the month, day and year. Since the user needs to set only time, we need to get the month, day and year when the alarm was set. We don't want to get them from the user as it would be an inconvenience. Instead, the application will get them from the `Calendar` utility class instead. Once the user sets the alarm time in the screen displayed in Listing 4.3, we'll just need to wait for the alarm to display a "*BEEP* *BEEP* *BEEP*" message when the time requested reaches. Listing 4.4 represents the screen that is displayed when the alarm time reaches.

Listing 4.4: The screen when the alarm occurs

```
package com.scmadkit.ch04;
import javax.microedition.lcdui.*;
/**
 * This screen is displayed when the alarm occurs.
 *
 * @author Sathya.Srinivasan
 */
public class AlarmForm extends TextBox {
 public static final Command OK_COMMAND
                         = new Command("Dismiss", Command.OK, 1);
 /** Creates a new instance of AlarmForm */
 public AlarmForm() {
   super("ALARM!", "*BEEP* *BEEP* *BEEP*", 100, TextField.ANY);      ❶
   this.initialize();
 }
 /**
 * Initializes the UI objects of this screen.
 */
 private void initialize() {
     this.addCommand(OK_COMMAND);
 }
}
```

❶ The message that is to be displayed when the alarm time reaches

Now that we have the main screens out of the way, let us look at the code for creating the `TimerTasks`. In order to create a `Timer`, we need a `TimerTask` that goes along with it. The `run()` method of this class will be executed when the event occurs. Listing 4.5 represents the subclass of the `TimerTask` that we implemented to show the alarm screen at the scheduled time.

Listing 4.5: The task that will be executed when the alarm goes off

```
package com.scmadkit.ch04;
import java.util.TimerTask;
import javax.microedition.lcdui.Display;
import javax.microedition.lcdui.Displayable;
import javax.microedition.midlet.MIDlet;
/**
 * This is a customization of the TimerTask class
```

```
 * to show the alarm screen at the scheduled time.
 *
 * @author Sathya.Srinivasan
 */
public class AlarmTask extends TimerTask {
  private Displayable dis;
  private MIDlet midlet;
  /**
  * Sets the screen that should be displayed
  * when the scheduled event occurs.
  *
  */
     public void setDisplayable(MIDlet midlet, Displayable dis) {
       this.dis = dis;
       this.midlet = midlet;
     }
     public void run() {
       Display.getDisplay(midlet).setCurrent(dis);
  }
}
```

(1) This method is called at the scheduled time. In our case, we simply want to show the screen that was set earlier.

The `TimerTask` subclass that is shown in Listing 4.5 will be executed when the alarm goes off by simply showing the screen that was set earlier. The next step is to create another task for changing the time in the reference clock for every second. Listing 4.6 represents the subclass of the `TimerTask` that we implemented to mimic a clock and the interface that the corresponding display must implement.

Listing 4.6: A task to change the time and an interface that the corresponding display must implement

```
package com.scmadkit.ch04;
import java.util.Date;
import java.util.TimerTask;
import javax.microedition.lcdui.TextBox;
/**
 * This task acts like a clock. The task itself simply changes the
 * contents of the associated display with the current date.
 *
 * @author Sathya.Srinivasan
 */
public class ClockTask extends TimerTask {
  private TimeDisplay display;
  /** Creates a new instance of ClockTask */
  public ClockTask(TimeDisplay display) {
       this.display = display;
```

```
  }
  public void run() {
    display.setTime(new Date());           (1)
  }
}
package com.scmadkit.ch04;
import java.util.Date;
/**
 * Interface to an UI that sets the current time.
 *
 * @author Sathya.Srinivasan
 */
public interface TimeDisplay {
  /**
   * Sets the current time on the display.
   *
   * @param time The current time.
   */
   public void setTime(Date time);
}
```

(1) This method changes the contents of the display with the current date.

The `TimerTask` subclass that is shown in Listing 4.6 is used to change the contents of the associated display with the current date. It is implemented just to let us know the current date and time so that we know what we should set for the alarm time. Finally, we need the main application that ties all these pieces together. Listing 4.7 represents the main application that extends the `MIDlet` class and defines the lifecycle of the application.

Listing 4.7: The main application that calls the shots

```
package com.scmadkit.ch04;
import java.util.Date;
import java.util.Timer;
import javax.microedition.midlet.*;
import javax.microedition.lcdui.*;
/**
 * This is the main class that defines
 * the lifecycle of the application.
 * The AMS will call the startApp() method
 * when this application is launched.
 *
 * @author Sathya.Srinivasan
*/
public class AlarmMIDlet extends MIDlet implements CommandListener {
  private AlarmSetForm alarmSetForm = new AlarmSetForm();
  private AlarmForm alarmForm = new AlarmForm();
  private MainScreen mainForm = new MainScreen();
  private Timer timer = new Timer();
```

```
   private AlarmTask task;
   private ClockTask clock;
   private Timer clockTimer = new Timer();
 /**
  * Starts this application.
  */
 public void startApp() {
    // Adds this class as a listener to commands in various screens.
    mainForm.setCommandListener(this);
    alarmSetForm.setCommandListener(this);
    alarmForm.setCommandListener(this);
    // Sets the clock timer.
    clock = new ClockTask(alarmSetForm);
    clockTimer.scheduleAtFixedRate(clock, 1000, 1000);
    // Shows the main screen.
    Display.getDisplay(this).setCurrent(mainForm);
 }
 /**
  * Pauses this application. We don't have to do much here for this
  * example.
  */
 public void pauseApp() {
 }
 /**
  * This method is called when the application is destroyed by the
  * AMS. If a Timer has been set, we might want to cancel it before
  * closing the app.
  */
 public void destroyApp(boolean unconditional) {
    // Cancels any tasks in the timer.
    timer.cancel();
 }
 /**
  * This method is invoked whenever a command is executed by the
  * user, as this class has registered itself as a listener to all
  * the screens.
  */
 public void commandAction(Command c, Displayable d) {
    if(c == AlarmSetForm.OK_COMMAND) {
      mainForm.setString("Alarm has been set for "
                          + alarmSetForm.getAlarmTime());        1
      // The user wants to set the timer.
      // Cancels the currently running task, if any.
      if(task != null) {
          task.cancel();
          timer.cancel();
```

```
            }
            // Sets the timer task.
            task = new AlarmTask();
            task.setDisplayable(this, alarmForm);
            timer.schedule(task, alarmSetForm.getAlarmTime());
            // Goes back to the main screen.
            Display.getDisplay(this).setCurrent(mainForm);
        } else if (c == AlarmSetForm.CANCEL_COMMAND) {
            Display.getDisplay(this).setCurrent(mainForm);              (2)
        } else if (c == MainScreen.SET_ALARM_COMMAND) {
            Display.getDisplay(this).setCurrent(alarmSetForm);          (3)
        } else if (c == MainScreen.EXIT_COMMAND) {
            this.notifyDestroyed();                                     (4)
        } else if (c == AlarmForm.OK_COMMAND) {
            StringBuffer msg = new StringBuffer();
            msg.append("Last alarm occurred at ");
            msg.append(new Date(task.scheduledExecutionTime()));        (5)
            mainForm.setString(msg.toString());
            Display.getDisplay(this).setCurrent(mainForm);
        }
    }
}
```

(1) The user has just set the alarm and the display is changed.
(2) The user decides not to set the alarm, so the application goes back to main screen without setting the timer.
(3) The user wants to set the alarm.
(4) The user wants to quit the application, so a notification to the AMS that this application can be destroyed is sent.
(5) The user has just got an alarm and the text in the main screen is changed.

The MIDlet code shown in Listing 4.7 assembles all the classes that we have created so far and is the main entry to the alarm clock application. Last but not least, here's the application descriptor that goes along with the classes.

```
MIDlet-1: AlarmMIDlet, , com.scmadkit.ch04.AlarmMIDlet
MIDlet-Jar-Size: 6508
MIDlet-Jar-URL: SCMADKit.jar
MIDlet-Name: SCMAD Exam Guide
MIDlet-Vendor: McGraw-Hill
MIDlet-Version: 1.0
MicroEdition-Configuration: CLDC-1.1
MicroEdition-Profile: MIDP-2.0
```

Executing a piece of code based on an event is great. What if you want to start the application itself based on an event? This is where a new feature in MIDP 2.0 called push registry comes in.

4.6.2 Push Registry

Push registry is a simple but very powerful mechanism that can be used to start applications in a mobile device based on an external event. Unlike a `Timer` event, which is based on a certain point in time, push registry is based on an external event such as a short message received by the device, or even data received at a network port of the mobile device. This is called push registry because the events are pushed into the application from external sources. This is a truly asynchronous event.

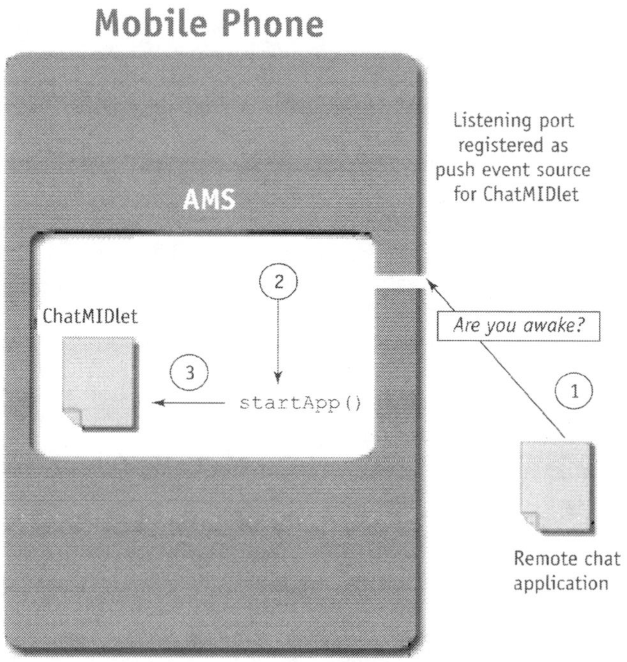

Figure 4.8 The sequence of a push event

In Fig. 4.8, we can see the sequence that occurs during a push event notification. In this figure, we have a `ChatMIDlet` that is configured to be started up when a chat message arrives on the specified listening port. The sequence that triggers the asynchronous execution of the `ChatMIDlet` goes as follows. First, the remote chat application, which certainly doesn't have to be a MIDlet, sends a chat message to a well-known port, one that everybody has agreed to use for this fictional chat protocol, on our mobile phone. Second, the AMS on our mobile phone sees that a message has arrived on one of the ports that it knows and the port is registered as a source of push events, and subsequently invokes `startApp()` on the associated MIDlet. Third, the `ChatMIDlet` begins execution, processes the incoming message, and, we presume, presents the user with an opportunity to respond to the message.

As you can see, this has many implications. On one hand, we can imagine the benefit of a powerful chat client that auto-starts when an incoming message arrives from a remote correspondent. This is great. On the other hand, unmonitored use of this feature can result in many spamming and privacy violations. Basically, a pushed event means that we are giving control over execution to external sources. The potential for security problems should be obvious. The sources of the external push events associated with an application can be specified either in the application descriptor (static declaration) or inside the program itself (dynamic declaration). In the following paragraphs, we will see how to register external push event sources.

Static Declaration

One way to register external event sources is to declare them in the application descriptor. If the connection sources are specified statically, AMS will check if the requirements for the requested connections can be satisfied fully before installing the application. Setting up the listening connections as per the application descriptor becomes part of the installation process. After all, the chat client sketched above wouldn't work very well if it wasn't able to set up a listening connection. If at least one requirement cannot be satisfied, the application will not be installed and the user will be notified of the errors appropriately. The following are the reasons why an application might not be installed because of the Rush Registry requirements.

- ❑ The port where the push events will be received by the application in the device is already reserved by another application.
- ❑ The requested protocol for the push event is not supported by the device.
- ❑ There are syntax errors in the `MIDlet-Push-<n>` attributes declared in the descriptor.
- ❑ Declaration of a MIDlet class in the `MIDlet-Push-<n>` attribute is not declared using a `MIDlet-<n>` attribute in the descriptor.

Now let's look at the details of declaring an external source of push events. Here's the syntax for declaring a push event in the application descriptor.

```
MIDlet-Push-<n>: <ConnectionURL>, <MIDletClassName>, <AllowedSender>
```

In the declaration, `n` is a sequence number that starts from 1. It has the same rules as that of the `MIDlet-<n>` declaration, in that the sequence should not break. If the sequence breaks, then only the contiguous set of entries starting from 1 will be considered. The rest will be ignored.

`<ConnectionURL>` is the URL that has the same syntax as that of the parameter in the `Connector.open` method. It takes the form `protocol://:port`.

`<MIDletClassName>` is the name of a `MIDlet` class that will be called when an event is received from the declared connection endpoint by AMS. The class should already be registered in the descriptor using a valid `MIDlet-<n>` declaration.

`<AllowedSender>` is a filter that can be used to limit the connection sources that can send events to the declared connection endpoint. Using this, the application provider can ensure that only approved sources can send events, thereby providing more security to the consumer and the application.

While the format of the sender is dependent upon the protocol used by the connection, it is typically an IPv4 (or IPv6) address in case of TCP/IP and UDP protocols. Apart from declaring specific addresses, you can also use the '*' and '?' wildcard characters. The '*' can be used to generalize a portion of the string, while the '?' can be used to generalize a single character. Thus, your declarations may be

192.168.0.1 (allows only 192.168.0.1)

192.168.0.* (allows all addresses from 192.168.0.1 to 192.168.0.255)

192.168.0.? (allows all addresses from 192.168.0.1 to 192.168.0.9)

* (allows all addresses)

Dynamic Declaration

The developer can also choose to programmatically configure external sources of push events. This dynamic declaration can be very powerful. The same rules are applied as above but the handling of problems is a bit different since the application is already installed and running. If the connection sources can't be configured, the application may throw an exception (for example, some other applications may be registered to listen for push events from the same source).

So, how do you decide whether to use static or dynamic declaration? As the static declaration is very strict and will not allow an application to be installed if requirements are not satisfied, it must be used carefully. If you think that your application can function even if the push events cannot be enabled, you should use dynamic declaration. This way, at least you are delivering most of your application to the consumer. On the other hand, if the use of push events pretty much lies at the center of your application's functionality, you might want to make sure that the application isn't installed if it can't use the push event mechanisms that it needs.

Exam Tip

If a static push connection declaration cannot be honored by the device, the application will not be installed.

Looking for connections

Before attempting to register a connection, an application might want to check if an endpoint is available or might simply want to see a list of all available connections in the device. The `listConnections` method of the `PushRegistry` class helps the application achieve this goal.

```
public static String[] listConnections(boolean available)
```

This method returns a list of all registered connections in the device or a subset of the registered connections that are available depending on the parameter passed.

Registering a connection

An application can dynamically register an endpoint with AMS for push registry using the `registerConnection` method of the `PushRegistry` class. The full syntax of the method is given below.

```
public static void registerConnection(String connection, String midlet,
String filter) throws ClassNotFoundException, IOException
```

As you can see, the parameters are the same as the `MIDlet-Push-<n>` attributes and have the same meaning as well.

The `ClassNotFoundException` will be thrown if the `MIDlet` fully-qualified class name as passed to the method cannot be found in the MIDlet suite or if no declaration can be found for that class in the descriptor file or the JAR manifest file.

The `IOException` will be thrown if the connection has already been reserved by another application in the device. Moreover, a `ConnectionNotFoundException` may be thrown if the protocol mentioned in the connection string URL is not supported by the device.

Apart from these caught exceptions, the method can also throw an `IllegalArgumentException` if the `connection` string or the `filter` string is `null`, or a `SecurityException` if the `MIDlet` does not have permissions to dynamically register a push connection.

Unregistering a connection

Being a good programmer that you are, you want to clean up the resources before your application exits. Right? The `unregisterConnection` is your method. Here's the syntax.

```
public static boolean unregisterConnection(String connection)
```

The `connection` parameter is the URL that represents the connection, including the protocol, host name and the port number. The return parameter indicates if the operation was successful or not. The method can optionally throw a `SecurityException` if the `MIDlet` attempts to unregister a connection registered by some other application (shame on you!).

So, we have looked at establishing a push registry connection that starts a MIDlet when an externally triggered event arrives. What else can we do with the push registry?

Registering Alarms

A nice feature in the push registry is the ability to register a class as an alarm. This use of the push registry is more like the event scheduling of the `Timer` class. It's not really a pushed event in the sense that the source doesn't come from an external source. It's more like a `Timer` event, but the event will cause an entire `MIDlet` to be executed rather than some arbitrary code written into the `run()` of a `TimerTask`. Using this method, a MIDlet in a MIDlet suite can request AMS to start another MIDlet in the same suite at a specified time. The general syntax of the method is:

```
public static long registerAlarm(String midlet, long time)
   throws ClassNotFoundException, ConnectionNotFoundException
```

The `midlet` parameter is the fully-qualified class name of MIDlet within the MIDlet suite that should be launched. As before, MIDlet must be declared in one of the `MIDlet-<n>` attributes in the descriptor file or the JAR manifest file.

The `time` represents the time when the application must be launched. The value is as returned by the `Date.getTime()` method.

The method returns the most recent time when the application would be launched. This method can throw a `ClassNotFoundException` if the passed `midlet` string is not valid or is not declared in one of the `MIDlet-<n>` attributes in the descriptor or manifest file. It can throw a `ConnectionNotFoundException` if the device does not support alarm-based application launch. It can also throw a `SecurityException` if the application does not have permissions to register an alarm.

The application can register an alarm for one or more MIDlets within a MIDlet suite, but can register only one alarm at a time for a MIDlet. That is, it cannot register the same MIDlet twice at two different start times. If done, the time mentioned in the second call would overwrite the time in the first call.

Interaction between Application and AMS

The push registry mechanism has a very close relation with AMS of the device as it depends on it to handle the incoming connections. The following are major responsibilities of AMS with respect to push registry:

- Listen for inbound connection notifications for the registered push connections, and perform necessary operations if the associated application is currently not running and a connection is requested.
- Shutdown currently running applications as required. Note that how AMS shuts down the application is platform-dependent.
- Start the MIDlet associated with the push connection.

When a MIDlet suite is deleted from the device, AMS will remove all registered push connections for that suite and will make them available to other applications.

Optionally, AMS may do the following:

- If the connection is a message-based connection, AMS may buffer the messages and deliver them to the application after starting it.
- If the connection is a stream-based connection, AMS will open the connection and hand it over to the application after starting it, but AMS does not guarantee that the connection will remain open. The connection time might be over before AMS had a chance to start the application.

☞ **Note:** AMS and the application handle the connection in a mutually exclusive manner. That is, once AMS has started the application and handed over the connection, it is no longer responsible for listening on that endpoint. It is the application's responsibility to reconnect if needed, close the connection, or do whatever it wants to do with it.

Summary

The MIDP 2.0 specification forms the core of the exam and hence that needs to be understood thoroughly. Most of the applications that you will be writing for mobile devices using Java ME will be based on this specification. In this chapter, we focused on the high-level concept of an application defined by the MIDP 2.0—MIDlet. The execution of MIDlets is controlled not by a `main` method entry point, but by the invocation of its various lifecycle methods by AMS. Understanding the lifecycle of a MIDlet is important for successful development for mobile phones, as well as successful performance in the exam.

In addition to the definition of the MIDlet lifecycle, the MIDP 2.0 governs the discovery, installation, execution and removal of MIDlet applications on a device. We examined the packaging of MIDlets and the various methods of providing an application descriptor that allows the agents in the various stages of discovery and installation to make informed decisions about their handling of the application. You need to have a solid understanding of the role of the descriptors in these stages of a MIDlet's life.

We also discussed some of the APIs that are tightly bound to the MIDlet's execution. In particular, we looked a couple of APIs related to events and notification. We examined the `Timer` class, by which MIDlet can schedule future events. We looked at a mechanism for handling events triggered from external sources. The push registry, while associated with only one class, is simple but powerful external event mechanism that allows events to be pushed down to the application from external Internet-based sources.

Now that you've got the basics, and if you downloaded the toolkit, you have what it takes to develop a strong familiarity with MIDlets. Write as many applications as you can to get a hands-on experience. Writing applications will go a long way in helping you remember the lifecycle of the application and questions related to the installation and troubleshooting.

References

1. MIDP 2.0(JSP-118) specification
   http://www.jcp.org/aboutJava/communityprocess/final/jsr118/
2. The MIDP 2.0 Push Registry
   http://developers.sun.com/techtopics/mobility/midp/articles/pushreg/
3. Invoking Platform Services in MIDP 2.0
   http://developers.sun.com/techtopics/mobility/midp/ttips/platformRequest/

Exercises

1. Write a MIDlet that can make a phone call to a pre-defined phone number (your home phone number) using the MIDlet's platform request API.
2. Create a JAD file for a MIDlet suite that has the following specifications:
   a. The name of the suite is "Super Application."
   b. The icon for the suite is "SuperApp.png"
   c. There are two applications in the suite:
      i. The first application name is "Superman". The main class for this application is com.superapp.Superman
      ii. The second application name is "Spiderman". The main class for this application is com.superapp.Spiderman
   d. The description for the suite is "Application for super heroes."
   e. When the suite is being uninstalled, the message "Do you want to kill the super heroes?" must be displayed to the user.

Review Questions

1. If a developer wants to deploy a MIDlet suite whose name is "`MyMidlet`" and whose main classes are "`MyMidlet1`" and "`MyMidlet2`", which of the following declarations can be used in the associated JAD file for successful installation of the suite?
   a. `MIDlet-1: MyMidlet1, MyMidlet1.png, MyMidlet1`
      `MIDlet-2: MyMidlet2, MyMidlet2.png, MyMidlet1`
   b. `Midlet-1: MyMidlet1, , MyMidlet1`
      `Midlet-2: MyMidlet2, , MyMidlet2`
   c. `MIDlet-1: MyMidlet1, , MyMidlet1`
      `MIDlet-2: MyMidlet2, , MyMidlet2`
   d. `MIDlet: MyMidlet1, MyMidlet2`
2. Which of the following attributes are mandatory in the manifest file?
   a. `MIDlet-Name`
   b. `MIDlet-Vendor`
   c. `MIDlet-Jar-URL`
   d. `MIDlet-Install-Notify`
3. A push connection can be registered for an application either through the descriptor files or programmatically inside the application.
   a. True
   b. False
4. Identify the missing states or methods related to the MIDlet lifecycle in the following diagram. For methods, it is sufficient to give the name of the method with two parentheses.

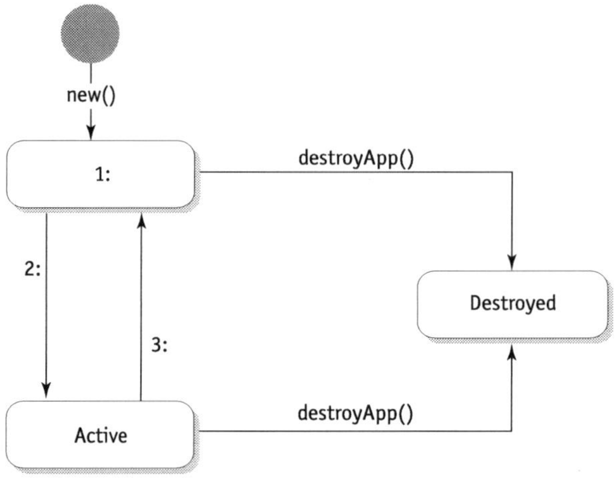

5. Identify the correct MIME type for JAD file.
   a. text/vnd.sun.j2me.app-descriptor
   b. text/vnd.sun.j2me.jad
   c. text/sun.j2me.app-descriptor
   d. text/vnd.sun.j2me. descriptor
6. What will happen when the following class is executed?

```
public class HelloMIDlet extends MIDlet {
   public static void main(String[] args) {
      System.out.println("Hello World! - From main method");
   }
   public void startApp() {
      System.out.println("Hello World! - From start method");
   }
   public void pauseApp() {
      // Nothing here
   }
   public void destroyApp(boolean unconditional) {
      // Nothing here either.
   }
}
```

   a. The message "Hello World!–From main method" will be printed on the console.
   b. The message "Hello World!–From start method" will be printed on the console.
   c. The program will throw an `IllegalStateException` because the `main` method cannot be declared in a MIDlet.
   d. The program will not compile because the `main` method cannot be declared in a MIDlet.
7. Which of the following statements is true about the `platformRequest(String)` method of the `MIDlet` class?

a. This is a blocking method. The application will be paused until the request is completed.
b. This method can be used to perform an update on the currently running application without having a need to close the application.
c. It is possible to make phone calls using the underlying device's phone capabilities using this method.
d. An application cannot access the native file system using this method as per the specification.

8. Which of the following entries is a valid value for the `AllowedSender` attribute of a `MIDlet-Push-<n>` declaration?

a. 64.45.36.*
b. 201.245.2?4.*
c. 200.256.144.5
d. *

9. What will happen when an application attempts to register a push connection dynamically to an endpoint that has already been reserved by another application?

a. The endpoint will be unregistered with the previous application and will be registered with the new application.
b. The endpoint will still be registered with the previous application and the new application will get a `ConnectionNotFoundException`.
c. The endpoint will still be registered with the previous application and the new application will get an `IOException`.
d. The application will not even be installed in the device because AMS will check whether the application tries to create push connections for already reserved endpoints.

10. Which of the following statements is true about the responsibility of AMS related to push connections?

a. For message-based connection, AMS is guaranteed to deliver the messages received before the application has a chance to read messages from the connection.
b. For stream-based connection, AMS is guaranteed to keep the connection open until the application is ready to handle the stream.
c. Once a connection is handed off to the application, AMS is not responsible for the connection anymore, even if the connection gets disconnected.
d. AMS does not guarantee how the currently running application is terminated when another application is started due to a push request.

Review Answers

1. a and c. The `MIDlet-<n>` declaration consists of three parts—name of the MIDlet, an optional icon associated with the name, and the fully qualified class name of the MIDlet. The icon can be omitted, but the separator (comma) should still be present in the declaration. Option b is wrong because the name of the attribute is `MIDlet-<n>`and not `Midlet-<n>`. Attribute names are case-sensitive.

2. a and b. The `MIDlet-Name` and `MIDlet-Vendor` attributes are mandatory for a JAD file. The `MIDlet-Jar-URL` attribute is not applicable for the manifest file but is mandatory for the descriptor file. The `MIDlet-Install-Notify` attribute is an optional attribute for both of them.
3. True. Push connections can be registered for an application either statically through declarations in the descriptor file or dynamically using the methods in the `PushRegistry` class.
4. 1: Paused, 2: startApp(), 3: pauseApp(). The following diagram shows the complete picture.

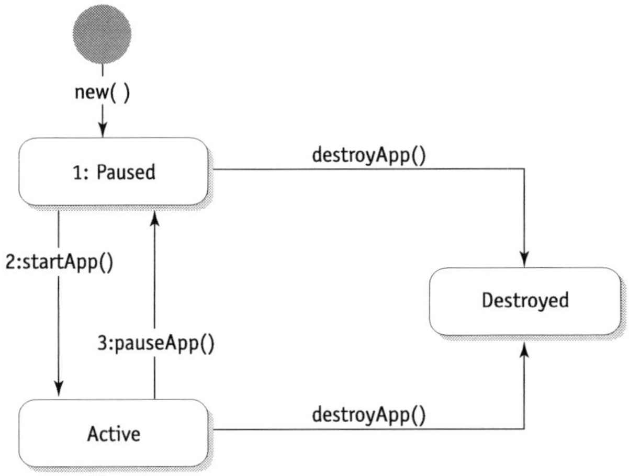

5. a. text/vnd.sun.j2me.app-descriptor is the correct MIME type for the JAD file.
6. b. The MIDP specification states that a MIDlet file should not have a "`public static void main`" method. However, if one is provided, it will be ignored and the MIDlet will be processed normally, which will result in the `startApp()` method being executed first.
7. c. The `platformRequest(String)` method is a non-blocking, non-queuing method. If multiple calls are made to this method in scenarios where the application must exit to honor the call, only the last request will be handled. While it is possible to update the currently running application using the `platformRequest(String)` method, the application must first exit before the update is performed. The update cannot be done while the application is running. Finally, there is no requirement in the specification to access the native file system as it may vary among implementations.
8. a, b, and d. Wildcards '*' and '?' are allowed in the IP address value of the `AllowedSender` attribute to mask either a part of the address or a single character in the address respectively. The '*' value can be used to represent any address. Option c is wrong because it contains an invalid number for an IP address which is 256.
9. c. If an application has already reserved an endpoint, any other application cannot register with the same endpoint dynamically. If there is an attempt, the application will get an `IOException`.

10. c and d. For message-based connections, AMS may store the messages and deliver them to the application before it hands the connection over, but is not required to do so. For stream-based connection, AMS will try to hand over the connection to the application as quick as possible, but will not make any attempts to prevent the connection from getting timed out.

Exam Notes

☞ Explain the specification guarantees for: browsing for MIDlet suites, transferring MIDlet suites using HTTP, push registries, basic authentication, installing and updating MIDlet suites, invoking MIDlet suites and deleting MIDlet suites.

Browsing MIDlet Suites

- AMS must provide facilities for the user to browse the installed MIDlets.

Transferring MIDlet Suites Using HTTP

- Appropriate permissions will be asked from the user if not defined in the descriptor.
- HTTP is used as a protocol for transferring the JAD and JAR files to the device.
- Appropriate header values such as the content-type should be set.

Push Registries

- Static push registries required by the MIDlet suite should be defined using the `MIDlet-Push-<n>` attributes in the JAD file.
- If the requested resources for the push registry attributes are not available, the application will not be installed.

Basic Authentication

- If the application requires basic authentication (401 – Unauthorized, 407 – Proxy authentication required HTTP responses during installation), the device should ask for the user's approval.

Installing MIDlet Suites

- User can cancel a MIDlet suite installation at any time without affecting anything.
- If the installation failed, AMS will supply a status code indicating the reason for the failure.
- The use of "`MIDlet-Install-Notify`" attribute of the JAD file.

Updating MIDlet Suites

- If an application is already installed, further installation of the application is treated as an update to the application installed in the device.
- The MIDP implementation must notify if the installation is an older, newer, or same version as the suite already installed in the device and must get confirmation from the user before the installation begins.
- An untrusted MIDlet suite cannot be updated to a trusted MIDlet suite.

Deleting MIDlet Suites

- When a MIDlet suite is deleted, all MIDlets and RMS data associated with this suite will be deleted.
- User will be prompted for confirmation.
- Individual MIDlet cannot be deleted from a MIDlet suite. The most atomic part is MIDlet suite.

☞ Identify correct and incorrect statements or examples about the MIDP application model, including: the MIDP execution environment, MIDlet suites, MIDlet suite packaging (including the manifest and the application descriptor), discovering available services on the device, and discovering which version of MIDP/CLDC is on the device.

MIDP Execution Environment

- MIDlet suites must not contain classes from CLDC or MIDP API.
- Installed application cannot override system classes/packages.
- Class files cannot be read as resources or extracted for reuse.
- JAD properties can be read using the `MIDlet.getAppProperty()` method.
- Non-class resources in the JAR can be read using the `Class.getResourceAsStream()` method.

MIDlet Suites

- A MIDlet suite must contain at least one class that extends the `MIDlet` class.
- The `MIDlet` class must have a no-args constructor.
- A class should not contain a standard `main` method. If present, the method must be ignored. The `MIDlet` class must be used instead. This is because the `main` method is the starting point for a CLDC application, but is overridden by the MIDP specification at the profile level.

MIDlet Suite Packaging

- A MIDlet suite contains a JAD file and a JAR file.
- One or more MIDlets may be present in a JAR file.

- The manifest file (`/META-INF/manifest.mf`) file inside the JAR file contains attributes used during the installation and execution of the suite.

MIDP/CLDC Version Discovery

- The version of the implemented MIDP specification can be obtained by calling the `System.getProperty("microedition.profiles")` or `MIDlet.getAppProperty("MicroEdition-Profile")` method if a JAD file is present.
- The version of the implemented CLDC specification can be obtained by calling the `System.getProperty("microedition.configuration")` or `MIDlet.getAppProperty("MicroEdition-Configuration")` method. This would typically be "`CLDC-1.0`" or "`CLDC-1.1`".

☞ Develop applications that correctly reflect a MIDlet's application lifecycle, including: the purpose of the MIDlet class, communication with the application management software, platform request API, valid MIDlet states and transitions, and the behavior that should and should not be implemented within different lifecycle methods (including the constructor).

Purpose of MIDlet Class

- The `MIDlet` class is the starting point for running a MIDlet suite.
- The class provides methods to AMS for managing the lifecycle of MIDlet. These will be used by AMS to change the lifecycle state of a MIDlet. They are `startApp()`, `pauseApp()` and `destroyApp(boolean)`.

MIDlet Communication with AMS

Method	*Description*
`notifyPaused()`	The MIDlet is ready to be paused.
`notifyDestroyed()`	The MIDlet is ready to be destroyed.
`resumeRequest()`	The MIDlet is ready to run again.

Platform Request API

- The method signature - `MIDlet.platformRequest(String url):boolean`
- This indicates that the requested URL should be handled.
- The MIDlet maybe in background while this is being done. If this is not possible, the device may wait till the MIDlet exits and might then handle the requested MIDlet.
- This is a non-blocking method.
- On platforms where the device has to exit to honor this request, if multiple requests are made, only last request will be handled. If not, multiple requests must be handled concurrently.

- A very typical use for this request is to install an update of the running application.
  - If the requested URL refers to an update to the requesting MIDlet, the application must be stopped to install the update.
  - If the requested resource is another MIDlet suite but not an update, it should be handled like a new install. The requesting MIDlet may or may not be stopped based on the device capability.
- Another use of the API is to make a phone call.
  - In this case, the URL should be of the form "`tel://msisdn-number`".
  - The request should be passed to the default phone application of the device.
  - Appropriate permissions must be requested from the user first.

Valid MIDlet States and Transitions

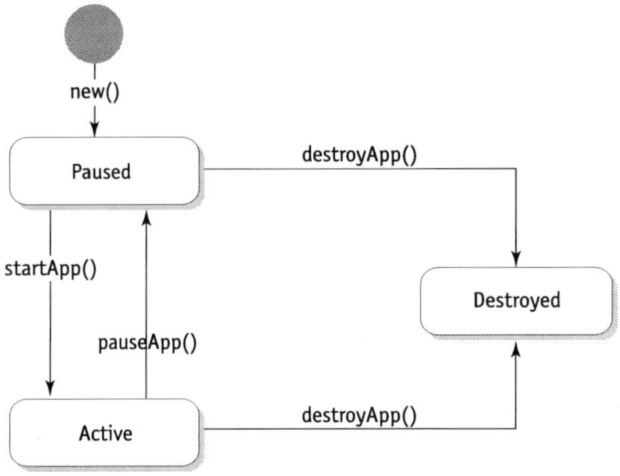

MIDlet Lifecycle Behavior

- MIDlet (or any other class in the suite) should not have a `static public void main(String[] args)` method. If present, the method will be ignored by AMS.
- MIDlet must not call the `System.exit()` method. If called, a `SecurityException` will be thrown.
- Call the `MIDlet.notifyDestroyed()` after calling the `MIDlet.destroyApp()` method if you want to close the application from inside the application. This is the one that notifies that `MIDlet` is ready to be destroyed.

☞ Deploy a MIDP 2.0 application with the correct use of JAD files and manifests.

Mandatory Attributes

- A JAD file does not have to be present to install a MIDlet. In such case, the MIDlet suite is treated as untrusted.

Attribute name	*Description*	*Manifest*	*JAD*
`MIDlet-Name`	The name of the MIDlet suite	Mandatory	Mandatory
`MIDlet-Version`	The version for this MIDlet suite	Mandatory	Mandatory
`MIDlet-Vendor`	The name of the vendor providing the MIDlet	Mandatory	Mandatory
`MIDlet-Jar-URL`	The URL of the JAR file	N/A	Mandatory
`MIDlet-Jar-Size`	The size of the attached JAR file	N/A	Mandatory
`MIDlet-<n>`	The description for each MIDlet in the form: `MIDletName, {Icon-URL}, MIDletClassName`	Mandatory in either one	Mandatory in either one
`MicroEdition-Profile`	The implemented profile needed. Typically MIDP-2.0	Mandatory in either one	Mandatory in either one
`MicroEdition-Configuration`	The minimum configuration needed. Typically CLDC-1.0 or CLDC-1.1	Mandatory in either one	Mandatory in either one

Optional Attributes

Attribute name	*Description*	*Where?*
`MIDlet-Icon`	The icon for the MIDlet suite	Manifest or JAD
`MIDlet-Data-Size`	The minimum memory space required by the application	Manifest or JAD
`MIDlet-Description`	The description for the MIDlet suite	Manifest or JAD
`MIDlet-Info-URL`	The URL where further information can be obtained about the MIDlet suite	Manifest or JAD
`MIDlet-Permissions`	Permissions required for the MIDlet suite	Manifest or JAD
`MIDlet-Permissions-Opt`	Optional permissions for the MIDlet suite	Manifest or JAD
`MIDlet-Install-Notify`	The URL where the success of installation is to be notified. The POST method of the HTTP protocol must be supported	Manifest or JAD
`MIDlet-Delete-Notify`	The URL where the success of deletion is to be notified. The POST method of the HTTP protocol must be supported	Manifest or JAD
`MIDlet-Delete-Confirm`	The confirmation message to be displayed to the user before the deletion of the MIDlet suite	Manifest or JAD
`MIDlet-Push-<n>`	Push Registry entries. Format is similar to `MIDlet-<n>` attribute	Manifest or JAD

☞ Given an installation failure, analyze the problem and develop possible resolutions.

Status code		*Status message* *Description*
900	Success	The MIDlet suite was installed successfully.
901	Insufficient memory	There is not enough memory to install the `MIDlet` suite. Try to reduce the `MIDlet-Data-Size` requirement if it is too high.

902	User cancelled	User cancelled the installation. Don't cancel next time!
903	Loss of service	Service for data transfer was lost. Maybe the service operator was not good. Try again.
904	JAR size mismatch	The size of the JAR does not match size mentioned in the JAD file. Correct the attribute value.
905	Attribute mismatch	At least the value of an attribute in JAR manifest does not match with that of a JAD attribute. Correct the attribute value mismatch (especially, `MIDlet-Vendor, MIDlet-Name`, and `MIDlet-Version`). If `MIDlet` is trusted, all `MIDlet-*` must match between JAR manifest and JAD entries.
906	Invalid descriptor	The JAD file is invalid. Correct the values. Some mandatory values might be missing and/or there are some bad entries in the JAD.
907	Invalid JAR	JAR file is invalid. The manifest cannot be extracted from the JAR. The JAR manifest does not have correct syntax or some mandatory attributes might be missing.
908	Incompatible configuration or profile	The configuration value for the `MicroEdition—Configuration` attribute or the profile value for the `MicroEdition-Profile` attribute is invalid.
909	Application authentication failure	The application could not be authenticated properly.
910	Application authorization failure	The installation is not authorized. An attempt was made to install an untrusted version of an installed, trusted suite. Permissions mentioned in the `MIDlet-Permissions` attribute cannot be satisfied.
911	Push registration failure	The static push registry entries could not be honored.
912	Deletion notification	Deletion notifications could not be sent successfully.

☞ Given a set of requirements, develop applications that correctly implement MIDP 2.0 support for delayed or scheduled activities using timers and background threads.

Timer and TimerTask

- These classes function roughly in the same manner as that of their counterpart classes in Java SE.
- The `TimerTask` is a `Runnable` class that can be used to do something upon being triggered by the `Timer` class.
  - The `scheduledExecutionTime()` returns the scheduled time of the last run of this task or the currently running task.
  - The `cancel()` method cancels the task if it has not run yet. If it is a repeating task, this will not run again.
- At least five `Timer` threads must be supported by a MIDP 2.0-compliant device.
- The `Timer` class is thread-safe.
- The `Timer.schedule` methods can be used to schedule tasks.

Method arguments	*Description*
`TimerTask task, Date time`	Schedules the task to be run at the specified time.
`TimerTask task, Date firstTime, long period`	Schedules the task to be run repetitively.
`TimerTask task, long delay`	Schedules the task to be run after a specified delay from the time of the call (in milliseconds).
`TimerTask task, long delay, long period`	Schedules the task to be run after a specified delay repetitively from the time of the call (in milliseconds).

- The `Timer.scheduleAtFixedRate()` methods can be used to schedule tasks at a fixed rate.

☞ Explain MIDP 2.0 push registry benefits and limitations, and describe its use in applications.

Push Registry Benefits

- Push registry can be used to start an application based on an external event received from a port that it is registered to.
  - If the application is not running or is paused when an event is received, AMS will start the application in the standard process. The application can then receive the message or stream using the standard process.
  - If the application is running, nothing happens since the application will already be listening for messages or streams anyway.
- Push registry can be used for `socket`, `datagram`, `sms` and `cbs` protocols.
- IPv4 and IPv6 URLs are supported.
- If an application is not running, the messages will be received by AMS and delivered to the application after starting it for `Message` connections.
- If an application is not running, the stream will be preserved by AMS and handed over to the application after starting it for `datagram` or `socket` connections, as long as the stream connection does not timeout.

Push Registry Limitations

- Two MIDlet suites cannot share the same push registry connection.
- If all the statically declared connections could not be registered successfully during installation of the application or if there are errors in the declaration, the application will not be installed.
- All implementations are not required to support push registry for protocols that typically support push registry. In such case, an attempt to register the connection will result in a `ConnectionNotFoundException`. For example, the system might support socket protocol, but not necessarily support push registry for the `socket` protocol.

Use of Push Registry in Applications

- When a push registry event is received by AMS, what happens to the currently running application (it cannot be the application to which the event is registered to, since push registry will not listen to events of the currently running application) is up to the implementation. It may pause or destroy the running application before starting the target application.
- If an application is running and has registered itself to the push registry for some events,
  - AMS will not listen for events for that application.
  - If the application calls the `Connection.close()` method, any events sent to that port will be lost (the push registry will not be listening as the application is currently running).
  - Once the application is destroyed, AMS will start listening for events for that application.
- An application can register itself for an alarm using the `registerAlarm(String class, long time)`.
  - The `class` should be a MIDlet in the currently running MIDlet suite.
  - Upon receipt of an event, the `class` will be notified when the `time` arrives.
  - At most, only one alarm can be registered per registry entry.
  - The MIDlet must be registered in the descriptor or the manifest file.

☞ Develop applications that correctly use MIDP 2.0 push registry including discovery, dynamic vs. static, and recognizing the types of connections that can and cannot be accepted.

Discovery of Push Registry

- The push registry and AMS is responsible only for starting a not-running application when an event that the not-running application has registered itself for in the push registry, is received by the device. It is the application's responsibility to retrieve the message from the connection.

Static Push Registry Declarations

- The following attributes must be present in the JAD or the manifest file of the JAR of the application.

Attribute	*Value Format*
MIDlet-Push-<n>	`<Connection-URL>, <MIDletClassName>, <AllowedSender>` where - `n` is a sequentially incrementing number from 1 with no breaks - `Connection-URL` is the URL to listen to of the form: `protocol://:port` - `MIDletClassName` is the class registered to receive the event. This should be declared in one of the `MIDlet-<n>` attributes. - `AllowedSender` is the address or address range of the senders permitted to send events. This is also called as a filter.

- If there is a break in the sequence number, only the contiguously numbered entries (starting from 1) are considered. The rest are ignored.
- If there is an error in the declaration, the application will not be installed.
- If the requested port is reserved or is restricted, the application will not be installed.
- If the `MIDletClassName` is not declared in one of the `MIDlet-<n>` attributes, the application will not be installed.

Dynamic Push Registry Declaration

- An application can be registered dynamically to the push registry by invoking the `static PushRegistry.registerConnection(String connection, String midlet, String filter)` method.
- The parameters are the same as that of the static declaration.

Part-3

Creating Mobile Applications

In this part, we are going to have fun with many APIs that can be used to build up full-blown mobile applications in the Java ME platform. The topics here include MIDP UI API to construct the forms, networking API to connect to other devices, MIDP Game API to develop Java ME games, RMS API to persistently store data in the device, and security mechanisms for the applications.

So let's have fun with all these cool APIs!

5
Chapter

A Face to Remember–The MIDP User Interface API

Exam Objectives

8.1 Given a scenario, develop MIDP 2.0-compliant user interfaces, recognizing portability requirements and limitations (e.g. double-buffering not guaranteed), and performance issues (e.g. using inner classes, freeing memory buffers, etc.). (Section 5.1)

8.2 Discuss the MIDP user interface high-level API including:
- ❖ Concurrency
- ❖ Portability
- ❖ Structure of the API
- ❖ Interplay with the application manager

(Section 5.2)

8.3 Explain the MIDP user interface low-level API including:
- ❖ Font support
- ❖ Repainting
- ❖ Coordinate system

(Section 5.6.3)

8.4 Given a set of requirements, develop interactive MIDP 2.0 user interface code with proper event handling (including both the high-level and low-level APIs, repainting and threading issues). (Section 5.3)

8.5 Identify correct and incorrect statements or examples about the classes (including the class hierarchy) within the javax.microedition.lcdui package. (Sections 5.4, 5.5 and 5.6)

8.6 Compare and contrast high-level and low-level APIs, including layout techniques. (Section 5.1)

8.7 Explain requirements, issues, class hierarchy, and relationships between items and screens. (Section 5.4.1)

INTRODUCTION

As the title implies, this chapter covers the packages that provide support for user interfaces. If you are developing MIDlets, as discussed in the previous chapter, you are going to depend on the MIDP's user interfaces mechanisms to provide the Graphical User Interface (GUI) components that will create the screen appearance of your application.

The target devices of JTWI are mobile phones. Not only mobile phones have a very limited set of display capabilities, but the interaction between users and their phones comes under a completely different set of restrictions and circumstances compared to the interaction between users and their personal computers. Even in Java SE, the platform was built with a goal in mind that portability is achieved as much as possible, certain portions of it still need to be tightly coupled with the personal computers. Particularly in the area of user interfaces, the Java SE's AWT and Swing packages assume some very specific parameters based upon typical desktop and laptop displays. They also assume mice and other common input devices, not to mention an ample supply of memory to support event handling mechanisms. Due to all these, it was not possible for MIDP to merely take a subset of these standard UI packages. As you will soon learn, MIDP defines an entirely new set of packages for programming user interfaces in mobile devices.

Let's start by examining the requirements for designing a user interface toolkit for mobile devices. Here are some of the obvious concerns:

- ❑ Limitations on the size of the screen
- ❑ Limitations on the way user can provide input (in many cases, no mouse or keyboard)
- ❑ Richness of the visual tools supported by the device
- ❑ The power of the device itself to render the user interface
- ❑ The amount of attention that the user can give to the application (driving a car is particularly distracting)

As we start to dig into the packages defined by MIDP, try to take note of the way these imperatives are reflected in the design and architecture of the key classes.

5.1 MIDP USER INTERFACE MODEL

Almost all mobile devices have a simple black and white or color screen based on a Liquid Crystal Display (LCD) technology. As a reminder of this, the MIDP UI package has been named as `javax.microedition.lcdui`. Before we dive in, we should look at an architectural overview of the UI packages.

Figure 5.1 depicts the most important classes in the `javax.microedition.lcdui` package.

☞ **Note:** In this UML dialect, abstract classes are represented by italicized names. There are more than three classes in the package, but these three abstract classes define the hierarchy of

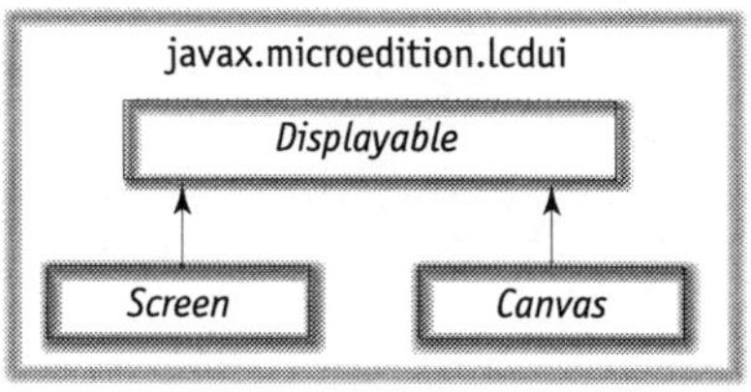

Figure 5.1 The `javax.microedition.lcdui` package overview

functionality for the package and everything else in the package will be a subclass of this hierarchy.

At the heart of the MIDP UI model is the `Displayable` class. Everything that can be displayed on a mobile device screen must extend the `Displayable` class. This abstract class provides the foundation for the functionality required by an object that can be drawn to the screen. It provides rendering methods and methods to support the MIDP's event handling mechanisms. Everything you do with UIs will involve subclasses of `Displayable`.

The next important thing to note about the MIDP UI packages is the division of UI components into high-level and low-level functionality. As we can see in Fig. 5.1, two abstract classes extend, or subclass, the seminal `Displayable` class. This creates a hierarchical fork in the package. Two classes extend `Displayable` to represent high- and low-level UI functionality. The high-level extension is `Screen`, and the low-level extension is `Canvas`. Both of these classes are still abstract. Since these classes are all abstract, we will never create an instance of any of them. The API provides concrete subclasses of `Screen` and `Canvas` which we will use in development. So, while everything we use will be a descendant of `Displayable`, either via the `Screen` or `Canvas` side of the family, we won't be working directly with these classes. Nonetheless, to understand the structure of the UI package, you need to be clear about the division between high-level `Screens` and low-level `Canvases`.

At this point, we should explain what we mean by high-level and low-level UI functionality. Actually, it's pretty simple. The high-level APIs provide high-level GUI components needed by most application developers. These include various menus, displays and interfaces; and the underlying implementation does the drawing for you. If you put one of these components in your application, you don't need to concern yourself with manually drawing the onscreen graphical appearance; this is handled in a professional manner by the implementation of the platform. Similarly, the event handling and user input is handled by the implementation. The application sees these UI details only on a high level. While the developer gives up control of the details, perhaps not knowing which key will be used to trigger a move left event, or exactly what color a button will be, the API is simpler and portability is guaranteed. Referring back to Fig. 5.1, the concrete classes that provide this functionality are all subclasses of the abstract `Screen`.

On the other hand, some applications need more low-level access to drawing and event handling. In particular, games need to have precise control over the rendering screen real estate, as well as specific control over keys and event handling. Since buttons are such a common feature of UIs, it is easy to generalize them into a high-level component. The onscreen appearance and behavior of a blood thirsty troll, being not quite as common, is left to the application developer. Referring again back to Fig. 5.1, access to the required low-level functionality comes through the classes on the `Canvas` side of the hierarchy. These classes give direct and full control over the key-driven events and over the drawing of screen graphics. However, with the use of some of this low-level functionality, portability might be lost. As a developer, you must keep this critical disadvantage in mind. And, indeed, there is a whole subpackage of support for game-oriented extensions of this class, but we will save those APIs for a later chapter.

For your convenient study, Table 5.1 summarizes the characteristics of the two branches of the inheritance hierarchy just described. If any of this is a bit fuzzy, you might come back to it after we visit the concrete subclasses that you will utilize as a developer. We will cover these classes in the coming sections.

Table 5.1 Differences between high-level and low-level MIDP UI API

High-level API	*Low-level API*
For business applications	For graphical applications
Typically made of pre-defined widgets like forms, text fields, buttons, scroll bars, etc.	Typically render graphic data pixel-by-pixel
More portable, as the device implementation is expected to render the pre-defined widgets in a consistent manner	Less portable, as the program directly interacts with the display mechanism of the device, which may not be consistent across different devices (such as aspect ratio, screen size, etc.)
Lesser control to different features of a device, to ensure consistency (user input is done through pre-defined widgets like buttons).	Full access to the basic features of the device (such as events based on individual keys)
All widgets extend the `Screen` class.	All classes extend the `Canvas` class. And the `Graphics` class provides the necessary functionalities.

As you might already be guessing, if you are familiar with AWT, or other desktop user interface toolkits, you will have to re-adjust your understanding of toolkits at a fundamental level. For one thing, in MIDP, there will never be more than one window at a time. Since the display of a mobile device is rather tiny, MIDP does not provide any support for multiple windows. Rather, only one window is visible at any given time. This is similar to looking at one card in a deck of stacked cards. In AWT terms, the MIDP UI might to be similar to a `Panel` that has a `CardLayout`.

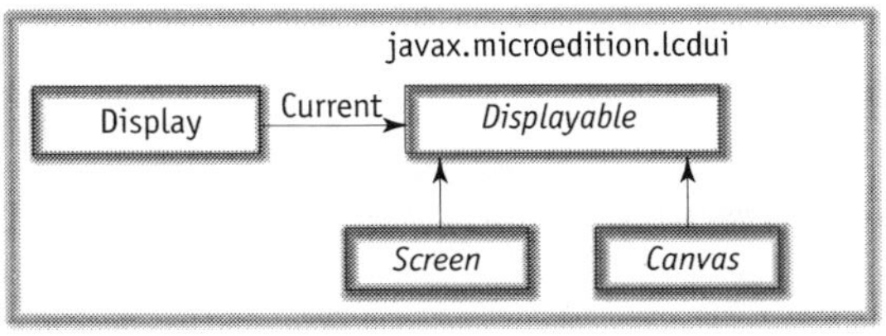

Figure 5.2 High-level UI classes in MIDP API

In Fig. 5.2, we again show the classes that define the hierarchy of the `javax.microedition.lcdui` package, but this time we introduce the `Display` class. The `Display` class is a helper class that allows the developer to get references to the objects that will be used in the application. This class provides access to the actual physical display of the device. Among other things, we can control which `Displayable` object is currently seen on the device. We noted earlier that MIDlets will always have a single onscreen component. This is depicted in Fig. 5.2. We can see that the `Display` class holds a reference, *current*, to an instance of `Displayable`. The object that *current* refers to is the object that represents the component that is currently visible on the device's display.

The `Display` class cannot be instantiated. However, every MIDlet application will have its own instance of the `Display` class, which can be obtained by calling the static

```
Display.getDisplay(MIDlet midlet)
```

method, where `midlet` is the main class in the application that extends the `MIDlet` class. Since the MIDP user interface follows the `CardLayout` pattern, an application can set the view to be displayed by calling the

```
display.setCurrent(Displayable displayable)
```

method, where `display` is an instance of the `Display` class associated with the application and `displayable` is the `Screen` or `Canvas` instance to be displayed.

Exam Tip

Even if there are multiple MIDlets in a MIDlet suite, only one MIDlet is viewable at a time, whose `Displayable` instance can be obtained using the `Display.getCurrent()` method.

Unique to the mobile device domain, the `Display` class also provides a couple of convenience methods that would flash the backlight of the display (using the `flashBacklight(int duration)` method) or vibrate the device itself (using the `vibrate(int duration)` method).

Let us now dive into the various classes available in the `javax.microedition.lcdui` API that form the core of the user interface mechanism of mobile Java applications.

5.2 CREATING HIGH-LEVEL USER INTERFACES

Depending on the rendering power of the machine in which an application is deployed or displayed, the presentation layer of an application can be either *thin* or *fat*. Web applications that are displayed in browsers have thin presentation consisting of built-in browser supplied widgets. Typically, the UI consists of an HTML- or XML-based semantic description of the graphic controls and their relative positioning, which is parsed and rendered with the built-in graphical units of the browser. This is high-level graphics functionality; there is certainly no access to the specific rendering of screen real estate. Furthermore, the presentation in the browser is typically decoupled from complex processing. It would normally be responsible for getting information from the user, sending it to a server, which would do the processing, and then displaying the results back to the user.

While this lack of control over the UI elements has certain disadvantages, it clearly means that the API is simple and portable. We provide a high-level description of a UI and each browser is left to render that UI as it will. This also allows the browsers to preserve their native look and feel, helping the user understand the UI through its similarity to other applications. How can we trust the browser to implement the controls we want? Good question! The Web standards that govern Web-based technologies, such as HTML, guarantee that a compliant browser will provide an implementation for each control. The specifications of the MIDP provide the same guarantee for our high-level UI packages.

Exam Tip

Classes in the high-level user interface category are portable. They are guaranteed to be displayed in a device-friendly manner with a device-friendly look and feel. Some low-level user interface features such as key events are also portable.

Figure 5.3 depicts the concrete subclasses of `Screen` that make up the high-level functionality of the `javax.microedition.lcdui` package. Recall from Fig. 5.1 that `Screen` is an abstract class that subclasses `Displayable`. Each of these subclasses is a built-in widget that you can use for your application's UI.

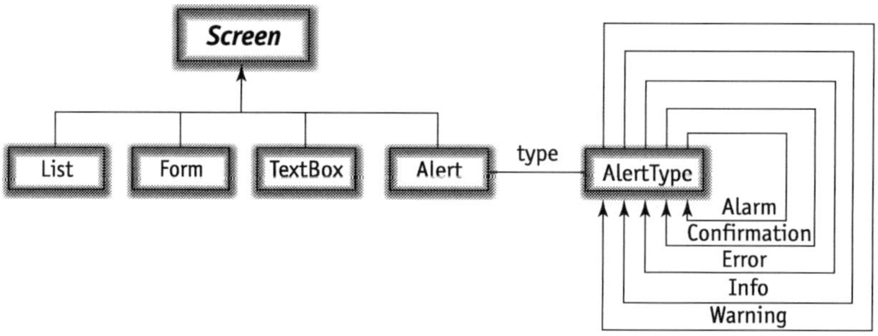

Figure 5.3 The `Screen` class and its subclasses

In general, the classes that extend the `Screen` class occupy the whole screen, except the `Alert` class, which is normally used as a popup window used for getting user confirmation or displaying warning or informational messages. Most of these class names should sound familiar. They provide functional counterparts to common desktop and HTML components. Table 5.2 shows the analogous components in these packages.

Table 5.2 High-level UI components in MIDP and their counterparts in other packages

Function	*MIDP*	*AWT*	*Swing*	*HTML*
Listing a bunch of options that user can select from	`List`	`List/ComboBox`	`JList/JComboBox`	`SELECT`
A container where a number of widgets can be organized to create a user input screen.	`Form`	`Panel/Frame`	`JPanel/JFrame`	`FORM`
A multi-line text input widget.	`TextBox`	`TextArea`	`JTextArea`	`TEXTAREA`
A popup window to display warning, error, or informational messages or to get user confirmation	`Alert`	`Dialog`	`JOptionPane`	`javascript:alert()`

With this table, you already know most of the features that would be provided by the UI widgets in MIDP. The main difference between these widgets and the ones that you are used to so far would be due to the limitations imposed on these widgets regarding screen space available for display. Let us look at these widgets in detail to see what those constraints are and how to use these widgets effectively to provide a pleasant user interface to your application. First, we'll cover the event handling mechanism that allows us to interact with the user.

5.3 ISSUING COMMANDS

In addition to visual components, the high-level API also defines a high-level event handling mechanism. Before we look at building nice screens and forms, let us look at how we can handle various device events, such as key presses, in order to trigger application actions. While this looks like a case of the 'cart before the horse', it would be helpful since some of the widgets implicitly have some events associated with them.

Unlike a typical desktop user interface, a mobile UI does not have too much space. The screen is small, and the keyboard is smaller. While there are some devices that have a full QWERTY keyboard, most do not have it. To make things worse, even the key layout is not exactly standard as device manufacturers have to combine style with purpose and some outrageous styles have outrageous screens and keys. The MIDP high-level UI specification addresses this problem by abstracting out the user interface components so that the device manufacturers are at liberty to construct the devices as they want but still comply with the specification.

Perhaps the most abstract of these UI components is the input mechanism. Instead of having a standard button or a menu, the MIDP abstracts the high-level user input into a generic action called the *command* (this is similar to the `Action` class in the Swing package). Basically, a command is just an action that a user can take in her interaction with the application. The MIDP implements several common actions in its `Command` class.

The application developer can specify the commands associated with a screen or a widget along with some characteristics that define its display features, purpose and perceived importance. Based on this information, the device implementation is at liberty to place it at the most logical place in the screen that gels with its native user interface. If necessary, we may specify that we want the implementation to pay more attention to a certain command such as "move left" or "exit". We then let the implementation decide which button will fulfill this functional role. It might be a completely different button, in a completely different location, on varying devices, but we are guaranteed that it will be some button. And, again, the user will be familiar with the button due to its consistence with other applications they use on the device.

Exam Tip

There is no guarantee how or where a `Command` will be placed on the screen of a device. This typically depends on the number of commands associated with the given screen, the type of the `Command`, and the priority of the `Command`.

A `Command` can be instantiated using one of the two constructors provided.

```
Command(String label, int commandType, int priority)
```

or

```
Command(String shortLabel, String longLabel, int commandType, int
priority)
```

Once the parameters are specified, they cannot be changed at runtime.

5.3.1 Displaying Command Text

The `label`, `shortLabel` and `longLabel` define what should be displayed as the text of the `Command` instance when displayed on the screen. The `shortLabel` normally takes precedence over the `longLabel`, which is optional. If both values are given, the device implementation might choose either of them depending on the available real estate.

5.3.2 Deciding on Command Type

The type of the `Command` is used by the device typically to place the `Command` at the appropriate place that will gel with other related commands present in the native interface to provide maximum convenience to the user. For example, if a device displays its back button on the left side of the screen, then a `Command` of type BACK will most probably be displayed on the left side also. The available `Command` types are listed in Table 5.3. These constants are defined in the `Command` class.

Table 5.3 Constants that can be used to describe a `Command` type

Command type	*Intention*
BACK	Go back to the previous screen.
CANCEL	Cancel the current action.
EXIT	Quit the application.
HELP	Get help for the given screen.
ITEM	Indicates that the command is associated with the specific item, not the whole screen.
OK	Confirm the current action (submit a form, etc.).
SCREEN	Application-specific command applicable to the current screen.
STOP	Stop the currently running process or operation (such as a network connection attempt).

☞ **Note:** The `Command` type itself does not result in any action or behavior. It is only a hint to the device implementation about the intent of the `Command` so that the implementation can place the `Command` in the most logical manner based on its look and feel guidelines.

5.3.3 Setting Command Priority

If a screen has multiple commands of the same type, how can the application let the implementation know that one command is more important than the other? This is where the *priority* attribute of a command comes into picture. The priority allows the user to hint to the implementation the relative importance of the command with respect to other commands on the screen. The priority is an integer, where a lower value indicates that the command is very important and a higher value indicates that the command is less important.

Exam Tip

The value of a priority is device-dependent. The MIDP 2.0 specification does not define any specific range of values for priority or even if it should be positive or negative. Only the relative comparison is defined (lower value means more important). It is possible to have multiple `Commands` with same priority.

Typically, priority is specified as a positive integer starting from 1, although it is not necessary to do so. It is good practice to have distinct priorities for different commands with the same type on the same screen, although it is not required. If the same priority is given for multiple commands of the same type, the device implementation will decide the order of placement (for example, it can place commands by the alphabetical order of labels or the order in which commands were added), which may result in different order for different implementations.

5.3.4 Attaching Commands to Screen

Once the `Command` objects are created as described above, the next step is to attach them to a screen. A `Command` can be associated with a `Displayable` class or to an `Item` class. This essentially means that a `Command` can be associated with any screen type (`Screen`, `Form`, or `Canvas`) and any `Item` (`TextField`, `ImageItem`, etc.).

`Commands` can be added or removed to/from the `Displayable` or `Item` objects using `addCommand(Command command)` and `removeCommand(Command command)` methods. As you can guess from the method name, multiple `Commands` can be added to the same `Displayable` or `Item`. If someone tries to remove a `Command` that is not in the `Displayable` or `Item` object, nothing will happen.

5.3.5 Listening for Commands

The last step in the whole `Command` business is to listen for the `Commands` that we have painstakingly created and attached so far. While it is possible to attach multiple commands to a screen, you can have only one listener per `Displayable` or `Item` instance to listen for the command events. This makes sense because you don't want multiple objects to take action based on the same event. Imagine what happens when two of your kids have access to the same TV remote control during prime time!

There are two listener interfaces defined for propagating command events—the `CommandListener` interface for `Commands` associated with a `Displayable` class and the `ItemCommandListener` interface for `Commands` associated with an `Item` class. Each of these interfaces has only one method.

```
CommandListener.commandAction(Command c, Displayable d)
ItemCommandListener.commandAction(Command c, Item i)
```

Both the interfaces let the implementation know which `Command` caused the event to occur and the associated `Displayable` or `Item` instance where the event occurred. The implementing class can use this information to take appropriate actions.

Now that we know how to define `Commands` and prepare for handling the events that they create, we can go on with creating the visual components of the UI.

5.4 CREATING USER INPUT FORMS

The Form is perhaps the most often used widget in the high-level section of the MIDP UI API. This visual widget provides a flexible tool that handles a wide range of interaction with the user. Again, if you think of it as equivalent to an HTML form, you can easily understand the role it plays in building a user interface between your application and the user. Subclassing Screen, Forms are high-level components that provide a flexible do-it-yourself mechanism that allows the developer to assemble their own collection of visual elements called Items. Let's jump right in and see how it's done.

If you prefer to liken the javax.microedition.lcdui package to other Java GUI packages, such as the AWT or Swing packages, that's fine. But there are some significant differences. For instance, if you liken the Form to an AWT Panel or Frame, you should bear in mind two major points of difference. First, the Form class doesn't allow the user to control the layout. Since different mobile devices can have radically different screens, it is left to the device implementation of the API to determine the best way to layout the components placed inside a Form. Again, the Form is located at a much higher level and is more equivalent to the high-level GUI component of HTML. We will learn a couple of things you can do to influence layout, but don't expect the kind of control you get from AWT or Swing components.

The second major difference is the automatic appearance of a scroll bar. A scroll bar is provided automatically if all the components of the Form cannot be fit inside a single view. In most cases, a Form scrolls only vertically and not horizontally. This is because it is much more convenient for a user to traverse in one direction instead of two directions in a mobile device. This, like most of the stuff you are learning, arises because of the resource constraints of the mobile device and their impact on UI design.

5.4.1 Dissecting Form

The Form is just a container. A Form should have something in it to be useful. In most cases, a Form would contain one or more instances of the Item class. More specifically, a Form will contain subclasses of the Item class. The Items provided by the platform all bear strong resemblance to common UI components from other platforms such as HTML. We think you find the learning curve to be quite gentle. Table 5.4 gives you a quick comparison of the subclasses of the Item class with other UI platforms.

Table 5.4 Item subclasses and their counterparts in other UI platforms

Function	*MIDP*	*AWT*	*Swing*	*HTML*
Abstract base class that defines a visual component that can be added into a container	Item	Component	JComponent	N/A

Non-editable string that typically provides information about an input component	`StringItem`	`Label`	`JLabel`	`Plain text`
Editable field that is used to get text information from the user	`TextField`	`TextField`	`JTextField`	`INPUT type= "text" (or) type="password"`
A group of selectable components that represents multiple choices, one of which needs to be selected by the user	`ChoiceGroup`	`RadioButton`	`JRadioButton`	`INPUT type = "radio"`
A graphical display that represents the progression of a long-running task	`Gauge`		`JProgressBar`	`N/A`
A non-interactive empty space that can be used for providing white space between components	`Spacer`	`Label with empty spaces`	`JLabel with` empty spaces or `Insets`	` ` as needed
Display for images	`ImageItem`	`Label or Panel`	`JLabel` or `JPanel`	`IMG`
Visual component to get date or time information from user	`DateField`	-	-	-
Basic component that can be customized	`CustomItem`	-	-	-
Accept a command from user	`Command` (does not extend from `Item` class)	`Button`	`JButton`	`INPUT type="button"`

The class diagram in Fig. 5.4 shows the relationship between the various components that we just mentioned.

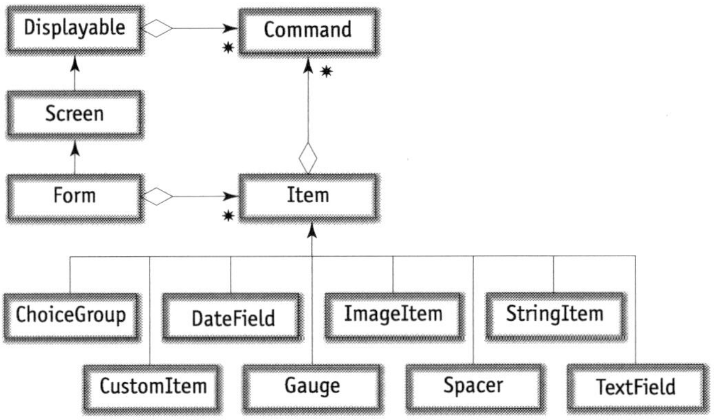

Figure 5.4 Relationships between Item and its subclasses

Exam Tip

It is very important from an exam perspective to understand the relationship between the various classes in the `javax.microedition.lcdui` package. They are good candidates for drag and drop style questions!

As you can see in Fig. 5.4, a `Form` can contain zero or more instances of the `Item` class (or its subclasses). You can see some of the specific classes, such as `TextField or Gauge`, that extend the `Item` class. Adding `Items` to the Form is simple. Just call the `form.append(Item item)` method. We will learn what each `Item` does in the upcoming sections. Before we go on, let's see what else we can observe in this class diagram. Can you see how the `Form` can have zero or more `Commands` attached to it? This might not be obvious if you're not familiar with UML, but the class diagram shows us that a `Form` is a descendant of `Displayable`. Because of this, the ability to hold `Commands` is inherited from `Displayable`. All descendants of `Displayable` will have this ability. The ability to hold `Items`, however, is unique to the `Form` subclass.

5.4.2 Laying Out Items

Before we go on to the details of the individual `Item`, we will look at the bits of layout control we have available to us in MIDP. In the AWT and Swing worlds, we have an overwhelming array of layout managers to handle the layout of components within a container. Unfortunately, we don't have such power in the MIDP world. But the MIDP UI does allow us a certain amount of layout control.

Since mobile devices have a much smaller width than traditional devices, the default layout mechanism will display elements from top-to-bottom growing vertically, with `Items` aligned to the left. However, an application can override this default behavior by specifying constraints on each `Item` added to a `Form` using the item's `setLayout` method. The following constants can be specified as a parameter to this method.

`LAYOUT_LEFT, LAYOUT_RIGHT` and `LAYOUT_CENTER` constraints can be used for the horizontal alignment of the `Item`.

`LAYOUT_TOP, LAYOUT_BOTTOM` and `LAYOUT_VCENTER` constraints can be used for the vertical alignment of the `Item`.

`LAYOUT_EXPAND` and `LAYOUT_SHRINK` suggest that the `Item` should occupy either the whole row or only its minimum width, respectively.

`LAYOUT_VEXPAND` and `LAYOUT_VSHRINK` suggest that the `Item` should occupy either the available vertical space or only its minimum height, respectively.

`LAYOUT_NEWLINE_BEFORE` and `LAYOUT_NEWLINE_AFTER` can be used to ask the layout manager to place the `Item` in a new row or to ensure that the `Item` should be last in its row, respectively.

LAYOUT_DEFAULT suggests that the Item placement should follow MIDP 1.0 layout convention while LAYOUT_2 suggests that the Item placement should use MIDP 2.0 directives.

These layout constraints are by no means the low-level control that we have in AWT. Again, they are more similar to the layout control available to traditional HTML designers. While the designer can't specify exactly where the components go, she can make some slight modifications to the built-in positioning. Now that we have looked at how the Items can be laid out in a Form, let us start analyzing each of the Item subclasses in detail.

5.4.3 Displaying Simple Text

The StringItem class is probably the simplest class in the package. The StringItem, obviously is a subclass of the Item. It is used to provide non-editable textual information to the user. While the StringItem is functionally equivalent to the Label class in AWT, the way it is displayed differs slightly. Apart from the text that needs to be displayed, you can also associate a label that goes with the text, which will typically be displayed in front of the text in a slightly different font style (although there is no guarantee).

Exam Tip

A StringItem is like a Label component in the java.awt package. It can be used to display a short piece of text and cannot be edited by the user.

Some label and text information must be provided to a StringItem when a new instance is created. Here are the constructors/methods that are provided in this class.

```
StringItem(String label, String text)
StringItem(String label, String text, int appearanceMode)
aStringItem.setText(String text)
```

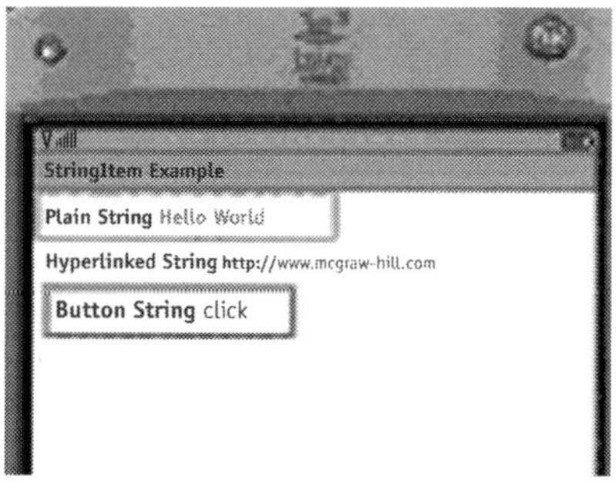

Figure 5.5 StringItem example

The appearanceMode can be one of three constants specified in the Item class—PLAIN, HYPERLINK, or BUTTON. As the name suggests, the mode lets the implementation know the intent of the text so that it is displayed accordingly. It is also possible to change the font of the text by calling the setFont(Font font) method.

In Fig. 5.5, we show some examples of StringItems. Each has some label text in bold, and some string text. The hyperlinked string gives an example of using the appearanceMode parameter to change the appearance of the text string.

5.4.4 Getting Text Information from User

One of the most common `Items` used in a `Form` is a `TextField`. A `TextField` can be used to get a short piece of text from the user. This component is equivalent to the HTML text input element, which people commonly refer to as a text field. There's also a big brother called `TextBox` that is equivalent to the HTML text box, but we will cover it specifically in a later section. This would be easy.

`TextFields` have several characteristics that we need to understand. First, they have specific numbers of visible characters displayed. Additionally, they follow a mini-MVC (Model-View-Controller) approach. That is, what you see in the display might not necessarily be what the model represents (the data sent back to the application). For example, a phone number might be displayed to the user in a locale-based format, such as (xxx) xxx-xxxx, but this is just the view of the data. When the data is sent to the application, it will be a simple series of ten digits.

Another characteristic of `TextFields` arises from the physical constraints of the keyboards. Phones usually do not have a full-fledged QWERTY-style keyboard. This means that most of the keys have overloaded values. To handle this, most devices employ a *predictive input* mechanism. This means that the device will try to guess the word based on the numeric keys typed by correlating it with an in-built dictionary.

To provide contextual hints to help the device predict the correct interpretation of the keystrokes, an application can set a *constraint* on the `TextField`. A number of pre-defined constraints are provided in the API. Table 5.5 outlines these constraints, gives their types and a short description of how they constrain the user's input. As well as being a hint to restricted keyboards about how to interpret overloaded key strokes, you might also think of this as a sort of low-level data validation. For instance, if we are collecting a zip code from the user, we can constrain the input to only numbers. Other cool built-in constraints support email and password entry.

Table 5.5 `TextField` constraints

Constraint	*Type*	*Description*
`ANY`	Restriction	There are no restrictions. User can type any character.
`DECIMAL`	Restriction	Only numbers, including an optional sign (+ or -) at the beginning and the decimal separator (a period "." or a comma ",") are allowed.
`EMAILADDR`	Restriction	Only characters acceptable as a valid email address are allowed.
`NUMERIC`	Restriction	Only numbers, including an optional sign at the beginning are allowed.
`PHONENUMBER`	Restriction	Valid characters allowed for a phone number. This may vary based on the device.
`URL`	Restriction	This constraint allows the user to enter a URL. Only valid URL characters are allowed.

INITIAL_CAPS_SENTENCE	Modifier	Hint that the initial letter of each sentence should be capitalized.
INITIAL_CAPS_WORD	Modifier	Hint that the initial letter of each word should be capitalized.
NON_PREDICTIVE	Modifier	Predictive text will be disabled. Use this if the data that the user might enter is not likely to be present in the in-built dictionary (like names).
PASSWORD	Modifier	The display will be masked with some character (say, *) while the user is entering the data.
SENSITIVE	Modifier	This is for sensitive input data like credit cards, where the device should not try to store the information in its in-built dictionary or any auto-complete mechanism that it might have.
UNEDITABLE	Modifier	This constraint displays text that cannot be edited. This works much like a `StringItem`.

In Table 5.5, you can see that there are two types of constraints: *restrictions* and *modifiers*. You can combine restrictions with modifiers to get powerful effects. You can combine a restriction and a modifier using the standard bitwise OR operator (|). For example, if you want the user to be able to enter a credit card number, you might set the restriction on the text field as follows.

```
textField.setConstraints(NUMERIC | SENSITIVE);
```

The above line implies that the text field can contain only numbers and that the information entered is sensitive.

In order to dynamically determine which constraint has been set on a text field, the `CONSTRAINT_MASK` constant can be used along with a bitwise AND operator (`&`). For example, in the above example, we can determine if the information is sensitive inside the program as follows.

```
if(textField.getConstraints() & TextField.CONSTRAINT_MASK ==
TextField.SENSITIVE) {
   // The information in the TextField is sensitive.
}
```

Exam Tip

Restrictive constraints can be combined only with modifier constraints. Both restrictive and modifier constraints cannot be combined with others in their own group.

In Fig. 5.6, we show the examples of `TextFields`, which we discussed before in Table 5.5. All twelve values listed in the table are shown in the figure to give you an idea how they look when they are implemented.

We should point out that the `TextBox`, the big brother of `TextField`, shares this set of constraints and related behaviors. We will refer back to this when we discuss the `TextBox` on its own. Apart from these constraints, the API also provides methods to manipulate the text in the widget. See Table 5.6.

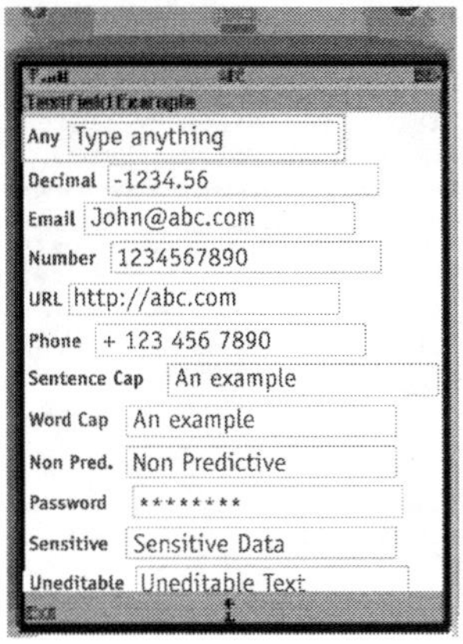

Figure 5.6 `TextField` example

Since mobile devices are available in various countries throughout the world, they might have in-built support for different languages. In cases where the application might want to explicitly set the language required to type the text, the `setInitialInputMode(String)` method can be used. The parameter passed to this method is a `String`, which can have one of the following formats.

`UCB_XXX` where `XXX` is the name of the character set defined in `java.lang.Character.UnicodeBlock` class in Java SE.

Example: `UCB_BASIC_LATIN, UCB_HIRAGANA`

`IS_XXX` where `XXX` is the name of the input subset defined in the `java.awt.im.InputSubset` class in Java SE.

Table 5.6 Managing text in a `TextField`

Method	*Description*
`delete(int offset, int length)`	Deletes the characters from the `TextField` according to the specified range.
`insert(char[] data, int offset, int length, int position)`	Inserts a range of the specified character array into the `TextField` at the specified position.
`insert(String text, int position)`	Inserts a string into the `TextField` at the specified position.
`getChars(char[] data)`	Copies an array of characters from the `TextField` into the specified array.
`setChars(char[] data, int offset, int length)`	Replaces the characters in the specified range of the `TextField` with the specified array.
`getString()`	Gets the contents of the `TextField` as a string.
`setString(String text)`	Replaces the contents of the `TextField` with the specified one.

Example: `IS_FULLWIDTH_LATIN, IS_KANJI`

`MIDP_XXX` where `XXX` is the character subset defined in MIDP.

Example: `MIDP_UPPERCASE_LATIN, MIDP_LOWERCASE_LATIN`

`X_XXX` where `XXX` is a user-defined subset. The prefix "`X_`" indicates a custom character set.

5.4.5 Adding Choice

Sometimes you might not want the user to type the data in free-text format. Instead, it would be preferable to provide the user a set of pre-defined options and ask him to select one of them. In such cases, the `ChoiceGroup` item can be useful. Unlike the Swing/AWT package, there is no separate implementation for a radio button (where you can select one out of several options) and a check box (where you can select one or more out of several options). Instead, it is left to the implementation to decide how to display the choices.

Exam Tip

There is no special implementation for a check box or a radio button in MIDP 2.0. It is up to the implementation to determine how to display a `ChoiceGroup` depending on the constraints placed on it.

The `Choice` interface implemented by the `ChoiceGroup` class (which also is implemented by the `List` class.) defines four selection models.

`EXCLUSIVE`

If the `ChoiceGroup` is defined in this mode, the user can only select one of the given options. Although it is up to the implementation, it may typically display the instance as a bunch of radio buttons.

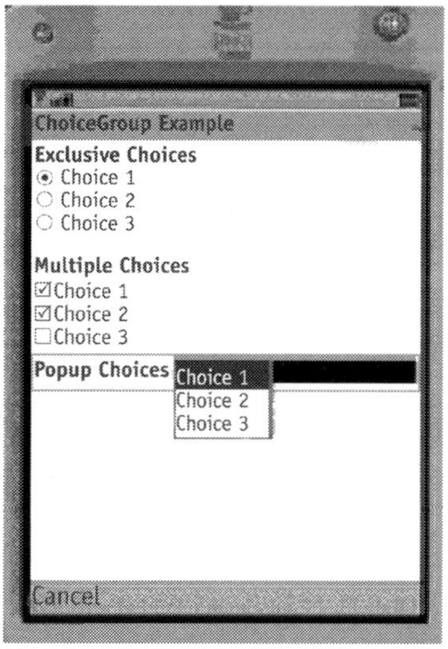

Figure 5.7 `ChoiceGroup` example

`IMPLICIT`

This selection model is not applicable to `ChoiceGroup` elements. We will discuss more about this when talking about `Lists`.

`MULTIPLE`

In this selection model, the user can select one or more options among the given ones. An implementation would typically render this instance as a bunch of check boxes.

`POPUP`

A popup `ChoiceGroup` acts in a manner similar to that of a `JComboBox` of the Swing API. It essentially provides a drop-down list of choices.

Figure 5.7 illustrates how various options are displayed on the screen.

You can manage the choices in the choice group by the following methods available in the `ChoiceGroup` class; see Table 5.7.

Table 5.7 Managing choices in a `ChoiceGroup`

Method	*Description*
`append(String element, Image image)`	Adds an element to the end of the list. An optional image can be provided (`null` if not needed).
`insert(int location, String element, Image image)`	Adds an element at the specified location. Other elements will be adjusted accordingly.
`set(int location, String element, Image image)`	Replaces the element at the specified location with the new element.
`delete(int location)`	Deletes the element at the specified location. Other elements will be adjusted accordingly.
`deleteAll()`	Deletes all the elements in the group.

When you want to get information from a `ChoiceGroup`, you can use one of the following methods to see whether one or more choices have been selected or if you simply want to get the name of some choice. See Table 5.8.

Table 5.8 Getting information from a `ChoiceGroup`

Method	*Description*
`getSelectedIndex()`	Gets the index of the element that has been selected. This returns –1 if there are no elements in the item or if the user is allowed to select multiple options.
`isSelected(int location)`	Checks if the element at the specified location has been selected.
`getSelectedFlags(boolean[] arrayToPopulate)`	Populates the given array with the state of the elements in the item. The array should at least be as long as the number of elements in the group. If longer, the other elements will be set to false. If shorter, an `IllegalArgumentException` will be thrown. The method also returns the number of elements selected.

We can now build a `Form` that collects text that the user enters or predefined values that the user chooses. Now, we will begin to look at some `Items` with more specialized uses.

5.4.6 Setting up Date with User

One of the major issues with the Swing framework (as of Java SE 6 version at least) is the lack of a customized date field that can be provided to the user to get date and time information. While date information can be entered in a text field, always there is a problem in parsing the date if it is entered as such, as a date can be entered in different formats at different locales. To ease this issue, the MIDP API provides a `DateField` item, which is customized to take date and time information.

The `DateField` is simple to use. There are only two settings needed from the programmer, one of them being optional. The mandatory setting—input mode—is used to determine what type of date information is required from the user. There are three options.

`DATE` to obtain day, month, and year information. Time will be set to 00:00:00.

`TIME` to obtain hour and minute information. Date will be set to January 1, 1970.

`DATE_TIME` to obtain both date and time information. However, only hours and minutes information will be accurate. The seconds part may not be reflected correctly.

An optional `TimeZone` object can be passed to a `DateField` constructor to specify the default time zone that should be used by the widget.

The screens in Fig. 5.8 show how the field will be displayed in various modes.

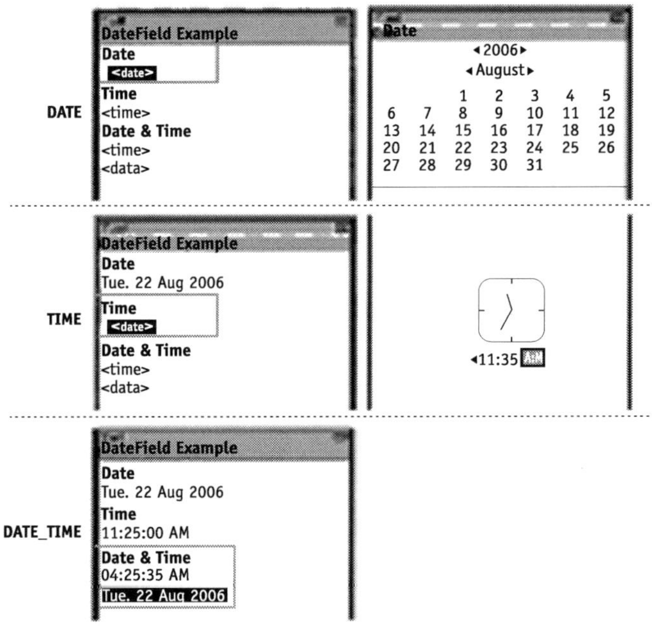

Figure 5.8 `DateField` example

The application can get the date from this field using the `getDate()` method, which would return a `java.util.Date` object. Similarly, the application can also set the default date using the `setDate(java.util.Date)` method. Moreover, the application can get and set the input mode of the field using the `getInputMode()` and `setInputMode(int)` methods, respectively.

5.4.7 Gauging Progress of Action

One important function of a user interface is providing feedback to the user about the progress of an activity inside an application. Otherwise, it might mislead the user into thinking that the application has stopped responding or even worse, crashed unexpectedly. To avoid this problem, most applications (at least ones that have a respectable user interface) provide some sort of a progress bar when a long-running activity is being performed. MIDP provides an `Item` called `Gauge` to provide the user information about the progress of an activity in an application.

A `Gauge` can be either interactive or non-interactive. In an interactive mode, the user is capable of setting the value. An example would be when you want the user to select a value within a finite range. This is similar to the `JSlider` class in Java SE's Swing. Alternatively, a `Gauge` can be used to simply display the state of a variable or the progress of an action. Almost all mobile phones come with two non-interactive `Gauges` by default—the battery indicator and the signal strength indicator. This is similar to the `JProgressBar` class in Java SE's Swing.

The interactive nature of a `Gauge` can be set in the constructor when the `Gauge` is initialized. The syntax of the constructor is

```
Gauge(String label, boolean interactive, int maxValue, int initialValue)
```

Interactive Gauges

Interactive `Gauges` must have a defined initial value and a maximum value, and the initial value must be lesser than or equal to the maximum value. The minimum value is always 0. The application can set the intermediate value using the `setValue` method anytime. The value set must be between 0 and `maxValue`. The interactive `Gauge` knows how much time the job will take and provides a measured visual representation of the progress of the task.

Non-interactive Gauges

Non-interactive `Gauges` are more interesting than the interactive ones. To begin with, they can have either a definite range or indefinite range. If the application needs a non-interactive `Gauge` with an indefinite range, then the `maxValue` must be a special constant defined in the `Gauge` class called, not surprisingly, `INDEFINITE`.

In case of an indefinite range, the value passed to the `setValue` method takes a new meaning. The special values shown in Table 5.9 are defined in the `Gauge` class to be used for a non-interactive gauge with indefinite range. These `Gauges` represent jobs of undefined lengths of time.

Table 5.9 Non-interactive indefinite `Gauge` values

Constant	*Description*	*Example*
`CONTINUOUS_RUNNING`	The represented activity is long-running. The application does not know when the action might finish.	The application is about to request a connection to an external server.
`CONTINUOUS_IDLE`	The represented activity is not doing anything or is in a wait state.	The application has sent a request to an external server and is waiting for a response.
`INCREMENTAL_UPDATING`	The represented activity has progressed in its activity, but does not know when it will complete. In this case, every time `setValue (INCREMENTAL_UPDATING)` is called, the state of the `Gauge` will change.	The application is downloading a file of unknown size. However, it did download 'x' bytes of information.
`INCREMENTAL_IDLE`	The represented activity is in between progress.	The application has just downloaded 'x' bytes and is in the process of downloading another 'y' bytes, but has not done so.

Figure 5.9 displays a snapshot of `Gauges` initialized in various modes.

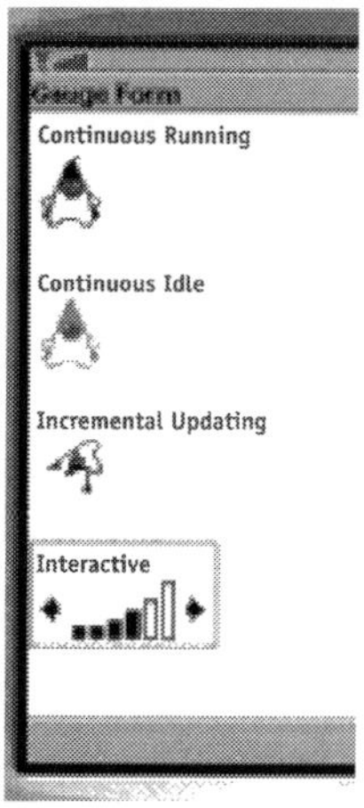

Figure 5.9 `Gauge` example

Note that the `Gauge` displayed here uses a graphical Duke figure to represent the progress of the job. Not all phones use this graphic. Many will simply use a progress bar. Like all of the high-level components, the actual look and feel of the component is implementation-specific. But rest assured, if you put a `Gauge` on your `Form`, there will be some kind of graphical representation of the progress. As for the Duke `Gauge`, he shakes his head constantly in the continuous running mode and does other similar cute things for the other modes.

5.4.8 Spacing Out Items

While an implementation would normally do an excellent job of layout of the `Items` in a `Form`, it might be preferable sometimes to introduce deliberate empty spaces between `Items` for the sake of clarity or to provide visual grouping of related items in a `Form`. A `Spacer` item can be used for this purpose.

A `Spacer` is essentially a `StringItem` that does not have any text. The constructor accepts a minimum width and height for the instance. Any dimension greater than the dimension that can be displayed on the device will automatically be reverted to the maximum allowed dimension of the device.

Since a `Spacer` is a non-interactive, non-informational element, the default features provided in the `Item` class don't make any sense. To be specific, a `Spacer` cannot have any associated `Command` (since it is non-interactive) and cannot have any label (since it is non-informational). Any attempt to set the label or the command to a `Spacer` will fail with an `IllegalStateException`.

Exam Tip

A Spacer is non-interactive and non-informational. It cannot have either a command or label associated with it. Any attempts to do so will result in an `IllegalStateException`.

Figure 5.10 shows a `Spacer` between two items.

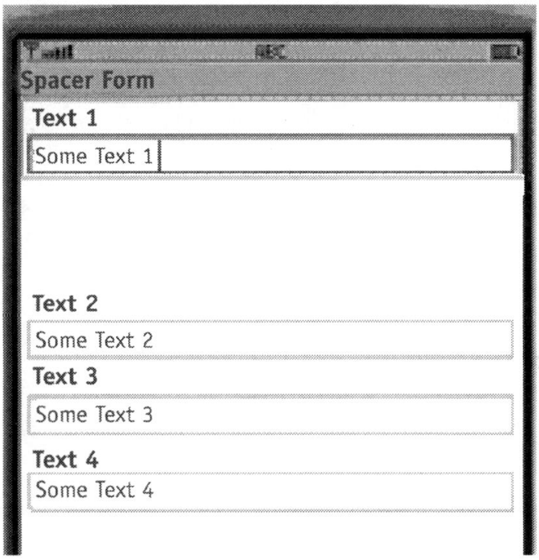

Figure 5.10 `Spacer` example

In this figure, a `Spacer` of 50 pixels high is placed between `TextField` items `Text1` and `Text2`, while there is no `Spacer` item between `TextField` items `Text3` and `Text4`.

5.4.9 Projecting Image

If a picture is normally worth a thousand words, it must be worth a million words when your display is 96 × 54. The `ImageItem` class can be used to represent an image in a form. Each `ImageItem` instance represents an image object.

Creating Image

An `Image` represents any graphical data. In MIDP, graphical data are classified under two categories—mutable images, where the user or application can dynamically make changes to the contents of the image, or immutable images, where the image is for display purpose only.

An `Image` can be created using one of the several static `createImage` methods available in the `Image` class. Table 5.10 tells you the purpose of each of these methods.

Table 5.10 Creating an `Image`

Method Signature	*Description*
`createImage(byte[] imageData, int imageOffset, int imageLength)`	Creates an immutable image from the given byte array.
`createImage(Image source)`	Creates an immutable image from another `Image`.
`createImage(Image image, int x, int y, int width, int height, int transform)`	Creates an immutable image from another `Image`, which is really a crop of the original image based on the given dimensions.
`createImage(java.io.InputStream stream)`	Creates an immutable image from a data stream. The data should be encoded in a format recognized by the implementation. All MIDP-compliant devices will support PNG format.
`createImage(int width, int height)`	Creates a mutable image of specified dimensions.
`createImage(String name)`	Creates an immutable image from the named resource.
`createRGBImage(int[] rgb, int width, int height, boolean processAlpha)`	Creates an immutable image from an ARGB data sequence, where each entry is of the form 0×AARRGGBB.

In RGB images, if `processAlpha` is set to `true`, the first (higher order) byte represents the transparency of the image, where 00 means the image is fully transparent and FF means the image is fully opaque. If `processAlpha` is set to `false`, then the first byte is ignored.

If the implementation does not support image morphing, semitransparent pixels will be replaced with fully transparent pixels. In other words, one image will overwrite the other image in overlapping areas.

The `transform` parameter can be used to transform the orientation of the source image data. The following values are acceptable. The values are defined the `Sprite` class, which will be discussed in the Game API chapter.

- `Sprite.TRANS_NONE`—Makes no transformation
- `Sprite.TRANS_ROT90`—Rotates the image clockwise by 90 degrees.
- `Sprite.TRANS_ROT180`—Rotates the image clockwise by 180 degrees.
- `Sprite.TRANS_ROT270`—Rotates the image clockwise by 270 degrees.
- `Sprite.TRANS_MIRROR`—Mirrors the image along its vertical axis.

- `Sprite.TRANS_MIRROR_ROT90`—Mirrors the image along its vertical axis and rotates the image clockwise by 90 degrees.
- `Sprite.TRANS_MIRROR_ROT180`—Mirrors the image along its vertical axis and rotates the image clockwise by 180 degrees.
- `Sprite.TRANS_MIRROR_ROT270`—Mirrors the image along its vertical axis and rotates the image clockwise by 270 degrees.

When a mutable image is created, it is not drawn on the screen directly. In order to draw directly on the screen, you should use the `Canvas` class instead. Now that we have an idea how to create and use an `Image`, let's get back to our `ImageItem` class.

Displaying Image

The `ImageItem` class itself is simply a wrapper around the `Image` class that allows the `Image` to be embedded into a `Form`. The following constructors are used to create an `ImageItem`.

```
ImageItem(String label, Image image, int layout, String altText)
ImageItem(String label, Image image, int layout, String altText,
        int appearanceMode)
```

The `layout` parameter is the same as that discussed earlier when we talked about laying out items in a form. The `appearanceMode` parameter determines how the `ImageItem` is displayed and can be one of `Item.BUTTON`, `Item.PLAIN`, or `Item.HYPERLINK`.

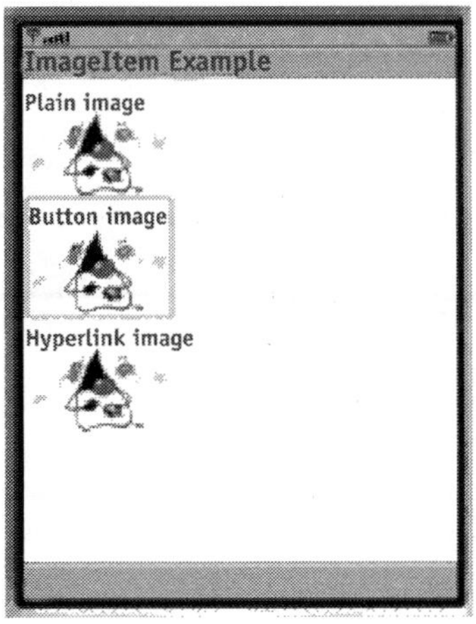

Figure 5.11 `ImageItem` example

Like in websites, if an image is being downloaded from an external source, it might take some time before it is displayed on the screen. Till then, it is a good practice to display some information about the image being downloaded as a placeholder. Such placeholder information can be provided in the `altText` parameter.

The following screenshot in Fig. 5.11 shows how an `Image` is displayed on a form using the `ImageItem` class.

So far, we looked at the various pre-defined `Item` classes that have been provided to us by the MIDP 2.0 specification. What if none of them satisfies our needs or if we want to differentiate ourselves with a very jazzy user interface? The MIDP specification does consider this and gives us the `CustomItem` class, which can be—you guessed it—used to define custom `Item` objects.

5.4.10 Creating Custom Widgets

A custom-made `Item` object is normally created if the pre-defined `Items` do not reflect the user needs or if they do not fit with the application's theme. A `CustomItem` can be made visually different and can have a finer control over input events, while the other `Item` objects cannot.

Now we have covered all the `Items` that can be added to a `Form`. `Forms` provide a high-level mechanism for collecting a custom assembly of `Items`. For many applications that simply want to collect data from the user in a standard fashion, the `Form` will serve wonderfully. As we noted before, the `Form` is one of the direct subclasses of `Screen`, thus making it one of the core high-level components. But there are some more high-level components at our disposal. In the next section, we will go on to discuss some of the other descendents of `Screen`, siblings of the `Form`.

5.5 OTHER HIGH-LEVEL UI COMPONENTS

Recall that the UI components of the `javax.microedition.lcdui` are split into a basic hierarchy of two prongs. One side of the prong is the high-level components that all descend from the `Screen` class. The other side of the prong is the low-level descendants of the `Canvas` class. In the previous section, we took a long detailed look at the `Form` class, a high-level component and descendant of `Screen`. The `Form` allowed us to build our own UI's out of a high-level set of components known as `Items`. While the `Form` may be the most central figure in the high-level components, there are other useful high-level components as we can see in Fig. 5.3. In this section, we will look at these other high-level components. Consider, as we look at them, that, just like `Form`, they are concrete subclasses of `Screen`. First, we will look at the `Alert`.

5.5.1 Alerting User

Alerts are the tiny popup windows that come up in an application either to warn you about something or to ask for your confirmation regarding an action. In the computer literate world of the 21st century, your grandmother could probably spot an alert. The `Alert` class is MIDP's version of an alert.

An alert can be displayed in two modes—timed or modal. A timed alert is shown on the screen for a pre-determined time and goes away automatically. A good example would be a splash screen. On the other hand, a modal alert requires user confirmation in order to disappear. A good example would be an error indicating that the application could not connect to a network resource.

Although the `Alert` class itself is simple, it comes with a number of rules that you should familiarize yourself with in order to know how to use it properly. Before we go into the details, let us first see how we can create an `Alert`.

Creating Alert

An alert can be created by simply invoking the constructor of the class with a title to be displayed on the window as in `Alert(String title)`. A more useful constructor looks like this.

```
Alert(String title, String text, Image image, AlertType type)
```

As you can guess, the `title` will be displayed on the title bar of the window, the `text` will be displayed at the center of the `Alert` box, the `image` that typically indicates the nature of the alert is displayed on the side of the text, and the `type` indicates what type of an alert box this really is.

Five pre-defined `AlertType` instances can be used to indicate the nature of the `Alert`.

```
1. ALARM
2. CONFIRMATION
3. ERROR
4. INFO
5. WARNING
```

The `AlertType` can also be used to associate a sound to be played for each type. The `playSound(Display)` method can be used to hint the device to play the appropriate sound.

☞ **Note:** The sound itself is not customizable. It is pre-determined and is left to the device to pick the right sound. Since it is pre-determined, you might not get any sound for a custom `AlertType`. As it can be seen from the method signature, the display used (obtained from `Display.getDisplay(midlet)`) should be passed as a parameter to the method.

Alerts with Image

The image displayed on the `Alert` can be mutable or immutable. If the image is mutable, the image displayed would be a snapshot obtained when the `getImage()` method was called on the `Image` object. Even if the image changes after the `getImage()` method is called, it will not be reflected on the `Alert`, since it already has the snapshot.

Timed Alerts

As mentioned earlier, alerts can be setup so that they can go away after a certain time. This behavior is controlled by four factors.

1. If no timeout is specified on an `Alert`, the default timeout is set by the device. This can be obtained by calling the `getDefaultTimeout()` method.
2. The `setTimeout(int)` method can be used to set the time for which to display the `Alert`. A special value `Alert.FOREVER` can be used to indicate that the alert should be dismissed by the user manually.

3. If the text displayed in the alert is so long that a scroll bar is needed, the implementation will provide a scroll bar, but the `Alert` will automatically become modal even if a timeout has been specified, as the user now has to take time to scroll through the information.
4. If the alert contains more than one command (typically a command translates to a button on the alert, like a "Yes" button and a "No" button), the alert automatically becomes modal even if a timeout has been specified, as the user has to make an explicit decision.

Alert Commands

Each alert comes by default with one in-built command, which is defined as the `Alert.DISMISS_COMMAND` constant. The user can add custom commands by using the `addCommand(Command)` method. Similarly, the user can remove custom commands by using the `removeCommand(Command)` method.

The `DISMISS_COMMAND`, however, is controlled by the implementation. An application cannot explicitly add or remove the `DISMISS_COMMAND`. It is removed automatically when a custom command is added to the `Alert` or added automatically when all custom commands are removed from the `Alert`.

Thus, an `Alert` is guaranteed to have at least one command associated with it.

If there is only one command associated with an `Alert` and the `Alert` has been set to timeout, then the timeout action will be equivalent to the user pressing the single command on the `Alert`.

Alert Listeners

The application can listen to the commands on the `Alert` by registering a `CommandListener` using the `setCommandListener(CommandListener)` method. There can at most be one listener associated with an alert. If a custom alert is not specified, the implementation will automatically define one listener for the alert to handle the `DISMISS_COMMAND`.

In some cases, it might be desirable to go to a different screen than the one from where the alert was displayed as soon as the user makes a selection on the alert. The `setCurrent (Alert alert, Display display)` method in the `Display` class (NOT the `Alert` class) can be used to achieve this.

If an `Alert` does not have a custom command listener, then the implementation will automatically perform the necessary action to display the desired screen. However, if a custom listener is defined on the alert, then it is up to that listener to make the appropriate change.

Using Indicators

Finally, it is also possible to attach a `Gauge` to an alert to indicate the progress of an event. However, there are quite a few restrictions.

The Gauge must be non-interactive. While there is no specific reason given for this restriction, it should be fine, since in most cases gauges are used in an alert to let the user know that the program is attempting to do something such as downloading a file or connecting to a network. Since the Gauge must be non-interactive, it must also not contain any commands or listeners associated with it. The Gauge cannot be shared among Alerts. Each Alert must have its own instance. The Gauge must also not have a label. This restriction is mainly due to the extremely tiny space available to an Alert box (since it is normally less than half the size of the screen itself). As Alerts automatically become modal if the size is large, this is sensible, as you don't want a modal Alert for a non-interactive Gauge.

Along the same note, the preferred dimensions of the Gauge must not be set so that the implementation can adjust the size of the Gauge at runtime depending on how much display size it has. For the same reason, the layout of the Gauge must be LAYOUT_DEFAULT to give more flexibility to the implementation to resize the Gauge if needed.

Since an Alert is a subclass of the Displayable class, it also inherits the Ticker feature. While an application can set a Ticker on an Alert (although in most reason there is no need to do so), the implementation can choose not to display it due to space restrictions. As a result, the application should not rely on this feature to display anything important.

Two other high-level classes are also children of the Screen class. Let us now have a closer look at them.

5.5.2 Getting More Text

If you think a TextField just does not cut it for you and that you need more space, you can always opt to go for a TextBox. A TextBox is a larger version of the TextField and takes the whole of the screen rather than just a part. As a result, it inherits from the Screen class rather than the Item class.

Since the data entered in a TextBox may be more than what can be displayed, the implementation will automatically provide a scroll bar if needed.

One important consideration that must be given when using a TextBox is the maximum number of characters that can be stored in it. While the application can set the maximum number of characters that can be stored in a TextBox, there may be an implementation constraint that can override this requirement. The maximum number of characters that can be stored can be obtained using the getMaxSize() method of the TextBox. Ideally, the application must check this value before changing it to ensure that it is always within the bounds.

This becomes more apparent when you look at the setMaxSize(int maxSize) method. This method, unlike a typical set method, returns an integer that represents the actual maximum size of the TextBox, which may be smaller than the requested size.

Exam Tip

The maximum number of characters set on a `TextBox` may be smaller than the maximum size desired, due to implementation constraints. It is better to check the `getMaxSize()` method to check the maximum possible size (or check the return value of the `setMaxSize` method) and take necessary precautions.

Apart from these differences, a `TextBox` is similar in functionality to a `TextField`. It shares input constraints and input modes with the `TextField`. Please refer back to the discussion of `TextField` for a detailed account of how these constraints work.

The `TextBox` also contains a few extra methods that can be used to insert or remove a piece of `String` at an arbitrary position. See Table 5.11.

Table 5.11 Managing text in a `TextBox`

Method	*Description*
`delete(int offset, int length)`	Deletes the characters from the `TextBox` according to the specified range.
`insert(char[] data, int offset, int length, int position)`	Inserts a range of the specified character array into the `TextBox` at the specified position.
`insert(String text, int position)`	Inserts a string into the `TextBox` at the specified position.
`getChars(char[] data)`	Copies an array of characters from the `TextBox` into the specified array.
`setChars(char[] data, int offset, int length)`	Replaces the characters in the specified range of the `TextBox` with the specified array.
`getString()`	Gets the contents of the `TextBox` as a string.
`setString(String text)`	Replaces the contents of the `TextBox` with the specified one.

We can clearly see that the methods provided in Table 5.11 are exactly the same as those provided in Table 5.6 since the `TextBox` is a larger version of the `TextField`. Let us now move on to another alternative for making a choice—the `List`.

5.5.3 Listing Choices

If you want to provide the user a list of options outside a `Form`, `List` is the class for you. A `List` is very similar to the `ChoiceGroup` class that we saw earlier, except that it is used outside the context of a `Form`. Again, it is a direct subclass of `Screen`. However, it does implement the same `Choice` interface as the `ChoiceGroup`. Functionally, there's not much difference between the two choice components. The real difference is in the fact that `List` is made to exist as a `Screen` itself, while the `ChoiceGroup`, being a subclass of `Item`, is made to exist within a `Form`.

We will go over the differences that you need to keep in mind when making your choice between the two classes. The biggest difference is that a `List` occupies the whole display. That is why it is a subclass of `Screen`. `Form` also subclasses `Screen` and occupies the whole display.

One of the functional differences is that the `POPUP` mode, part of the `Choice` interface, cannot be used with a `List`.

Another functional difference, perhaps the most important difference, involves event handling. This option is NOT available in the `ChoiceGroup` class. A `List` has the ability to invoke an action based on a selection through the `Command` and `CommandListener` mechanisms that we saw earlier. The `List` class comes with a default command called `SELECT_COMMAND` which is invoked when a `List` is created in `IMPLICIT` mode and when a selection is made. Any `CommandListener` associated with the `List` can listen for this command and take appropriate action. In order to implement event handling on a `List`, you only need to create the `List` in the `IMPLICIT` mode, by passing the `Choice.IMPLICIT` to the `List` constructor, and then implement the event handling in the `CommandListener` that you associate with the `List`.

It is also possible for the application to set an explicit command by using the `setSelectCommand(Command)` method if it does not want the default `SELECT_COMMAND`.

Exam Tip

The implementation must ensure that no command is invoked if a `list` is empty.

5.6 CREATING LOW-LEVEL USER INTERFACES

We have now covered the high-level UI components. Now, we move on to the low-level portion of the API that provides more direct access to screen rendering and event handling. Instead of choosing abstract components that will be rendered according to the implementation, you will now be able to draw on the screen yourself. Instead of handling abstract commands that the implementation maps to its own set of specific keys, you will now be able to listen directly to primitive key events. Again, referring back to Fig. 5.1, we are now visiting the low-level side of the class hierarchy, all of which descend from the `Canvas` class. The low-level API begins with the `Canvas` class, a peer to the `Screen` class that all of the high-level classes inherit from. Again, both `Screen` and `Canvas` are direct subclasses of the `Displayable` class.

Although the `Canvas` class itself provides most of the basic functionalities needed to interact with the user interface of a device, it is abstract in itself. While the `javax.microedition.lcdui` package provides many concrete subclasses of the abstract `Screen` class, it offers only one subclass of `Canvas`, the `GameCanvas` class. Unless you write your own subclass of `Canvas`, you will always work with `GameCanvas` when developing low-level UIs. However, `GameCanvas` provides a rich set of game-specific functionality for the developer that goes far beyond the general graphics mechanisms of the `Canvas`. In this section, we will address the graphics mechanisms available to all `Canvas` subclasses via their inheritance from the `Canvas`. We will cover the special functionality of the `GameCanvas` in the next chapter.

5.6.1 Interacting with Keys

Since mobile devices mostly function as cell phones and since their size is much more limited than a PDA or a laptop, the keyboard is quite different from the standard devices. We just can't be sure of what keys a particular device will offer. In order to carve out some stability, MIDP focuses on defining some constants that can be bound to a minimal set of keys that we can expect to find on any compliant device. These constants are provided by the `Canvas` class. There are two sets of keys defined: those related to the device's use as a phone and those related to the device's use as a game machine.

Phone-based Keys

The keys – `KEY_NUM0, KEY_NUM1`, ..., `KEY_NUM9, KEY_POUND, KEY_START`– represent the standard numeric keypad of a cell phone. These keys are covered by the ITU (International Telecommunications Union) specification.

Given that a new model comes out every other day, how is this model extensible? What if a manufacturer wants to provide more keys or simply intends to provide a standard QWERTY keyboard with the cell phone (some models already do)? Fear not. The keys (at least the ITU keys) represent the Unicode values of the characters that they represent. Thus, if the manufacturer wants to add more keys, all he has to do is to ensure that the key codes for the keys are the Unicode values of the keys they represent. That said, in order to be compliant with the MIDP specification, it is always a good idea to work within the constraints of the specification.

Game-based Keys

Apart from these keys, the class also defines a few more constants that map to standard game play keys. These constants define the following game play keys: `UP, DOWN, RIGHT, LEFT, FIRE, GAME_A, GAME_B, GAME_C, and GAME_D`.

Just now, I mentioned that the key values represent the Unicode values of the keys. What about the game keys then? They don't really have a Unicode equivalent, do they? Absolutely not. The game keys are symbolic keys rather than actual keys. In fact, this is not exactly low-level key handling, but it's a necessary logical layer to help standardize the key set across disparate devices. While it is possible to have an exclusive game key in some devices, frequently the game keys are mapped onto the standard keys of the device. The logical layering allows this.

Methods are provided to resolve the mapping. The `getKeyCode(int gameAction):int` and `getGameAction(int keyCode):int` methods can be used to convert the key code of a game constant to the key code of the actual key it represents on the keyboard and vice versa. It must be noted that multiple keys can be mapped to the same game action (different choices for different types of people, for example). In such cases, only one (any one) of the mapped values will be returned.

Key Events

We know what keys are available in the device. Now, how do we respond to key presses? The `Canvas` provides in-built support for key event callbacks, a.k.a. event-listener methods. This is similar to the methods defined in the `KeyListener` class of the Java AWT package.

There are three methods defined for key events.

1. `keyPressed(int keyCode)`
2. `keyReleased(int keyCode)`
3. `keyRepeated(int keyCode)`

The first two methods are simple—one is triggered when a key is pressed and one when a key is released. What about the third? The `keyPressed` event does not differentiate between a key pressed for a short period of time and a key pressed for a longer period. While this is fine when standard keys (like numbers when a phone call is made) are pressed, it might not be sufficient for games, where the user might want to keep holding the `FIRE` button for continual firing action. As a result, the `keyRepeated` event is provided to indicate a key being pressed repeatedly or simply kept down for a long period.

While this might sound reasonable, simpler devices might not be able to differentiate between a long press and a short press. Hence, the support for `keyRepeated` event is optional and can be verified programmatically by calling the `hasRepeatEvents()` method.

Exam Tip

The `keyRepeated` event can be used to check for keys pressed repeatedly or for a long time. This feature is not mandatory and its support can be verified by calling the `hasRepeatEvents()` method.

Another important thing to note is that no explicit listeners are needed to listen for key events. The `Canvas` class has in-built event listening mechanism, and one needs to just override the event delivery methods to take advantage of these low-level events. This is true in case of pointer events also, as we shall see in the next section.

5.6.2 Interacting with Pointers

While most mobile phones do not have mice or other pointer-based inputs, some devices covered by MIDP, such as PDA-integrated mobile phones, do have that support. Keeping this in mind, the `Canvas` class provides support for pointer-based events, but pointer support is clearly an optional feature in MIDP.

Exam Tip

Pointer support in a MIDP-compliant device is optional. As a result, some devices may not execute code in the pointer event methods, so applications should not rely on execution of such callback methods.

Just because it's optional, it doesn't mean that you shouldn't use it. You just need to view it as an extra functionality and cover your bases in the case that the pointer support is unavailable. The application should use the `hasPointerEvents()` and `hasPointerMotionEvents()` methods to check if the support is available and take appropriate steps based on the response.

The pointer events themselves are a simplified version of the events that you might have seen in the `MouseEvent` and `MouseMotionEvent` of the Java AWT package. There are three callback methods defined in the `Canvas` class.

1. `pointerDragged(int x, int y)`
2. `pointerPressed(int x, int y)`
3. `pointerReleased(int x, int y)`

As stated earlier, there is no need to explicitly add a listener to a `Canvas` to listen for pointer events. It is sufficient to just override these methods and provide the appropriate implementation.

5.6.3 Creating Graphics

As we have said, the low-level APIs provide the developer with direct control over rendering graphics on the screen. Now we will discuss the mechanisms for doing so. If you have experience in AWT, you probably started with some examples about drawing "Hello World!" on a `Panel`. Maybe you even drew a few rectangles and triangles. If so, you can rejoice now! The MIDP `Canvas` class provides similar support to arbitrarily draw pixels on the `Canvas` using a similar `Graphics` class. The `Graphics` class represents the drawing context and provides the functionality to draw to the screen.

Exam Tip

For a Canvas, the only way to get the associated Graphics object is by overriding the paint method.

Drawing Text

The Graphics class provides some simple methods to draw text directly on the screen. The drawString(String str, int x, int y, int anchor) method can be used to draw a string from the (x, y) point specified. The drawSubstring(String str, int offset, int length, int x, int y, int anchor) method is a variation that allows the application to draw a portion of the string determined by the offset and length values provided.

For finer control, the Graphics class provides the drawChar(char character, int x, int y, int anchor) and drawChars(char[] data, int offset, int length, int x, int y, int anchor) methods to draw individual character(s).

Depending on the type of font, different characters may have different widths and lengths. In order to provide consistency, the application can also specify an anchor point, which refers to the relative position from which to translate coordinates in the string. The pre-defined values of anchor points – TOP, BOTTOM, LEFT, RIGHT, BASELINE and HCENTER can be combined with bitwise OR operator (|) to determine where the coordinate should be considered with respect to the text. For example, a value of BOTTOM | LEFT implies that the anchor point should be on the left at the bottom line of the font. Figure 5.12 shows these anchor locations.

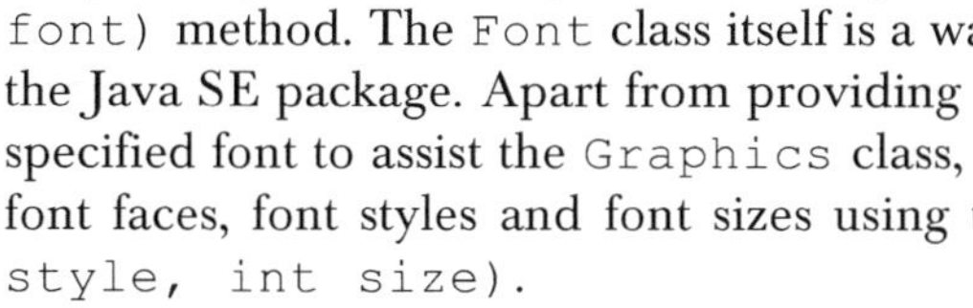

Figure 5.12 Font anchor point values

Speaking of fonts, they can be changed *before* drawing the text using the setFont(Font font) method. The Font class itself is a watered down version of the Font class available in the Java SE package. Apart from providing methods to get the dimensions of character in the specified font to assist the Graphics class, the Font class also provides support for different font faces, font styles and font sizes using the static method getFont(int face, int style, int size).

Exam Tip

Fonts in MIDP UI are characterized by face (MONOSPACE or PROPORTIONAL), style (PLAIN, BOLD, ITALIC, or UNDERLINED) and size (SMALL, MEDIUM, or LARGE). Applications can only use these pre-defined constants and cannot set custom font faces, styles, or sizes.

Due to the constrained nature of the target devices, the font sizes and styles are not absolute, such as "12", "14", etc. or "Verdana", "Times New Roman". Instead, they are pre-defined constants that refer to font groups and relative font sizes that could be interpreted appropriately by the target device. The constants in Table 5.12 are already available in the `javax.microedition.lcdui.Font` class for this purpose.

Table 5.12 `Font` constants that represent different font face, style and size categories

Type	*Constant*	*Description*
Font face	`FACE_MONOSPACE`	Fixed-length font, such as Courier New. Example: `This is a monospace text.`
	`FACE_PROPORTIONAL`	Variable-length font, such as Times New Roman. Example: This is a proportional font.
Font style	`STYLE_BOLD`	Text in a thicker font. Example: **This is bold**.
	`STYLE_ITALIC`	Text in a slanted font. Example: *This is in italics*.
	`STYLE_PLAIN`	Text that does not have any special characteristics. Example: This is plain.
	`STYLE_UNDERLINED`	Text that has a line under it. Example: This is underlined.
Font size	`SIZE_LARGE`	Font with a size larger than normal.
	`SIZE_MEDIUM`	Font with a normal size. This typically is the standard font size used in the device.
	`SIZE_SMALL`	Font that has a size smaller than normal.

As you can see, the constants themselves don't specify how *exactly* the text is going to look. They just describe the characteristics of the text that the device implementation must consider while drawing the text.

Drawing Figures

There are a number of `drawXXX` methods provided in the `Graphics` class that can be used to draw simple figures such as rectangles, circles, squares, etc. This is similar to the ones you would find in the `java.awt.Graphics` class.

Table 5.13 shows a list of such methods and their use.

Table 5.13 Drawing methods in the Canvas class

Method	*Description*
`drawLine(int x1, int y1, int x2, int y2)`	Draws a line from (x1, y1) to (x2, y2).
`drawRect(int x, int y, int width, int height)` `fillRect(int x, int y, int width, int height)`	Draws/Fills a rectangle whose top-left corner is (x, y) and that is `width` pixels wide and `height` pixels high.
`drawRoundRect(int x, int y, int width, int height, int arcWidth, int arcHeight)` `fillRoundRect(int x, int y, int width, int height, int arcWidth, int arcHeight)`	Draws/Fills a rectangle but rounds off the edges with an arc that covers a rectangle of specified `width` and `height`.
`fillTriangle(int x1, int y1, int x2, int y2, int x3, int y3)`	Draws a triangle of specified coordinates and fills it with the current color.
`drawArc(int x, int y, int width, int height, int startAngle, int arcAngle)` `fillArc(int x, int y, int width, int height, int startAngle, int arcAngle)`	Draws/Fills an arc covering a rectangle of specified dimensions. The arc is drawn from the startAngle (0 being the 3 o'clock position) and extends till the `arcAngle` degrees. If the `arcAngle` is a positive value, the rotation will be in counter-clockwise direction. If it is a negative value, the rotation will be in clockwise direction.

One can also change the style of the lines being drawn using the `setStrokeStyle(int style)` method. The styles available by default are `SOLID` and `DOTTED`.

Before you start using these methods, let me explain the coordinate system used by the `Graphics` class.

Coordinate System

A coordinate system is a mechanism used to describe a point in space. For example, the point (0, 0) in a simple mathematical graph would refer to the junction of the X-axis and the Y-axis. In most drawing software including this `Graphics` API, the coordinate (0, 0) refers to the top-left corner of the screen on which something needs to be drawn. The values increase from left to right and from top to bottom.

Sometimes, you might not always want to start from the top-left corner. You may want to draw figures in other areas of the screen but might still want to keep your numbers with reference to the base origin (0, 0). For example, let us say you want to draw a square of size 4. The coordinates will then be (0, 0), (0, 4), (4, 0), and (4, 4). Now let us say that you want to draw another square, but with (5, 5) as the top-left corner coordinate. For this you'd have to redraw the rectangle with new coordinates (5, 5), (5, 9), (9, 5), and (9, 9). This essentially needs some thinking on your part to translate the coordinates to the new origin. To simplify this issue, the `Graphics` class also provides a translation method.

The `translate(int x, int y)` method can be used to change the coordinate origin of the `Graphics` instance the application is working with. Once this method is called, the values in the future calls to `drawXXX` methods will be interpreted based on this origin.

An important point to note is that the `translate` method call is cumulative. That is, if you call the method twice, the new coordinate will be the sum of the values in the calls. Thus, two calls with values (4, 3) and (5, 4) will change the coordinate origin from (0, 0) to (9, 7).

☞ **Note:** MIDP specifies only minimum size of a screen. Different devices may have different screen sizes. As a result, applications must not rely on absolute coordinate values. If absolute coordinates are essential, applications must first check the dimensions of the device and translate the coordinates accordingly.

Manipulating Canvas

The `Graphics` class also provides a few methods to manipulate structures that have been drawn on it. You can copy a portion of the canvas to another portion using the `copyArea` method. You can also clip a portion of a canvas. To do this, you have to first define a 'clip' rectangle using the `setClip(int x, int y, int width, int height)` method. Once the rectangle is defined, you can specify the area to be clipped using the `clipRect (int x, int y, int width, int height)` method. The resulting visible area will be the intersection of the two rectangles.

Painting Canvas

As stated earlier, an application can draw on the `Canvas` by putting custom code inside the `paint(Graphics)` method and by using the `Graphics` object that is passed to the `paint` method. Since MIDP is defined for resource-constrained devices, the `paint` method has some special rules and characteristics compared to the `paint` method you might see in the AWT or Swing package.

The most important characteristic is how painting calls are handled. The `paint` method is typically called when the `Canvas` is made visible or switched from another screen, or if a portion of the `Canvas` has changed. Since repainting pixels may hog resources, the painting is not done immediately. Rather, the implementation queues the painting calls and then performs the painting in a bulk fashion. This has a few implications on what the application can assume about painting.

When a `paint` method is called, there is no guarantee that the painting will happen immediately. The `paint` method must never be called directly by the application. Instead, the `repaint` method must be called. The application must not hold any local reference to the `Graphics` object passed to the `paint` method. If an application wants to force the painting to happen immediately, it must call the `serviceRepaints()` method, which will trigger the repainting process.

Since `serviceRepaints()` triggers painting, it is a blocking method and will not return till the painting is completed. Moreover, as it is going to wait for the painting to complete, it must not hold any locks that might be needed by the `paint` method itself. This is because the thread that might do the painting method may be different from the thread where the `serviceRepaints()` method was called, and if the `serviceRepaints()` method holds the lock needed by the `paint` method, there will be a deadlock.

One of the mechanisms that a MIDP implementation might use in repainting screens is a technique called double buffering. Double buffering is essentially writing the contents of the screen (that is, the pixels) in memory before copying them over to the screen. The major advantage of double buffering is the elimination of screen flicker, which is caused when the screen goes blank when existing contents of the screen are erased and before new contents are copied. Apart from this, double buffering also enables the implementation to process multiple `paint` calls in a batch. For example, if multiple actions are performed on the screen that warrants a screen repaint, the implementation can render the pixels in memory for the calls first and then copy the final contents to the screen. Thus, the screen will be repainted only once instead of multiple times. As you can see, the features we described above facilitate such a mechanism. However, it is to be noted that double buffering is only optional and not mandatory.

Exam Tip

Double buffering removes screen flicker when screens are repainted. However, it is not necessary for an implementation to use double buffering for repainting screens.

Avoiding Deadlocks

We mentioned earlier that a `paint` method should not be called directly and that the `repaint` method should be called instead. We also mentioned that the `serviceRepaints()` method should be called to process the pending `paint` calls immediately and that the thread calling the `serviceRepaints()` method should not hold any locks, as the `serviceRepaints()` method might need the same lock, which may result in a deadlock situation.

That said, is there a way we can guarantee that no locking will happen even if the thread calling the `serviceRepaints()` method has a lock that the method needs or if we don't even know if the thread has the lock in question or not? There is.

A simple way to avoid a locking situation is to call methods synchronously. While this approach is not desirable in many places as it may cause bottlenecks, it does make sense in some specific situations such as when handling input events or when handling multiple paint requests.

MIDP provides a generic mechanism to queue user requests along with system events via the `Display.callSerially(Runnable r)` method. Essentially, what happens is that the `run` method of the passed `Runnable` implementation is called after pending events and paint requests are performed, ensuring that there are no conflicts.

> **Exam Tip**
>
> The `Display.callSerially(Runnable r)` method can be used to schedule user events such as repaints to be performed serially along with input events and system paint requests to avoid deadlocks.

It does not matter from which thread the `callSerially` method is called, because the concern here is the `Runnable` instance, not the method itself. As a result, the `callSerially` method will not wait till the `run()` method of the `Runnable` instance is executed. Like typical callback method, it is a good practice to not have any long-running operations on the `run()` method, since that might cause new events to wait till the method is executed fully. It is preferable to put such long-running operations in another thread and start it from the `run()` method so that the `run()` method can return quickly.

Working with Color

With the `Graphics` object, one can use RGB (Red-Green-Blue) colors. It is possible to render individual pixels based on their color composition, get the color composition of the individual pixels, and get grayscale value of the color being used.

Table 5.14 lists the methods that manipulate color.

Table 5.14 Color methods in the Graphics class

Method	*Description*
`drawRGB(int[] rgbData, int offset, int scanLength, int x, int y, int width, int height, boolean processAlpha)`	Draws colors in Red-Blue-Green encoding format with extra option for setting the transparency level.

`getRedComponent()`
`getGreenComponent()`
`getBlueComponent()`
	Gets the individual color components of the current color used in the `Graphics`.

`getColor()`
`setColor(int rgb)`
`setColor(int red, int green, int blue)`
	Gets the current color of the `Graphics` instance or sets the color that the `Graphics` instance should use.

`setGrayscale(int value)` `getGrayscale()`	Gets or sets the grayscale value of the color used.
`getDisplayColor(int color)`	Gets the color that will be displayed for the color requested (the color displayed may be different from the color requested due to resolution limitation of the device)

This completes the coverage of the low-level `Canvas` class. If you need to control the on-screen rendering of your application, you must use the `Canvas` and the `Graphics` based techniques described above. This should provide more than adequate control for the specialized graphics needs of games and other graphics-based applications. In addition to these techniques, the `GameCanvas` class provides a very rich set of specialized graphics functionality to support game development. This functionality is so rich that we have dedicated the next chapter to game development using the `GameCanvas` class and other related classes. In this section, we have only covered the lowest level mechanism by which all `Canvas` subclasses render themselves to the screen.

Summary

The MIDP UI API, while posing quite a few constraints due to the limitations of the underlying device, nevertheless provides a wide variety of options, sufficient for a designer to show his creative genius. If the constraints are followed properly and best practices are adhered to, the user will see a seamless integration of the application with the device's look and feel, providing a pleasant user experience.

You should now have a clear understanding of the MIDP UI model. In particular, you should understand the difference between the high-level UI packages. Every top-level object that can be drawn to the screen descends from `Displayable`. The first two subclasses of `Displayable` define the split between high-level and low-level functionality. These classes are, respectively, `Screen` and `Canvas`. For the exam, make sure you understand the two distinct purposes of each of these family branches.

The high-level and low-level APIs provide different types of display and different types of event handling. The high-level APIs provide access to abstract representations of display and events, while the low-level provides direct access to screen rendering and primitive key events. For instance, the high-level event handling utilizes the `Command` class while the low-level event handling addresses the events generated from the real keys of the device. You need to know the details of each of them.

A word to the wise, you should familiarize yourself with the details of the API itself, as the exam will contain quite a few code snippets. As always, it is a good idea to write some sample applications to get a feel of the API. There's a bit of conceptual stuff in this chapter, but this is primarily a hands-on section. So, get out your emulators and write some code.

If you recall from our discussion of the low-level `Canvas` class, we have postponed discussion of the single concrete subclass of this branch of the hierarchy. The `GameCanvas` extends `Canvas` and provides a rich set of additional functionality to support development of games. This class, along with a set of helper classes, remains in their own package `javax.microedition.lcdui.game`. The next chapter explores developing game applications with this package.

References

1. MIDP 2.0(JSR-118) specification
   http://www.jcp.org/aboutJava/communityprocess/final/jsr118/
2. J2ME 101, Part 1: Introduction to MIDP's high-level user interface
   http://www-128.ibm.com/developerworks/edu/j-dw-java-j2me1-i.html
3. MIDP user interface
   http://www.javaworld.com/javaworld/jw-05-2005/jw-0516-midp.html

Exercises

1. Develop an application that contains two interactive `Gauges`, three `TextFields`, where the current values of the two `Gauges` must be set into the two `TextFields`, the sum of which must be set into the third `TextField`.
2. Create different types of `ChoiceGroups` and display the label of the selected element in an `Alert`. See the result and analyze the difference.

Review Questions

1. Which mode of selection is not possible in a `List` item?

   a. `IMPLICIT` b. `MULTIPLE`

   c. `POPUP` d. `EXCLUSIVE`

2. Identify the correct statement regarding how painting is done on MIDP application screens.

   a. When the `repaint` method of a `Canvas` instance is called, it will be painted immediately.

   b. The call to the `paint` method is made synchronously from inside the `repaint` method to ensure that the screen is painted properly before processing any other request.

   c. A `Canvas` will be painted when the `repaint` method is called, regardless of whether it is visible or not.

   d. When the `serviceRepaints()` method of a `Canvas` instance is called, all pending `repaint` requests will be processed immediately.

3. Identify the appropriate missing pieces in the MIDP UI high-level class hierarchy.

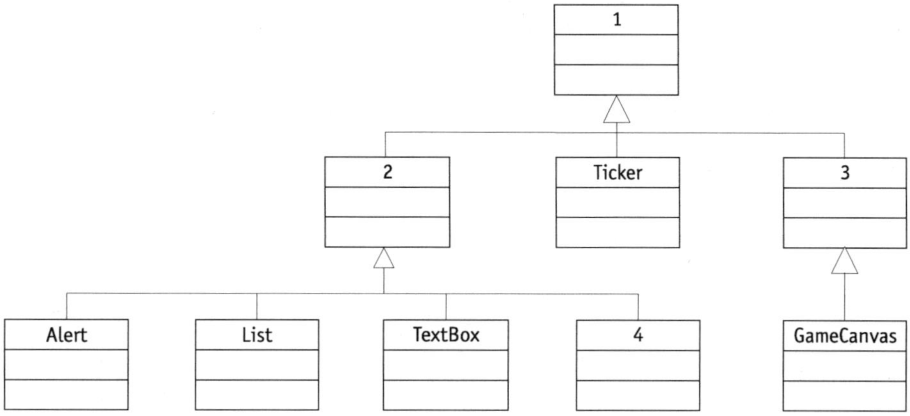

a. `Displayable`
b. `Display`
c. `Screen`
d. `Form`
e. `Canvas`
f. `Graphics`
g. `Item`

4. Which of the following values are valid modes for a `TextField`?
   a. `NUMERIC`
   b. `EMAIL_ADDRESS`
   c. `PHONE`
   d. `ANY | PASSWORD`
5. Which of the following statements are true with regard to buffering and concurrency in a MIDP application?
   a. As the processing capacity of mobile devices is limited, MIDP requires that all compliance devices provide double-buffering mechanism for optimal user experience.
   b. All pending paint operations will be performed immediately when the `callSerially(Runnable r)` method is called in the associated `Display` instance before running the passed instance.
   c. The `callSerially(Runnable r)` method will wait till the associated `Runnable` instance completes its `run()` method execution.
   d. It is possible that a deadlock may occur if the thread calling the `serviceRepaints()` method shares a lock that is used by the `paint` method.
6. How will the data be displayed when the `Form` described in the code is displayed?

```
public class FontForm extends Form {
    public class FontForm() {
        super("Font Example");
        this.initialize();
    }
    private void initialize(){
        Font font = Font.getFont(Font.FACE_MONOSPACE,
                                 Font.SIZE_LARGE,
```

```
                                        Font.STYLE_BOLD);
        StringItem string = new StringItem("Greeting", "Hello World!");
        string.setFont(font);
        this.append(string);
    }
}
```

a. A `StringItem` with the label "Greeting" and text "Hello World!" will be displayed with the default font dimensions of the device.
b. A `StringItem` with the label "Greeting" and text "Hello World!" will be displayed and the "Hello World!" text will have a Courier-like font face in bold style with a large font size.
c. A runtime exception will be thrown.
d. The program will not compile because one of the parameters is invalid.

7. How does the `Screen` class in MIDP differ from the `Canvas` class in terms of functionality?
   a. The `Screen` class uses event callbacks for listening to user input whereas the `Canvas` uses listener classes.
   b. The `Canvas` class can change the way it can paint itself on the screen whereas the device implementation determines how the elements of a `Screen` class are painted on the screen.
   c. The `Canvas` class can handle pointer devices if available while the `Screen` class cannot.
   d. The `Screen` class must handle `repaint` calls while the device implementation handles repaint requests on behalf of the `Canvas` class.
8. Which of the following statements is true with regard to event handling mechanisms in a MIDP application?
   a. A MIDP display extending the `Screen` class will not have any access to key events.
   b. It is not possible to use mouse or similar pointer-based devices in a MIDP application as they are not guaranteed to be available in all mobile devices.
   c. The MIDP API provides special mapping for game events for specific keys in a mobile device to facilitate gaming applications.
   d. All key events are always handled asynchronously.
9. Which of the following statements are true about how a MIDP application can be displayed on a mobile device screen?
   a. Only one screen can be visible at a given time for an application.
   b. An application can have multiple windows visible at the same time.
   c. It is not possible to programmatically access native mobile device features such as vibration and backlight from a MIDP application.
   d. Any screen that can be displayed in a MIDP application can have a `Ticker` placed on it.

10. What are the valid responsibilities of a class that extends the `CustomItem` class to create a custom widget?
    a. The subclass must provide the minimum content dimensions of the widget.
    b. The subclass must define the various interaction modes that will be accepted by the subclass.
    c. The subclass must notify any listeners on the `CustomItem` that its state has changed.
    d. The subclass must notify the `CommandListener` instances about a command action for `Command.SCREEN` type commands.

Review Answers

1. c. `POPUP` option is valid only for `ChoiceGroup` items, not for `List` items.
2. d. When a `repaint` method is called, the implementation may decide to batch some of the calls for better performance since the desired regions to be painted on different calls may overlap with each other. Call to the `paint` method from inside the `repaint` method is always done asynchronously. If the canvas is not visible, if it has zero or negative area or if the area to be painted is outside the bounds of the `Canvas`, the `repaint` method call will be ignored.
3. 1 – a, 2 – c, 3 – e, 4 – d.

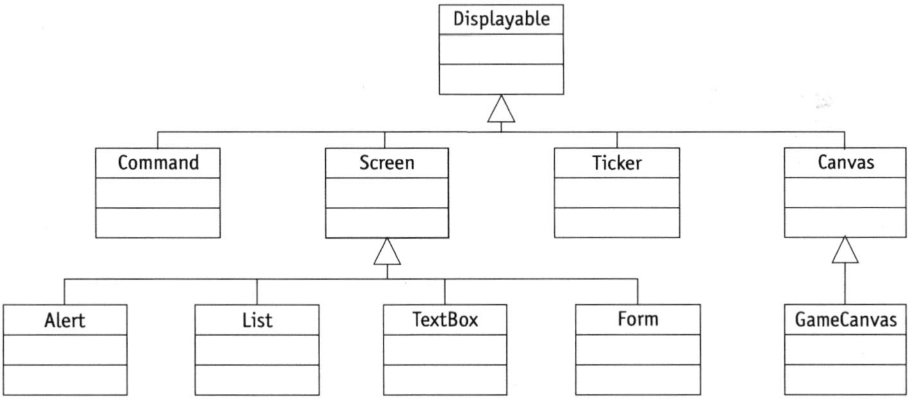

4. a and d. The valid constraint for specifying an email address field is `EMAILADDR`. The valid constraint for specifying a phone number is `PHONENUMBER`.
5. b and d. Double buffering is not guaranteed in the MIDP specification, since some mobile applications may have very limited memory and might not be able to hold too much information in memory. The `callSerially` method will never block for the `Runnable` instance to run, as the call to the `run()` method of the `Runnable` instance will occur independently of the call to the `callSerially` method.

6. c. The program will compile because all the `Font` constants are valid. However, the program will throw an `IllegalArgumentException` indicating that the style passed is illegal. This is because the signature of the `Font.getFont` method is `Font.getFont(int face, int style, int size)`. In the code, the parameters for style and size have been switched, resulting in an error.
7. b and c. High-level API such as `Screen` has access to user input only through listener mechanisms like `CommandListener` and `ItemStateListener`, while low-level API like `Canvas` has direct access to key events and pointer events via callback methods. Since `Canvas` is a low-level API, it has to manage paint calls and input device event callbacks by itself. In case of high-level API like `Screen` and its subclasses, the way the widget is displayed is dependent on the device implementation and cannot be modified by the application.
8. a and c. Classes extending the `Screen` class are considered a part of the abstract high-level UI API. Such screens include `Form`, `TextBox`, etc. These classes get user input using the `Item` classes and `Command` objects and hence do not need access to input device events directly. Also, all key events are handled synchronously or sequentially to ensure that repeat strokes are captured faithfully and in proper order.
9. a and d. The user interface of a MIDP application is similar to that of a pack of cards. An application can contain a number of screens, but only one is visible at any time. This screen can be obtained by calling `Display.getDisplay(midlet).getCurrent()`, where `midlet` is the main class of the MIDP application that extends the `MIDlet` class. There are a couple of convenient static methods in the `Display` class, namely `Display.flashBacklight(int duration)` and `Display.vibrate(int duration)` that allow the application to control the backlight and vibration facilities of the underlying device (if available).
10. a and c. Since a `CustomItem` can have any shape, it must implement the callback methods that will be used by the `Layout` managers providing information about the minimum area that its contents will occupy. Note that this is different from the minimum sizes as defined in the `Item` class, which defines the physical limitations of the `Item`. The content area excludes the space allotted for label, borders, etc. The subclass must also invoke the `Item.notifyStateChanged()` method to notify the `Item`'s `ItemStateListener`, not the `CommandListener`, whenever the state of the `Item` has changed so that any listeners listening on the events can take appropriate action. Interaction modes such as key events and pointer events are defined by the device implementation. The `CustomItem` can use the `getInteractionModes()` method to determine the available interaction modes.

Exam Notes

☞ Given a scenario, develop MIDP 2.0-compliant user interfaces, recognizing portability requirements and limitations (e.g., double-buffering not guaranteed), and performance issues (e.g., using inner classes, freeing memory buffers, etc.).

Portability Requirements

- The display of the application should be device-independent. Since devices have varying screen sizes, care has to be taken so that absolute coordinates are not used, and even if used, they are adjusted taking the screen size of the device into consideration.
- Availability of input devices (for example, pointing devices) should not be assumed as they might not be available in some devices (like cell phones).

Limitations

- Only one `Displayable` is visible at a given time.

Performance Issues

- Image buffers must be used sparingly.
- The `Graphics` object must be created once before displaying and should be reused thereafter.

☞ Discuss the MIDP user interface high-level API including concurrency, portability, structure of the API, and interplay with the application manager.

High-level API

- High-level APIs are used to provide access to UI components in a device-independent manner. These APIs are typically used by business applications that need forms for input.

Concurrency

- UI API is thread-safe.
- Implementation generally does not hold locks to visible objects and hence any object can be used as a lock for synchronization.

Portability

- High-level APIs are portable across devices since the implementation takes care of rendering.

Structure

- Used by business applications.
- Drawing of components on the device display is performed by the implementation.
- Applications cannot define visual appearance of components.
- Primitive interactions like navigation and scrolling are handled by the implementation (like scrolling of a really long `List`).

- No access provided to input devices for key presses and releases.
- All `Screen` subclasses fall under the high-level API category.

Interplay with Application Manager

- The following guarantees are given by AMS.
  - The `Display.getDisplay(MIDlet)` method can be called from the start of the MIDlet till it is destroyed (from the constructor to the `destroyApp()` call of the MIDlet).
  - The `Display` object is the same throughout the lifecycle of a MIDlet run.
  - The `Displayable` set using `Display.setCurrent` will not be changed by AMS.
- The following behaviors are assumed by AMS with respect to the application.
  - The application may set the first screen in the `startApp()` method. Since this method can be called multiple times (application may be paused and resumed), initialization should not be performed in this method (should be done in the constructor instead).
  - The application should release as many threads as possible in the `pauseApp()` method.
  - The application should delete created objects using the `destroyApp()` method.

☞ Explain the MIDP user interface low-level API including font support, repainting and coordinate system.

Low-level API

- Low-level APIs provide access to the more basic features of the device, like drawing on the screen and the screen coordinates. These APIs are not necessarily portable for this reason (each device might have different screen size) and hence must be used with caution. Typically, game applications use these APIs.
- Used by game applications.
- Full control of the device display is available to the application.
- Access provided to input devices for key presses and releases.
- `Canvas` (and `GameCanvas`) and `Graphics` fall under the low-level API category.
- There are some parts in low-level APIs which are device-independent abstractions and hence portable (like key definitions). It is preferable to use these as much as possible.

Font Support

- Implementation and support for fonts is device-specific. If the requested font type is not available, the nearest font is returned.
- Fonts can be requested using the following constants with the `getFont(int face, int style, int size)` method.
  - By size: `SIZE_SMALL`, `SIZE_MEDIUM`, or `SIZE_LARGE`

  - ♦ By face: `FACE_PROPORTIONAL`, `FACE_MONOSPACE`, or `FACE_SYSTEM`
  - ♦ By style: `STYLE_PLAIN`, `STYLE_BOLD`, `STYLE_ITALIC`, or `STYLE_UNDERLINED`.

Repainting

- The `paint(Graphics g)` method has to be implemented by a `Canvas` subclass.
- The `repaint` method queues up a request for repaint. The `serviceRepaints()` method schedules the repainting thread.

Coordinate System

- While using coordinates, use the `Canvas.getWidth()` and `Canvas.getHeight()` to find out the screen area of the device and adjust accordingly to provide maximum portability.
- The origin (0, 0) is defined at the upper-left corner of the display.
- The width and height of the display can be obtained using `Canvas.getWidth()` and `Canvas.getHeight()` methods.
- Pixel ratio is 1:1. That is, the gaps between two horizontal pixels and two vertical pixels are the same.

☞ Given a set of requirement, develop interactive MIDP 2.0 user interface code with proper event-handling (including both the high-level and low-level APIs, repainting and threading issues).

High-level Event Handling

- High-level APIs use `Command` objects and `CommandListener` to listen to abstract actions.
  - ♦ The `Command` is an abstract action that can be displayed in a device-specific manner by the implementation.
  - ♦ The `CommandListener` can be used to find out if the user invoked a `Command`, and if so, which `Command` was invoked and act appropriately.
  - ♦ The `ItemCommandListener` can be used to listen to commands invoked on `Item` objects.
  - ♦ The `ItemStateListener` can be used to listen to state changes in `Item` objects.
- All UI callbacks are serialized.
- `Timer` events are not considered as UI events.
- There can be only one type of listener associated with a 'listenable' object. For example, there cannot be two `CommandListeners` for the same `Displayable` object.
- The `CommandListener` interface
  - ♦ `public void commandAction(Command c, Displayable d);`
- The `ItemCommandListener` interface
  - ♦ `public void commandAction(Command c, Item i);`

- The `ItemStateListener` interface
  - `public void itemStateChanged(Item item);`

Low-level Event Handling

- Low-level APIs include events for key presses and key releases.
- Events for pointer actions are available if such an input device is present in the device.
- Key events in the `Canvas`
  - `public void keyPressed(int keyCode);`
  - `public void keyReleased(int keyCode);`
  - `public void keyRepeated(int keyCode);`
    - May not be available for all devices.
    - Can be checked using `hasRepeatEvents()` method.
- Pointer events in the `Canvas`. This may not be available in all devices.
  - `public void pointerPressed(int x, int y);`
  - `public void pointerReleased(int x, int y);`
  - `public void pointerDragged(int x, int y);`
  - The availability of pointer events can be checked using `hasPointerEvents()` and `hasPointerMotionEvents()` methods.

Repainting Issues

- Repainting is done automatically for `Screen` objects (high-level APIs) but not for `Canvas` objects (low-level APIs).
- For `Canvas`, repainting is done asynchronously.
- Multiple `repaint` requests can be clubbed together during the actual repaint by the device.
- Repaint is actually triggered only by the `Canvas.serviceRepaints()` call.
- `repaint` call is only a request.

Threading Issues

- Caller of the `Canvas.serviceRepaints()` method must not hold any locks needed by the `paint` method.
  - Since the `paint` method called by the `serviceRepaints()` method may work on a thread other than the originating thread, it might want to obtain a lock. If the caller of the `serviceRepaints()` method has the same lock, there will be a deadlock.
- The `Display.callSerially(Runnable r)` method can be called to ensure that the `Runnable` implementor's `run()` method is called in serial order along with other events.
- Typically used by animations to ensure that repaints are properly done.

☞ Identify correct and incorrect statements or examples about the classes (including the class hierarchy) within the javax.microedition.lcdui package.

Classes in javax.microedition.lcdui Package Displayable

- A `Displayable` can have a title, a `Ticker` and a set of `Command` objects associated with it.
- When a `Displayable` is made visible using the `Display.setCurrent()` method, the previous one is replaced.
- Title may contain line breaks.

Display

- There is only one `Display` object for a MIDlet.
- `Display.vibrate(int duration)` to request a vibration operation.
- `Display.flashBacklight(int duration)` to request a backlight flashing effect operation.

Command

- The type of `Command` determines where the `Command` will be placed in a `Screen`.

Command type	*Intention*
`BACK`	Go back to the previous screen.
`CANCEL`	Cancel the current action.
`EXIT`	Quit the application.
`HELP`	Get help for the given screen.
`ITEM`	Indicates that the command is associated with the specific item, not the whole screen.
`OK`	Confirm the current action (submit a form, etc.).
`SCREEN`	Application-specific command applicable to the current screen.
`STOP`	Stop the currently running process or operation (such as a network connection attempt).

- The priority value of a `Command` determines the ordering of multiple commands in a `Screen`.
  - ♦ The lower the priority value of a `Command`, the higher its importance.

Canvas

- Key constants are defined for the ITU-T keypad (`KEY_NUM0`, …, `KEY_NUM9`, `KEY_POUND`, `KEY_STAR`).

- Key constants are defined for game keys (UP, DOWN, LEFT, RIGHT, FIRE, GAME_A, GAME_B, GAME_C, GAME_D).

Choice

- A Choice can be IMPLICIT, EXPLICIT, MULTIPLE, or POPUP (valid only for ChoiceGroup, not for List).
- The state of a selected element in a Choice remains with it even if elements are added or removed in the Choice.
- The CommandListener method should return immediately since commands may be queued and multiple threads might not be used by the implementation, which will result in the method becoming a bottleneck.

Alert and AlertType

- If an Alert is set to be a timed alert and too much data is given such that it cannot be displayed fully in a screen (scrolling will be enabled automatically), then the Alert becomes a modal alert.
- An Alert has an implicit Command called DISMISS_COMMAND.
  - If more than one Command is added to the Alert, the Alert automatically becomes modal.
  - If all user Commands are removed from the Alert, the DISMISS_COMMAND is automatically added.
  - If an explicit user Command is added, then the implicit DISMISS_COMMAND is removed.
- A Gauge can be added to an Alert using the setIndicator() method to show progress.
  - The Gauge added must be non-interactive.
  - The Gauge must not be owned by another container.
  - It must not have any Commands.
  - It must not have an ItemCommandListener.
  - Its label must be null.
  - Its preferred width and height must be unlocked.
  - Its layout must be LAYOUT_DEFAULT.
- If there is a Ticker in an Alert, it may not be displayed on all devices.
- If an explicit CommandListener is added, then the implicit listener is disabled.
- Timeout in an Alert is specified in milliseconds or can be Alert.FOREVER.
- AlertTypes are INFO, WARNING, ERROR, CONFIRMATION, and ALARM.

ChoiceGroup

- ChoiceGroup is displayed typically as a radio-button or drop-down menu for Choice.EXPLICIT type and check boxes for Choice.MULTIPLE type.

- Elements in a `ChoiceGroup` must be non-null.
- `Choice.IMPLICIT` type is not allowed.

DateField

- `DateField` can be in `DATE`, `TIME`, or `DATE_TIME` mode.

Form

- An `Item` can be contained in only one `Form`. Otherwise, an `IllegalStateException` will be thrown.
- The `Form` grows vertically when new `Items` are added. Typically, more than one element is present in a single row only when there is enough space.

Gauge

- A `Gauge` can be interactive or non-interactive.
- A non-interactive `Gauge` can have a definite or indefinite range. An interactive `Gauge` always has a definite range.
- `Gauge` update types have special meaning for non-interactive `Gauges` with indefinite range.

Constant	*Description*	*Example*
`CONTINUOUS_RUNNING`	The represented activity is long-running. The application does not know when the action might finish.	The application is about to request a connection to an external server.
`CONTINUOUS_IDLE`	The represented activity is not doing anything or is in a wait state.	The application has sent a request to an external server and is waiting for a response.
`INCREMENTAL_UPDATING`	The represented activity has progressed in its activity, but does not know when it will complete. In this case, every time `setValue(INCREMENTAL_UPDATING)` is called, the state of the `Gauge` will change.	The application is downloading a file of unknown size. However, it did download 'x' bytes of information.
`INCREMENTAL_IDLE`	The represented activity is in between progress.	The application has just downloaded 'x' bytes and is in the process of downloading another 'y' bytes, but has not done so.

ImageItem

- Used to add a mutable or immutable `Image` to a `Form`.
- If an `Image` is mutable, a snapshot of the `Image` at the time of calling `ImageItem.setImage` is used. This snapshot is not changed even if the underlying mutable `Image` is modifed unless an explicit `ImageItem.setImage` call is made again.

List

- An item selection in an `IMPLICIT List` can be found by listening to the `List.SELECT_COMMAND` command.
- A `List` can be of type `Choice.EXPLICIT`, `Choice.IMPLICIT`, or `Choice.MULTIPLE`. But it cannot be `Choice.POPUP`.

Spacer

- The `Spacers` are used to space out other `Items` in a `Form`.
- `Commands` cannot be added to `Spacers`. Hence the methods `addCommand` and `setDefaultCommand` have been overridden to always throw an `IllegalStateException`.

TextField

- Display of the contents of a `TextField` may be different from the data. For example, a phone number may be displayed as (123) 456 7890, whereas the data might be 1234567890.
- ANDable text constraints `PASSWORD`, `UNEDITABLE`, `SENSITIVE`, `NON_PREDICTIVE`, `INITIAL_CAPS_WORD`, and `INITIAL_CAPS_SENTENCE`.

☞ Compare and contrast high-level and low-level APIs, including layout techniques.

Difference between High-level and Low-level APIs

High-level API	*Low-level API*
All classes extend the `Screen` class.	All classes extend the `Canvas` class.
Cannot listen to input events directly. Must use the `Command` class or the event listener classes.	Can listen to keystrokes and pointer events via callbacks provided in the `Canvas` class.
Cannot draw directly on the screen.	Can draw directly on the screen using the `Graphics` object passed in the `paint` method of the `Canvas` class.
No need to worry about rendering data.	Must explicitly provide rendering code by overriding the `paint` method.
Thread-safe	Typically thread-safe, except in case of `serviceRepaints()` calls, which may result in a deadlock.
Cannot access input devices.	Can access input devices using the callback methods.
Portable. Widgets are displayed according to the underlying device look and feel.	Portable to an extent. Use of screen coordinates needs careful planning.

☞ Explain requirements, issues, class hierarchy, and relationships between items and screens.

Class Hierarchy and Relationship in javax.microedition.lcdui Package

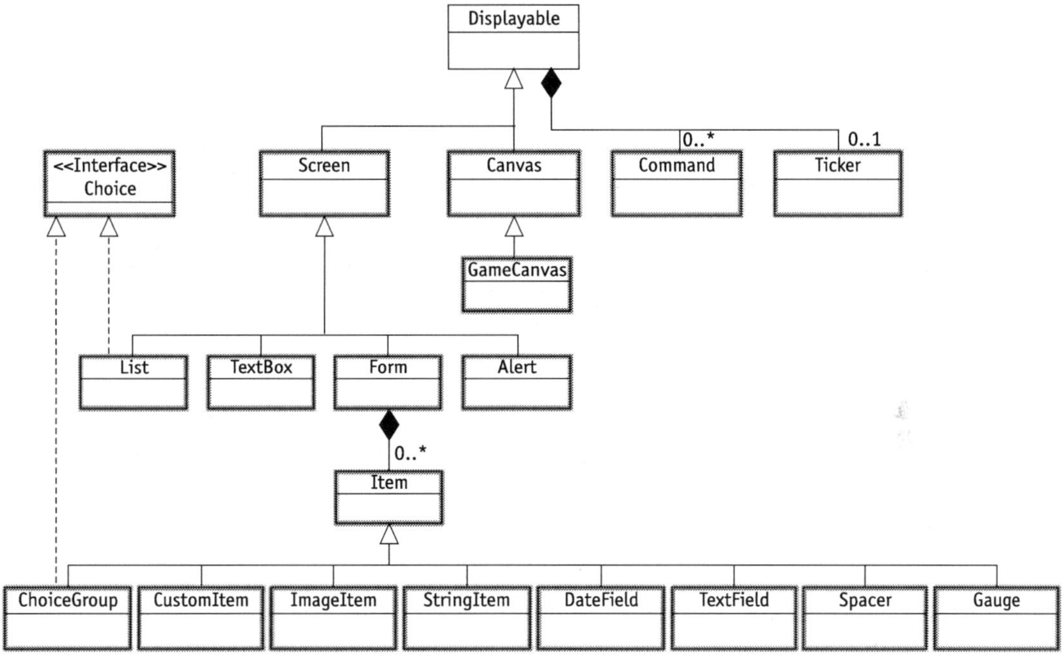

6

Chapter

Playing Games Using the MIDP Game API

Exam Objectives

5.1. Given a scenario, develop code using the MIDP Game API package to improve performance and reduce application size. (Section 6.5)

5.2. Compare and contrast the use of MIDP's GameCanvas class and the MIDP low-level Canvas. (Section 6.1)

5.3. Given a set of requirements, develop code using MIDP's LayerManager class. (Section 6.2.2)

5.4. Given a set of requirements, develop code using MIDP's Layer, Sprite, and TiledLayer classes. (Sections 6.2.1, 6.3 and 6.4)

INTRODUCTION

In 1982, inspired by my Commodore 64's *Larry Bird versus Doctor J* game, I sent a letter of inquiry off to Electronic Arts (EA). At that time, I was 12 years old and the now humongous software company was still small enough to send a hand-written letter back explaining that they currently had no openings, for a 12-year old in particular, and that if I really wanted to write games I should do my math homework and get a computer science degree in college. Well, I eventually took my math seriously and got a degree, but I still don't work for EA. At any rate, games have been at the core of consumer computing from day one, and the market is increasing. In fact, now we have the opportunity to start writing fairly impressive games for mobile phones. What's the world coming to?

In the previous chapter, we learned to create user interfaces with the classes of the MIDP's `javax.microedition.lcdui` package. This chapter covers the gaming-specific portion of that API. If you recall from that chapter, the MIDP's UI platform was divided between sets of classes geared toward low-level and high-level functionality. To refresh ourselves, all classes that represent something that can be seen on the display of the device inherit from the abstract `Displayable`. Two subclasses of `Displayable` are provided to initiate the division between high-level and low-level UI classes. The high-level subclass of `Displayable` is the `Screen` class. The low-level subclass is the `Canvas` class. The `Screen` class provides convenient access to abstract UI functionality, allowing quick development and cohesive look-and-feel, through such classes as `Form`. The low-level `Canvas` provides access to low-level rendering of the screen and low-level handling of the device key events.

For games, the low-level control is a must have. With that in mind, the game API is built on the low-level branch of the family. The central `GameCanvas` is a subclass of `Canvas`. The game API provides a brief set of classes that provide game-specific access to low-level graphics and event handling. Additionally, the API provides some mid-level support for common graphical techniques employed by gaming developers. This mid-level support includes specialized classes to control sprite and background images, as well as cycle-based rendering sequences. We will learn about each of these in this chapter.

For the exam, you need to know how to develop applications using these APIs. So, in addition to the API architecture and details, we'll look at some detailed code examples. But first we need to cover the class hierarchy. To start, let's look at the five classes of the `javax.microedition.lcdui.game` package. They are `GameCanvas`, `Layer`, `LayerManager`, `Sprite` and `TiledLayer`. In the next section, we'll look at each in detail.

6.1 GAMECANVAS: SETTING STAGE FOR THE GAME

In some sense, games are plays where you control one of the actors. If a game is a play, then we must have a stage. The `GameCanvas` class acts as a stage of a MIDP game, on which elements of a game are located. In this role, `GameCanvas` provides basic functionality for the screen of a game. As we hinted at in the introduction, the game API is built on the low-level MIDP UI classes. So, `GameCanvas` leverages the low-level control of that API by extending the low-level `Canvas` class. We examined the low-level graphical capabilities of the `Canvas` in the previous chapter. As you might recall, we access that functionality by overriding the `paint` method of the class and using the `Graphics` object passed in to that method to draw to the screen. On top of this, `GameCanvas` adds game-related functionality to support a slightly higher-level model of game development.

As we learned in the previous chapter, every class that can be displayed on the screen must extend `Displayable`. If you trace the class hierarchy, you can easily see that `GameCanvas` is a descendent of `Displayable`. So, `GameCanvas` represents our screen. All of the UIs of the games that we develop under the MIDP will fit in `GameCanvas`. As you can see, the game API is just a part of the MIDP UI. If it's been a while since you read the MIDP UI chapter, it might help to refresh your memory on the details about the MIDP UI model. For instance, do you know the difference between high-level and low-level graphics functionality? If not, perhaps you should go back and reread the summary of that chapter. But if you're ready, let's get to the details of the `GameCanvas` class.

6.1.1 Dedicated Buffer and Dimensions

For each `GameCanvas` instance created, a dedicated buffer is also created for that `GameCanvas` instance. Since there will be a unique buffer for each `GameCanvas` instance, it is highly recommended to re-use the one that was created once, in order to minimize the memory usage of a game.

The `Graphics` instance returned from `getGraphics()` method of a `GameCanvas` instance represents the contents of the buffer that was dedicated to that `GameCanvas` instance and the modification on the contents of the buffer is done only through that `Graphics` instance. No other external influence can affect the contents of the buffer.

Initially, the buffer is filled with white pixels, but it will get dirty when the application starts to draw things on the `Graphics` instance of `GameCanvas`. The size of the dedicated buffer is set to the maximum dimensions of `GameCanvas`. However, the area of `GameCanvas` that can be flushed by the flush operation is the remaining area after the area taken by a `Ticker`, `Commands` and so forth. If those elements take more area on `GameCanvas`, there will be less area left for the dimensions of `GameCanvas`. Therefore, the area that will be affected during the flush operation is limited to the current dimensions of `GameCanvas`.

Why don't we just create a MIDlet to clearly see the difference between the `GameCanvas` without a `Ticker` and the one with a `Ticker`? We will create a MIDlet that will display as shown in the screenshots of Fig. 6.1. The left screenshot shows a `GameCanvas` that does not contain a `Ticker`, while the right screenshot shows a `GameCanvas` with a `Ticker`.

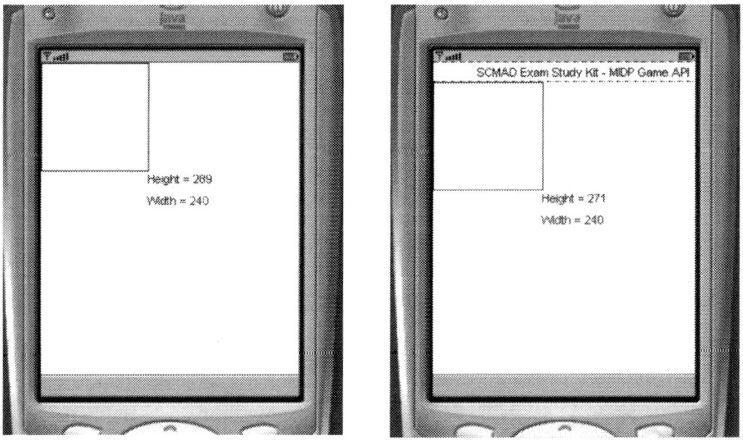

Figure 6.1 The screens that show the effects of other UI elements on the current dimensions of the `GameCanvas`

Listing 6.1 clarifies the current dimensions of a `GameCanvas`, which highly depend on the space that other UI elements on the `GameCanvas` occupy.

Listing 6.1: The `GameCanvas` to print out its own width and height

```
package com.scmadkit.ch06;
import javax.microedition.lcdui.game.GameCanvas;
import javax.microedition.lcdui.Graphics;
/**
 * This GameCanvas draws a white background rectangle,
 * draws a small blue rectangle whose top-left is
 * at (0, 0) position of the GameCanvas
 * and draw two strings about its own height and width.
 *
 *
 * @author Ko Ko Naing
 */
public class AreaGCanvas extends GameCanvas {
  /**
   * Creates a new instance of AreaGCanvas
   */
  public AreaGCanvas() {
      /* Calls the constructor of the GameCanvas */
      super(false);
  }
  /**
   * Render the GameCanvas
   * @param myGraphics Graphics
   */
  public void paint(Graphics myGraphics) {
      /* Sets the current color to white */
      myGraphics.setColor(255, 255, 255);
      myGraphics.fillRect(0,
                          0 ,
                          this.getWidth(),
                          this.getHeight());                      ❶
      /* Sets the current color to blue */
      myGraphics.setColor(0, 0, 255);
      myGraphics.drawRect(0, 0, 100, 100);                        ❷
      /* Draws a string about the current width of the GameCanvas */
      myGraphics.drawString("Width = " + this.getWidth(), 100, 120,
                                Graphics.TOP | Graphics.LEFT);
      /* Draws a string about the current height of the GameCanvas */
      myGraphics.drawString("Height = " + this.getHeight(), 100, 100,
                                Graphics.TOP | Graphics.LEFT);
  }
}
```

❶ Fills a rectangle to the maximum size of the `GameCanvas`

❷ Draws a rectangle with width and height of 100 pixels each

The GameCanvas subclass that we implemented in Listing 6.1 is to draw a rectangle that takes up the whole canvas, a small blue rectangle, and to display the current width and height of the GameCanvas. Once we are done with our own class that extends GameCanvas, we will need to create a MIDlet to test the effect caused by adding a Ticker on that class as in Listing 6.2.

Listing 6.2: The MIDlet to test the effect caused by adding a `Ticker` to `GameCanvas`

```
package com.scmadkit.ch06;

import javax.microedition.midlet.*;
import javax.microedition.lcdui.*;

/**
 * This MIDlet is to test the effect caused
 * by adding a Ticker on the GameCanvas.
 *
 *
 * @author Ko Ko Naing
 */
public class AreaMIDlet extends MIDlet {
  private Display myDisplay;
  private AreaGCanvas areaGCanvas;
  private Ticker myTicker;
  /**
  * Creates a new instance of AreaMIDlet
  */
  public AreaMIDlet() {
     /* Gets the Display object of this MIDlet */
     myDisplay = Display.getDisplay(this);
     /* Creates a new instance of AreaGCanvas */
     areaGCanvas = new AreaGCanvas();
  }
  /* Signals that the MIDlet has entered the Active state */
  protected void startApp() {
     //myTicker = new Ticker
                  ("SCMAD Exam Study Kit - MIDP Game API");   (1)

     /* Sets the Ticker to the AreaGCanvas */
     areaGCanvas.setTicker(myTicker);

     /* Sets the AreaGCanvas as the current display */
     myDisplay.setCurrent(areaGCanvas);
  }
  protected void destroyApp(boolean unconditional) {}
  protected void pauseApp() {}
}
```

(1) Uncomment to see the difference

The MIDlet in Listing 6.2 is just to display the `GameCanvas` subclass that we created in Listing 6.1. You might want to test the effect caused by adding a `Ticker` to our `GameCanvas` by uncommenting the line "`myTicker =new Ticker("SCMAD Exam Study Kit-MIDP Game API");`". Now that you have an idea how extra UI elements added to `GameCanvas` can affect the painting area of `GameCanvas`, why don't we move on with some interesting features of a `GameCanvas`? The next section discusses one of the key features of `GameCanvas`, key events suppression.

6.1.2 Suppression of Key Events

The `GameCanvas` class has a special feature, where game key events can be suppressed or prevented from being generated to the `GameCanvas` instance. Suppressing the game key events on a `GameCanvas` may improve performance, because system calls such as `keyPressed`, `keyReleased` and `keyRepeated` are ignored. The suppression of the key events can affect only on the `GameCanvas` instance, which was created by passing the `boolean` value `true` into its constructor and is visible on the screen.

Being the `boolean` parameter of the constructor set to be `true`, the suppression mechanism of a `GameCanvas` starts when the `GameCanvas` is visible on the screen and stops when it is hidden. Key events can be prevented from being generated only for the keys that are defined as game keys in a certain device. As for other keys, key events will still be generated as usual. Listing 6.3 demonstrates game key suppression.

Listing 6.3: The `GameCanvas` to print out its key event triggers to the console.

```
package com.scmadkit.ch06;
import javax.microedition.lcdui.game.GameCanvas;
public class KeySuppressionGCanvas extends GameCanvas {
    /**
     * Creates a new instance of KeySuppressionGCanvas
     */
    public KeySuppressionGCanvas(boolean isSuppressed) {
        /* Calls the constructor of the GameCanvas */
        super(isSuppressed);
        /* Checks to see if the device supports repeating key events */
        if(!hasRepeatEvents()) {
            System.out.println("Repeating key events not supported.");
        }
    }
    public void keyPressed(int keyCode) {                        ❶
        System.out.println("A key is pressed.");
    }
    public void keyReleased(int keyCode) {                       ❷
        System.out.println("A key is released.");
    }
    public void keyRepeated(int keyCode) {                       ❸
```

```
        System.out.println("A key is repeated.");        3
    }
  }
```

1. Called when a key is pressed
2. Called when a key is released
3. Called when a key is repeated if the device supports repeating key events

The `GameCanvas` subclass that we implemented in Listing 6.3 is to display a string in the console to see if a key has been pressed, released, or repeated (or pressed for a certain period).

☞ **Note:** Not all implementations support the `keyRepeated` event. So it is important to check whether the device supports it or not using the `hasRepeatEvents()` method. If the method returns false, the `keyRepeated` method will never be called.

As usual, once we are done with our own class that extends the `GameCanvas`, we will need to create a MIDlet to test the effect caused by key suppression parameter on an instance of `GameCanvas` as in Listing 6.4.

***Listing 6.4: The MIDlet to test the effect caused by key suppression parameter on an instance of* `GameCanvas`.**

```
package com.scmadkit.ch06;
import javax.microedition.midlet.*;
import javax.microedition.lcdui.*;
/**
 * This MIDlet is to test the effect caused
 * by key suppression parameter
 * on an instance of GameCanvas.
 *
 *
 * @author Ko Ko Naing
 */
public class KeySuppressionMIDlet extends MIDlet {
   private Display myDisplay;
   private KeySuppressionGCanvas keySuppressionGCanvas;
   private boolean isSuppressed;
   /**
   * Creates a new instance of KeySuppressionMIDlet
   */
   public KeySuppressionMIDlet() {
      /* Gets the Display object of this MIDlet */
      myDisplay = Display.getDisplay(this);
      /*
       * Sets the boolean value that is to be passed
       * into GameCanvas constructor
       */
      isSuppressed = false;                                    1
```

```
        /* Creates a new instance of a KeySuppressionGCanvas */
        keySuppressionGCanvas = new
                            KeySuppressionGCanvas(isSuppressed);
    }
    /* Signals that the MIDlet has entered the Active state */
    protected void startApp() throws MIDletStateChangeException {
        /* Sets the GameCanvas as the current display */
        myDisplay.setCurrent(keySuppressionGCanvas);
    }
    protected void destroyApp(boolean unconditional) {}
    protected void pauseApp() {}
}
```

(1) Set this to true to see the key suppression effect

When the MIDlet in Listing 6.4 is executed, pressing any keys will result in generating key events and the corresponding messages will be printed to the console. This demonstrates the scenario when suppression of key events in the `GameCanvas` is disabled. But when the `isSuppressed` value is set to `true`, and the code is executed again, the result of the key event suppression can be seen easily, as the keys are pressed, released and repeated (if repeating key events is supported by the device).

6.1.3 Flushing Graphics

The `GameCanvas` class contains two overloaded methods to flush the contents of the off-screen buffer to the device display.

```
public void flushGraphics()
public void flushGraphics(int left, int top, int width, int height)
```

The first method just flushes the contents of the entire off-screen buffer to the device display and the flushed area covers the maximum dimensions of `GameCanvas`.

However, the second method flushes the rectangular region that is specified in the parameters of the methods. If the specified region is larger than the area of `GameCanvas`, the intersected region between the two areas will be flushed. If the width or height parameter is set to the value less than 1, nothing will be flushed, and the method will return suddenly.

Exam Tip

In both the methods, the contents of the off-screen buffer will not be modified because of the flush operation. The same pixels will be flushed, if the method is called again.

The methods will not return until the flushing operation is completed. Therefore, it is safe to modify the contents of the same buffer and re-use it anywhere else.

The methods will return suddenly without flushing anything, if its GameCanvas is not currently shown on the display or the flush operation cannot be started in a busy system environment.

6.1.4 Important Role of Graphics Class

The getGraphics() method of the GameCanvas class returns a Graphics instance that represents the GameCanvas. The returned Graphics instance writes pixels to the off-screen buffer of the GameCanvas. Graphics instances that are returned from the getGraphics() method of a GameCanvas are the only ones who are authorized to write pixels to the off-screen buffer of that GameCanvas.

Exam Tip

A Graphics instance is just to render the pixels into the off-screen buffer of its GameCanvas instance. The actual update on the display with the rendered pixels does not occur until one of the flushGraphics methods is called. Flushing the buffer does not modify the contents of the buffer, meaning that the rendered pixels are not cleared because of the flush operation.

Since a new Graphics instance is returned every time this getGraphics() method is called, it is highly recommended to obtain the needed Graphics instance(s) before the game starts and keep the instance(s) for re-use during the execution of the game. Even though many new Graphics instances can be returned from calling the getGraphics() method, they all will render to the same off-screen buffer of the GameCanvas that they come from. Figure 6.2 illustrates the redundant nature of multiple Graphics objects obtained from a GameCanvas's getGraphics().

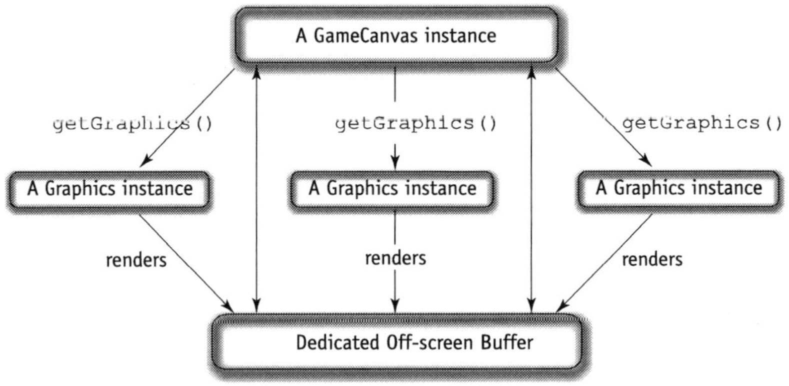

Figure 6.2 Graphics instances and the off-screen buffer of the GameCanvas

The newly returned `Graphics` instance possesses the following characteristics:

1. The destination canvas to render the pixels is its one and only associated `GameCanvas`.
2. The clip region of the `Graphics` covers the entire buffer, the maximum dimensions of the `GameCanvas`.
3. The current color to render the pixels is black.
4. The font to type on the display is the same as the font returned from `Font.getDefaultFont()`.
5. The stroke style is `Graphics.SOLID`.
6. As we might already have known, the origin of the coordinate system is at the top-left corner of the system.

6.1.5 Comparison to MIDP Low-level Canvas Class

We will now cover some differences between `GameCanvas` and its superclass `Canvas`. `GameCanvas` provides many powerful features for game development that simply don't exist in `Canvas`. These features make development much easier than if we had to do everything with the lowest-level `paint` method. However, if not used properly, these advantages can become pitfalls. For example, creating a new instance of `GameCanvas` each time will decrease performance of the application due to the creation of a new unique buffer. It is very important to re-use the existing `GameCanvas` once created.

As we study the advanced features of `GameCanvas`, we need to keep a mental list of pros and cons. With power, comes responsibility. Due to the resource constraints of the target devices, the penalties for misuse are much more visible. In this section, we'll highlight the key differences between the two classes with an eye toward noting the pros and cons that might be associated with selecting which level of functionality might be more appropriate for your own applications.

Painting Behaviors

The `Canvas` class only has two overloaded `repaint` methods; one of which is used to paint the whole `Canvas` and the other is used to paint a specific region on the `Canvas`. But those repaint calls are just to request the system software to paint the screen. The `repaint` method call and the actual `paint` method call occur asynchronously, meaning that `repaint` method will not block and wait `paint` to finish and return.

In contrast, the `GameCanvas` class has ability to paint the screen whenever it wants, without the need to request the system to call a repaint for it. The two overloaded `flushGraphics` methods of the `GameCanvas` class will not return until the screen is updated with the pixels contained in the off-screen buffer of `GameCanvas`.

Latching Technique

The GameCanvas class contains a useful method, getKeyStates(), which can retrieve the states of the physical game keys. Latching behavior of this method can guarantee that every single key press is caught in a typical game loop, even though the loop runs slower than the key presses.

However, some devices may not have ability to query the keypad hardware directly. Then the state returned by the getKeyStates() might fall behind the actual state of the physical keys. There is also another issue, where some devices cannot recognize the simultaneous press on multiple keys. Nevertheless, the latching technique provided by the getKeyStates() method of the GameCanvas class offers a big advantage in retrieving the key press without missing any in a gaming environment.

Now that we have covered the salient points of GameCanvas, we will look at the helper classes of the package that provide the advanced game functionality.

6.2 LAYER AND LAYERMANAGER: THE GAME'S BACKDROP

If GameCanvas is the stage, the Layer class provides the structure for building the visual backdrop for the game. A Layer represents a visual element of a game including sprite graphics or background image fields. Layer is an abstract class that contains the basic methods that all visual elements of a game should possess in order to access information such as size, location and visibility. The game API provides two subclasses of Layer to implement more specific functionality for the developer. The Sprite class represents sprite graphics. The sprites are the little monsters and characters of the game, the ones that chase each other around. The TiledLayer class represents stuff like the background. Fields of scrollable background image are perfect for the TiledLayer.

Typically, you will create a variety of Layer objects and assemble them together on GameCanvas. The details of rendering can get complicated with z-orders and changing positions, but the game API provides a helper class to make the process easier. As the name says, the LayerManager manages a series of layers that are under its control. By automating the rendering process, the LayerManager automatically renders the layers that are located in a game to obtain a desired game view, resulting in the simplification of the management of several layers for a game. Now, we will look at the details of the Layer and LayerManager.

6.2.1 Layer Class

The Layer class of the MIDP Game API is an abstract class which represents a visual element of a game. The class contains basic common methods that all of its subclasses inherit. But all of Layer subclasses must implement a paint(Graphics) method in a suitable way to render themselves. Basically, a developer will paint to the Layer and then assemble one or more layers on GameCanvas to get the desired effect. Each Layer is like a sheet of clear plastic upon which you can draw various pieces of a visual scene. This allows you to separate elements by drawing them on different plastic sheets (`Layers`). To combine them, you can stack them up and they look as if they are all part of the same drawing. It sounds a bit complicated at first, but it won't after some concrete examples that we will examine shortly.

Exam Tip

The horizontal and vertical position of a layer is always relative to the coordinate system of the `Graphics` object passed to the `paint` method of the `Layer` class. That coordinate system is usually referred to as the painter's coordinate system in the MIDP 2.0 specification. The coordinate system is based on the top-left corner of the layer.

Table 6.1 lists all of the methods located in the `Layer` abstract class.

Table 6.1 Methods of the Layer class

Method	*Description*
`public int getWidth()`	Returns the width of the layer.
`public int getHeight()`	Returns the height of the layer.
`public int getX()`	Returns the horizontal position of the layer's top-left corner in the painter's coordinate system.
`public int getY()`	Returns the vertical position of the layer's top-left corner in the painter's coordinate system.
`public boolean isVisible()`	Returns `true`, if the layer is visible. Otherwise, returns `false`.
`public void move(int dx, int dy)`	Moves the layer to the specified distance, corresponding to the layer's top-left corner.
`public abstract void paint(Graphics g)`	Paints the layer, if it is visible.
`public void setPosition(int x, int y)`	Sets the position of the layer to the coordinate specified, corresponding to the layer's top-left corner.
`public void setVisible(boolean visible)`	Makes the layer visible, if `true` is passed into the method. Passing `false` makes the layer invisible.

As you can see, the methods of the `Layer` class mostly relate to its rendering and positioning. This class is truly a visual element.

6.2.2 LayerManager Class

The `LayerManager` is just a helper class that tries to minimize some of the overhead related to assembling a set of `Layers` for a game. The `LayerManager` keeps track of the `Layers` and their order. It also manages the complexities of rendering the various Layers to the screen in an efficient manner.

List of Layers

Layers can be added to a LayerManager and they all are maintained in that LayerManager as items in an ordered list. They can be inserted, appended and removed from the LayerManager.

The Layers are mounted over one another inside the LayerManager like a pile of papers. As you can see in Fig. 6.3, the Layer that is located at the index number 0 is the layer that is closest to the user, while the Layer that is located at the highest index number of the list is furthest away from the user. The indices of the Layers are always maintained in a way that is continuous. Even if a layer in the middle of the LayerManager is removed, the indices of the Layers will be adjusted automatically to maintain the continuous numbering.

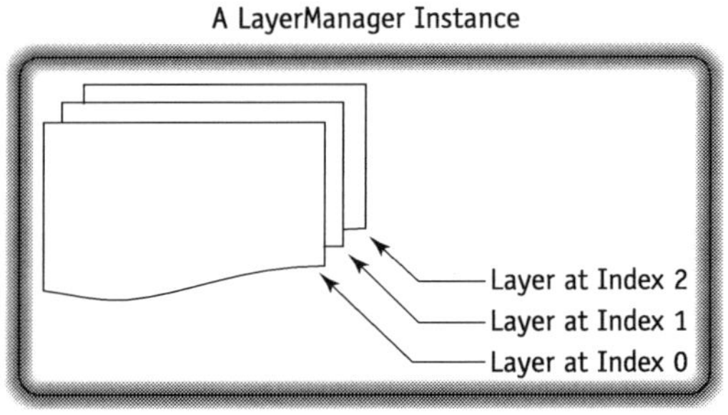

Figure 6.3 Visual diagram to see how Layers are ordered in a LayerManager

View Window

The Layers in the LayerManager are typically much larger than a single physical display. This makes sense in terms of games. Usually, the game occurs in some logical world that is explored one screenfull at a time by a user-controlled character; when the character reaches one of the screen boundaries, the screen scrolls to reveal a new screenfull of the game world. The portion of the full game world that we see on the screen at any given instant is known as the *view window*. The view window defines the portion of the layers that will be shown to the user.

The size of the view window determines the visible area where the user can see things and it is usually fixed at the size that is suitable for the display screen. The position of the view window is relative to the coordinate system of the LayerManager and changing the position can simulate the scrolling and panning effect on the user's view of a game scene. For instance, simply moving the view window to the left can result in scrolling the game scene to the left.

The positions of the layers in a LayerManager is relative to the coordinate system of the LayerManager itself, and the position of the view window set using setViewWindow(int x, int y, int width, int height) is also relative to the coordinate system of the LayerManager. However, when painting on the screen using paint(Graphics g, int x, int y), the location of the view window to be painted is relative to the origin of the Graphics instance.

Table 6.2 summarizes the methods of LayerManager.

Table 6.2 Methods of the LayerManager class

Method	*Description*
public void append(Layer l)	Appends the specified layer at the highest index in the LayerManager. If the specified layer has already been in the LayerManager, it is removed from the LayerManager before being appended to the LayerManager.
public void insert(Layer l, int index)	Inserts the specified layer into the specified index in the LayerManager. If the specified layer has already been in the LayerManager, it is removed from the LayerManager before being inserted to the LayerManager.
public void remove(Layer l)	Removes the specified layer. The method does nothing, if the specified layer is not in the LayerManager.
public Layer getLayerAt(int index)	Returns the layer located at the specified index in the LayerManager.
public int getSize()	Returns the number of the layers contained in the LayerManager.
public void paint(Graphics g, int x, int y)	Renders the LayerManager's view window at the specified location, corresponding to the Graphics object's top-left corner.
public void setViewWindow (int x, int y, int width, int height)	Sets the view window on the LayerManager as the width and height specified, corresponding to the LayerManager's top-left corner.

As you can see, LayerManager has methods that support adding and removing Layers. It also has methods to set the view window, thereby controlling the portion of the game world that is shown to the user.

6.3 SPRITES: THE GAME'S ACTORS

Now we will know about the actors of our play. In the game world, these guys are usually monsters and fairies. In the real world, as opposed to the virtual world, a sprite could be any of a broad group of Tolkien-esque creatures such as elves, fairies, brownies, ghosts, dwarves and certainly hobbits. Remember Mario Brothers? I think Mario and Luigi were probably gnomes or dwarves, certainly not elves. Nowadays, the characters are more likely to be humans with futuristic assault weapons, but that's another, somewhat dismaying, story.

The Sprite class extends the Layer class directly and it acts as a main character in a game. The main attribute of a Sprite, as opposed to its non-specialized ancestor Layer, is that it can move around on the screen. To support this, the `Sprite` class has several features that help a developer provide animation. A `Sprite` holds several raw frames that can be utilized to generate an animation sequence. A `Sprite` also provides easy access to graphical transformations such as rotation and flipping. As `Sprite` is a subclass of the `Layer` class, it also inherits all methods of the `Layer` class that manipulate its size, location and visibility.

6.3.1 Raw Frames for a Sprite

Raw frames that will be used to render a `Sprite` are arranged in row-oriented way, in which frames are ordered from left to right in a row-by-row basis. All frames must be in a single `Image` object that can be mutable or immutable. By mutable, it means that the `Image` object is modifiable, while an immutable `Image` is not modifiable.

If there is only one frame in an `Image` object and the `Sprite` will be rendered with that single frame, the image can contain a frame with any width and height within its boundary. However, if more than one frame will be used to render a `Sprite`, the image must contain a series of equally-sized frames with a specified width and height. Figure 6.4 shows a series of frames of a dancing stick man figure.

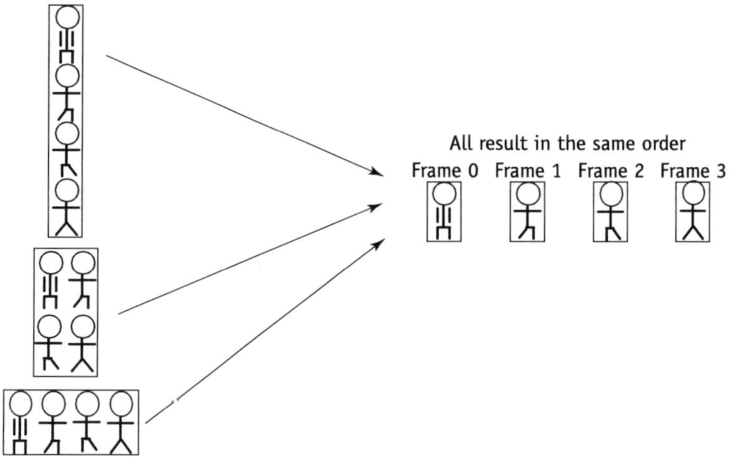

Figure 6.4 Various arrangements of the raw frames in an `Image` and their resulting order

In Fig. 6.4, we can see the possible row-based arrangements of the frames in an `Image` object, and their corresponding indices. We have three arrangements. These arrangements include four rows of one frame, two rows of two frames, and one row of four frames. This row-based arrangement is the structure of the `Image` object, but it doesn't necessarily affect the animation sequence. In these four arrangements, the indices of the frames are the same. The indices will be used in the animation sequence, so these row-based arrangements all would render the same sequence.

> **Exam Tip**
>
> The indices are in zero-based numbering and the frames are ordered in row-oriented way that numbers the frames across the first row, then the second row and so forth.

6.3.2 Frame Sequence of Sprite

If we wanted to change the animation sequence, we would need to change the frame indices. Unfortunately, this would be problematic at best. In order to support changing animation sequences, the `Sprite` class provides us with a logical animation sequence that is mapped to the raw frame indices. A *frame sequence* of a `Sprite` orders the raw frames that are to be displayed one by one. By default, the frame sequence is the same as the sequence that is ordered in the row-oriented way of the raw frames in the image. Thus the length of the default frame sequence is equal to the number of raw frames in the image.

Using the `setFrameSequence(int[])`, `nextFrame()` and `prevFrame()` methods, the frames can be displayed as specified in the sequence order specified in the array of indices. It can be easily done by just creating an array of frame indices as an `int` array and passing it into the `setFrameSequence(int[])`. Those methods operate only on the indices of the frame sequence of the array, not on the indices of the raw frames.

Frame sequence indices may be defined in any order as desired. The only restriction is that the frame sequence passed in must have at least one frame index in its `int` array and the indices in the frame sequence must be valid raw frame indices of the image. Frame indices inside the frame sequence may be specified in any order; they may be omitted, repeated, and reversed.

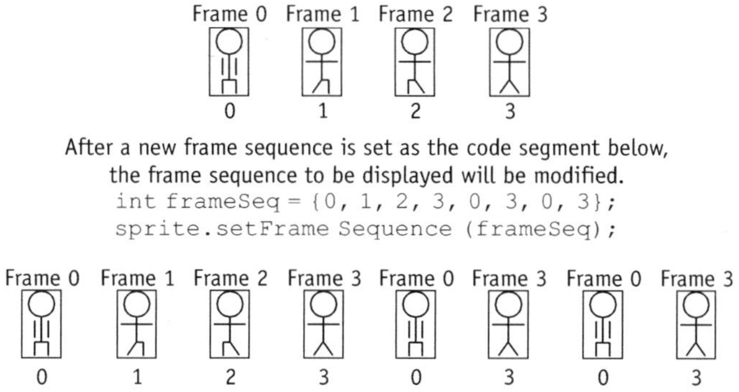

Figure 6.5 Frame sequence modification effect on a `Sprite`

The following code example in Listing 6.5 clarifies the way the frame sequence works on a

Sprite. It reflects the frame sequence shown in Fig. 6.5.

Listing 6.5: The GameCanvas to display an animated Sprite according to its frame sequence

```
package com.scmadkit.ch06;

import javax.microedition.lcdui.game.*;
import javax.microedition.lcdui.*;
import java.io.IOException;

/**
 * This SpriteSeqGCanvas draws a rectangle with white background,
 * append a Sprite into the LayerManager and render the LayerManager.
 * The Sprite will be an animated person on the display,
 * rotating its frame sequence.
 *
 *
 * @author Ko Ko Naing
 */
public class SpriteSeqGCanvas extends GameCanvas implements Runnable
{
  Sprite sprite;
  LayerManager layerManager;
  Thread thread;
  /**
   * Creates a new instance of SpriteSeqGCanvas
   */
public SpriteSeqGCanvas() {
  /* Calls the constructor of GameCanvas */
  super(false);
  try {
     sprite = new Sprite
             (Image.createImage("/res/man1.png"), 30, 60);        ❶
     int[] spriteSeq = {0,1,2,3,0,3,0,3};                          ❷
     /* Sets the frame sequence to the Sprite */
     sprite.setFrameSequence(spriteSeq);
     /* Creates a LayerManager instance */
      layerManager = new LayerManager();
     /* Appends the Sprite into the LayerManager */
     layerManager.append(sprite);
  } catch (IOException ioe) {
     System.out.println("I/O Access Error.");
  }
 }
 /**
  * Renders the GameCanvas
  * @param myGraphics Graphics
  */
```

```
    public void paint(Graphics myGraphics) {
        /* Sets the current color to white */
        myGraphics.setColor(255, 255, 255);
        /* Fills a rectangle to the maximum size of the canvas */
        myGraphics.fillRect(0, 0, this.getWidth(), this.getHeight());
        /* Renders the LayerManager's view window */
        layerManager.paint(myGraphics, 100, 100);
    }
    /**
     * Creates a new thread for this SpriteSeqGCanvas instance
     * and start the thread instance
     */
    public synchronized void start() {
        thread = new Thread(this);
        thread.start();
    }
    public void run() {
        while (true) {
            sprite.nextFrame();
            //sprite.prevFrame();                                        ③
            /* Repaints the canvas */
            repaint();
            /* */
            try {
             Thread.sleep(500);                                          ④
            } catch (InterruptedException err) {
               System.out.println(err.getMessage());
            }
        }
    }
}
```

1. Creates a `Sprite` instance using an image
2. Creates a frame sequence to be displayed
3. Comment the first line and uncomment the second line to see the difference
4. Waits for a while, before changing to a new frame

The `GameCanvas` subclass that we implemented in Listing 6.5 draws a rectangle with white background, appends a `Sprite` into the `LayerManager` and renders the `LayerManager`. The `Sprite` will be an animated person on the display, rotating its frame sequence. But we still need to create a MIDlet to test the effect caused by changing the frame sequence of a `Sprite` as in Listing 6.6.

Listing 6.6: The MIDlet to test the effect caused by changing the frame sequence of a

Sprite

```
package com.scmadkit.ch06;

import javax.microedition.midlet.*;
import javax.microedition.lcdui.*;

/**
 * This MIDlet is to test the effect caused
 * by changing the frame sequence of a Sprite.
 *
 *
 * @author Ko Ko Naing
 */
public class SpriteSeqMIDlet extends MIDlet {
    private Display myDisplay;
    private SpriteSeqGCanvas spriteSeqGCanvas;

    /**
     * Creates a new instance of SpriteSeqMIDlet
     */
    public SpriteSeqMIDlet() {
        /* Gets the Display object of this MIDlet */
        myDisplay = Display.getDisplay(this);
        /* Creates a new instance of GameCanvas */
        spriteSeqGCanvas = new SpriteSeqGCanvas();
    }

    /* Signals that the MIDlet has entered the Active state */
    protected void startApp() {
        spriteSeqGCanvas.start();                                    (1)

        /* Sets the GameCanvas as the current display */
        myDisplay.setCurrent(spriteSeqGCanvas);
    }
    protected void destroyApp(boolean unconditional) {}
    protected void pauseApp() {}
}
```

(1) Starts the `GameCanvas` thread

The MIDlet in listing 6.6 creates an instance of the `GameCanvas` subclass that we developed in Listing 6.5 and starts the thread. We can also reverse the frame sequence displayed by commenting the "`sprite.nextFrame();`" and uncommenting the line "`sprite.prevFrame();`". The animation will run backward then.

In addition to the methods that we used in the code example, the `Sprite` class still has some more useful methods to manipulate the frames. The `setFrame(int)` and `getFrame()` method can also be used to set a known frame index to the current frame and get the current index in the frame sequence. The `getFrameSequenceLength()` retrieves the number of frame sequence indices located in that frame sequence. Now that we are familiar with basic sprite animation technique using frame sequence of a `Sprite`, let's go forward with another interesting feature that you can use to move your animated sprite around.

6.3.3 Reference Pixel of a Sprite

A traditional way to place a UI element or an image on a canvas in a Java ME game or even in Java SE applications is to use top-left corner of the element or the image. Methods such as `setPosition(int x, int y)`, `getX()` and `getY()` can be used to get and set the position of a `Layer`, which is relative to the painter's coordinate system. A subclass of the `Layer` class, the `Sprite` class, includes methods which can specify an arbitrary point to position itself, rather than to position itself at the traditional top-left corner. That arbitrary point is called *reference pixel.*

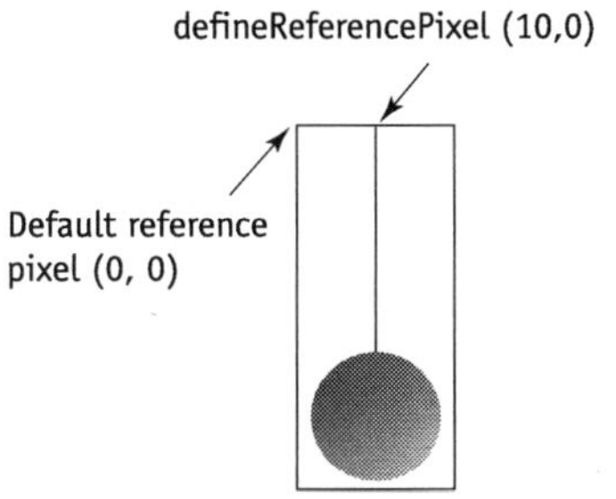

Figure 6.6 Default reference pixel and a newly defined reference pixel of a `Sprite`

By default, the reference pixel of a `Sprite` will be at the top-left corner of the untransformed `Sprite`. The reference pixel of a `Sprite` can be defined by using the method `defineReferencePixel(int x, int y)`. But the `Sprite` should be in the untransformed frame to define a reference pixel properly. If the `Sprite` has been transformed before defining a reference pixel, the reference pixel defined on the transformed `Sprite` will be relative to the top-left corner of the untransformed `Sprite`. Because the top-left corner of the `Sprite` may change after the `Sprite` is transformed. Therefore, the developer might be confused with the resulting position of the `Sprite` later in the game development. We will discuss about the `Sprite` transformation in the next section. Figure 6.6 shows a `Sprite` with a defined reference pixel. In this case, we have set the reference pixel to the top of the chain on a hanging ball.

A reference pixel may also be defined outside of the `Sprite`'s bounds, as necessary. Then the location of a reference pixel can be inquired using the methods `getRefPixelX()` and `getRefPixelY()`. After defining a reference pixel for the `Sprite`, we need to use the `setRefPixelPosition(int x, int y)` method to position the `Sprite` in the painter's coordinate system, based on the reference pixel defined. Figure 6.7 shows the hanging ball, with its reference point as defined in Fig. 6.6, being positioned to various pixel positions.

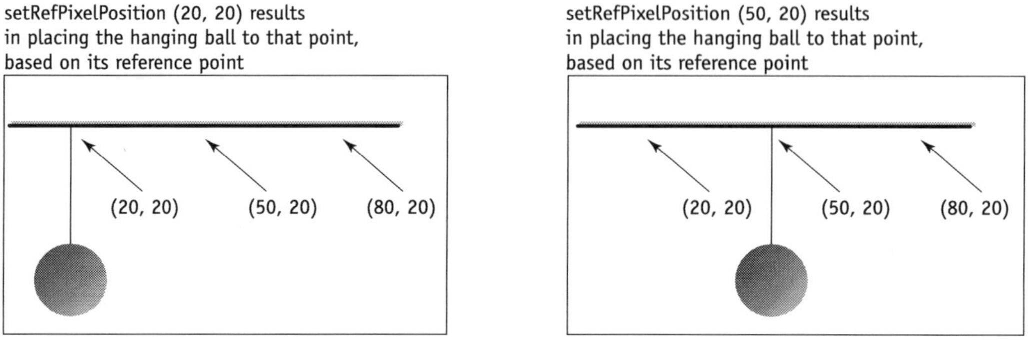

Figure 6.7 Use of reference pixel in positioning the `Sprite`

These techniques are good for moving the sprite around. We will now examine some techniques for changing the appearance of the `Sprite`.

6.3.4 Sprite Transformation

In addition to the various methods available for a `Sprite` to display its frames and to move its reference pixel, a `Sprite` can be mirrored and rotated in multiples of 90 degrees using `setTransform(int transConstant)`. There are eight predefined transformation constants available in the `Sprite` class. Table 6.3 lists all of the predefined constants available for `Sprite` transformation.

Table 6.3 Predefined constants for `Sprite` transformation
(Notice the shaded region of the arrow to recognize the effect)

Constant	*Description*	*Resulting sprite*
`Sprite.TRANS_NONE`	No transformation applied	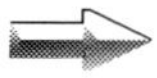
`Sprite.TRANS_ROT90`	Rotate the `Sprite` to clockwise 90 degrees	
`Sprite.TRANS_ ROT180`	Rotate the `Sprite` to clockwise 180 degrees	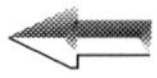
`Sprite.TRANS_ ROT270`	Rotate the `Sprite` to clockwise 270 degrees	
`Sprite.TRANS_MIRROR`	Vertically mirror the `Sprite`	
`Sprite.TRANS_MIRROR_ROT90`	Vertically mirror the `Sprite` and rotate it to clockwise 90 degree	

`Sprite.TRANS_MIRROR_ROT180`	Vertically mirror the `Sprite` and rotate it to clockwise 180 degrees	
`Sprite.TRANS_MIRROR_ROT270`	Vertically mirror the `Sprite` and rotate it to clockwise 270 degrees	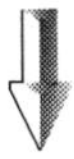

During the transformation process, the reference pixel of the `Sprite` does not change and stays remain at the same place. To avoid the future confusion on the position of the reference pixel, it is highly recommended to define a reference pixel for a `Sprite` before making any transformation on the `Sprite`. After defining a new reference pixel for a `Sprite`, the transformation process will choose the reference pixel as the center point in transforming the `Sprite`. Figure 6.8 illustrates this.

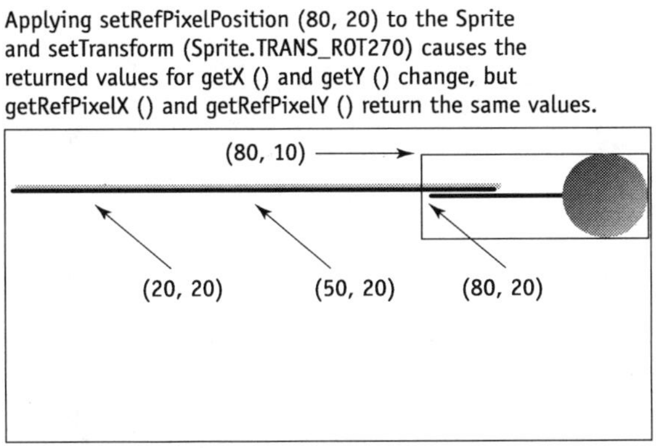

Figure 6.8 Results of transforming a `Sprite` after defining and setting a reference pixel to it

The most important thing to note here is that the `getRefPixelX()` and `getRefPixelY()` will always return the same values no matter how we transform the `Sprite` using the `setTransform` method. But the `getX()` and `getY()` methods will return the values that represents the top-left corner of the `Sprite`. In the next section, we will discuss another important topic in game development, the detection of sprite collisions.

6.3.5 Sprite Collision

For game applications, the detection of collisions between the monsters and fairies is a core functionality. Keeping this in mind, a `Sprite` can be checked for collision with another element such as an `Image` object, a `Sprite` object or a `TiledLayer`. There are three versions of the overloaded `collidesWith` method to accomplish this check. All of them are straightforward. Table 6.4 summarizes the three methods to check for a collision and a method to define a collision rectangle for a `Sprite`.

Table 6.4 Three `collidesWith` methods and a method to define a collision rectangle of the `Sprite` class

Method	*Description*	*Pixel-level collision*	*Non-pixel-level collision*
`collidesWith(Image image, int x, int y, boolean pixelLevel)`	Checks for a collision between the `Sprite` and the specified image. The specified method parameters `x` and `y` are used to position the image. Both the `Sprite` and the image must be visible to be able to collide. Transformation of the `Sprite` is automatically accounted for.	Collision will be detected, only when opaque pixels of both elements collide. Opaque pixels outside the `Sprite`'s collision rectangle will be ignored.	Collision will be detected when the defined collision rectangle of the `Sprite` intersects with the image's bounds.
`collidesWith(Sprite sprite, boolean pixelLevel)`	Checks for a collision between the `Sprite` and the specified sprite. Both of the `Sprite`s must be visible to be able to collide. Transformation of the `Sprite` is automatically accounted for.	Collision will be detected, only when opaque pixels of both elements collide. Opaque pixels outside the `Sprite`'s collision rectangle will be ignored.	Collision will be detected when the defined collision rectangles of the `Sprite` intersect.
`collidesWith (TiledLayer tiledLayer (TiledLayer pixelLevel)`	Checks for a collision between the `Sprite` and the specified `TiledLayer`. Both the `Sprite` and the `TiledLayer` must be visible to be able to collide. Transformation of the `Sprite` is automatically accounted for.	Collision will be detected, only when opaque pixels of both elements collide. Opaque pixels outside the `Sprite`'s collision rectangle will be ignored.	Collision will be detected when the defined collision rectangle of the `Sprite` intersects with a non-empty cell in the `TiledLayer`.
`defineCollisionRectangle (int x, int y, int width, int height)`	Defines the `Sprite`'s collision rectangle, being relative to untransformed `Sprite`'s top-left corner. By default, the collision rectangle is located at the same place as the `Sprite`. The rectangle may be smaller or larger than the default rectangle.	If the collision rectangle is made larger than the default rectangle, the pixels outside the bounds of the `Sprite` are treated as transparent.	Collision will be detected when the defined collision rectangle of the `Sprite` intersects with other elements as mentioned above.

Let's try to put our theories into practice by developing a small MIDlet to see how the `Sprites` collide with/without pixel-level detection as in Fig. 6.9. The screenshot in Fig. 6.9(a) was taken when pixel-level detection was not applied, and that in Fig. 6.9(b) when pixel-level detection was applied.

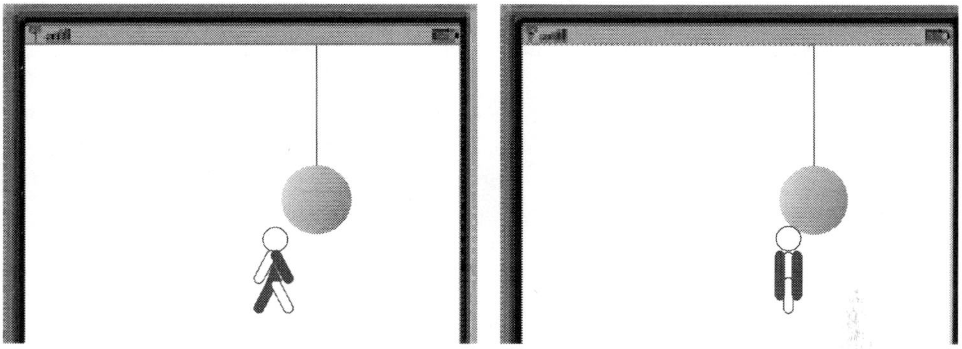

(a) (b)

Figure 6.9 `Sprite` collisions with/without pixel-level detection

Listing 6.7 demonstrates the sprite collisions using the `collidesWith(Sprite sprite, boolean pixelLevel)` method as shown in Fig. 6.9.

Listing 6.7: The `GameCanvas` to display the collision between two `Sprites`

```
package com.scmadkit.ch06;

import javax.microedition.lcdui.game.*;
import javax.microedition.lcdui.*;
import java.io.IOException;

/**
 * This SpriteCollisionGCanvas draws a rectangle,
 * with white background, appends two Sprites
 * into the LayerManager, renders the LayerManager,
 * and checks if the two Sprites collide.
 *
 *
 * @author Ko Ko Naing
 */
public class SpriteCollisionGCanvas
              extends GameCanvas implements Runnable {
    Sprite manSprite;
    Sprite ballSprite;
   LayerManager layerManager;
   Thread thread;

   /**
```

```
    * Creates a new instance of SpriteCollisionGCanvas
    */
   public SpriteCollisionGCanvas() {
   /* Calls the constructor of GameCanvas */
   super(false);
   try {
      /* Creates a Sprite instance for a walking stick man */
      manSprite = new
           Sprite(Image.createImage("/StickManWalk.png"), 21, 43);
      /* Places the man at an appropriate position */
      manSprite.setPosition(0, 100);
      /* Creates a Sprite instance for a hanging ball */
      ballSprite = new
            Sprite(Image.createImage("/HangingBall.png"), 21, 106);
      /* Places the ball at an appropriate position */
      ballSprite.setPosition(150, 0);
      /* Creates a frame sequence to be displayed */
      int[] spriteSeq = {0,1};
      /* Sets the frame sequence to the walking man Sprite */
      manSprite.setFrameSequence(spriteSeq);
      /* Creates a LayerManager instance */
      layerManager = new LayerManager();
      /* Appends the Sprites into the LayerManager */
      layerManager.append(manSprite);
      layerManager.append(ballSprite);
    } catch (IOException ioe) {
       System.out.println("I/O Access Error.");
    }
}
/**
  * Renders the GameCanvas
  * @param myGraphics Graphics
  */
public void paint(Graphics myGraphics) {
    /* Sets the current color to white */
    myGraphics.setColor(255, 255, 255);
    /* Fills a rectangle to the maximum size of the canvas */
    myGraphics.fillRect(0, 0, this.getWidth(), this.getHeight());
    /* Renders the LayerManager's view window */
    layerManager.paint(myGraphics, 0, 0);
}
/**
 * Creates a new thread for this SpriteCollisionGCanvas instance
```

```
     * and start the thread instance
     */
    public synchronized void start() {
       thread = new Thread(this);
       thread.start();
    }

    public void run() {
       while (true) {
          if(!manSprite.collidesWith(ballSprite, true)) {       ❶
             manSprite.nextFrame();                              ❷
             manSprite.setPosition(
                      manSprite.getX()+10, manSprite.getY());
          }

          /* Repaints the canvas */
          repaint();

          /* Waits for a while, before changing to a new frame */
          try {
          Thread.sleep(500);
          } catch (InterruptedException err) {
             System.out.println(err.getMessage());
          }
       }
    }
}
```

❶ Set the parameter to `false` to see the non-pixel-level collision effect

❷ Detects the collision of the two `Sprites`. If they don't collide, the man keeps on walking. If they do, the man stops walking

The `GameCanvas` subclass that we just created contains two `Sprites` in its `LayerManager`: the one that represents a walking stickman and the other that represents a hanging ball. The walking man walks until his head hits the ball. When pixel-level collision is used, the man stops walking only when his head hits the ball. But when pixel-level collision is not used, the man stops walking even when his head is about to hit the ball. As you can guess, this is because if the pixel-level detection is not applied, the collision will occur even when the default collision rectangle of the man `Sprite` touches the default collision rectangle of the ball `Sprite`.

But we still need to create a MIDlet to put our `GameCanvas` class into action. The MIDlet code in Listing 6.8 does similar work as other MIDlets that we created earlier in the chapter.

Listing 6.8: The MIDlet to test the `Sprite` collision

```
package com.scmadkit.ch06;

import javax.microedition.midlet.*;
import javax.microedition.lcdui.*;
```

```
/**
 * This MIDlet is to test the Sprite collision.
 *
 *
 * @author Ko Ko Naing
 */
public class SpriteCollisionMIDlet extends MIDlet {
  private Display myDisplay;
  private SpriteCollisionGCanvas spriteCollisionGCanvas;
  /**
   * Creates a new instance of SpriteCollisionMIDlet
   */
  public SpriteCollisionMIDlet() {
    /* Gets the Display object of this MIDlet */
    myDisplay = Display.getDisplay(this);
    /* Creates a new instance of SpriteCollisionGCanvas */
    spriteCollisionGCanvas = new SpriteCollisionGCanvas();
   }
  /* Signals that the MIDlet has entered the Active state */
  protected void startApp() {
     /* Starts the GameCanvas thread */
     spriteCollisionGCanvas.start();                              ❶
     /* Sets the GameCanvas as the current display */
     myDisplay.setCurrent(spriteCollisionGCanvas);
  }
  protected void destroyApp(boolean unconditional) {}
  protected void pauseApp() {}
}
```

❶ Starts the `GameCanvas` thread

The MIDlet in Listing 6.8 is just to test the `Sprite` collision scenarios from the `GameCanvas` subclass that we developed in Listing 6.7. It creates an instance of the `GameCanvas` subclass that we developed in Listing 6.7 and starts the thread.

Now that we have learned all about `Sprites` and we can create actors for our play, we can focus on creating stunning graphics for their imaginary worlds.

6.4 TILEDLAYER: A SCENE FOR OUR PLAY

Perhaps we are pushing our theatrical metaphor a bit too far. Well, if you grant us creative license, we will continue towards success on the SCMAD exam, if not towards literary greatness. The `TiledLayer` class represents the background scene of a game. While the main function of a `Sprite` is animation, the main function of a `TiledLayer` is to provide atmosphere and texture. Generally, the user doesn't scrutinize the background. Furthermore, the graphical nature of the background is often repetitive.

Take for example the rocky wall of a subterraneous tunnel, a common gaming background. Imagine you are a fairy, named Hamlet, whose mission is to collect diamonds from the nooks and crannies of this underground region. Ah, but it's not so simple, a variety of goblins and trolls chase after you in the hopes of ripping you apart and eating your delicate elven flesh. As you run for your life, you notice something odd about the stones in the tunnel wall. It seems that the wall is made up of a repeating set of stones. Every ten feet or so, you think that you notice a repeated stone. You stop to check, but the troll that has been hot on your heels, call him Claudius if you will, quickly arrives and gobbles you up. The moral of the story – If anyone takes the time to closely examine your masonry, a troll will eat them.

A large visual background scene of a game can be created easily using the `TiledLayer` class. This class builds fields of visual imagery by repeating a set of frames, thereby eliminating the need to render a huge image. A `TiledLayer`, like a `Sprite`, holds a set of image frames called *tiles*. The tiles of a single image can be used to build a very large scrolling background scene without taking up as much memory as a huge image.

6.4.1 Tiles of an Image

Tiles are like raw frames of a `Sprite`. They can be arranged in a way that raw frames of a `Sprite` are arranged in Fig. 6.4, row-oriented way. But one big difference between indices of the tiles and raw frames of a `Sprite` is that the former starts from 1, while the latter starts from 0. There is a reason for that. We will see later on why indices of tiles need to start from 1, rather than 0.

An `Image` object to be broken up into tiles can be mutable or immutable. By mutable, it means that the `Image` object is modifiable, while an immutable `Image` object is not modifiable. A series of tiles must be built up equally in size from a single image. These tiles are considered as static tiles, because the association between the tiles and the image data is fixed. A static tile is created when a `TiledLayer` is instantiated, and it can be changed later using the method `setStaticTileSet(Image image, int tileWidth, int tileHeight)`.

Animated tiles can also be created using `createAnimatedTile(int staticTileIndex)` method and `setAnimatedTiled(int animatedTileIndex, int staticTileIndex)` method. An animated tile is a virtual tile that is dynamically associated with a static tile. It works almost the same way as animating a `Sprite`. The appearance of an animated tile is that of the static tile that is currently associated with the animated tile. This technique is very useful and resource-efficient in animating large repeating scenes of a game. Initially creating an animated tile using `createAnimatedTile(int staticTileIndex)` will return the index to be used in the future identifying the new animated tile. The animated tile indices are always negative, beginning from -1 and continuously getting smaller and smaller, for instance, -2, -3 and so forth. After an animated tile has been created, it is associated to a static tile. Then the static tile associated with the animated tile can be changed by specifying the animated tile index and the desired static tile index into the `setAnimatedTiled(int animatedTileIndex, int staticTileIndex)` method.

6.4.2 Cells of a TiledLayer

Cells of a `TiledLayer` are equally sized and they are placed into the grid of the `TiledLayer`. The constructor of the `TiledLayer` class has two parameters to specify the number of rows and columns in the grid as well as two parameters to specify the width and height of a tile along with a parameter to specify an image.

```
TiledLayer(int columns, int rows, Image image, int tileWidth, int
tileHeight)
```

Contents of each cell are specified by means of a tile index, where positive numbers for static tiles, negative numbers for animated tiles and 0 for an empty cell. The empty cell is transparent and all cells initially contain index 0. `setCell(int col, int row, int tileIndex)` and `fillCells(int col, int row, int numCols, int numRows, int tileIndex)` can be used to change the contents of the cells. A cell must be set to only one tile, while a tile may be applied to many cells.

We have now covered all the classes of the `javax.microedition.lcdui.game` package. You now have the tools to create the graphical component of your MIDlet game applications. Before closing on the subject, the next section will discuss some performance issues related to these tools.

6.5 OPTIMIZING GAME SIZE AND PERFORMANCE

Successful applications for mobile devices demand more than just a how-to knowledge of the APIs. The success of these applications often comes down to a thin margin of available resources that can impact performance negatively. As a developer of applications for mobile phones, you should always look for ways to tweak performance in your favor. The following sections address several opportunities for such tuning within the game API. For this resource-constrained platform, these tuning strategies are certainly as important as the package's class hierarchy.

6.5.1 Tuning the GameCanvas

Several performance tweaks can be made to `GameCanvas`, the stage for a game. Every `GameCanvas` instance has its own unique off-screen buffer. Therefore, it is highly recommended to create one at the beginning of the game cycles and re-use it during the execution of the game so that the memory usage can be the minimum.

Using key events suppression feature of `GameCanvas` class may also improve overall performance of a game by the fact that the system calls to `keyPressed`, `keyReleased` and keyRepeated methods are no longer needed. If you don't plan to field these events with your own logic, why don't we just shut down the event listening system by suppressing the key events?

Since a new Graphics object is created every time you call the GameCanvas's getGraphics() method, it is highly recommended to create as little amount of Graphics objects as possible and re-use them smartly. The recommended practice is to obtain a Graphics object during initialization and then keep the reference throughout the game's execution. This is much, much faster than recreating an object each time you need to render something.

6.5.2 Tuning the Layers

A couple of tweaks can be made to the Layer as well. These tweaks mainly focus on the paint(Graphics g) method of the Layer class. Since this is an abstract method, all implementations will occur in subclasses of Layer. Hence, the recommendations discussed in this section are actually applied to subclasses of Layer and their implementations of paint(Graphics g).

Since paint(Graphics g) method will do nothing if its Layer instance is not visible, the application should avoid calling the implementation of the method to eliminate the overhead in just making a method call and getting nothing from it. And it is highly recommended to make use of clipping and translation features of the Graphics class to control and limit the area, where the Layer is going to be rendered so that the whole screen does not need to be rendered unnecessarily.

6.5.3 Tuning the LayerManager

The paint(Graphics g, int x, int y) method of the LayerManager class ignores the Layers that are located in the region that is completely outside of the clip region of the Graphics instance that is passed into the method. Since the clip region may extend beyond the bounds of a Layer, it is suggested to make sure that rendering operations affect only to the region within the Layer's bounds.

6.5.4 Tuning the Sprites

It is better to use a Sprite with many raw frames of an Image object than to use several Sprites, in order to create animation. It is highly recommended to define a reference pixel for a Sprite before any transformation is applied to the Sprite to reduce later confusions for developers, because the reference pixel is defined relative to the coordinate system based on the initially untransformed state of a Sprite.

As mentioned earlier, Layer-related improvements are also applied to its subclass, Sprite. Since the paint(Graphics g) method will do nothing if its Sprite instance is not visible, the application should avoid calling the method to eliminate the overhead in just making a method call and getting nothing from it.

6.5.5 Tuning the TiledLayer

Static tiles of a `TiledLayer` can be modified using `setStaticTileSet(Image image, int tiledWidth, int tiledHeight)` method. A call should be made to the method very carefully, because it consumes memory and time to load up a new image again into its grid of cells. It is highly recommended to use animated tiles, if possible, rather than animating tiles with our own effort using the `setStaticTileSet` method back and forth. Frequently calling that method will decrease the overall performance of a game.

Summary

MIDP 2.0 Game API provides five classes: `GameCanvas`, `Layer`, `LayerManager`, `Sprite` and `TiledLayer` to make the game development easy and robust. This API builds upon the standard MIDP low-level UI classes such as `Graphics` and `Image` to make a perfect game development environment. The Game API classes provide convenient game-specific functionality to supplement the low-level capabilities of the MIDP UI.

Although it might cause you pain to recall, we likened a game application to a play in order to clarify the roles of the various classes of the game API. The `GameCanvas` class acts as a stage of a MIDP game, on which elements of a game are located, and provides basic functionality for the screen of a game. On this stage, we paint our background with the `TiledLayer` class that utilizes a set of tiles to create realistic and efficient textures. If it helps you remember the details of this class, you might try to remember the story of the ill-fated fairy Hamlet who, while fleeing from Claudius the troll, stopped to examine the stones in the tunnel wall.

And, of course, Claudius and Hamlet both appear courtesy of the `Sprite` class, without which the functional capabilities of their animated pursuits would be much more work for a developer. A `Sprite` can be rendered using one of several raw frames from a single image. Those raw frames can be used to simulate `Sprite` animation. Additionally, `Sprites` support some basic graphical transformations such as rotation and flipping.

Do not forget that both `Sprites` and `TiledLayers` are subclasses of the abstract `Layer` class. This class provides both of its subclasses with their basic functionality as visual elements of a game application. The `LayerManager` class acts as a manager who takes care of layers under its control. It can be considered as a place where layers are maintained carefully and rendered accordingly.

As always, the exam demands that you understand the APIs on a practical level. We recommend that you write some games. There's no other way to get a true feel of the platform. And as you write the games, make sure and employ the performance tuning techniques we introduced for each of the game API classes. This practical stuff is all covered on the exam. And remember, don't stop to look at the rocks if a troll is chasing you!

We have now completed the user interface packages. At this point, we have covered the MIDlet application model as well as the full set of user interface packages. Now that we have the basics of MIDlet application development covered, it's time to start learning how to do the Java ME versions of the basics, such as networking and data storage. That's what we will do in the next two chapters. We'll start with networking.

References

1. MIDP 2.0(JSR-118) Specification
   http://www.jcp.org/aboutJava/communityprocess/final/jsr118/
2. J2ME 101, Part 2: Introduction to MIDP's low-level user interface
   http://www-128.ibm.com/developerworks/edu/j-dw-java-j2me2-i.html
3. Creating 2D Action Games with the Game API
   http://developers.sun.com/techtopics/mobility/midp/articles/game/
4. MIDP 2.0: The Game API
   http://www.microjava.com/articles/techtalk/game_api?content_id=4271
5. Game Canvas Basics
   http://developers.sun.com/techtopics/mobility/midp/ttips/gamecanvas/

Exercises

1. Combine the listings provided in the chapter and build a small 2D animation game.
   a. To do a `Sprite` exercise, for example, create a bird `Sprite` and animate its flying movement. Create a tree image and detect whether the bird `Sprite` collides the tree image or not by using any of the `collidesWith` methods that we discussed earlier.
   b. To do a `TiledLayer` exercise, for example, create an outdoor scenery using an image editor, arrange its tiles and try to render both static tiles and animated tiles on the game scene.
   c. To do a `LayerManager` exercise, for example, try to set view window using methods available in the `LayerManager` class and try out some of the `Layer` manipulation methods.
   d. To do a `GameCanvas` exercise, for example, flush the `Graphics` using both of the two `flush` methods and play around with `getKeyStates()` method.

Review Questions

1. In order to improve the overall game performance by updating only a small area of the game scene, there is a way to flush the desired data in the off-screen buffer to the display. Which of the following methods can be used to achieve this?

a. The `serviceRepaints` method from the `Canvas` class should be called, and the `setClip` method of the `Graphics` class should be applied to set a clip region on the `Graphics` object.
b. Since the `flushGraphics` method of the `GameCanvas` class will ignore transparent pixels when flushing to the display, transparent pixels should be created as much as possible.
c. The `flushGraphics(int, int, int, int)` method of the `GameCanvas` class can be used to flush a specified region of the off-screen buffer to the display.
d. We need to implement our own mechanism to limit the flushed region resulting by calling the `flushGraphics` method.

2. Identify the two characteristics of a `Graphics` instance returned from the `getGraphics()` method of the `GameCanvas` class.
   a. Every single `Graphics` instance returned from the `getGraphics()` method of the `GameCanvas` class writes to the same off-screen buffer of its `GameCanvas`.
   b. Only one `Graphics` instance will be created, even though the `getGraphics()` method of the `GameCanvas` class is called several times.
   c. The stroke style of a newly created `Graphics` instance is dotted stroke style.
   d. The clip region of the `Graphics` instance covers the maximum area of its associated `GameCanvas`.
3. True or False: `LayerManager` extends `Layer`, providing additional methods to manage the layers under its control.
   a. True
   b. False
4. Identify the correct property of the layers of a `LayerManager`.
   a. Layers are grouped together in a `LayerManager` on x-axis line.
   b. Layers are grouped together in a `LayerManager` on y-axis line.
   c. Layers are grouped together in a `LayerManager` on z-axis line.
   d. Layers are grouped together in a `LayerManager` in an arbitrary way.
5. Which of the following is true about the raw frames of a `Sprite`?
   a. Raw frames are arranged in an `Image` object in a top-to-bottom and column-by-column basis.
   b. The `Image` object to be used to create raw frames must be immutable.
   c. Raw frames can vary in size (that may be in width or height).
   d. The index of the first raw frame is 0.
6. Assuming that there are four raw frames for the Sprite, what will happen when the following code segment is executed?

```
int[] seq = {1,2,0,3,2};
Image i = Image.createImage("/mickey.png");
Sprite s = new Sprite(image, 20, 20);
```

```
s.setFrameSequence(seq);
LayerManager lm = new LayerManager();
lm.append(s);
Layer lRetrieved = (Sprite)lm.getLayerAt(0);
```

a. The code cannot be compiled.
b. A `ClassCastException` will be thrown at the last line.
c. An `IllegalArgumentException` will be thrown when the `setFrameSequence(int[])` method is called.
d. The code executes fine and `lRetrieved` will have the same object reference as the `Sprite s`.

7. Match the classes in group one to the descriptions in group two.

Group One:
- `GameCanvas`
- `Layer`
- `LayerManager`
- `Sprite`
- `TiledLayer`

Group Two:
- Represents a visual element in a game
- Creates large areas of graphical content without the resource usage as in a large `Image` object
- Provides the basic screen functionality
- Simplifies game development by automating the rendering process
- Represents basic animated element that can display one of several graphical frames

8. Identify the two valid transformation predefined constants available for a `Sprite`.
   a. `Sprite.TRANS_ROT90`
   b. `Sprite.TRANS_ROT90_MIRROR`
   c. `Sprite.TRANS_MIRROR_ROT90`
   d. `Sprite.TRANS_ROT150`
9. True or False: There are four overloaded `collidesWith` methods in `Sprite` class to check a collision with another `Sprite`, an `Image` object, a `LayerManager` object, and a `TiledLayer`.
   a. True b. False
10. Identify a method that is overridden by the `GameCanvas` class from `Canvas` class.
    a. `public void paint(Graphics g)`
    b. `public void flushGraphics(int x, int y, int width, int height)`
    c. `public int getKeyStates()`
    d. `public Graphics getGraphics()`

Review Answers

1. c. The GameCanvas class provides us with a very convenient way to flush a specific region of the game scene just to update the needed area as well as to improve the performance of a game.
2. a. and d. Though new Graphics instances are created every time getGraphics() method is called, they all will render pixels to the same off-screen buffer of the GameCanvas, from which they are created. The stroke style of a newly created Graphics instance is the solid stroke style.
3. b. Only Sprite and TiledLayer extend Layer in MIDP Game API. LayerManager extends Object and has its own methods to handle the layers under its control.
4. c. Layers are mounted over one another inside the LayerManager like a pile of papers. Therefore, it seems that they are placed on z-axis line.
5. d. The first index number of raw frames for a Sprite is 0. However, the first index number of tiles for a TiledLayer is 1.
6. d. The code can successfully be compiled and no exception will be thrown during the execution. The method parameter for the setFrameSequence(int[]) is valid and casting a Layer to a Sprite is perfectly legal.
7. GameCanvas–Provides the basic screen functionality

   Layer–Represents a visual element in a game

   LayerManager–Simplifies game development by automating the rendering process

   Sprite–Represents basic animated element that can display one of several graphical frames

   TiledLayer–Creates large areas of graphical content without the resource usage as in a large Image object
8. a. and c. TRANS_MIRROR_ROT90 and TRANS_ROT90 are the correct choices. The rotation of a Sprite goes in multiples of 90, so there is no room for TRANS_ROT150. TRANS_ROT90_MIRROR is an invalid constant.
9. b. There are only three overloaded collidesWith methods. There is no collidesWith method to check a collision with a LayerManager.
10. a. Since every subclass must implement abstract methods of its superclass, GameCanvas class must implement the abstract paint(Graphics) method of its superclass Canvas.

Exam Notes

☞ Given a scenario, develop code using the MIDP Game API package to improve performance and reduce application size.

Performance Improvements

- Most of the implementation of the API in the devices will be done at the native code level. So the performance will be significantly better.

- API is set in such a way that hardware acceleration can be done easily in the implementation.
- Images for animation and layers are stored in a single buffer and are rendered after every game cycle. Hence, the number of `paint` calls are reduced.
- Make sure that only the affected pixels are drawn in a screen, not the whole screen.
- If you use only the `GameCanvas.getKeyStates()` method to query the keys pressed by the user, initialize the `GameCanvas` object using the `GameCanvas(true)` constructor to suppress events listeners generated for game keys.
- Reuse a `GameCanvas` object since a buffer is created for each `GameCanvas` instance. Creating multiple instances will result in multiple buffers, which is bad for performance.
- Call `GameCanvas.getGraphics()` method to get the `Graphics` object before starting the game and re-use the object again, since each call gets a new instance of the `Graphics` object.
- A `Layer` should not be rendered if it is not visible.
- Use `TiledLayer.setCell(int, int, int, int)`, `TiledLayer.fillCells(int, int, int, int, int)` and `TiledLayer.setStaticFileSet(Image, int, int)` methods sparingly as they affect performance.

Application Size Reduction

- Amount of work done in Java has been reduced significantly by letting the native code do most of the work. Hence, the size of the application will be very small.
- Reuse a `GameCanvas` object to minimize heap usage of memory.

☞ Compare and contrast the use of MIDP's `GameCanvas` class vs. the MIDP low-level `Canvas`.

GameCanvas

- A dedicated off-screen buffer is created for each `GameCanvas` instance. Whatever is drawn on the `Canvas` is first stored in this buffer and then flushed to the screen by calling the `GameCanvas.flushGraphics` method.
- Contents of the buffer are modified by calls to the object and by no-one else (like the system, etc.).
- Buffer size is the maximum size of the `GameCanvas`. But the flush size maybe smaller depending on the presence of other objects on the screen (`Ticker`, `Commands`, etc.).
- Calling the `GameCanvas(true)` constructor while creating an instance of `GameCanvas` will only suppress the event listeners for game keys. Event listener methods can be used to listen to other methods. Also the suppression will be effective only when the canvas is visible.
- If keys are pressed while the canvas is being hidden, they will be queued up till the canvas becomes invisible and will be sent to the application when the canvas becomes visible again.
- Some devices may not detect multiple keys pressed at the same time properly.
- `flushGraphics()` method is a blocking, atomic operation. The application can render the next frame immediately after the return of this method.

- When `flushGraphics(int x, int y, int width, int height)` is called, only the intersecting non-zero region is flushed.
- Flushing the buffer does not clear the buffer. It only renders the pixels on the screen. The pixels are still there in the buffer.
- Default color of a `Graphics` object is black with a `SOLID` stroke, and has the default `Font`.
- Game keys are `UP`, `DOWN`, `LEFT`, `RIGHT`, `FIRE`, `GAME_A`, `GAME_B`, `GAME_C`, and `GAME_D`.
- The return value of the `getKeyStates()` method can be ANDed (bitwise & operator) with the game key constants to find out if a key was pressed or not (If the result is 1, key is pressed).
- If a key is kept pressed while the canvas is being shown (made visible), then that key will not be recorded as pressed. It has to be released and pressed again for the `getKeyStates()` to take note of the key press.
- Calling the `getKeyStates()` method will clear the previous state values of all the game keys.

Differences between GameCanvas and Canvas

- `GameCanvas` has an off-screen buffer to improve performance.
- Extra game key press constants are defined in the `GameCanvas` for the keys described above.
- The new `getKeyStates()` method can be used to get the state of keys pressed without querying each of them.

☞ Given a set of requirements, develop code using MIDP's `LayerManager` class.

LayerManager

- `LayerManager` maintains an ordered list of `Layer` objects to be displayed. `Layers` can be added, inserted, or removed from the `LayerManager` when needed.
- The `Layer` at index 0 will be the closest to the user and the `Layer` with the maximum value will be the farthest from the user.
- The indexes are always contiguous. If a layer is removed, the others will be rearranged in such way that the continuity is maintained (much like the behavior of an `ArrayList`).
- A portion of the `LayerManager` can be made visible through the view window. To pan the `LayerManager`, simply move the view window's coordinates. This can be done by invoking the `paint(Graphics g, int x, int y)` method and by changing the x and y values.
- `append(Layer layer)` can be used to add a `Layer` to the `LayerManager`.
  - The `Layer` appended will have the highest index (farthest from user).
  - If the `Layer` is previously present, it will be removed. If a `Layer` x was at position 2 of a 5-layer `LayerManager`, appending the same `Layer` will result in the `Layer` having

a new index of 4 (since the index will reduce when the `Layer` is removed first before being appended).

- `insert(Layer layer, int index)` will insert a `Layer` at the given position. If it is previously present, that `Layer` will be removed.
- `paint(Graphics g)` method will paint the `Layers` in the descending order first (`Layer` with highest index first).
- Only the intersection between the view region and the `Graphics` region will be rendered.
- `Layers` outside the intersection region might not be rendered for performance reasons.
- Default values for the view window are `0`, `0`, `Integer.MAX_VALUE`, `Integer.MAX_VALUE`.

☞ Given a set of requirements, develop code using MIDP's `Layer`, `Sprite` and `TiledLayer` classes.

Layer

- This is an abstract class.
- The `paint(Graphics g)` method should be overridden to paint this `Layer`. The implementation should check to make sure that the `Layer` is painted only if it is visible.

Sprite

- `Sprite` is typically used to display a moving object in a game screen.
- This sub-class of `Layer` can be used to animate images.
- The images in this layer can be flipped (like how your image flips if you stand in front of a mirror—along the vertical axis) and rotated by multiples of 90° (90°, 180°, 270°).
- The frames used by `Sprite` are present in a single image passed while creating the `Sprite` object. The frames can be arranged inside the image in any rectangular format (for example, 1×4, 2×2, 4×1). The total width and height of the image should be a multiple of the width and height of a single frame. All frames should have the same dimensions.
- Frames are numbered starting from 0.
- A frame sequence inside the `Sprite` is the order in which the frames should be rendered. The sequence can be different from the sequence of frames in the image.
- The default frame sequence is the same as the sequence generated from the image. The sequence is generated by counting frames in the image from left-to-right and top-to-bottom.
- Frames should be manually switched using the `nextFrame()` and `prevFrame()` methods. This is circular and so calling `prevFrame()` on the first frame will give the last frame in the sequence and vice versa.
- The size of the sequence need not be the same as that of the total frames. Hence, frames can be repeated, ignored, jumbled, etc.
- A "no-effect" can be created by showing the same frame again and again.
- A reference pixel is used to determine the pivot, using which image transformations (like rotations) can be made.

- `defineReferencePixel(int x, int y)` defines the pixel which will serve as a reference pixel. `setReferencePixel(int x, int y)` will move the `Sprite` in such a way that that pixel will be displayed in the specified location on the screen.
- There are methods to check if the given `Sprite` collides with an `Image` or a `TiledLayer`. Setting the `pixelLevel` parameter to true will detect collision only if opaque pixels of the two objects collide. `Sprite` MUST be visible.
- A collision rectangle defines the area in this `Sprite` that will be used for intersection in the collision detection methods. Default area is the same as that of the Sprite itself.
- `getFrameSequenceLength()` gets the frames in the sequence. `getRawFrameCount()` gets the total number of frames available in the `Sprite`. The former may not be equal to the latter.
- The array passed in the `setFrameSequence(int[] sequence)` is copied. Hence, changes made to the array after the call will have no impact on the set sequence.
- Calling the `setImage(Image image, int frameWidth, int frameHeight)` will cause a new frame set to be loaded into the `Sprite`.
  - If the new `Image` contains more frames than the current `Image`,
    - The current frame remains unchanged.
    - If the defined frame sequence is a custom sequence, it remains unchanged. If it is default, the frame sequence will be reset to the default sequence of the new `Image`.
  - If the new `Image` contains less frames than the current `Image`,
    - The current frame will be set to the 0th frame.
    - The frame sequence will be set to the default frame sequence of the new `Image`, regardless of whether the current frame sequence is default or not.
  - The reference pixel is unchanged in its definition as well as its location.
    - If the frame size is different, the top-left coordinate will be shifted such that the reference pixel will remain stationary.
    - If the frame size is different, the collision rectangle will be reset to the new size of the `Sprite` (which would be the size of the frame).

TiledLayer

- `TiledLayer` is typically used to show the background of a game screen (rolling mountains and stuff).
- The tiles for the object are provided in the same way as in a `Sprite`, through an Image containing frames arranged in a rectangular fashion.
- Tiles are indexed, starting from 1. (This is different from a `Sprite`, where the indexing starts from 0.)
- Tiles can be animated by specifying a virtual index number with a tile and putting it in the sequence. This is useful to show effects like rippling water on a lake, etc.

- Animated indexes are always negative, beginning with –1 and should be consecutive. A tile is associated with an animated index by calling the `setAnimatedTile(int animatedIndex, int staticIndex)` method.
- Unlike a `Sprite` which contains a frame sequence, a `TiledLayer` is identified by a grid where the tiles can be placed. The grid dimensions are specified in the constructor.
- Creating an animated tile
  - Set the initial tile using `TiledLayer.createAnimatedTile(int staticTile)` method. This returns the negative animation index for this tile.
  - Set the second tile to create the animation for the cell using the `TiledLayer.setAnimatedTile(int animationIndex, int staticTile)`.
  - Example tiles would be one tile having water wave at the top of the image and another tile having water wave at the bottom of the image. Showing them one after the other will create the impression of the wave moving.
- If the index of a cell is 0, then nothing will be displayed on that cell (no image).
  - A new set of tiles can be set in the `TiledLayer` by using the `setStaticTileSet(Image image, int tileWidth, int tileHeight)` method.
  - If the number of tiles in the new `Image` is greater than the current one, the animated tiles and the grid will be preserved.
  - If the number of tiles in the new `Image` is less than the current one, all animated tiles will be erased. The grid contents will be reset to 0.

7

Chapter

Connecting to the Outside World

Exam Objectives

4.1 Write code using the Generic Connection framework specified by CLDC, recognizing its characteristics, use, classes, and interfaces. This may include identification of the class hierarchy and relationships of the Generic Connection framework. (Section 7.1)

4.2 Write code for MIDP 2.0 networking, and issues and limitations related to Hypertext Transfer Protocol (HTTP), HTTPS, and Transmission Control Protocol/Internet Protocol (TCP/IP) sockets and datagram, recognizing which connections are required and which are optional, as well as comparing the issues related to TCP/IP and User Datagram Protocol (UDP) datagrams. (Section 7.2)

4.3 Write code using the MIDP 2.0 classes in the javax.microedition.io package, including code that correctly opens, closes, and uses a network connection, using the implications of network blocking operations, scheme, connection number limitations, and character encoding. (Section 7.3)

4.4 Given a problem scenario, troubleshoot networking issues for MIDP 2.0. (Section 7.4)

INTRODUCTION

To have an application of some worth on a mobile phone, it's necessary to have access to networking capabilities. Indeed, this is true for almost all applications in Java editions these days. And, as we mentioned earlier in this book, Java has been from its inception a network-aware technology at every level. Java SE has had rich support for networking from the beginning. I recall how it felt like cheating when I was doing my networking homework in Java rather than C. I don't think my professor realized the inherent networking functionality of the Java APIs. I got an A.

The networking capabilities of Java SE, while being great, just don't work for the micro world. Mostly, they are too large to fit within the memory restrictions of micro devices. Even without the memory consideration, the networking circumstances of micro devices just don't fit into the normal system. Many do not natively handle TCP/IP communications and rely on Internet gateways that they can access through their native wireless networks. Others support infrared and Bluetooth technologies, and everything else under the sun. Ultimately, the specifics of device communication facilities are too extensive to address specifically in APIs to the degree seen in Java SE.

The solution for mobile phones covered in the exam comes at two levels: the configuration level and the profile level. At the configuration level, we have a generalization of connection types known as Generic Connection Framework (GCF). This framework specifies generic interfaces for I/O and network connections. It is defined in CLDC. The framework, as specified by CLDC, provides no specific implementations and makes no specific protocol requirement of the implementation. This work is left to the profile level. In our case, MIDP 2.0 steps in by providing the implementations of GCF and making several requirements in regards to supported protocols.

In this chapter, we discuss GCF, the various protocols that are supported in MIDP 2.0, writing networking code with APIs and troubleshooting that code.

7.1 GCF AT A GLANCE

By saying that the framework is generic in nature, the CLDC specification expert group means that the framework supports input/output and networking functionalities in a general and extensible way. Software frameworks are common place design patterns of today's techno-logical world that support clean and efficient extensibility. Software frameworks, in general, aim at creating the skeletal structure of a software system while deferring on specific implementation of the actual work to be done. In the case of GCF, the deferred implementations are the details of protocol-specific network communication. The framework seeks only to define the types of objects involved and the collaborative relationships among those objects. They typically accomplish this by providing an infrastructure of abstract classes or interfaces that must be extended or implemented when providing support for specific functionality, such as HTTP. The design pattern magic of a framework is that the repetitive tasks of the domain are handled by the framework in a consistent and proven fashion, while the end developer is left to focus on the specifics of their own work.

It should be no surprise, then, to find a framework positioned at the configuration layer. Configurations, as a conceptual piece of the Java ME architecture, seek to provide a low-level set of functionality across as broad section of devices as possible. In terms of I/O and networking, the extreme variance and rate of flux among device native capabilities provides a significant challenge. Rather than trying to provide specific functionality, CLDC tries merely to lay down a sound framework of interfaces that will represent the common connection types in a generic fashion. The implementation details are to be provided by profiles. This allows the configuration to kill two birds with one stone by providing a convenient and extensible framework for developers while simultaneously establishing a proven set of rules that all implementations must obey.

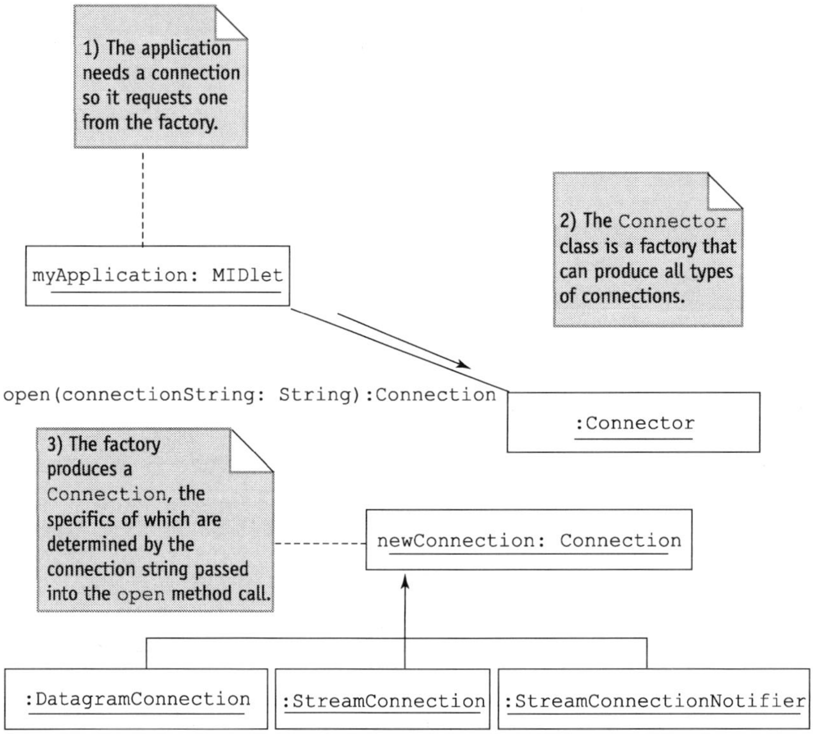

Figure 7.1 Illustration of how GCF works

Figure 7.1 provides an introductory glance into the infrastructure established by GCF. In this collaboration diagram, we can see the level at which GCF works. It specifies a number of interfaces and defines their working relationships, while wholly abstaining from the sultry details of actual protocols. By defining interfaces, GCF can define behavioral rules and relationships for all as yet unspecified implementations. The only thing in this diagram that is not an interface is the `Connector` class, and it is a factory. But a factory is an odd sort of class at best. Factories are typically not instantiated as objects and provide static methods which impose another form of structure, on behalf of the framework, by specifying the channels by which actual instances of the interfaces can be obtained.

In this introductory sketch of GCF, we can see that the framework articulates the types and roles of the I/O domain. First, if an application, most likely a MIDlet, needs a connection, it must request one from the `Connector` factory. Second, the factory will parse the format of the connection string, a format specified by the framework via its definition of the factory's method signatures, and produce an appropriate `Connection`. Thirdly, all connections that the factory returns must implement the `Connection` interface, or one of its subinterfaces. This framework, though not large in its number of classes, clearly established the infrastructure of connection creation and manipulation.

7.1.1 GCF Characteristics

Now we will look at the specific details of GCF with an eye toward understanding how its characteristics work toward creating a flexible and extensible framework. We discuss in this section the following GCF characteristics:

- ❑ the use of a generic connection string parameter
- ❑ the non-specification of individual networking protocols
- ❑ the hierarchy of the GCF interfaces and classes

Each of these characteristics is essential for a mobile application developer to understand. So let's discuss them in detail.

Using Connection String Parameter

In a resource-constrained environment, it is difficult for CLDC to contain all of the class libraries included in Java SE and Java EE platforms in a small mobile device with a few hundred kilobytes of total memory space. Therefore, the CLDC specification expert group designed GCF by eliminating many protocol-specific Java SE networking and I/O classes and by generalizing them to support the extensibility of protocols at the profile level.

GCF, in the absence of specific libraries for different types of connections, defines a specific static method for instantiating all types of connections. The reuse of this method for various types of connections depends upon the generic format of its connection string. The format given below is the general format of the connection string parameter that needs to be passed during the creation of a connection using GCF.

```
Connector.open("<scheme>:<address>;<parameters>");
```

<scheme> identifies the communication protocol that will be used between the mobile device and the remote device, <address> identifies the address of the remote device, and <parameters> identifies the parameters that are needed to open a connection such as username and password for user authentication or baud rate for transmission rate agreed between the two devices.

Let's look at a couple of examples:

To open an HTTP connection to a Web server, use

```
Connector.open("http://www.google.com");
```

To open a socket connection to a remote device, use

```
Connector.open("socket://192.168.0.5:2136;user=john;pass=nhoj");
```

To open a communication port such as Infrared (IrDA) port, use

```
Connector.open("comm:com1;baudrate=115200");
```

It is the responsibility of the device implementation itself to take care of the connection string that is passed in. The binding of communication protocol to our application is done at runtime by determining the substring before the first colon (:).

☞ **Note:** The static `open` method belongs to the `Connector` class. This class provides an interface to the implementation-specific connection resources. This is a very important class. We will discuss the `Connector` class and its powerful static methods in Section 7.1.2.

Absence of Specific Networking Protocols

The goal of GCF is not to provide any specific functionality, but merely to provide a solid framework that will work in a consistent manner under the specific needs of various specific target devices. Therefore, the CLDC specification neither mandates any specific networking protocol implementations nor specifies any supported networking protocols. It is the responsibility of the profile-level specifications, such as MIDP or IMP, to mandate specific networking protocol implementations. When the profiles want to add support for a specific network protocol, they must extend one of the interfaces of GCF. Figure 7.2 shows how profile-level networking protocol implementations extend GCF to provide specific networking support.

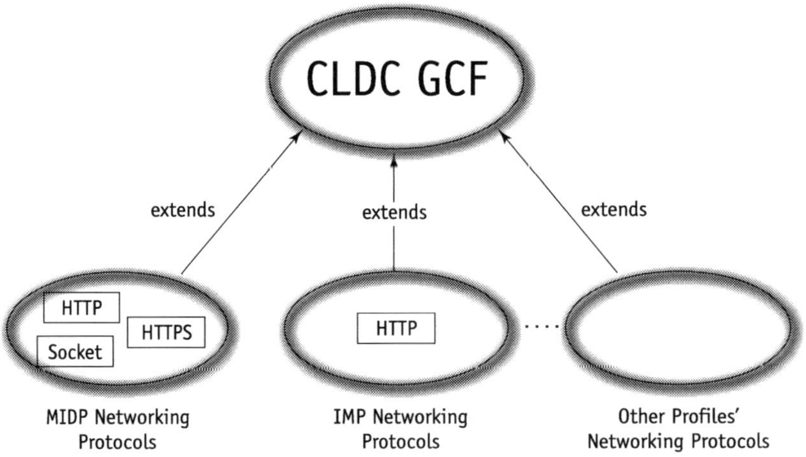

Figure 7.2 Specific implementations extend interfaces of the Generic Connection framework

☞ **Note:** IMP, Information Module Profile, is a strict subset of MIDP. It is not a part of the SCMAD exam objectives. It is displayed in the diagram just to clarify the extensibility concept of GCF.

Now we know that GCF needs to be extended to support specific networking protocols at the profile level before we develop any network applications. The next section will examine the hierarchy of interfaces that are the points of extension for GCF.

Understanding Framework Hierarchy

We have seen how GCF remains agnostic to protocol-specific details through its use of the connection string parameter and the absence of specific networking protocols. We can now turn to examining the interfaces that make up the hierarchy itself. How can there be an API to a framework that doesn't implement anything? Well, the framework is mostly made up of interfaces that define the behaviors that the implementations will take. Indeed, if you think about it, this is the purpose of an interface in the first place. If the concrete classes that provide the details for the specific connection types implement one of the generic connection interfaces, they can be handled the same way regardless of their protocol or internal details. Application code will not need to know anything about the internals. A generic connection can be treated programmatically in a consistent manner despite its internal details.

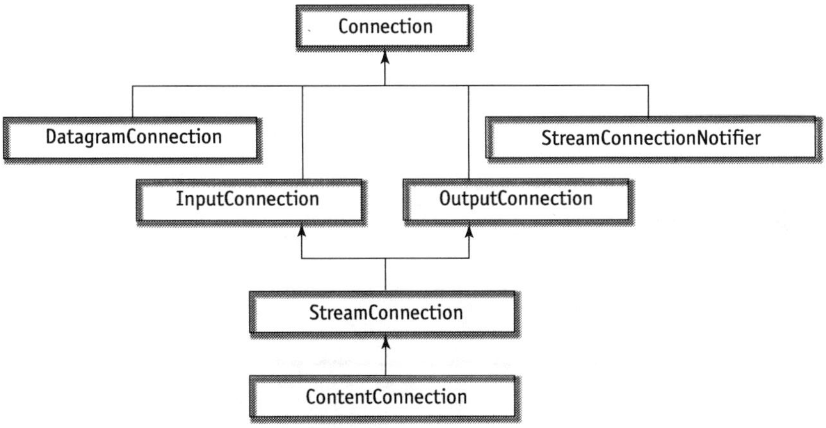

Figure 7.3 Hierarchy of the GCF interfaces

GCF contains a hierarchy of seven connection interfaces as shown in Fig. 7.3. Note that the `StreamConnection` extends both the `InputConnection` and `OutputConnection` to combine the functionality into a single interface for two directional streams. These are the basic connection interfaces that profile-level implementations must extend to provide support for specific networking protocols. Table 7.1 provides a brief description of the purpose of each interface.

Table 7.1 Basic interface types and their specific GCF interface mappings

Interface purpose	*GCF Interface*
A basic serial input connection	`InputConnection`
A basic serial output connection	`OutputConnection`
A datagram-oriented connection	`DatagramConnection`
A circuit-oriented connection	`StreamConnection`
A notification mechanism to inform a server of client-server connections	`StreamConnectionNotifier`
A basic web server connection	`ContentConnection`

Exam Tip

The mapping between basic interface types and the actual GCF interface is a must-know knowledge for the exam. The exam usually contains several tricky questions related to those basic connection types and the mapping with actual GCF interfaces.

While these interfaces do most of the work of creating the structure of GCF, some other important classes provide key functionality for working with the framework. These helper classes include the `Connector` class, the `ConnectionNotFoundException` class and the `Datagram` interface for datagram packets. We'll discuss these classes in the next section, and then we'll take a closer look at all the interfaces in Section 7.1.3.

7.1.2 GCF Classes

There are two classes in GCF of the CLDC specification: the `Connector` class and the `ConnectionNotFoundException` class. They are provided as support staff for the central set of interfaces that establish the structure of the framework.

Connector Class

The `Connector` class is a factory class that can be used to create and open new `Connection` objects and input/output streams. The `Connector` class has altogether seven methods: three overloaded `open` methods to create and open `Connection` objects, and four convenience methods to create and open input/output streams.

All the three overloaded `open` methods take a connection string as one of the parameters. Three of them also return a reference to a `Connection` interface, which is the base interface of all other interfaces available in GCF. Table 7.2 summarizes these three overloaded `open` methods and the variances in their method signatures.

Table 7.2 Summary of the three overloaded `open` methods

Overloaded `open` *method*	*Connection string*	*Access mode*	*Timeout flags*
`open(String connString)`	<scheme>:<address>;<parameters>	`Connector.READ_WRITE`	false
`open(String connString, int mode)`	<scheme>:<address>;<parameters>	`Connector.READ`, `Connector.WRITE` or `Connector.READ_WRITE`	false
`open(String connString, int mode, boolean isTimeout)`	<scheme>:<address>;<parameters>	`Connector.READ`, `Connector.WRITE` or `Connector.READ_WRITE`	true or false

Each of the parameters of the `open` methods can affect the attributes of the connection that is going to be opened. The extra parameters are fairly straightforward. If you need to control the access mode or the timeout characteristic, you can use the appropriate version. Let's examine each method more closely.

```
static Connection open(String connString)
```

The first method, `open(String connString)`, can be used to create and open a connection. The created connection will have the default setting for the access mode and timeout exception flag.

```
static Connection open(String connString, int mode)
```

The second overloaded method, `open(String connString, int mode)`, should be used to apply an access mode to a connection that is going to be created, if an access mode flag needs to be set explicitly during the creation of the connection. There are three access modes available in the `Connector` class:

- ❑ `Connector.READ` (to make the connection read-only)
- ❑ `Connector.WRITE` (to make the connection write-only)
- ❑ `Connector.READ_WRITE` (to make the connection both readable and writable)

Depending on the protocol of the connection that is to be opened, this `mode` parameter must be set properly. Otherwise, an `IllegalArgumentException` will be thrown at runtime. For example, a connection for a bar-code reader of a mobile device should not be created with write-only access mode using `Connector.WRITE`, but with a read access mode using either `Connector.READ_WRITE` or `Connector.READ`. By default, `Connector.READ_WRITE` is used in opening a new connection. It means that the first overloaded `open(String)` method uses `READ_WRITE` mode automatically during the creation of a connection.

```
static Connection open(String connString, int mode, boolean isTimeout)
```

If it is certain that our application can handle a timeout exception, we can specify a `boolean` parameter in the third overloaded method as `true` to indicate that our application can handle a timeout exception if it is thrown from the device implementation. A device implementation may throw an `InterruptedIOException` exception when it detects a timeout condition during the creation of a connection, meaning that it takes more than a certain timeout period specified by the device implementation to open a connection. However, we cannot guarantee that such exception will actually be thrown from the device implementation. It is device-dependent.

Exam Tip

`InterruptedIOException`, not `TimeoutException`, might be thrown from the device implementation when it detects a timeout condition during the creation of a connection. There is no such `TimeoutException` in CLDC.

If the timeout `boolean` parameter is not set when the first overloaded `open(String)` method or the second overloaded `open(String, int)` method is used, no exception will be thrown from the implementation even if a timeout condition is detected.

The `Connector` class also contains four convenience methods for obtaining a stream directly from the factory, thus eliminating the need to handle the `Connection` directly when what you really need is just the stream. Table 7.3 summarizes these four convenience methods:

Table 7.3 Summary of the four convenience input/output stream-related methods

Convenience input/output stream-related method	*Purpose of the method*
`static InputStream openInputStream(String connectionUrl)`	To create and open a connection input stream
`static OutputStream openOutputStream(String connectionUrl)`	To create and open a connection output stream
`static DataInputStream openDataInputStream (String connectionUrl)`	To create and open a connection data input stream
`static DataOutputStream openDataOutputStream (String connectionUrl)`	To create and open a connection data output stream

Table 7.4 demonstrates the step saved by using the convenience method. In one code snippet, the `Connection` is obtained first. In the second, this step is avoided by using the convenience method.

Table 7.4 Saving time with convenience methods

Not using an input/output stream convenience method	*Using one of the input/output stream convenience methods*
`String url = "http://www.mcgraw-hill.com";`	`String url = "http://www.mcgraw-hill.com";`

`StreamConnection connectionObj = (StreamConnection)Connector.open(url);` `InputStream inputStreamObj = connectionObj.openInputStream();`	`InputStream inputStreamObj = Connector.openInputStream(url);`

☞ **Note:** By using the convenience methods, we cannot get a reference to the connection itself and therefore we cannot access methods or attributes which are specific to the connection.

Now you know everything you need to know for the exam topics related to the `Connector` class of GCF. But there is one more class left in GCF to discuss. That is one and only one exception class located in the GCF, `ConnectionNotFoundException`.

ConnectionNotFoundException Class

The only exception class, `ConnectionNotFoundException`, of GCF will be thrown when the target specified in the connection string parameter cannot be found, or the communication protocol specified is not supported. Figure 7.4 shows the elements of the connection string that can trigger this exception.

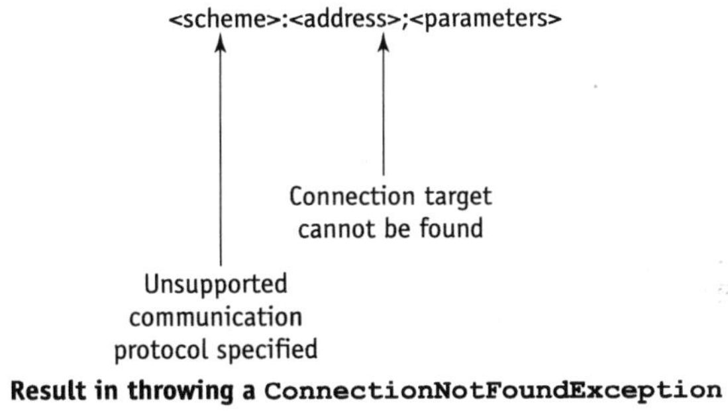

Figure 7.4 Invalid items in the connection string, which can cause `ConnectionNotFoundException` to be thrown

For example, assuming that a MIDlet contains a code segment as follows:

```
String param = "telephony:operator=brain.read;target=mary.jones";
Connection conn = Connector.open(param);
```

If telephony protocol is not supported in a device, an attempt to call the `open` method will cause a `ConnectionNotFoundException` to be thrown.

Similarly, assuming that a MIDlet contains a code segment as below:

```
String param = "http://www.non-existing.com;param1=value1";
Connection conn = Connector.open(param);
```

If the target address "//www.non-existing.com" cannot be found during the execution of the `open` method, a `ConnectionNotFoundException` will be thrown by the method.

Now that we've covered the helper classes of the framework, we will move on to the details of the central figures of GCF, the interfaces.

7.1.3 GCF Interfaces

Back in Fig. 7.3, we saw that there are seven connection interfaces in GCF. The `javax.microedition.io` package also contains the `Datagram` interface which represents a datagram unit. The exam expects you to know the methods available in GCF interfaces. But don't worry. In the next sections, you'll get some hands-on practice with each of them. Recall that GCF strives to provide a set of generic interfaces that will be able to handle the full breadth of specific connections that might occur in the real devices. With this in mind, the crux to understanding the framework is learning the correlation between each interface and its real-world connection type. If you understand this, you will easily remember the details of the interfaces themselves.

Connection Interface

This is the base interface for all types of connection interfaces available in GCF. A connection can be opened using any of the three overloaded `static` methods of the `Connector` class that we discussed earlier. The `Connection` interface contains only one method, which is `close()`.

The following is the method signature of the `Connection`'s `close` method:

```
public void close() throws IOException
```

Exam Tip

If there is an attempt to access I/O-related methods of the closed connection, an `IOException` will be thrown.

But there will be no effect, if the closed connection is closed again and again.

Even though a connection is closed, the streams that were previously opened from the connection will remain open until they are closed by the `close()` method of the streams themselves. It means that closing the connection will not automatically close the streams associated with it and the streams are still usable. However, access to the closed connection will cause an `IOException` to be thrown.

InputConnection Interface

This connection interface is of basic serial input connection type. Use it to open a stream to read data from a serial connection. Its two methods are:

```
public InputStream openInputStream() throws IOException
public DataInputStream openDataInputStream() throws IOException
```

The first method is used to open an abstract input stream, which represents an input stream of bytes. However, if you need a data input stream that supports primitive Java data types, use the second method.

OutputConnection Interface

This connection interface is of basic serial output connection type. Use it to open a stream to write data to a serial connection. Its two methods are:

```
public OutputStream openOutputStream() throws IOException
public DataOutputStream openDataOutputStream() throws IOException
```

The first method is used to open an abstract output stream, which represents an output stream of bytes. However, if a data output stream that supports primitive Java data types is needed, the second method should be used.

StreamConnection Interface

This connection interface extends both `InputConnection` and `OutputConnection` interfaces. It can be considered as the starting point for classes which support two-way communications in a single place. Use this connection interface to test simple basic input and output connections at the same point. One thing to note is that this interface does not define any methods. It only inherits the methods from its ancestors: `Connection`, `InputConnection` and `OutputConnection`.

> **Exam Tip**
>
> Every `StreamConnection` can have at most only one input stream and output stream.
>
> An attempt to open an additional input stream or output stream will cause an `IOException` to be thrown. Opening a `DataInputStream` is considered as opening an input stream. In the same way, opening a `DataOutputStream` is considered as opening an output stream.
>
> An attempt to open a new input stream or a new output stream after they have been once closed will cause an `IOException` to be thrown.
>
> Thread synchronization should be taken care of as appropriate when methods of `StreamConnection` are called from another thread. `close()` is the one and only method that can be called without the need of consideration for thread synchronization.

ContentConnection Interface

This connection interface extends `StreamConnection` interface. Use its methods to get basic information related to the content that is passed in. Its three methods are:

```
public String getType();
public String getEncoding();
public long getLength();
```

As the name of each method indicates, the type, encoding and length of the content contained in the connection can be retrieved by using each method, respectively.

StreamConnectionNotifier Interface

This connection directly inherits from the base `Connection` interface and has only one method, `acceptAndOpen()`. Use this connection interface when a notification for an incoming `StreamConnection` is needed.

> **Exam Tip**
>
> The `acceptAndOpen()` method will block the application until a client connection is available and connected to the current running application.

DatagramConnection Interface

This connection interface inherits the base `Connection` interface (see Fig. 7.3) and it is totally different from all the other connection types. Packets, called datagrams, are delivered through the `DatagramConnection` and are represented by the `Datagram` interface.

`DatagramConnections` are stateless network connections, as opposed to connections that manage the ongoing session of communication. The stateless connection does not have any sort of connection management. Indeed, it can hardly be said to be a connection at all. This means that such thing as the success of a datagram's delivery is unknown. But being stateless has its benefits as well. Without the overhead of connection-state management, `DatagramConnections` are much more efficient means of transmitting data over a network, meaning that they are faster than stream- or circuit-oriented connections.

`DatagramConnection` defines the following methods.

```
public Datagram newDatagram(int size)
public Datagram newDatagram(int size, String address)
public Datagram newDatagram(byte[] buffer, int size)
public Datagram newDatagram(byte[] buffer, int size, String address)
public void send(Datagram datagram)
public void receive(Datagram datagram)
public int getMaximumLength()
public int getNominalLength()
```

The first four methods can be used to create a new `Datagram` instance from the `DatagramConnection`. Then the `Datagram` can be sent or received via the `send(Datagram)` or `receive(Datagram)` methods. The last two methods retrieve the maximum length (size) of a datagram, which can be created using the first four methods and the nominal length (size) of the datagram that is stored into the data buffer, respectively.

Datagram Interface

The `Datagram` interface contains the data to be sent over a `DatagramConnection`. It extends both `DataInput` and `DataOutput` interfaces. The interface contains methods to manage the *address, length, data buffer* and *offset* of the datagram as listed in Table 7.5.

Table 7.5 Datagram methods

Method	*Description*
`public String getAddress()`	Gets the address of the datagram
`public void setAddress(String address)`	Sets the address of the datagram
`public void setAddress(Datagram reference)`	Sets destination address of the datagram by copying the address of another datagram
`public String getLength()`	Gets the length of the data in the datagram `public void setLength(String length)` Sets the length of the data in the datagram `public byte[] getData()` Gets the array of bytes that is contained in the datagram
`public void setData(byte[] data, int offset, int length)`	Sets the array of bytes starting from the specified offset to the specified length
`public int getOffset()`	Gets the offset of the byte array in the datagram
`public void reset()`	Resets the offset of the datagram to the beginning of the byte array.

Exam Tip

There is no address-related class in CLDC specification, as in the standard Java SE networking API. The address is set in the `Datagram` object itself. If the datagram is received from another device, the address stored inside the `Datagram` object is the address of that device. If the datagram is to be sent, the address stored inside the `Datagram` object is the address of the device that is going to send the datagram.

Now you know everything you should know for the exam about GCF. As mentioned in the previous sections, GCF is located at the configuration level, in CLDC to be specific. The goal of GCF is to establish a framework for the handling of network connections. Toward this end, GCF defines interfaces and some helper classes but leaves protocol-specific implementations to the profile layer. The next section will discuss the profile-level implementations that are utilized in JTWI and tested on the exam.

Can you anticipate what specific protocol support the JTWI's specified profile might deem necessary? Mobile phones are the target devices of JTWI, so what kind of connections will they need to support? Well, if you don't have an answer, we'll give you one in the next section.

7.2 MIDP 2.0 PROTOCOL IMPLEMENTATIONS

JTWI specifies the MIDP 2.0 as its required profile. After we have learned about the CLDC's GCF, we should realize that we can expect to find a set of classes, implementing the interfaces of GCF, and providing support for specific network protocols. Indeed, we can. The MIDP 2.0 specification supports several networking protocols such as HTTP, HTTPS, TCP/IP Sockets, UDP Datagrams and so forth. The figure given below shows the relationship of the MIDP connections and the GCF connections.

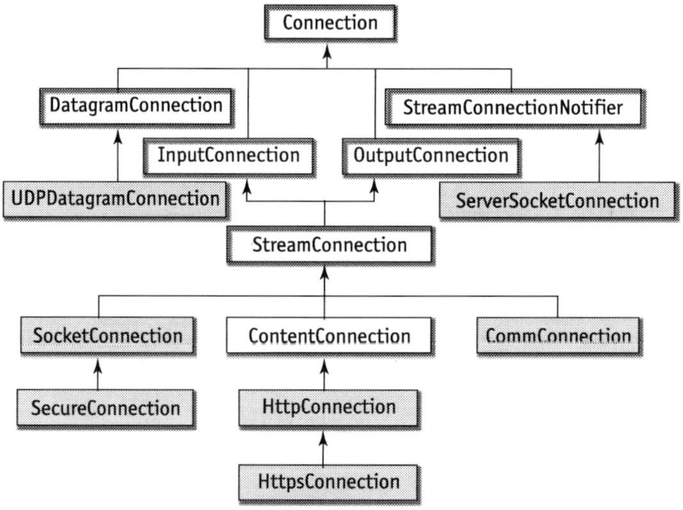

Figure 7.5 Hierarchy of MIDP 2.0 networking interfaces, in addition to the CLDC's GCF

In Fig. 7.5, the interfaces that are in shaded rectangles are located at the profile level, MIDP 2.0 in this case. The interfaces that are in white rectangles are located at the configuration level, CLDC 1.1 in this case. The following section will examine these classes and look at how to use them in our code.

7.2.1 MIDP 2.0 Specification Requirements

First, the MIDP 2.0 identifies two protocols as particularly important to mobile devices. The specification mandates that HTTP and HTTPS must be supported by all of the MIDP 2.0 implementations, while any other protocols in the specification are optional to be supported. Table 7.6 summarizes which connection interfaces are required and which are optional.

Table 7.6 List of connection interfaces, which are required and optional in MIDP 2.0 specification

Required Connections	*Optional Connections*
`HttpConnection` – Hypertext Transfer Protocol	`SocketConnection` – TCP/IP Socket
`HttpsConnection` – Secure Hypertext Transfer Protocol	`ServerSocketConnection` – TCP/IP Server Socket
	`SecureConnection` – Secure Socket Layer
	`UDPDatagramConnection` – UDP Datagram
	`CommConnection` – Logical Serial Communication

Security is very important in mobile devices for a variety of reasons. In order to provide network access to a MIDP 2.0 application, permissions must be granted by the user as appropriate. Permissions act as guards to prevent applications from accessing the outside world without the user knowing it. Since network access from a mobile phone often incurs a monetary fee, we definitely don't want to allow applications open access to network resources. Table 7.7 lists the permission names that can be used to provide network access for a MIDP 2.0 application.

Table 7.7 List of connection types and permissions needed to use them in a MIDP 2.0 application

Connection type	*Permission needed*
`HttpConnection`	`javax.microedition.io.Connector.http`
`HttpsConnection`	`javax.microedition.io.Connector.https`
`SocketConnection`	`javax.microedition.io.Connector.socket`
`ServerSocketConnection`	`javax.microedition.io.Connector.serversocket`
`SecureConnection`	`javax.microedition.io.Connector.ssl`
`DatagramConnection in client mode`	`javax.microedition.io.Connector.datagram`
`DatagramConnection in server mode`	`javax.microedition.io.Connector.datagramreceiver`
`CommConnection`	`javax.microedition.io.Connector.comm`

The permissions listed above are to be specified in `MIDlet-Permissions` and `MIDlet-Permissions-Opt` of the application descriptor as appropriate, indicating that a certain connection type is necessary or optional for a MIDP 2.0 application to be able to operate in a proper manner. Connection types listed in `MIDlet-Permissions` are essential for the MIDP 2.0 application to be able to operate in a proper manner. Otherwise, it will not operate properly. However, connection types listed in `MIDlet-Permissions-Opt` are optional and the MIDP 2.0 application will be able to operate properly without them. In this case, the application might run in a limited manner, for instance, a game can be played as single-player mode rather than online two-player mode, in which a network access is needed.

If you are not clear on how to specify the permissions and where to specify them properly, don't worry about the details for now. The permissions follow the MIDlet security model which we will discuss at length in Chapter 9 (Securing Wireless Applications).

7.2.2 HTTP

In case you are unfamiliar with the central protocol of the Web, let's have a crash course. HTTP is a stateless protocol that communicates via request-response pairs. The parameters of the request must be set before the request is sent to the remote server machine. As seen in Fig. 7.6, an HTTP connection must be in one of the three states during its lifetime. These states are as follows:

- ❑ Setup state–in which request parameters to be sent can be set
- ❑ Connected state–in which the request has been sent to the remote server machine and a response is expected
- ❑ Closed (Final) state–in which the connection has been closed and nothing can be done on the connection

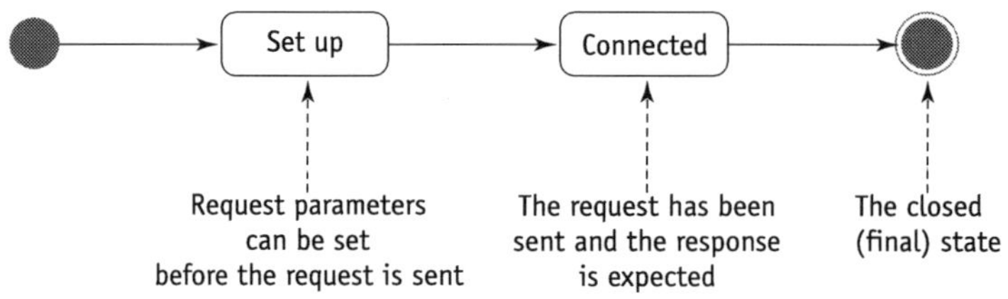

Figure 7.6 The three lifecycle states of an HTTP connection

The MIDP 2.0 specification supports a subset of HTTP, which can be implemented using both IP and non-IP. In the case where there is no built-in support for IP in a mobile device, a gateway is needed to serve as a bridge to connect between the non-IP device and the HTTP server.

HTTP 1.1 is the version of HTTP that MIDP 2.0 implementation must support. An HTTP connection can be created by using the connection string that starts with the scheme "http".

The `HttpConnection` interface is located in `javax.microedition.io` package, and the typical format of the connection string to create an instance of `HttpConnection` is

```
http://host[:port][params]
```

where `//host` = hostname or IP address, `port` = numeric port number, `params` = semicolon-preceded list of parameters, and [ ] = item located inside a pair of square brackets are optional.

7.2.3 HTTPS

HTTPS, Secure HTTP, is just an extension of HTTP, which can be used to securely exchange the files on the Internet. MIDP 2.0 release contains the support for HTTPS connection with the `HttpsConnection` interface. In addition to the `IOException` that might be thrown during the failure or interruption of an I/O operation, `CertificateException` might be thrown in the situation, where various failures occur during the establishment of the secure link.

> **Exam Tip**
>
> **Unlike `IOException`, `CertificateException` is not located in the `java.io` package, but in the `javax.microedition.pki` package. But `CertificateException` extends `IOException`.**

An HTTPS connection can be created by using the connection string that starts with the scheme "https". The `HttpsConnection` interface is located in `javax.microedition.io` package, and the typical format of the connection string to create an HTTPS connection is

```
https://host[:port][params]
```

where `//host` = hostname or IP address, `port` = numeric port number, `params` = semicolon-preceded list of parameters, and [ ] = item located inside a pair of square brackets are optional.

7.2.4 TCP/IP Sockets

TCP/IP socket connection is a stream- or circuit-based connection. A TCP/IP socket communication is analogous to a client-server communication, where the `SocketConnection` interface defines the client socket stream connection and the `ServerSocketConnection` interface defines the server socket stream connection. The server socket connection must wait and listen for the client connections to come in.

A socket connection can be created by using the connection string that starts with the scheme "socket". A socket connection needs explicit identification for the host portion and the port number portion in the connection string. The `SocketConnection` interface is located in `javax.microedition.io` package, and the typical format of the connection string to create a socket connection is

```
socket://host:port
```

On the other hand, a server socket connection can be created by using the connection string in the format given below. The port number portion can be omitted. An instance of `ServerSocketConnection` interface will be returned, when it is passed to the `open` method of the connection factory, the `Connector` class. In the case where the number is omitted, the system will allocate a suitable port for the application.

```
socket://[:port]
```

where `//host` = hostname or IP address, `port` = numeric port number, and [ ] = item located inside a pair of square brackets are optional.

7.2.5 UDP Datagrams

UDP datagram connection is defined by the `UDPDatagramConnection` interface in the MIDP 2.0 specification. Since the `UDPDatagramConnection` interface extends the `DatagramConnection` interface from GCF, it inherits all properties that are available in the `DatagramConnection` interface.

The primary goal of a UDP datagram connection is to send the data efficiently to the remote device, where delivery and order of the data at the arrival are not that important. And there is no mechanism to protect duplication of the data sent. But this type of connection can send data faster than a socket connection. Therefore, UDP datagram connections are useful in multimedia-based applications such as online game applications and music streaming applications. Table 7.8 compares the differences between socket connection and datagram connection in terms of speed and data-related issues.

Table 7.8 Comparisons between TCP/IP socket connection and UDP datagram connection

Issues	*TCP/IP socket connection*	*UDP datagram connection*
Speed	LOWER	HIGHER
Reliability	YES	NO
Data Ordering	YES	NO
Duplication Protection	YES	NO
Connection Type	Connection-oriented	stateless

A UDP datagram connection can be created by using the connection string that starts with the scheme "datagram" as in the creation of basic datagram connection in GCF. A UDP datagram connection needs explicit identification for the host portion and the port number portion in the connection string. The `UDPDatagramConnection` interface is located in `javax.microedition.io` package, and the typical format of the connection string to create a UDP datagram connection is

```
datagram://host:port
```

On the other hand, a UDP datagram receiver connection can be created using the connection string in the format given below. The port number portion can be omitted. In the case where the number is omitted, the system will allocate a suitable port for the application.

```
datagram://[:port]
```

where //`host` = hostname or IP address, `port` = numeric port number, and [ ] = item located inside a pair of square brackets are optional.

7.2.6 Logical Serial Communication

Logical serial communication is newly added in MIDP 2.0. This communication channel can be used to provide the device network access via local serial ports such as Infrared, RS-232 modem port, etc. The connection is defined by `CommConnection` interface, which, as we can see in Fig. 7.5, extends `StreamConnection` and inherits all of the properties from it. The `CommConnection` is located in `javax.microedition.io` package, and the typical format of the connection string to create an instance of `CommConnection` is

```
comm:port_id[params]
```

where `port_id` = port identifier that is logically configured in the device and [ ] = item located inside a pair of square brackets are optional.

We have now covered different types of `Connections` implemented by MIDP 2.0. In next section, we will begin looking at how to write code that uses these `Connections`.

7.3 WORKING WITH CONNECTION

Now that we have seen the specific connection types supported by the MIDP 2.0, we need to learn how to create these connections. If you recall from the GCF discussion, connections are obtained through the `static` methods of the `Connector` class. This is a factory class that instantiates the concrete connections that implement the GCF's interfaces. A network connection can be created using one of the three overloaded `open` methods available in the `Connector` class.

A connection must be properly opened and closed in a MIDP application so that the application will run in a proper manner and the resources will be efficiently used and effectively freed. In the coming subsections, we'll cover all the connection lifecycle phases: opening, using and closing.

7.3.1 Opening Connection

Again, the `Connector` class is a connection factory, from which different types of connections can be opened. The general format of the connection string that must be passed into one of the three overloaded `open` methods of the `Connector` class is

```
Connector.open("<scheme>:<address>;<parameters>");
```

Table 7.9 MIDP 2.0 connection interfaces, their protocol descriptions and connection strings

Connection interface	*Connection type*	*Connection string*	*Example of connection string*
`HttpConnection`	HTTP	http://host[:port][params]	http://mcgraw-hill.com:88;user=john ;pass=nhoj
`HttpsConnection`	HTTPS	https://host[:port][params]	https://mcgraw-hill.com;user=mary ;pass=yram
`SocketConnection`	TCP/IP Socket	socket://host:port	socket://192.168.0.44:8840
`ServerSocketConnection`	TCP/IP Server	socket://[:port]	socket://:8840
`SecureConnection`	Secure Socket Layer	ssl://host:port	ssl://mcgraw-hill.com:556
`UDPDatagramConnection`	UDP Datagram	datagram://[:port] or datagram://host:port	datagram://:6651 or datagram://123.144.157.88:6652
`CommConnection`	Logical Serial Communication	comm:port_id[params]	comm:com1;baudrate=9600 ;bitsperchar=7

host = hostname or IP address

port = numeric port number

params = semicolon-preceded list of parameters

[ ] = item located inside a pair of square brackets are optional

Exam Tip

Parameters appended to the end of a connection string are preceded by a semicolon (;).

A general way to open a connection,

```
<ConnInt> myConnection = (<ConnInt>) Connector.open(<ConnString>);
```

where `<ConnInt>` corresponds to a connection interface in the first column of Table 7.9 and `<ConnString>` corresponds to the connection string in the same row.

We'll look at each of the MIDP 2.0-specific connection interfaces in the next section.

7.3.2 Using Connection

Now that we've got a connection, we need to use it. The exam covers the way to write code for various connections available in the MIDP 2.0 specification, so you need to know the details of creating the connections as well as working with these connections.

HttpConnection Interface

The `HttpConnection` interface contains a bunch of methods and constants related to a HTTP connection. Most of the methods are for retrieving information about a HTTP connection. The following methods are the only two setter methods in the `HttpConnection` interface:

```
setRequestMethod(String method)
setRequestProperty(String key, String value)
```

Exam Tip

The only two setter methods: `setRequestMethod(String method)` and `setRequestProperty(String key, String value)` can be called only in the *setup* state of a HTTP connection. After the *setup* state, if the connection is in the *connected* state, an attempt to call these two methods will cause an `IOException` to be thrown. Of course, why do we need to set the request-related information into a HTTP connection that is already in the *connected* state? Once the request has been sent and a response is being expected from the server, the properties and method of the request cannot be modified anymore.

Table 7.10 lists the methods that can lead the connection to the *connected* state from the *setup* state. The setup state can be thought of as the time in which the request is configured. Methods invoked in this manner, such as `setRequestProperty`, typically set header values. As soon as the method requires data to be exchanged with the server, in either direction, the connection transforms to the connected state. Most of the methods that cause the transition are from the `HttpConnection`, while some of them are from its super interfaces such as `ContentConnection` and `InputConnection`.

Table 7.10 Methods that cause transition of an HTTP connection from the *setup* state to the *connected* state

Method	*Method location and its description*
`public InputStream openInputStream()` `public DataInputStream openDataInputStream()`	`InputConnection` – to receive the data that is in the response

`public String getLength()`
`public String getType()`
`public String getEncoding()`
	`ContentConnection` – to retrieve basic information about the content being passed in the connection

`public String getHeaderFieldKey(int n)`
`public String getHeaderField(int n)`
`public String getHeaderField(String name)`
`public String getHeaderFieldDate(String name, long def)`
`public String getHeaderFieldInt (String name, int def)`
	`HttpConnection` – to retrieve header-related information

`public String getResponseMessage()` `public int getResponseCode()`	`HttpConnection` – to retrieve response-related information

`public long getDate()`
`public long getExpiration()`
`public long getLastModified()`
	`HttpConnection` – to retrieve date-related information

Table 7.11 shows methods that can be called from either the setup or connected state. Note that these do not require information from the response.

Table 7.11 Methods that can be called while the connection is in the *setup* or *connected* state

Method	*Method location and its description*
`public void close()`	`Connection` – to close the connection

`public String getProtocol()`
`public String getURL()`
`public String getHost()`
	`HttpConnection` – to retrieve basic information about the content being passed in the connection

`public String getPort()`
`public String getQuery()`
`public String getRef()`
`public String getFile()`
	`HttpConnection` – to retrieve header-related information

`public String getRequestMethod()` `public String getRequestProperty(String key)`	`HttpConnection` – to retrieve request-related information

After an output stream has been opened by calling `openOutputStream` or `openDataOutputStream` method, the connection is still in the setup state. Even though the data has been written to the stream, the request is not sent yet. Perhaps we have written some headers to the output stream, but the entire request has not been sent yet, so the connection is still in the setup state. However, if a method listed in Table 7.10 is called, the request will be sent and a response can be expected from the server. These methods require information from the response, so we should expect that the request must be sent at that point. Once these methods have been called and the connection moves to the connected state, any attempt to modify the request method or properties through `setRequestMethod` and `setRequestProperty` methods will be ignored. In the connected state, these methods will throw an `IOException`.

When an output stream is flushed by calling the `flush()` method of the `OutputStream` or `DataOutputStream` interfaces, the request parameters are sent along with the data that was written to the stream. When an output stream is closed by calling the `close()` method of `OutputStream` or `DataOutputStream` interfaces, the connection enters the connected state. After closing all the streams that were opened from the connection and closing the connection itself, the connection enters the closed state, and it is the end of its life.

Listing 7.1 shows how to connect to a Web server using the `Connector` class and how to use the `HttpConnection` interface to retrieve the information related to an HTTP connection.

Listing 7.1: The MIDlet to test the functionality of the HttpConnection interface and its methods

```
package com.scmadkit.ch07;

import java.io.*;
import javax.microedition.midlet.*;
import javax.microedition.io.*;

/**
 * This MIDlet is to test the functionality
 * of the HttpConnection interface and its methods.
 *
 *
 * @author Ko Ko Naing
 */
public class HTTPMIDlet extends MIDlet {
   /**
    * Creates a new instance of HTTPMIDlet
    */
   public HTTPMIDlet() {
   }
   /* Signals that the MIDlet has entered the Active state */
   protected void startApp() {
       /**
        * Declares an HTTP connection, an input stream and
        * a connection string
        */
      HttpConnection httpConnection = null;
      InputStream inputStream = null;
      String connStr = "http://www.google.com/wml";

      try {
         /* Opens a HTTP connection using the Connector class */
         httpConnection = (HttpConnection)Connector.open(connStr);

         /* Sets the request method for the HTTP connection */              (1)
         httpConnection.setRequestMethod(HttpConnection.POST);
        /* Sets the request properties for the HTTP connection */
```

```
        httpConnection.setRequestProperty("Last-Modified",
                                      "15 Nov 2004 12:45:24 GMT");
        httpConnection.setRequestProperty("User-Agent",
                          "Profile/MIDP-2.0 Configuration/CLDC-1.1");   ❶
        httpConnection.setRequestProperty("Accept-Charset",
                                              "iso-8859-5");
        /**
        * Opens the input stream associated with the connection
        */                                                              ❷
        inputStream = httpConnection.openInputStream();

        /* Gets the content type of the connection */
        String contentType = httpConnection.getType();
        doSomethingWithType(contentType);

        /* Gets the content length of the connection */
        int contentLength = (int) httpConnection.getLength();

        /* Reads the data from the input stream */
        if (contentLength > 0) {
          int bytesread = 0;
          int totalBytesRead = 0;
          byte[] dataArr = new byte[contentLength];
          while ((totalBytesRead != contentLength)                      ❸
                  && (bytesread != -1)) {
             bytesread = inputStream.read(dataArr, totalBytesRead,
                         contentLength - totalBytesRead);
             totalBytesRead += bytesread;
          }
          doSomethingWithData(dataArr);
       }
   } catch (ConnectionNotFoundException cnfe) {
       System.out.println("The connection target cannot be found");
   } catch (IOException ioe) {
       System.out.println("I/O access error");
   } catch (ClassCastException cce) {
        System.out.println("Invalid connection string for a HTTP
connection");
   } finally {
      if (inputStream != null) {
         try {
            inputStream.close();
         } catch (IOException ioe) {
            System.out.println("I/O access error");
         }
      }
      if (httpConnection != null) {
```

```
            try {
               httpConnection.close();
            } catch (IOException ioe) {
               System.out.println("I/O access error");
            }
         }
      }
   }
   protected void destroyApp(boolean unconditional) {}
   protected void pauseApp() {}

   private void doSomethingWithData(byte[] data) {
      // Do something with the retrieved data
      // ...
   }

   private void doSomethingWithType(String contentType) {
      // Do something with the retrieved content type
      // ...
   }
}
```

1. Configures the HTTP connection
2. Sends the request and receives the response
3. Processes the response data in the input stream

Let's go through the example. The first thing we do is create a connection string with the URL for Google and pass it to `Connector`'s factory method, which gives us our `HttpConnection`. After that, we are in the setup state for several lines. During this state, we set the method and several request headers. So far, we are just configuring our connection.

```
httpConnection = (HttpConnection)Connector.open(connStr);
httpConnection.setRequestMethod(HttpConnection.POST);
httpConnection.setRequestProperty("Last-Modified",
                                   "15 Nov 2004 12:45:24 GMT");
httpConnection.setRequestProperty("User-Agent",
                     "Profile/MIDP-2.0 Configuration/CLDC-1.1");
httpConnection.setRequestProperty("Accept-Charset", "iso-8859-5");
```

After we have setup the connection, we are ready to send the request and receive the response. The following line belongs to the connected state. When the input stream is retrieved, the request is completed and the connected state is begun. This makes sense. The input stream contains the response data so it should seem obvious that by this point, we have sent the request and received the response.

```
inputStream = httpConnection.openInputStream();
```

Once we have the response, we need to process it. The following iteration reads and processes the response data from the input stream.

```
if (contentLength > 0) {
    int bytesread = 0;
    int totalBytesRead = 0;
    byte[] dataArr = new byte[contentLength];

    while ((totalBytesRead != contentLength) && (bytesread != -1)) {
     bytesread = inputStream.read(dataArr, totalBytesRead,
                                  contentLength - totalBytesRead);
     totalBytesRead += bytesread;
    }
   doSomethingWithData(dataArr);
}
```

After we have processed the data, we enter the *closed (final)* state when the connection is closed in the `finally` block. Again, using an HTTP Connection is a three-state process: setup, connected and closed. Next, we will look at secure HTTP connections.

HttpsConnection Interface

The `HttpsConnection` interface extends the `HttpConnection` interface to add support for the secure version of the protocol. The new interface adds only two methods, described in Table 7.12.

Table 7.12 `HttpsConnection`-**specific methods**

Method	*Description*
`public int getPort()`	Returns the port number associated with this connection. The default HTTPS port number is 443, and it will be returned if no port number is specified in the string passed to `Connector.open`.
`public SecurityInfo getSecurityInfo()`	Returns the `SecurityInfo` object that is associated with this connection only if the connection has been successfully established.

Listing 7.2 shows how to connect to a Web server using the `Connector` class and how to use the `HttpsConnection` interface to retrieve the information related to an HTTPS connection. If a secure link cannot be established due to errors related to certificates, a `CertificationException` will be thrown during the `open` method call.

Listing 7.2: The MIDlet to test the functionality of the `HttpsConnection` interface and its methods

```
package com.scmadkit.ch07;

import java.io.*;
import javax.microedition.midlet.*;
import javax.microedition.io.*;
import javax.microedition.pki.*;
/**
 * This MIDlet is to test the functionality
 * of the HttpsConnection interface and its methods.
 *
 * @author Ko Ko Naing
 */
public class HTTPSMIDlet extends MIDlet {
   /**
   * Creates a new instance of HTTPSMIDlet
   */
   public HTTPSMIDlet() {
   }
   /* Signals that the MIDlet has entered the Active state */
   protected void startApp() {
      /**
      * Declares an HTTPS connection, an input stream,
      * a connection string and a security information
      */
    HttpsConnection httpsConnection = null;
    InputStream inputStream = null;
    String connStr = "https://www.YourSecureServer.com";
    SecurityInfo securityInfo = null;
    try {
      /* Opens a HTTPS connection using the Connector class */
      httpsConnection =(HttpsConnection) Connector. open (connStr);     1
      /**
```

```
* Sets the request method for the HTTPS connection
* The following call can be omitted, because the
* default request method is GET
*/
httpsConnection.setRequestMethod(HttpsConnection.GET);
/* Sets the request method for the HTTPS connection */
httpsConnection.setRequestProperty("Last-Modified",
              "15 Nov 2004 12:45:24 GMT");
httpsConnection.setRequestProperty("User-Agent",
              "Profile/MIDP-2.0 Configuration/CLDC-1.1");
httpsConnection.setRequestProperty("Accept-Charset",
              "iso-8859-5");
/**
* Opens the input stream associated with the connection
  */
inputStream = httpsConnection.openInputStream();
/* Gets the content type of the connection */
String contentType = httpsConnection.getType();
doSomethingWithType(contentType);
/* Gets the content length of the connection */

int contentLength = (int) httpsConnection.getLength();
/* Reads the data from the input stream */
if (contentLength > 0) {
   int bytesread = 0;
   int totalBytesRead = 0;
   byte[] dataArr = new byte[contentLength];


   while ((totalBytesRead != contentLength)
              && (bytesread != -1)) {
      bytesread = inputStream.read(dataArr, totalBytesRead,
              contentLength - totalBytesRead);
      totalBytesRead += bytesread;
```

```
        }
        doSomethingWithData(dataArr);
    }
        /**
         * Retrieves the security info associated with the
         * connection
         */
    securityInfo = httpsConnection.getSecurityInfo();
     /**
        * Retrieves the certificate associated with the
        * connection
        */
        Certificate certificate
                = securityInfo.getServerCertificate();
        doSomethingWithCertificate(certificate);
    }  catch (CertificateException ce) {
            System.out.println("The secure link cannot be established");
    } catch (ConnectionNotFoundException cnfe) {
            System.out.println("The connection target cannot be found");
    } catch (IOException ioe) {
            System.out.println("I/O access error");
    } catch (ClassCastException cce) {
            System.out.println("Invalid connection string for a
HTTPS connection");
    } finally {
            if (inputStream!= null) {
               try {
                  inputStream.close();
               } catch (IOException ioe) {
                  System.out.println("I/O access error");
               }
            }
            if (httpsConnection != null) {
               try {
                  httpsConnection.close();
```

3

4

```
            } catch (IOException ioe) {
                System.out.println("I/O access error");
            }
        }
    }
  }
  protected void destroyApp(boolean unconditional) {}
  protected void pauseApp() {}
  private void doSomethingWithData(byte[] data) {
     // Do something with the retrieved data
     // ...
  }
  private void doSomethingWithType(String contentType) {
     // Do something with the retrieved content type
     // ...
  }
  private void doSomethingWithCertificate(Certificate certificate) {
     // Do something with the retrieved certificate
     // ...
  }
}
```

1. Configures the HTTPS connection
2. Sends the request and receives the response
3. Processes the response data in the input stream
4. Retrieves the security information and certificate associated with the connection

As you can see, using an HttpsConnection differs little from using an HttpConnection. An HTTPS connection contains all properties that can be seen in an HTTP connection. The difference is that data being transferred in an HTTPS connection are encrypted, and HTTPS uses port 443, instead of port 80 used by HTTP.

SocketConnection Interface

A socket can be created by explicitly specifying the host and port number to the connection string. Listing 7.3 shows how to connect to a server socket stream connection using the Connector class and how to use the SocketConnection interface to retrieve the information related to a socket connection and echo the retrieved message back to the server.

Listing 7.3: The MIDlet to test the functionality of the SocketConnection interface and its methods

```
package com.scmadkit.ch07;

import java.io.*;
import javax.microedition.midlet.*;
import javax.microedition.io.*;
/**
 * This MIDlet is to test the functionality
 * of the SocketConnection interface and its methods.
 *
 *
 * @author Ko Ko Naing
 */
public class SocketMIDlet extends MIDlet {
/**
* Creates a new instance of SocketMIDlet
*/
   public SocketMIDlet() {
   }
   /* Signals that the MIDlet has entered the Active state */
   protected void startApp() {
   /**
   * Declares a socket connection, a data output stream,
   * and a connection string
   */
      SocketConnection socketConn = null;
      DataOutputStream dOutputStream = null;
      String connStr = "socket://124.120.220.169:5000";
      try {
         /**
         * Opens a socket connection using the Connector class      1
         */
         socketConn = (SocketConnection)Connector.open(connStr);
```

```
        /* Sets a socket option for the socket connection */
        socketConn.setSocketOption(SocketConnection.KEEPALIVE, 3);      1
        /**
          * Opens the output stream associated with the connection
          */                                                           2
        dOutputStream = socketConn.openDataOutputStream();

        /* Gets address information */
        String localAddress = socketConn.getLocalAddress();
        int localPort = socketConn.getLocalPort();

        /* Writes the data to the output stream */
        dOutputStream.writeUTF("Hi, I'm from  "                        3
                    + localAddress + ":" + localPort);
    } catch (ConnectionNotFoundException cnfe) {
      System.out.println("The connection target cannot be found");
    } catch (IOException ioe) {
      System.out.println("I/O access error");
    } catch (ClassCastException cce) {
      System.out.println("Invalid connection string for a socket
connection");
    } finally {
      if (dOutputStream!= null) {
        try {
          dOutputStream.close();
        } catch(IOException ioe) {
          System.out.println("I/O access error");
        }
      }
      if (socketConn != null) {
        try {
          socketConn.close();
        } catch(IOException ioe) {
            System.out.println("I/O access error");
```

```
          }
       }
    }
  }
  protected void destroyApp(boolean unconditional) {}
  protected void pauseApp() {}
}
```

1. Configures the socket connection
2. Sends the request and receives the response
3. Writes the data to the output stream

In Listing 7.3, we see a similar pattern to the previous connection examples. A connection string is defined and passed to `Connector.open`. This is no different from what we've seen. But the following line sets one of the configurable options exposed through the `SocketConnection` interface.

```
socketConn.setSocketOption(SocketConnection.KEEPALIVE, 3);
```

After the connection is obtained and configured, we get an output stream from the connection with the following line:

```
dOutputStream = socketConn.openDataOutputStream();
```

Now, we have a stream for writing the data to the connection. With this in hand, we can just write the string we want as in the following line:

```
dOutputStream.writeUTF("Hi, I'm from "
                         + localAddress + ":" + localPort);
```

In this code, we just write the address information of the device to the output stream. The connected server will receive the data through its input stream. In the next section, we will discuss the `ServerSocketConnection` interface which can be used to represent a listening server for incoming socket connections.

ServerSocketConnection Interface

A server socket can be opened either by specifying a port number in the "socket://:port" format or by passing just "socket://" as the connection string. In the latter case, the system will allocate an available port for the connection and the port allocated can be retrieved by calling `getLocalPort()` method.

> **Exam Tip**
>
> `ServerSocketConnection` **interface does not extend** `SocketConnection` **interface. It extends** `StreamConnectionNotifier` **interface.**

The `acceptAndOpen()` method of its ancestor, `StreamConnectionNotifier`, returns a `SocketConnection` instance. Then it can be used to communicate with the incoming remote device.

Exam Tip

Local hostname can be retrieved using `System.getProperty("microedition.hostname")`, in addition to the host address returned from `socketConnection.getLocalAddress()` or `serverSocketConnection.getLocalAddress()`.

Listing 7.4 shows how to accept an incoming socket stream connection using the `acceptAndOpen()` method and how to use the `SocketConnection` interface to retrieve the information related to a socket connection and print the message out to the console.

Listing 7.4: The MIDlet to test the functionality of the `ServerSocketConnection` interface and its methods

```
package com.scmadkit.ch07;


import java.io.*;
import javax.microedition.midlet.*;
import javax.microedition.io.*;
/**
 * This MIDlet is to test the functionality
 * of the ServerSocketConnection interface and its methods.
 *
 *
 * @author Ko Ko Naing
 */
public class ServerSocketMIDlet extends MIDlet {
   /**
    * Creates a new instance of ServerSocketMIDlet
    */
   public ServerSocketMIDlet() {
   }
   /* Signals that the MIDlet has entered the Active state */
   protected void startApp() {
```

```
/**
* Declares a server socket connection, a socket
* connection and a data input stream
*/
ServerSocketConnection ssConnection = null;
SocketConnection socketConn = null;
DataInputStream dInputStream = null;
try {
   ssConnection = (ServerSocketConnection)
            Connector.open("socket://:5000");                  1
   socketConn = (SocketConnection)
            ssConnection.acceptAndOpen();                      2
   /* Sets socket options for the socket connection */
   socketConn.setSocketOption(SocketConnection.KEEPALIVE, 5);  3
   socketConn.setSocketOption(SocketConnection.DELAY, 0);
   socketConn.setSocketOption(SocketConnection.LINGER, 5);

   /* Opens the input stream associated with the connection */
   dInputStream = socketConn.openDataInputStream();
   /* Gets address information*/
   String localAddress = ssConnection.getLocalAddress();
   int localPort = ssConnection.getLocalPort();
   String remoteAddress = socketConn.getAddress();
   int remotePort = socketConn.getPort();
   /* Reads the data from the input stream */
   String message = dInputStream.readUTF();
   if (message != null && !message.equals("")) {
      String tempMessage = localAddress + ":" + localPort
                     + " received \"" + message                4
                     + "\" from " + remoteAddress
                     + ":" + remotePort;
      System.out.println(tempMessage);
   }
} catch (ConnectionNotFoundException cnfe) {
```

```
            System.out.println("The connection target cannot be found");
        } catch (IOException ioe) {
            System.out.println("I/O access error");
        } catch (ClassCastException cce) {
            System.out.println("Invalid connection string for a socket
connection");
    } finally {
            if (dInputStream!= null) {
                try {
                    dInputStream.close();
                } catch (IOException ioe) {
                    System.out.println("I/O access error");
                }
            }
            if (socketConn != null) {
                try {
                    socketConn.close();
                } catch (IOException ioe) {
                    System.out.println("I/O access error");
                }
            }
        }
    }
    protected void destroyApp(boolean unconditional) {}
    protected void pauseApp() {}
}
```

1. Opens a server socket connection
2. Accepts and opens a socket connection to communicate
3. Configures the socket connection
4. Reads the data from the input stream

Again, first we use a connection string to obtain a `ServerSocketConnection`. This is similar to all the other examples we have seen. Since this is a server, we will obtain a socket connection once we have received a request at the server port. The following line accepts the request and creates the `SocketConnection`.

```
socketConn = (SocketConnection) ssConnection.acceptAndOpen();
```

From here, the code is similar to the `SocketConnection` example. Some socket options are configured for the connection, an input stream is obtained, and we read some data from the connection. Then we just write the data to the system output to see the data that the connected socket connection sent.

SecureConnection Interface

A secure socket stream connection can be created by explicitly specifying the host and port number to the connection string. In the same way as `HttpsConnection`, if a secure link cannot be established due to errors related to certificates, a `CertificationException` will be thrown during the `open` method call or `openXXXStream` method call of the `Connector` class.

Listing 7.5 shows how to connect to an Secure Sockets Layer (SSL) server using the `Connector` class and how to use the `SecureConnection` interface to retrieve the information related to a secure socket stream connection.

Listing 7.5: The MIDlet to test the functionality of the* `SecureConnection` *interface and its methods

```
package com.scmadkit.ch07;

import java.io.*;
import javax.microedition.midlet.*;
import javax.microedition.io.*;
import javax.microedition.pki.*;
/**
 * This MIDlet is to test the functionality
 * of the SecureConnection interface and its methods.
 *
 *
 * @author Ko Ko Naing
 */
public class SecureMIDlet extends MIDlet {
    /**
     * Creates a new instance of SecureMIDlet
     */
    public SecureMIDlet() {
    }
```

```
/* Signals that the MIDlet has entered the Active state */
protected void startApp() {
   /**
    * Declares a secure ssl connection, an input stream,
    * an output stream and a security information
    */
   SecureConnection secureConn = null;
   DataInputStream dInputStream = null;
   DataOutputStream dOutputStream = null;
   SecurityInfo securityInfo = null;
   try {
      /**
       *Opens a secure connection using the Connector class
       */
      secureConn = (SecureConnection)
               Connector.open("ssl://icicibank.com");
/* Sets socket options for the secure connection */
      secureConn.setSocketOption(SecureConnection.KEEPALIVE, 3);
      secureConn.setSocketOption(SecureConnection.LINGER, 3);
      /**
       * Opens the input stream
       * associated with the connection
       */
      dInputStream = secureConn.openDataInputStream();


       /**
       * Opens the output stream
       * associated with the connection
       */
      dOutputStream = secureConn.openDataOutputStream();
      /* Retrieves address information*/
      String localAddress = secureConn.getLocalAddress();
      int localPort = secureConn.getLocalPort();
      String remoteAddress = secureConn.getAddress();
```

1

2

```
        int remotePort = secureConn.getPort();
        /**
        * Retrieves the security information
        * associated with the connection
        */
        securityInfo = secureConn.getSecurityInfo();
        /**
        * Retrieves the security protocol information
        * associated with the connection
        */
        String protocolName = securityInfo.getProtocolName();
        String protocolVersion = securityInfo.getProtocolVersion();
        /* Reads the data from the input stream */
        String message = dInputStream.readUTF();
        if (message != null && !message.equals("")) {
        String tempMessage = localAddress + ":" + localPort
                        + " received \"" + message
                        + "\" from " + remoteAddress
                        + ":" + remotePort
                        + " using " + protocolName
                        + " version-" + protocolVersion;
          dOutputStream.writeUTF(tempMessage);
        }
      } catch (CertificateException ce) {
        System.out.println("The secure link cannot be established");
      } catch (ConnectionNotFoundException cnfe) {
        System.out.println("The connection target cannot be found");
      } catch (IOException ioe) {
        System.out.println("I/O access error");
      } catch (ClassCastException cce) {
        System.out.println("Invalid connection string for a secure
socket stream connection");
    } finally {
      if (dInputStream != null) {
```

❸ (annotates the security information retrieval lines)

❹ (annotates the data reading and response lines)

```
            try {
                dInputStream.close();
            } catch (IOException ioe) {
                System.out.println("I/O access error");
            }
        }
        if (dOutputStream != null) {
            try {
                dOutputStream.close();
            } catch (IOException ioe) {
                System.out.println("I/O access error");
            }
        }
        if (secureConn != null) {
            try {
                secureConn.close();
            } catch (IOException ioe) {
                System.out.println("I/O access error");
            }
        }
      }
    }
    protected void destroyApp(boolean unconditional) {}
    protected void pauseApp() {}
}
```

1. Configures the secure socket connection
2. Opens an input stream and an output stream
3. Retrieves the security information and protocol information
4. Reads the data, modifies it and writes it back

The above code simply implements an echo application using a secure socket. In the following lines, we obtain the security information about the connection, and use it to build our echoed response.

```
String protocolName = securityInfo.getProtocolName();
String protocolVersion = securityInfo.getProtocolVersion();
```

```
/* Read the data from the input stream */
String message = dInputStream.readUTF();
if (message != null && !message.equals("")) {
    String tempMessage = localAddress + ":" + localPort
                + " received \"" + message
                + "\" from " + remoteAddress
                + ":" + remotePort
                + " using " + protocolName
                + " version-" + protocolVersion;
    dOutputStream.writeUTF(tempMessage);
}
```

The echo message that we write back to the output stream contains details regarding the security protocol information of the connection. It is a bit more interesting than traditional echo applications, but still nothing too entertaining. As an example, however, it works just fine. Also, note how the `catch` blocks are set up to catch security exceptions that might have been thrown during the creation of the socket.

UDPDatagramConnection Interface

Like its direct superinterface, `DatagramConnection` interface, `UDPDatagramConnection` interface can be opened by explicitly specifying the host and port number for an outbound UDP datagram connection, or by omitting both the host and port number, for an inbound UDP datagram connection.

Listing 7.6: The MIDlet to test the functionality of the **`UDPDatagramConnection`** ***interface and its methods***

```
package com.scmadkit.ch07;
import java.io.*;
import javax.microedition.midlet.*;
import javax.microedition.io.*;
/**
 * This MIDlet is to test the functionality
 * of the UDPDatagramConnection interface and its methods.
 *
 *
 * @author Ko Ko Naing
 */
```

```
public class UDPMIDlet extends MIDlet {
   /**
   * Creates a new instance of UDPMIDlet
   */
   public UDPMIDlet() {
   }
   /* Signals that the MIDlet has entered the Active state */
   protected void startApp() {
      /**
      * Declares a UDP connection and a datagram
      */
      UDPDatagramConnection udpDatagramConnection = null;
      Datagram datagram = null;
      try {
         /* Opens a UDP connection using the Connector class */
         udpDatagramConnection = (UDPDatagramConnection)
                  Connector.open("datagram://:5500");
         /* Instantiates the datagram with the size of 200 bytes */
         datagram = udpDatagramConnection.newDatagram(200);
         /* Retrieves address information */
         String localAddress = udpDatagramConnection.getLocalAddress();
         int localPort = udpDatagramConnection.getLocalPort();
         /* Receives the datagram from the connection */
         udpDatagramConnection.receive(datagram);
         doSomethingWithDatagram(datagram);
      } catch (InterruptedIOException ioe) {
         System.out.println("I/O operation interrupted");
      } catch (ConnectionNotFoundException cnfe) {
         System.out.println("The connection target cannot be found");
      } catch (IOException ioe) {
         System.out.println("I/O access error");
      } catch (ClassCastException cce) {
         System.out.println("Invalid connection string for a socket connection");
```

```
        } finally {
            if (udpDatagramConnection != null) {
                try {
                    udpDatagramConnection.close();
                } catch(IOException ioe) {
                    System.out.println("I/O access error");
                }
            }
        }
    }
    protected void destroyApp(boolean unconditional) {}
    protected void pauseApp() {}
    private void doSomethingWithDatagram(Datagram datagram) {
        // Do something with the retrieved datagram
        // ...
    }
}
```

1. Configures the UDP datagram connection
2. Receives and processes the datagram

Notice how GCF has established a pretty solid routine for the handling of network connections? It makes for boring reading, but easy development. So, we first obtain our connection by passing the connection string to the factory method of `Connector`. Then, just for fun, we obtain some information about the connection with the following two lines.

```
String localAddress = udpDatagramConnection.getLocalAddress();
int localPort = udpDatagramConnection.getLocalPort();
```

Since we created an inbound connection by failing to specify a host, we can't expect to write anything to our connection. So, the next line of importance is one that reads a datagram from the connection.

```
udpDatagramConnection.receive(datagram);
```

Well, someone sent us a datagram. We can't just throw it away, so we might as well:

```
doSomethingWithDatagram(datagram);
```

We could have just as easily created a connection to send datagrams to someone else. To do this we would have specified the host and remote port in the connection string. Well, we would leave this for you as an exercise.

CommConnection Interface

CommConnection interface directly extends StreamConnection interface and defines a logical serial port connection, where bytes are transferred serially. However, it is not necessary to be a physical serial port such as RS-232 modem port. IrDA infrared communication port can be configured as a logical serial port in the operating system of the device so that it can be simulated as a physical serial port.

> **Exam Tip**
>
> The best way to discover the current baud rate of a CommConnection is using the getBaudRate() method of the CommConnection interface.
>
> Setting baud rate request parameter in the connection string results the same as setting the baud rate using setter method of the connection.

A CommConnection instance can be created by explicitly specifying a port identifier and configuration parameters, each of which is preceded with a semicolon (;). Valid identifiers can be retrieved through the use of System.getProperty ("microedition. commports") method call. The method will return a comma-separated list of logical serial ports configured in the device.

Listing 7.7: The MIDlet to test the functionality of the CommConnection interface and its methods

```
package com.scmadkit.ch07;
import java.io.*;
import javax.microedition.midlet.*;
import javax.microedition.io.*;
/**
 * This MIDlet is to test the functionality
 * of the CommConnection interface and its methods.
 *
 *
 * @author Ko Ko Naing
 */
public class CommMIDlet extends MIDlet {
    /**
    * Creates a new instance of CommMIDlet
    */
```

```
public CommMIDlet() {
}
/* Signals that the MIDlet has entered the Active state */
protected void startApp() {
  /**
  * Declare a serial communication connection and an input
  * stream variables
  */
  CommConnection commConn = null;
  InputStream inputStream = null;
  try {
     /**
     * Open the serial communication connection using the
     * Connector class
     */                                                      ❶
     commConn = (CommConnection)
             Connector.open("comm:com0;baudrate=9600");
     /**
     * Open the input stream associated with the connection
     */
     inputStream = commConn.openInputStream();
     /* Retrieve baud rate information */
     int baudRate = commConn.getBaudRate();
     doSomethingWithBaudRate(baudRate);
     /* Read the data from the input stream */
     int charRead = 0;
     while (true) {
        StringBuffer buffer = new StringBuffer();
        charRead = 0;
        while (charRead != '\r') {                            ❷
           charRead = inputStream.read();
           buffer.append((char) charRead);
        }
        System.out.println(buffer.toString());
```

```
            }                                                              ❷
        } catch (ConnectionNotFoundException cnfe) {
              System.out.println("The connection target cannot be found");
        } catch (IOException ioe) {
              System.out.println("I/O access error");
        } catch (ClassCastException cce) {
              System.out.println("Invalid connection string for a serial
communication connection");
        } finally {
            if (inputStream != null) {
              try {
                inputStream.close();
              } catch(IOException ioe) {
                System.out.println("I/O access error");
              }
            }
            if (commConn != null) {
              try {
                commConn.close();
              } catch(IOException ioe) {
                System.out.println("I/O access error");
              }
            }
        }
      }
      protected void destroyApp(boolean unconditional) {}
      protected void pauseApp() {}
      private void doSomethingWithBaudRate(int baudRate) {
        // Do something with the retrieved baudrate
        // ...
    }
}
```

❶ Configures the comm connection

❷ Receives and processes the data from the input stream

While still not that exciting, this code demonstrates the power of GCF. In this example, we are not working with a network protocol. We are opening a connection to a logical serial comm port on the device. Nonetheless, we still do pretty much the same sequence of steps. We first obtain the connection from the `Connector` factory method. We then get the input stream, read the data, and write it to the system's standard output. Now that we've learned how to open and use the various connections supported by the MIDP, we should see about cleaning up.

7.3.3 Closing Connection

To close a connection, `close()` of the base `Connection` interface must be called. The following code snippets show a typical example of how to close a connection properly.

```
try {
   /* Closes the inputstream for the connection, if opened */
   if(inputStream != null)
      inputStream.close();
   /* Closes the outputstream for the connection, if opened */
   if(outputStream != null)
      outputStream.close();
   /* Closes the connection and this is the end of its life */
   connection.close();
   /**
   * If any other codes down here try to call a method
   * on the closed connection, an IOException will be thrown.
   */
} catch(IOException ioe) {
   /* Handles the thrown exception here */
}
```

Note that `close()` is so simple because it is a part of the framework. It is implemented by the `Connection` interface itself. This functionality will be inherited by all of the subinterfaces, whether they are HTTP connections or serial port connections or any other types of connections.

In the next few sections we will discuss some issues that are common to all types of connections. These tips will help improve the I/O code that you write in your MIDlets.

7.3.4 Dealing with Some Limitations of Network Connection

Whenever `Connector.openXXX` method is called, a MIDlet that is interacting with the user can cause the system to block the calling thread and ask the user for the permission to open a networking connection. It can make the application hang waiting for the method to return.

Though it might need a bit effort to handle this situation, it is better to see the application and system run smoothly without being blocked. The most basic and easiest way to tackle this problem is to call `Connector.openXXX` method in a separate thread, rather than the UI thread that is currently interacting with the user.

7.3.5 Character Encoding

The `InputStreamReader` class and the `OutputStreamWriter` class of CLDC 1.1 specification contain the following two constructors, where character encoding can be specified for character input stream and character output stream:

```
new InputStreamReader(InputStream inputStream, String encoding);
new OutputStreamWriter(OutputStream outputStream, String encoding);
```

If the second parameter is specified and is a valid usable encoding in the device, it will become a character encoding to be used in the streams created. If the specified encoding value is not supported by the system, an `UnsupportedEncodingException` will be thrown. However, if the other constructors, where encoding value needs not to be specified, are used, the default character encoding of the system will be used in those streams. The default character encoding of a system can be retrieved through the use of `System.getProperty("microedition.encoding")` method call. The default value is "ISO-8859-1". It means that all devices that claimed to be CLDC 1.1 compliant support ISO Latin-1 characters range.

7.4 NETWORK TROUBLESHOOTING

Connecting to the outside world produces more problems than doing things only in one device. In this section, we'll take a look at how to troubleshoot a few common errors that occur with networking code.

java.lang.SecurityException

Methods `open`, `openDataInputStream`, `openDataOutputStream`, `openInputStream` and `openOutputStream` methods of the `Connector` class

Causes Security violation occurs due to the user's denial on permission or the application does not have the right to use the API

Solutions Grant appropriate permission for the application

java.lang.IllegalArgumentException

Methods `open`, `openDataInputStream`, `openDataOutputStream`, `openInputStream` and `openOutputStream` methods of the `Connector` class

Causes Invalid request parameters or inappropriate arguments have been passed into a method

Solutions Make sure valid request parameters are being passed and valid values of arguments are being passed into the methods

java.io.InterruptedIOException

Methods `open(String, int, boolean)` method of the `Connector` class, receive and send methods of `DatagramConnection` interface

Causes The I/O operation has been interrupted or the timeout expires

Solutions Resend the data again upon receiving errors or reduce the datagram size

java.io.EOFException

Methods `readXXX` methods of the `DataInputStream` class

Causes An end of file or end of stream has reached, while data is being read to the stream

Solutions Always check the end-of-file condition before reading the data

java.io.IOException

Methods All methods on a closed connection and `open` method of `InputStreamConnection` or `OutputStreamConnection` interface, when an input or output stream has been opened or closed once

Causes Calling methods of a closed connection, opening an input or output stream twice or opening a new input or output stream again once it is closed

Solutions Make sure not to open an input or output stream twice, not to open a new input or output stream again once it is closed and not to call methods of a closed connection

javax.microedition.io.ConnectionNotFoundException

Methods `open`, `openDataInputStream`, `openDataOutputStream`, `openInputStream`, and `openOutputStream` methods of the `Connector` class

Causes The connection target could not be found or the protocol type is not supported

Solutions Make sure that the connection target is reachable and find out the supported protocols

javax.microedition.pki.CertificateException

Methods `open`, `openDataInputStream`, `openDataOutputStream`, `openInputStream` and `openOutputStream` methods of the `Connector` class

Causes A secure link cannot be established while opening a HTTPS connection or a secure socket stream connection

Solutions Validate the certificates supplied by the server

Summary

In this chapter we covered a lot of functionality in just a few interfaces and even fewer classes. We saw how the JTWI's configuration and profile work together to provide a full set of I/O and networking APIs for mobile application developer. What we discussed, whether you realized it or not, has been a perfect lesson in the conceptual architecture of Java ME. Consider this a case study in the roles of configurations and profiles. As we review what we learned, notice the roles that the configuration and profile play and how they work together.

First of all, GCF is specified in the JTWI's configuration, the CLDC 1.1. The goal of this configuration-level framework is to provide a flexible, reusable structure for the handling of I/O and networking resources within the applications that might be developed on the broad range of micro devices supported by CLDC. It implements no specific protocols, but lays the framework for easy extension.

The JTWI's profile, the MDIP 2.0, provides those extensions by implementing a set of protocols deemed to be vital to mobile devices. These protocols include HTTP, HTTPS, TCP/IP socket, SSL, UDP datagram and logical serial communication port. These specific implementations fit into GCF and are handled according the GCF's specified practices, such as instantiating through the factory methods of the `Connector` class. We also looked at the problems that can occur in network-related applications and covered some troubleshooting techniques.

For the exam, make sure that you understand the conceptual order of GCF. While you certainly need to know the class hierarchy of GCF, this is mostly conceptual stuff. On the other hand, when it comes to the specific implementations of the MIDP-level stuff, you better know the details. Again, practice with some coding if you want to feel confident that you have mastered the code-level details required concerning such things as creating and working with the various connection types. Sometimes I/O and networking can be boring, but there's nothing that will smooth your life as a developer more than a master of these packages.

We now can write MIDlets that have robust user interfaces and network connectivity. In Chapter 8, Record Management Store (RMS), we will discuss a topic of importance to all applications – data storage.

References

1. CLDC 1.1(JSR-139) specification
   http://www.jcp.org/aboutJava/communityprocess/final/jsr139/index.html
2. MIDP 2.0(JSR-118) specification
   http://www.jcp.org/aboutJava/communityprocess/final/jsr118/index.html

3. The Generic Connection Framework
   http://developers.sun.com/techtopics/mobility/midp/articles/genericframework/
4. J2ME Low-Level Network Programming with MIDP 2.0
   http://developers.sun.com/techtopics/mobility/midp/articles/midp2network/
5. MIDP Network Programming using HTTP and the Connection Framework
   http://developers.sun.com/techtopics/mobility/midp/articles/network/

Exercises

1. Write additional code to build up full-blown applications for various connection types, provided in Section 7.3.2 (using a connection).
   a. `HttpConnection`–Connect to "http://www.google.com/wml" and see what will be returned
   b. `HttpsConnection`–Find a website where https:// protocol is being used and try to access from the MIDlet
   c. `SocketConnection` and `ServerSocketConnection`–Try to connect the two devices using the provided socket connection examples
   d. `SecureConnection`–Find a website where ssl:// protocol is being used and try to access from the MIDlet
   e. `UDPDatagramConnection`–Use the datagram connection example provided in the book and try to connect the two devices
   f. `CommConnection`–Use serial communication connection example available in the Sun's Java ME Wireless Toolkit and try to connect the two devices

Review Questions

1. Assuming that File Transfer Protocol (FTP) is not supported by the device, what will happen when the following code segment is executed?

```
String param = "ftp://ftp.google.com";
Connection ftpConnection = Connector.open(param);
```

   a. A warning message will be popped up to the user
   b. The `Connector.open(param)` will return `null`
   c. A `ConnectionNotFoundException` will be thrown
   d. The code will not be compiled
2. True or False: `DatagramConnection` interface is of circuit-oriented connection type.
   a. True
   b. False

3. Which of the following connection interfaces are optional that are not mandated in MIDP 2.0 specification?
   a. `HttpConnection`
   b. `CommConnection`
   c. `HttpsConnection`
   d. `SocketConnection`
   e. `ContentConnection`
4. Which of the following state sequence is the correct sequence for an HTTP connection to pass through?
   a. *setup, connected, closed*
   b. *setup, pending, connected, closed*
   c. *setup, connected, pending, closed*
   d. *setup, connected, pending, unconnected, closed*
5. True or False: `HttpsConnection` interface extends `SecureConnection` interface.
   a. True
   b. False
6. Which of the following connection strings can be used to create a TCP/IP server socket connection?
   a. serversocket://:8840
   b. socket://192.168.0.5:8840
   c. serversocket://192.168.0.5:8840
   d. socket://:8840
7. Assuming that datagram connection is supported, what will happen when the following code segment is executed?

```
String param = "datagram://";
UDPDatagramConnection datagramConnection =
(UDPDatagramConnection)Connector.open(param);
```

   a. A `ConnectionNotFoundException` will be thrown
   b. The code will not be compiled
   c. An available port will be allocated for this connection
   d. The `Connector.open(param)` will return `null`
8. Identify the correct statements about the `connection.close()` method.
   a. Calling `close()` method on the connection that has been closed has no effect
   b. There is an `open` method in the `Connection` interface along with the `close()` method of the `Connection` interface
   c. Even though the `Connection.close()` has been called, the input or output stream that has been opened before on that connection will still be open
   d. When a connection has been closed, an attempt to access the methods of the connection will cause an `IllegalAccessException` to be thrown
9. Identify the characteristic(s) of a UDP datagram connection.
   a. Delivery of datagrams is reliable.
   b. Duplicate datagrams transfer is protected.
   c. Data transmission in UDP datagram connection is faster than in TCP/IP connection.
   d. Ordering of datagrams is guaranteed.

10. Identify the exception that will be thrown, when a secure link cannot be established using `HttpsConnection`.

    a. `ConnectionNotFoundException` b. `InterruptedException`

    c. `CertificateException` d. `IllegalAccessException`

    e. `SecurityException`

Review Answers

1. c. `ConnectionNotFoundException` will be thrown during the execution, when the communication protocol specified is not supported, or the target specified in the connection string parameter cannot be found.
2. b. `DatagramConnection` interface is not of circuit-oriented connection type, but of datagram- or packet- oriented type.
3. b and d. MIDP 2.0 implementation must provide support for `HttpConnection` and `HttpsConnection` interfaces, and ContentConnection interface is part of GCF defined by the CLDC specification. `CommConnection` and `SocketConnection` are optional connections that the implementation might provide support.
4. a. An HTTP connection must exist in one of the three states throughout its lifetime: *setup*, *connected* and *closed.*
5. b. `HttpsConnection` interface extends `HttpConnection` interface, not `SecureConnection` interface. HTTPS is just a security-enhanced version of HTTP.
6. d. socket://<port> format is used to create a TCP/IP server socket connection by passing it into the `Connector.open` method.
7. c. The system will find an available port and allocate it to the connection, when no host and port is specified in the connection string of the `Connector.open`.
8. a and c. There is no `open` method in the `Connection` interface and an `IOException` will be thrown, when there is an attempt to access the closed connection.
9. c. Delivery and ordering of datagrams in a UDP datagram connection is not guaranteed and there is no mechanism to protect the duplicate datagrams in this kind of connection.
10. c. `CertificateException` will be thrown, when a secure link cannot be established for an HTTPS connection. It extends the `java.io.IOException`, but is located in `java.microedition.pki` package.

Exam Notes

☞ Write code using GCF specified by CLDC, recognizing its characteristics, use, classes and interfaces. This may include identification of the class hierarchy and relationships of GCF.

GCF

- GCF has been designed to provide maximum flexibility to its implementation while preserving uniformity. The following steps are typically followed to set up a connection using GCF classes.
  1. Create a URL to connect to. This is a string of the form `[schema]:[host][:port]`
  2. Use the factory class `Connector` to create a connection

     ```
     Connector.open(String url,
                    {int mode},
                    {int timeout}): Connection
     ```

     - The optional `mode` parameter can be `READ`, `WRITE`, or `READ_WRITE`
     - The default mode is `READ_WRITE`
     - If an unsupported mode is used, an `IllegalArgumentException` will be thrown.
     - Timeout can be used to specify that the caller wants to know about timeouts. If `true`, the protocol may throw an `InterruptedIOException` when timeout occurs. This is only a suggestion to the implementation and is not guaranteed.
  3. Cast the return value (a `Connection`) to the appropriate sub-interface of the `Connection`. The `Connector` framework will create an appropriate sub-interface based on the protocol given in the passed URL.
  4. Use the following methods to get the streams for the `Connection`:

     ```
     Connection.getInputStream()
     Connection.getOutputStream()
     Connection.getDataInputStream()
     Connection.getDataOutputStream()
     ```

  5. Subinterface-specific methods can be used to get further information from the stream.
  6. Use the `Connection.close()` method to close the stream.
  7. Once an `InputStream` or `OutputStream` (or its `Data` counterparts) is obtained, attempts to get another one of the same type will throw an `IOException`. For example, you cannot call `Connector.openInputStream` twice.

GCF Interfaces

- CLDC does not support any network-specific protocol. Only generic interfaces are provided by the CLDC, which are expected to be subclassed (or subinterfaced) by the profiles.
- The URL for a connection should be of the format `[protocol]:[host][:port][;parameters]`
- `Connector`
  - A factory to provide `Connection` interface implementations.
  - The `Connector` creates the suitable implementation based on protocol portion of the URL passed in its `open` method. The `protocol` portion is the substring of the URL from the beginning to the first occurring colon (:).

- ♦ Convenience methods for opening connection streams are also present. They have the same behavior as their counterparts in `Connection` subinterfaces.
- `Connection`
  - ♦ The superinterface that represents the most generic connection type.
  - ♦ The `open` method is not provided here as the `Connector` class should be used to create and open a connection.
- `InputConnection` (Serial input connection)
  - ♦ Implemented by devices from where the data can be read.
  - ♦ Provides the `openInputStream` and `openDataInputStream` methods.
- `OutputConnection` (Serial output connection)
  - ♦ Implemented by devices to which the data can be written.
  - ♦ Provides the `openOutputStream` and `openDataOutputStream` methods.
- `StreamConnection` (Circuit connection)
  - ♦ Implemented by devices that provide two-way communication.
  - ♦ Combines the `InputConnection` and `OutputConnection` interfaces.
- `ContentConnection` (Content-based connection like a web server connection)
  - ♦ A sub-interface of the `StreamConnection` that provides extra methods for getting content information, like type, length and encoding.
- `StreamConnectionNotifier` (Server portion of a client-server connection)
  - ♦ Implemented by server connections.
  - ♦ Accepts connections and notifies of the incoming connection. The `acceptAndOpen()` method is defined here.

MIDP Characteristics

- The baud rate specified in the `CommConnection` is only a suggestion. The device may set whatever is possible. The actual baud rate can be obtained using the `CommConnection.getBaudRate()` method.
- If no host or port is given in the URL of a `SocketConnection` or a `ServerSocketConnection` (socket://), the device will assign the next available free port. This can be obtained using the `getLocalPort()` method. The host name will also be assigned automatically. This will typically be the system property "`microedition.hostname`" if available.
- If the host portion is not specified in a datagram URL, the connection is treated as a server connection (that is, it can receive datagrams). If the host portion is specified, the connection is treated as a client connection (that is, it can send datagrams).
  - ♦ In the server mode, the port is the port where data is received. This is the port for both sending and receiving data.
  - ♦ In the client mode, the port is the port in the target system where the data is to be sent. The reply-to port is dynamically allocated.

- The `DatagramConnection.receive(Datagram)` is a blocking call.
- Length of a `Datagram`
  - When the `Datagram` is being sent, this represents the length of data to be sent.
  - Before receiving the `Datagram`, this represents the length of bytes to receive.
  - After receiving the `Datagram`, this represents the length of bytes received.
- The `Datagram.reset()` method resets the data of the `Datagram` (length, offset, and buffer).

Class Hierarchy Relationships

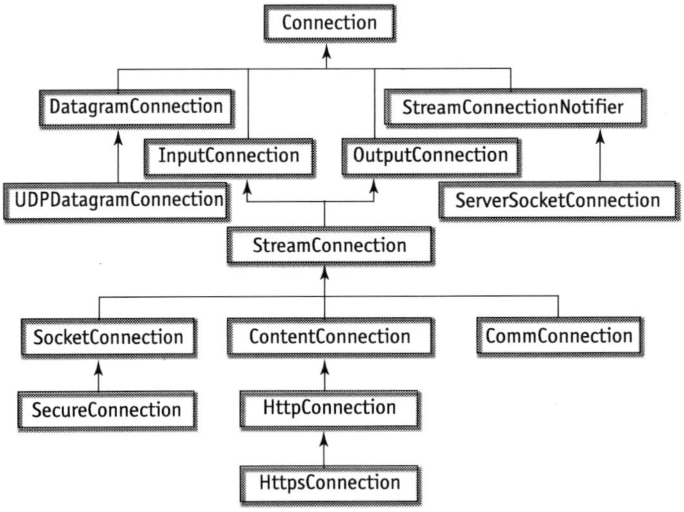

Figure 7.7 Hierarchy of MIDP 2.0 Networking interfaces, in addition to the CLDC's GCF

- In Fig. 7.7, shaded rectangles are the interfaces that are located at the profile level, MIDP 2.0 in this case.
- White rectangles are the interfaces that are located at the configuration level, CLDC 1.1 in this case.

☞ Write code for MIDP 2.0 networking, and issues and limitations related to HTTP, HTTPS and TCP/IP sockets and Datagrams, recognizing which connections are required and which are optional, as well as comparing the issues related to TCP/IP and UDP Datagrams.

Protocols Supported by MIDP 2.0

URL Format	*Protocol*	*Connection Subclass*
http://host[:port][params]	HTTP 1.1	`HttpConnection`
https://host[:port][params]	HTTPS	`HttpsConnection`

ssl://host:port	Secure Socket Layer (SSL)	`SecureConnection`
socket://[:port]	TCP/IP Server Socket	`ServerSocketConnection`
socket://host:port	TCP/IP Socket	`SocketConnection`
datagram://[host:port]	UDP	`UDPDatagramConnection`
comm:port_id[params]	Communication Devices (Ex. RS-232 Serial, IrDA)	`CommConnection`

Mandatory Connections

- `HttpConnection`
- `HttpsConnection`

Optional Connections

- `UDPDatagramConnection`
- `SocketConnection`
- `ServerSocketConnection`
- `CommConnection`
- `SecureConnection`

Issues with TCP/IP and Datagram Connections

- Delivery of data and duplicate protection is not guaranteed in UDP. Delivery is guaranteed in TCP/IP.
- The destination address is specified inside the `Datagram` for a UDP connection. It is specified in the connection for a TCP/IP connection.

☞ Write code using the MIDP 2.0 classes in the javax.microedition.io package, including code that correctly opens, closes and uses a network connection, using the implications of network blocking operations, scheme, connection number limitations and character encoding.

Opening Network Connection

- A connection can be created in one of the following ways:
  - ♦ `Connection connection = Connector.open("protocol://host:port;paramList");`
  - ♦ `Connection connection = Connector.open("protocol://host:port;paramList", Connector.READ);`
  - ♦ `Connection connection = Connector.open("protocol://host:port;paramList", Connector.WRITE, true);`
  - ♦ `InputStream in = Connector.openInputStream("protocol://host:port;paramList");`

- `DataInputStream dataIn = Connector.openDataInputStream("protocol://host:port;paramList");`
- `OutputStreamout = Connector.openOutputStream("protocol://host:port;paramList");`
- `DataOutputStream dataOut = Connector.openDataOutput Stream("protocol://host:port;paramList");`

- Typically, the connection returned in the first three options is typecast into an appropriate subinterface to get more information about the connection.

Examples of Valid URLs

URL	*Protocol Type*	*Connection Interface*
comm:com0;baudrate=19200	Serial connection protocol, typically to an RS-232 or IrDA port	`CommConnection`
http://www.google.com:80	HTTP	`HttpConnection`
https://www.verisign.com:8080	HTTPS	`HttpsConnection`
socket:// or socket://:8840	TCP/IP Server Socket	`ServerSocketConnection`
socket://192.168.0.44:8840	TCP/IP Socket	`SocketConnection`
datagram://123.144.15.88:6651	UDP	`UDPDatagramConnection`
ssl://icicibank.com:556	Secure Socket Layer	`SecureConnection`

Closing Connection

- Connections can be closed using the `Connection.close()` method.
- If a `Connection` is already closed, then calling this method has no effect.
- If the associated streams are open, then this method will wait till they are closed.
- In this case, the Stream objects can still be accessible, but an attempt to access a method of the `Connection` interface (or its subinterface) will result in an `IOException` to be thrown.
- This method is thread-safe.

☞ Given a problem scenario, troubleshoot networking issues for MIDP 2.0.

Exception	*Method*	*Reason*
ConnectionNotFoundException	All Connector's open methods and their variations	The connection target could not be found or the protocol type is not supported.
InterruptedIOException	Connector's open(String, int, boolean) and Datagram Connection's receive() and send()	The I/O operation has been interrupted or the timeout expires.
EOFException	DataInputStream's readXXX() methods	An end of file or end of stream has been reached, while data is being read to the stream.
IOException	All methods on a closed connection and open() method of InputStream Connection or OutputStream Connection interface	Calling methods of a closed connection, opening an input or output stream twice or opening a new input or output stream again once it is closed.
CertificateException	All Connector's open methods and their variations	A secure link cannot be established while opening a HTTPS connection or a secure socket stream connection
SecurityException	All Connector's open methods and their variations	Security violation occurs due to the user's denial on permission or the application does not have the right to use the API
IllegalArgumentException	All Connector's open methods and their variations	Invalid request parameters or inappropriate arguments have been passed into a method

8

Chapter

Persisting Data Using the Record Management System (RMS)

Exam Objectives

6.1 Develop code that correctly implements handling, sharing and removing RecordStores within MIDlet suites. (Section 8.1)

6.2 Develop code that correctly implements adding, retrieving, modifying, and deleting individual records in a RecordStore, and converting RecordStore record data to and from byte arrays, and that reflects performance implications. (Section 8.2)

6.3 Identify correct and incorrect statements or examples about filtering, comparing, event listening, and enumerating records in a RecordStore. (Section 8.3)

INTRODUCTION

Any reasonably complex application tends to have a need for its own space to store persistent data. Even a game needs a place to store persistent data. For instance, the player who can have Hamlet collect the most diamonds before Claudius the troll eats him should have this feat recognized in a hall of fame that lists the top ten high scores. Or perhaps Hamlet wants to save his game when he reaches a new level in the troll filled tunnels. Persistent storage is a fundamental element of any computing platform.

But persistent storage presents perhaps the biggest resource challenge to all micro devices. These devices certainly do not have the luxury of huge storage areas that desktop systems or enterprise systems enjoy. It hasn't been all that long since we had to conserve on persistent storage in the realm of personal computers. A few years ago, hard drives measured in GB were as fantastic as trolls. Now, of course, we have portable music devices that humble some of the hard drives I still have in my closet. For our purposes, MIDP 2.0 specifies a mechanism for persistent data storage called Record Management System (RMS). It specifies a modest 30KB of data space for an application—extremely tiny compared to desktop/enterprise systems. While this amount may be small, the ability to store even a small amount of persistent data can be employed to powerful effects.

The RMS model for data storage, as one might guess from the name, centers around the concept of a record. A record is simply the lowest-level unit of data storage and it holds a byte array. A collection of records are stored together in a container called record store. You could think of a record store as equivalent to a file in a flat file database system. Each record is roughly equivalent to each line in a flat file. In terms of namespace, a record store is associated with a MIDlet suite so that a record store's device-wise unique name consists of the name of its MIDlet suite plus its own name. The records within a record store are then indexed on a 1-based system. Access to an individual record store can be configured so that the data is available only to the suite under whose namespace it belongs, or so that it is visible to all suites on the device. This is up to the developer.

As with many aspects of the MIDP, the implementation is left entirely to the device manufacturer. In this case, we have no idea how the data will be persisted, although we can be sure that is probably not on a floppy. The MIDP simply defines the classes that expose the implementation's functionality in a platform-dependent manner. The classes for the RMS are contained in `javax.microedition.rms` package of the MIDP API. Figure 8.1 gives an overview of these classes. We will go through these classes in detail throughout this chapter.

8.1 RECORD STORES

As we said in the introduction, the RMS model centers around the concept of a record store. It should not come as a surprise then that the central class of the RMS API is the `RecordStore` class. The `RecordStore` class represents a collection of records, each of which is actually a byte array. Again, a record store is analogous to a file in a flat file type of database. In a flat file, the lowest-level unit of data storage is the line. Indeed, in flat file systems these lines are often referred to as records. Before we go on to the details of how to create and store actual data, we should first get familiar with the mechanisms for creating/opening, examining and closing record stores themselves.

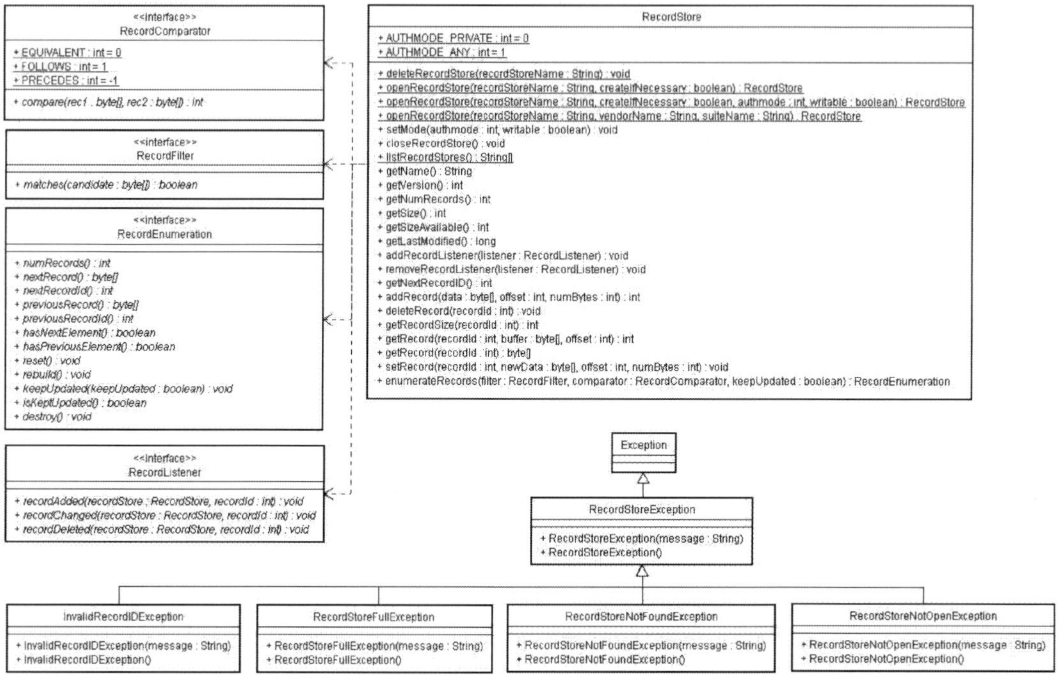

Figure 8.1 `javax.microedition.rms` package of RMS

8.1.1 Creating/Opening Record Stores

Before we can do anything, we need to know how to create and access record stores. The following `static` method in the `RecordStore` class can be used to achieve this.

```
public static RecordStore openRecordStore(String recordStoreName,
                                          boolean createIfNecessary)
                                   throws RecordStoreException,
                                          RecordStoreFullException,
                                          RecordStoreNotFoundException,
                                          IllegalArgumentException
```

Let's break this down gently. The `recordStoreName` is the name that we want to give to the record store. This is a simple string that makes sense to the application and, more importantly, the person who is going to maintain the application.

Typically, Java is very generous with names. You can often find lengthy method names. In fact, many encourage the use of long and descriptive names to make the code more readable.

However, in case of Java ME, we cannot take such liberty due to resource constraints. While no performance impact comes in having long method names, it does have a resource impact when record store names are long, as they are stored in the device memory, where each byte really counts.

As a result, the MIDP specification restricts the name of a record store to 32 characters. If the name of the record store passed into the method contains more than 32 characters or if it is a `null` or an empty string, this method will throw an `IllegalArgumentException`.

Exam Tip

The name of a record store must be 1 to 32 characters long. If it is empty, `null`, or more than 32 characters long, an `IllegalArgumentException` will be thrown.

The `createIfNecessary` flag indicates whether a new record store needs to be created if one with such name does not exist already in the device. By setting this flag to `true`, an application can create a new record store. If the flag is set to `false` and if the record store does not exist, a `RecordStoreNotFoundException` will be thrown.

If there is not enough space in the device for creating a new record store, a `RecordStoreFullException` will be thrown.

For any other fault that prevents the device from completing the application's request, a `RecordStoreException` will be thrown.

As mentioned earlier, the name of a record store is made unique by combining the name passed with the values of the `MIDlet-Vendor` and `MIDlet-Name` attributes, where `MIDlet-Vendor` represents the person or company that created the application and `MIDlet-Name` represents the name of the MIDlet suite.

Until MIDP 1.0, all record stores were considered the exclusive property of the application that created the record store. That is, if there is a bunch of applications in the device, they cannot access any other application's record store other than their own. MIDP 2.0 introduced the concept of shared record stores, which we will discuss in the following subsection.

8.1.2 Shared Record Stores

As the name implies, shared record stores are record stores that can be shared across applications installed in a device. To provide this feature, a new overloaded `openRecordStore` method was added to the `RecordStore` class.

```
public static RecordStore openRecordStore (String recordStoreName,
                                           boolean createIfNecessary,
                                           int authmode,
                                           boolean writable)
```

```
                                    throws RecordStoreException,
                                           RecordStoreFullException,
                                           RecordStoreNotFoundException,
                                           IllegalArgumentException
```

As you can see, the method signature does not differ much except for the addition of two new parameters. So, let's just look at the new parameters in detail.

The `authmode` parameter means authorization mode. This tells the level of visibility of a record store. There are two possible modes.

`AUTHMODE_PRIVATE` indicates that the record store is the exclusive property of the application that creates it. Sounds familiar? It should. With this mode, the record store behaves exactly in the same way as it would have if it had been created using the previous `openRecordStore` method with only two parameters.

`AUTHMODE_ANY` indicates that the record store can be accessed by other applications. Note that other applications mean any other application, including those written by other developers or companies. Hence, you must be careful before opening the doors of your record store as this might pose a potential security risk.

If the record store with the given name already exists, the authorization mode is ignored and a reference to the existing record store is returned. In other words, you cannot trick fiddling around with the authorization mode using this method once a record store has been created.

Exam Tip

There are only two possible values for the `authmode` parameter—`AUTHMODE_PRIVATE` or `AUTHMODE_ANY`. An attempt to pass any other value (since this is an integer) will result in an `IllegalArgumentException`.

However, you can change the authorization mode of a record store after it has been created. For this you must call the following method.

```
public void setMode(int authmode, boolean writable)
                                 throws RecordStoreException,
                                        SecurityException,
                                        IllegalArgumentException
```

Calling this method comes with a caveat. Only the application that created the record store can change the authorization mode of the record store. This is quite reasonable, as you don't want any other application to suddenly make the record store private and deny access to the application that created it!

If an application attempts to do such a blasphemous act, a `SecurityException` will be thrown by the implementation.

Exam Tip

Only the application that created the record store can modify the authorization mode of the record store. If attempted by any other application, a `SecurityException` will be thrown.

The `IllegalArgumentException` will be thrown from the `setMode` method if the authorization mode is not one of the two values described above.

The uniqueness of the name becomes apparent when we look at the method an application must use to open a record store that was not created by it or, in other words, a record store that was shared by another application.

```
public static RecordStore openRecordStore(String recordStoreName,
                                         String vendorName,
                                         String suiteName)
                                  throws RecordStoreException,
                                  RecordStoreNotFoundException
```

Here, the `vendorName` represents the vendor of the MIDlet suite that created the record store and `suiteName` represents the name of the MIDlet suite that created the record store.

One thing we have not mentioned so far is the `writeable` parameter of the overloaded `openRecordStore` method and the `setMode` method. As you can guess, it indicates if other applications can write to the shared record store. If this parameter set to `true`, other applications can write to the record store. If it is set to `false`, other applications can read from the record store but not write to it.

8.1.3 Record Store Features

Once we have some actual record stores to work with, we might find that we need to obtain some information about a particular record store. The `RecordStore` class itself contains a number of methods that can be used to obtain some meta-information regarding the store. These methods range from getting generic information on the record store like its name, version and so forth to more specific information like the size of a record in the record store.

Naming

Since many applications can access the record stores in a device, there must be a way to uniquely identify each record store. To achieve this, a convention is followed for naming the record stores.

The name of a record store is constructed based on the following pieces of information:

- The name provided by the user
- The value of the `MIDlet-Vendor` attribute of the application that created the record store

- The value of the `MIDlet-Name` attribute of the application that created the record store

The name of a record store can be obtained at runtime by invoking the following method:

```
public String getName() throws RecordStoreNotOpenException
```

As can be inferred from the method signature, the method will work only if the record store in question has already been opened.

Exam Tip

The name of a record store is uniquely identified using a combination of the record store's name and the values of the `MIDlet-Name` and `MIDlet-Vendor` attributes of the application that created the record store.

Versioning

A record store maintains the number of times it has been modified. A record store is considered to be modified if

- A record has been added to the record store
- A record has been deleted from the record store
- A record has been updated in the record store

Interestingly, no specific requirements have been set in the specification about the convention for the version. All the specification says is that the version number should increase upon successive modifications by a constant value and that the increment should be a positive value.

In a simple implementation, the first version may be 0 and may increment by 1 for every modification, but this is not guaranteed.

The current version number of a record store can be obtained by invoking the method

```
public int getVersion() throws RecordStoreNotOpenException
```

As can be inferred from the method signature, the method will work only if the record store in question has already been opened.

The application can also get the time when the record store was last modified by invoking the method

```
public long getLastModified() throws RecordStoreNotOpenException
```

The return value is in the format similar to that of the time returned by the `System.currentTimeMillis()` method.

Listing Record Stores

You can obtain a list of all the record stores owned (or created) by an application by calling the method

```
public static String[] listRecordStores()
```

Note that this will return only the record stores owned by the application, not including the ones that are created by other applications but visible to the application. In other words, shared record stores that can be accessed by the application (as will be discussed later in this chapter) will not be listed in the array. If the application does not own any record stores, the method would return `null`.

Getting the Size

The `RecordStore` class API provides some handy convenience methods to figure out the amount of space consumed by the record store and the amount of space that is available in the device. This can be used effectively by the application in managing its data. For example, before attempting to store any data, the application can check if enough memory is available and warn the user if there is not enough space.

While the exception handling mechanism can also be used to achieve the same result by checking for an exception when an attempt is made to store a record, the previous approach would be more effective and potentially have a better performance.

To get the amount of space occupied by the record store, the method

```
public int getSize() throws RecordStoreNotOpenException
```

can be called. The value returned by the method indicates the size of the record store including any overhead space in *bytes*.

To get the amount of space remaining in the device, the method

```
public int getSizeAvailable() throws RecordStoreNotOpenException
```

can be called. The value returned by the method indicates the additional space available (less the overhead space required for storing a record or record store) in *bytes*. Figure 8.2 illustrates the meaning of the two methods.

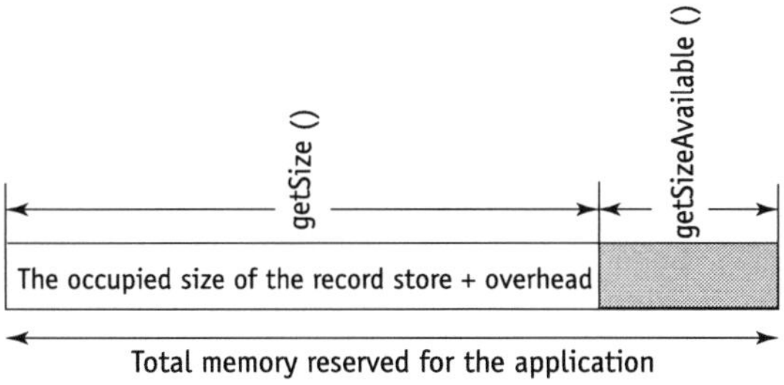

Figure 8.2 The meaning of the `getSize()` and `getSizeAvailable()` methods

Since space required for overhead is not indicated in the return value, the application should provide some leeway around the return value.

Getting Information about Records

Once a record store has been created and is in use, an application that accesses the store might want to get some meta-information about the records contained in the record store. The `RecordStore` class provides a bunch of convenience methods for this. The following table provides a list of these methods and explains why they are there. For all the methods mentioned below, the record store should have been opened already. Otherwise, a `RecordStoreNotOpenException` will be thrown.

Table 8.1 Methods that get information about records in a record store

Method signature	*Rationale*
`int getNumRecords()`	Gets the number of records currently in the record store.
`int getNextRecordID()`	Returns the ID that would be assigned when a record is added to the store. If multiple record stores are used with related information (much like a simple relational database where multiple tables are connected through the corresponding primary keys), it would be essential for the application to know the ID (primary key) that would be assigned to the record so that the record in the other store can refer to it appropriately. This need arises mainly because record ID for a record cannot be set manually by the application. It is automatically assigned by the record store implementation (like sequence numbers in a database) This method also throws a `RecordStoreException` if any other issue (other than record store not being open) happens.

We made some references that record store should be open before we call some of the methods. We should now see how to close a record store.

8.1.4 Closing Record Stores

After we finish working with our record store, the civil thing to do would be to close it. Closing a record store is a relatively simple activity. All you need to do is call the `closeRecordStore()` method on the `RecordStore` object.

If the record store is already closed, it will throw a `RecordStoreNotOpenException`. If it cannot be closed for any other reason, it will throw a `RecordStoreException`. One important thing to keep in mind is that the `closeRecordStore()` method should be called as many times as the `openRecordStore()` method is called on the same record store. Until then, the record store will not actually be closed.

Now that we have successfully figured out how to create, open and close record stores, let's see how we can populate the store with records and retrieve it.

8.2 C.R.U.D!

Now that we know how to work with record stores, we need to learn how to create and store the data that goes in and comes out of the record stores, records in our case. Any persistence mechanism must support four basic operations:

1. Create data
2. Retrieve data
3. Update data
4. Delete data

RMS is no exception to this requirement. The methods to perform these operations are present in the `RecordStore` class.

8.2.1 Creating Records

As mentioned earlier, the data we store in a record store is called a record. In reality, a record is an array of bytes. The signature of the method that adds a record to a record store presents this point very clearly.

```
public int addRecord(byte[] data, int offset, int numBytes)
                                throws RecordStoreNotOpenException,
                                       RecordStoreException,
                                       RecordStoreFullException,
                                       SecurityException
```

The `data` itself is a simple array of bytes. It is possible to use a single byte array to represent multiple records in order to avoid having a number of byte arrays in the application. For this reason, the other two parameters are provided. The `offset` represents the index of the first byte to be considered for storage. The `numBytes` represents the total number of bytes to store from the `offset` point.

It is also possible to have an empty record (a record that contains no data). To achieve this, you just have to pass `null` as the `data` parameter in the method.

Each CRUD operation in RMS is blocking and atomic. That is, the method will not return until the operation is performed (or an exception is thrown). The return value of the method represents the ID that has been assigned to the record that was just added into the system. RMS does not allow an application to set the ID of a record. Instead, it assigns one automatically every time a record is added to a record store. In order to make the ID unique, a simple sequencing mechanism is used. The first record ID begins with 1 and is incremented by one every time a new record is added into the record store. If a record is deleted, the ID of the deleted record cannot be reused. The ID is just lost forever.

Exam Tip

All record operations are atomic and blocking.
The record ID is assigned automatically by RMS and is a sequence number beginning with 1.
If a record is deleted, the record ID cannot be reused.

Creating records in the form of byte arrays, to me, is somewhat similar to writing programs in assembly language after having spent years in learning Java! While from a library perspective, it makes a lot of sense to provide an API that is as flexible as possible, such a method might be too cumbersome for a typical application.

There are several ways to work around with this issue. Let's have a look at them, shall we?

Creating String Records

The first complex data structure that comes to mind is a simple `String` object. Fortunately, it's easy to convert `String` objects to its constituent bytes. The `String` class has a method as follows:

```
public byte[] getBytes()
```

It can't get simpler than that! All the application has to do is invoke the method on the `String` object that it wants to store and pass the result as a parameter to our `addRecord` method.

This is fine for `String` objects. How about a more complex scenario like a record having multiple fields (similar to multiple columns' values in a single row of a table), each being a different data type?

Creating Records with Different Data Types

The `java.io` package in the CLDC API contains two classes called `ByteArrayOutputStream` and `DataOutputStream`. The `ByteArrayOutputStream`, as the name implies, is capable of taking a byte stream and converting it into a byte array. A stream is a different representation of data to which the elements of data (bytes) can be written sequentially. It is possible to feed one type of stream into another type of stream and provide a higher level of abstraction. The `DataOutputStream` is one such stream, which can be connected to a `ByteArrayOutputStream`. The `DataOutputStream` in turn provides methods that can be used to convert primitive data types and `String` objects into their corresponding bytes. The best part about this conversion is that the stream automatically figures out where one value ends and another one begins when different data types are written to the stream.

This concept can be used as our advantage to store primitive data types into a record store and even different values of data types in the same record. Let's take a look at the following code snippets as an example.

```
ByteArrayOutputStream bout = new ByteArrayOutputStream();
DataOutputStream out = new DataOutputStream(bout);
out.writeInt(expense.getType().getId());
out.writeLong(expense.getDate());
out.writeUTF(expense.getDescription());
out.writeDouble(expense.getAmount());
byte[] bytes = bout.toByteArray();
```

This way of creating records is much more convenient from the application's perspective. Now that we have added a record to the record store, it would be a good idea to find out how to get it back.

8.2.2 Retrieving Records

There are two methods in the `RecordStore` class that let us retrieve records from a record store. Let's look at the first one.

```
public byte[] getRecord(int recordId)
                        throws  RecordStoreNotOpenException,
                                RecordStoreException,
                                InvalidRecordIDException
```

Quite simple, right? You pass in a record ID and you get back a bunch of bytes that the record represents. The most important thing to note here is that the data returned is a copy of the data stored inside the device, not a reference to the location. That is, if you modify the contents of the returned array, the actual contents stored in the device will not be altered.

If the record does not contain any data, the method will return `null`. On the other hand, if the record ID passed is invalid or not present in the record store, an `InvalidRecordIDException` will be thrown.

In addition, there is a more complex method that can be used to retrieve the data and put it in an existing byte array.

```
public int getRecord(int recordId, byte[] buffer, int offset)
                throws RecordStoreNotOpenException,
                       RecordStoreException,
                       InvalidRecordIDException
```

In this case, instead of getting the byte array back, we want the method store the byte array returned into an array that we already have. The `buffer` represents the array where we want to copy the data retrieved from the record store and the `offset` tells the method the starting position in the array from where it'll start replacing the contents with the new data. The return parameter represents the number of bytes that were copied into the array. This can be used to determine the size of the data that was retrieved.

Retrieving String Records

In the previous section, we explained how a `String` object could be stored as a record in a record store. Let's see how to retrieve such a record from the record store.

The `String` object once again comes to the rescue. A `String` object can be easily constructed from a byte array using one of its constructors.

```
public String(byte[] bytes)
```

All we have to do is get the byte array from the record store using the `getRecord` method and pass the returned value to the constructor of the `String` class and voila! We have a `String` object in our hand.

Retrieving Records with Different Data Types

In the previous section, we explained how a record having elements of different data types could be created. Let's see how we can retrieve them from the record store.

In order to do this, we simply do the reverse of what we did previously. There are two complementary classes called `ByteArrayInputStream` and `DataInputStream` in the `java.io` package of the CLDC API. The `ByteArrayInputStream` takes in a byte array and converts it into a byte stream. The `DataInputStream` can then be placed on top of the `ByteArrayInputStream`. Then, the application can use the methods in the `DataInputStream` class to retrieve the underlying bytes as primitive data types or `String` objects.

If the byte stream represents different data types, the corresponding methods must be called in the same order in order to retrieve the data accurately. The key point to note here is the order of retrieval. If the methods are called in a different order, the methods might return inaccurate values or might even throw exceptions. Let's take a look at the following code snippets as an example.

```
ByteArrayInputStream bin = new ByteArrayInputStream(record);
DataInputStream in = new DataInputStream(bin);
long date = in.readLong();
String description = in.readUTF();
double amount = in.readDouble();
```

The code example assumes that the record is composed of three fields: a date field of `long` type, a description field of `String` type and an amount field of `double` type. If the fields are read from the stream in a different order, inaccurate values might be returned. Figure 8.3 displays the fields of different data types in a record.

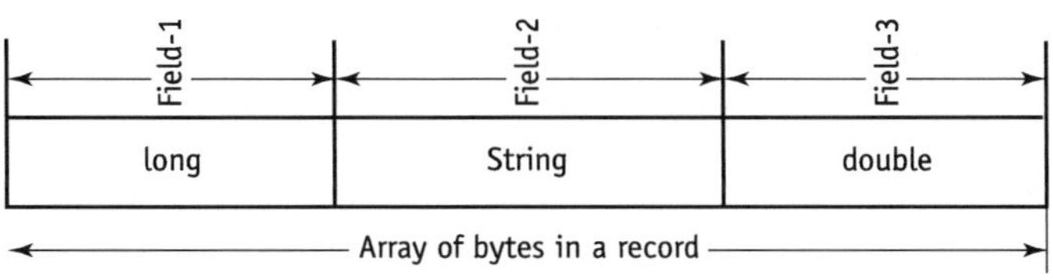

Figure 8.3 Fields of a record containing different data types

Now that we know how to create and retrieve records from a record store, let's take a look at how we can update existing records in a record store.

8.2.3 Updating Records

We have created the data for a record and have retrieved it successfully. The next potential operation would be to update or modify the data in a record. The signature of the method to do this is quite similar to the one that we use to add a record into the record store.

```
public void setRecord(int recordId, byte[] newData,
                      int offset, int numBytes)
        throws RecordStoreNotOpenException,
                      InvalidRecordIDException,
                      RecordStoreException,
                      RecordStoreFullException,
                      SecurityException
```

The `recordId` represents the ID of the record to be modified. The `newData` contains the byte array that would replace the existing data. If only a portion of the array needs to be copied to the record in the record store, the `offset` parameter can be used to specify the starting index in the array from where the data should be copied. The `numBytes` represents the number of bytes to be copied from the `offset` index.

From the exceptions that could be thrown by the method, one interesting point can be noted. If we replace an existing record with a new record, why do we need to declare `RecordStoreFullException`? It is because of two possible reasons: The metadata information might require more space, and more importantly, the data that is being replaced is larger than the data that is already there. That's right. RMS does not pose any restriction on the size of the data to be replaced except that the size should not be so large that it cannot fit on the storage space. Conversely, what happens if the data being replaced is shorter than the one being replaced? No worries. The calls, if made using the streams, do not get affected.

It is important to note that RMS does not have any locking mechanism for thread-safe operations. While each call is guaranteed to be atomic, that does not mean that an application will have a corruption-free data when it uses multiple threads. For example, if there are two threads in an application, both modifying the same record in the same record store, the data that finally gets stored in the record may vary depending on which thread wrote first and which one wrote last. It is up to the application to ensure that the desired data is written to the record store.

We should be able to create, retrieve and update records in a record store by now. The last operation that we need to go for is deleting records which we won't need anymore in the future.

8.2.4 Deleting Records

We have come to the last CRUD operation—deleting records. This simple method takes in a record ID and deletes the appropriate record.

```
public void deleteRecord(int recordId)
                throws RecordStoreNotOpenException,
                       InvalidRecordIDException,
                       RecordStoreException
```

The exceptions are quite intuitive. For the call to succeed, the record store should be open, the passed ID should be valid, and nothing catastrophic should happen.

As mentioned earlier, once a record is deleted, the ID of the record cannot be reused. It is lost into oblivion forever for that record store.

We have covered all the basic operations that we need to manage a record store. Now let's see the other classes that the API provides, which can be used for getting the most out of record stores.

8.3 ADVANCED FEATURES

The following set of features work on top of a record store to provide additional capabilities like going through the records in an iterative fashion, filtering records based on some criteria, comparing two records for equality, and listening for record store changes.

8.3.1 Listening to Record Events

It might be desirable sometimes to listen for changes to a record store and act accordingly. One such scenario might be when two applications sharing a record store are active at the same time and want to know if the other application modified the contents of the shared record store.

For this, a simple event listener mechanism, very similar to the ones you see in the `java.awt.event` package, is used. The RMS API provides an interface called the `RecordListener` that an application can implement if it is interested in listening for record store changes. An implementing application must override the following methods:

```
public void recordAdded(RecordStore recordStore, int recordId)
public void recordChanged(RecordStore recordStore, int recordId)
public void recordDeleted(RecordStore recordStore, int recordId)
```

As the names suggest, these methods are triggered when a record is added to the record store, a record is modified in the record store and a record is deleted from the record store respectively. The parameters provide a handle to the record store itself and give us the identifier of the record that was affected.

An application that has implemented this interface can register to a record store by passing itself as a parameter to the record store using the following method:

```
public void addRecordListener(RecordListener listener)
```

At any time, if the application wishes to stop listening for events, it can do so by invoking the following method in the record store by passing itself as the parameter:

```
public void removeRecordListener(RecordListener listener)
```

The `RecordEnumeration` interface that we shall see next, uses the listener to update itself.

8.3.2 Enumerating Records

One of the most common things that an application would want to do with its record store is to go through its contents. The RMS API provides a special interface to do this—the `RecordEnumeration` interface.

You can get an implementation of this interface for a record store by invoking the following method on the record store:

```
public RecordEnumeration enumerateRecords(RecordFilter filter,
                                          RecordComparator comparator,
                                          boolean keepUpdated)
                                    throws RecordStoreNotOpenException
```

As you can see, the method takes in instances of two other classes that we have not come across so far—the `RecordFilter` and the `RecordComparator`. Let's forget those classes for this section. We'll cover them later. These two parameters are optional and hence, we can pass `null` to both of them.

Going through Records

The method returns a `RecordEnumeration` interface implementation that can be used to go through the records in a record store. As with a typical iteration mechanism, the order in which the records are returned is not defined. That is, don't expect the returned records to be sorted in any way.

Exam Tip

`RecordEnumeration` is bidirectional. It is possible to go forward and backward through the iteration. If the `RecordComparator` object passed is `null`, the order of the records enumerated is not defined.

The iteration is bidirectional. That is, you can iterate forward or backward. There are four simple methods provided in the `RecordEnumeration` interface that let us do this.

```
public boolean hasNextElement()
public boolean hasPreviousElement()
public byte[] nextRecord() throws InvalidRecordIDException,
                                  RecordStoreNotOpenException,
                                  RecordStoreException
public byte[] previousRecord() throws InvalidRecordIDException,
                                      RecordStoreNotOpenException,
                                      RecordStoreException
public int nextRecordId() throws InvalidRecordIDException
public int previousRecordId() throws InvalidRecordIDException
```

Looking at these methods, some potential error scenarios pop up in our mind. What if we call the `previousRecord()` right after we open a record store? What if we call the `hasNextElement()` or `hasPreviousElement()` before we open a record store?

If you call the `previousRecord()` right after you open a record store, the last element in the record store is returned. Then you can keep calling `previousRecord()` till the first element is reached, after which there will be no more elements. This sounds reasonable as the `RecordEnumeration` is supposed to be bidirectional.

If the `hasNextElement()` or `hasPreviousElement()` method is called before the corresponding record store is opened, it will return `false`.

One difference between the `nextRecord()` and the `nextRecordId()` is that the first method returns a copy of the record and the second method returns the ID of the record. Note that both methods will result in the `RecordEnumeration`'s internal pointer moving forward. That is, if there are records, say, 1 & 2 in the record store and you call the `nextRecordId()` and then call the `nextRecord()`, the first method will return 1 and the second method will return the contents of the record with the ID 2. The same concept is applied to `previousRecord()` and `previousRecordId()` methods as well.

Now that we have looked at the essentials, let's go behind the scenes and understand how the `RecordEnumeration` actually works. A `RecordEnumeration` implementation internally contains a list of record IDs that it can go through. This list of IDs is created when the `RecordEnumeration` implementation is created (which would be when the `enumerateRecords` method of the `RecordStore` instance is called). Whenever the enumeration methods are called, the list pointer is updated appropriately.

Updating Enumeration's Index

At this point, you are probably getting a nagging feeling. If a separate list is constructed when the `RecordEnumeration` implementation is created first, how is it maintained later on? For example, after the `RecordEnumeration` implementation is obtained, what will happen to the list when one of the records is deleted from the underlying record store? This is a typical scenario when indexes are created off a data store.

The `RecordEnumeration` interface cleverly passes the buck to the programmer. If you go back and look at the parameters of the `enumerateRecords` method in the `RecordStore`, you will see a third parameter called `keepUpdated`. As the name suggests, this parameter can be used to let the `RecordEnumeration` implementation know whether it must constantly keep updating its record store.

Let's say we want the `RecordEnumeration` to be accurate at all times. Therefore, we set the `keepUpdated` parameter to `true`. Now, how does the `RecordEnumeration` keep its indexes current? Remember the `RecordListener` interface that we discussed some time back where we said that it could be used to listen for changes in a record store. Well, the `RecordEnumeration` implementation implements the interface and registers itself as a listener to the `RecordStore` that it represents. Now, whenever the enumeration is notified of the change in the record store, it rebuilds its list and hence, stays current.

One important thing to note here is that the whole process of rebuilding the indexes can be quite time-consuming (and memory-consuming), depending on the size of the record store and the frequency of the changes made to the record store. So, one should be very careful before turning this option on.

Exam Tip

The resources consumed by the `RecordEnumeration` implementation can be freed by calling its `destroy()` method. Use this method after you are done using the enumeration for optimal performance.

If you don't want to update the enumeration all the time but still want to keep the enumeration current manually, there is another option. Set the `keepUpdated` parameter to `false` when getting the `RecordEnumeration` and call the `rebuild()` method of the `RecordEnumeration` whenever you need to update the enumeration's indexes.

There is also a mechanism to revert the indexes back to its original state – the state when the `RecordEnumeration` was first created. This can be done by calling the `reset()` method of the enumeration.

It is also possible to turn on or off the automatic index update by calling the `keepUpdated(boolean keepUpdated)` method of the enumeration. At any point, you can also check if the enumeration has its automatic update turned on by calling the `isKeptUpdated()` method.

Exam Tip

The index of a record enumeration can be automatically updated by setting its `keepUpdated` parameter to `true`. However, this comes at a price. Turning the parameter on may severely hurt the performance of the record enumeration.

Finally, when the associated record store is closed, the `RecordEnumeration` becomes invalid. After this, any method invoked on the enumeration will throw a `RecordStoreNotOpenException`, even if the record store is opened again. All the condition methods will return `false`.

Earlier, we mentioned that the enumeration returns records in no specific order. What if we want the records to be returned in a specific order? The next section discusses how to achieve this.

8.3.3 Comparing Records

To control the order of the records returned by a `RecordEnumeration`, the `RecordComparator` interface could be used. The `RecordComparator` works in a fashion similar to that of the `Comparator` interface in the Java Collections Framework. It contains one single method

```
public int compare(byte[] rec1, byte[] rec2)
```

The method can return one of three pre-defined values:

- `EQUIVALENT`, if the records contain the same value
- `PRECEDES`, if `rec1` precedes `rec2`
- `FOLLOWS`, if `rec1` follows `rec2`

You can pass an instance of a `RecordComparator` interface implementation to the `enumerateRecords` method to control the order of records returned by the enumerator.

Ordering records is quite similar to the `ORDER BY` clause in a SQL statement. It controls the order in which results are returned from a search. Going by this analogy, what happens if you want to include a SQL-like `WHERE` clause? The `RecordFilter` comes to the rescue.

8.3.4 Filtering Records

A `RecordFilter` interface implementation can be passed to the `enumerateRecords` method while getting the record store's enumerator to control the records returned by the enumerator.

The interface, once again, contains one single method

```
public boolean matches(byte[] candidate)
```

What all the implementations have to do is analyze the candidate passed and say whether it should be filtered. If it should be filtered, the method should return `true` (the candidate matches the filter condition) and if it should not be filtered, the method should return `false` (the candidate does not match the filter condition).

If a filter is used while getting the `RecordEnumeration` implementation, the enumeration would consult the filter before returning a record. Thus, the enumeration will act like a SQL `SELECT` statement with a `WHERE` clause. The beauty of this architecture is that for different types of `WHERE` clauses, you can create different implementations of the `RecordFilter` interface and pass the appropriate one to the `enumerateRecords` method as required. This makes implementing different types of search queries very easy.

Now that we know everything we should know about records, record stores and advanced features that come with RMS, let's put all pieces together to complete the puzzle and clearly see the picture of RMS.

8.4 PUTTING IT ALL TOGETHER

We have talked about a lot of classes and interfaces in this chapter. One good way to remember all these is to actually put them in a working example so that it sticks to the mind. So, let's try to create a simple application that uses a record store and see how all these classes and interfaces are used in real world.

8.4.1 Problem Definition

We are going to build a simple expense tracker application that can be used to keep track of expenses incurred on a vacation. Since a vacation implies being away from your home, a mobile device is an ideal target platform to deploy the application.

An expense has three attributes.

1. Type of expense (a pre-defined list)
2. The amount (in dollars)
3. The date when the expense was made

Assume that there already is user interface for this expense tracking software (we have discussed the user interface in the MIDP UI chapter). Our task is to create a storage mechanism where the expenses incurred can be stored safely and reliably.

The following queries can be performed on the database.

1. Add an expense
2. Delete an existing expense
3. Get all expenses
4. Get all expenses based on the expense type
5. Get the most expensive expenses

Let's create an interface to abstract the storage mechanism from the rest of the system.

8.4.2 Implementation

Before we implement the way to access the data, let's first create an interface that would define the methods that the implementation should, er..., implement.

Listing 8.1: The* `IExpenseDAO` *interface

```
package com.scmadkit.ch08;

import javax.microedition.rms.*;

/**
 * This interface provides the API that must be implemented by the
 * DataAccessObject that would store/retrieve/delete records in the
 * underlying persistence system.
 *
 * @author Sathya.Srinivasan
 * @version 1.0
 */
public interface IExpenseDAO {
  //~ Methods ---------------------------------------------

  /**
   * Adds a record into the record store.
   *
   * @param expense The expense to be added into the record store.
   *
   * @return The expense object containing newly-created ID in the
   * record store
   *
   * @throws   RecordStoreException If the record cannot be added for
   *           unexpected reasons.
   * @throws   RecordStoreNotOpenException If the record store cannot
   *           be created.
   * @throws   RecordStoreFullException If the record store does not
   *           have enough space.
   */
  public Expense add(Expense expense)
              throws RecordStoreException,
                     RecordStoreNotOpenException,
                     RecordStoreFullException;

  /**
   * Gets all the records in the record store.
   *
   * @return All the stored expenses as an array.
   *
   * @throws RecordStoreNotOpenException If the record store cannot
   *         be opened.
```

```
 * @throws RecordStoreException If the array cannot be created for
 *         any other reason.
 */
public Expense[] allRecords()
                 throws RecordStoreNotOpenException,
                        RecordStoreException;

/**
 * Deletes the passed record.
 *
 * @param expense The expense to be deleted.
 *
 * @throws RecordStoreException If the record cannot be deleted
 *         for unexpected reasons.
 * @throws RecordStoreNotOpenException If the record store cannot
 *         be opened.
 * @throws InvalidRecordIDException If the expense passed contains
 *         an invalid id.
 */
public void delete(Expense expense)
             throws RecordStoreException,
                    RecordStoreNotOpenException,
                    InvalidRecordIDException;

/**
 * Gets the most expensive expenses.
 *
 * @param recordsToReturn The number of expenses to return.
 *
 * @return  An array of most expensive expenses. If the number of
 *          records in the record store is less than the records
 *          requested, all records in the record store sorted by
 *          the expense amount in descending order will be returned.
 *
 * @throws  RecordStoreException If the records cannot be
 *          retrieved for unexpected reasons.
 * @throws  RecordStoreNotOpenException If the record store cannot
 *          be opened.
 */
public Expense[] mostExpensiveExpenses(int recordsToReturn)
                 throws RecordStoreException,
                        RecordStoreNotOpenException;

/**
 * Gets the records based on a certain record type.
 *
 * @param type The type of expense to be used as a filter.
 *
```

```
     * @return An array of expenses that match the passed criteria.
     *
     * @throws RecordStoreException If the records cannot be
     *         retrieved for unexpected reasons.
     * @throws RecordStoreNotOpenException If record store cannot
     *         be opened.
     */
    public Expense[] recordsFor(ExpenseType type)
                      throws RecordStoreException,
                             RecordStoreNotOpenException;
}
```

As you can see, an expense has been represented in the API as a data structure. So, let's define the structure.

Listing 8.2: The **`Expense`** *data structure*

```
package com.scmadkit.ch08;
/**
 * This class is a data structure that represents an Expense.
 *
 * @author Sathya.Srinivasan
 * @version 1.0
 */
public class Expense {
   //~ Instance fields ——————————————————————
   private ExpenseType type;
   private double amount;
   private int id;
   private long date;
   private String description;
   //~ Constructors ————————————————————————-
     /**
    * Creates a new Expense object.
    *
    * @param type Type of expense.
    * @param amount The amount incurred in this expense.
    * @param date The date when the expense happened.
    */
   public Expense(ExpenseType type, double amount, long date) {
      this.setType(type);
      this.setAmount(amount);
      this.setDate(date);
      this.setDescription(description);
   }
   //~ Methods ———————————————————————
   /**
    * Sets the amount for this expense.
```

```
 *
 * @param amount The amount incurred in this expense.
*/
public void setAmount(double amount) {
  this.amount = amount;
}

/**
 * Gets the amount for this expense.
 *
 * @return Amount incurred in this expense.
 */
public double getAmount() {
   return amount;
}

/**
 * Sets the date when this expense happened.
 *
 * @param date The date when this expense happened.
 */
public void setDate(long date) {
   this.date = date;
}

/**
 * Gets the date when this expense happened.
 *
 * @return Date when this expense happened.
*/
public long getDate() {
   return date;
}

/**
 * Sets the ID of this expense.
 *
 * @param id ID of this expense.
 */
public void setId(int id) {
   this.id = id;
}

/**
 * Gets the id for this expense.
 *
 * @return ID for this expense.
 */
public int getId() {
```

```
        return id;
    }

    /**
     * Sets the type of this expense.
     *
     * @param type Type of this expense.
     */
    public void setType(ExpenseType type) {
        this.type = type;
    }

    /**
     * Gets the type of this expense.
     *
     * @return Type of this expense.
     */
    public ExpenseType getType() {
        return type;
    }

    /**
     * Sets the description for this expense.
     *
     * @param description Description for this expense.
     */
    public void setDescription(String description) {
        this.description = description;
    }

    /**
     * Gets the description for this expense.
     *
     * @return Description for this expense.
     */
    public String getDescription() {
        return this.description;
    }

    /**
     * A readable version of this Expense.
     *
     * @return Readable version of this Expense.
     */
    public String toString() {
        StringBuffer buffer = new StringBuffer();
        buffer.append(this.getDate());
        buffer.append(',');
        buffer.append(this.getType().toString());
```

```
      buffer.append(',');
      buffer.append(this.getDescription());
      buffer.append(',');
      buffer.append(this.getAmount());
      return buffer.toString();
   }
  }
```

The `Expense` class needs an `ExpenseType`, which contains a list of pre-defined expense types.

Listing 8.3: The `ExpenseType` enumeration

```
package com.scmadkit.ch08;

/**
 * This class represents an enumeration of the expense types used in
 * this application.
 *
 * @author Sathya.Srinivasan
 * @version 1.0
 */
public class ExpenseType {
  //~ Static fields/initializers ——————————————

  /** Indicates a breakfast expense. */
  public static final ExpenseType BREAKFAST =
                                    new ExpenseType(1, "Breakfast");
  /** Indicates a lunch expense. */
  public static final ExpenseType LUNCH =
                                    new ExpenseType(2, "Lunch");
  /** Indicates a dinner expense. */
  public static final ExpenseType DINNER =
                                    new ExpenseType(3, "Dinner");
  /** Indicates a gas expense. */
  public static final ExpenseType GAS = new ExpenseType(4, "Gas");
  /** Indicates an entertainment expense. */
  public static final ExpenseType ENTERTAINMENT =
                                    new ExpenseType(5, "Entertainment");
  /** Indicates a miscellaneous expense. */
  public static final ExpenseType MISCELLANEOUS =
                                    new ExpenseType(6, "Miscellaneous");
  //~ Instance fields ——————————————————————-

  private String description;
  private int id;

  //~ Constructors ————————————————————————-

  /**
```

```
 * Creates a new ExpenseType object.
 *
 * @param id ID for this instance.
 * @param description Description for this instance.
 */
public ExpenseType(int id, String description) {
    this.setId(id);
    this.setDescription(description);
}

//~ Methods ——————————————————————————

/**
 * Sets the description for this instance.
 *
 * @param description Description for this instance.
 */
public void setDescription(String description) {
    this.description = description;
}
/**
 * Gets the id of this instance.
 *
 * @return ID of this instance.
 */
public int getId() {
    return id;
}

/**
 * Gets an instance of the ExpenseType class based on the passed
 * id. This is used to reconstruct the object when getting it from
 * the database.
 *
 * @param id The id of the type.
 *
 * @return The instance representing the id.
 *
 * @throws IllegalArgumentException If the passed id is invalid.
 */
public static ExpenseType getInstance(int id) {
    switch(id) {
        case 1:
            return BREAKFAST;
        case 2:
            return LUNCH;
        case 3:
            return DINNER;
```

```
            case 4:
                return GAS;
            case 5:
                return ENTERTAINMENT;
            case 6:
                return MISCELLANEOUS;
            default:
                throw new IllegalArgumentException("Invalid ID " + id);
        }
    }
    /**
     * Provides a readable version of this instance.
     *
     * @return A human-readable version of this instance.
     */
    public String toString() {
        return description;
    }
    /**
     * Sets the id for this instance.
     *
     * @param id ID for this instance.
     */
    private void setId(int id) {
        this.id = id;
    }
}
```

Now we have all the required classes. It's time to implement the interface. Our implementation of the interface is supposed to implement four methods. Let's look at them one by one.

Adding Records

In order to add the records, we need the object that needs to be added. The only assertion that we need to make in this method is to ensure that the passed object is not `null`.

Listing 8.4: Adding records to a **`RecordStore`**

```
package com.scmadkit.ch08;

import javax.microedition.rms.*;

public class ExpenseDAO implements IExpenseDAO {
   private static final String STORE_NAME = "expenseTracker";

   public Expense add(Expense expense)
                throws RecordStoreException,
```

```
                          RecordStoreNotOpenException,
                          RecordStoreFullException {
      if (expense == null) {
         throw new IllegalArgumentException("Expense cannot be null");
      }
      RecordStore store = RecordStore.openRecordStore(STORE_NAME, true);
      try {
         byte bytes[] = ExpenseUtility.convertToBytes(expense);
         int id = store.addRecord(bytes, 0, bytes.length);
         expense.setId(id);
      } catch(IOException e) {
         throw new RecordStoreException("Could not process record."
                                        + " REASON:"
                                        + e.getMessage());
      }
      store.closeRecordStore();
      return expense;
   }
}
```

The program checks if a record store of the name "`expenseTracker`" is already present in the RMS. If not, it creates one (the `createIfNecessary` parameter is set to `true`). If an expense is successfully added to the store, it sets the ID indicating the location of the expense in the record store in the passed object and returns it back to the application.

We saw the mechanism to convert an `Expense` object into its constituent bytes in the previous section. Let's have a quick look at that code again.

Listing 8.5: Converting an* `Expense` *object into an array of bytes

```
package com.scmadkit.ch08;

import java.io.*;

/**
 * This is an utility class that can perform some generic functions
 * on an Expense object.
 *
 * @author Sathya.Srinivasan
 * @version 1.0
 */
public final class ExpenseUtility {
   /**
    * Converts an Expense object to a byte array.
    *
    * @param expense The expense object to be converted.
    *
    * @return An array of bytes representing the passed object.
    *
```

```
   * @throws IOException If the object cannot be converted.
   */
  public static final byte[] convertToBytes(Expense expense)
                              throws IOException {
    ByteArrayOutputStream bout = new ByteArrayOutputStream();
    DataOutputStream out = new DataOutputStream(bout);
    out.writeInt(expense.getType().getId());
    out.writeLong(expense.getDate());
    out.writeUTF(expense.getDescription());
    out.writeDouble(expense.getAmount());
    return bout.toByteArray();
  }
}
```

The method uses the `DataInputStream` and `ByteArrayInputStream` objects to convert the object contents into bytes.

Now, let's implement the second method.

Deleting Records

The delete method just needs an `Expense` object to delete. Once again, the only assertion that needs to be made is to see if the passed `Expense` object is a non-`null` object. This time around, we also expect that the `Expense` object will contain an ID that can be used to delete that particular record.

Listing 8.6: Deleting a record from a record store

```
package com.scmadkit.ch08;

import javax.microedition.rms.*;

public class ExpenseDAO implements IExpenseDAO {
  public void delete(Expense expense)
                throws RecordStoreException,
                       RecordStoreNotFoundException,
                       InvalidRecordIDException {
      if(expense == null) {
        throw new IllegalArgumentException("Expense cannot be null");
        int id = expense.getId();
        RecordStore store = RecordStore.openRecordStore(STORE_NAME, false);
        store.deleteRecord(id);
        store.closeRecordStore();
      }
   }
}
```

Since this is a delete operation, the program should not try to create a new record store if one does not exist. Hence, in this case, the `createIfNecessary` parameter is set to `false`.

If the application tries to open the record store when it has not been created yet, the method will throw a RecordStoreNotFoundException.

Once the record store is opened, the application attempts to delete the record by invoking the deleteRecord method on the record store. If the expense passed does not have a valid ID, the method will throw an InvalidRecordIDException.

Finally, we should remember to close the record store.

All this is fine. These are basic operations. Let's try to write something useful queries on the records that we have dutifully added to the record store.

Getting All Records

We have defined three methods in the interface. The first method gets all the records stored in the record store. This could be used to display all the expenses to the user.

The next method gets all the records matching a record type. A good example for this would be to get a list of all Gas-related expenses.

The other method is for returning the most expensive expenses made. For example, the user might want to get the top 10 expenses and see if they could have been avoided.

For the first method, we need to just go through all the records without any fuss. The simplest version of the RecordEnumeration instance can do this for us.

Listing 8.7: Getting all records from a record store

```
package com.scmadkit.ch08;
import javax.microedition.rms.*;
public class ExpenseDAO implements IExpenseDAO {
   public Expense[] allRecords()
                    throws RecordStoreNotOpenException,
                          RecordStoreException {
        RecordStore store = RecordStore.openRecordStore(STORE_NAME,
        false);
        RecordEnumeration enumeration = store.enumerateRecords(null,
        null, false);
        int size = store.getNumRecords();
        Expense expenses[] = new Expense[size];
        int count = 0;
        try {
           while(enumeration.hasNextElement()) {
               int id = enumeration.nextRecordId();
```

```
            byte record[] = store.getRecord(id);
      expenses[count++]=ExpenseUtility.convertToObject(record);
          }
      } catch(IOException e) {
          throw new RecordStoreException("Could not read records."
                                 + " REASON: "
                                 + e.getMessage());
      }
      enumeration.destroy();
      store.closeRecordStore();
      return expenses;
  }
}
```

Since we are getting records from an existing record store, we can pass `false` to the "`createIfNecessary`" parameter of the `openRecordStore` method.

As we are getting all the records, we do not need any filtering or comparison mechanisms. Hence, the first two parameters passed to the `enumerateRecords` method that represent a comparator and a filter can be `null`.

As we have decided to return an array, we should first find out the size of an array. Since we are returning all the records in the record store, this is quite easy to figure out. The `RecordStore` class contains a method called `getNumRecords()` that would do this for us.

Finally, we need to loop through the records in the record store and construct the objects. Let us assume that we do not want to return a partial set of records if something bad happens while going through the loop. Let's throw an exception in case if something happens instead.

One thing may look strange to you inside the loop. The code first gets the ID of the next record from the enumeration and then gets the record based on the ID from the record store. Why the two-step process? Why not simply get the record using the `nextRecord()` method of the `RecordEnumeration` interface?

In this particular implementation, we want to store the ID of the record in the `Expense` object. The return value of the `nextRecord()` method would only give the contents of a record, not its ID. Moreover, this implementation is useful from a learning perspective as it touches upon different methods.

We have already looked at the code that would convert a byte array into an `Expense` object previously. Let's have a look at that again.

Listing 8.8: Converting a byte array into an* `Expense` *object

```
package com.scmadkit.ch08;
```

```
import java.io.*;
/**
 * This is a utility class that can perform some generic functions on
 * an Expense object.
 *
 * @author Sathya.Srinivasan
 * @version 1.0
 */
public final class ExpenseUtility {
 /**
 * Converts a byte array into an Expense object.
 *
 * @param record The byte array to be used.
 *
 * @return   An Expense object constructed from the passed byte
 *           array.
 *
 * @throws   IOException If the object cannot be created from the
 *           byte array.
 */
 public static final Expense convertToObject(byte record[])
                        throws IOException {
   ByteArrayInputStream bin = new ByteArrayInputStream(record);
   DataInputStream in = new DataInputStream(bin);
   ExpenseType type = ExpenseType.getInstance(in.readInt());
   long date = in.readLong();
   String description = in.readUTF();
   double amount - in.readDouble();
   Expense expense = new Expense(type, amount, date);
   expense.setDescription(description);
   return expense;
 }
}
```

Now that we know how to get records from a record store, let's go for a more complex variant—getting records that match a certain criteria.

Getting Records Based on Criteria

Our next method wants us to get a list of records based on a specific `ExpenseType`. This means that we have to go through all the records, but filter them so that the records that do not match the given `ExpenseType` are not returned. This should immediately remind you of an interface in the RMS package—the `RecordFilter` interface. So, let's create a `RecordFilter` implementation called `ExpenseTypeFilter` that would meet our needs.

Listing 8.9: Filtering records based on a criterion

```
package com.scmadkit.ch08;

import java.io.IOException;
import javax.microedition.rms.RecordFilter;
/**
 * Filters a record based on a given expense type.
 *
 * @author Sathya.Srinivasan
 * @version 1.0
 */
public class ExpenseTypeFilter implements RecordFilter {
    //~ Instance fields ------------------------------
    private ExpenseType expenseType;
    //~ Methods ----------------------------------
    /**
     * Sets the expense type to be used in this filter.
     *
     * @param type The {@link ExpenseType} to be used in this filter.
     */
    public void setExpenseType(ExpenseType type) {
        this.expenseType = type;
    }
    /**
    * Checks if the passed byte array matches the criteria.
    *
    * @param record The record to be checked if it meets
    * the criteria.
    *
    * @return true if the record matches the criteria.
    *            false otherwise.
    */
```

```
    public boolean matches(byte record[]) {
        try {
            Expense expense = ExpenseUtility.convertToObject(record);
            return (expense.getType() == expenseType);
        } catch (IOException e) {
            return false;
        }
    }
}
```

Since the filter is supposed to be based on a certain expense type, we need to pass the expense type to be used as a filter while creating the filter object.

The class simply overrides the method that should be overridden from the `RecordFilter` interface. It converts the passed array of bytes using the now familiar `convertToObject` method in the `ExpenseUtility` class. Since the `ExpenseType` object is an enumeration, we can simply use the == operator instead of the `equals` method, as the same object will be passed throughout the application. Since the `convertToObject` method can throw an exception, we need to handle that here. Although the case should never arise as we are handling a well-defined set of bytes, we can simply return `false` in case an exception occurs.

Now, all we need to do is use this class in our `ExpenseDAO` class.

```
public class ExpenseDAO {
    public ExpenseTypeFilter filter = new ExpenseTypeFilter();
    /**
     * Gets records based on a certain record type.
     *
     * @param type The type of expense to be used as a filter.
     *
     * @return An array of expenses that match the passed criteria.
     *
     * @throws RecordStoreException If the records cannot be
     *          retrieved for unexpected reasons.
     * @throws  RecordStoreNotOpenException If the record store cannot
     *          be opened.
     */
  public Expense[] recordsFor(ExpenseType type)
                          throws RecordStoreException,
                             RecordStoreNotOpenException {
```

```
        if(type == null) {
            throw new IllegalArgumentException("Expense cannot be null");
        }
        filter.setExpenseType(type);
        RecordStore store = RecordStore.openRecordStore(STORE_NAME,
                                                               false);
        RecordEnumeration enumeration
                             = store.enumerateRecords(filter, null, false);
        Vector matchedRecords = new Vector();
        try {
            while(enumeration.hasNextElement()) {
                int id = enumeration.nextRecordId();
                byte record[] = store.getRecord(id);
                matchedRecords.add(
                    ExpenseUtility.convertToObject(record));
            }
        } catch(IOException e) {
            throw new RecordStoreException("Could not read records."
                                           + " REASON: "
                                           + e.getMessage());
        }
        enumeration.destroy();
        store.closeRecordStore();
        Expense[] expenses = new Expense[matchedRecords.size()];
        for(int i=0;i<expenses.length;i++) {
            expenses[i] = (Expense) matchedRecords.elementAt(i);
        }
        return expenses;
    }
}
```

You might have noticed a few things that were not done in the implementation of the `allRecords()` method. The first one would be use of a `Vector` class. Where did that come from? If you remember, we determined the size of the array to be returned previously by looking up the value of the getNumRecords() method. We cannot use the same thing now because this method returns the total number of records in the record store, while we might be returning only a subset. The only dynamic array that is provided in the CLDC specification is Vector. Therefore, we are going to use that here.

The only other change in this method compared to the allRecords() method is that we are passing the filter that we have added to this class. While the class itself needs not be created every time the recordsFor method is called, we do have to set the expenseType that is passed to the method in the filter object.

We are finally down to the last method—the one that gets the most expensive expenses.

Getting Records in Specific Order

To get the most expensive expenses, we need to compare the amount of each expense, sort the whole list in descending order of the amount and return only the top 'n' records. Once again, the concept of comparison triggers something in our brain—the RecordComparator interface.

In a fashion similar to that of the RecordFilter, let's create a class called MostExpensiveComparator that implements the RecordComparator interface.

Listing 8.10: Comparing records to determine the sorting order

```
    package com.scmadkit.ch08;
    import java.io.IOException;
    import javax.microedition.rms.RecordComparator;
    /**
    * Compares records and provides the order according to the amount
in
    * the Expense in descending order.
    *
    * @author Sathya.Srinivasan
    * @version 1.0
    */
 public class MostExpensiveComparator implements RecordComparator {
    //~ Methods ———————————————————
    /**
    * Compares two expense records.
    *
    * @param record1 The first record to be compared.
```

```
     * @param record2 The second record to be compared.
     *
     * @return PRECEDES if the first record is more expensive than the
     *              second record. FOLLOWS if the first record is less
     *              expensive than the second record. EQUIVALENT
     *              if the expenses are the same.
     */
    public int compare(byte record1[], byte record2[]) {
        Expense expense1 = null;
        Expense expense2 = null;
        try {
            expense1 = ExpenseUtility.convertToObject(record1);
        } catch(IOException e) {
            return FOLLOWS;
        }
        try {
            expense2 = ExpenseUtility.convertToObject(record2);
        } catch(IOException e) {
            return PRECEDES;
        }
        double amount1 = expense1.getAmount();
        double amount2 = expense2.getAmount();
        if(amount1 > amount2) {
            return PRECEDES;
        } else if(amount1 < amount2) {
            return FOLLOWS;
        } else {
            return EQUIVALENT;
        }
    }
}
```

The implementation itself is quite simple. We take two records passed to us, convert them into `Expense` objects, compare the amounts, and return the pre-defined `PRECEDES`,

FOLLOWS, or EQUIVALENT values if the first record has an amount greater than, lesser than, or equal to the second record's amount.

Now let's see how we can use this class in our ExpenseDAO class.

```
public class ExpenseDAO {
    private MostExpensiveComparator comparator = new
MostExpensiveComparator();
    /**
    * Gets the most expensive expenses.
    *
    * @param recordsToReturn The number of expenses to return.
    *
    * @return    An array of most expensive expenses. If the number of
    *             records in the record store is less than the records
    *             requested, all records in the record store sorted by
    *             the expense amount in descending order will be returned.
    *
    * @throws RecordStoreException If the records cannot be
    *           retrieved for unexpected reasons.
    * @throws RecordStoreNotOpenException If the record store cannot
    *           be opened.
    */
public Expense[] mostExpensiveExpenses(int recordsToReturn)
                    throws RecordStoreException,
                       RecordStoreNotOpenException {
    if(recordsToReturn <= 0) {
        throw new IllegalArgumentException(
                    "Records to return must be greater than 0.");
    }
    RecordStore store = RecordStore.openRecordStore(STORE_NAME, false);
    int totalRecords = store.getNumRecords();
    Expense expenses[] = new
Expense[(recordsToReturn<totalRecords)
                        ? recordsToReturn
                        : totalRecords];
```

```
        RecordEnumeration enumeration = store.enumerateRecords(null,
                                                  comparator, false);
        int count = 0;
        try {
            while(enumeration.hasNextElement()) {
                int id = enumeration.nextRecordId();
                byte record[] = store.getRecord(id);
    expenses[count++]=ExpenseUtility.convertToObject(record);
                if(count == expenses.length) break;
            }
        } catch(IOException e) {
            throw new RecordStoreException("Could not read records. "
                                          + " REASON: "
                                          + e.getMessage());
        }
        enumeration.destroy();
        store.closeRecordStore();
        return expenses;
    }
}
```

The implementation is quite similar to the `recordsFor` method implementation. We create another class-level attribute called `comparator`, since the `comparator` object is the same across multiple method invocations.

Instead of passing a filter, we pass the comparator this time around to the `enumerateRecords` method.

You might have also noticed that we have not used the `Vector` this time around. This is simply because we know the size of the array to return. If the requested number of records is less than the total number of records in the record store, we should return the requested number of records. If it is greater than or equal to the number of records in the record store, we can simply return all the records (sorted, of course) in the record store. Either way, we know the number of records to return.

Other than these variations, the implementation is quite similar to the other methods, as the `RecordEnumeration` does the job for us in conjunction with the `RecordComparator` implementation.

Thus, we have the complete implementation of the `IExpenseDAO` interface.

Summary

RMS is a primitive, but flexible mechanism to provide persistence to your Java ME application. The RMS model centers around the concept of a collection of records called record store. These record stores exist within the namespace of a single MIDlet suite and can be shared or held private. In this chapter, we looked in depth at the techniques for creating record stores and storing data records within them.

In particular, we examined the methods of the `RecordStore` class that allow us to create and access record stores. Some of these methods allow us to set access rules on the record stores so that we can share or not share the data as desired. We also looked at the methods involved in writing and reading actual records to and from the record stores. Make sure that you know how to write code that executes each phase of the C.R.U.D. cycle.

In some ways, RMS is a simple API. However, we need to make sure that we have practical experience in using it. Much of the practical application comes through the higher-level functionality provided by the various interfaces such as the `RecordFilter`, `RecordComparator` and `RecordEnumeration`. These interfaces provide powerful tools for manipulating sets of records. You should feel comfortable with knowing how and when to apply these tools to specific situational needs.

As always, the developer of mobile phone applications must keep performance in mind. Some of the options in some classes, like the `keepUpdated` option in the `RecordEnumeration`, while helpful, can be detrimental to the overall performance of the application. Use these options judiciously to get the most out of these classes.

For the exam, we recommend going through the vacation expense application provided in this chapter. In fact, write your own application that utilizes RMS in a similar fashion to the expense application. Again, the API is simple on the surface, but practical knowledge of its use is paramount for the exam.

References

1. MIDP 2.0(JSR-118) specification
   http://jcp.org/aboutJava/communityprocess/final/jsr118/
2. MIDP Database Programming Using RMS: a Persistent Storage for MIDlets
   http://developers.sun.com/techtopics/mobility/midp/articles/persist/
3. J2ME Record Management Store
   http://www-106.ibm.com/developerworks/wireless/library/wi-rms/
4. Databases and MIDP, Part 1: Understanding the Record Management System
   http://developers.sun.com/techtopics/mobility/midp/articles/databaserms/

Exercises

1. Write the storage classes for a "TO DO List" application. The application stores all the 'to do' items for the user. Each entry in the list contains the following attributes.
   a. Date Created (long)
   b. Priority (byte—ranging from 1–5)
   c. Completed? (boolean)
   d. Description (String)
   e. Date Due (long)

   You can write a console-based UI to test the application.

Review Questions

1. What will happen when the following method is called?
   ```
   RecordStore.openRecordStore("ARecordStoreWithAReallyReallyLongName",
                                               true);
   ```
   a. A record store with the given name is created if it does not exist already.
   b. If a record store already exists, a `RecordStoreAlreadyOpenException` will be thrown.
   c. An `IllegalArgumentException` will be thrown.
   d. The program will not compile because the method takes in only one parameter.
2. True or False: An application cannot create record stores that can be shared.
   a. True
   b. False
3. Which of the following are valid return values of the method in the `RecordComparator` interface?
   a. `FOLLOWS`
   b. `EQUAL`
   c. `SUCCEEDS`
   d. `EQUIVALENT`
4. Select the correct signature of the method that an implementing class should override from the `RecordFilter` interface.
   a. `public boolean matches(byte[] record)`
   b. `protected boolean matches(byte[] record)`
   c. `public int matches(Object record)`
   d. `public boolean matches(Object record)`
5. True or False: The `closeRecordStore` method of a `RecordStore` object should be called the same number of times as the `openRecordStore` method of a `RecordStore` for proper operation.

a. True

b. False

6. What will be the value of the `hasRecord` variable when the following code snippet is executed?

```
// The record store "store" is a valid record store and has one
// record.
RecordStore store = RecordStore.openRecordStore("store", false);
RecordEnumeration enumeration = store.enumerateRecords(null, null,
                                                        false);
store.closeRecordStore();
boolean hasRecord = enumeration.hasNextElement();
```

a. True

b. False

c. The code will not compile

d. The code will throw a `RecordStoreNotOpenException`

7. Which of the following might not have a significant impact in improving the performance of a `RecordEnumeration` instance and the application that uses it?

a. Setting the `keepUpdated` parameter of a `RecordEnumeration` instance to `false`.

b. Iterating through the enumeration forward using `hasNextElement()` method instead of backwards using `hasPreviousElement()` method.

c. Calling the `RecordEnumeration`'s `destroy()` method once the application is done using it.

d. Setting the filter and comparator methods to `null` while instantiating a `RecordEnumeration` from a `RecordStore`.

8. Identify the methods that need to be overridden in the `RecordListener` interface.

a. `recordAdded(RecordStore recordStore, int recordId)`

b. `recordRemoved(RecordStore recordStore, int recordId)`

c. `recordUpdated(RecordStore recordStore, int recordId)`

d. `recordChanged(RecordStore recordStore, int recordId)`

9. Which of the following are used to uniquely identify a record store in a shared environment?

a. The `MIDlet-Name` attribute value of the application that created the record store.

b. The `MIDlet-Vendor` attribute value of the application that created the record store.

c. The `MIDlet-Version` attribute value of the application that created the record store.

d. A unique internal record store number that is created and maintained by AMS.

10. What will happen when the following code snipped is executed.

```
RecordStore store = RecordStore.openRecordStore("store", true,
AUTHMODE_ANY, true);
```

a. A record store with the name "store" will be created. Only the application that created the record store can access it. The application has permission to add, remove, or read records.
b. A record store with the name "store" will be created. Only the application that created the record store can access it. The application has permission only to read records. It cannot add or delete records to the application.
c. A record store with the name "store" will be created. All applications in the device can access the record store. All the application that created the record store can read, write, or delete records from the record store.
d. A record store with the name "store" will be created. All applications in the device can access the record store. Only application that created the record store can read, or write records to the record store. Other applications can only read from the record store.

Review Answers

1. c. The name of a record store cannot exceed 32 characters. If it does, then an `IllegalArgumentException` will be thrown. The passed name contains 37 characters.
2. b. It is possible to create record stores that can be shared across applications. Refer to Section 8.1.2 Sharing record stores for further details.
3. a and d. The valid return values of the compare method of a `RecordComparator` interface are `PRECEDES`, `FOLLOWS` and `EQUIVALENT`.
4. a. The correct signature of the `matches` method in the `RecordFilter` interface is `public boolean matches(byte[] record)`.
5. a. "A record store will not actually be closed until `closeRecordStore` is called as many times as `openRecordStore` was called. In other words, the MIDlet needs to make a balanced number of close calls as open calls before the record store is closed". So, the `closeRecordStore` method should be called as many times as the `openRecordStore` method is called so that all resources are properly released.
6. b. Since the record store associated with the `RecordEnumeration` is closed before the `hasNextElement()` is called, the `RecordEnumeration` becomes invalid. Any call made on the `hasNextElement()` or the `hasPreviousElement()` methods would return false and other operations will throw a `RecordStoreNotOpenException`.
7. b. The direction of loop iteration (forward or backward) does not have a significant impact on the performance of a `RecordEnumeration`, whereas the rest of the options do.
8. b and d. The following are the methods that are defined in the `RecordListener` interface.

```
// Triggered when a record is added to the record store.
public void recordAdded(RecordStore recordStore, int recordId)
// Triggered when a record in the record store is updated.
public void recordChanged(RecordStore recordStore, int recordId)
// Triggered when the record in the record store is deleted.
public void recordDeleted(RecordStore recordStore, int recordId)
```

9. a and b. A record store is uniquely identified using a combination of the name of the record store (passed when the record store is created), the value of the `MIDlet`-Name attribute of the application that created the record store, and value of the `MIDlet-Vendor` attribute of the application that created the record store.
10. c. This method signature is used to create a shared record store. The first parameter indicates the name of the record store. The second parameter (`createIfNecessary`) tells that the record store should be created if it does not already exist. The third parameter (`authmode`) indicates that the record store can be shared with other applications (since the value is set to `AUTHMODE_ANY` instead of `AUTHMODE_PRIVATE`). Finally, the fourth parameter `(writable)` indicates that other applications can write to the record store.

Exam Notes

☞ Develop code that correctly implements handling, sharing and removing RecordStores within MIDlet suites.

Handling Record Store

- A MIDlet suite can have multiple record stores.
- Record stores remain persistent across multiple invocations.
- Each record store should have a unique name in a MIDlet suite.
- The names of record stores are case-sensitive and cannot exceed 32 characters.
- The MIDlet suite is identified by the `MIDlet-Vendor` and `MIDlet`-Name attributes.
- No locking operations are provided.
- Record store operations are atomic, synchronized and serialized.
- Time stamp format is same as that of `System.currentTimeMillis()`
- Records are `byte` arrays.
- Records are identified by an integer record ID.
- Record ID starts with 1 and increases by 1 monotonically.
- `RecordStore.getVersion()` returns a number indicating the number of times a change (add, delete, or change) has been made on it.

Opening Record Store

- `static RecordStore.openRecordStore(String name, boolean create)`
  - Created if one is not already available.
  - Name cannot exceed 32 characters.
  - `RecordStoreFullException` if there is no space.
  - `RecordStoreNotFoundException` if there is no record store by the given name and if the `create` parameter is `false`.
  - `RecordStoreException` if there is a general error.

Closing Record Store

- `RecordStore.closeRecordStore()` removes all listeners and makes the `RecordEnumeration` invalid.
- Number of open calls and close calls should be the same for proper functioning.
- `RecordStoreNotOpenException` is thrown if you attempt to close an already closed store.

Sharing Record Store

- Sharing of records is possible only from MIDP 2.0.
- `RecordStore.openRecordStore(String name, boolean create, int authMode, boolean writable)`
- If `authMode` is `AUTHMODE_PRIVATE`, it is same as the normal open.
- If `authMode` is `AUTHMODE_ANY`, the `RecordStore` opened will be shared with other MIDlet suites.
- If the `authMode` is `AUTHMODE_ANY` and you try to access a record store opened using `AUTHMODE_PRIVATE`, the `RecordStore` is NOT shared.
- Untrusted MIDlet suites can share record stores.
- `RecordStore.openRecordStore(String name, String vendor, String suite)`
    - Opens a shared `RecordStore`.
    - If requested `RecordStore` was opened using `AUTHMODE_PRIVATE`, this succeeds only if this requesting `MIDlet` has the same vendor and suite as the `MIDlet` that created the requested `RecordStore`.
    - If requested `RecordStore` was opened using `AUTHMODE_ANY`, it always succeeds.

Removing Record Store

- If a MIDlet suite is removed, all associated record stores will be removed.
- `static RecordStore.deleteRecordStore(String storeName)`
    - Only a MIDlet in the `MIDlet` suite that created the record store can delete the record store.
    - If the record store is open when an attempt is made to delete it, then a `RecordStoreException` is thrown.
    - `RecordStoreNotFoundException` is thrown if there is no record store with the given name.
    - No delete events are sent to listeners.

☞ Develop code that correctly implements adding, retrieving, modifying and deleting individual records in a RecordStore, and converting RecordStore record data to and from byte arrays, and that reflects performance implications.

Adding Records

- `int addRecord(byte[] data, int offset, int numBytes)`
- data may be an empty array or `null`.
- `numBytes` may be zero.
- `RecordStoreNotOpenException` thrown if the record store is not open.
- `RecordStoreFullException` thrown if there is no space in the device.
- `RecordStoreException` is thrown for general errors.
- `SecurityException` is thrown if the operation is not allowed.

Retrieving Records

- `RecordStore.getRecord(int recordId):byte[]` gets the data for the given ID.
- `InvalidRecordIDException` is thrown if the passed ID is invalid.
- `RecordStore.getRecord(int recordId, byte[] data, int offset):int` gets the data for the given ID and copies it to the passed array. The return value represents the number of bytes read from the offset.
  - `InvalidRecordIDException` is thrown if the passed `ID` is invalid.
  - `ArrayIndexOutOfBoundsException` is thrown if the given array is smaller than the record.
- `RecordStore.getRecordSize(int recordId)` returns the size of the data.

Modifying Records

- `RecordStore.setRecord(int recordId, byte[] newData, int offset, int numBytes)`
  - Overwrites the existing data.
  - `SecurityException` is thrown if the operation is not allowed.

Deleting Records

- `RecordStore.deleteRecord(int recordId)` deletes a given record from the store.
- The record Id of the deleted record will not be reused.

Converting Record Store Data to Byte Arrays

```
byte[] data = recordStore.getRecord(recordId);
ByteArrayInputStream byteIn = new ByteArrayInputStream(data);
DataInputStream in = new DataInputStream(byteIn);
int someInt = in.readInt();
int someString = in.readUTF();
```

Converting Record Store Data from Byte Arrays

```
int someInt = 1;
String someString = "Hello";
ByteArrayOutputStream byteOut = new ByteArrayOutputStream();
DataOutputStream out = new DataOutputStream(byteOut);
out.writeInt(someInt);
out.writeUTF(someString);
byte[] data = byteOut.toByteArray();
recordStore.addRecord(data, 0, data.length);
```

- If the data contains only one `String`, then the `String.getBytes()` method can be used instead of `ByteArrayStreams`.

Performance Implications

- Adding a `RecordFilter` can have performance implications on a `RecordEnumeration`.
- Setting the `keepUpdated` flag on a `RecordEnumeration` will have severe performance implications as the index of the enumeration will be rebuilt each time the underlying `RecordStore` is changed.
- Adding a `RecordListener` to a `RecordStore` might have an impact on the performance of the `RecordStore`.

☞ Identify correct and incorrect statements or examples about filtering, comparing, event listening and enumerating records in a record store.

Record Filter

- `boolean matches(byte[] candidate)`
- The candidate should be considered as read-only.

Record Comparator

- `int compare(byte[] candidate1, byte[] candidate2)`
- `EQUIVALENT` should be returned if the candidates are equal.
- `PRECEDES` should be returned if `candidate1` precedes `candidate2`.
- `FOLLOWS` should be returned if `candidate1` follows `candidate2`.

Record Listener

- `void recordAdded(RecordStore store, int recordId)` invoked if a record is added.
- `void recordChanged(RecordStore store, int recordId)` invoked if a record is changed.

- `void recordDeleted(RecordStore store, int recordId)` invoked if a record is deleted.
- `RecordStore.addRecordListener(RecordListener listener)` can be used to register a listener to a `RecordStore`.

Record Enumeration

- `RecordStore.enumerateRecords(RecordFilter filter, RecordComparator comparator, boolean keepUpdated)` is used to get an enumeration for a `RecordStore`.
- `RecordEnumeration` keeps an internal list of record ids which is a snapshot of the IDs in the `RecordStore` when the enumeration is created first.
- If the associated `RecordStore` is closed, the `RecordEnumeration` becomes invalid.
- If an operation is performed on a `RecordEnumeration` after the `RecordStore` is closed, the record may return an invalid ID or throw a `RecordStoreNotOpenException`, even if the `RecordStore` is opened later.
- During enumeration, if some records are deleted, the enumeration might still return the invalid IDs (if it is not set to listen for updates).
- During enumeration, if some records are added, the enumeration might not return the new IDs (if it is not set to listen for updates).
- First call to `nextRecord()` will return the record data from the first record in the enumeration's sequence.
- First call to `previousRecord()` will return the record data from the last record in the enumeration's sequence.
- An `IllegalStateException` is thrown if the `RecordEnumeration` is accessed after `RecordEnumeration.destroy()` has been called.
- If the `keepUpdated` is true, then the index of the `RecordEnumeration` is updated after every change to the underlying `RecordStore`. This `RecordEnumeration` is registered as a listener to the `RecordStore`.
- Having the `keepUpdated` parameter as true might severely affect the performance of the application.
- `keepUpdated(true)` == `rebuild()`
- The byte array returned by `nextRecord()` method is only a copy. Changes made to the array will not be reflected in the data stored in the `RecordStore`.
- Calling `numRecords()` will force the enumeration to recrate the indexes.
- After calling `nextRecord()` or `nextRecordId()`, the enumeration is advanced to the next available record.
- After calling `previousRecord()` or `previousRecordId()`, the enumeration is advanced to the previous available record.
- The `reset()` method will cause the internal indexes to be restored to the same set that was created when the enumeration was instantiated.

9

Chapter

Securing Wireless Applications

Exam Objectives

3.1 Given a set of requirements, design and build applications given CLDC-specified application-level security, including the sandbox model. (Section 9.1)

3.2 Identify correct and incorrect statements or examples about untrusted MIDlet suites. (Section 9.2)

3.3 Explain trusted MIDlet suite security authorization and permissions, including the process for MIDlet suite signing. (Section 9.2)

3.4 Explain requirements and process of using X.509 public key infrastructure (PKI) authentication for MIDlet suites. (Section 9.3)

INTRODUCTION

From its inception, the Java platform has been integrated with network capabilities so that it can support the concept that "The Network is the Computer". This is becoming truer and truer with each passing days. The fact that we now develop applications to run on mobile phones seems to provide yet another profound revelation of this concept. And as we all know, being connected means exposure to security threats. Increasingly, we are spending our time in protecting our computers from various viruses and malicious software entities. In view of this, security has become an expected core element of the JTWI's model for delivering applications to mobile phones.

This chapter covers the security requirements specified in various component specifications of JTWI. It discusses a variety of security mechanisms that are defined at a variety of levels. We will see the application-level security mandated by the CLDC 1.1, and learn about the high-level MIDP's security model of trusted and untrusted MIDlet suites. We will also cover a digital signing technology recommended by MIDP.

9.1 CLDC SECURITY PROVISIONS

CLDC makes some specifications regarding security. As one might expect of the configuration layer, the security specifications made by CLDC make security assertions at a pretty fundamental level. Figure 9.1 shows the layers of Java ME architecture with the configuration-level security concerns of CLDC. They address such core issues as the Virtual Machine (VM) and the low-level application model.

☞ **Note:** This is the CLDC concept of an application, bytecodes that execute in the VM—not the lifecycle-based MIDlet.

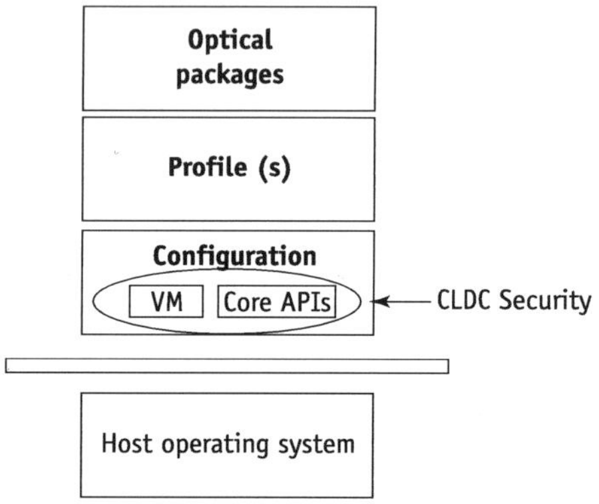

Figure 9.1 CLDC-level security concerns

The security concerns of CLDC can be divided into three different levels: low-level security, application-level security and end-to-end security. The low-level and end-to-end security issues are not covered by the SCMAD exam as they are not in the control of the developer. We will discuss about them briefly before examining the application-level security that is covered by the exam.

Exam Tip

Low-level security and end-to-end security are not part of the SCMAD exam. They are mentioned here just to inform you that there are three different levels in the security model defined by CLDC.

The low-level security addresses security issues at the level of JVM. The security requirements at this level pertain more to the implementers of compliant JVMs than to developers. Indeed, developers have no access to these details. The end-to-end security pertains to the transfer of data between a mobile device and a remote device. It guarantees that information transmission is protected along the way to the remote device from the mobile device. Some sorts of encryption techniques need to be considered to achieve this security model. However, end-to-end security is outside the scope of the CLDC specification because it is the responsibility of the profile-level implementation to take care of the security issues between end-to-end services. This, then, is also clearly out of the control of the developer.

9.1.1 Application-level Security

The developer has some responsibilities over configuration-level security and s/he must understand the application-level security defined by CLDC. The application-level security concerns three main issues: sandbox model, system class protection and dynamic class loading. Each of these will be discussed in detail in the following sections.

Sandbox Model

A sandbox security model is based upon the notion of containment. You might think about it like this. Kids love to play in sand, but parents hate to clean it up. The obvious solution is to build some small walls that can isolate the mercurial matter within the confines of a well-defined barrier. The sandbox model of security provides a similar structure for the Java application. In some ways, it's a simple, brute force type of solution, but it works. The general idea is that a Java application is a powerful thing that might be able to do some things you don't want it to do. Typically, these malicious things include villainous use of the file system or network resources. The sandbox security model simply tries to confine the application and limit its range in the same way that the walls of a sandbox confine the sand and limit its spread.

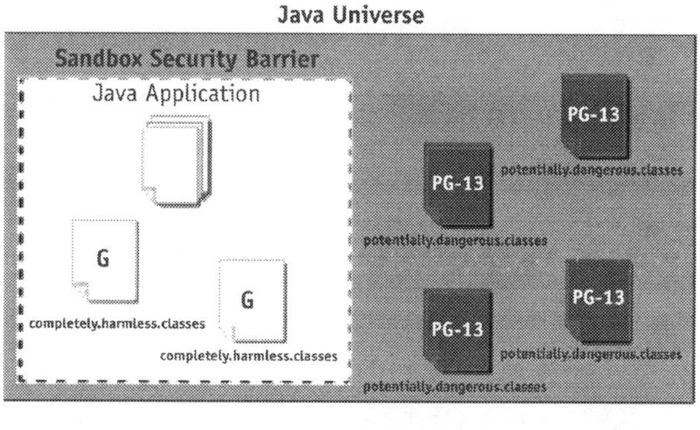

Figure 9.2 The sandbox security model

Basically, the sandbox model puts restrictions on the things an application can do. Figure 9.2 illustrates the simplicity of this model. The walls of the sandbox simply bar access to restricted APIs. The following bullet points indicate the specific strategies that CLDC uses to impose a sandbox security model on Java applications executing in compliant devices:

- Class files must be properly verified as valid Java classes.
- The downloading, installation and management of Java ME applications on the device takes place in such a way to prevent the system class loading mechanism of the virtual machine from being altered or bypassed by application programmer.
- The application programmer has access only to a closed and predefined set of Java APIs as defined by CLDC, MIDP and manufacturer/vendor-specific classes.

- The application programmer has no access to native functions that are not part of Java APIs as defined by CLDC, MIDP and manufacturer/vendor-specific classes. The application programmer does not even see the set of native functions accessible to the virtual machine.

While the sandbox model provides security by putting a barrier around the application that allows only a limited set of safe functionality, other security steps must be taken to ensure that the application can do no harm. The next sections will discuss restrictions mandated by the CLDC specification in protecting system classes and loading dynamic classes.

System Class Protection

Obviously, if we are going to run Java applications on mobile phones, dynamic downloading of applications must be supported. As we saw in the CLDC chapter, support for this functionality is part of the CLDC specification. This requirement carries with it some serious security concerns. The CLDC implementation must make sure that a downloaded application does not contain classes that alter, extend, override or add any classes to the protected system packages such as `java.*`, `javax.microedition.*` or other profile-specific or manufacturer/vendor-specific packages. If these classes were overridden, all efforts at security are futile.

This requirement can be enforced by the implementation in a couple of ways. Primarily, the system classes themselves must take precedence over user classes when looking for classes. This then implies that class file lookup order must not be manipulated by application programmer in any means. Class file lookup order is implementation-dependent and it is outside the scope of the CLDC specification to define class file lookup order for an implementation.

Dynamic Class Loading

Another important restriction that prevents the application itself from loading extraneous classes is that a Java ME application can load classes only from its own JAR file. This ensures that classes in each application live on their own without harming classes of other applications. Moreover, this makes sure that a third-party application cannot access the protected or private components of the Java classes that a manufacturer/vendor or a service provider may have provided as part of the system applications.

Exam Tip

Memorize the three application-level security issues defined by CLDC. The ability to identify these is required for the exam.

Now we are all set with security-related topics for the configuration level, CLDC in this case. The next section discusses profile-level security-related topics mentioned in the MIDP 2.0 specification.

9.2 UNTRUSTED AND TRUSTED MIDLET SUITES

At the profile level, the MIDP 2.0 implements its own security mechanisms. These mechanisms define protected APIs and functions available to MIDlet applications. An application must have the appropriate permissions to access these protected APIs and functions. The MIDP security model is built on the distinction between trusted and untrusted MIDlet suites. In this section, we will learn how MIDP controls access to protected resources by the distinction between trusted and untrusted applications.

9.2.1 Protected APIs and Functions

The whole security model of the MIDP 2.0 evolves around the idea that certain APIs may expose security vulnerabilities. A good example would be the various networking capabilities exposed through the API. Network access is always a good way for trouble to start. In order to stop the trouble before it begins, the APIs that give access to networking capabilities are determined to be protected resources. An API or function is characterized as protected by virtue of the existence of a named permission associated with that API or function. In the section on trusted applications, we will explore these concepts in depth. For now, just understand that some of the APIs and functions available to MIDlets might have had permissions defined for them, thus making them protected APIs or functions.

9.2.2 Untrusted MIDlet Suites

The mechanism for handling untrusted suites is quite simple. If a suite is untrusted, it is simply restricted from accessing protected APIs and functions. By definition, if the origin and integrity of a MIDlet suite can not be verified, that MIDlet suite is categorized as untrusted. Untrusted MIDlet suites must run in a MIDP version of the sandbox security model. This is not the same sandbox as defined in CLDC, but it is a sandbox. Basically, an untrusted MIDlet suite is allowed to run, but it cannot access any of the protected APIs or functions. The only variance in this requirement is that a very small set of restricted functions may be allowed with explicit user authorization. Table 9.1 lists the APIs for which a user can grant permissions to an untrusted MIDlet suite.

Table 9.1 List of APIs that can be accessed by untrusted MIDlet suites with explicit user confirmation

API	*Description*
`javax.microedition.io.HttpConnection`	HTTPS networking protocol access
`javax.microedition.io.HttpsConnection`	HTTPS networking protocol access

The next Table, 9.2, lists the APIs that are open to untrusted MIDlet suites without any user intervention. These are unprotected APIs. They have been deemed to contain no security risks.

Table 9.2 List of APIs that can be accessed by untrusted MIDlet suites without explicit user confirmation

API	*Description*
`javax.microedition.midlet`	MIDlet Lifecycle API
`javax.microedition.rms`	Record Management System API
`javax.microedition.lcdui`	User Interface API
`javax.microedition.lcdui.game`	Game API
`javax.microedition.media`	Multimedia API for playback of sound
`javax.microedition.media.control`	

Exam Tip

Be prepared to memorize the list of APIs that can be accessed by untrusted MIDlet suites with or without explicit user confirmation. The exam usually asks you to identify them in a way or another.

Incidentally, MIDP 1.0-compliant MIDlet suite is considered as untrusted MIDlet suite in a MIDP 2.0 implementation. MIDP 1.0 restricts each MIDlet suite to run in a closed sandbox environment, in which MIDlets are not allowed to access sensitive APIs or functions of the device. In MIDP 2.0, it is still applicable and all MIDlet suites that are developed according to the MIDP 1.0 specification are considered as untrusted MIDlet suites. Therefore, every MIDP 2.0 implementation must support the execution of MIDP 1.0-compliant MIDlet suites as untrusted MIDlet suites. You might have noticed that JAR manifest or application descriptor (JAD) coming along with untrusted MIDlet suites does not include explicit entries to request permissions. Security permissions and its related concepts will be discussed in the following sections in detail.

9.2.3 Trusted MIDlet Suites

Now we will look at the security mechanism for trusted MIDlet suites. Unfortunately, it's not as simple as the untrusted model. Most of the complexity in it comes from the flexibility of the model. So we should be glad. As with all flexible models, we need to spend some time getting to know the lay of the land. Welcome to another introduction to a conceptual architecture. It's been a long dry spell for the engineers, but finally we have returned to the cleanliness of the conceptual realm. Unfettered by the drudgery of actual code, we can once again soar into the abstract realm of parsed syntax and rigorous word choice. Table 9.3 defines the key terms of this new conceptual architecture.

Table 9.3 Definitions related to trusted MIDlet suites concept

Term	*Description*
Permission	A named permission defined by an API or function to prevent it from being used without authorization
Protection domain	A set of *allowed* and *user* permissions that may be granted to a MIDlet suite
Protection domain root certificate	A certificate associated with a protection domain that device implementation implicitly trusts to verify and authorize MIDlet suites
Trusted MIDlet suite	A MIDlet suite for which the authentication and integrity of the JAR file can be trusted by the device and bound to a protection domain

These terms, which we will cover shortly, chart the conceptual model of the trusted MIDlet suite security process. These terms define the components of the conceptual mechanisms by which trusted MIDlets are granted access to sets of the protected APIs and functionality. The granting of access is not a wholesale matter. There is a high degree of granularity and configurability in the process. In fact, this flexibility accounts for most of the complexity. Now, let's look at these terms in detail.

Permissions

As we said before, permissions represent the means by which we recognize an API or function as protected. This means that permissions are in some ways the most important concept in the security model. Without the presence of permissions, nothing would be recognized as protected. Where there is security, there definitely is permission that can be used to access the protected area.

In precise terms, permission is simply a named item that is associated with a protected API or function. It is this association that marks the API or function as protected. If any application wants to access a protected resource, it must have been granted that specific permission. More on the granting process in a bit. Recall that some APIs are not protected. These unprotected APIs will simply not have an associated permission. To determine if an API or a function has associated with a permission, we can consult the API documentation.

Figure 9.3 shows a MIDlet that is attempting to access the `javax.microedition.io.Connector` factory methods for creating various `Connection` types. As you might expect, network resources are all considered protected resources. The API defines a separate permission for each protocol implemented. In order to open an HTTP connection, the MIDlet must have the permission defined for that protocol. To open a server socket, another specific permission is needed.

In Fig. 9.3, the MIDlet has been granted permissions for several protocols. Note that the protocol namespace mirrors the package and class namespace. The MIDlet has the permission for HTTP connections, so its call to open an HTTP connection is approved. Since the MIDlet doesn't have a permission for a server socket, and one is defined in the API (javax.microedition.io.Connector.serversocket), its attempt to open a server socket connection is denied.

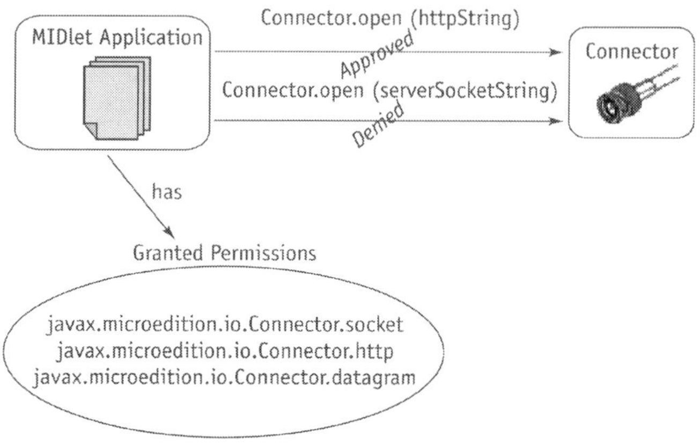

Figure 9.3 A MIDlet requesting protected resources

Note, a permission can be defined for an entire class, thus making the entire class protected, or it can be defined for a specific function within the class. For instance, the `Connector.open` method gives access to network connections of various protocol types. Each of these protocol types is protected by a permission. For instance, the permission associated with the ability of this method to return a server socket is `javax.microedition.io.Connector.serversocket`. On the other hand, the entire `PushRegistry` class is covered with a class-level permission named `javax. microedition.io.PushRegistry`.

Exam Tip

The exam usually contains questions that ask you to determine whether an application has access to certain protected APIs or functions or not by providing you the JAD or manifest file of the application containing the requested permission names.

As you might have noticed from the above examples, permissions are matched to APIs by a mirroring of the namespace hierarchy of the Java packages. The name of the permission itself is preceded by a full package name that identifies the package or class with which the permission is associated. Since they must mirror the package names, it follows that the set of valid characters for naming permissions is the same as for defining Java package names and class names. Capitalization conventions for permission names should also be the same as those for Java package names. And, of course, the names of the permissions are case-sensitive.

Each API in the MIDP 2.0 specification defines permissions for its own protected functions. However, the APIs that are outside the MIDP 2.0 specification must define permissions for their sensitive functions and specify the behavior of the APIs when they are deployed on a MIDP 2.0-compliant device. For example, Wireless Message API 1.1 specification includes an appendix (Appendix D) that discusses the topic related to the deployment of WMA interfaces on a MIDP 2.0 platform.

Protection Domains

Protection domains are the entry points for granting specific permissions to MIDlet suites. Every trusted MIDlet suite must belong to a single, defined protection domain. The protection domain is associated with the origin of the MIDlet suite. Recall that if a MIDlet suite's origin can't be determined, it will be automatically viewed as untrusted. Now, we know why. If the origin of a MIDlet suite is not known, its protection domain certainly can't be determined.

Each protection domain is associated with a set of permissions that may be granted to a MIDlet suite of that domain. The associated permissions are further classified as either *allowed* or *user* permissions. An allowed permission is simply granted to every MIDlet suite that is identified as belonging to the protection domain. User permissions are permissions that are granted to the MIDlet suite that belongs to the domain only with explicit authorization by the user, such as clicking 'yes' on a dialog box. Protection domains are defined by protection domain owners, such as device manufacturers, carriers and MIDP implementers. Protection domain owners are the ones who specify how the device identifies and verifies a MIDlet suite that claims to be trustable. If the suite can be verified, it is bound to a protection domain. The definition of protection domains are a detail of the MIDP implementation on the device. For now, just assume that the protection domain exists. Figure 9.4 illustrates an example of protection domains in a mobile device and some MIDlet suites bound to those protection domains.

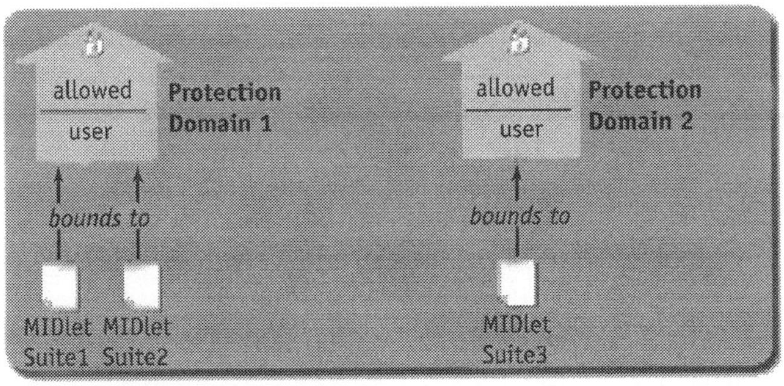

Figure 9.4 Protection domains and MIDlet suites bound to them

Before a MIDlet suite can be trusted, it must be bound to a protection domain. Before it can be bound to a protection domain, it must be verified. This process generally includes a verification of the origin of the MIDlet suite JAR as well as verification of the integrity of the JAR. Obviously, the verification process is the lynch pin of the security model. Later, we will discuss a mechanism that can be used to identify trusted MIDlet suites by signing and verification processes of X.509 PKI. This is the mechanism that MIDP 2.0 specification mandates the implementers to follow, in order to recognize trusted MIDlet suites by signing and verifying them.

9.2.4 Process of Granting Permissions

Now we will examine the process by which a MIDlet suite attempts to become a trusted suite attached to a protection domain and enabled with a set of permissions that will allow it to execute to its fullest capacity. First, we will sketch the process and then go into more detail on the various elements of the process. The responsibility of the MIDlet suite lies in declaring the permissions that it will need in order to function. This is the job of the developer obviously. When a suite is loaded onto a device, the device must examine the suite to determine whether it can bind it to one of its known protection domains. If it cannot, there is no hope for granting permissions. If the MIDlet suite can be bound to a domain, we can move on to determining whether its requested permissions may be granted. Once a MIDlet suite is bound to a protection domain, we can compare the permissions it requests with the permissions associated with the protection domain. Obviously, the requested permissions need to be granted in the MIDlet suite's protection domain. If all of the requested permissions are associated with the MIDlet suite's domain, it will be allowed to enter the device and execute. Sounds simple? That was just the summary. Now we will discuss it in detail.

Requesting Permissions for MIDlet Suite

In order to figure out whether a MIDlet suite has the permissions it needs to execute on the device, it must present a list of the permissions it requires in its JAD and/or JAR manifest file. These requested permissions can be identified as *critical* or *optional.* If any of the critical permissions cannot be granted, the application will be refused. However, if any of the optional permissions cannot be granted, the application will still be accepted, though it may execute in a limited capacity. The following attributes are used to identify the requested permissions.

MIDlet-Permissions attribute A MIDlet suite that must access certain protected APIs or functions to be able to run correctly needs to list the corresponding critical permissions in its `MIDlet-Permissions` attribute. The permissions listed in `MIDlet-Permissions` attribute are critical to the functionality of the MIDlet suite, and the MIDlet suite cannot run properly without them.

MIDlet-Permissions-Opt attribute If a MIDlet suite can operate with or without accessing certain protected APIs or functions, the permission names for those APIs or functions should be listed in `MIDlet-Permissions-Opt` attribute. The MIDlet suite will run in a limited manner, if the requested permissions listed in `MIDlet-Permissions-Opt` attribute cannot be granted to the MIDlet suite. For instance, a game can be played in single-player mode rather than online two-player mode, in which a network access is needed and the permission requested for network access has not been granted to the MIDlet suite.

A MIDlet suite can request multiple permissions needed in any of `MIDlet-Permissions` and `MIDlet-Permissions-Opt` attributes in its JAD and/or manifest file. Both `MIDlet-Permissions` and `MIDlet-Permissions-Opt` attributes can contain a list of one or more permission names. Those permissions must be delimited by a comma. Leading and trailing whitespaces and tabs among them are ignored. For example,

```
MIDlet-Permissions: javax.microedition.io.PushRegistry,
                    javax.microedition.io.Connector.http
MIDlet-Permissions-Opt: javax.microedition.io.Connector.https,
                    javax.microedition.io.Connector.ssl
```

Exam Tip

The exam usually asks you to determine whether the MIDlet suite will be accepted or not based on the given protection domains and requested permissions by the suite.

Once the developer has identified the necessary critical and optional permissions and described them in the JAD and/or manifest file, it's up to the mechanisms on the device's implementation to determine whether the application can be accepted, and in what capacity. Let's see how it works!

Identifying Permissions on Device

First, we need to make sure that the requested permissions even exist on the device's implementation of the APIs. Mathematically, we can say that the pre-defined set of permissions on the device is the union of all permissions defined for every single protected API or function on the device. It may sound trite, but we must be explicit about some things. After all, we are in the conceptual realm of rigorous word choice and parsed syntax. It's certainly possible that an application would request a permission that is not defined in any of the APIs supported by the device. We must be prepared. In fact, if a MIDlet suite requests a critical permission that doesn't exist on the device, the MIDlet suite will be refused. If it requests an optional permission that doesn't exist on the device, this alone won't prohibit the application from being installed.

Once the set of permissions known to the device is collected, we can proceed. The first step is to compare the requested permissions with the set of actual permissions associated with all the various APIs on the device. If a critical requested permission does not exist on the device, the MIDlet suite is refused. If an optional requested permission does not exist on the device, the MIDlet suite may continue with the permission granting process.

Binding to Protection Domain

Again, every trusted MIDlet suite must be bound to a protection domain to be able to be authorized. The protection domain defines two sets of permissions for its member suites: those that are allowed without further mediation and those that depend on explicit user authorization. When a MIDlet suite arrives with its set of requested permissions, it is time to resolve them against the permissions defined in the protection domain. For a MIDlet suite to be accepted, all of its critical requested permissions must be granted via the mechanisms of the protection domain. The optional requested permissions may be granted or not granted. They will not prevent the execution of the MIDlets in the MIDlet suite, though they might alter its capabilities.

Allowed permissions If a MIDlet suite requests a permission that is one of the *allowed* permissions of the protection domain, there is no problem. This permission is simply granted with no further mediation.

User permissions If a MIDlet suite requests a permission that is a *user* permission of the domain, it is up to the user to determine whether the permission will be granted. There is a bit of flexibility to the granularity of the user's authorizations for these permissions.

The three user interaction (authorization) modes are `blanket`, `session` and `oneshot`. Once the `blanket` access mode is granted for a protected API or function, the API or function can be accessed by the MIDlet suite anytime it wants. The `blanket` access mode will end when the MIDlet suite is uninstalled or the user modifies the permission. But when the `session` access mode is granted to a protected API or function, there is no need to prompt the user to ask for the permission until the MIDlet suite terminates. If the MIDlet suite restarts and tries to access the protected API or function again, the user must be prompted with a list of choice, whether to grant or deny permission for access to the MIDlet suite again. The `oneshot` access mode is valid only for each time the user grants access to a protected API or function. If the MIDlet suite tries to invoke the protected API or function, the user must be prompted again.

It is up to device implementers how to let the user choose user permission access mode. The user should be provided with a straightforward description for permissions so that they won't get confused in making decision. Each `user` permission has a default user interaction mode and it can also be associated with other available user interaction modes. Tradeoff between usability and user notification needs to be considered when choosing `blanket`, `session` or `oneshot` interaction mode. The `blanket` interaction mode provides the user with the highest usability, while the `oneshot` mode provides the user with the highest amount of notifications when the MIDlet suite

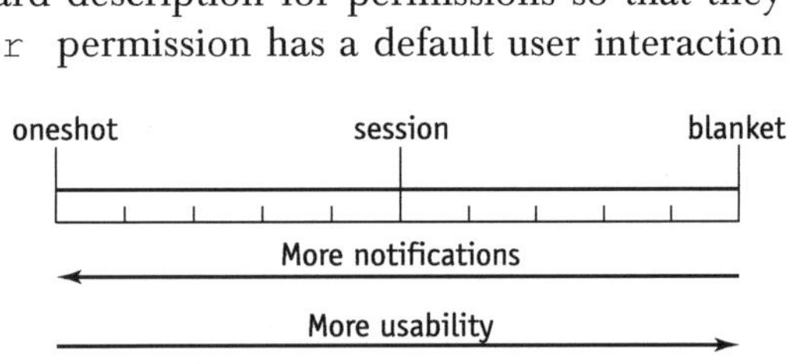

Figure 9.5 Tradeoff between usability and notification

tries to access a protected API or function. Figure 9.5 illustrates the tradeoff between usability and user notification that might exist when choosing the user interaction modes.

In the end, if all of the critical requested permissions have been granted, either as *allowed* permissions of the protection domain, or as *user* permissions granted through explicit user authorization, the MIDlet suite may execute.

☞ **Note:** Within a protection domain, each permission must be located either in the set of allowed permissions or in the set of user permissions, but not in both sets.

Summarizing the Process

After all of that lengthy engineer talk, a short practical list of steps would be nice for us. The following bullet list outlines the steps involved in a MIDlet suite's journey from obscurity to a trusted relationship with the device and its user.

- The MIDlet suite must be bound to a protection domain.
- The CRITICAL and OPTIONAL permissions are retrieved from the JAD or manifest file. If they are defined in both places, they must be identical.
- If any of the CRITICAL requested permissions are unknown to the device, i.e., one of the requested permissions is not in the set of permissions on the device, the MIDlet suite is rejected.
- If any of the OPTIONAL requested permissions are unknown to the device, i.e., one of the requested permissions is not in the set of permissions on the device, the permission will not be granted. Note, the MIDlet suite may still be accepted.
- If any of the CRITICAL requested permissions are not present in the protection domain that the MIDlet suite is bound to, the MIDlet suite is rejected.
- If any of the OPTIONAL requested permissions are not present in the protection domain that the MIDlet suite is bound to, the permission will not be granted. Note, the MIDlet suite may still be accepted.
- If any of the requested permissions are from `user` permissions set of the protection domain, the user must be prompted for authorization according to one of three modes, i.e. `blanket`, `session` and `oneshot`. It is the device implementation that needs to provide a way to make request to the user and receive response from the user.
- The total set of granted permissions is the intersection of the requested permissions with the granted permissions defined in the protection domain (`Allowed` plus `user` granted permissions).
- If a MIDlet suite's requested permissions are in the set of granted permissions, it may execute.
- Finally, if the MIDlet suite tries to access something it doesn't have the appropriate permission for, a `SecurityException` will be thrown during the execution.

You should now understand the security model by which MIDlet suites are classified as trusted or untrusted. The untrusted model is simple. The MIDlet suite runs in a strict sandbox. For trusted MIDlet suites, a complex process of binding to protection domain and granting of permissions ensues. Ultimately, execution depends upon whether all of the requested permissions can be granted.

9.2.5 Authorization Model of MIDP 2.0

The authorization model of the MIDP 2.0 is designed based on the relationships among the elements that have been just discussed. The following points summarize the four elements that participate in establishment of the basic authorization of a MIDlet suite.

- A set of permissions, which is requested by the MIDlet suite in `MIDlet-Permissions` and `MIDlet-Permissions-Opt` attributes.
- A set of permissions, which is a union of permissions for each protected API or function on the device.
- Protection domain, which consists of a set of `allowed` and `user` permissions.
- The user, who may be prompted to grant or reject permissions.

9.2.6 Assumptions by MIDP 2.0

- MIDlets do not need to care about the security policy of the implementation, but some security exceptions that might be thrown when using protected API or function.
- A MIDlet suite is bound to a single protection domain and its permissible actions.
- Internal representation of protection domains and permissions is implementation-specific.
- User interface to display the authentication results and configuration settings is implementation-specific.
- Device implementation must protect the security policy and protection domain information stored in the device from viewing or modification except by authorized parties.
- If the security policy for a device is static and does not allow use of some protected APIs or functions, the implementation of unused and inaccessible security functions may be removed.
- Security policy should be just to restrict access from an implementation and must not be used to avoid implementing certain functionalities. For example, unimplemented protocols under GCF must throw `ConnectionNotFoundException`.

Earlier, we hinted that there was a process by which the MIDlet suite's origin and JAR integrity could be verified so that a device could have confidence in the identity of MIDlet suite prior to binding it to a protection domain. In some ways, this verification step is the most important step in the process. If the verification process is invalid, none of the mechanisms mentioned above will do much good. MIDP makes some recommendations regarding this critical phase. The recommended process for verification is discussed in the following section.

9.3 SIGNING AND AUTHENTICATING MIDLET SUITES BASED ON X.509 PKI

PKI mechanisms provide tools for verifying the origin and integrity of JARs transferred over the Internet. In particular, PKI can be used to digitally sign a data object such as a MIDlet suite. We can use this to verify both the identity of who sent the MIDlet suite and that the suite has not been altered in transit. A signed MIDlet suite may become a trusted one by identifying the signer of the MIDlet suite and binding it to a protection domain. After this is done, the MIDlet suite can begin the process of attempting to get the permissions it requires. But before any of the permissions is allowed by the user, we must first be able to use the digital signature to verify the origin and integrity. The next sections will discuss how developers and distributors of MIDlet suites can sign and authenticate their products, and how device implementations can process those signatures on their end. This process is based on X.509 PKI.

First, we will have a quick primer in the workings of a PKI system. A PKI revolves around the concept of keys. PKI uses what is known as an asymmetric cryptography process. This means that if one key is used to encode, a different key is used to decode. Older, symmetric systems used a single key for both encoding and decoding. Anyone who wants to be a mover and a shaker in the PKI world needs to get a pair of keys for themselves, one public and one private key. In case it's not obvious, you never show your private key to anyone, while your public key is widely distributed. There is no correspondence between a key's classification as public or private and its functional use as an encoding or decoding device. The only rule is that if one is used to encode, the other is used to decode. For some processes, the private key is used for encoding. In other processes, the public key is used for encoding.

In mathematical terms, the key is actually just an input parameter to the encryption function. Typically, the encryption function takes two inputs: a key and a data object. The output is an encrypted version of the data object. It is pretty simple. Decoding the encrypted data object is also simple. We need, again, two inputs: a key and the encrypted data object. The key that we need for decryption should be different from the key that we used in the encryption process. For example, if Bob's public key was used to encrypt the data object, Bob's private key must be used to decrypt the data object. Again, the private key could have been used for encryption and the public key for decryption.

The only remaining issue, as far as our security concerns go, is the manner in which we obtain the public key of other users. This is critical. If we can't be sure of the public key, our use of it has almost no meaning. Let's say that our friend encrypted and emailed us a document. If she used her private key to encrypt the document, we must have her public key to decrypt the document. No other key will work. One of the nice things about this is that we can know with certainty that this document was indeed sent by her. In other words, we don't have to worry that the document was intercepted and maliciously altered. Perhaps the document originally pledged undying love, but was intercepted by a rival and altered into a bitter Dear John letter. Oh, the treachery. But if her public key opens the document, we know her private key locked it.

But how do we know that the public key we have is truly hers. This is an electronic key after all. If it were a secret code that she had whispered quietly into our ear one moonlit night—I remember that sweet night even now—then we could be fairly sure of ourselves. But, this is the age of virtual romance, and PKI is an Internet standard after all. It's most likely we will obtain our friend's public key electronically. So, we need to have a way of gaining confidence in the true identity of the public keys we obtain and use.

This role is filled by certification authorities. Certification authorities are trusted third-party organizations that certify the identities of public keys. The process they use is quite simple. Someone who wants to use PKI registers with a certification authority. They get a pair of keys, and a certificate. The certificate is a document that contains the public key, the name of the person associated with that key, and a digital signature. We will explain the digital signature soon, but for now it is suffice to say that it is the means by which the integrity of the other information in the certificate is known to be correct. Instead of just sending us her public key over the dangerous airways of the Internet, our friend sends us her certificate. With her certificate in hand, we can examine the digital signature, through a process to be explained in next few paras, to know for sure that the included key belongs to her. After doing this, we will know that the contents of the letter are true representation of the contents of her heart.

The scenario described above, wherein our friend encrypts the true feelings of her heart, represents the most obvious use of encryption: making sure that no one else can read the sensitive data contained in some object. But the scenario above also began to hint at another use of PKI: digital signing of data objects to guarantee their origin and integrity. This is what we will do with our MIDlet suites. We don't really care if someone intercepts and reads our MIDlet suites, but we want to guarantee to our end-users that the MIDlet suite has not been intercepted and tampered with in some malicious intention. For these purposes, we don't want to encrypt the suite itself, we just want to guarantee its origin and the integrity of its contents. This is done by digitally signing the suite.

Digital signatures generally work in the following way. Rather than wasting time in encoding the entire data object, we first obtain a hash code, or a message digest, for the data object. A hash code is obtained via a hash function that produces a unique and small identifier for a given data object. No other data object can produce this same identifier from the hash function. Next, the signer uses her private key to encrypt the hash code. Now, she bundles the original data object with the encrypted hash code and a certificate containing her public key. If this data object is our MIDlet suite, the bundle will be the JAR file. We can now say that this bundle has been digitally signed.

If this digitally signed bundle is sent to someone, they can reverse the process to determine whether the bundled contents are what they seem to be. First, the certificate is examined to determine the identity of the public key it contains. We said earlier that the certificate is digitally signed by the certification authority. The public keys of the certification authorities are widely available. My web browser, for instance, comes with dozens built in. Examining the certificate amounts to using the public key of the certificate authority to decode the certificate. Once we do this, we know exactly whose public key we have.

We then use this public key to decrypt the hash code that was in the bundle. Next we take the original data object from the bundle and run the hash function on it by ourselves. We take the hash code obtained from this and compare it to the decrypted hash code from the bundle. If they match, the data object we have just received has not been altered. If it had been altered, it would not have produced the same hash code. Note, we also know, through the certification process, the precise origin of the data object. A process like this will be used to digitally sign and authenticate MIDlet suites. Now, let's look at the details.

9.3.1 Signing MIDlet Suites

As we have described in our overview of a PKI system, there are several important pieces in the security model of X.509 PKI. These pieces include public and private keys, certificates (issued by certificate authorities and containing public keys), a signer and, of course, the MIDlet suite. We'll discuss how each of them takes part in the process one by one.

Before we start, we should make a note about JAD and manifest redundancy. As we have mentioned several times, JAD and the manifest may contain duplicate information. However, we must note, now, that JAD is outside of the security of the signed JAR. If these two documents contain conflicting information, we have a problem. Because of this, we must articulate some rules that apply when the values defined in these two documents do not agree.

Attributes defined in the manifest of the JAR are secure since they are protected by the signature of the MIDlet suite. However, attributes defined in JAD are not secure. Values of the attributes defined in JAD must be the same as those of the corresponding attributes in the manifest of JAR for a trusted MIDlet suite. Otherwise, the suite must not be installed. Therefore, if an attribute appears in the manifest of JAR, it must not be overridden by a different value from JAD. This is to protect the MIDlet suite from modification of sensitive attribute values by outside parties. The `MIDlet.getAppProperty(String attrKey)` method returns the value specified in the manifest of JAR, if the attribute, `attrKey` in this case, is defined in the manifest. Otherwise, the value of the corresponding attribute specified in the application descriptor, if any, will be returned.

Exam Tip

MIDP 1.0 does not mandate that the attribute values in JAD and the manifest of JAR should be equal. That is only needed in the MIDlet suites that are signed and authenticated using X.509 PKI mechanism. MIDP 1.0 even gives higher priority to JAD attribute values over manifest attribute values.

Now let's look at the specific steps in the PKI security process. Assuming you are the signer of the MIDlet suite, the first thing you will need to do is obtain a certificate from a certification authority. You need to check the authorization policy of the device. The device must ultimately hold the public key from the certification authority, associated with a protection domain as the root certificate. The certificate has to comply with the RSA X.509 specification. You may obtain certificates from more than one authority. If more than one certificate is put into the MIDlet suite JAR, they must all contain the same public key.

Next, the signer will put her certificate(s) into the application descriptor as a certification path. A certification path includes the signer's certificate plus zero or more chained certificates. These other certificates represent other parties that have agreed to verify the MIDlet suite. The root certificate, that ultimately resolves the whole chain, is found on the device. It can also be found in removable storage. The root certificate is the public key from the certification authority. Note that more than one certification path can be inserted into the MIDlet suite. This simply represents multiple ways of authenticating the MIDlet suite. If more than one path is available, you would get a second chance if, for instance, the root certificate for the first one wasn't on the device. Again, you need to check the authorization policy of the device so that you can be sure of the root certificates on the device.

Certificates are base64-encoded. This encoding is simply a way of putting the data into an ASCII format for inclusion in JAD. While it makes the information more obfuscated to a human, it is by no means an encryption. All of the certificates from all the paths are put into JAD. Each certificate is associated with an attribute name built according to the following syntax.

```
MIDlet-Certificate-<n>-<m>: <base64 encoding of a certificate>
```

Here, `<n>` is the number of the path to which this certificate belongs and `<m>` is the position of the certificate in that path. Think of a two dimensional array, 1-based, where each element of the first array holds a certification path that is itself an array of certificates. For the first certification path, `n = 1` and is incremented for each additional path. The verification process will examine the paths in the sequence defined by this parameter. The signer's own certificate will always be the first in the chain. Thus, `m = 1` when the certificate holds the signer's key. The other certificates in the chain are indexed according to their logical sequence.

Now, the signer is ready to make the RSA SHA-1 digital signature. Recall that this signing process calculates a hash code for the MIDlet suite and then encrypts that hash code with the signer's private key. But a signing tool, such as the Java `jarsigner`, does all of this for you. Once the signature has been created, it must be base64-encoded and inserted into JAD under the attribute name `MIDlet-Jar-RSA-SHA1`. Once this is done, the MIDlet suite is considered signed. Nothing else needs to be done by the signing party. Next, we'll see how the implementation verifies the signature and, thus, authenticates the MIDlet suite.

9.3.2 Authenticating MIDlet Suites

When a MIDlet suite is downloaded into the device, the implementation must first decide if the MIDlet suite is signed. This is as simple as checking for the presence of the `MIDlet-Jar-RSA-SHA1` attribute in JAD. The value associated with this attribute, as we just learned, is the digital signature. If there is no such attribute, the MIDlet suite is simply installed as an untrusted MIDlet suite. If there is a signature, we must start the process of verifying that signature.

First, the signer's certificate must be verified. Recall from our earlier discussion of PKI that if the identity of the public key can't be verified, the whole process is moot. There can be more than one certification path, but we will start with the path at index 1, as specified by the format of the JAD certificate attribute. Each certificate in the path must be decoded from the base64 encoding. Next, the chain is resolved according to the X.509 process. The root certificates of the protection domains are used in the attempt to resolve the chains. When the chain is resolved, the MIDlet suite is bound, as a trusted suite, to the protection domain from which the root certificate that resolved the chain was taken. Regardless of the number of chains, the MIDlet suite is bound to the protection domain for the first chain that resolves. If no chain resolves, the suite is not installed.

Assuming that one of the certification paths has resolved, and thus verified the signer's certificate, we can move on to verifying the digital signature and the integrity of the MIDlet suite JAR. This process requires the signature itself as well as the public key of the signer and a hash code. The signature is in the JAD under the `MIDlet-Jar-RSA-SHA1` attribute. The public key is in the certificate verified in the preceding step. The hash code will be produced, using a hash function, from JAR and compared to the hash code in the signature. To get the hash code, the signature is first decoded from base64, and then decrypted using the signer's public key. If the hash codes match, we have confirmed that the MIDlet suite has not been altered in transit. At this point, we have verified the identity of the signer and we have confirmed the integrity of JAR itself. The results of verification steps have a direct impact on authorization of the MIDlet suite. Table 9.4 summarizes the verification results based on the initial states of the MIDlet suite.

Table 9.4 MIDlet suite verification results based on the initial states of the MIDlet suite installation process

Initial state	*Verification result*
JAD is not present and JAR is downloaded	Authentication cannot be performed, the MIDlet suite JAR can be installed as an untrusted MIDlet suite
JAD is present, but JAR is unsigned	Authentication cannot be performed, the MIDlet suite JAR can be installed as an untrusted MIDlet suite
JAR is signed, but no root certificate is present	Authentication cannot be performed, the MIDlet suite JAR cannot be installed

JAR is signed, but a certificate on a certification path is expired	Authentication cannot be performed, the MIDlet suite JAR cannot be installed
JAR is signed, but a certificate on a certification path is rejected for any other reasons except expiration	JAD is rejected, the MIDlet suite JAR cannot be installed
JAR is signed and certificate path is validated, but signature verification is failed	JAD is rejected, the MIDlet suite JAR cannot be installed
JAR is signed, certification path is validated and signature is verified	The MIDlet suite JAR can be installed as a trusted MIDlet suite

What now? This discussion has been so complex you might have forgotten the whole MIDlet suite security model. Remember the trusted and untrusted suites? At this point, with the signer's identity and the integrity of the JAR both ready, we have a trusted MIDlet suite in our hands. It seems like so much has been accomplished, with all of the hash codes and asymmetric encryption, but really we've only just begun the MIDlet suite security process. What happens now is that the trusted MIDlet suite starts the process of requesting permissions for the APIs it needs to use. This was the process we covered in the first half of this chapter. Now you've come full circle. Congratulations!

We'll tie up a couple of loose ends before we end, one about caching and one about split-VM implementations. First of all, the implementation's authorization process is allowed to cache results from the above calculations for re-use, but care must be taken to maintain the security of this information. Lastly, it's possible that a split-VM implementation might have its own security process, due to a conversion of the MIDlet suite JAR into a device-specific format. The details of these processes are not covered by MIDP.

Summary

In this chapter, we have seen a variety of security mechanisms provided within the realm of the JTWI specification for mobile phone applications. Admittedly, this chapter has been heavy on the conceptual language. Unfortunately, this is the nature of security mechanisms. If it doesn't suit your nature, you might as well bite the bullet and learn it. Besides, the abstract security concepts discussed in this chapter are found throughout the field of computer science and technology these days. Mastery of these topics will serve you far beyond the scope of this exam.

Some of the security occurs at the configuration layer's core implementation of the Java platform and some of it occurs at the profile layer's implementation of the MIDlet application model. At the configuration layer, the CLDC security model consists of three levels: low-level security, application-level security and end-to-end security. While the CLDC addresses security at the virtual machine and network transit levels, you are only responsible for its application-level security provisions. Low-level security is also called virtual machine security and end-to-end security is the responsibility of the profile-level implementation. If you recall, the application-level security provisions implement a sandbox model for security. Basically, this model confines the application by limiting the classes that it can execute. For the test, you need to be familiar with the set of classes that can be accessed within the sandbox and the mechanisms for enforcing the bounds of the sandbox.

At the profile layer, all MIDlet suites based on MIDP 1.0 are considered as untrusted ones, while the MIDP 2.0 defines a model based upon trusted and untrusted MIDlet suites. This model defines permissions that help protect APIs and functions from unauthorized access. You need to understand the steps involved in the determination of the set of permissions ultimately granted to a MIDlet suite. For instance, you should clearly understand the role of the protection domain in this process. You should also know the difference between critical and optional requested permissions and the mechanisms by which a MIDlet suite specifies these requests.

The MIDP 2.0 also specifies a PKI implementation to be used in the verification of MIDlet suites. Applications can be signed and authorized using X.509 PKI. "Signing a MIDlet suite" steps include creating a signer certificate, inserting certificates into the application descriptor and creating the digital signature of the JAR. "Authorizing a MIDlet suite" steps include verifying the signer certificate, MIDlet suite signature and JAR.

Now you are at the end of the Part III, where you learned how to create mobile applications using MIDP UI, Game API, networking API, RMS and security-enhanced techniques. The coming part will discuss optional features that you can add to your mobile applications to make them more creative using Mobile Media API and more robust using Wireless Messaging API.

References

1. MIDP 2.0(JSR-118) specification
   http://www.jcp.org/aboutJava/communityprocess/final/jsr118/
2. MIDP Application Security 3: Authentication in MIDP
   http://developers.sun.com/techtopics/mobility/midp/articles/security3/index.html
3. Secure Java MIDP Programming Using HTTPS with MIDP
   http://developers.sun.com/techtopics/mobility/midp/articles/https/index.html

Review Questions

1. Which of the following ensures that poorly organized class files do not break the system or maliciously encoded class files do not harm the device in any situation?
   a. Application-level security
   b. End-to-end security
   c. Low-level security
   d. Sandbox security
2. Which of the following is the statement that is not related to application-level security?
   a. An application can load classes only from its own JAR file.
   b. An application containing malicious codes or ill-formed class files cannot access the system resources.

c. Information transmission made by an application is protected along the way to the remote device from the mobile device.

d. An application to be downloaded cannot contain code that alter, extend, override or add any classes to protected system packages.

3. True or False: Applications built that are based on MIDP 1.0 are recognized as untrusted MIDlet suites.

   a. True

   b. False

4. Which one of the following method calls does not need explicit user confirmation to access?

   a. `HttpConnection.openInputStream()`

   b. `HttpsConnection.getPort()`

   c. `HttpConnection.getURL()`

   d. `MIDlet.checkPermission(String permission)`

5. Which of the following definition refers to protection domain?

   a. A set of *allowed* and *user* permissions that may be granted to a MIDlet suite

   b. A set of permissions available on the device

   c. A set of permissions defined by the certificate authority

   d. A set of permissions requested by a MIDlet suite

6. Which of the following attributes can be used to request permissions for a MIDlet suite?

   a. `MIDlet-Permissions`

   b. `MIDlet-Permissions-Optional`

   c. `MIDlet-Permissions-Mandatory`

   d. `MIDlet-Permissions-Opt`

7. Which of the following are user interaction modes available for *user* permissions?

   a. `application` b. `oneshot`

   c. `blanket` d. `session`

   e. `request`

8. Which of the following step is included in MIDlet suites signing process?

   a. Verifying signer certificate

   b. Inserting the RSA SHA-1 signature of JAR

   c. Verifying MIDlet suite signature

   d. Installing MIDlet suite

9. How do you specify multiple permissions in the application descriptor?

   a. By separating with commas (,)

   b. By separating with semi-colons (;)

   c. By separating with white spaces ( )

   d. There is no way that we can specify multiple permissions.

10. In which initial state can we install a MIDlet suite?
    a. JAD is not present and JAR is unsigned.
    b. JAR is signed and a certificate on a certification path is expired.
    c. JAR is signed, certificate path is validated and signature verification is failed.
    d. JAR is signed and root certificate is missing.

Review Answers

1. c. Ensuring that poorly organized class files do not break the system or maliciously-encoded class files do not harm the device in any situation is the responsibility of the low-level security.
2. c. End-to-end security, not application-level security, makes sure that information transmission made by an application is protected along the way to the remote device from the mobile device.
3. a. MIDP 1.0 does not have trusted MIDlet suites concept. So MIDP 1.0 applications are considered as untrusted ones.
4. d. Access to classes located in the `javax.microedition.midlet` package does not need explicit user confirmation, but `javax.microedition.io.HttpConnection` and `javax.microedition.io.HttpsCOnnection` classes do need it.
5. a. Protection domain contains a set of *allowed* and *user* permissions that may be granted to a MIDlet suite.
6. a. and d. `MIDlet-Permissions` and `MIDlet-Permissions-Opt` must be used to request critical and optional permissions for a MIDlet suite.
7. b., c., and d. `oneshot`, `blanket` and `session` are the three interaction modes available for *user* permissions.
8. b. Inserting the RSA SHA-1 signature of the JAR is one of the steps included in MIDlet suite signing process.
9. a. Multiple permissions can be specified in `MIDlet-Permissions` for critical permissions or `MIDlet-Permissions-Opt` for optional permissions by separating each permission with a comma(,).
10. a. Only in the state, where JAD is not present and JAR is unsigned, a MIDlet suite will be installed as untrusted one. The rest of the states violate the requirements for a trusted MIDlet suite. Signed MIDlet suite is the MIDlet suite that claims to be trusted one, but the later conditions do not let the MIDlet suite to be installed.

Exam Notes

☞ Given a set of requirements, design and build applications with CLDC-specified application-level security, including the sandbox model.

CLDC Application-level Security

- Application-level security means that a Java application can access only the libraries, resources and other components that the device on which the application is installed and the Java environment that it runs in allows it to access.
- The sandbox model means that the device cannot use libraries or resources other than those defined by the configurations, profiles and other classes supported by the device (say, optional packages like Bluetooth API).
- Requirements by the CLDC sandbox model:
    - Classes must be verified to be valid by the CLDC pre-verifier and runtime verifier.
    - Application programmer cannot modify the class loading mechanism. Custom class loading mechanisms are not allowed in CLDC.
    - Only a closed set of pre-defined profiles (like MIDP, WMA) are available to the programmer (you cannot use third-party libraries willy-nilly unless supported by the device!).
    - Application programmer cannot write or use native code that is not part of the pre-defined packages (there is no `Runtime.exec()` method). Libraries containing native code cannot be downloaded into a device (unless it is a part of J2ME or that supplied by the device manufacturer).
- Application programmer cannot override the `java.*`, `javax.microedition.*`, or other profile-specific or manufacturer-specific packages. That is, you cannot spoof a Java package (say, you cannot have a class called `java.lang.String`, which you wrote, in your package).
- Application programmer cannot modify the class lookup order by rearranging the JAR files and paths present in the `classpath` variable (you typically cannot set the `classpath` of a CLDC!).
- By default, a Java application can load application classes only from its own JAR file.
- No end-to-end security mechanism (like encryption) is defined in CLDC. That responsibility is left to the profile implementations.

☞ Identify correct and incorrect statements or examples about untrusted MIDlet suites.

Untrusted MIDlet Suites

- All MIDP 1.0 applications in a MIDP 2.0 environment are considered as untrusted MIDlet suites.
- An untrusted MIDlet suite is a MIDlet suite whose origin or JAR file integrity cannot be verified.
- The following APIs are accessible to untrusted MIDlet suites, **without explicit user confirmation:**

API	Description
`javax.microedition.rms`	Record Management Store API
`javax.microedition.midlet`	MIDlet lifecycle API
`javax.microedition.lcdui`	User Interface API
`javax.microedition.lcdui.game`	Game API
`javax.microedition.media`	
`javax.microedition.media.control`	Audio playback API

- The following APIs are accessible to untrusted MIDlet suites, **with explicit user confirmation:**

API	Description
`javax.microedition.io.HttpConnection`	http protocol handler
`javax.microedition.io.HttpsConnection`	https protocol handler

- If the user does not give permission, a `SecurityException` will be thrown.

☞ Explain trusted MIDlet suite security authorization and permissions, including the process for MIDlet suite signing.

Trusted MIDlet Suites Authorization

- The concept of trusted MIDlet suites was introduced in MIDP 2.0.
- A MIDlet suite is considered trusted if it is signed and verified using a mechanism such as X.509 PKI.
- Authorization model of the MIDP 2.0 contains the following participating elements:
  - A set of *allowed* and *user* permissions granted to a MIDlet suite.
  - A set of permissions requested by the MIDlet suite in its `MIDlet-Permissions` and `MIDlet-Permissions-Opt` attributes.
  - A set of permissions for each protected API.
  - The user who may be asked to grant permissions.
- The MIDlet does not need to be aware of security permissions. It need to be only worried about whether a `SecurityException` is thrown or not while executing a method.
- How the user is asked for permission is implementation-dependent.
- The permission information in a device cannot be viewed or modified.
- A `SecurityException` cannot be thrown because of an unimplemented functionality. It should only be used to throw errors because of lack of permission or authorization. For example, if a protocol is not implemented, it should throw a `ConnectionNotFound Exception`, not `SecurityException`.

Trusted MIDlet Suites Permission

- Permissions are typically specified both at the class level and at the function level.
- Permission names have a hierarchy similar to Java package names.
  - A permission must have the same prefix as that of the package name.
  - If a permission is for a specific class, the permission name prefix must be same as that of the class name. For example, if you want to define permissions for a class `com.company.module.Foo`, the permission name must begin with `com.company.module.Foo`, say, like `com.company.module.Foo.read`.
- Permissions defined in the `MIDlet-Permissions` attribute are the permissions, without which the MIDlet suite cannot operate.
- Permissions defined in the `MIDlet-Permissions-Opt` attribute are the permissions, with or without which the MIDlet suite can operate, but probably with a reduced functionality (for example, a single-player game instead of an online two-player game).
- Permissions defined in these attributes are separated by commas (,).
- *Allowed* permissions are those, which do not need explicit user confirmation.
- *User* permissions are those, which need explicit user confirmation.
- A permission can be a *user* permission or an *allowed* permission, but not both.
- *Allowed* permission has the value "`allow`" in the policy file.
- *User* permission can have one of three values:
  - "`blanket`" means once the permission is defined by the user, it remains that way for the life of the application (from install to uninstall) till explicitly changed.
  - "`session`" means once the permission is defined by user, it remains that way for that run of the application (from start of the MIDlet suite to stop).
  - "`oneshot`" means the permission has to be defined by user for every invocation of API.
- The implementation should (but not a must) provide these options to the user. An option to deny must be provided too.

Granting Permissions to Trusted MIDlet Suites

- The `MIDlet-Permissions` and `MIDlet-Permissions-Opt` attribute values must be identical in the JAD file and the manifest. If not, the MIDlet suite must not be installed.
- If CRITICAL requested permissions are not known to the device, the MIDlet suite must not be installed.
- If CRITICAL requested permissions are not present in the protection domain, the MIDlet suite must not be installed.
- If a permission requested is a *user* permission, the user must explicitly provide permission.
- Permissions granted to a MIDlet is:
  (Requested Permissions) $\cap$ (User Permissions $\cup$ Allowed Permissions)
- A `SecurityException` must be thrown if the user did not grant permission to an API.

MIDlet Signing Process

Signing a MIDlet suite involves the following steps:

Creating Certificate

- At least X.509 certificates must be supported.
- The signer (the application programmer) requests a certificate from a Certificate Authority (CA) using the standard signing procedure. The CA creates an RSA X.509 certificate and sends it back to the signer.

Inserting Certificates in JAD

- The certificate path (except the root certificate portion) should be inserted into JAD using `base64` encoding standard (without line breaks).
  - ♦ The attribute name for the path is of the form `MIDlet-Certificate-<n>-<m>`, where `n` = `1` for the first certification path and to be increased for extra certificates and `m` = `1` for the signer certificate and to be increased for intermediate certificates.

Creating JAR Signature and Adding to JAD

- The signature of the JAR is created with the signer's private key.
- The signature is encoded using `base64` algorithm and added as value to the attribute `MIDlet-Jar-RSA-SHA1` in the JAD file.

MIDlet Authentication Process

Authenticating a MIDlet suite involves the following steps:

Verifying Signer Certificate

- The attribute values are checked for presence and verified.
- Appropriate certificate definition is matched with the root certificates installed in the device.

Verifying MIDlet Suite Signature and JAR

- The public key of the verified certificate is used along with the signature from the `MIDlet-Jar-RSA-SHA1` attribute value and the SHA-1 digest of the JAR file to verify the MIDlet suite signature.

MIDlet Suite Installation

Initial State	*Installed?*	*Trusted?*
JAD not present, JAR is unsigned or signed	Yes	No
JAD present, JAR is unsigned	Yes	No
JAR signed but no root certificate present in device	No	-

JAR signed, certificate expired	No	-
JAR signed, certificate rejected	No	-
JAR signed, certificate valid, but signature fails	No	-
JAR signed, certificate valid, signature verified	Yes	Yes

☞ Explain requirements and process of using X.509 PKI authentication for MIDlet suites.

- See Section 9.3.2 (Authenticating MIDlet Suites).

Part-4

Working with Optional Features

In the Java ME platform, optional features like Wireless Message API (WMA) and Mobile Media API (MMAPI) can't be overlooked. Believe it or not, the secondary purposes of most of the mobile phone users today are to send and receive wireless messages or to listen to some music and watch some video clips, while the primary purpose is to make and receive phone calls.

This final part of the book covers these two optional features. So why don't we get our hands dirty by playing around with these?

10

Chapter

Working with Multimedia: MIDP 2.0 Media API and Mobile Media API (MMAPI)

Exam Objectives

10.1 Given a set of requirements, develop code using MMAPI's support for tone generation. (Section 10.2)

10.2 Given a set of requirements, develop code that correctly uses MIDP support for sound including:

- ❖ Audio playback
- ❖ Tone generation
- ❖ Media flow controls (start, stop)
- ❖ Media type controls (volume, tone)
- ❖ Media capabilities using "Manager", "Player", and "Control" objects
- ❖ Recognizing the difference between required and optional features

(Sections 10.3, 10.4, 10.5 and 10.6)

10.3 Develop code that correctly uses MMAPI support for playback and recording of media, including:

- ❖ The use of the "DataSource", "Player", and "Manager" objects
- ❖ Support for audio and video capture and playback
- ❖ System properties queries
- ❖ Recognizing the difference between required and optional features

(Sections 10.3, 10.4, 10.5 and 10.6)

10.4 Identify correct and incorrect statements or examples about the media class hierarchies in both MIDP 2.0 and MMAPI 1.1. (Section 10.7)

INTRODUCTION

Two of the most powerful modes of communication are audio and visuals. From the start, computer graphics and sound capabilities have been the hallmark of a good application. In fact, they may be the number one selling point for many consumer devices. Since many devices do not yet support rich multimedia functionality, the media APIs of JTWI come in two flavors: the required MIDP 2.0 Media API and the optional MMAPI 1.1.

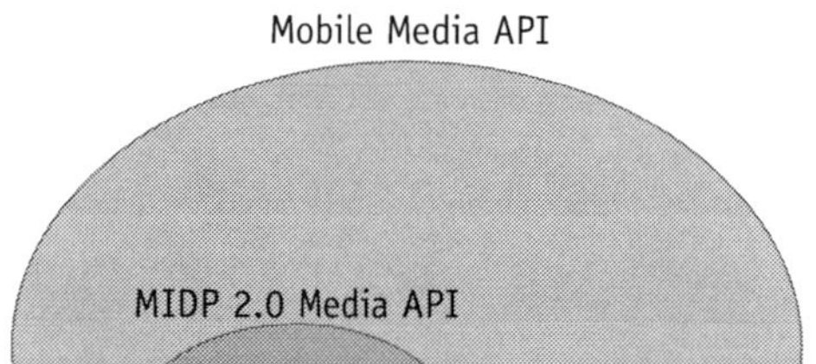

Figure 10.1 MIDP 2.0 Media API subsets MMAPI

These flavors, however, are really part of the same API. MMAPI can be considered as a true API. It establishes a framework for handling media content and provides support for a wide range of media types. As seen in Fig. 10.1, the MIDP 2.0 Media API is a subset of MMAPI. The subset tries to meet the more modest needs of less media rich devices. We will cover the details in this chapter, but in a nutshell, the subset supports only the audio functionality of the superset.

Because the MIDP 2.0 is a required component specification of JTWI, its Media API is obviously a required API. In other words, the subset of functionality it defines will be present on all JTWI-compliant implementations. If an implementation chooses to support functionality not covered by this subset, such as video, it must be through the MMAPI 1.1. This is the conditional requirement.

☞ Just because a device has native video capabilities doesn't mean the implementation has to support them. But if they do choose to expose the video capabilities to the Java platform, it must be exposed through MMAPI.

For the exam, you need to be clear on this relationship between the MMAPI 1.1 and the MIDP 2.0 Media API. Since the MIDP Media API is a strictly upward compatible subset of MMAPI, it makes sense from a logical perspective to discuss MMAPI first and then note where the MIDP subset differs. This is what we will do in this chapter. Section 10.7 addresses the differences between the two APIs. We suggest that you take a look at this section now. And you might want to take an occasional glance as you read through the details of MMAPI.

10.1 UNDERSTANDING MMAPI

MMAPI is structured around two classes: `DataSource` and `Player`. We can view the interaction of a device with multimedia content as occurring in two phases. The first phase occurs when the content data is delivered to the device via some protocol. The second phase is when the content data is handled by a media player. The `DataSource` class represents the protocol-based procurement of the content data, be it a music or video file. The `DataSource` hides the details from the developer. The `Player` class knows how to handle the content. In addition to these key classes, there is a `Manager` class. The `Manager` class provides static factory methods for obtaining `Players` to handle a variety of media types. It's a pretty simple model, and in this chapter we will learn the details of how to work with it. Let's take a quick tour of the packages and classes of the API.

There are three main packages in the MMAPI. The first package contains the main interfaces such as `Player`, `Control` and the `Manager` class. This small package is the `javax.microedition.media` package.

The next package, `javax.microedition.media.control`, contains implementations of the `Control` interface found in the core package. These implementation classes represent a variety of controls that a `Player` can provide to control the play of a media type. Such controls include obvious things like `VolumeControl`, `ToneControl` and `TempoControl`.

The last package is the `javax.microedition.media.protocol` package. This package contains the important abstract class `DataSource` that represents some sort of protocol-based source for media content data. This package also includes an interface for the stream of data that comes from a `DataSource`. This interface is called `SourceStream`.

Believe or not, that almost covers everything that we need to know for the exam in MMAPI. Figure 10.2 provides an overview of the interplay between the various classes and interfaces present in the `javax.microedition.media` package.

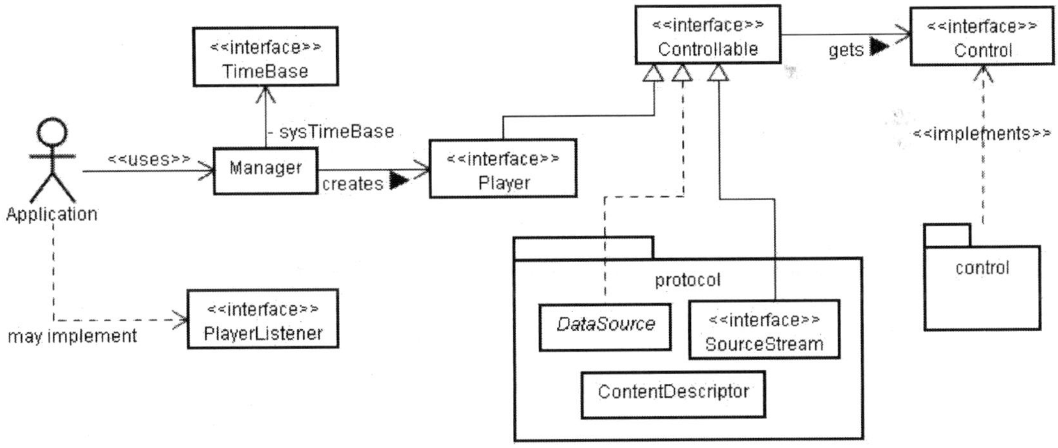

Figure 10.2 Interaction between the major components in MMAPI

For now, just note that the application works primarily with the `Manager`, the factory methods of which will provide the various `Players` that will handle our media files. Of course, there's more to it than that. But a high-level sketch of the framework is good for an introduction. Now that we have covered the basics, let's go into the details of each of these components.

10.2 GENERATING SIMPLE TONES

The media handling capabilities of MMAPI are quite rich. But sometimes you just want to make a beep. Before we go on to the full `DataSource` and `Player` model, let's take a look at a convenience method provided by the `Manager` class for making simple tones. One of the simplest things that can be done with the Media API is to create monotones. A monotone is a single note played over a period of time. A sequence of monotones can be used to generate simple music. Typically, such monotones are used as basic ring tones in a mobile phone. Of late, polyphonic tones (multiple notes at the same time), generally in MIDI format, are used for creating more realistic ring tones, but here we are looking at the simplest tone, the monotone.

Support for monotones is present in both MMAPI and MIDP Media API. The method that can be used to create a tone is:

```
Manager.playTone(int note, int duration, int volume) throws MediaException
```

where

- ❑ `note` is a value between 0 and 127 (64 being the C note)
- ❑ `duration` defines the number of milliseconds that the note must be played
- ❑ `volume` is a relative value in percentage between 0 (silent) and 100 (loudest)

This method does not really do much except generating a simple monotone for a specific duration at a specific volume. This is most commonly used to generate a beep or a single-tone alarm from the device.

Listing 10.1 is an example of how a simple monotone can be generated using the `playTone` method:

Listing 10.1: Generating a simple tone using the Manager class

```
package com.scmadkit.ch10;

import javax.microedition.midlet.*;
import javax.microedition.media.*;
import javax.microedition.media.control.ToneControl;
public class SimpleToneMIDlet extends MIDlet {
   protected void startApp() {
      try {
         Manager.playTone(ToneControl.C4, 5000, 100);        ❶
      } catch (MediaException me) {
```

```
                me.printStackTrace();
            }
        }
        protected void pauseApp() {}
        protected void destroyApp(boolean _boolean){}
}
```

(1) Plays a middle C note with the loudest volume for five seconds

The `playTone` method used in Listing 10.1 will play the note that is represented by the `ToneControl.C4` constant, a middle C note. We will discuss the details of the `ToneControl` interface later in this chapter. Since the duration of the tone is specified as 5000 in the second parameter, it is equivalent to five seconds. The third parameter, 100, represents the loudest possible volume of the device.

With a bit of musical talent, you can actually create some interesting music with this convenience method. It's at least rewarding to get some sound out of the device with relatively little work. But, ultimately this is obviously limited. So, let's get back to the full rich media model of MMAPI.

10.3 DEFINING SOURCE OF MEDIA

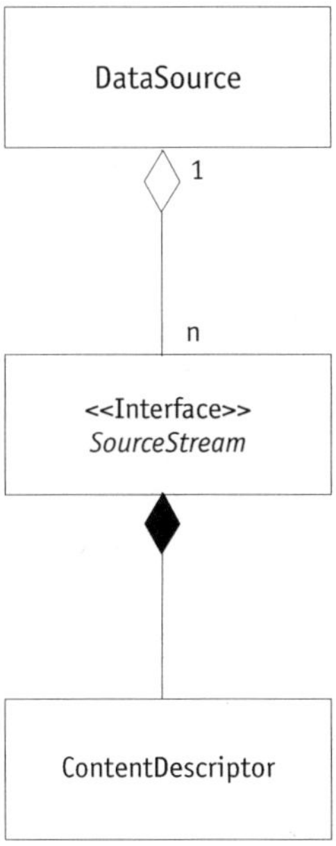

Figure 10.3 Classes representing media

As a starting point for our coverage of MMAPI, we provide overviews of the most important components of the media framework. First, we will look at the classes that represent the media itself. Data that is to be played in a mobile phone can be described in two important ways. First, it has a source location. It generally originates from two possible sources—from a file located in the device itself (like a MIDI file for a ring tone) or as a stream from an external location (like a URL of a song that needs to be played). Second, it has a format, such as MP3, MIDI, WAV, MPEG, etc. Figure 10.3 shows the relationship of the classes that describe media content.

MMAPI defines the `DataSource` class to represent—not surprisingly—the source of the data that needs to be played. The `DataSource` class uses the `SourceStream` interface to describe the actual data and the `ContentDescriptor` class to describe the format of the data. For now, just note that a `DataSource` has one or more `SourceStreams` that represent its data. Each of the `SourceStreams` has a `ContentDescriptor` that describes its data. Let us look at each of these pieces in detail.

10.3.1 Describing Source

An instance of the `DataSource` class is constructed using a `String` called the *locator string*. The locator string defines the origin of the data, in a specific format, as shown below.

```
scheme:scheme-specific-part
```

While this format may look simple, this can be used to specify lots of information. scheme defines the type of protocol used. Two schemes have been defined in MMAPI so far. More schemes can be defined by device vendors, specific to their device families. However, it is the application's responsibility, in that case, to ensure that the application does not crash if it is installed on a device from a different vendor.

The defined schemes are `capture` (to capture live media) and `rtp` (for real-time streaming).

Capturing Live Media

The *locator string* for the live-media capture can be further expanded as

```
capture://<device>[?<params>]
```

where `<device>` is one of

- "audio"
- "video"
- "audio_video" or
- a custom device name (an alphanumeric string)

and `<params>` is a URL-like parameter string of the form:

```
key=value[&key=value[&key=value...]]
```

Table 10.1 provides some of the parameters that can be used in capturing audio streams.

Table 10.1 Parameters used in capturing audio streams

Parameter	*Description*
encoding	Type of encoding algorithm used. For example, "pcm", "ulaw", "gsm".
rate	Bit rate of the audio stream (in bits per second). For example, "96000", "11025", "8000".
bits	Number of bits used
channels	A positive integer

Table 10.2 provides some of the parameters that can be used in capturing video snapshots.

Table 10.2 Parameters used in capturing video snapshots

Parameter	*Description*
encoding	Type of encoding algorithm used. For example, "gray8", "rgb888", "bgr888", "rgb565".
width	Width of a frame (in pixels)
height	Height of a frame (in pixels)
fps	Frames per second

The following are some of the *locator string* examples for capturing live media:

```
capture://audio
```
(Default audio)

```
capture://audio?encoding=pcm
```
(Audio in PCM format)

```
capture://devmic0?encoding=pcm&rate=11025&bits=16&channels=1
```
(Audio from a custom device - devmic0)

```
capture://video
```
(Default video)

```
capture://video?encoding=gray8&width=160&height=120
```
(Video snapshot with 'gray8' encoding, 160 pixel wide and 120 pixels high)

```
capture://devcam0?encoding=rgb888&width=160&height=120&fps=7
```
(Video from a custom device - devcam0)

```
capture://mydev?myattr=123
```
(Custom device with a custom parameter)

> **Exam Tip**
>
> Remember the format for the *locator string*. While you might not be questioned about the exact values represented in the string, you are expected to know the syntax of the string.

Capturing RTP (Real-Time Protocol) Streams

RTP is a public standard for streaming media. The RTP *locator string* takes a more familiar URL-like syntax as below.

```
rtp://<address>[:<port>][/<type>]
```

where

- <address> and the optional <port> define IP address of the source
- <type> is one of "audio", "video", or "text"

Apart from these generic syntaxes, the javax.microedition.media.Manager class has two pre-defined constants—MIDI_DEVICE_LOCATOR and TONE_DEVICE_LOCATOR for MIDI audio and tone sequence-based audio, respectively—that are built into all MMAPI-compliant devices.

Apart from getter methods for getting the *locator string* (getLocator()), content type (getContentType()), and streams associated with the source (getStreams()), the DataSource class also defines the following lifecycle methods as listed in Table 10.3.

Table 10.3 Lifecycle methods in the `DataSource` class

Method	*Use*
`void connect()`	Connects to the data source described by the locator string.
`void disconnect()`	Disconnects from the data source and frees relevant resources.
`void start()`	Initiates data transfer.
`void stop()`	Terminates data transfer.

While the source data can also be described as a traditional `java.io.InputStream`, it is better to define the source using the `DataSource` class for the following reasons:

- It provides API (via the `SourceStream` interface) to randomly seek bytes in the stream.
- It supports the concept of a transfer size. This is especially useful for video, where data is typically transferred as frames of fixed length.
- The `DataSource` class implements the `Controllable` interface that is extended by the `SourceStream` interface, thereby providing a mechanism to specify the controls that can be used while playing the associated media.

Now that we have defined the source, let's proceed to look at reading them.

Apart from getting the source of the data from external resources using the `DataSource` class and from pre-defined device resources using the *locator string*, it is also possible to get the resource information from a JAR file or even from a record stored in the application's RMS.

Listing 10.2 illustrates how media content data can be played from a JAR file.

Listing 10.2: Playing media obtained from a JAR file

```
package com.scmadkit.ch10;
import java.io.*;
import javax.microedition.midlet.*;
import javax.microedition.media.*;
public class InputStreamToneMIDlet extends MIDlet {
   protected void startApp() {
      /**
      * Notice that in MIDP 2.0, the wav format is mandatory
      * only in the case that the device supports sampled audio.
      */
      try {
         InputStream is =
            getClass().getResourceAsStream("/audio.wav");          ❶
         Player p = Manager.createPlayer(is, "audio/X-wav");       ❷
         p.start();
```

```
        } catch (IOException ioe) {
           ioe.printStackTrace();
        } catch (MediaException me) {
           me.printStackTrace();
        }
     }
     protected void pauseApp() {}
     protected void destroyApp(boolean _boolean){}
  }
```

(1) Retrieves the media content from the specified location

(2) Creates a Player from the Manager class and plays the media content

In Listing 10.2, an input stream is created using the `getResourceAsStream` method of the `Class` class. And, to create a `Player`, the input stream is passed into the version of the `createPlayer` method of the `Manager` class that can accept an input stream. Then the media content is played using the created `Player`.

Here's another example in Listing 10.3 that illustrates how media content data stored in an RMS can be played using MMAPI.

Listing 10.3: Playing media obtained from an RMS source

```
package com.scmadkit.ch10;

import java.io.*;
import javax.microedition.midlet.*;
import javax.microedition.media.*;
import javax.microedition.rms.*;

public class RMSToneMIDlet extends MIDlet {
   protected void startApp() {
      try {
         RecordStore rs;
         int recordId;

         // ...
         // Initiates the record store                  (1)
         // Initiates the record id
         // ...

         InputStream is =
            new ByteArrayInputStream(rs.getRecord(recordId));   (2)
         Player p = Manager.createPlayer(is, "audio/X-wav");
         p.start();                                             (3)
```

```
            } catch (IOException ioe) {
                ioe.printStackTrace();
            } catch (MediaException me) {
                me.printStackTrace();
            } catch (RecordStoreException rse) {
                rse.printStackTrace();
            }
        }
        protected void pauseApp() {}
        protected void destroyApp(boolean _boolean){}
    }
```

1. Sets up the record store that contains the media content
2. Retrieves the media content from the specified record
3. Creates a `Player` from the `Manager` class and plays the media content

In Listing 10.3, an input stream is created using a `ByteArrayInputStream` constructor, into which the array of bytes returned from the `getRecord` method of the `RecordStore` class is passed. And, to create a `Player`, the input stream is passed into the version of the `createPlayer` method of the `Manager` class that can accept an input stream. Then the media content is played using the created `Player`.

Though the examples that we've seen in the listings are pretty straightforward, we have at least got an idea how to play media content from different sources. Next, we will be looking at the way how to describe the media content that we have in hand.

10.3.2 Describing Content

If `DataSource` describes the source of the media, `ContentDescriptor` describes the content type of the media. This is a fairly simple class that manages one single `String` – the content type and provides mechanisms to set the value (through the constructor) and get the value (via a getter method). If the content type is `null`, it means that the content details are unknown. As we saw in Fig. 10.3, the `ContentDescriptor` is held by the `SourceStream`, which we are going to see next.

10.3.3 Reading Data from DataSource

The `SourceStream` interface defines methods that can be used to read data from a source defined by the `DataSource` class. Implementations of this interface can be obtained from the corresponding `DataSource` using the method:

```
public SourceStream[] getStreams()
```

While a `DataSource` may be associated with multiple streams, there will typically be just one stream. Data contained in a `SourceStream` can be accessed randomly. The interface provides methods to read data `(read(byte[] b, int off, int len))`, seek to a specified position `(seek(long where))`, and tell the current position of the reader in the stream `(tell())`.

As mentioned earlier, the interface also provides a method called `getTransferSize()` to get the size of a logical chunk of data that is being transferred. In case of video transfers, this will typically be the amount of data contained in a single frame.

So far, we have successfully defined the source of data and mechanisms on how to read the data. Now comes the most important part—playing the data we just read.

10.4 GETTING MEDIA PLAYER

We have created our `DataSource` and prepared to read the data, now it is show time. Well, almost. First, we need to look at the factory methods, which allow us to obtain an appropriate `Player` for our media type. The starting point to playing media content is the `javax.microedition.media.Manager` class. This class provides the factory methods to create a `Player` instance that can be used to play media content. The `Manager` also provides access to some high-level information about the capabilities of the device itself.

A `Player` class can be obtained from the `Manager` using one of the three `createPlayer` methods defined in the `Manager` class. Each method takes in a parameter that describes the source of the data that should be played. The following are the signatures of the `createPlayer` methods defined in the `Manager` class, and Table 10.4 lists all the parameters that might be passed into the methods. As you can see, it is possible to create a `Player` in a variety of ways.

```
public static Player createPlayer(DataSource dataSource)
    throws java.io.IOException, MediaException

public static Player createPlayer(String locatorString)
    throws java.io.IOException, MediaException

public static Player createPlayer(InputStream inputStream,
            String type)
    throws java.io.IOException, MediaException
```

Table 10.4 Parameters used for getting a `Player` instance

Parameter	*Description*
`dataSource`	Used to create a `Player` instance using the provided `DataSource` object. The `DataSource` object defines the source of the data, the content type, and the streams associated with the source.

`locatorString`	Is a no-frills version of the `DataSource`, typically (although not necessarily) used to denote simpler media types, such as MIDI files or tone sequences.
`inputStream`	Used to create a `Player` instance based on the data streamed through the given stream. The `type` parameter (a `String`) is also passed along with the `InputStream` instance to indicate the type of content being streamed. If the type is `null`, then the `Player` will try to determine the type based on the contents of the stream (typically, based on some header information, if present).

Since MMAPI doesn't require implementation of any particular media types or protocols, the `Manager` provides a couple of convenience methods to determine the protocols and media types supported by the implementation.

```
public String[] getSupportedContentTypes(String protocol)
public String[] getSupportedProtocols(String contentType)
```

A single protocol may support streaming of a variety of media content types. This can be seen in the `protocol` string parameter of the content type method above. The first returns the supported content types for a given protocol. The second returns the supported protocols for a given content type. If a `null` parameter is passed to these methods, the API will return all the content types or protocols supported by the device, respectively.

Exam Tip

You might be asked some tricky questions based on null values passed to some of the methods in MMAPI. It is important to remember the default behavior of such methods.

☞ In the JTWI chapter, we discussed a few extra requirements that it imposes upon MMAPI. For instance, the HTTP protocol is required. Refer back to that chapter to see what other requirements are made on MMAPI.

Finally, the `Manager` class also provides a method called `getSystemTimeBase()` to get the default timescale used by the device. This method returns a `TimeBase` instance, which can be used to get the current time of the `TimeBase` in *microseconds*.

Exam Tip

In devices that cannot calculate time in *microseconds*, the implementation must provide appropriate conversion to return the time in *microseconds*.

Now that we've got what we need to play media content, a `Player`, let's go ahead and play some.

10.5 PLAYING MEDIA

Finally, it's show time. Perhaps the most important man in MMAPI is the `javax.microedition.media.Player` interface. This interface defines the lifecycle of a media being played. As we have just seen, the `Player` implementation is obtained from the `Manager` based on media source. The player obtained can then be used to load, start, stop, or loop back the media originating from the source. Figure 10.4 illustrates the state transitions of a `Player`.

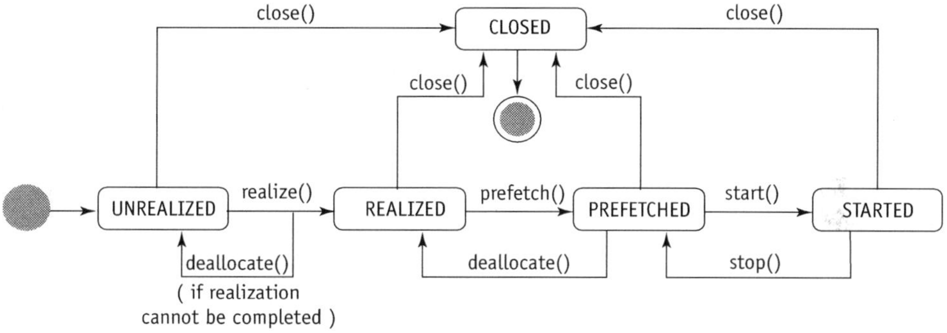

Figure 10.4 State transitions of a `Player`

As can be seen in Fig. 10.4, a `Player` has a distinct lifecycle, defined by various states of the media handling process. Lifecycle definition is important for the media because of the asynchronous and time-consuming nature of various media-related functions, particularly the acquisition of the content.

Exam Tip

The state diagram (and the contents) of the `Player` is one of the most important aspects of MMAPI from exam perspective. Try to understand and memorize the diagram in Fig. 10.4. You will get questions ranging from missing states to the state a `Player` would get to when a method is called.

Now we will examine each of these states in detail.

10.5.1 Initializing Player

When a `Player` is initialized, it goes into the `UNREALIZED` state. At this point, the `Player` does not have any information about the media it might be playing. This is equivalent of powering up a stereo system or a DVD player. The system is ready, but is not doing anything yet.

During this state, the application cannot invoke any of the methods in the `Player` that can be used to obtain information about the media being played or about the media itself, for the simple reason that there is no media to inquire about in the first place. The following methods, as a result, will throw an `IllegalStateException`, when called on an unrealized `Player`.

Table 10.5 Methods that cannot be invoked when a `Player` is in the UNREALIZED state

Method	*Purpose*
`String getContentType()`	Gets the type of content that is currently being played.
`void setTimeBase(TimeBase timeBase)`	Sets the `TimeBase` for the media being played. This is used for synchronizing multiple streams using one `TimeBase`.
`TimeBase getTimeBase()`	Gets the `TimeBase` currently being used by the `Player`.
`long setMediaTime(long time)`	Skips the media to the specified time.
`Control[] getControls()`	Gets controls supported by the `Player`.
`Control getControl(String)`	Gets the `Control` implementation for the specified control.

The `Player` can be transitioned from the `UNREALIZED` state to the `REALIZED` state by calling the `realize()` method on the `Player`.

The `TimeBase` interface can be used to synchronize the internal time of `Player` implementations obtained from different data sources so that they can be rendered in harmony. Listing 10.4 is an example.

Listing 10.4: Synchronizing `Players` using the `TimeBase` class

```
package com.scmadkit.ch10;
import java.io.*;
import javax.microedition.midlet.*;
import javax.microedition.media.*;
public class TimeBaseToneMIDlet extends MIDlet {
  protected void startApp() {
    Player p1, p2;
    try {
      p1 = Manager.createPlayer(
            "http://localhost:8080/audio.mid");        1
      p1.realize();
      p2 = Manager.createPlayer(
            "http://localhost:8080/video.mpg");        2
      p2.realize();
```

```
            p2.setTimeBase(p1.getTimeBase());                    ③
            p1.prefetch();
            p2.prefetch();
            p1.start();
            p2.start();
        } catch (IOException ioe) {
            ioe.printStackTrace();
        } catch (MediaException me) {
            me.printStackTrace();
        }
    }
    protected void pauseApp() {}
    protected void destroyApp(boolean _boolean){}
}
```

① Creates a `Player` using the media content from the specified Web URL

② Creates another `Player`

③ Sets the `TimeBase` of the first `Player` to the second `Player`

The code in the Listing 10.4 creates two `Players` that will be used to play two multimedia contents at the same time. This is accomplished by setting a `Player`'s `TimeBase` to another `Player`. First, we need to explicitly call the `realize()` method to put the `Players` into the `REALIZED` state. Because if the `setTimeBase` method is called when a `Player` is in the `UNREALIZED`, `STARTED` or `CLOSED` state, an `IllegalStateException` will be thrown. After setting the `TimeBase`, the `prefetch()` and `start()` method for each `Player` are called to play the contents simultaneously. Pretty simple?

Now that we have initialized our `Players`, let's move forward to retrieve some useful information about the media content before actually playing the media content.

10.5.2 Getting Media Information

Getting the media information is performed in two stages. In the first stage, the `Player` tries to get information about the source where the data can be found and tries to connect to it. Once that is done, the `Player` is said to be in the `REALIZED` state. As connecting to resources either locally (as a file) or externally (as Internet resources) might have I/O overheads, this method may be a time-consuming operation. While designing the system, your application should try to minimize user irritation by showing a progress bar or something equivalent.

In some cases, the user or the application might want to cancel the process of realization. In such cases, the application might call the `deallocate()` method to send the `Player` back to the `UNREALIZED` state. If the `Player` is allowed to complete the realization process, it will never go back to the `UNREALIZED` state.

Once the `Player` moves to the `REALIZED` state, it can get local resources like internal memory buffers and will try to fill the buffers by downloading information from the source. The `Player` will also try to acquire control of the audio or video mechanism in the device. This is done by calling the `prefetch()` method. Once this process is complete, the `Player` will move to the `PREFETCHED` state.

If, for some reason, the required device resources could not be obtained (say, some other application is using it), this method will throw a `MediaException`. The `Player`'s state remains in the `REALIZED` state. The application may call the `prefetch()` method at a later time to get the device resources.

If need be, it is possible to go from the `PREFETCHED` state back to the `REALIZED` state by calling the `deallocate()` method on the `Player`. This might normally be needed if the application wants to pause the `Player` and relinquish the control of the device to other applications that might need it urgently (say, a phone call when a song is being played).

For convenience, it is also possible to call the `prefetch()` method when the `Player` is in the `UNREALIZED` state. In such cases, the `prefetch()` method will internally call the `realize()` method, thereby making the appropriate transition.

Exam Tip

If any of the transition methods are called when they are in the wrong state, the call will be ignored. For example, if `realize()` is called when the `Player` is in the `PREFETCHED` state, the call will be ignored. An exception to this rule is that if any method is called when the device is in the `CLOSED` state, an `IllegalStateException` will be thrown.

If any of these methods are called when they are already in their respective states (like `start()` is called when the `Player` is in the `STARTED` state), the calls will be ignored. The only exception to this rule is if `prefetch()` is called when the `Player` is in the `PREFETCHED` state. If invoked, the `Player` will try to get the resource handles to reduce startup time.

Now that we have downloaded the data and have acquired the necessary device resources, let's see how to play the media.

10.5.3 Playing Media

Once the `Player` has downloaded the media content and acquired the device resources necessary to play the media, it can start the process of playing the media. This is done by calling the `start()` method of the `Player`. When this method is called, the `Player` moves to the `STARTED` state.

The `Player` will move back to the `PREFETCHED` state, when one of the following events occurs:

- The `stop()` method on the `Player` is invoked.
- The end of the media content reaches.
- A pre-defined stop time for the `Player` has reached (similar to the sleep-timer in a stereo system).

While the `Player` is in the `STARTED` state, the following methods must not be invoked. If invoked, the methods will throw an `IllegalStateException`.

Table 10.6 Methods that cannot be invoked when `Player` is in the `STARTED` state

Method	*Purpose*
`void setTimeBase(TimeBase timeBase)`	As the `Player` is currently playing, changing the `TimeBase` will impact the playing time and hence is not allowed.
`void setLoopCount(int count)`	As the `Player` is currently playing, changing the loop counter will affect the internal pointers of the `Player` and hence is not allowed.

Here's an example in Listing 10.5, showing how a media can be played in a loop.

Listing 10.5: Playing the media in a loop

```
package com.scmadkit.ch10;

import java.io.*;
import javax.microedition.midlet.*;
import javax.microedition.media.*;

public class LoopToneMIDlet extends MIDlet {
   protected void startApp() {
      try {
         Player p = Manager.createPlayer(
                  "http://localhost:8080/audio.wav");      ❶
         p.setLoopCount(5);
         p.start();                                        ❷
      } catch (IOException ioe) {
         ioe.printStackTrace();
      } catch (MediaException me) {
         me.printStackTrace();
      }
   }
   protected void pauseApp() {}
   protected void destroyApp(boolean _boolean){}
}
```

❶ Creates a `Player` using the media content from the specified Web URL

❷ Sets the number of loop count for the `Player` to five and plays the media content

In Listing 10.5, a `Player` is created from the source at the specified web URL, the location of the file 'audio.wav' on the local machine in this case (make sure you have your web server up and running on your machine while testing this). Then, the amount of loops that the media content will play is set to five on the created `Player`. After the loop is set, the `start()` method is called to put the `Player` into the `STARTED` state. You will hear the music play repeatedly for five times.

Exam Tip

You might encounter some tricky questions in the exam regarding methods that must not be invoked when the `Player` is in a given state. While reading code snippets, check the state of the `Player` whenever you come across any of the above-mentioned methods and ensure that it is proper to call those methods during that state.

Apart from these methods, calling the `close()` method on the `Player` at any time will send the `Player` to the `CLOSED` state. At this state, the `Player` would have relinquished control of the device resources that it had acquired (like the speaker) and will also release any resources it had acquired to fetch the media (like a network connection).

Once the `Player` has been started, it is possible to 'skip' the media by calling the `setMediaTime()` method. This method takes in a time in *microseconds* (one *microsecond* is one millionth of a second). For example, if the media being played is 5:00 minutes long and 2:30 minutes have elapsed already, calling `setMediaTime(4 * 60 * 1000 * 1000)` will 'skip' the media to 4:00th minute in the media. This method also returns another time – the time in the media, to where the device actually skipped. This is because some devices might not accurately skip in *microseconds* and may approximate it to the nearest value. Setting the media time to less than 0 or greater than the duration of the media will move the player pointer to the start of the media or end of the media, respectively.

There are two other convenience methods provided in the `Player` class:

- `getMediaTime()` returns the current playtime of the media in *microseconds.*
- `getDuration()` returns the total playtime of the media in *microseconds.*

The final step in successfully playing media content in MMAPI is to stop the `Player` and clean up the resources. Let's have a look at the methods that will help us do this.

10.5.4 Stopping Media

A playing media can be stopped at anytime by calling the `stop()` method. This will transition the `Player` to the `PREFETCHED` state, where it can be resumed by calling the `start()` method. Note that calling `start()` after calling `stop()` resumes the playing and does not make the `Player` start from the beginning of the media. This is equivalent of hitting and releasing the 'Pause' button in your stereo system.

Finally, when the application is done playing the media to its heart's content, it should call the `close()` method to release all associated resources that were used for getting media content and in playing the media. Once the `Player` is in the `CLOSED` state, it cannot come back to any other state. Effectively, a new `Player` has to be created if the same media needs to be played again. Calling any other method on the closed `Player` will result in an `IllegalStateException`.

Optionally, the application might want to listen to these state changes as and when they happen to provide appropriate messages to the user, so that the user does not get bored out of his skull while waiting for the media to load. How can we do that?

10.5.5 Listening for Player States

MMAPI provides a `PlayerListener` interface to listen to state changes of a `Player`. While it might not be as interesting as listening to a nice bit of music, it can be pretty helpful in improving user interaction with the application by providing appropriate messages during the course of the `Player`.

The `Player` interface itself defines `addPlayerListener()` and `removePlayerListener()` to register and unregister a listener to or from the `Player`. The `PlayerListener` interface provides one single method.

```
public void playerUpdate(Player player, String event, Object eventData)
```

The `event` is one of many constants defined in the `PlayerListener` interface. Table 10.7 lists some of the constants pertaining to the state changes that we have discussed so far. We will discuss the other events as necessary.

Table 10.7 Events generated due to state changes of a `Player`

Event	*Reason*
`STARTED`	Is fired when the `Player` changes its state from `PREFETCHED` to `STARTED`
`STOPPED`	Is fired when the `Player` changes its state from `STARTED` to `PREFETCHED` because the `stop()` method is called explicitly.
`END_OF_MEDIA`	Is fired when the `Player` changes its state from `STARTED` to `PREFETCHED` because the `Player` has played the media completely.
`STOPPED_AT_TIME`	Is fired when the `Player` changes its state from `STARTED` to `PREFETCHED` because the media time is equal to the time specified using the `setStopTime()` method (found in `StopTimeControl` that will be explained later).
`CLOSED`	Is fired when the `Player` transitions to the `CLOSED` state.
`ERROR`	Is fired when an unexpected error occurs while attempting to play the media content. The `Player` automatically goes into the `CLOSED` state.

So far, we have looked at getting the resources to play media using MMAPI and in playing the acquired media. Let's try to tie everything together with an example.

10.5.6 Playing Media—An Example

Listing 10.6 illustrates a detailed example of how a media can be played using the `Player` interface and how its methods work.

Listing 10.6: Playing audio content using MMAPI

```
package com.scmadkit.ch10;
import java.io.*;
import javax.microedition.midlet.*;
import javax.microedition.media.*;
import javax.microedition.media.control.*;
public class AudioPlayerMIDlet extends MIDlet {
   static final long SECS_TO_MICROSECS = 1000000L;
   protected void startApp() {
      try {
         /* Creates a player */
         Player p = Manager.createPlayer(
                  "http://localhost:8080/world.mid");
         p.realize();
         p.addPlayerListener(new MyListener());          ❶
         VolumeControl vc = (VolumeControl)
                     p.getControl("VolumeControl");
         if (vc != null)
         vc.setLevel(100);                                ❷
         p.setMediaTime(10 * AudioPlayerMIDlet.SECS_TO_MICROSECS);   ❸
         /**
          * Guarantees that the player can
          * start with the smallest latency
          **/
         p.prefetch();
         /* Non-blocking start */
         p.start();
      } catch (IOException ioe) {
         ioe.printStackTrace();
      } catch (MediaException me) {
         me.printStackTrace();
```

```
      }
    }
    protected void pauseApp() {}
    protected void destroyApp(boolean _boolean){}
}
class MyListener implements PlayerListener {
    public void playerUpdate(Player p, String event, Object data) {
      if (event == PlayerListener.END_OF_MEDIA) {
        System.out.println("Done processing!");
        try {
          p.setMediaTime(
            5 * AudioPlayerMIDlet.SECS_TO_MICROSECS);
          p.start();                                                    ④
        } catch (MediaException me) {
          me.printStackTrace();
        }
      }
    }
}
```

① Adds an instance of `PlayerListener` to the `Player`

② Grabs volume control for the `Player` and sets the volume to the maximum

③ Sets a start time

④ Runs every time the `Player` reaches the end of the media content being played

The code provided in Listing 10.6 is just to stick all the techniques that we have discussed in the previous sections. It shows how to implement the `PlayerListener` interface to listen to the events generated on a `Player`. And it also shows how to get a control, `VolumeControl` in this case, as well as how to start playing media content at a specified media time. Now that we know how to play some music using MMAPI, Listing 10.7 illustrates how video media can be played using MMAPI.

Listing 10.7: Playing video content using MMAPI

```
package com.scmadkit.ch10;
import java.io.*;
import javax.microedition.lcdui.*;
import javax.microedition.midlet.*;
import javax.microedition.media.*;
import javax.microedition.media.control.*;
```

```
public class VideoPlayerMIDlet extends MIDlet {
   protected void startApp() {
      try {
         Player p = Manager.createPlayer(
                    "http://localhost:8080/lions.mpg");      ❶
         p.realize();
         VideoControl vc = (VideoControl)
                    p.getControl("VideoControl");
         if (vc != null) {
            Form form = new Form("video");                    ❷
            form.append((Item)vc.initDisplayMode(
                          vc.USE_GUI_PRIMITIVE, null));
            Display.getDisplay(this).setCurrent(form);
         }
         /* Non-blocking start */
         p.start();
      } catch (IOException ioe) {
         ioe.printStackTrace();
      } catch (MediaException me) {
         me.printStackTrace();
      }
   }
   protected void pauseApp() {}
   protected void destroyApp(boolean_boolean){}
}
```

❶ Creates a video `Player` using the media content from the specified Web URL

❷ Retrieves the video control from the Player and sets it into the current display

The code in Listing 10.7 shows how to create a `Player` that can be used to playback video content. The `VideoControl` of the `Player` is retrieved and set into a `Form`, which is set as the current display on the screen. You are all set to play the video content using the code example. But make sure that the video content is really accessible in your server, 'lions.mpg' in this case.

Now that we know how to play media content, we can become greedy. How do we get to make the `Player` play in the right manner? In other words, how do we control how the `Player` plays the media?

10.6 CONTROLLING PLAYER

The lifecycle transition methods control the simple start and stop of a `Player`. A `Player` also exposes a set of `Controls` available for controlling the actual playing of the media. Like `DataSource` and `SourceStream`, the `Player` interface extends the `Controllable` interface. Each `Player` comes with a pre-defined set of `Control` subinterfaces that can be used by the application to control how the `Player` plays the media. As we saw earlier, the `Controllable` interface defines two methods: `getControl(String controlType)` and `getControls()`.

`getControl(String controlType)` is to get a `Control` based on the class name passed into the method. This class name should be fully qualified (that is, with the whole package name). If not, it is assumed to be in the `javax.microedition.media.control` package. If multiple classes implement the requested interface, one of them (any one) will be returned.

`getControls()` is to get an array of `Controls` that are associated with the given `Player`. All the `Control` interfaces in MMAPI are defined inside the `javax.microedition.media.control` package. The interfaces can be broadly classified into three categories—audio controls, video controls and general controls that are independent of the media type.

Figures 10.5 and 10.6 provide a high-level and detailed overview of the various controls provided by MMAPI. We will look into each of these controls in more detail in the following sections.

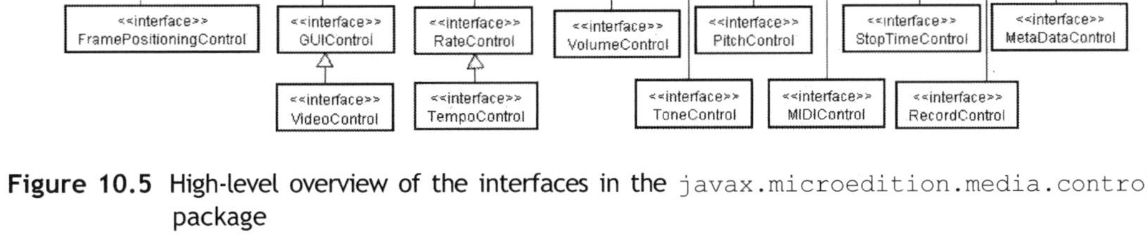

Figure 10.5 High-level overview of the interfaces in the `javax.microedition.media.control` package

10.6.1 General Controls

These controls provide functionality that applies to all media types.

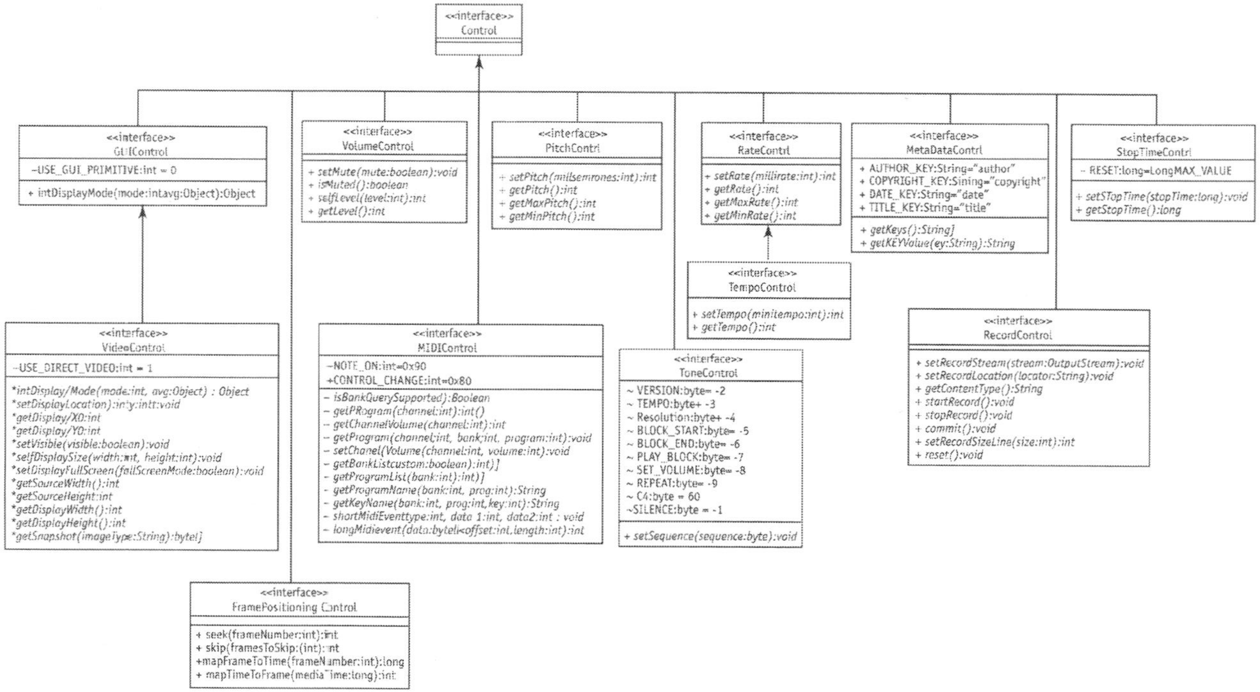

Figure 10.6 Detailed class diagram of the `Controls` in MMAPI

MetaDataControl

This control can be used to get some generic information about the meta-information provided in the media stream. A set of pre-defined keys provided in the control can be used to retrieve information. Table 10.8 summarizes these pre-defined keys.

Table 10.8 Keys provided in the `MetaDataControl` interface

Key	*Description*
`AUTHOR_KEY`	Author information provided in the media stream, if available.
`COPYRIGHT_KEY`	Copyright information provided in the media stream, if available.
`DATE_KEY`	Date (typically the date when the media was recorded) information provided in the media stream, if available.
`TITLE_KEY`	Title of the media stream, if available.

The interface itself provides two methods to retrieve information based on these keys as listed in Table 10.9.

Table 10.9 Methods provided in the `MetaDataControl` interface

Method	*Function*
`String[] getKeys()`	Gets all the key names defined in this interface.
`String getKeyValue(String key)`	Gets the value of the parameter identified by the key name.

For example, this interface may be extended by an MP3 `Player` to provide the values defined in the ID3 tag of the MP3 media.

StopTimeControl

This control provides a mechanism to set a pre-defined stop time for the `Player`. The most important use for such control is to provide a 'sleep-timer' feature to the `Player`, although it does not fully work that way. Unlike a normal 'sleep-timer' feature where the time refers to the time that must elapse before the media player stops, this time refers to the time in the media when the `Player` should stop.

For example, if the media being played is 5 minutes long, the time set by this control must be between 0 and 5 minutes. Therefore, the time is not for the `Player` (regardless of the various media being played), but rather for the specific stream that is currently playing in the media.

If a `Player` was stopped because the `Player` has played the media for the duration specified by this interface, then a `STOPPED_AT_TIME` event will be fired by the `Player`. If the stop time needs to be removed, then the time can be set to the pre-defined constant `RESET` provided in this interface. Table 10.10 lists the methods defined in this interface.

Table 10.10 Methods provided in the `StopTimeControl` interface

Method	*Function*
`void setStopTime(long stopTime)`	`stopTime` is the media time at which the player should be stopped (*in microseconds*) or `RESET` if the existing time needs to be removed.
`long getStopTime()`	Gets the current stop time (or `RESET` if no stop time has been set so far).

We know how to stop or pause the media. Looking back at our remote controls, we will see where the fast-forward and rewind buttons are.

RateControl

The speed of the media being played by the `Player` can be controlled using the `RateControl` interface. This interface provides fine-grained control over the speed at which the media is played. The `setRate(int)` method in this interface allows the caller to specify the change needed in terms of a *milli-percentage* value, or one thousandth of a percentage change.

For example, if the caller wants to double speed at which the media is currently playing, he should pass a 200,000 to this method (200% of the current speed). The rewind functionality is achieved by simply specifying a negative value in the same manner.

In addition to the `setRate` method and its corresponding `getRate()` method, the `getMaxRate()` and `getMinRate()` methods can be used to get the limits supported by the `Player` implementation.

Next, we'll look at an advanced feature common to both audio and video media—the ability to record the media.

RecordControl

Devices that are capable of recording audio or video data would implement this optional interface provided in MMAPI. The interface provides some generic methods independent of the media content or format by treating the media data as a byte stream. It is left to the implementation to provide appropriate metadata associated with the stream (while committing the data) and media-capturing device to provide appropriate header information.

When the `startRecord()` method in this interface is called, the `Player` will immediately start recording the media currently being played. It is always a good idea to start the recording first and then start the `Player` itself to ensure that all of the media is captured fully. In addition, if the media has not started playing, the recording will automatically go into a 'pause' mode until the media starts playing. As a result, no awkward pauses will be recorded. The data being captured will be streamed through the `OutputStream` provided by the `setRecordStream()` method prior to recording the media.

When the `stopRecord()` method is called, the recording will not be *stopped*, but rather will be *paused*. Calling `startRecord()` will resume the recording. Finally, the `commit()` method should be called to complete the recording.

Exam Tip

The `stopRecord()` method does not stop the recording, but rather pauses the recording. To ensure proper recording, recording must be started before the media is played.

Figure 10.7 displays the sequence diagram that provides the typical sequence of steps in recording a media.

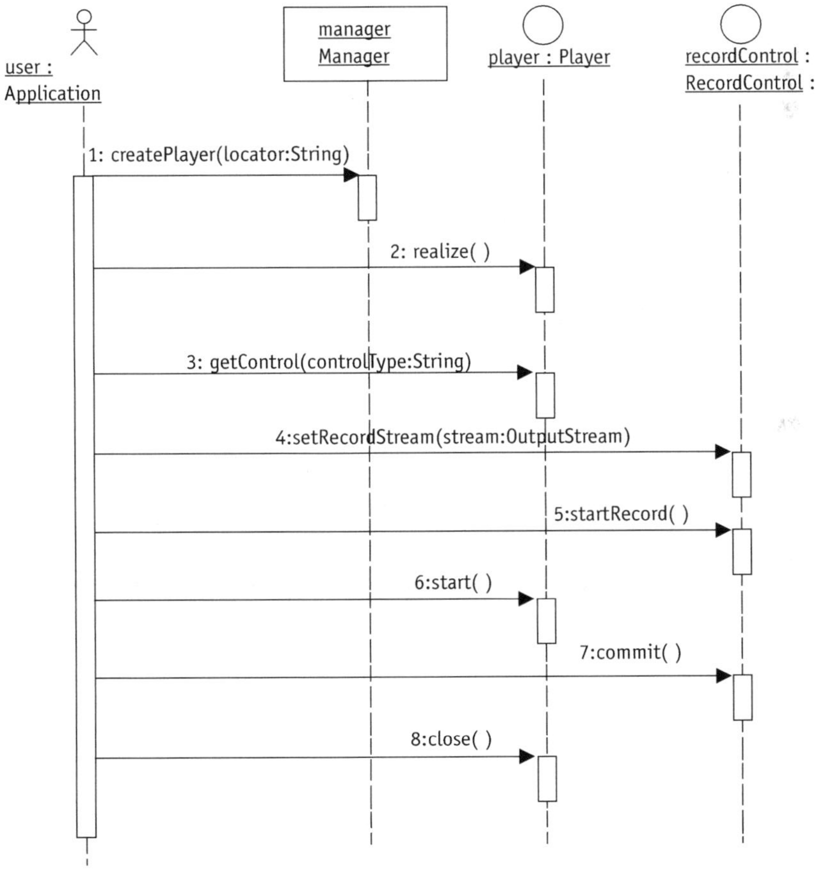

Figure 10.7 Sequence diagram for recording media using MMAPI

Table 10.11 gives a more thorough list of the methods provided in this interface.

Table 10.11 Methods provided in the `RecordControl` interface

Method	*Function*
`void setRecordStream(OutputStream stream)`	Sets the stream where the recorded data should be sent.
`void setRecordLocation (String locator)`	Sets the location of the recorded output data.
`String getContentType()`	Gets the content type of the recorded output data.
`void startRecord()`	Starts the recording.
`void stopRecord()`	Pauses the recording.
`void commit()`	Completes the current recording. This implicitly calls the `stopRecord()` method.
`void reset()`	Erases the data that has been captured so far. This method implicitly calls the `stopRecord()` method.
`void setRecordSizeLimit(int size)`	Determines the amount of information to be recorded. The recording will be stopped automatically when the number of bytes specified here has been reached. Setting the size to `Integer.MAX_VALUE` will remove any limit on the recording and will record the data till the end of the media or till there is enough space, whichever comes first.

The `RecordControl` fires `RECORD_STARTED`, `RECORD_STOPPED`, or `RECORD_ERROR` events to any listeners implementing the `PlayerListener` interface to indicate that the recording has started, stopped, or encountered an error, respectively.

With the general controls out of our way, let us take a closer look at the ones that are used most often—the audio controls.

10.6.2 Audio Controls

Audio controls are used to control the various audio parameters of the `Player` such as volume, pitch and tempo. The controls under this category are also used to control various audio formats such as tone sequences and MIDI.

Let us look at these controls in detail.

VolumeControl

Perhaps the most important and most used control in this category is the `VolumeControl` interface, which, as it implies, controls the volume of a `Player`. The volume is expressed as a percentage of the maximum volume that can be produced by the underlying device, as each device may have different capabilities. As a result, you should not think that keeping the volume at 100% would blow your ears away.

The percentage scale itself is linear. Hence, the `Player` at 50% volume would be half as loud as 100% volume. If the value passed is less than 0 or greater than 100, the value is set to 0 or 100, respectively.

Apart from this relative volume control, there is also a shortcut to *mute* the speaker. When a device is set to *mute*, the volume remains the same, but no sound is generated. Thus, when the *mute* option is removed, the device regains the volume that it had before it was set to *mute*.

Table 10.12 Methods provided in the `VolumeControl` interface

Method	*Function*
`void setLevel(int level)`	Sets the volume level of the `Player`. The level should be a value between 0 and 100, a percentage of the maximum volume.
`int getLevel()`	Gets the current volume level of the `Player`.
`void setMute(boolean isMuted)`	If `isMuted` is `true`, then the `Player` will not generate any sound. If `false`, the `Player` will resume at the volume it had before it was muted.
`boolean isMuted()`	Indicates if the `Player` is currently in the muted state or not.

The interface also provides a `VOLUME_CHANGED` event to any `PlayerListener` implementations on the `Player` every time the volume level is changed or if the *muted* state of the `Player` is changed.

PitchControl

In musical terms, pitch refers to the frequency of the audio being played. In general, it implies shrillness, such as a high-pitched voice (extremely shrill and mostly annoying) and low-pitched voice.

Exam Tip

For the exam, you are not required to have a degree in music. So, the exam would typically test you more on the syntax of the code and the applicability of certain methods rather than the musical soundness behind the code.

The `PitchControl` interface can be used to adjust the pitch of the audio being played. The control will change the pitch of the audio relative to the current pitch set in the `Player`. Thus, a positive value passed to the `setPitch(int)` method in the interface will relatively increase the pitch by the passed value and a negative value will relatively decrease the pitch by the passed value. The value passed is in *milli-semitones* (One milli-semitone is one thousandth of a semitone).

In addition to the setPitch method and its corresponding getPitch() method, the getMaxPitch() and getMinPitch() methods can be used to get the limits supported by the Player implementation.

TempoControl

In musical terms, tempo refers to the speed at which the audio is perceived and is denoted in *beats per minute (bpm).* The tempo of the media being played can be changed using the setTempo method of the TempoControl interface. The value passed is in *milli-tempo*—that is, one thousandth of a tempo, to allow fractional beats. Thus, 120 bpm would be 120,000 *milli-tempo.* As tempo typically varies within a music piece (slow to fast, for example), some audio formats such as MIDI (Musical Instrument Digital Interface) will encode the tempo in the media data itself. In such cases, the tempo set by the user will be overridden by the tempo present in the media data itself, if needed. Not surprisingly, the current playback tempo can be retrieved using the getTempo() method of the interface.

Tempo is closely associated with the rate at which the media being played, which is controlled by the RateControl interface. In fact, so strong is the bond that the TempoControl extends the RateControl interface. The difference between TempoControl and RateControl is that the TempoControl controls the musical speed of the audio, while the RateControl controls the physical speed of the media being played.

In effect, the musical tempo of the media can be calculated as follows.

```
Tempo bpm = (TempoControl.getTempo()/1000) *
(RateControl.getRate()/100000)
```

☞ The setTempo and getTempo methods do not affect or reflect the rate of the media playback, meaning that setting or getting the tempo will not change the value returned by the getRate method and vice versa.

Listing 10.8 is an example for the use of TempoControl in playing MIDI files.

Listing 10.8: Playing MIDI files

```
package com.scmadkit.ch10;
import java.io.*;
import javax.microedition.midlet.*;
import javax.microedition.media.*;
import javax.microedition.media.control.TempoControl;
public class MIDIPlayerMIDlet extends MIDlet {
   protected void startApp() {
      try {
         Player p = Manager.createPlayer(
                    "http://localhost:8080/world.mid");
```

```
            p.realize();
            // Grabs the tempo control.
            TempoControl tc =
               (TempoControl)p.getControl("TempoControl");
            tc.setTempo(300000); // 300 beats/min
            p.start();
         } catch (IOException ioe) {
            ioe.printStackTrace();
         } catch (MediaException me) {
            me.printStackTrace();
         }
      }
      protected void pauseApp() {}
      protected void destroyApp(boolean _boolean){}
   }
```

In Listing 10.8, after creating a MIDI player using the static `createPlayer` method, the `Player` is realized to put it into the `REALIZED` state. Then a `TempoControl` is retrieved and the tempo is set to run 300 beats per minute. Pretty fast music playback, uh? Try to adjust the value to see the difference in the speed of the music playback. The next section covers more about the MIDI format and the control used to work on MIDI music playback – `MIDIControl`.

MIDIControl

The MIDI format is a special audio format aimed for musical instruments such as keyboards, guitars, etc. This format is being used worldwide to represent synthesized music in an extremely compact manner with a lot of flexibility. Most professional (and even amateur) electronic instruments support this format.

The format provides the ability to define music in 16 channels. Channels are similar to tracks of music—that is different instruments playing at the same time. For example, in a rock concert, the keyboard will be in a channel, drums in a separate channel, guitar in another channel and so on. Each channel can define its own music parameters such as volume, tempo, pitch, etc. Apart from musical data, the format also provides supports for *control messages* that can be used to dynamically change the way the data should be interpreted.

The `MIDIControl` interface in MMAPI provides support for the MIDI format. Since the ability to play the MIDI format is a bit sophisticated, this control has not been incorporated into the MIDP 2.0 Media API. In the `MIDIControl` interface, a single musical instrument represented in the format is called as a *program.* Related *programs* (such as string instruments) are grouped together into *banks.* Each *bank* can have at most 128 *programs.* Figure 10.8 illustrates the conceptual terms of MIDI.

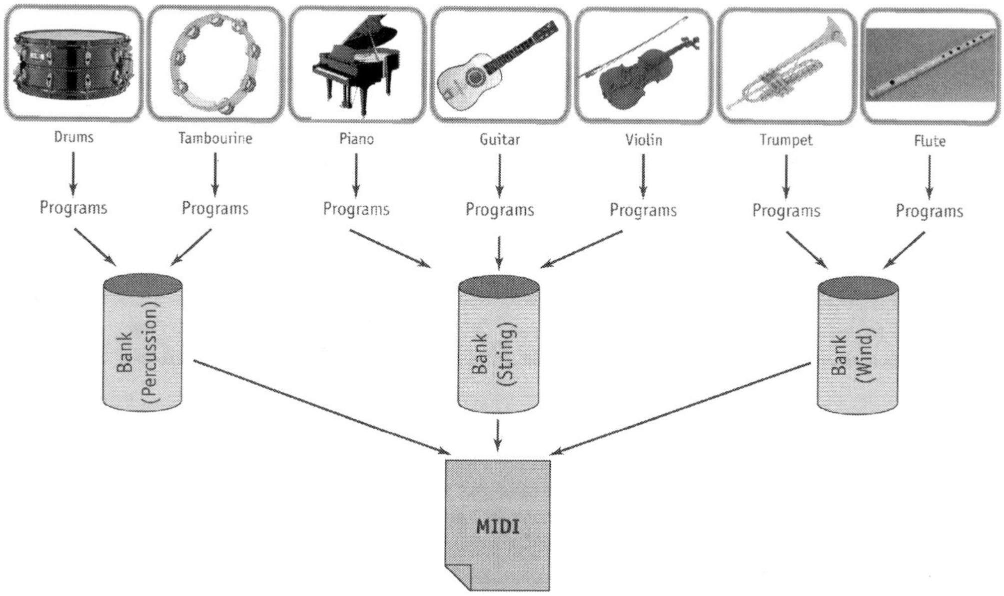

Figure 10.8 MIDI Concept

The `MIDIControl` interface provides methods to get information about *banks* and *programs*. Table 10.13 provides a list of those methods and their purposes.

Table 10.13 Getting information about MIDI banks and programs

Method	*Purpose*
`boolean isBankQuerySupported()`	Checks if the synthesizer can be queried for *bank* information.
`int[] getBankList(boolean isCustom)`	*Banks* can be internal or custom. Internal *banks* are provided by the instrument manufacturer whereas custom banks are loaded into the instrument. This method gets a list of either internal or custom *banks* of the instrument based on the passed `isCustom` flag.
`int[] getProgramList(int bank)`	Gets a list of all the programs (or instruments) in the given bank.
`String getProgramName (int bank, int program)`	Gets the name of specified program in the specified bank.
`String getKeyName(int bank, int program,int key)`	Gets the name of a key for a given key of a program in the specified bank.

Apart from the methods to get information about the MIDI *banks* and *programs*, the API provides methods to control the volume in a channel and the instrument used in the channel. Table 10.14 describes those methods and their purposes.

Table 10.14 Controlling channel information of a MIDI device

Method	*Purpose*
`int getChannelVolume(int channel)`	Gets the volume of the given channel.
`void setChannelVolume(int channel, int volume)`	Sets the volume of the channel. The volume is a value between 0 and 127. The volume set using this method may be overridden by volume control events. While each channel has its own volume, there is also a master volume for the instrument across all channels. The effective volume of a channel is a product of its volume and the master volume.
`void setProgram(int channel, int bank, int program)`	Sets the instrument to be used by a given channel in the program of the bank specified.
`int[] getProgram(int channel)`	Gets the instrument currently being used in the channel specified.

As mentioned earlier, the MIDI format allows control events to be sent to the instrument dynamically as messages. An application can programmatically send a short event or a long event.

Short events are 2- or 3- byte events and can be sent using this method.

```
public void shortMidiEvent(int type, byte data1, byte data2)
```

where

- `type` is a value from 0x80 to 0xFF, except 0xF0 and 0xF7, which are reserved
- `data1` is the first data byte for 2- and 3- byte events (from 0 to 127)
- `data2` is the second data byte for 3 byte events (from 0 to 127)

Long events are typically system messages or a series of short events. The following method is used for sending long events.

```
public int longMidiEvent(byte[] data, int offset, int length)
```

where

- `data` is the array of bytes to send. Note that the contents are not validated for correctness
- `offset` is the beginning position in the array from where the data should be sent
- `length` is the number of bytes to be sent starting from the `offset` position

The method returns the actual number of bytes sent and –1 if there was an error sending the message.

Exam Tip

Remember the upper and lower values that can be used for various parameters. Volume ranges from 0–127 (not 0–100 like `VolumeControl`), channels range from 0–15, and programs range from 0–127.

The exam's intent is to test on your MMAPI skills, not your ability to program using the MIDI format. So, have a basic understanding of the concepts about the MIDI format, but concentrate more on the API.

ToneControl

Earlier we saw how to use a convenience method of the `Manager` class to play a single tone. Now we will learn how to play a series of tones. The `ToneControl` interface in MMAPI can be used to play a sequence of tones in a specific order as opposed to a single tone.

There is only one single method in the `ToneControl` interface.

```
public void setSequence(byte[] sequence)
```

where

- `sequence` is a sequence of bytes that need to be played

The `ToneControl` interface defines a mini-language for writing the byte sequence that needs to be played. The details of the notation are explained in detail in the API. However, here's an overview to help you understand the notation better (also enough to be useful for the exam).

The data described in a tone sequence typically fall under one of the following four categories provided in Table 10.15.

Table 10.15 Tone sequence format

Event type	*Format*	*Description*
Tone Event	note, duration	Defines a single tone and the amount of time (based on resolution and tempo) it should be played.
Block Event	`PLAY_BLOCK`, block_id	Indicates that the data defined in a block with the id 'block_id' should be played (a positive integer).
Volume Event	`SET_VOLUME`, volume	Indicates that the volume should be changed to the given volume from this point onwards. (a value between 0 and 100).
Repeat Event	`REPEAT_EVENT`, n, 'Tone Event'	Indicates that the tone event defined must be repeated n times. (a value between 2 and 127).

You might be wondering what a block is and where exactly a block is defined. Prior to defining the tone sequence as mentioned above, you can also define some meta-information. Table 10.16 lists different types of meta-information that can be specified in a tone sequence.

Table 10.16 Tone sequence header information

Event type	*Format*	*Description*
Version	VERSION, number	Defines the version for the sequence.(a positive integer)
Tempo	TEMPO, modifier	Defines the tempo (in *beats per minute*) used in the sequence. (a value between 5 and 127)
Resolution	RESOLUTION, resolution	Defines the number of notes that can be packed into a beat. For example, 8 means each note is $1/8^{th}$ of a beat long. (a value between 1 and 127)

Block Definition	BLOCK_START, number, sequence_event, BLOCK_END, number	Defines a block of music. The sequence event contained in the block can be a combination of the events mentioned in Table 10.15. A block is a reusable piece of music, much like how a code is pulled out as a private method so that it can be called from multiple places inside the class.

Now that we have our basics straight, let's look at an example that ties all these pieces together in Listing 10.9.

Listing 10.9: Generating a sequence of tones using **`ToneControl`**

```
package com.scmadkit.ch10;
import java.io.*;
import javax.microedition.midlet.*;
import javax.microedition.media.*;
import javax.microedition.media.control.ToneControl;
public class MIDIPlayerMIDlet extends MIDlet {
   protected void startApp() {
      /**
      * "Mary Had A Little Lamb" has "ABAC" structure.
      * and the tone sequence uses block to repeat "A" section.
      */
      /* set tempo to 30 bpm */
      byte tempo = 30;
      byte d = 8; // eighth-note
      byte C4 = ToneControl.C4;; // a middle C
      byte D4 = (byte)(C4 + 2); // a whole step          ❶
      byte E4 = (byte)(C4 + 4); // a major third
      byte G4 = (byte)(C4 + 7); // a fifth
      byte rest = ToneControl.SILENCE; // rest
      byte[] mySequence = {
         ToneControl.VERSION, 1, // version 1
         ToneControl.TEMPO, tempo, // set tempo
         ToneControl.BLOCK_START, 0, // start define "A" section
         E4,d, D4,d, C4,d, E4,d, // content of "A" section   ❷
         E4,d, E4,d, E4,d, rest,d,
         ToneControl.BLOCK_END, 0, // end define "A" section
         ToneControl.PLAY_BLOCK, 0, // play "A" section
         D4,d, D4,d, D4,d, rest,d, // play "B" section
```

```
            E4,d, G4,d, G4,d, rest,d,
            ToneControl.PLAY_BLOCK, 0, // repeat "A" section      ❷
            D4,d, D4,d, E4,d, D4,d, C4,d // play "C" section
        };
        try{
            Player p = Manager.createPlayer(
                        Manager.TONE_DEVICE_LOCATOR);
            p.realize();
            ToneControl c =
                (ToneControl)p.getControl("ToneControl");         ❸
            c.setSequence(mySequence);
            p.start();
        } catch (IOException ioe) {
            ioe.printStackTrace();
        } catch (MediaException me) {
            me.printStackTrace();
        }
    }
    protected void pauseApp() {}
    protected void destroyApp(boolean _boolean){}
}
```

❶ Prepares notes for the tone sequence

❷ Sets up an array of bytes and arranges the notes for the tone sequence

❸ Gets the `ToneControl` of the `Player` and sets the prepared tone sequence

The code provided in Listing 10.9 is just to illustrate the way the tone sequence can be programmed. It needs a reasonable amount of knowledge related to music to put the notes into an organization to play a full-blown tone sequence, but fortunately you don't need such knowledge for the exam. Just emphasize on how notes and blocks can be defined and how to set a sequence into the `ToneControl` of a `Player`.

This is the last audio-related control that you need to study for the exam. The next section will take you to another interesting category of controls—video controls.

10.6.3 Video Controls

So far, we have looked into various audio controls. Let's now move from the radio era to the TV era. Video media, being visual in nature, requires a visual interface for the user. The MMAPI defines a special control that can be used by media that needs a user interface—the `GUIControl`.

GUIControl

The `GUIControl` provides a Graphical User Interface (GUI) for users to view any media. In simpler terms, it provides a screen. While the control looks simple enough, it provides the most important function of returning an appropriate UI component where the data can be painted and shown to the user. Since the API itself needs to be generic and be devoid of implementation details, the only method in this interface returns a generic `java.lang.Object`.

```
public Object initDisplayMode(int mode, Object arg)
```

The `Object` returned by this method will be a subclass of `java.awt.Component` for devices that support the Java AWT package or a subclass of `javax.microedition.lcdui.Item`, for devices that support MIDP. If a device supports both MIDP and AWT, the second argument can be used by the application to choose one among the available options. The argument, in such cases, must be a `String` that refers to the fully qualified class name of the base class—`java.awt.Component` or `javax.microedition.lcdui.Item`.

The mode is an extension mechanism provided by the API to allow future implementations to provide more sophisticated user interface types. Currently, there is only one mode supported—`USE_GUI_PRIMITIVE`.

> **Exam Tip**
>
> **The only one mode supported in the `GUIControl` interface is `USE_GUI_PRIMITIVE`. The return value and the second argument of the `initDisplayMode()` are determined based on the mode passed to the `initDisplayMode()` method.**

Figure 10.9 illustrates a simple scenario that explains how a `GUIControl` can be embedded in the user interface of a mobile device.

The `GUIControl` is a generic superinterface that must be extended by other interfaces that are more specific to the type of media being displayed. In order to display video content, MMAPI provides a sub-interface of `GUIControl` called `VideoControl`.

VideoControl

The `VideoControl` interface extends the `GUIControl` interface and provides more useful methods related to video content.

First, the `VideoControl` provides one more mode called `USE_DIRECT_VIDEO` for the `initDisplayMode(int, Object)` method that you are now familiar with. This mode is supported only by platforms that support the `javax.microedition.lcdui.Canvas` class. In this mode, the second argument passed to the `initDisplayMode` should be the `Canvas` where the video should be rendered.

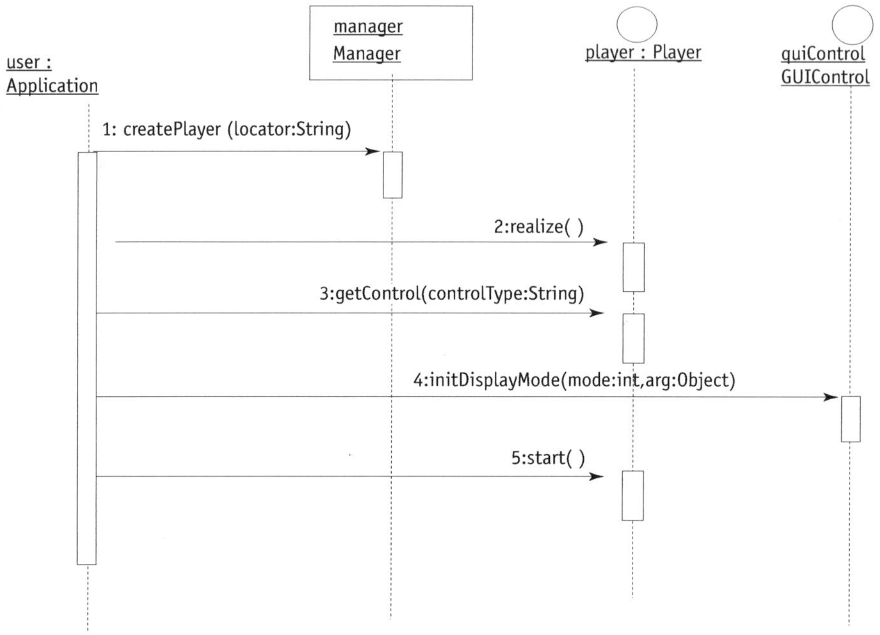

Figure 10.9 Sequence diagram for displaying video using the `GUIControl` interface

Let us take a quick look at the differences between the `USE_GUI_PRIMITIVE` and the `USE_DIRECT_VIDEO` mode in Table 10.17.

Table 10.17 Differences between the `USE_GUI_PRIMITVE` and `USE_DIRECT_VIDEO` modes

Mode	*Second argument to* `initDisplayMode`	*Return Value of* `initDisplayMode`
`USE_GUI_PRIMITIVE`	Fully qualified class name of the object that would render the media.	An instance of the class passed as the argument. For AWT, this would be a subclass of `java.awt.Component`. For LCDUI, this would be a subclass of `javax.microedition.lcdui.Item`.
`USE_DIRECT_VIDEO`	An instance of a subclass of `javax.microedition.lcdui.Canvas`. Supported only in LCDUI screens.	`null`

The interface also provides a number of getter and setter methods to get information about the media content being displayed and control how the media content is displayed. Table 10.18 provides a list of features provided by this interface along with the methods used to achieve the functionality.

Table 10.18 Features provided by the `VideoControl` interface

Feature	*Methods used*
Visibility	`setVisible(boolean isVisible)` can be used to specify if the screen showing the video should be shown or hidden.
Size of the frame	`getDisplayHeight()`, `getDisplayWidth()`, `setDisplaySize(int width, height)` can be used to get or set the actual dimensions of the frame being played. `getSourceWidth()`, `getSourceHeight()` can be used to get the dimensions of the frame defined in the media source.
Frame coordinates	`getDisplayX()`, `getDisplayY()`, `setDisplayLocation(int x, int y)` can be used to get or set the coordinates of the video being displayed relative to the upper left-hand corner of the GUI object on which it is displayed.
Full screen	`setDisplayFullScreen(boolean isFullScreenMode)` can be used to make the video occupy the viewable area of the device's screen.
Snapshot	`byte[] getSnapshot(String imageType)` can be used to get a snapshot of the frame currently being displayed encoded in a specific type, as defined by the `imageType` parameter. MMAPI implementations must at least support the PNG image format. Other formats maybe optionally supported by various implementations.

Listing 10.10 is an example that illustrates various methods provided in the `VideoControl` interface.

Listing 10.10: Displaying video using `VideoControl` *API*

```
package com.scmadkit.ch10;

import java.io.*;
import javax.microedition.lcdui.*;
import javax.microedition.midlet.*;
import javax.microedition.media.*;
import javax.microedition.media.control.VideoControl;

public class VideoSnapshotMIDlet extends MIDlet {
   protected void startApp() {
      try {
         Player p = Manager.createPlayer(
                  "http://localhost:8080/lion.mpg");
         p.realize();
         Form form = new Form("video");
         VideoControl vc =
            (VideoControl)p.getControl("VideoControl");
         if (vc != null) {
```

```
                form.append((Item)vc.initDisplayMode(
                               vc.USE_GUI_PRIMITIVE, null));       ❶
                Display.getDisplay(this).setCurrent(form);
            }
            p.start();
            Thread.currentThread().sleep(5000);                    ❷
            byte[] pngImage = vc.getSnapshot(null);
            doSomethingWithImage(pngImage);
        } catch (IOException ioe) {
            ioe.printStackTrace();
        } catch (MediaException me) {
            me.printStackTrace();
        } catch (InterruptedException ie) {
            ie.printStackTrace();
        }
    }
  protected void pauseApp() {}
  protected void destroyApp(boolean _boolean){}
  private void doSomethingWithImage(byte[] pngImage) {
  // Do something with the retrieved image
  // ...
  }
}
```

❶ Retrieves the video control from the `Player` and sets it into the current display

❷ Waits for five seconds and takes a snapshot

Sound familiar with the code in Listing 10.10? It is almost the same as that in Listing 10.7 except that this one shows you how to take a snapshot of the video being played using the `VideoControl` retrieved from the `Player`. After the `Player` is put into the `STARTED` state using the `start()` method, the application sleeps for five seconds before taking a snapshot of the video that is being played. It's that simple. Once you've got the byte array that contains the image data, you can display it as appropriate using the classes available in MIDP UI API.

We have so far figured out how video can be rendered on a mobile device using MMAPI. What if we need better control over the video being rendered?

FramePositioningControl

Video data is typically composed of frames. For example, a simple video can be created by showing 24 or 30 frames within a second. As a human eye is capable of identifying a break when a sequence of images are shown only if the number of images shown per second is less than 16, the eye registers the sequence of images as one continuous stream.

The `FramePositioningControl` interface can be used to control the precise positioning of a frame in a video. As mentioned above, there is a correlation between the number of frames in a video and the amount of time the media can be played. For instance, a video file containing 48 frames can be played in 2 seconds, if the frame rate is 24 fps (*frames per second*).

Frames are normally numbered starting from 0. The `FramePositioningControl` interface provides the `seek(int frameNumber)` and `skip(int frameNumber)` methods to go to an absolute frame in the media or skip a specified number of frames from the current frame of the media.

In some situations, the `Player` may not be able to accurately determine the time elapsed based on a given frame number or the frame number based on the elapsed media time. The `FramePositioningControl` provides the `mapFrameToTime (int frame)` and `mapTimeToFrame(long time)` to allow the `Player` to provide the appropriate conversion that can be used further by the application.

This covers the various controls that are defined by MMAPI to control various aspects of audio and video media that can be played on a mobile device. Most importantly, the API provides enough hooks to future implementations. As we explained in the introduction to this chapter, MMAPI is only a conditionally required component specification of JTWI. But the MIDP 2.0 Media API is definitely required, and it's a true subset of MMAPI. We will now discuss the differences between MMAPI and the MIDP 2.0 Media API subset.

10.7 DIFFERENCES BETWEEN MMAPI AND MIDP MEDIA API

According to the JTWI 1.0 specification, MMAPI is a conditionally required specification. MMAPI is not required unless the implementation supports the advanced media features covered by that API. Many devices, due to their limited capabilities, will not implement MMAPI. In order to service the lesser media needs of these devices, and still maintain a consistent handling of media throughout JTWI, a strict subset of MMAPI has been identified for inclusion in the MIDP 2.0. This subset is known as the MIDP 2.0 Media API. It is fully compliant and upwardly compatible with MMAPI. Since the MIDP 2.0 is a required component specification, you must be aware of differences between MMAPI as a whole and the MIDP subset. Fortunately, these differences are quite easily summarized.

Table 10.19 provides a list of feature differences between the MIDP media subset and MMAPI.

Table 10.19 Differences between Media API in MIDP and MMAPI

Feature	*Media API in MIDP*	*MMAPI*
Controls	Audio only (`ToneControl` and `VolumeControl`)	Audio, video and other graphics
Synchronized playback	Not possible	Possible using the `TimeBaseControl` interface
Media protocols	Custom protocols are not supported	Custom protocols can be defined using the `DataSource` class
Multiple media streams	Not possible	Possible using `DataSource` class and the `SourceStream` interface

Summary

Playing songs, taking pictures and watching movies are the bells and whistles that sell mobile phones. With this in mind, it would be hard to propose a standard for developing applications on mobile phones without addressing the rich set of media supported by many of the target devices. On the other hand, some devices do not have these rich media feature sets. In order to address this, JTWI makes MMAPI a conditionally required component specification. JTWI says that if a device exposes the media features through the Java language, it must implement MMAPI in so doing. If the device simply doesn't have, or want to expose, a rich set of media features, MIDP provides a simpler subset of MMAPI.

In this chapter, we introduced the media playing framework of MMAPI. Like GCF of CLDC, the framework of MMAPI provides a flexible set of interfaces and abstract classes for which protocol and media type specific implementations can be provided by the manufacturers or JTWI implementers. While MMAPI does not require any specific implementations, JTWI does make a few requirements including support for HTTP and MIDI files. You should consult the JTWI chapter to review the additional requirements it imposes on MMAPI. (Remember when we said you would have to reread that chapter at a later time? Well, now is the time.)

As per the specifics of MMAPI, you should know the interfaces and abstract classes that structure the framework. It is important to understand the interaction between the `Player` and the `Manager`. The `Manager` provides the factory methods to obtain a `Player` that can be used to play digital media obtained from a specified location. You should now know how to acquire a `Player` for a given media type or `DataSource`. You should also understand the functionality provided by the various implementations of the `Control` interface. For the exam, you must understand the lifecycle of the `Player`.

As always, we encourage you to write some code. It's the best way to learn the practical knowledge of the API demanded by the exam. The next, and last, chapter covers the very hot technology of WMA. This important required component specification of JTWI provides functionality for such things as text messaging.

References

1. Mobile Media API, version 1.0
   http://www.jcp.org/aboutJava/communityprocess/final/jsr135/
2. The J2ME Mobile Media API
   http://developers.sun.com/techtopics/mobility/midp/articles/mmapioverview/
3. The Basics of the MMAPI for Java Developers
   http://www.awprofessional.com/articles/article.asp?p=375708&rl=1

Review Questions

1. Which of the following interfaces are not available in the media API defined in the MIDP 2.0 specification, but are available in the broader MMAPI?

   a. `VolumeControl` b. `ToneControl`

   c. `MIDIControl` d. `VideoControl`

2. What will happen when the following code snippet is executed? Assume that the URI defined is valid.

```
try {
   Player p = Manager.createPlayer("http://server.com/music.wav");
   p.start();
   p.setLoopCount(5);
} catch (IOException ioe) {
   ioe.printStackTrace();
} catch (MediaException me) {
   me.printStackTrace();
}
```

   a. The media will be downloaded and played once.
   b. The media will be downloaded and played 5 times.
   c. The media will be downloaded and played 6 times.
   d. An `IllegalStateException` will be thrown because the loop count is set after the `Player` has been started.
   e. A `MediaException` will be thrown because the `Player` has not been realized or prefetched.

3. Which of the following methods will correctly play a tone at a middle C note at 50% volume for one second?

   a. `Manager.playNote(ToneControl.C4, 1000, 50)`
   b. `Manager.playTone(ToneControl.C4, 1000, 50)`

c. `Manager.playTone(ToneControl.C4, 1000, 0.5)`
d. `Manager manager = new Manager();`
   `manager.play(1, 50, ToneControl.C4);`

4. What will happen when the following code is executed? Assume that `mySequence` has been properly defined elsewhere.

```
try {
  Player p = Manager.createPlayer(Manager.TONE_DEVICE_LOCATOR);
  p.realize();
  ToneControl tc = (ToneControl)p.getControl("ToneControl");
  tc.setSequence(mySequence);
  p.start();
} catch (IOException ioe) {
  ioe.printStackTrace();
} catch (MediaException me) {
  me.printStackTrace();
}
```

a. The sequence specified in `mySequence` will be played successfully.
b. An `IllegalStateException` will be thrown because the `prefetch()` method was not called before calling the `realize()` method.
c. The outcome is dependent upon the device where it is run, as it is not guaranteed that the `ToneControl` interface will be available in all devices.
d. An `IOException` will be thrown because the `close()` method was not called at the end.

5. Which of the following statements is true about the `StopTimeControl` interface?
a. This control is used to stop a `Player` after playing for the specified number of seconds.
b. This control is used to stop a `Player` after it has played the current media until the time specified.
c. This control is used to synchronize play times of different media.
d. The `setStopTime` method defined in this control would throw an `IllegalArgumentException` if the value provided were beyond the playtime of the currently playing media.

6. What will happen when the following code is executed? Assume that the device supports MIDI playback and that the locator string is valid.

```
Player p;
TempoControl tc;
try {
    p = Manager.createPlayer("http://server.com/tune.mid");
    p.realize();
    // Grab the MIDI control.
    mc = (MIDIControl)p.getControl("MIDIControl");
    mc.setChannelVolume(0, 110);
    p.start();
} catch (IOException ioe) {
```

```
    ioe.printStackTrace();
  } catch (MediaException me) {
    me.printStackTrace();
  }
```

a. The player will play the given MIDI file successfully at the given volume.
b. An `IllegalArgumentException` will be thrown as the volume requested is beyond the valid range.
c. The volume of the first channel will be set to a value corresponding to 110, but may change if there are volume control events defined inside the MIDI data being played.
d. An `IllegalStateException` will be thrown because the `prefetch()` and `realize()` methods of the `Player` were not called before the `start()` method.

7. Which of the following are the valid states of a `Player`?

a. `UNREALIZED`
b. `RUNNING`
c. `STARTED`
d. `PREFETCHED`
e. `READY`

8. What will happen if the following snippet of code is executed?

```
try {
  Player p = Manager.createPlayer("capture://audio");
  p.realize();
  RecordControl rc = (RecordControl)p.getControl("RecordControl");
  ByteArrayOutputStream output = new ByteArrayOutputStream();
  rc.setRecordStream(output);
  rc.startRecord();
  Thread.currentThread().sleep(1000);
  p.start();
  Thread.currentThread().sleep(5000);
  rc.commit();
  p.close();
} catch (IOException ioe) {
  ioe.printStackTrace();
} catch (MediaException me) {
  me.printStackTrace();
} catch (InterruptedException ie) {
  ie.printStackTrace();
}
```

a. The program will record the audio from the default audio mechanism of the device for 5 seconds.
b. The program will record totally for 6 seconds. The first second will be blank and the next 5 seconds will be the audio received from the default audio mechanism.
c. The program will throw an `IllegalStateException` because the `startRecord()` was called before the `Player` was started.
d. The program will throw an `IOException` because the locator string is invalid.

9. What features with respect to obtained media from a source are available in MMAPI that are not available in MIDP 2.0 Media API?
   a. Ability to define custom protocols
   b. Ability to get streaming media
   c. Ability to randomly seek a position in the source data
   d. Support for frame-delimited data.
10. Which of the following methods, if invoked, will throw an `IllegalStateException` when a `Player` is in the `STARTED` state?
   a. `setTimeBase`
   b. `start`
   c. `setLoopCount`
   d. `deallocate`

Review Answers

1. c and d. The media API for MIDP is a subset of the broader MMAPI aimed to provide some basic support to devices that do not have sophisticated multimedia abilities. As a result, only the `VolumeControl` and `ToneControl` interfaces are defined in the MIDP specification to support media playback.
2. d. The `setLoopCount` method cannot be called when a `Player` is in the `STARTED` state (because the `start()` method was called), to provide a consistent loop count behavior. The program would loop for 5 times if lines 3 and 4 are swapped.
3. b. The correct signature for playing a single note using the `Manager` is
   ```
   public static void playTone(int note, int duration, int volume)
   ```
   where
   - `note` is calculated using the formula:
     ```
     note = ln(freq/8.176)* 17.31234049066755 = 1/(ln(2^(1/12)))
     ```
   - `duration` is the time the note should be played, specified in milliseconds.
   - `volume` is a percentage of the maximum volume, a number between 0 and 100.
4. a. The sequence defined in `mySequence` will be played successfully. The code will not throw an `IllegalStateException` because calling the `start()` method will implicitly call the `realize()` and `prefetch()` methods as needed. `ToneControl` support is a mandatory control that must be available in all MMAPI-compliant devices and MIDP 2.0-compliant devices, and hence we can be assured of its availability. The `Player` will automatically be stopped when the `Player` has finished playing the sequence and hence, there is no need to call the `close()` method, although it is a good idea.
5. b. The `StopTimeControl` interface is used to stop the `Player` after it has played its current media after a specified period of time. As a result, the time specified in the interface is the time relative to the media being played, not an absolute time. If the time passed to the method is beyond the media time, it will automatically be adjusted to the start or the end time of the media.

6. c. The value of the volume in a `MIDIControl` ranges from 0 to 127, and hence the value passed is valid. While the device will try to keep the volume at the specified level during playback, it might be overridden if a volume change event is specified in the media itself. Hence, choice A is incorrect.
7. a, c, and d. The valid states of a `Player` are `UNREALIZED`, `REALIZED`, `STARTED`, `STOPPED` and `CLOSED`.
8. a. The program will record the audio from the default audio capture device for 5 seconds. The `capture://audio` locator string refers to the default audio capture mechanism of the device. The `Player` will be in a stand-by mode until some media is playing. As a result, for the first second, it will not record anything, as the media has not started playing.
9. a, c, and d. The `DataSource` class can be used to define custom protocols. It also provides methods via the `SourceStream` interface to randomly seek data in the stream and provides support for frame-delimited data, which can be very useful for video streams. Both `DataSource` and `SourceStream` are not available in MIDP 2.0 Media API.
10. a and c. If the `Player` is playing some media, the application cannot change the `TimeBase` used by the `Player` to play the media or the number of times the `Player` should loop through the media, to provide consistent and predictable behavior. If the `start()` method is called when the `Player` has been started already, the method call will be ignored. If the `deallocate()` method is called when the `Player` is in the `STARTED` state, it will implicitly call the `stop()` method and stop the `Player`.

Exam Notes

☞ Given a set of requirements, develop code using MMAPI's support for tone generation.

Tone Generation

- Simple monotonic tones can be produced using the `Manager.playTone(int note, int duration, int volume)` method.
  - `note` can vary from 0 to 127
  - `duration` is expressed in milliseconds
  - `volume` can vary from 0 to 100 (percentage of the actual volume)
- More complex tones can be played by getting a tone sequence player.
  - `Player p = Manager.createPlayer(Manager.TONE_DEVICE_LOCATOR)`
  - A tone sequence player MUST implement `ToneControl` and SHOULD implement `VolumeControl` and `StopTimeControl` interfaces.
- A monotonic tone sequence is a byte array and has the following structure:
  - Version definition (`ToneControl.VERSION, 1`)
  - Tempo definition (`ToneControl.TEMPO, {5-127}`)
  - Resolution definition (`ToneControl.RESOLUTION, {1-127}`)

- Block definition (`ToneControl.BLOCK_START, {block number}, {tone values}, BLOCK_END, {same block number}`)
- Sequence events should be one of the following:
  - Tone Event—A single tone of the form: `{note value, tone duration}`
  - Volume Event—indicates volume to be set from this point forward and has two consecutvie bytes in the form: `{ToneControl.SET_VOLUME, volume value}`
  - Repeat Event—repeats a given tone: `{ToneControl.REPEAT, multiplier, note}`, where `multiplier` should be between 2 and 127
  - Block Event—plays a pre-defined block: `{ToneControl.PLAY_BLOCK, block number}`

- The byte sequence can be set using the `ToneControl.setSequence(byte[] sequence)` method.
  - The method can be called only if the `Player` is not in the `PREFETCHED` or `STARTED` state. Otherwise, an `IllegalStateException` will be thrown.
- The constant `ToneControl.C4` defines the middle C.
- The constant `ToneControl.SILENCE` should be used to create a pause.
- Multiplying the tempo by four gives the bpm.
- `VolumeControl` can be used to set the volume of a `Player`.
  - The volume level can be between 0 and 100, inclusive. If the set value is less than 0, it will be treated as 0 and if the set value is greater than 100, it will be treated as 100.
  - When a `Player` is unmated from the muted state, the volume will return to what was there previously before the `Player` was muted.
- `StopTimeControl` can be used to stop a `Player` after it has played its current media after a specified period of time. This is something like setting the sleep timer in a TV or stereo.
  - The `Player` is guaranteed to stop at most before 1 second after the specified time.
  - If the `Player` is running while the stop time is being set and the `Player` has already crossed the requested time, it will be stopped immediately.
  - Once the `Player` is stopped, the stop time is reset. It can also be reset manually using the `RESET` constant.
  - If the stop time has been set on the `Player`, calling the `setStopTime(int time)` will cause an `IllegalStateException` to be thrown.

☞ Given a set of requirements, develop code that correctly uses MIDP support for sound including audio playback, tone generation, media flow controls (start, stop), media type controls (volume, tone), and media capabilities using "`Manager`", "`Player`", and "`Control`" objects, recognizing the difference between required and optional features.

MIDP 2.0 Media Support

- Since MIDP 2.0 might be supported by devices that do not have the need to provide extensive media support, the media requirements in MIDP 2.0 is a strict subset of the

MMAPI 1.1 specification. Hence, whatever under MIDP 2.0 is totally compatible with MMAPI 1.1.

- MIDP 2.0 media supports *audio only.* All graphic and video controls are excluded.
- Custom protocols via `DataSource` *are not supported.*
- MIDI playback is not mandated and so the `Player.MIDI_DEVICE_LOCATOR` is not present.
- Operations and functions are exactly the same as that of MMAPI 1.1.

Class	*Function*	*Difference w.r.to MMAPI 1.1*
`Manager`	Factory to create `Players`	No support for `DataSource`
`Player`	Plays media data	Subset of features. No MIDI support
`Control`	Interface for media controls	-
`ToneControl`	Controls tone sequence format	-
`VolumeControl`	Controls volume	-
`Controllable`	Superinterface of the `Player`	No `SourceStream` subinterface
`PlayerListener`	Listener for `Player` events	Subset of features

☞ Develop code that correctly uses MMAPI support for playback and recording of media, including the use of the "`DataSource`", "`Player`", and "`Manager`" objects, support for audio and video capture and playback, system properties queries, recognizing the difference between required and optional features.

DataSource

- `DataSource` is an abstract class that can be extended to create custom streaming content.
- The `Manager.createPlayer(DataSource ds)` method can be used to create a Player object from a specified `DataSource`.
- `DataSource` extensions are preferable over the standard `InputStream` objects since these support random seeking capabilities. That is, you can go to a specified time in the content using this class, which is not possible if you use `InputStream`.
- `DataSource` also supports the concept of a transfer size, which is more suitable for framed content like video.
- The typical sequence of operations in a `DataSource` object is
  - `DataSource(String locator)` to create an object from a given locator URL.
  - `DataSource.connect()` to connect to the source.
  - `DataSource.getStreams():SourceStream[]` to get one or more streams associated with this `DataSource`. Typically, there will be only one stream.
  - `DataSource.start()` to start the transfer of data.
  - `DataSource.stop()` to stop the transfer of data.
  - `DataSource.disconnect()` to disconnect from the source.

- The `SourceStream.getTransferSize()` can be used to find the size of a block of data transferred. This information can be used to set appropriate buffer size while calling the `SourceStream.read(byte[] byte, int offset, int length)` method.

Manager

- The `Manager` is a factory class that creates `Players` based on the content type of an associated stream.
- The `Manager.createPlayer` method can take in a locator URL (a `String`), a `DataSource` object, or an `InputStream` object which will have information about the source.
- The `Manager` also has a simple method `Manager.playTone` to play a tone.
- Convenience constants `MIDI_DEVICE_LOCATOR` and `TONE_DEVICE_LOCATOR` can be used to get a MIDI (`audio/midi`) or tone sequence (`audio/x-tone-seq`) `Player`.
- `Manager.getSupportedContentTypes(null)` will give *all* the content types supported by this `Manager`. If a valid `String` is passed, it gives the content types supported for the requested protocol.
- `Manager.getSupportedProtocols(null)` will give *all* the protocols supported by this `Manager`. If a valid `String` is passed, it gives the protocols supported for the requested content type.
- The locator URL string is of the format: `<scheme>://<scheme-specific-part>`.
- The `Manager.getSystemTimeBase()` gets a implementation-independent time base that can be used by the `Players`.

Locator URL	*Content Type*
`device://tone`	Tone sequence (`TONE_DEVICE_LOCATOR`)
`device://midi`	MIDI (`MIDI_DEVICE_LOCATOR`)

Player

- A `Player` renders a time-based media data (audio, video, etc.)
- Lifecycle of a `Player` can be understood using the following diagram:

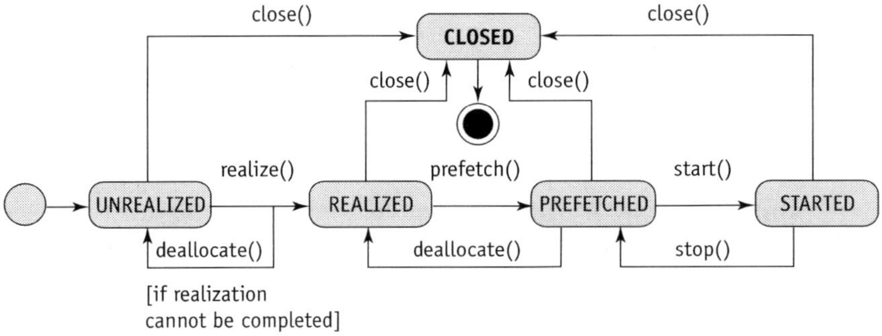

- The `Player.setMediaTime(long)` can be called to randomly place the pointer to a specific time. This is similar to, say, fast forwarding/reversing the data to the xth minute of play.
- Loop count set by the `setLoopCount(int)` method can be between 1 and 127. –1 will cause indefinite looping. 0 is not allowed.

UNREALIZED State

- The `Player` does not have information about the data.
- The following methods *cannot* be invoked (will cause an `IllegalStateException`):
  - `getContentType`
  - `set/getTimeBase`
  - `setMediaTime`
  - `getControls`
  - `getControl`
- The `Player.realize()` method is used to realize the `Player`.
  - This is a time-consuming method since it takes time to get information about the data source.
  - While the `Player` is being realized, the `deallocate()` method can be called to stop the realization and move the `Player` back to the `UNREALIZED` state if needed.

REALIZED State

- The `Player` has enough information about the data that it can play.
- Once the `Player` is realized, it *never* returns to the `UNREALIZED` state.
- The `Player.prefetch()` method can be used to move the player to the `PREFETCHED` state.
  - This is a time-consuming method since the `Player` might try to get as much information or data as possible to minimize the start time of the `Player`.
  - If this method is called before realizing the `Player`, the `Player.realize()` method is implicitly called.

PREFETCHED State

- The `Player` has all the information needed and is ready to be started.
- When a `Player` is stopped, it returns to this state.
- The `Player` can be started using the `Player.start()` method.
  - If this method is called before the `Player` is in the `PREFETCHED` state, the `Player.prefetch()` method is implicitly called.
  - If the `Player` was stopped previously by calling the `Player.stop()` method, the `Player` will start playing from where it left off. In essence, this is equivalent of pressing the PAUSE button in a stereo.

STARTED State

- The `Player` has started playing. This method is a *non-blocking* method and returns as soon as the `Player` has started playing. The playing itself happens in the background.
- The following methods will throw an `IllegalStateException` if invoked.
  - `setTimeBase`
  - `setLoopCount`
- If a loop count is set, then once the end of the data has reached, the `Player` will loop back to the beginning and start all over once again till there are no more loops.
- If the `Player.stop()` method is called, the `Player` returns to the `PREFETCHED` state.

CLOSED State

- This state can be reached by calling the `Player.close()` method when the `Player` is in the `UNREALIZED`, `REALIZED`, `PREFETCHED`, or `STARTED` state.

Audio and Video Capture

- Audio and video capture can be done using a `Player` that implements the `RecordControl` interface.
- The capture can be done by the following steps:
  - Realize the `Player` using the `Player.realize()` method
  - Get the `RecordControl` interface of the `Player` using the `Player.getControl("RecordControl")` method
  - Set the `RecordControl`'s stream using the `RecordControl.setRecordStream` or `RecordControl.setRecordLocation` method
  - Start the `RecordControl` using the `RecordControl.start()` method
  - Start the `Player` using the `Player.startRecord()` method
  - Stop the `Player` using the `Player.stop()` method
  - Stop the `RecordControl` using the `RecordControl.stopRecord()` method
  - Commit the data captured using the `RecordControl.commit()` method
- If the `Player` is not running and the `RecordControl.startRecord()` is called, it will be on stand-by till the player has actually started running. So there will be no *empty-recording.*
- The `RecordControl.reset()` method can be used to erase the captured content.

System Properties

Property	*Description*
`supports.mixing`	`true` if mixing is supported. `false` otherwise. Mixing means that at least two tones can be played simultaneously using any combination of the `Manager.playTone` and the audio playback methods
`supports.audio.capture`	`true` if audio capture is supported. `false` otherwise
`supports.video.capture`	`true` if video capture is supported. `false` otherwise
`supports.recording`	`true` if recording is supported. `false` otherwise
`audio.encodings`	space-separated, supported audio encodings
`video.encodings`	space-separated, supported video encodings
`video.snapshot.encodings`	space-separated, supported image encodings for video capture

☞ Identify correct and incorrect statements or examples about the media class hierarchies in both MIDP 2.0 and MMAPI 1.1.

Class Hierarchy in MIDP 2.0 and MMAPI 1.1

- `Controllable` is the base interface.
  - `Player` implements the interface and plays media data.
  - `SourceStream` implements the interface and provides custom protocol support. *Not in MIDP 2.0.*
  - `DataSource` is a class used to provide custom media protocols. *Not in MIDP 2.0.*
- `Manager` class is a factory to get `Player` implementations.
  - Default constants provided for tone sequence `(TONE_DEVICE_LOCATOR)` and MIDI `(MIDI_DEVICE_LOCATOR)` playback. *MIDI is not supported in MIDP 2.0.*
- `Player` class is used to play media data. An implementation is obtained from the `Manager` factory.
  - `TimeBase` is used by the `Player` to track time.
- `Control` is the superinterface for all controls that can be implemented by a `Player`. Only the identified controls are supported in MIDP 2.0.
  - Audio Controls
    - `ToneControl` controls the tone seqeuence format. *Supported in MIDP 2.0.*
    - `VolumeControl` controls the `Player`'s volume. *Supported in MIDP 2.0.*
    - `MIDIControl` controls MIDI playback.
    - `PitchControl` controls the pitch of a MIDI note.
    - `TempoControl` controls the tempo of a MIDI note.
  - Video Controls
    - `VideoControl` controls video media playback.
    - `FramePositioningControl` controls the framing of video.

- General Controls
  - `StopTimeControl` allows you to set a preset stop time. This is like a sleep-time.
  - `RateControl` is used in conjunction with `TimeBase` to calibrate time used by `Player`.
  - `GUIControl` is used to display a user interface for the associated `Player`.
  - `RecordControl` is used to record the media played by the `Player`.
  - `MetaDataControl` can be used to get some general meta-data information about the media content.
- `PlayerListener` is a listener interface that can be implemented and registered to a `Player` to listen to the `Player`'s events.

11

Chapter

Sending Messages Using the Wireless Messaging API

Exam Objectives

11.1 Describe the WMA's basic support for sending and receiving messages, and the Generic Connection Framework. (Section 11.1)

11.2 Explain the WMA's support for Short Message Service (SMS) and Cell Broadcast capabilities. (Sections 11.2 and Section 11.3)

11.3 Identify correct and incorrect statements or examples about WMA including the WMA addressing scheme, client vs. server connections, WMA-related exceptions, WMA-related security issues, message size limitation, message creation, sending, synchronous compared to asynchronous message receipt, and the relationship between WMA and Push Registry. (Section 11.4)

INTRODUCTION

At the starting of this book, we might have said that text messaging on mobile phones was very popular throughout the world, but still hadn't quite caught on in the United States. Well, now you can vote for your favorite American Idol with SMS text messaging. The Wikipedia entry on the subject includes sections discussing the political and social implications of SMS. It is pretty clear that text messaging has become a significant consumer force, if not a full blown world wide phenomenon. With this in mind, JTWI identifies WMA 1.1 as a mandatory component specification.

In this chapter, we will examine the WMA model for supporting message-based network communications. WMA builds upon the GCF we discussed earlier in this book. As we have seen, GCF was built to be a generic, extensible model that could be adapted to implementations of a variety of specific networking protocols. WMA provides a set of interfaces and classes to extend the framework of GCF in the direction of message-based protocols like SMS and Cell Broadcast Service (CBS).

Note, in the spirit of extensible frameworks, the core classes of WMA do not themselves implement any specific protocols; they merely extend the interfaces and classes of GCF in the direction of message-based protocols. If you recall, GCF provides the `Connection` interface as a generic abstraction of the functionality of various I/O connections. The WMA `MessageConnection` interface extends the GCF `Connection` interface to provide additional functionality for message-based protocols. Seeking only to extend the flexibility of GCF towards messaging, WMA leaves the specific implementation unspecified.

However, JTWI tightens some of the optional elements of WMA, thus making it a requirement for compliant devices to provide WMA implementations to support SMS and CBS. In this chapter, then, we will first examine the interfaces and classes that comprise the WMA extension of GCF. Since the generic nature of the interfaces makes it hard to see the details in action, we will hop right into some detailed explanation and examples of the SMS and CBS implementations. After we have the practical footing from those sections, we will return again to wrap up some of the details of the WMA classes.

11.1 WMA PACKAGE OVERVIEW

CLDC defines, at the configuration layer of the Java ME architecture, GCF as a flexible and extensible model for implementing various types of input and output. On a mobile phone, these sources of I/O typically turn out to be network connections based on a variety of protocols. When we discussed GCF previously, we noted that it provides a `Connection` interface to represent a generic sort of connection. We also noted that GCF did not require any specific protocols be implemented. So, without some further specification, there wouldn't be much functionality, just an empty framework. GCF is supposed to shape the usage of I/O, not provide the actual implementations. Actual implementations are provided at the profile layer, or in additional packages. For instance, MIDP provides the implementations to support HTTP and other protocols common to its target devices.

As we said in the introduction, WMA further extends the generic structure of GCF towards the needs of message-based protocols. We will now look at the interfaces and classes that it provides in the service of this goal. These classes belong to the `javax.wireless.messaging` package. This package contains a scant five interfaces: `Message`, `TextMessage`, `BinaryMessage`, `MessageConnection` and `MessageListener` interfaces. Figure 11.1 displays the hierarchy of WMA and its relationship to GCF.

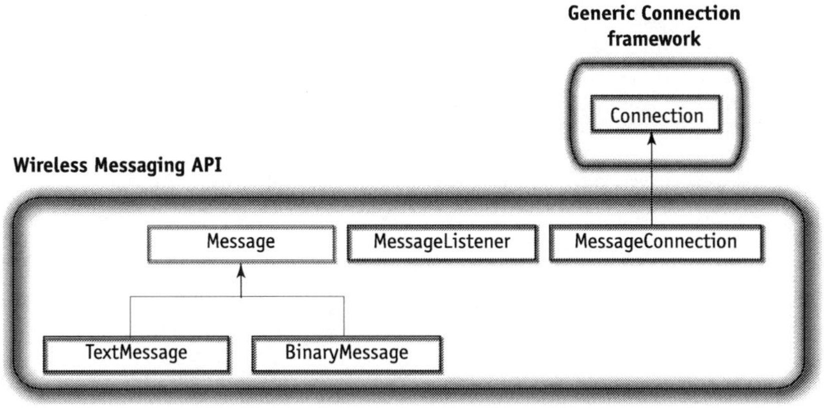

Figure 11.1 Overview of the Wireless Messaging API Hierarchy

The `MessageConnection` interface is the central figure in this package—it extends the `Connection` interface of GCF—but we will delay discussion about it for a bit. First, we will look at the `Message` interface and its sub-interfaces. Then, when we discuss the `MessageConnection`, we can build upon our knowledge of the `Message` interfaces to examine real examples of using the `MessageConnection` to send actual `Messages`.

11.1.1 Message Interface

A class that implements the `Message` interface represents a wireless message. Every wireless message contains an address part and a data part. Since different types of message-based protocols carry differing types of payload data, the methods to manipulate the data part of a message are not defined in the `Message` interface. The `Message` interface only has methods to manipulate addresses and timestamps; it is a base interface meant to be extended by other more specific interfaces. The data payload is supposed to be manipulated by the subinterfaces that extend the `Message` interface, because different types of data part need to be manipulated by different subinterfaces of the base `Message` interface. Table 11.1 lists the methods that are defined in the `Message` interface.

Table 11.1 Methods of the `Message` interface

Method	*Description*
`public java.util.Date getTimestamp()`	This method returns the date, on which the message has been sent.
`public String getAddress()`	This method returns the address that has been associated to the message.
`public void setAddress(String address)`	This method sets the specified address to associate with the message.

The class provided in Listing 11.1 can be used as a utility class to get and print timestamp and address of a message to the console and to set an address to associate with the message.

Listing 11.1: A utility class that shows how the methods of the Message interface can be applied

```
package com.scmadkit.ch11;
import javax.wireless.messaging.Message;
/**
 * This class is to get and print timestamp
 * and address of a message to the system console,
 * and to set a new address to associate with the message.
 *
 * @author Ko Ko Naing
 */
public class MessageUtil {
    /**
     * Print the timestamp of the message
     */
    public static void printTimestamp(Message message) {
        java.util.Date timestamp = message.getTimestamp();
        System.out.println("Timestamp of the message:" + timestamp);
    }
    /**
     * Print the address of the message
     */
    public static void printAddress(Message message) {
        String address = message.getAddress();
        System.out.println("Address of the message:" + address);
    }
    /**
     * Set and print a new address to the message
     */
    public static void setAddress(Message message, String address) {
        System.out.println("The original address of the message is"
                           + message.getAddress());
        System.out.println("The address to be set into the message is"
                           + address);
        message.setAddress(address);
        System.out.println("The new address of the message is"
                           + message.getAddress());
    }
}
```

11.1.2 TextMessage Interface

The `TextMessage` interface extends the `Message` interface and is to represent a text message. Therefore, it contains methods to manipulate the text payload: `getPayloadText()` and `setPayloadText(String)`. There is no data validation built-in in the `setPayloadText(String)` method, meaning that the validity of the `String` value passed into the method will not be verified by the method. It is the responsibility of the application developer to validate the value before passing it into the method. Since the `TextMessage` interface extends the `Message` interface, it inherits all of the address and timestamp-related methods from the `Message` interface. Object instances that implement the `TextMessage` interface act like containers that just store the text data that is passed into its setter method.

One thing that needs to be considered is character encoding. Text messages that are represented by this interface concern only with the `Strings` that are encoded in Java. Device implementation is responsible for the conversion of the `Strings` into a suitable encoding for the messaging protocol used for a text message. It is obvious that different protocols will use different encoded character sets. An application needs to be aware of the character sets that can be recognized by the protocol. Otherwise, the characters transmitted may not be correct at the receiving device. Therefore, it is highly recommended to make sure that the character encoding used is recognized by the messaging protocol so that characters are transmitted correctly at the receiving device. Table 11.2 lists the methods that are defined in the `TextMessage` interface, excluding the methods that it inherits from the `Message` interface.

Table 11.2 Methods of the `TextMessage` interface

Method	*Description*
`public String getPayloadText()`	This method returns the text data payload that is in the message.
`public void setPayloadText(String text)`	This method sets the text data payload into the message.

The class provided in Listing 11.2 can be used as a utility class to get and print text payload of a text message to the console and to set a new text payload into the message.

Listing 11.2: A utility class that shows how the methods of the* `TextMessage` *interface can be applied

```
package com.scmadkit.ch11;
import javax.wireless.messaging.TextMessage;
/**
 * This class is to get and print text payload
 * of a text message to the system console,
 * and to set a new text payload into the message.
 *
```

```
    * @author Ko Ko Naing
    */
public class TextMessageUtil {
      /**
       * Print the text payload of the message
       */
   public static void printTextPayload(TextMessage textMessage) {
      String payloadText = textMessage.getPayloadText();
      System.out.println("Text payload of the message :"
                        + payloadText);
   }
   /**
    * Set and print a text payload to the message
    */
   public static void setTextPayload(TextMessage textMessage,
                                     String payloadText) {
      System.out.println("The original text payload of the message
                        is" + textMessage.getPayloadText());
      System.out.println("The text payload to be set into the message
                        is" + payloadText);
      textMessage.setPayloadText(payloadText);
      System.out.println("The new text payload of the message
                        is" + textMessage.getPayloadText());
   }
}
```

11.1.3 BinaryMessage Interface

The `BinaryMessage` interface extends the `Message` interface and is to represent a binary message. Therefore, it contains methods to manipulate binary data payload: `getPayloadData()` and `setPayloadData(byte[])`. There is no data validation built-in in the `setPayloadData(byte[])` method, meaning that the validity of the array of bytes value passed into the method will not be verified by the method. It is the responsibility of the application developer to validate the value before passing it into the method. Since the `BinaryMessage` interface extends the `Message` interface, it inherits all of the address and timestamp-related methods from the `Message` interface. Object instances that implement the `BinaryMessage` interface act like containers that just store the binary data that is passed into its setter method. Table 11.3 lists the methods that are defined in the `BinaryMessage` interface, excluding the methods that it inherits from the `Message` interface.

Table 11.3 Methods of the `BinaryMessage` interface

Method	*Description*
`public byte[] getPayloadData()`	This method returns the binary data payload that is in the message as an array of bytes.
`public void setPayloadData(byte[] data)`	This method sets the binary data payload into the message with an array of bytes.

The class provided in Listing 11.3 can be used as a utility class to get and print binary payload of a binary message to the console and to set a new binary payload into the message.

Listing 11.3: A utility class that shows how the methods of the BinaryMessage interface can be applied

```
package com.scmadkit.ch11;
import javax.wireless.messaging.BinaryMessage;
/**
 * This class is to get and print binary payload
 * of a binary message to the system console,
 * and to set a new binary payload into the message.
 *
 * @author Ko Ko Naing
 */
public class BinaryMessageUtil {
  /**
   * Print the binary payload of the message
   */
  public static void printBinaryPayload(BinaryMessage binaryMsg){
   byte[] payloadData = binaryMsg.getPayloadData();
   System.out.println("Binary payload of the message :"
                 + payloadData);
   }
   /**
    * Set and print a binary payload to the message
    */
   public static void setBinaryPayload(BinaryMessage binaryMsg,
                                        byte[] payloadData) {
   System.out.println("The original binary payload of the message
                       is" + binaryMsg.getPayloadData());
   System.out.println("The binary payload to be set into the
                       message is" + payloadData);
   binaryMsg.setPayloadData(payloadData);
   System.out.println("The new binary payload of the message is"
                       + binaryMsg.getPayloadData());
  }
}
```

It is worth noting, to help one understand the nature of the framework, that it would be the role of adapter specifications—the additional specifications that might outline the implementations of other protocols—to create new extensions of the `Message` interface. This is not the role of the application developer; it is the role of the implementers of device functionality.

The next section will discuss the `MessageConnection` interface, the key player in the WMA.

11.1.4 MessageConnection Interface

The `MessageConnection` interface provides the most fundamental functionalities available in WMA such as creating messages, sending messages, receiving messages and so forth. Specifically, the interface contains two methods for creating a new message and a method each for sending a message, for receiving a message, for calculating the number of segments in the messaging protocol that will be needed to send a specified message and for registering a `MessageListener` instance that can be used to notify the device platform of an incoming message. Table 11.4 lists the methods that are defined in the `MessageConnection` interface.

Table 11.4 Methods of the `MessageConnection` interface

Method	*Description*
`public javax.wireless.messaging. Message newMessage(String type)`	This method constructs a new `Message` instance of a specified type.
`public javax.wireless.messaging.Message newMessage(String type, String address)`	This method constructs a new message instance of a specified type and initializes the message with a specified destination address.
`public int numberOfSegments (javax. wireless.messaging.Message message)`	This method returns the number of segments in the messaging protocol that will be needed to send a specified message.
`public void send (javax.wireless. messaging.Message message)`	This method sends a specified message.
`public javax.wireless.messaging Message receive()`	This method receives a message.
`public void setMessageListener (javax.wireless.messaging. MessageListener listener)`	This method registers a `MessageListener` instance that can be used to notify the device platform of an incoming message.

The following two code examples show how to use the `MessageConnection` to send and receive messages. Note, the `MessageConnection` can be created to be a client or a server connection. A client connection is created with a URL string that identifies the remote address to which all messages will be sent. A server connection is created with a URL that identifies a local port and can receive and send messages. The `MIDlet` class provided in Listing 11.4

shows how the `MessageConnection` interface, created as a client connection, can be used to send SMS text messages.

Listing 11.4: A `MIDlet` class that shows how methods of the `MessageConnection` interface can be used to send text messages

```
package com.scmadkit.ch11;
import javax.microedition.midlet.*;
import javax.microedition.io.*;
import javax.microedition.lcdui.*;
import javax.wireless.messaging.*;
import java.io.IOException;
/   **
    * This MIDlet is to send a text message
    * to a recipient device by using SMS MessageConnection.
    *
    * @author Ko Ko Naing
    */
public class SMSSenderMIDlet extends MIDlet implements CommandListener,
Runnable {
    /** Current display of the application */
    Display display;
    /** UI command to send a message */
    Command sendCommand = new Command("Send", Command.ITEM, 1);
    /** UI command for exit the application */
    Command exitCommand = new Command("Exit", Command.EXIT, 2);
    /** UI box where users can type a message */
    TextBox messageBox;
    /** The address of the recipient device */
    String destiDevice;
    /** The port on the recipient device */
    String destiPort;
    /** SMS message connection to send text messages */
    MessageConnection smsConnection = null;
    /** SMS Connection String */
    String connectionString;
    /**
     * Create a new instance of a SMSSenderMIDlet
     */
public SMSSenderMIDlet() {
    /** Get the address of the recipient device from JAD */
    destiDevice = getAppProperty("Destination-Device");
    /** Get the port on the recipient device from JAD */
    destiPort = getAppProperty("Destination-Port");
```

```
        display = Display.getDisplay(this);
    }
    /**
     * Signal that the MIDlet has entered the Active state
     * @throws MIDletStateChangeException
     */
    protected void startApp() throws MIDletStateChangeException {
        connectionString = "sms://" + destiDevice + ":" + destiPort;
        try {
            /** Open the message connection */
            smsConnection =
            (MessageConnection) Connector.open(connectionString);
        } catch(IOException ioe) {
            ioe.printStackTrace();
        }
        messageBox = new TextBox(" Enter Message", null, 65535,
                                 TextField.ANY);
        messageBox.addCommand(exitCommand);
        messageBox.addCommand(sendCommand);
        messageBox.setCommandListener(this);
        display.setCurrent(messageBox);
    }
    /**
     * Respond to UI commands from the user
     * @param c UI command requested by the user
     * @param s Screen that initiatizes the user request
     */
    public void commandAction(Command c, Displayable s) {
        try {
            if (c == exitCommand) {
                destroyApp(false);
                notifyDestroyed();
            } else if(c == sendCommand) {
                /** Send the message using a separate thread */
                new Thread(this).start();
            }
        } catch (Exception ex) {
            ex.printStackTrace();
        }
    }
        /**
         * Send the message using another Thread so that
         * we don't need to worry about UI freezing problem
         */
```

```
    public void run() {
        try {
            /** Create a new text message */
            TextMessage textMessage = (TextMessage)
            smsConnection.newMessage(MessageConnection.TEXT_MESSAGE);
            textMessage.setPayloadText(messageBox.getString());
            /** Send the text message */
            smsConnection.send(textMessage);
        } catch (Exception e) {
            e.printStackTrace();
        }
    }
    public void destroyApp(boolean unconditional) {
        if (smsConnection != null) {
            try {
                /** Close the message connection */
                smsConnection.close();
            } catch (IOException ioe) {
                ioe.printStackTrace();
            }
        }
    }
    public void pauseApp() {}
}
```

The `MIDlet` class provided in Listing 11.5 shows how the `MessageConnection` interface can be created as a server connection and used to receive SMS text messages. This example uses the blocking `receive()` method to field incoming messages in blocked, looping manner. There is also an event-based method for fielding incoming messages, but we use the blocking `receive()` method in this example.

Listing 11.5: A `MIDlet` class that shows how methods of the `MessageConnection` interface can be used to receive text messages

```
package com.scmadkit.ch11;
import javax.microedition.midlet.*;
import javax.microedition.io.*;
import javax.microedition.lcdui.*;
import javax.wireless.messaging.*;
import java.io.IOException;
/**
 * This MIDlet is to receive text messages
```

```
 * by using SMS MessageConnection.
 *
 * @author Ko Ko Naing
 */
public class SMSReceiverMIDlet extends MIDlet implements
CommandListener {
    /** UI command to exit the application */
    Command exitCommand = new Command("Exit", Command.EXIT, 1);
    /** UI Alert to display received text messages */
    Alert alert;
    /** Current display of the application */
    Display display;
    /** The port on which we listen for SMS messages */
    String listeningPort;
    /** SMS message connection to receive text messages */
    MessageConnection smsConnection;
    /** The message received from an SMS message connection */
    Message message;
    /**
     * Create a new instance of a SMSReceiverMIDlet
     */
    public SMSReceiverMIDlet() {
        /** Get the port on which we listen for SMS messages */
        listeningPort = getAppProperty("Incoming-Port");
        display = Display.getDisplay(this);
        }
        /**
         * Signal that the MIDlet has entered the Active state
         * @throws MIDletStateChangeException
         */
    public void startApp() {
        alert = new Alert("SMS Receiver MIDlet");
        alert.setTimeout(Alert.FOREVER);
        alert.addCommand(exitCommand);
        alert.setCommandListener(this);
        alert.setString("Listening on port " + listeningPort + "...");
        display.setCurrent(alert);
        /** SMS connection to be read */
        String connectionString = "sms://:" + listeningPort;
        try {
            while(true) {
                if(smsConnection == null) {
```

```
                /** Open the message connection. */
                smsConnection = (MessageConnection)
                                     Connector.open(connectionString);
            }
            message = smsConnection.receive();
            if (message != null) {
                String senderAddress = message.getAddress();
                alert.setTitle("From:" + senderAddress);
                alert.setString(((TextMessage)
                                       message).getPayloadText());
                display.setCurrent(alert);
            }
        }
    } catch (IOException ioe) {
        ioe.printStackTrace();
    }
}
public void pauseApp() {}
public void destroyApp(boolean unconditional) {
    if (smsConnection != null) {
        try {
            /** Close the message connection */
            smsConnection.close();
        } catch (IOException ioe) {
            ioe.printStackTrace();
        }
    }
}
/**
 * Respond to UI commands from the user
 * @param c UI command requested by the user
 * @param s Screen that initiatizes the user request
 */
public void commandAction(Command c, Displayable s) {
    try {
        if (c == exitCommand) {
            destroyApp(false);
            notifyDestroyed();
        }
    } catch (Exception ex) {
        ex.printStackTrace();
    }
}
}
```

11.1.5 MessageListener Interface

As we noted before, in the last code example, a server `MessageConnection` can use the blocking `receive()` method, typically written in a server loop, to field incoming messages, or it can use an event-based system. The `MessageListener` interface provides an event-based mechanism for the application to be notified of incoming messages. If you want to receive notification of incoming messages, you must implement the `MessageListener` interface. When a message is received, the `notifyIncomingMessage(MessageConnection)` method of the `MessageListener` interface is called. That is the only method in the `MessageListener` interface. This mechanism is called asynchronous message receiving mechanism. We will discuss this mechanism in detail in the Section 11.4.6.

Table 11.5 Methods available in the `MessageListener` interface

Method	*Description*
`public void notifyIncomingMessage (javax.wireless.messaging.Message Connection connection)`	This method is called by the device platform, when an incoming message arrives to a specified `MessageConnection`, to which the `MessageListener` is registered.

The `MIDlet` class provided in Listing 11.5 shows how an application can make use of the `MessageListener` interface to notify of incoming messages, without being blocked by the `receive()` method call of the `MessageConection`, which we don't know how long it will take to fully download the whole message to the device. By creating a separate `Thread` and receiving message from that `Thread`, the application will not be blocked by `receive()` method call and it will be able to keep on going with its execution, while on the other side, the message is being received by another separate `Thread`.

Listing 11.6: Asynchronous-message-receiving version of the* `MIDlet` *class from Listing 11.5

```
package com.scmadkit.ch11;
import javax.microedition.midlet.*;
import javax.microedition.io.*;
import javax.microedition.lcdui.*;
import javax.wireless.messaging.*;
import java.io.IOException;
/**
 * This MIDlet is to receive text messages asynchronously
 * by using SMS MessageConnection and the MessageListener interface.
 *
 * @author Ko Ko Naing
 */
```

```
public class AsynchronousSMSReceiverMIDlet extends MIDlet implements
CommandListener, MessageListener, Runnable {
    /** UI command to exit the application */
    Command exitCommand = new Command("Exit", Command.EXIT, 1);
    /** UI Alert to display received text messages */
    Alert alert;
    /** Current display of the application */
    Display display;
    /** The port on which we listen for SMS messages */
    String listeningPort;
    /** SMS message connection to receive text messages */
    MessageConnection smsConnection;
    /** The message received from an SMS message connection */
    Message message;
    /**
     * Create a new instance of a AsynchronousSMSReceiverMIDlet
     */
    public AsynchronousSMSReceiverMIDlet() {
        /** Get the port on which we listen for SMS messages */
        listeningPort = getAppProperty("Incoming-Port");

        display = Display.getDisplay(this);
    }
    /**
     * Signal that the MIDlet has entered the Active state
     * @throws MIDletStateChangeException
     */
    public void startApp() {
        alert = new Alert("Asynchronous SMS Receiver MIDlet");
        alert.setTimeout(Alert.FOREVER);
        alert.addCommand(exitCommand);
        alert.setCommandListener(this);
        alert.setString("Listening on port" + listeningPort + "...");
        display.setCurrent(alert);

        /** SMS connection to be read */
        String connectionString = "sms://:" + listeningPort;

        /** Open the message connection */
        if (smsConnection == null) {
            try {
                /** Open the message connection */
                smsConnection = ( MessageConnection)
                                     Connector.open(connectionString);
                smsConnection.setMessageListener(this);
```

```
            } catch (IOException ioe) {
                ioe.printStackTrace();
            }
        }
    }
    public void pauseApp() {}
    public void destroyApp(boolean unconditional) {
        if (smsConnection != null) {
            try {
                /** Close the message connection */
                smsConnection.close();
            } catch (IOException ioe) {
                ioe.printStackTrace();
            }
        }
    }
    /**
     * Respond to UI commands from the user
     * @param c UI command requested by the user
     * @param s Screen that initiatizes the user request
     */
    public void commandAction(Command c, Displayable s) {
        try {
            if (c == exitCommand) {
                destroyApp(false);
                notifyDestroyed();
            }
        } catch (Exception ex) {
            ex.printStackTrace();
        }
    }
    /**
     * Called when a new message arrives
     * @param messageConnection The connection on which the message is
     * received
     */
    public void notifyIncomingMessage( MessageConnection
                                        messageConnection) {
        new Thread(this).start();
    }
    public void run() {
        try {
            message = smsConnection.receive();
```

```
            if (message != null) {
               String senderAddress = message.getAddress();
               alert.setTitle("From:" + senderAddress);
               alert.setString(((TextMessage)message).getPayloadText());
               display.setCurrent(alert);
            }
         } catch (IOException ioe) {
            ioe.printStackTrace();
         }
      }
   }
```

11.2 UNDERSTANDING SMS ADAPTER SUPPORT

Now we will look at the implementations that are required by JTWI. First, we will look at Short Message Service, usually known among mobile phone users as "SMS".

11.2.1 SMS Message Structure

GSM and CDMA, the two major standards for mobile phone communication, use differing message structures. CDMA SMS message structure can be found in the CDMA IS-637 standard documentation. Since it is out of scope for the exam, we will not discuss it here. However, let's take a shallow look at the GSM SMS message structure.

The GSM SMS message is composed of a fixed header and a field called `TP-User-Data`. The `TP-User-Data` field in turn contains the payload of the message and an optional header. The optional header is in a field called `User-Data-Header`. A field in the fixed header indicates whether optional header is in the `TP-User-Data` field or not. Figure 11.2 illustrates the general structure of a GSM SMS message.

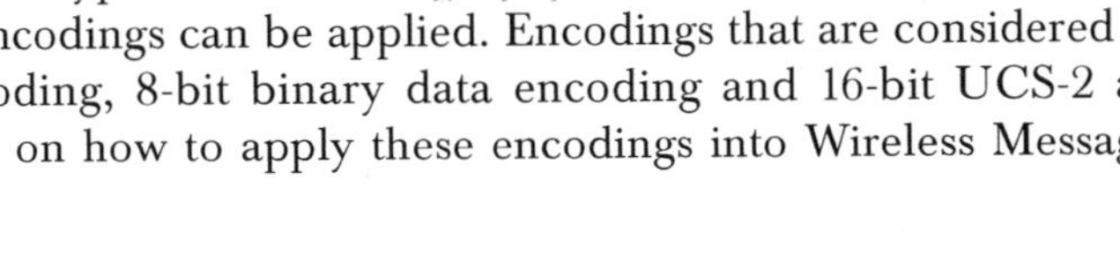

Figure 11.2 Structure of GSM SMS message

Depending on the type of the message payload contained in the `TP-User-Data` field, different types of encodings can be applied. Encodings that are considered most important are 7-bit alphabet encoding, 8-bit binary data encoding and 16-bit UCS-2 alphabet encoding. Detailed discussion on how to apply these encodings into Wireless Messaging API will come later.

11.2.2 SMS Message Payload Length

As you can see in Fig. 11.2, the length of an SMS message payload highly depends on the spaces taken by optional headers of `TP-User-Data` field. The more header information specified in the optional header portion, the fewer payloads can be filled into a message. For example, if the optional header information contains additional port number information, taking up more space in the `User-Data-Header` field, the SMS message can contain lesser amount of payload.

However, the message that an application sends to other devices can still be so long that it cannot fit into a single SMS message. In this case, device implementation is responsible to take care of message splitting and concatenation using the concatenation feature of the GSM standard specification. This mechanism works behind the scenes and is invisible from the application. It means that the concatenation feature of the GSM standard will automatically split the message payload that is considered very large into multiple SMS messages before sending it to the remote device. Upon receiving the messages, this feature automatically concatenates the received SMS messages into a fully resembled payload and passes it to the application. Therefore, total message payload length can be very long, but the remote device will receive multiple SMS messages. It is also important to keep in mind that the encoding applied on the payload content also affects the maximum length of an SMS message.

11.2.3 SMS Message Payload Concatenation Feature

There are two mechanisms defined in the GSM standard specification to concatenate SMS messages. Device implementation is free to use any of the two mechanisms in sending messages, while it must be able to accept messages with both mechanisms. It makes sense that if a receiving device can accept messages with both mechanisms, the sending device just needs to use one of them to send messages.

A WMA implementation needs to support at least 3 SMS messages to be received and concatenated to form a fully resembled payload for the application. In the same way, up to 3 SMS messages must be supported by a WMA implementation in sending messages. However, device implementation is free to raise this limit. But applications should be developed in a way that messages that will take up more than 3 SMS messages are not allowed to be sent. This is because we do not know whether the receiving device is able to handle such amount of messages using its concatenation feature or not. The `numberOfSegments (Message message)` method of the `MessageConnection` interface can be used to check the number of segments that will be needed to send a specified message in a certain messaging protocol. If it returns a number more than 3, we should reconsider whether to send this message or to reduce the message payload.

The CDMA IS-637 SMS protocol uses a different mechanism to concatenate the messages that are very large. But the mechanism works in a very similar manner as the GSM SMS concatenation feature for segmentation and reassembly of split messages. For example, the minimum amount of the CDMA SMS split messages is 3 to be consistent with the GSM SMS adapter.

Exam Tip

The exam usually contains tricky questions on the maximum amount of SMS protocol messages supported in sending an SMS message and the minimum amount of SMS protocol messages supported by the implementation in receiving an SMS message.

11.2.4 SMS Message Addressing Scheme

GSM SMS and CDMA SMS messages use the same addressing scheme and use `"sms://"` as communication protocol in URL connection strings. Table 11.6 describes the syntax of the URL connection strings for SMS messages.

Table 11.6 BNF notation for the syntax of the URL connection strings for SMS messages

String specified		*Definition*
smsurl	::=	`"sms://"` address_portion
address_portion	::=	foreign_host_address | local_host_address
local_host_address	::=	port_number_portion
port_number_portion	::=	":" digits
foreign_host_address	::=	msisdn | msisdn port_number_portion
msisdn	::=	"+" digits | digits
digits	::=	digit | digit digits
digit	::=	"0" | "1" | "2" | "3" | "4" | "5" | "6" | "7" | "8" | "9"

Some examples of valid SMS URL connection strings are:

```
sms://:1234
sms://+123456789:1234
sms://+123456789
```

When one of the URL connection strings listed above is passed into the `Connector.open` method, the method must return an object implementing the `MessageConnection` interface. If the first URL connection string is used, the connection returned will be in server mode with capability to send and receive SMS messages. But if the second or third URL connection string is used, the connection returned will be in client mode, which can only send SMS messages. Now it's time to learn the semantics of the items specified in an SMS URL string. The next section will be on this topic.

Specifying SMS Recipient Addresses and Port Numbers

In the syntax of the URL string discussed above, the "`msisdn`" portion of the string represents the recipient phone number and the port number portion of the string represents the port number that can identify an application. If the port number is specified in the address, the `TP-User-Data` field of an SMS message contains a `User-Data-Header` with the port number information of the application. For example, if the address for a message is specified as "`sms://+123456789:1234`", then the receiving device will try to find an application that is associated with the port number "`1234`" and deliver the message to that application. If a connection string containing both the phone number and the port number is specified during the creation of the connection, it is considered as opening a client mode connection. Figure 11.3 illustrate the meaning of the client mode connection string.

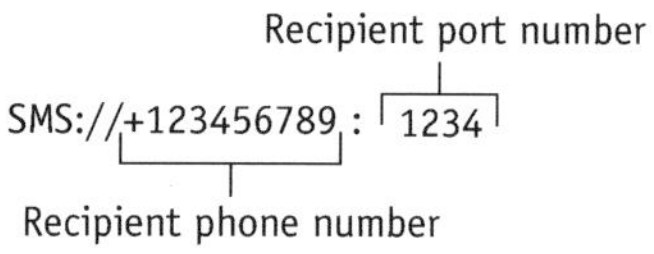

Figure 11.3 Illustration of client mode connection string

However, if the address for a message is specified as "`sms://:1234`" to opens a server mode connection, the port number "`1234`" is associated to the application that open the connection and it will be used for receiving messages from other applications. If a connection string containing only the port number is specified during the creation of the connection, it is considered as opening a server mode connection. Figure 11.4 illustrates the meaning of the server mode connection.

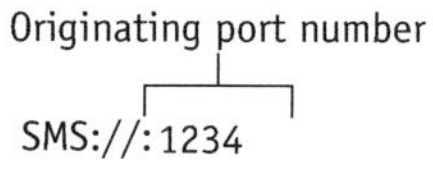

Figure 11.4 Illustration of server mode connection string

If you do not know about the client and server mode connections, don't worry about them right now. They will be discussed in detail in the next section. For now, let's get back to port number-related business.

There are certain restrictions in allocating port numbers for receiving applications. It is of first-in-first-out type. The first application that allocates a certain port number will be considered to be the owner of the port number. If an application attempts to allocate the same port number and open a connection using the same port number that has been allocated by the first application, an `IOException` will be thrown. Similarly, if any non-Java application in the device has allocated the port number and a Java application attempts to allocate the same port number, an `IOException` will be thrown.

The port numbers are split into ranges, one of which is controlled by IANA. If we want to ensure that our application will always be able to use a certain port number, we can register the port number with IANA so that the port number will always be reserved for our application only. Otherwise, we can just randomly select a port number from any available range that is not controlled by IANA and allocate it for our application. In this case, we need to ensure that `IOException` is properly handled by the application, in case another application might have been using the same port number.

There also are restrictions related to allocating port numbers in sending messages. Certain port numbers are reserved for restrictive access and it is not allowed for Java applications to send SMS messages to those port numbers. Device implementation is responsible to throw a `SecurityException`, when an application attempts to send a message to any of those port numbers, for example, 2923 for WAP WTA secure session service and 49999 for WAP OTA configuration.

If a feasible port number is not specified in the connection string, the `TP-User-Data` field does not contain the application port number information. Java applications cannot receive this kind of message. So the receiving device will handle the message by itself. Device implementation might provide the user with normal text message for SMS messages that do not contain application port number information.

In the CDMA IS-637 SMS protocol, there is no port number or application identifier that can be used to distinguish the applications. Another mechanism, called WAP WDP, is used to achieve this purpose. We will not go for further discussion on this mechanism here, since it is beyond the scope of this book.

We now know how to specify connection string in opening a connection. Let's go ahead and learn how to open connections with different modes.

Client Mode Connection Versus Server Mode Connection

Messages can be sent using either client or server mode connection. But messages can only be received using server mode connections.

When a client mode connection is used for sending a message, the originating port number is usually set by the device implementation and any messages received to this port number are not delivered to the connection. It means that client mode connections cannot be used for receiving messages. Some examples of connection strings for client mode connections are `sms://+123456789:1234` and `sms://+123456789`.

Exam Tip

Remember Fig. 11.3 clearly mentions that the port number that might be specified in the client mode connection string is the recipient port number, not the originating port number.

When a server mode connection is used for sending a message, the originating port number is specified in the connection string, for example, `sms://:1234` and `sms://:9876`. Then the port number will be set to the port number of the connection. Someone might come up with a question, asking "So where do we set the address and the port number of the recipient device for sending messages from a server mode connection?" The answer is that we need to set the address of the recipient address and the port number in the message that is to be sent manually using `aMessage.setAddress(String)` method call. This is not a case in the client mode connections, where recipient address and/or the recipient port number are already set, while opening the connection. Recall Figs 11.3 and 11.4, if necessary.

Since the application port number is already set in a server mode connection, the recipient does not need to explicitly set the address of the sender to reply back. The `getAddress()` method call on the message received will return the phone number and the port number of the sender. Therefore, whenever any response from recipients is expected, connections should be opened in server mode.

An application can open multiple connections at the same time and those connections can be both client and server mode. It means that there is no such restriction that an application must have client mode connections only or server mode connections only.

11.2.5 Handling Received SMS Messages

When SMS messages have been received by a certain application, they are usually removed from the temporary storage space such as SIM/ME memory. Therefore, it is the responsibility of the application to save the received messages by itself using any mechanisms available for the application, for example, RMS facility of the MIDP API, if the messages need to be stored persistently on the device.

The ordering of the SMS messages sent is not guaranteed in the GSM SMS protocol. They might be sent in any order. However, ordering is handled properly when a large message is split into multiple messages and they are automatically concatenated back into a single SMS message. So the split SMS messages are seen as only one at the end.

But if an application sends multiple SMS messages (not the split multiple message of a large message), the ordering of the messages arrived to the recipient might be different from the ordering of the messages sent. In this case, the application must take care of this by itself to know which message is sent first and which is next. However, device implementation must make sure that the order, in which the messages that are delivered to the application, is the same as the order that the message were received to the device.

11.2.6 Finding out SMSC Address

Before we go further and learn how to find out SMS Center (SMSC) address, it is not a bad idea to discuss what it is and why we need to find its address. SMSC is the place where messages sent are stored temporarily. SMS is a store-and-forward protocol. This switching method is suited to mobile phones because of the unreliable availability of mobile phones. A sent message is stored at SMSC until it can be delivered. SMSC checks whether the recipient device is on the network or not. If the device is on the network, it will directly deliver the messages to the recipient. Otherwise, it will store the messages for a certain period of time. Once the device is back on the network, it will forward the messages to the recipient. Therefore, SMSC address might be needed by applications to send the SMS messages to recipients.

The WMA 1.1 specification mandates that the SMSC address used for sending SMS messages must be made available using `System.getProperty` method with the property name specified as `wireless.messaging.sms.smsc`. Therefore, we can retrieve the address of the short message service center by calling `System.getProperty ("wireless. messaging.sms.smsc")`. It will return a number starting with a plus sign (+) followed by a series of digits.

11.2.7 SMS Message Types

We have already known that SMS messages can be sent and received using either the `TextMessage` or the `BinaryMessage` type of the Wireless Messaging API. If the `TextMessage` type is used, the GSM default 7-bit alphabet or the 16-bit UCS-2 alphabet encoding must be used to encode the payload contained in the `TP-User-Data` field. One question might be raised, asking which one to use. If the string that is to be put into the content area of the `TP-User-Data` field contains only the characters that can be found in the default GSM 7-bit alphabet, the default GSM 7-bit alphabet encoding must be applied to the payload. On the other hand, if the string that is to be set into the content area of the `TP-User-Data` field contains the characters that cannot be found in the default GSM 7-bit alphabet, the 16-bit UCS-2 alphabet encoding must be applied to the payload.

As for the `BinaryMessage` type, the 8-bit binary data encoding must be applied to the payload.

This is the last section, where we talk about SMS adapter support provided by the WMA 1.1 specification. The next section will discuss another popular service, CBS adapter support provided by the WMA 1.1 specification.

11.3 UNDERSTANDING CBS ADAPTER SUPPORT

The other protocol required by JTWI is CBS, which allows messages to be broadcast to every mobile station that is listening or subscribed to a base station. CBS is a unidirectional data service, where receivers cannot send the response back to the base station, meaning that it is receiving-only. The two main important topics related to CBS will be discussed in the next sections in detail: the GSM CBS message structure and its addressing scheme.

11.3.1 CBS Message Structure

The type of a CBS message can be determined using its `Message-Identifier` field, which is used to select topics to subscribe to. The `Message-Identifier` field is comparable to a port number, though it is not. In the same way as SMS server mode connection, CBS applications can receive messages of a certain topic by opening a connection using the URL connection string as the address scheme defined in the next section.

11.3.2 CBS Message Addressing Scheme

GSM CBS messages uses `"cbs://"` as communication protocol in its URL connection string. Table 11.7 describes the syntax of the URL connection strings for CBS messages.

Table 11.7 BNF notation for the syntax of the URL connection strings for CBS messages

String specified		*Definition*
cbsurl	::=	`"cbs://"` address_portion
address_portion	::=	message_identifier_portion
message_identifier_portion	::=	":" digits
digits	::=	digit | digit digits
digit	::=	"0" | "1" | "2" | "3" | "4" | "5" | "6" | "7" | "8" | "9"

Some examples of valid CBS URL connection strings are:

```
cbs://:1234
cbs://:4321
```

In the syntax of the URL connection string mentioned above, the `message_identifier_portion` represents the message identifier for the CBS messages that the application is willing to receive. The `MessageConnection` instance returned from calling the `Connector.open` method with the URL connection string as above can only be used to receive CBS messages. An `IOException` will be thrown, if the application tries to send a message using this `MessageConnection` instance.

11.3.3 CBS Message Types

Cell broadcast messages use the same encodings used in GSM SMS messages. Device implementation will take care of the conversion from messages encoded using the default GSM 7-bit alphabet or the 16-bit UCS-2 alphabet to `TextMessage` instances and from messages encoded using 8-bit binary to `BinaryMessage` instances.

One thing to note about the CBS messages is that they do not contain any timestamps set to their address portion of the message. So whenever the `Message.getTimestamp()` method is called, `null` value will always be returned from the method call for any received CBS messages.

Now we are all set with the two messaging protocols—SMS and CBS. There are only a few things left that we need to look at for us to be confident with WMA-related exam objectives.

11.4 BACK TO WMA IN GENERAL

Now that we've looked at the specific details of the two JTWI required protocol implementations, we will return to the WMA framework to clear up some loose ends. These loose ends include such important items as WMA-related exceptions, WMA-related security issues, and message size limitation. Some sections are like summaries of the topics that we have already covered as side effects of covering the specific protocols. For example, addressing scheme and client versus server connections are the topics that we have learned in Sections 11.2 and 11.3. We will cover them again briefly to give a formally thorough treatment.

11.4.1 Addressing Scheme

The GSM SMS and the CDMA SMS use the same URL connection string syntax. Both of them use "`sms://`" as the communication protocol in the URL connection string. Refer to Section 11.2.4 for the detailed discussion of the URL connection string syntax for SMS messages. In general, if we specify the recipient phone number in opening a connection, the connection will become a client mode connection. If we do not, then the connection will become a server mode connection. The port number is optional in opening client mode connection. If a port number is not specified in opening a client mode connection, the message will be delivered to the default SMS application that is running on the recipient device. But if we do specify the port number, the message will be delivered to the Java application that allocated this port number for its own use.

The GSM CBS can only be run in receiving mode. The connection opened for CBS messages will not be able to send messages to any other devices. The string "`cbs://`" is used as the communication protocol of the URL connection string. Section 11.3.2 discusses the syntax of GSM CBS connection string in detail.

11.4.2 Client Versus Server Connections

Table 11.8 summarises the differences between client mode connection and server mode connection.

Table 11.8 Differences between client mode connection and server mode connection

Client Mode Connection	*Server Mode Connection*
Used for sending messages only	Used for sending as well as receiving messages
Used when reply from the other party is not expected	Used when reply from the other party is expected
`IOException` will be thrown, if the `receive()` is called	`receive()` method call is eligible
Port number specified in the connection string is of the recipient	Port number specified in the connection string is of the sender application
Recipient phone number and port number are specified in the connection string	Recipient phone number and port number need to be specified using `setAddress(String)` of the message, since the connection string does not contain recipient information

11.4.3 WMA-related Exceptions

Exceptions are unavoidable in many situations; therefore we should take a look at the ways to handle them peacefully. In this section, we'll see what exceptions should be expected, how they happen and how to handle them.

ConnectionNotFoundException

Methods

- `open` methods of the `Connector` class

Causes

- The connection target could not be found or the protocol type is not supported

Solutions

- Make sure that the connection target is reachable and find out the supported protocol

InterruptedIOException

Methods

- `open(String, int, boolean)` method of the `Connector` class
- `receive` and `send` methods of the `MessageConnection` interface

Causes

- The I/O operation has been interrupted or the timeout expires

Solutions

- Resend the data again upon receiving errors or reduce the message size

IOException

Methods

- `send`, `receive` and `setMessageListener` methods of the `MessageConnection` interface, when the connection has been closed
- `receive` and `setMessageListener` method on a client mode connection
- `send` and `receive` method, when the message could not be sent or received, because of the network failure
- `open` methods of the `Connector` class, when the specified port number has been bound to another application

Causes

- Sending messages, receiving messages and registering a message listener on a closed connection
- Trying to register a listener or trying to receive messages on a client mode connection
- Network failure occurs during sending and receiving messages
- Opening a connection that uses a port number that has been allocated by another application

Solutions

- Make sure not to send, receive and set message listener on a closed connection
- Make sure not to call server mode connection-related methods on a client mode connection
- Make sure the network is fine
- Make sure the specified port number has not been bound to any other application yet

NullPointerException

Methods

- `send` method of the `MessageConnection` interface

Causes

- The message being passed into the method is `null`

Solutions

- Make sure the message is not `null`

SecurityException

Methods

- `open` methods of the `Connector` class

- receive, send and setMessageListener methods of the MessageListener interface

Causes

- The communication protocol passed is not supported while opening a connection or the port number specified is reserved for restrictive use only while receiving messages, sending messages or registering a message listener

Solutions

- Find out what communication protocols are supported in the device and find out which port numbers are restrictive

11.4.4 WMA-related Security Issues

Will we be able to send and receive messages without consideration of any security issues? Of course, not. We need to consider the permissions that will be needed to perform the requested operation. Applications must be granted enough permission to send and receive messages. However, device implementation is free to implement any kinds of mechanisms for granting permissions. In the following sections, we will see what permissions are needed for opening connections and what permissions are needed for sending and receiving messages.

Specifying Permissions for Opening Connections

To open a connection, an application needs to be granted with an appropriate permission to access the MessageConnection interface. If the permission is not granted to the application before accessing the MessageConnection interface, calling any of the Connector.open methods will throw a SecurityException. Table 11.9 indicates the permissions defined for each adapter protocol, SMS and CBS, to open a connection.

Table 11.9 Permissions needed for opening connections

Permission	*Adapter protocol*
javax.microedition.io.Connector.sms	Short message service (SMS)
javax.microedition.io.Connector.cbs	Cell broadcast service (CBS)

Specifying Permissions for Sending and Receiving Messages

In addition to the permissions for opening a connection, an application also needs permissions to send and receive messages. If the permission is not granted to the application before sending or receiving messages, calling the messageConnection.send(Message) or the messageConnection.receive() method will throw a SecurityException. Table 11.10 indicates the permissions needed to send and receive messages.

Table 11.10 Permissions needed for sending and receiving messages

Permission	*Adapter protocol*
`javax.wireless.messaging.sms.send`	Short message service (SMS)
`javax.wireless.messaging.sms.receive`	Short message service (SMS)
`javax.wireless.messaging.cbs.receive`	Cell broadcast service (CBS)

Hold on. Even after specifying appropriate permissions for sending and receiving messages, we cannot send or receive any types of messages to any recipients we want. Device implementation may not allow certain types of messages and/or sending messages to certain recipients. By recipients, we mean both device addresses and/or application identifiers such as port numbers in a device. If an application attempts to send restricted messages and/or to restricted recipients, device implementation may throw a `SecurityException` even after the application is granted the permissions to open a connection and the permissions to send messages.

Therefore, we should not assume that being able to send a message to a recipient implies that we can send any kinds of messages to any addresses. Hence, our applications should be able to peacefully handle `SecurityException` that might occur, while opening a connection, sending or receiving messages. The next section will discuss how to be aware of the size limitation of a message while working on the messages with the Wireless Messaging API.

11.4.5 Message Size Limitation

Section 11.2.2 and Section 11.2.3 discussed the SMS message payload length and the SMS concatenation feature to handle large SMS messages. An SMS message can be so long that it cannot fit into a single SMS message. Device implementation is responsible to take care of message segmentation and reassembly using the concatenation feature of the GSM standard specification.

A WMA implementation needs to support at least 3 SMS messages to be received and concatenated to form a fully resembled payload for the application. In the same way, up to 3 SMS messages must be supported by a WMA implementation in sending messages. However, device implementation is free to raise this limit. But applications should be developed in a way that messages that will take up more than 3 SMS messages are not allowed to be sent. This is because we do not know whether the receiving device is able to handle such amount of messages using its concatenation feature or not. Therefore, it is highly recommended to keep the limit of the message up to the size that can be fit into 3 SMS messages.

11.4.6 Synchronous Versus Asynchronous Message Receiving Mechanisms

Normally, an application will be waiting for an incoming message using the `messageConnection.receive()` method in the application itself. This mechanism is called synchronous message receiving mechanism and the method `receive()` will block any other methods till the message is completely received by the application, even though it may take unacceptable time to return from the method.

Wireless Messaging API contains an asynchronous message receiving mechanism, in which the application will not be blocked during the message retrieval period. The `notifyIncomingMessage(MessageConnection)` method of the `MessageListener` interface can be used to achieve this goal. It is a non-blocking method call. If an instance of the class that implements the `MessageListener` interface is registered to the `MessageConnection` that will be used to receive messages, the `notifyIncomingMessage` method of the `MessageListener` instance will be invoked when a message is received from the `MessageConnection` that is registered to. After the `notifyIncomingMessage` method has been invoked, it should return as quick as possible to avoid blocking call. Therefore, message receiving process should be done in a separate thread which should have been created in the `notifyIncomingMessage` method. Refer to code Listing 11.6 to recall how to implement this mechanism. By using this mechanism, the methods will not be blocked during the message retrieval period and the application can continue to execute its code, while another thread is retrieving the message.

If multiple messages are to be received by the application successively, device implementation may call the `MessageListener` instance from multiple threads in parallel. To avoid unexpected results, the application must be ready to handle the situation and implement any synchronization technique in its code.

11.4.7 Relationship between WMA and PushRegistry

In the MIDP chapter, we learned about the `PushRegistry`. The `PushRegistry` allows a server type connection to listen for specific connections that are registered to specific MIDlets. When a given connection arrives, the MIDlet is invoked. Once an application has been started, it opens the incoming connection and read/write data to that connection as usual. For more detailed explanation about the `PushRegistry`, refer to Chapter 4 (The MIDlet: A Different Kind of Application).

As explained earlier, the `PushRegistry` exists at the heart of security-critical terrain. Thus, an array of permissions is required to enable this functionality. The MIDlet suite that wants to register itself to the push registry must request the permission to use the push registry as well as the permission to open the connection. In addition, if a MIDlet needs to read and/or write data to and from the connection, the suite must also request the permissions for the send and receive methods.

Specifying WMA Push Registration Entry

Push registration entries can be found either in JAD or can be created dynamically at execution time through the use of `PushRegistry` class. A push registration entry in JAD contains the URL connection string which identifies the messaging protocol and the port number of the incoming message connection, the MIDlet name and the filter field. The filter field indicates which senders are allowed to send messages that trigger the registered MIDlet name. Asterisk (*) and question mark (?) can be used to specify the senders in the filter field as wild cards. As usual, an asterisk (*) means that zero or more digits can be matched to senders' addresses and a question mark (?) means that one or more digits must be matched to senders' addresses.

SMS messaging protocol will match the MSISDN (Mobile Station International ISDN Number or, generally speaking, phone number) portion of the connection string against the specified filter field. The port number that might follow the MSISDN (phone number) will not be considered in matching with the filter field of the push registration entry. The plus sign that usually sit in front of the MSISDN (phone number) will also be considered in matching with the filter field.

For example,

```
MIDlet-Push-1: sms://:1234, MySmsMIDlet, +123456789
MIDlet-Push-2: sms://:1234, MyAnotherSmsMIDlet, 123456789
```

The sender needs to have a plus sign in its address to be able to launch the MIDlet named `MySmsMIDlet`. If not, the MIDlet named `MyAnotherSmsMIDlet` will be launched.

However, CBS messaging protocol does not care about the filter field. The filter field is usually set to an asterisk (*) to indicate that any sender will be allowed to send messages to launch the specified MIDlet.

For example,

```
MIDlet-Push-1: cbs://:9876, MyCbsMIDlet, +123456789
MIDlet-Push-2: cbs://:8765, MyAnotherCbsMIDlet, *
```

The two push registration entries above work in a very similar way. Without the need to consider the filter field, `MyCbsMIDlet` will be launched if the port number of the incoming message connection is 9876, while `MyAnotherCbsMIDlet` will be launched if the port number of the incoming message connection is 8765.

Understanding WMA Push Registry Connections Behaviors

The SMS messaging protocol has a mechanism that can explicitly buffer the messages, until an application retrieves them and deletes them when it is done with the messages. After a message has been received by the device but not passed the specified filtering criteria of the push registration entry, AMS has the right to delete them. AMS has been discussed in Chapter 4 (The MIDlet: A Different Kind of Application).

When an application has been initiated by the push notification, the application should read and process all the buffered messages reserved for it from the temporary storage space. In case the application is unable to read and process the messages when it is started or the user chooses not to start the application, the device implementation has the right to delete the messages from the buffer when necessary. For example, the device implementation may delete the messages when the buffer becomes full or some other buffer-related operations need to be done.

Summary

Prior to JTWI, the Wireless Messaging Protocol was a mere optional package in the world of Java ME. Now, it has stepped front and center. This mandatory component specification of JTWI will no doubt be one of the most used in the real world of mobile phone application development. And you certainly must know it for the exam.

By now, you should have a good understanding of how the specifications work. This chapter revisits, if indirectly, the concepts of flexibility as introduced in the configuration layer, GCF. In this chapter, we have seen how WMA extends GCF with its own set of flexible interfaces geared towards message-based protocols. The WMA package includes the following interfaces: `Message`, `TextMessage`, `BinaryMessage`, `MessageConnection` and `MessageListener`. Make sure you understand how these packages, as extensions of GCF, formally structure the implementation and use of specific message-based protocols. But make sure you understand that they leave the implementation to someone else!

In terms of specific protocol implementations, JTWI specifies two—SMS and CBS. We covered the details of these implementations as they pertain to the application developer. For the exam, you need to know both the practical, code-level use of these protocols via the WMA's framework interfaces, and the implementation details that bubble up with implications at the code level. Such items include the methods for obtaining the SMSC address from within the Java environment.

Make sure you know the details of using the WMA interfaces. Of particular importance are the differences between client and server connection types, both in their usage and in the differing mechanisms for creating them. You need to understand the URL-based addressing scheme, the WMA exceptions and WMA-related security issues. If you consider the example of setting up an SMS-based PushRegistry invoked application, with all of its security concerns, you will probably find yourself exercising a great deal of exam knowledge. It's a good subject for some sample code writing, which is always a good idea.

This is the last chapter of the book and we wish you all the best for your exam. But don't forget. You can still refer to this book even after passing the exam.

References

1. WMA 1.1(JSR-120) Specification
   http://jcp.org/aboutJava/communityprocess/final/jsr120/index2.html
2. Extend J2ME to Wireless Messaging
   http://www-128.ibm.com/developerworks/wireless/library/wi-extendj2me/

3. The Wireless Messaging API
http://developers.sun.com/techtopics/mobility/midp/articles/wma/
4. Mobile P2P messaging, Part 1
http://www-128.ibm.com/developerworks/wireless/library/wi-p2pmsg/
5. Nokia Series 40 Developer Platform 2.0 Specification
http://sw.nokia.com/id/1d0f16ac-ff5f-4b4d-bf63-5fcb21b2e1a6/Series_40_DP_2_0_Specification_v1_0_en.pdf

Review Questions

1. Which one of the following statements correctly defines the `MessageListener` interface?
   a. The interface that provides a mechanism for the application to be notified of incoming messages.
   b. The interface that provides a mechanism for the application to be notified of outgoing messages.
   c. The interface that provides a mechanism for the application to be notified of deleting messages.
   d. The interface that provides a mechanism for the application to be notified of updating existing messages.
2. Which of the following are the three methods located in the `Message` interface?
   a. `getHeader()`
   b. `getTimestamp()`
   c. `setTimestamp(Date)`
   d. `getAddress()`
   e. `setAddress(String)`
3. Which one of the following statement is true about the messaging functionality of WMA?
   a. Messaging functionality of WMA works exactly the same as the UDP datagram functionality of GCF.
   b. Messaging functionality of WMA is of store-and-forward nature.
   c. Application should send as many messages as possible to the recipient to make sure messages arrived to the destination device.
   d. Since character encoding is managed by the device implementation, we can apply any character encoding to the text message that is to be sent to the recipient and characters will properly be decoded at the recipient.
4. True or False: Unlike `setPayloadData(byte[])` of the `BinaryMessage` interface, `setPayloadText(String)` of the `TextMessage` interface does verify the validity of the string value that is passed into the method.
   a. True
   b. False

5. Which three of the following are the possible encoding techniques that will be used in GSM SMS messages?
   a. 7-bit alphabet encoding
   b. 16-bit UCS-2 alphabet encoding
   c. 8-bit binary data encoding
   d. 16-bit UTF-24 alphabet encoding
   e. 8-bit alphabet encoding
6. Which one of the following connection string can be used to create a CBS `MessageConnection`?
   a. `cbs://:8840`
   b. `cbs://192.168.0.5:8840`
   c. `cbs://+123456789:8840`
   d. `cbs://123456789:8840`
7. What will happen when the following code segment is executed and the port number 9876 is reserved for restrictive use only? Assume that the recipient is connected to the network and SMS messaging protocol is supported on the device.

```
String param = "sms://+987654321:9876";
MessageConnection msgConnection =
                                    (MessageConnection)Connector.open(param);
Message message =
                  msgConnection.newMessage(MessageConnection.TextMessage);
message.setPayloadText("Hello World!");
msgConnection.send(message);
```

   a. A `ConnectionNotFoundException` will be thrown from the send(message) method.
   b. A `SecurityException` will be thrown from the `send(message)` method.
   c. A `IOException` will be thrown from the `send(message)` method.
   d. The code will not be compiled.
8. Identify a valid permission name that will be needed for sending or receiving messages.
   a. `javax.wireless.messaging.sms.send`
   b. `javax.microedition.io.sms.receive`
   c. `javax.microedition.io.cbs.receive`
   d. `javax.wireless.messaging.cbs.send`
9. True or False: The mechanism that make use of `notifyIncomingMessage(Message)` method of the `MessageListener` to implement non-blocking method call is called asynchronous message receiving mechanism.
   a. True
   b. False

10. Which two of the following push registration entries will allow any phone numbers that starts with +60 to send SMS messages to launch the specified MIDlet? Assume that the incoming phone number contains a plus sign followed by nine digits.
    a. `MIDlet-Push-1: sms://:1234, MySmsMIDlet, +60???????`
    b. `MIDlet-Push-1: cbs://:1234, MySmsMIDlet, +601234567`
    c. `MIDlet-Push-1: cbs://:1234, MySmsMIDlet, *`
    d. `MIDlet-Push-1: sms://:1234, MySmsMIDlet, +601234???`
    e. `MIDlet-Push-1: sms://:1234, MySmsMIDlet, *`

Review Answers

1. a. The `MessageListener` interface is the interface that provides a mechanism for the application to be notified of incoming messages.
2. b. d. and e. `setTimestamp(Date)` and `getHeader()` methods are not of the `Message` interface.
3. b. Messaging functionality of WMA works very similar to the UDP datagram functionality of GCF, but there are some differences between them. Application should not send unnecessary messages since it might cost a certain amount of fee to the end user. Even though we can apply any character encoding to the text message that is to be sent to the recipient and device implementation will convert them as appropriate, we should only use the character encoding sets that is supported by the messaging protocol. Otherwise, the message will contain incorrect characters.
4. b. Both `setPayloadData(byte[])` of the `BinaryMessage` interface and `setPayloadText(String)` of the `TextMessage` interface do not check the validity of the value that is passed in.
5. a. b. and c. There is no such 16-bit UTF-24 alphabet and 8-bit alphabet encodings support in wireless messaging API.
6. a. cbs://<port> format is used to create a CBS `MessageConnection` by passing it into the `Connector.open` method. Since CBS connection cannot be used to send messages, it makes sense that we cannot specify a recipient address in the connection string.
7. b. If the specified port number is an restrictive one that is reserved for a privileged service, a `SecurityException` will be thrown from the send(message) method to indicate that security violation has been occurred.
8. a. The prefix for the permission names must be `javax.wireless.messaging`, not `javax.microedition.io`. There is no permission named `"javax.wireless. messaging.cbs.send"` and CBS connections cannot be used to send messages.
9. a. The ordinary message receiving mechanism that uses `receive` method to receive the message in its own thread is called synchronous message receiving mechanism and it will block any other method call until it receives the whole message.
10. d. and e. A question mark (?) represents one digit and an asterisk (*) represents zero or more digits.

Exam Notes

☞ Describe the WMA's basic support for sending and receiving messages, and the GCF.

GCF

- The `MessageConnection` interface, which can be used for sending and receiving `Messages`, derives from the `java.microedition.io.Connection` interface.
- An implementation of the `MessageConnection` interface can be obtained from the `Connector` factory, which returns a `Connection` interface and then typecast to `MessageConnection` interface.
- The messaging functionality is similar to the datagram functionality of the GCF in that:
  - It allows opening a connection using a `String` address
  - The connection can be opened either in client mode or in server mode.
- The `MessageConnection` should be closed using the `close()` method.
- If a `MessageConnection.newMessage(...)` method is called after closing the connection, the return value will be an implementation of the interface `Message` and not a sub-interface, even if asked for.
- The `MessageConnection` does not support the stream-related methods. If invoked, it will throw an `IllegalArgumentException`.

Sending Message

- A `MessageConnection` implementation is obtained by calling `Connector.open(String name)` method and typecasting the return value to a `MessageConnection`.
- For sending a message, the name should be of the form: `"scheme://target"`. Typically this would be something like `"sms://+1234567890"`.
  - The schema name (here, `"sms"`) can be anything, as defined by the mobile device implementation.
  - In this case, the `Connection` is said to be in the client mode.
  - The number represents the phone number where the message is to be sent.
  - The `Connector.open(String name, int mode)` can be used to represent the mode of connection. The mode can be `READ`, `WRITE`, or `READ_WRITE`.
  - If an attempt is made to open a connection in `READ` mode, where it is not possible to read anything (say, a printer), then it will throw an `IllegalArgumentException`.
  - The `Connector.open(String name, int mode, int timeouts)` can be used if the underlying implementation supports timeouts. If a timeout occurs, an `InterruptedIOException` will be thrown back.

- The `Message` to be sent should be created with the same instance of the `MessageConnection` interface using the `MessageConnection. newMessage (String type, String address)` method.
    - The `type` can be `MessageConnection.TEXT` (or the `String` "text") or `MessageConnection.BINARY` (or the `String` "binary").
    - The `type` is case-sensitive.
    - There can be other types supported by the mobile device. But they should have the format similar to the package name convention and should contain at least one period (.).
    - The `address` parameter is optional. If not mentioned, the address used to create the `MessageConnection` is used.
- An `IllegalArgumentException` can be thrown if:
    - The `Message` to be sent is not in the right format.
    - Does not contain valid information.
    - The `type` is not correct.
    - The payload exceeds the maximum allowed length.
    - The `Message` is not of the right type (this can happen if a different `MessageConnection` is used, rather than the one used to create the `Message`).
- An `InterruptedIOException` is thrown if the connection is closed before the `Message` is successfully sent.
- A `NullPointerException` is thrown if the `Message` is `null`.
- `Messages` can be sent in client mode as well as server mode. In the server mode, the destination address will be the same as the originating address when the connection is initially created.

Receiving Message

- An application can listen for messages only in the server mode.
- For receiving a message, the connection string should be of the form "`scheme://:port`". Typically, this would be something like "`sms://:5432`".
- If an attempt is made to start listening on a port already reserved or in use, the open method will throw an `IOException`.
- A `Message` can be received by invoking the `MessageConnection.receive` method. This is a blocking call and will wait till a `Message` comes to the application.
- An instance of `MessageListener` can be used to register to listen for incoming `Messages`. When a `Message` comes to the port where the application is listening, the `notifyIncomingMessage` method will be invoked.
- A `MessageListener` instance can be registered to the `MessageConnection` using the `setMessageListener(MessageListener listener)` method.
- The application has the responsibility to receive the message using the `MessageConnection.receive` method once notified.

- The `notifyIncomingMessage` should be a quickly returning method and the `Message` should not be received in the same thread. A separate thread should be used to invoke the `receive` method.
- The implementation may call the listener from multiple threads for multiple messages that arrive closely. The application should synchronize to handle this.
- An `IOException` can occur if the receive method is called when the connection was opened in the client mode.
- The application is responsible for persisting a received message (say, using RMS) if needed.

☞ Explain the WMA's support for SMS and Cell Broadcast capabilities.

WMA Support for SMS

- SMS is supported both in GSM and CDMA network.
- `TextMessages` should be encoded in GSM-7 bit or UCS-2 16 bit encodings. If a character is present in the message that is not in GSM-7 bit encoding, the message should be automatically treaded as UCS-2 16 bit encoding.
- If a port number is not mentioned in the address of a `Message` being sent, it will be sent to the default application of the device. If the port number is present, it will be sent to the application that is listening on that port of the device.
- Long messages can be split and concatenated. A minimum of 3 splits should be supported by the device.
- It is advised to limit the splits to 3. The number of splits of a given `Message` can be found out by calling the `numberOfSegments(Message)` method of the `MessageConnection`.
- SMS messages can be sent or received. The standard WMA rules are applied with regard to client and server modes.
- Some ports are restricted and if an attempt is made to use them, a `SecurityException` will be thrown.
- The SMSC address should be available in the system property `wireless. messaging. sms.smsc.` It is a phone number in the msisdn format.

WMA Support for CBS

- In a CBS, the base station of the service provider can broadcast a message, which can be viewed by all the subscribers to that base station.
- The address of a CBS message takes the form: `"cbs://port"`, where port is the port number where the message will be received.
- The `Message` can be `BinaryMessage` or `TextMessage`, but can only be received by an application and cannot be sent. If the send method is called with a CBS address, `IOException` will be thrown.

☞ Identify correct and incorrect statements or examples about WMA including the WMA addressing scheme, client vs. server connections, WMA-related exceptions, WMA-related security issues, message size limitation, message creation, sending, synchronous vs. asynchronous message receipt, and the relationship between WMA and Push Registry.

WMA Addressing Scheme

Message Type	*Address Format*
GSM/CDMA SMS in client mode	`sms://msisdn[:port]`
GSM/CDMA SMS in server mode	`sms://:port`
GSM CBS (only server mode)	`cbs://:port`

`msisdn` is a phone number of the format: `+1234567890`

`port` is a simple port number

- If the `port` is not given in the SMS client mode, the message will be sent to the device's default message handling mechanism.
- If the `port` is given, the message will be sent to the Java application meant to receive it.

Client vs. Server Connections

- Client connections can be used to send messages only. If the receive method is called, it will throw an `IOException`.
- Server connections can be used to send and receive messages. If a server connection is used to send a message, the recipient can reuse the address present in the message received from that connection.

WMA-related Exceptions

Exception	*Reason for throwing the exception*
`IllegalArgumentException`	The message to be sent is too long. The connection type is not supported for the operation. The message to be sent is invalid or incorrect.
`InterruptedIOException`	The connection was closed while sending or receiving data. Timeout is caused if timeout is specified during open call.
`IOException`	receive method is called in client mode.
`NullPointerException`	The message to be sent is `null`.
`SecurityException`	send or receive message is not permitted. There is an attempt to use a restricted or reserved port as a receiving port.

WMA-related Security Issues

- As sending and receiving SMS messages may incur a charge, user should be asked for permission before attempting to send or receive a message.
- Permission may depend on the type of message and the address used.
- The application may be restricted from sending/receiving certain types of messages and/or to certain addresses.
- Permission to send one message does not mean that successive messages will be granted permission.
- `SecurityException` may be thrown if an operation is attempted without proper permission.
- Granting permissions on devices with MIDP 1.0 is left to the user.
- Permissions on granted on devices implementing MIDP 2.0 are based on protocols.

Creating Messages

- The `Message` to be sent should be created with the same instance of the `MessageConnection` interface using the `MessageConnection.newMessage (String type, String address)` method.
  - The `type` can be `MessageConnection.TEXT_MESSAGE` (or the `String "text"`) or `MessageConnection.BINARY_MESSAGE` (or the `String "binary"`).
  - The `type` is case-sensitive.
  - There can be other `types` supported by the mobile device. But they should have the format similar to package name convention and should contain at least one period (.).
  - The `address` parameter is optional. If not mentioned, the address used to create the `MessageConnection` is used.
- An `IllegalArgumentException` can be thrown if:
  - The `Message` to be sent is not in the right format.
  - Does not contain valid information.
  - The `type` is not correct.
  - The payload exceeds the maximum allowed length.
  - The `Message` is not of the right type (this can happen if a different `Message Connection` is used, rather than the one used to create the `Message`).

Sending Messages

- See `MessageConnection` Interface (11.1.4).

Synchronous vs. Asynchronous Message Receipt

- Messages can be received synchronously using the `MessageConnection.receive` method. This is a blocking call and will not return till a message is received, even though it may take years!

- Messages can be received asynchronously by creating a class implementing the `MessageListener` interface and registering an instance of the class to the connection using the `MessageConnection.setMessageListener(MessageListener)` method.
  - The `notifyIncomingMessage(MessageConnection)` method of the `MessageListener` instance is invoked when a message is received.
  - The `notifyIncomingMessage(MessageConnection)` implementation should return very quickly and should not get the message by calling `MessageConnection.receive` in the same thread. This should be done in a separate thread.
  - If many messages come in a short period of time, the VM may notify the application of the messages in multiple simultaneous threads. The application should be able to handle the situation by itself and synchronize the messages accordingly.

Relationship between WMA and PushRegistry

- WMA applications can make use of `PushRegistry` to launch the application if a message is received when the application is not running or when another MIDlet is running.
- Permission should be obtained by the application to use the `PushRegistry` apart from the standard permissions to open connections, and to read/write messages.
- Permission entry for push registrations related to WMA is of the form:
  - `MIDlet-Push-n: (sms|cbs)://:port, classname, address`
  - The last entry indicates the source address of the message for which permission is granted. For all addresses, the wildcard (*) maybe used.
  - For `cbs` connections, the address is always (*).
- All successfully received messages will be buffered till they are read and deleted by the application.
- If the application does not read and delete messages upon startup, the device may delete the messages if it becomes necessary (say, buffer is full).

A

Appendix

Developing Mobile Applications Using Sun Java Wireless Toolkit

In order to test the sample code provided with this book, you will have to install Sun Java Wireless Toolkit on your machine. At the time we are writing this book, the latest version of the Sun Java Wireless Toolkit is 2.2. Sun Java Wireless Toolkit is formerly known as J2ME Wireless Toolkit and the name has been changed with an introduction of version 2.3. However this book uses version 2.2, since version 2.3 is still in beta. This appendix will help you install Sun Java Wireless Toolkit, and create and run J2ME projects.

A.1 WHAT ARE THE REQUIREMENTS OF TOOLKIT?

Before we move forward to the installation of the toolkit, let's have a look at the requirements for the toolkit so that it can run on your machine without any problem.

A.1.1 Hardware Requirements

Minimum hardware requirements are:

- 50 MB hard disk space
- 128 MB RAM
- 800 MHz Pentium III CPU or equivalent

A.1.2 Software Requirements

Minimum software requirements are:

- Microsoft Windows XP or Linux-x86
- Java™ 2 SDK, Standard Edition(J2SE SDK), version 1.4.2 for development, or Java™ 2, Standard Edition Runtime Environment (JRE), version 1.4.2 for just running applications

A.2 WHERE TO GET TOOLKIT?

You can find the Sun Java Wireless Toolkit version 2.2 on the website http://www.kokonaing.com. It is located under the `Downloads` section of the website and the file name is `j2me_wireless_toolkit-2_2-windows.exe`. You can even download it from http://java.sun.com/products/sjwtoolkit/, in case you might want to see if there is a newer version of the toolkit available.

A.3 HOW TO INSTALL TOOLKIT?

You don't need much effort to install the toolkit on your machine, once you have the installation file ready with you. So let's go ahead and install the toolkit on Windows XP platform. You can install it on Linux platform as well, if you wish.

Double-clicking on the `j2me_wireless_toolkit-2_2-windows.exe` will initiate the installation process. After clicking a few steps, you will be asked to specify the location of the J2SDK or JRE version 1.4.2. The installation will automatically find one for you, if you have one already installed on your machine, as it should be before you install the toolkit.

Then you will be asked to specify the location to install the toolkit. By default on Windows XP, it will be `C:\WTK22`. It is recommended to use the default location that is specified by the toolkit, if you don't have any reason to move it to somewhere else.

A.4 MENUS OF TOOLKIT

You will see menus shown in Fig. A.1, after you are done with the installation of the toolkit.

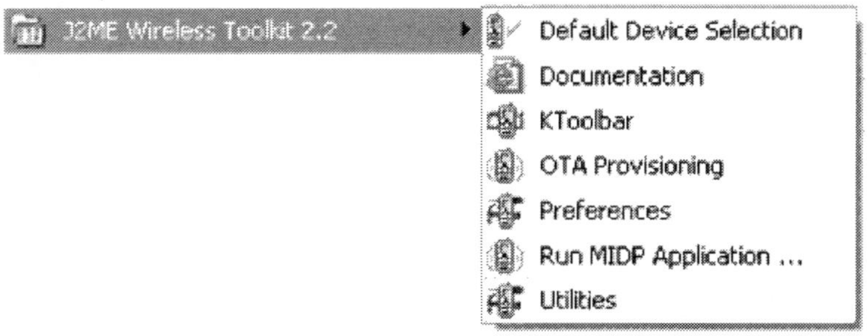

Figure A.1 Menus of the toolkit

Default Device Selection Menu

This menu lets you to choose the default device that will be used in many of the toolkit simulation features.

Documentation Menu

This menu launches the documentation related to the Sun Java Wireless Toolkit; including FAQs, Toolkit User's Guide and Toolkit Basic Customization Guide.

KToolbar Menu

This menu is the menu that you will definitely click the most. It will launch the main application, in which you can create projects, open existing projects, build and run projects and so forth.

OTA Provisioning Menu

This menu lets you emulate the OTA installation steps as in the real device. This is just to let you test with the toolkit's emulator, before installing your applications on your real device. The detailed OTA installation process will be covered in the Appendix C.

Preferences Menu

This menu lets you adjust your preferences in using the toolkit; including network configuration, performance setting, security domain assigning and so forth.

Run MIDP Application Menu

This menu lets you run MIDP application that you have created before, without launching the main KToolbar application. Upon clicking on this menu, you will be asked to specify the JAD file of your application. Once you have selected a JAD file, the MIDP application will be launched using the default device that you have chosen before using the Default Device Selection menu.

Utilities Menu

This menu contains many utilities that you can use to clear your database, monitor memory and network, signing MIDlets, managing certificates and so forth.

A.5 DIRECTORY STRUCTURE OF TOOLKIT

Figure A.2 shows the directory structure of your Sun Java Wireless Toolkit application. Among the directories, the most important directories are apps and lib.

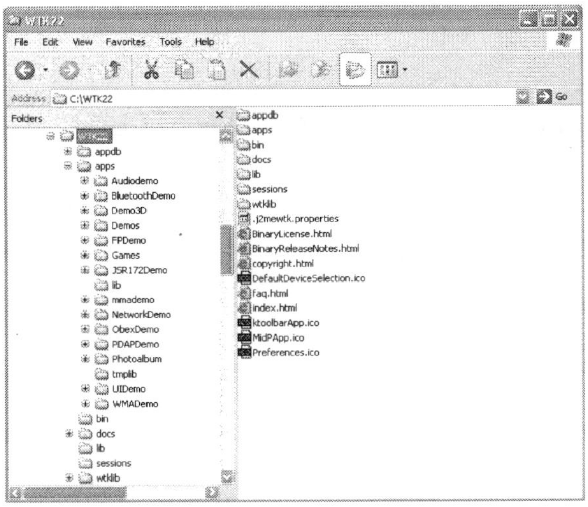

Figure A.2 Directory structure of Sun Java Wireless Toolkit

Apps Directory

All of your projects are kept in this directory and each subdirectory located under this directory corresponds to a project that you created in KToolbar application. The toolkit comes with sample projects which you can try to play around with them, in addition to the source code that comes with this book.

Lib Directory

This directory contains the class libraries that you will need to build projects such as MIDP library, CLDC library, WMA library and so forth.

A.6 HOW TO RUN EXISTING PROJECTS?

Running existing projects is very easy in Sun Java Wireless Toolkit. After opening the KToolbar application, you will see the list of existing projects in a popup window opened as in Fig. A.3, upon clicking on the Open Project menu.

Figure A.3 Opening a J2ME project in Sun Java Wireless Toolkit

When you select and open one of the projects from the list, the toolkit loads the selected project into its environment as shown in Fig. A.4. Then you can just click on the Run menu to run the loaded project.

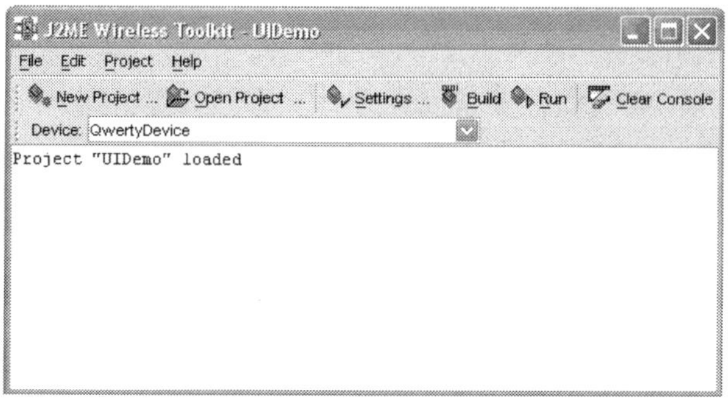

Figure A.4 Loading a J2ME project in Sun Java Wireless Toolkit

Running a project is that easy, as you have just seen. One thing to note is that running a project just runs the project without compiling the source files in the project again. So it just pulls the classes that have been compiled before and uses them to run the project.

So now it is time to go forward to learn how to create a new project in Sun Java Wireless Toolkit.

A.7 HOW TO CREATE NEW PROJECT?

Creating a new project is not that difficult, though people might think it is. Upon clicking on the New Project menu, you will be asked to specify the project name and the MIDlet class name that is going to be a MIDlet which will be launched when you run the project. Figure A.5 shows how the popup looks like. We are going to create a traditional project that we might have created in Programming 101 course. That is `HelloJ2MEProject`.

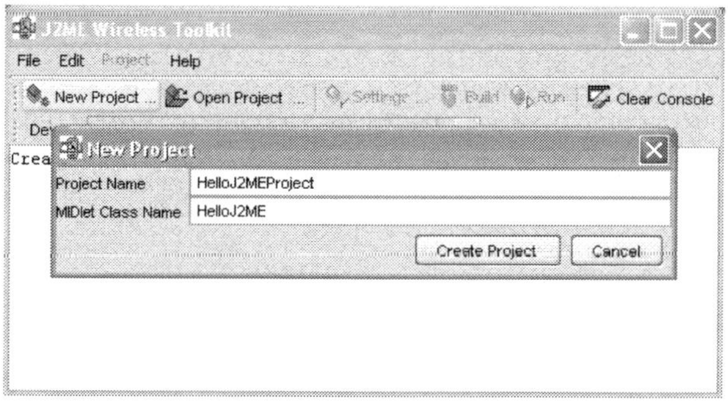

Figure A.5 Creating a J2ME project in Sun Java Wireless Toolkit

Then you will be prompted with a popup window, asking you to specify settings for the project that you are creating such as supported CLDC version, optional APIs used and so forth. Don't worry about them much. Just select the CLDC 1.1 in Configurations section and use default settings for others.

Now you have successfully created a J2ME project using Sun Java Wireless Toolkit. But you might wonder where the created MIDlet class file is located in the project directory. Figure A.6 shows the directory structure of your recently created `HelloJ2MEProject` project under the apps directory of the toolkit.

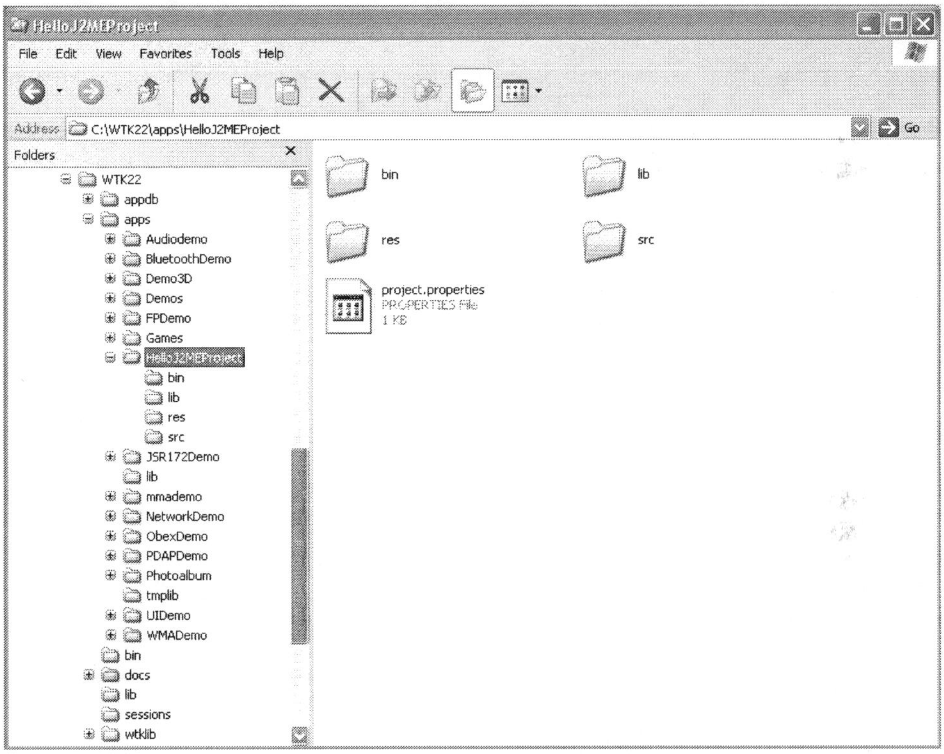

Figure A.6 Directory structure of the "HelloJ2MEProject" project

You just need to put the `HelloJ2ME` MIDlet source code file into the `src` directory. After building the project using the KToolbar successfully, you will be able to run the project by clicking on the Run menu of the KToolbar.

That's it! Now you can run the sample code provided with this book, in the same way as the procedures mentioned above.

B

Appendix

A Sample Java Application Descriptor (JAD) File

The following listing contains all the eligible attribute-value pairs for a JAD file. We have annotated each category that attributes belong to in the listing so that you can easily classify them according to the categories in one place. However, we left out any application-specific attributes that might be declared in a real application's JAD file. This listing is just to help you recall the JAD-related topics that we have discussed in the book in a blink of an eye.

```
MIDlet-Name: MyMIDletSuiteName
MIDlet-Version: 2.5
MIDlet-Vendor: MyVendorName
MIDlet-Jar-URL: http://www.mcgraw-hill.com/jars/MyApplication.jar
MIDlet-Jar-Size: 5678
```
①

```
MIDlet-1: MyMIDletOne, /logo/MyMIDletOneIcon.png,
         com.mcgraw-hill.scmad.appendB.MyMIDletOne
MIDlet-2: MyMIDletTwo, /logo/MyMIDletTwoIcon.png,
          com.mcgraw-hill.scmad.appendB.MyMIDletTwo
MIDlet-3: MyMIDletThree, /logo/MyMIDletThreeIcon.png,
         com.mcgraw-hill.scmad.appendB.MyMIDletThree
MicroEdition-Profile: MIDP-2.0
MicroEdition-Configuration: CLDC-1.1
```
②

```
MIDlet-Description: This MIDlet suite contains MyMIDletOne,
MyMIDletTwo, and MyMIDletThree. They are dummy MIDlets just to
clariy the usage of JAD attributes.
```
③

```
MIDlet-Icon: /logo/MyMIDletSuiteIcon.png
MIDlet-Info-URL: http://www.mcgraw-hill.com/mymidletsuite/info.html      ③

MIDlet-Data-Size: 1024                                                   ④

MIDlet-Permissions: javax.microedition.io.PushRegistry,
javax.microedition.io.Connector.datagramreceiver,
javax.microedition.io.Connector.serversocket,
javax.microedition.io.Connector.socket                                   ⑤
MIDlet-Permissions-Opt: javax.microedition.io.Connector.http,
javax.microedition.io.Connector.ssl,
javax.microedition.io.Connector.comm

MIDlet-Push-1: socket://:79,
com.mcgraw-hill.scmad.appendB.MyMIDletOne, 192.168.40.*                  ⑥
MIDlet-Push-2: datagram://:50000,
com.mcgraw-hill.scmad.appendB.MyMIDletThree, 192.18.122.??

MIDlet-Install-Notify:
http://www.mcgraw-hill.com/mymidletsuite/install.html?application=
MyMIDletSuiteName&version=2.5
MIDlet-Delete-Notify: http://www.mcgraw-hill.com/mymidletsuite/
delete.html?application=MyMIDletSuiteName&version=2.5                    ⑦
MIDlet-Delete-Confirm: Do you really want to delete MyMIDletSuiteName
from your device?

Any application-specific attributes that do not begin with MIDlet- or
MicroEdition-                                                            ⑧
```

① MIDlet suite attributes (Mandatory)
② Individual MIDlet attributes (Mandatory in JAD or manifest)
③ Additional MIDlet suite information (Optional)
④ Minimum persistent data size required by the MIDlet suite (Optional)
⑤ Security attributes (Optional)
⑥ Push registration entries (Optional)
⑦ Notification attributes (Optional)
⑧ Custom attributes (Optional)

C

Appendix

Over-the-Air (OTA) Provisioning

Chapter 4, "MIDlet: A Different Kind of Application," introduced you to the lifecycle of a MIDlet suite in Section 4.4. You should know how to deploy, discover, install, update and remove a MIDlet suite–at least theoretically–by now. This appendix guides you through the lifecycle of a MIDlet suite by using the OTA provisioning feature available in Sun Java Wireless Toolkit's emulator.

C.1 WHAT IS OTA PROVISIONING?

Before we move forward to OTA provisioning, we need to know what exactly it is. Let's take a few seconds to discuss various methods that are widely used to install Java ME applications, beginning with a dedicated wired connection and wrapping up with OTA provisioning, after which we'll go into greater detail on this subject.

C.1.1 Dedicated Wired Connection

When a dedicated wired connection is used in the installation process, you need a USB cable or some kind of cable that can provide a reliable connection between a laptop or desktop computer and the mobile device. This type of connection should be used mostly with PDA devices, which need to synchronize the user's data with a computer periodically. A cabled connection should be used to install applications from a computer. Many cell phones today have such connectivity with a computer as well. This type of installation is somewhat straightforward because users can easily go through the installation process provided in the devices' user's guides.

C.1.2 Bluetooth™ Wireless Connection

Bluetooth™ is a technology that can be used only within a short range and is intended to replace a cable connection. The primary advantages of the Bluetooth™ technology are its capability to handle both data and voice transmissions at the same time, low power consumption, and low cost. But this technology will not work in a long-range area, meaning that the devices must be in a short distance from each other to be able to communicate. This is another channel that can be used to install MIDlet suites, but MIDP 2.0 specification does not mandate this technology.

C.1.3 IrDA™ Connection

IrDA™ is a technology that applies infrared light waves to transmit data to and from participating devices. Unlike Bluetooth™, the main disadvantage of this technology is that the IrDA™ ports of the two devices must be pointed to one another without any barriers between them. This is also another channel that can be used to install MIDlet suites, but MIDP 2.0 specification does not mandate this technology.

C.1.4 OTA Provisioning

OTA provisioning is the process in which a wireless network is used as a medium to deliver the applications. It gets its name from the fact that the installation process takes place over the air. Deploying, discovering, installing, updating and removing an application are done across the wireless network to and from the provisioning server and the mobile device. HTTP 1.1, or a session protocol that implements HTTP 1.1 protocol, is used in transferring a MIDlet suite and its associated JAD file. The "Over the Air User Initiated Provisioning Specification" section was not included in MIDP 1.0 Specification. The OTA provisioning mechanism is so generic and dominant that it is included in MIDP 2.0 as part of the specification. Therefore, MIDP 2.0-compliant devices must implement the functional requirements for the OTA provisioning mechanism mandated by the MIDP 2.0 specification.

C.2 HOW DOES OTA PROVISIONING WORK?

Basically the steps mentioned in Section 4.6.2, "Discovering an Application," correspond to the steps in OTA provisioning. Figure C.1 shows the steps of OTA provisioning.

Mobile Device

Provisioning Server

Returns the JAR of the application

Confirms the installation

Returns the JAD of the application

Selects an application
Returns the list of applications
Browses the list of applications

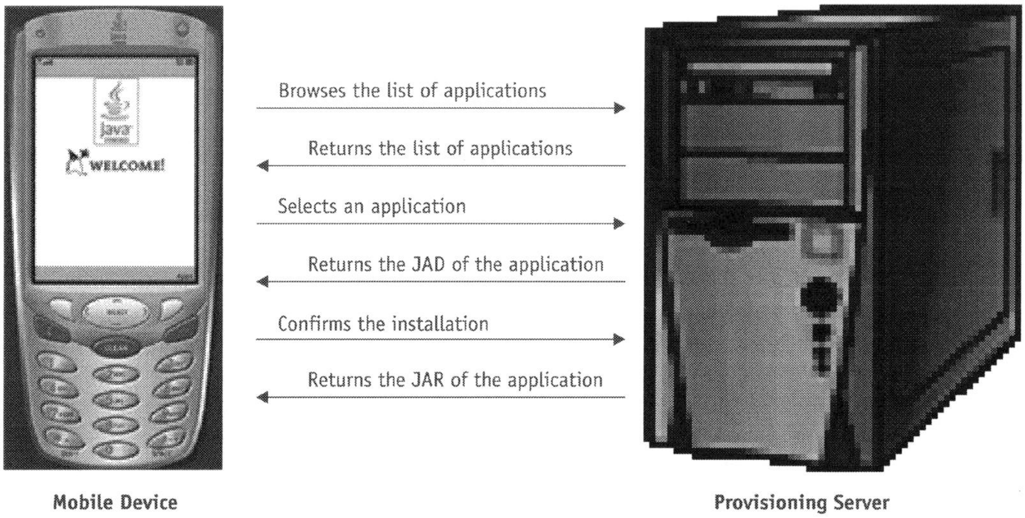

Figure C.1 MIDlet suite installation steps in OTA provisioning

C.3 GETTING STARTED

You will see the "OTA Provisioning" menu as shown in Fig. C.2, after you are finished with the installation of the toolkit as mentioned in Section A.3.

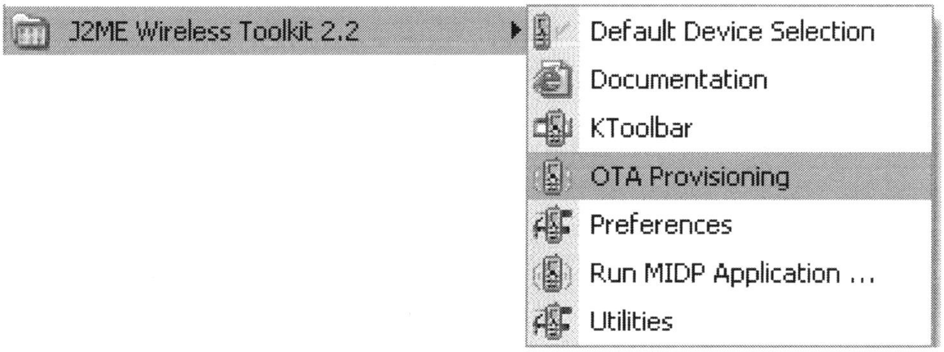

Figure C.2 "OTA Provisioning" menu of Sun Java Wireless Toolkit

Upon clicking on the "OTA Provisioning" menu of the toolkit, you'll see the startup screen in Fig. C.3 on the emulator.

Figure C.3 Startup screen on "OTA Provisioning" emulator

C.4 DEPLOYING APPLICATIONS

Before we can download the applications from the server, the content providers must place the MIDlet suites on their Web servers and make them available for download via their websites. Let's place GreetingSuite.jad, GreetingSuite.jar, GoodbyeSuite.jad, GoodbyeSuite.jar and list_apps.html that can be downloaded from the website http://www.kokonaing. com into a Web server and make them accessible at http://localhost:8080 <file_name>.<file_extension>.

list_apps.html contains the following content and is for browsing the list of applications available on the server:

```
<html>
   <head>
       <title>midlet suites list</title>
  </head>
  <body>
    <a href="http://localhost:8080/GreetingSuite.jad">Greeting Suite</a>
    <a href="http://localhost:8080/GoodbyeSuite.jad">Goodbye Suite</a>
   </body>
</html>
```

Now we have already deployed applications and files needed to be involved in the OTA provisioning steps. Note that the Web server must be running before we continue with the next sections.

C.5 DISCOVERING APPLICATIONS

Upon clicking the Apps menu on the startup screen as shown in Fig. C.3, we will see the list of applications installed on the device. In Fig. C.4, only one application was previously installed on the emulator: "Install Application," which is a system application.

Figure C.4 The list of applications previously installed on "OTA Provisioning" emulator

Clicking on the Menu and Launch commands will take us to the screen where we can type the Web address. Fig. C.5 shows how the screen flows on the toolkit's emulator.

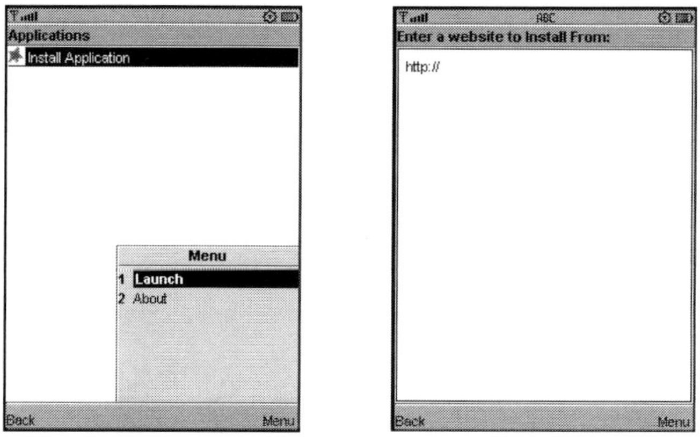

Figure C.5 Launching "Install Application" application on "OTA Provisioning" emulator

After you type the address in the textbox and click on the Menu and Go commands, the OTA Provisioning emulator will connect you to the address as specified in the URL field and try to download the HTML page that contains the list of applications available on the server. Fig. C.6 shows a series of changes on the emulator screen while connecting to the Web server.

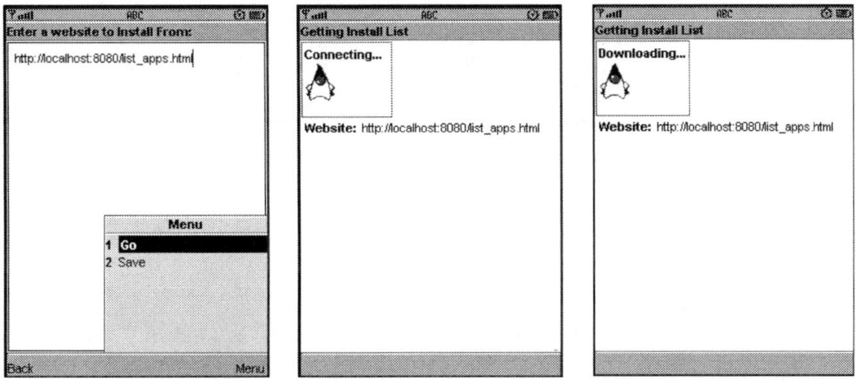

Figure C.6 Connecting to the Web server from OTA Provisioning emulator

After the emulator has retrieved the HTML page, it lists all the applications that end with .jad in the href value of <a> tag and displays the string between <a> and </a> as the name of a MIDlet suite. Figure C.7 shows that there are two MIDlet suites available on the server for download, which correspond to the HTML page that we deployed in Section C.4, "Deploying an Applications."

Figure C.7 The list of applications available on the Web server

Now that we have discovered the applications that are available on the Web server, the next step is to select and install an application from the list onto the device.

C.6 INSTALLING APPLICATIONS

After selecting an application and clicking on the Install menu, you will see a series of changes on the emulator screen as shown in Fig. C.8 while downloading an application from the Web server. According to the steps shown in Fig. C.1, the Web server will return the JAD of the selected application and display the information contained in the JAD to the user. Then the user can confirm whether or not to go on with the installation process.

Figure C.8 Downloading JAD from the Web server

Upon you click the Install menu, the installation process continues and the emulator downloads the actual JAR file from the Web server onto the device as shown in Fig. C.9.

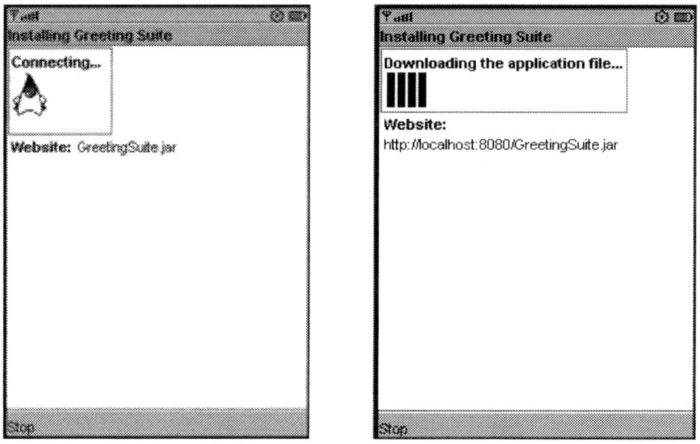

Figure C.9 Downloading the MIDlet suite (JAR) from the Web server

After the JAR has been successfully downloaded onto the device, the device will verify the downloaded JAR. If the verification process succeeds, the JAR will actually be installed on the device. Figure C.10 shows a series of changes on the emulator screen while verifying and installing the JAR file onto the device.

Figure C.10 Verifying and installing the MIDlet suite (JAR) on OTA Provisioning emulator

After the application has been installed on the device, you'll see the application appears in the list of applications on the main screen of OTA Provisioning emulator as shown in Fig. C.11.

Figure C.11 The list of applications installed on OTA Provisioning emulator

Now that you have installed an application, the next section shows you various scenarios that you might face while updating an existing application that was previously installed on the device, and how to deal with them.

C.7 UPDATING APPLICATIONS

To update an application, you need to select the application that you want to update first and click on the Menu and Update commands as shown in Fig. C.12.

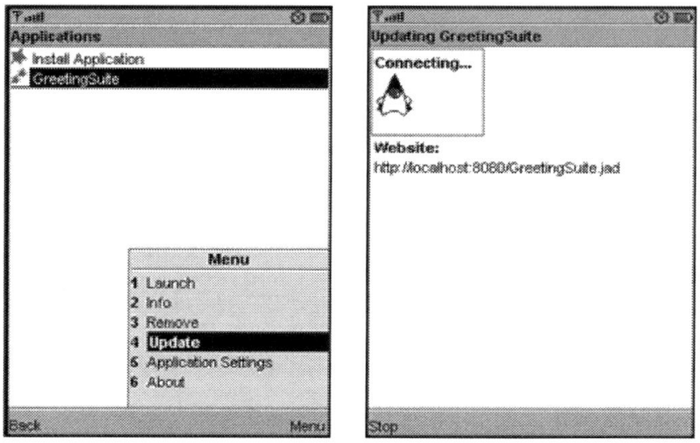

Figure C.12 Updating an application from OTA Provisioning emulator

Depending on whether the updating application is an older, a newer, or the same version as the application on the Web server, the updating screen on the emulator will vary as shown in Fig. C.13. Figure (a) shows that the application on the Web server is an older version; figure (b) shows that the application on the Web server is a newer version; and figure (c) shows that the application on the Web server is the same version as the one that is already on the device.

(a) (b) (c)

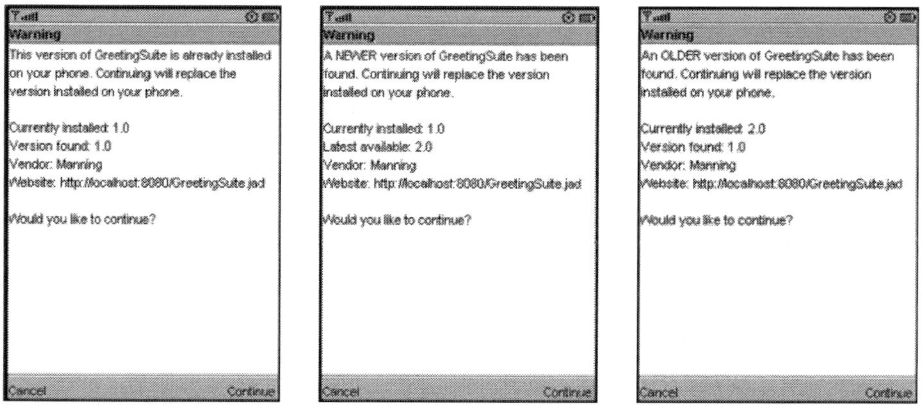

Figure C.13 Version information of an application displayed on OTA Provisioning emulator

After you click on the Continue command, the updating process continues by downloading the actual JAR file onto the device and verifies the downloaded application. If the verification process succeeds, the JAR will actually be updated on the device. Figure C.14 shows a series of changes on the emulator screen while verifying and updating the JAR file onto the device.

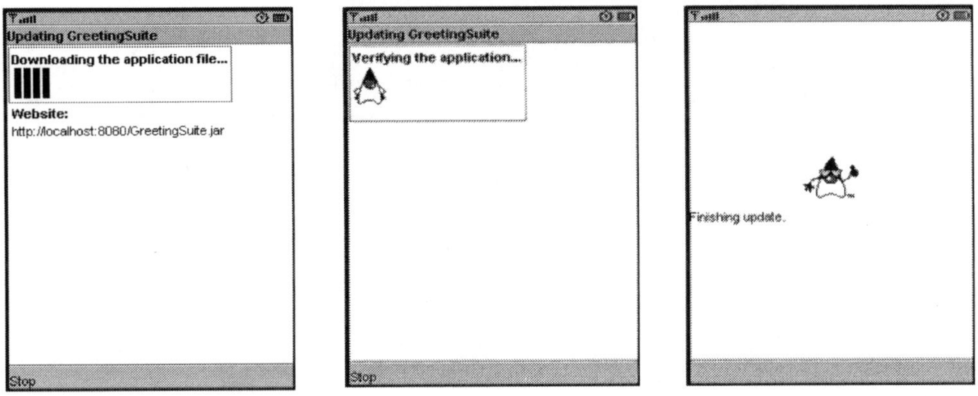

Figure C.14 Verifying and updating the MIDlet suite (JAR) on OTA Provisioning emulator

Now that we have successfully updated our application with the version that is on the Web server, we will finally see the last screen as in Fig. C.15, confirming that the update has been successful.

Figure C.15 Confirmation that the MIDlet suite (JAR) has been updated on OTA Provisioning emulator

C.8 REMOVING APPLICATIONS

To remove an application, we need to select the application that we want to remove first and click on the Menu and Remove commands as shown in Fig. C.16.

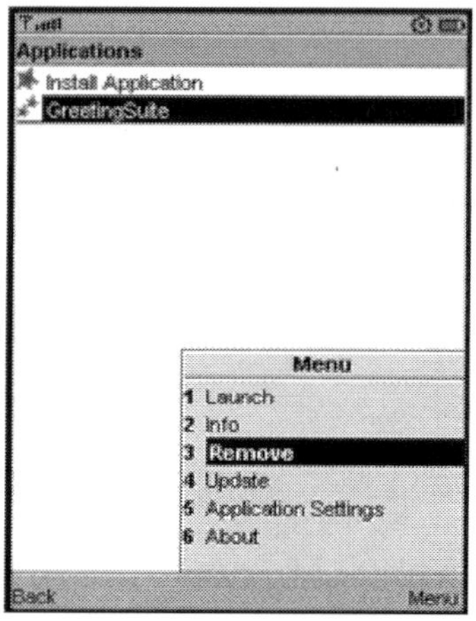

Figure C.16 Removing an application from OTA Provisioning emulator

When you click the Remove command from the menu, the emulator prompts you to confirm that you really want to remove the application as shown in Fig. C.17. It also lists all the MIDlets that are contained in the suite, since all of them will be removed from the device along with the suite.

Figure C.17 Confirming the removal of the application from OTA Provisioning emulator

Upon clicking the Remove command, the application immediately gets removed from the device, and the emulator takes you back to the screen that shows the list of applications installed on the device as in Fig. C.18.

Figure C.18 The list of applications left on OTA Provisioning emulator

We have passed through all the lifecycle stages of a MIDlet suite using the OTA provisioning feature available in Sun Java Wireless Toolkit's emulator. Now you can play around with the MIDlet suites that you have by placing them on your Web server and trying to install them on the toolkit's emulator.

Index

16-bit UCS-2 alphabet encoding 431, 437
7-bit alphabet encoding 431, 437
8-bit binary data encoding 431, 437

A
Abstract Window Toolkit (AWT) 5
`AcceptAndOpen()` method 256
Access modes 229
Addresses 417
Addressing Scheme 439
Alarm application 96
`Alert` class 153
Allowed permissions 337, 339, 342
Animated tiles 209, 210
Animation sequence 196, 197
API Fragmentation 6, 14
`Append(Layer)` method 195
Application environment 9
Application Management Software (AMS) 82
Application-level security 332, 333
Asymmetric cryptography process 345
Asynchronous message receiving mechanism 428, 444
Authenticating MIDlet suites 349

B
Base station 437
Base64-encoded certificates 348
Basic interface types 228
Basic serial input connection 228, 232
Basic serial output connection 228, 233
Basic web server connection 228
`BinaryMessage` interface 416, 420
  example 421
  methods 421
`BinaryMessage` type 437
Binding to a protection domain 342
`Blanket` 342
Blocking method 428

C
`Calendar` class 99
`Canvas` class
  `ServiceRepaints()` method 165
Canvas repaint methods 191
Canvas versus Screen 183
CBS adapter support 437
CBS connection strings 438
CBS Message Addressing Scheme 438
CBS Message Structure 438
CBS Message Types 438
`cbs://` 438, 439
CDMA IS-637 SMS protocol 432, 435
certificate 346
`CertificateException` class 239, 248, 259, 271
Certification authorities 346–348

Certification path 348–349
Chained certificates 348–349
Character encoding 270, 419
ChatMidlet 105
Choice interface 144
ChoiceGroup class 144, 157
Circuit-based connectin 239
Circuit-oriented connection 228
Clarifications 19
  application requirement 22
  device requirements 21
  for Clocks 25
  for Multi-threaded Applications 24
Class File Verification 54
Class-level permission 338
CLDC 43
CLDC 1.0 and CLDC 1.1, differences 50
CLDC Requirements 25
  basic-Latin 26
  ISO Latin-1 26
  latin-1 Supplement 26
CLDC Exception Handling 61
CLDC Error Handling 64
CLDC Library 55
  additional Utility Classes 59
  calendar and Time Classes 59
  collection Classes 57
  data Type Classes 56
  input/Output Classes 57
  property Support 60
  system Classes 56
  weak Reference 59
CLDC security 332
Client mode SMS 434
Client-server communication 239
Client Versus Server Connections 435, 439
Close() method 232, 269
Closing connection 269
CollidesWith methods 203, 204
CollidesWith(Sprite, boolean) method 205, 207
Collision detection 203
Collision rectangle 203, 207
Color class 166
Command class 134
  command priority 135
  constants 135
CommandListener class 136
CommConnection connection string 241
CommConnection example 266
CommConnection interface 236, 241, 266
Component Specifications 16
  conditionally required 17
  mandatory 17
  minimum configuration 17
Conceptual Architecture 7
Configuration 8
Configurations, profiles, and optional packages 7
Connected Device Configuration (CDC) 8
Connected Limited Device Configuration (CLDC) 8
Connected Limited Device Configuration (see CLDC)
  exception and Error Handling 52
  hardware Requirements 46
  high Level Goals 45
  Java ME Requirements 47
  object Finalization 52
  scope 48
  software Requirements 47
Connection interface 225, 232
Connection notification mechanism 228
Connection string 225–226, 242
ConnectionNotFoundException class 231, 271
ConnectionNotFoundException class 440
ConnectionNotFoundException exception 93
Connector class 224, 228, 242
  convenience methods 230
  open methods 228–229

open(String) method 225–226
openDataInputStream(String) method 230
openDataOutputStream(String) method 230
openInputStream(String) method 230
openOutputStream(String) method 230
Connector.READ constant 229
Connector.READ_WRITE constant 229
Connector.WRITE constant 229
ContentConnection interface 227, 233
getEncoding() method 234
getLength() method 234
getType() method 234
CreateAnimatedTile(int staticTileIndex) method 209
Critical permissions 340

D

Daemon Threads 53
Sata payload 417
Data validation 419
Datagram 240
Datagram addressing 235
Datagram interface 234
methods 235
DatagramConnection interface 227, 234
methods 234
Datagram-oriented connection 228
DataInput interface 235
DataInputStream class 233
DataOutput interface 235
DataOutputStream class 233
DataSource class 365, 366
getStreams() method 370
DateField class 146
Decryption 345
Default character encoding 270
DefineReferencePixel(int, int) method 201
Device authorization policy 348
Digital signature 346, 349
Display class 131
Displayable class 130
getCurrent() method 131
callSerially() method 166
Dynamic class loading 333

E

Empty cell 210
Encryption function 345
Encryption 345
End-to-end security 332
Enterprise Edition, EE 5
EOFException class 271
Equally-sized frames 196
Event-based mechanism 428
Expense tracker application 301

F

FillCells(int, int, int, int, int) method 210
Floating point support 50
Font class 162
Forms 137
layout 138
Frame 196
height 196
index 200
sequence indices 197
sequence 197
width 196
FreeMemory() method 66

G

Game performance 210
Game scene 194, 209
GameCanvas and Ticker 184
GameCanvas versus Canvas 183, 191
GameCanvas 183

dedicated buffer 184, 190
dimensions 184
flush operation 184, 189, 190
flushGraphics() method 189
flushGraphics(int, int, int, int) method 189
getGraphics() method 190
getGraphics() method 211
getKeyStates() method 192
graphics 184, 190
hasRepeatEvents() method 187
key suppression 187
keyPressed(int) method 187
keyReleased(int) method 187
keyRepeated(int) method 187
latching technique 192
painting behaviors 191
tuning 210
GameCanvas(boolean) constructor 187
Garbage Collection 65
Gauge class 147
GCF Characteristics 225
GCF extensions 226
GCF Interface hierarchy 227
GCF Interfaces 232
Generic Connection framework 223
getAddress() method 235, 417
getBaudRate() method 266
getData() method 235
getEncoding() method 234
getFrame() method 200
getFrameSequenceLength() method 200
getHeight() method 193
getLayerAt(int) method 195
getLength() method 234
getLocalPort() method 255
getMaximumLength() method 234
getNominalLength() method 234
getOffset() method 235
getPayloadData() method 420
getPayloadText() method 419
getPort() method 248
getRefPixelX() method 201, 203
getRefPixelY() method 201, 203
getSecurityInfo() method 248
getSize() method 195
getTimestamp() method 417, 438
getType() method 234
getWidth() method 193
getX() method 193, 201, 203
getY() method 193, 201, 203
Graphic coordinates 163
Graphics object re-use 211
GSM concatenation feature 432, 443
GSM SMS message structure 431

H

Handling SMS messages 436
Hash code 346, 349
Hash function 346
High-level API vs. Low-level API 130
HTTP 1.1 238
HTTP 238
closed (Final) state 238
connected state 238
lifecycle states 238
setup state 238
HttpConnection connection string 239
HttpConnection example 245
HttpConnection interface 236, 239, 243
methods 243
HTTPS conncetion 239
https 239
HttpsConnection connection string 239
HttpsConnection example 248
HttpsConnection interface 236, 239, 248
Hypertext Transfer Protocol 237
methods 248

I

IANA ranges 435
Identifying device permissions 341
IllegalArgumentException class 229, 270
Image class 150
  createImage() method 150
Image Formats
  color depth 28
  JFIF 19, 28
  JPEG (Joint Photographers' Expert Group) 18, 28
  PNG (Portable Network Graphics) 18, 28
Image object 196
Immutable image 196, 209
In-device verification 55
Indices of tiles 209
InputConnection interface 227, 232
  openDataInputStream() method 233
  openInputStream() method 233
InputStreamReader class 270
Insert(Layer, int) method 195
InterruptedIOException class 230, 271, 440
IOException class 232–233, 239, 243, 271, 434–435, 438, 441
IP and non-IP 238
isVisible() method 193
Item class hierarchy 138

J

JAD attributes 347
JAR manifest attributes 347
Java Application Descriptor (JAD) 21, 84, 85
Java ME Architecture 6, 11
Java Technology for the Wireless Industry (see JTWI)
java.io.ByteArrayInputStream class 57
java.io.ByteArrayOutputStream class 57
java.io.DateInputStream class 57
java.io.DataOutputStream class 57
java.io.InputStreamReader class 57
java.io.OutputStreamWriter class 57
java.lang.Class class 56
java.lang.Double class 57
java.lang.Error Class 64
java.lang.Float class 57
java.lang.NoClassDefFoundError class 64
java.lang.Object class 56
java.lang.OutOfMemoryError class 64
java.lang.ref. Reference class 59
java.lang.ref.WeakReference class 59
java.lang.Runnable class 56
java.lang.Runtime class 56
java.lang.String class 56
java.lang.StringBuffer class 56
java.lang.System class 56
java.lang.Thread class 56
java.lang.Throwable class 56
java.lang.VirtualMemoryError class 64
java.util.Enumeration class 57
java.util.Hashtable class 57
java.util.Stack class 57
java.util.Vector class 57
javax.microedition.io.Connector.cbs permission 442
javax.microedition.io.Connector.comm 237
javax.microedition.io.Connector.datagram 237
javax.microedition.io.Connector.datagramreceiver 237

javax.microedition.io.Connector.http 237
javax.microedition.io.Connector.https 237
javax.microedition.io.Connector.serversocket 237
javax.microedition.io.Connector.sms permission 442
javax.microedition.io.Connector.socket 237
javax.microedition.io.Connector.ssl 237
javax.microedition.lcdui package 129
javax.microedition.media package 363
javax.microedition.pki package 239
javax.microedition.rms package 284
javax.wireless.messaging.cbs.receive permission 443
javax.wireless.messaging.sms.receive permission 443
javax.wireless.messaging.sms.send permission 443
JCP (Java Community Process) 4
JSR (Java Specification Request) 4
JTWI
  Methodology of JTWI 16

K
Key events suppression 210
Keys
  events 159
  game 158
  phone 159
Kilo Virtual Machine (KVM) 5
Kilobyte Virtual Machine 52

L
Layer 192
  class 193
  graphics 193
  index 194
  method 193
  paint(Graphics) method 192, 211
LayerManager 192
  coordinate system 194
  methods 195
  paint(Graphics, int, int) method 211
  setViewWindow(int,int,int, int) method 194
  tuning 211
  view window 194
Layers 192, 211
  position of 194
Limitations of network connection 269
Local hostname 256
Local serial ports 241
Logical Serial Communication 237, 241
Low-level security 332

M
Manager class 363
  playTone() method 364
Managing memory 65
Manifest attributes 347
Manifest file 85
Media sources
  JAR file 368
  RMS 369
Message digest 346
  example 418
  methods 417
Message interface 416
  example 418
  methods 421
Message payload 432
Message Size Limitation 443
Message_identifier_portion 438
Message-based protocols 416
MessageConnection client connection 422

MessageConnection interface 416, 422
  example 423
  methods 421
  permissions 442
MessageConnection server
  connection 422
Message-Identifier field 438
MessageListener interface 416, 428
  example 428
Microedition.configuration property 60
Microedition.encoding property 60
Microedition.jtwi.version 27
Microedition.platform property 60
Microedition.profiles property 60
Microseconds 372
MIDI 392
MIDlet Installation Codes 92
MIDlet Suite Attributes 86
  MicroEdition-Configuration 87
  MicroEdition-Profile 87
  MIDlet-<n> 87
  MIDlet-Data-Size 88
  MIDlet-Delete-Confirm 89
  MIDlet-Delete-Notify 89
  MIDlet-Description 88
  MIDlet-Icon 88
  MIDlet-Info-URL 88
  MIDlet-Install-Notify 89
  MIDlet-JAR-Size 87
  MIDlet-JAR-URL 86
  MIDlet-Name 86, 288
  MIDlet-Permissions-Opt 89
  MIDlet-Push-<n> 89
  MIDlet-Vendor 86, 288
MIDlet suite verification results 349
MIDlet 79
  destroyApp() method 81
  hello world 80
  lifecycle 80
  pauseApp() method 81
  startApp() method 81
  suite 84
MIDlet-Certificate-<n>-<m> 348
MIDlet-Data-Size 23
MIDlet-Jar-RSA-SHA1 attribute 348
MIDlet-Permissions attribute 340
MIDlet-Permissions 89, 238
MIDlet-Permissions-Opt
  attribute 340
MIDlet-Permissions-Opt 238
MIDP 1.0 security 336
MIDP 2.0 connection interfaces 242
MIDP 2.0 connection security 237
MIDP 2.0 Media API 362
MIDP 2.0 Networking interface
  hierarchy 236
MIDP 2.0 optional connections 237
MIDP 2.0 protocol implementations 236
MIDP 2.0 required connections 237
MIDP 2.0 security 335
  assumptions 344
  authorization model 344
MIDP 78
MMAPI vs. MIDP media API 401
MMAPI 362
Mobile Information Device Profile
  (MIDP) 9
Mobile Media API (MMAPI) 10
Mobile Media API (see MMAPI)
Move(int, int) method 193
mutable image 196, 209

N

Naming permissions 338
Network troubleshooting 270
Networking protocols 226
NewDatagram(byte[], int)
  method 234
NewDatagram(byte[], int,
  String) method 234
NewDatagram(int) method 234
NewDatagram(int, String)
  method 234

NewMessage(String) method 422
NewMessage(String, String) method 422
NextFrame() method 197, 199
Non-pixel-level collision 204, 207
NotifyIncomingMessage(Message Connection) method 428, 444
NullPointerException class 441
NumberOfSegments(Message) method 422, 432

O

Oneshot 342
Opaque pixels 204
Open methods 228
OpenDataInputStream() method 233
OpenDataInputStream(String) method 230
OpenDataOutputStream() method 233
OpenDataOutputStream(String) method 230
Opening connection 242
OpenInputStream() method 233
OpenInputStream(String) method 230
OpenOutputStream() method 233
OpenOutputStream(String) method 230
Optimizing game performance 210
Optimizing game size 210
Optional header 431
Optional packages 10
Optional permissions 340
Ordering of SMS messages 436
OutputConnection interface 227, 233
  openDataOutputStream() method 233
  openOutputStream() method 233
OutputStreamReader class 270

P

Packets 234
Paint(Graphics) method 192
Paint(Graphics, int, int) method 195
Painter's coordinate system 201
Payload data 417
Permission names 338
Permissions for MessageConnection interface 442
Permissions for Sending and Receiving Messages 442
Permissions on the device 341
Permissions 237
Permissions 337
Pixel-level collision 204, 207
Pixel-level detection 205
PKI concept 345–347
PlatformRequest() method 93
Player class 371
  State transitions 373
  initialization 373
  synchronization 374
Player controls 383
PlayerListener class 379
Playing audio 380
Playing in a loop 377
Playing video 381
Port allocation 434
Pre-verification 54
PrevFrame() method 199
Private key 345
Process of granting permissions 340
Profiles 9
Profile-level security 335
Protected API or function 337
Protected APIs and functions 335
Protection domain owners 339
Protection domain root certificate 337
Protection domains and MIDlet suites 339
Protection domains 337, 339

Public key 345, 349
PushRegistry class 444
  listConnections() method 107
  registerAlarm() method 109
  registerConnection() method 108
  unregisterConnection() method 108

R

Raw frames 196
  indices 197
Real Time Protocol (RTP) 367
Receive() method 422, 428
Receive(Datagram) method 234
Receiving SMS messages 436
Record
  creating records 291, 310
  deleting records 296, 311
  getting records 293, 312
  ID 292
  updating records 295
Record Store
  exceptions 285
  memory allocation 289
  name limit 285
  sharing 286
RecordComparator class 299, 300, 318
RecordEnumeration class 297, 321
RecordFilter class 301, 315
RecordListener class 296
RecordStore class 283
  closeRecordStore() method 290
  listRecordStores() method 289
  openRecordStore() method 284
Reference Implementation (RI) 4
Reference pixel 201, 203
Remove(Layer) method 195
Requesting permissions for a MIDlet suite 340
Requirements of JTWI 20
Requirements for JTWI 31
Requirements on minimum configuration: CLDC 24
Reset() method 235
Restricted APIs or functions 335
Restricted port numbers 435
Root certificate 348
Row-oriented 196, 209
RSA SHA-1 digital signature 348

S

Sandbox security model 333
Sandbox security model, MIDP version of 335
Screen class 132
Secure Hypertext Transfer Protocol 237
Secure Socket Layer 237
  (SSL) server 259
SecureConnection example 259
SecureConnection interface 236, 259
Security process summary 343
SecurityException class 270
SecurityException class 435, 441
SecurityInfo object 248
Send(Datagram) method 234
Send(Message) method 422
Serial port connection 266
Server mode SMS 434
ServerSocketConnection connection string 240
ServerSocketConnection example 256–258
ServerSocketConnection interface 236, 239, 255
Session 342
SetAddress(Datagram) method 235
SetAddress(String) method 235, 417
SetAnimatedTield(int, int) method 209
SetCell(int, int, int) method 210

SetData(byte[], int, int) method 235
SetFrame(int) method 200
SetFrameSequence(int[]) method 197–198
SetMessageListener(MessageListener) method 422
SetPayloadData(byte[]) method 420–421
SetPayloadText(String) method 419
SetPosition(int, int) method 193, 201
SetRefPixelPosition(int, int) method 201–203
SetRequestMethod(String) method 243
SetRequestProperty(String, String) method 243
SetStaticTileSet(Image, int, int) method 209
SetTicker(Ticker) method 186
SetTransform(int) method 202–203
SetViewWindow(int, int, int, int) method 194–195
SetVisible(boolean) method 193
Signing and authenticating MIDlet suites 345
Signing MIDlet suites 347
SMS adapter support 431
SMS client mode 434
SMS client versus server mode connection 435
SMS connection strings 433
SMS message addressing scheme 433
SMS message length 432
SMS message order 436
SMS message structure 431
SMS port allocation 434
SMS recipient address 434
SMS server mode 434
sms:// 439
sms://communication protocol 433
SMSC address 436
Socket connection versus datagram connection 240
Socket stream connection 239
Socket 239
SocketConnection connection string 240
SocketConnection example 253, 255
SocketConnection interface 236, 239, 252
Spacer class 149
Specific networking protocols, absence of 226
Standard Edition, SE 5
Sprite 195
  collision 203, 205, 207
  collision rectangle 204, 207
  reference pixel 201, 203
  TRANS_MIRROR 202
  TRANS_MIRROR_ROT180 203
  TRANS_MIRROR_ROT270 203
  TRANS_MIRROR_ROT90 202
  TRANS_NONE 202
  TRANS_ROT180 202
  TRANS_ROT270 202
  TRANS_ROT90 202
  transformation 202–203
Sprites tuning 211
Stateless network connections 234
Static tiles 209–210
Stopping media 378
Storage size 67
Store-and-forward protocol 437
Storing and Retrieving Data 23
Stream capture
  audio 366
  video 366
Stream-based connection 239
StreamConnection interface 227, 233
  acceptAndOpen() method 234

StreamConnectionNotifier
 interface 227, 233
Synchronous Versus Asynchronous Message
 receiving mechanisms 443
System class protection 333
System.currentTimeMillis
 method 25

T
TCP/IP Server Socket 237
TCP/IP Socket 237
TCP/IP Sockets 239
Technology Compatibility Kit (TCK) 4, 20
text/vnd.sun.j2me.app-
 descriptor 85, 91
TextBox class 156
TextField class
 MIDP user interface requirements 30
TextField constants 141
TextMessage interface 416, 419
 example 419
 methods 419
TextMessage type 437
Thread Groups 53
Ticker 184, 187
 class 186
Tile height 210
Tile index 210
Tile width 210
TiledLayer 208
 cells 210
 grid 210
 tuning 212
TileLayer(int, int, Image, int, int)
 constructor 210
Tiles Indices 209
Tiles 209
Timeout exception 229–230
TimeoutException class 230
Time Zone class
 CLDC Requirements 25
Timer class 95
TimerTask class 96
 cancel() method 96
Timestamps 417
TimeZone class
 CLDC Requirements 25
 java.lang.Thread class
 methods 419
Tone 364, 394
 Control classes 384
TotalMemory() Method 66
TP-User-Data field 431, 432, 435, 437
Trusted and Untrusted Applications 32
Trusted MIDlet suites 336

U
UDP Datagram connection 240
UDP Datagram receiver connection 241
UDP Datagram 237, 240
UDPDatagramConnection connection
 string 241
UDPDatagramConnection
 example 263
UDPDatagramConnection
 interface 236, 240, 263
Unprotected APIs and functions 336
UnsupportedEncodingException
 class 270
Untrusted and trusted MIDlet suites 335
Untrusted MIDlet suites 335
Usability and notification tradeoff 342
User permissions 337, 339, 342
User-Data-Header field 431, 432, 434
User-defined Class Loaders 53
Using connection 243
Using TimeZones 25
 encoding strings 26
 general requirements 27
 imaging requirements 28
 network requirements 27
 push Registry Alarms 28
 requirements on Profile: MIDP 26

V
Virtual tile 209
`VolumeControl` class

W
Width, frame 196
Wireless Messaging API Hierarchy 417
Wireless Messaging API (WMA) 10
`Wireless.messaging.sms.smsc` property 437
WMA and PushRegistry relationship 444
WMA package overview 416
WMA Push Registration Entry 444
WMA Push Registry Connections behaviors 445
WMA-related Exceptions 440
WMA-related Security Issues 442
Working with `Timers` 29
- user Interface Requirements 29
- requirements on Messaging Support: WMA 30
- requirements on Multimedia Support: MMAPI 31
- security Permissions 33
- trusting Applications 32

X
X.509 PKI 345

AUTHORS' PROFILES

Ko Ko Naing is currently a development manager with Itorama Consulting (Thailand) Ltd. He has been developing enterprise applications using Java EE and mobile applications using Java ME for the past six years. He is the lead author of JMADPlus, a Sun Certified Mobile Application Developer (SCMAD) certification exam simulation software from Enthuware.com Pvt. Ltd. Furthermore, he was a technical reviewer of SCMAD exam preparation kit and SCJA exam preparation kit from Whizlabs Software Pvt. Ltd. Ko Ko can be found frequently in certification discussion forums such as JDiscuss.com and JavaRanch.com. He is an active moderator at JDiscuss.com, mainly managing the SCMAD forum. Besides the SCMAD certification, he also holds several other certifications, including SCJP, SCWCD, SCBCD, SCMAD, SCJA, and CCNA. Ko Ko graduated from Assumption University, Thailand, with Bachelor and Master of Computer Science.

Sathya Srinivasan is currently a technical architect with BearingPoint, Inc., USA.. He has been working on Java related projects for more than six years and holds SCJP, SCWCD, and SCMAD certifications. He is also the co-author of the popular SCMAD Exam Simulator from Whizlabs Software Pvt. Ltd. When he finds time, Sathya also tries to be an active participant in various forums at JavaRanch.com, especially the SCMAD forum. He has a Master's degree in Computer Science. His current interests include researching on collaborative systems, knowledge management systems, and enterprise-level search engines.

Chad Davis, though currently a software developer, harbors a secret past life as an English major. He holds Master's degrees in both English Literature and Computer Science. In addition to this book, he is co-author of *Struts 2 in Action* by Manning Publications. With his wife Mary Turner, he owns and works for Blackdog Software, Inc. Though working on this book has provided many satisfying moments, he has particularly enjoyed reading numerous specifications of the Java Community Process, as well as a variety of RFCs. While this might sound tedious to many, he is a devoted student of the more obscure forms of meticulous articulation that have arisen at the hands of those masters of terse precision—the engineers. Without them, the world would be vague.

Sivasundaram Umapathy is currently a technical architect with Sella Synergy India Limited, the IT division of Gruppo Banca Sella, Italy. He is into J2EE technologies for the past eight years. He holds SCJP, SCBCD, SCWCD, SCMAD, SCEA, OCA and PMP certifications. He has co-authored the Whizlabs SCMAD simulator with Sathya. He has a Master's degree in Software Systems from BITS, Pilani and currently pursuing PGSEM from IIM, Bangalore. His current interests are enterprise architecture, security, open source and all things Agile.

Made in United States
Troutdale, OR
09/22/2026

54730546R00286